World Wise

Your passport to safer travel

Your Passport to SAFER TRAVEL

by Mark Hodson

and The Suzy Lamplugh Trust

The Leading Authority for Personal Safety

With the *World Wise* Directory of information for travellers

Regular updates on the *World Wise* website at www.suzylamplugh.org/worldwise

SECOND EDITION

Published by Thomas Cook Publishing
PO Box 227
Thorpe Wood
Peterborough
PE3 6PU
United Kingdom

First published 1998
Second edition 2001

ISBN 1-841572-32-2

Commissioning Editor: Deborah Parker

Text and cover design and illustrations: Amanda Plant

Text typeset in Flareserif, Impact and Arial using QuarkXpress for Windows

Printed in Italy by Rotolito Lombarda Spa

The Publishers acknowledge the assistance of the Youth Exchange Centre of the British Council in the publication of this book.

Supported by the European Commission's Youth for Europe Programme.

The Publishers acknowledge the contribution of The Prince's Trust towards the research upon which this book is based.

Contents

The Prince's Trust
Helping Young People to Succeed

The Prince's Trust aims to help young people to succeed by providing opportunities which they would otherwise not have.

We target those young people who, through disadvantage or lack of opportunity, are failing to reach their full potential. We help them fulfil their ambitions, improve their skills and make a real contribution to their community.

We achieve this through a nation-wide network which delivers practical advice and counselling, support for business start-ups, loans and grants, training, local projects, personal development and support for study outside school. We help both individuals and groups.

Our core target group is young people between the ages of 14 and 25. In some of our programmes, we also address the needs of those who are as young as 11 and up to the age of 30.

To find out how The Prince's Trust can help you, call 0800 842842.

ST. JAMES'S PALACE

I was delighted to learn that my Trust has lent its support to the production of this very useful book. Foreign travel is more accessible for young people than it has ever been, which is splendid, but there are hidden dangers for the unprepared that can mean foreign trips end in disaster.

This book will help young travellers gain more from their time abroad. It is a rich source of information, and includes details about the enormously different cultures and lifestyles that thrive in each country in the world. The book also includes an invaluable guide to personal safety. Equipped with this book, the reader will learn much more about the sights and sounds they experience as they go, while travelling wisely and safely.

I would like to thank everyone at The Suzy Lamplugh Trust, Thomas Cook Publishing and all those who assisted in making the whole project a reality. I am pleased that The Prince's Trust, by agreeing to support the research which lies behind it, has been able to play its part in helping young people to travel widely and with a greater sense of security.

Charles

Foreword

As a young man I was an intrepid explorer – and I still am. I am fortunate that my most recent jobs have taken me all over the world, but the seeds of my passion for travel were sown young. It is not an exaggeration to say that those early, solo journeys have shaped my life.

Experiencing new cultures and different ways of life can have a transformative effect upon an individual. These adventures open up the world, stretch horizons. But experience reminds me that not every expedition is all about the good times. There are dark moments – tricky confrontations and unhappy episodes which can have dismal consequences.

It is therefore a great pleasure for me personally, and as Director-General of the British Council, to support the second edition of this book. *World Wise: Your Pasport to Safer Travel* describes both the well-known and the lesser known hazards that many young travellers will face. We should all have the chance to explore the worlds beyond our own, but not every journey will be easy. This guide prepares the way. My warmest thanks to The Suzy Lamplugh Trust for keeping us aware.

David Green
Director-General
The British Council

Introduction

Our eldest daughter Suzy disappeared one sunny summer's day in 1986 during her normal everyday work. She has now been presumed murdered and declared dead. We never cease to miss her and remember her with great joy.

When Suzy rang me on the Friday before that dark Monday when she totally vanished from our lives, she told me with excitement of all the things which she was doing. 'Aren't you overdoing things, darling?' I asked. 'Come on Mum' she said 'life is for living – don't forget that!'

I never have, and I now live with that thought in my heart. Life is for living, but real living needs quality. This means living with the freedom to choose, be ourselves and yet respect and value each other. To be able to do this, we need to live without harassment and fear of danger; to go out and live life to the full and to do so safely.

This is why the mission of The Suzy Lamplugh Trust, set up in the name of our daughter, is to provide practical personal safety for everyone, everywhere, every day. Travelling abroad is such an important part of living life to the full that we felt we ought to explore the risks and possible pitfalls.

We always joked with our children, saying that they and their friends seemed hell-bent on getting their 'BTA' – Been to America/Africa/Australia/Asia – before setting out seriously to earn their living, but since my children explored the world there has been an increase in international travel by young people. Cheaper travel and simple means of transferring money bring more and more exotic destinations within easy reach and make it possible to stay away for longer and longer periods. Effectively planned and prepared for, international travel can be both an education and a challenging experience which opens the mind to both the diversity and common interests shared by countries and peoples across the world.

The vast majority of young people return home safely and with a sense of personal fulfilment and enrichment. However, sometimes things can go wrong: not just the media headline cases but the unreported incidents – theft, health problems, breaches of political or cultural codes for example – or there is a 'fortunate near miss'. These experiences can provoke great anxiety; at worst, they may have severe physical or psychological consequences (for the travellers and their families) which undermine the positive benefits.

It became clear that a major cause of problems has been the misunderstanding or ignorance of the differences between cultures. Social relations, food, dress, body language, hospitality, photography, amongst other factors, all need to be considered if insensitive behaviour, and sometimes potentially dangerous situations, are to be avoided.

The Suzy Lamplugh Trust commissioned a study which is the basis for *World Wise.* We are most grateful to Thomas Cook for publishing this excellent book. Its publication is supported by a website maintained by Oxford Brookes University, on behalf of The Suzy Lamplugh Trust. This makes available, on the internet, regularly updated, the directory of advice for over 220 countries at www.suzylamplugh.org/worldwise.

I have no doubt that while this book does raise awareness about the problems of personal safety, it will also encourage people to travel and will build up confidence in those who have not previously thought that international travel was for them. The book will also, I hope, give some peace of mind for those of us who are left behind!

Diana Lamplugh, OBE
Director, The Suzy Lamplugh Trust

About the authors

Mark Hodson

Mark Hodson has spent a total of 18 months backpacking around Asia and Latin America, and has visited some of the world's most notorious trouble spots from El Salvador and Nicaragua to the Philippines and Northern Pakistan.

He has worked in London, Hong Kong, New York, the Bahamas and Holland (where he lived in a tent and packed flower bulbs). He now writes for the Travel section of The Sunday Times.

The Suzy Lamplugh Trust

The Suzy Lamplugh Trust is the leading authority on personal safety, whose mission is to create a safer society and enable everyone to live safer lives. Registered charity number 802567.

The Trust encourages people to live life to the full and to travel with confidence – and to do so safely. It provides practical personal safety guidance for everyone, every day, everywhere.

Information about the Trust's resources and training may be obtained from: The Suzy Lamplugh Trust, PO Box 17818, London SW14 8WW. www.suzylamplugh.org

Other World Wise publications from The Suzy Lamplugh Trust

The World Wise Video features lively and realistic advice from young travellers, for young travellers, on how to enjoy travel safely.

The World Wise Teaching notes are an excellent resource for teachers. They have been developed to help teachers equip students to help themselves.

The World Wide Resource Pack includes the *World Wise Book*, the *World Wise Video* and the *Teaching Notes.* A complete solution for schools and young travellers with all the information they need to make sensible decisions.

Acknowledgements

The Suzy Lamplugh Trust is most grateful to:

The Prince's Trust, for enabling this book to be published by funding the research, and the initial directory, on which the book is based.

The British Council for providing funds to assist the actual publication of this book.

The Foreign and Commonwealth Office, for providing funds to put the Directory on the Internet and for it to be regularly updated.

Oxford Brookes University, for help, support and encouragement.

The Educational Broadcasting Services Trust, for doing so much to get the project off the ground.

Without the help of all these organisations, and indeed of Thomas Cook Publishing, this book would not have come about. We thank you all.

This book has its origins in research conducted on behalf of The Suzy Lamplugh Trust by Oxford Brookes University. This involved interviews with travellers under the age of 25. Many of their experiences are included in this book, through the quotes reproduced in the text.

We would like to thank all those listed below who have contributed to the book through their own words:

Emma Amies
Ady Bungay
Juliet Coombe
Cheryl Cowling
Anna Davies
Brendan Fox
Faith Hagerty
Will Hagerty
Jo Kennedy and Liz Hardy
Diana Lamplugh
Stephanie Miles
Jean-Paul Penrose
Nathan Pope
Victoria Powers
Fiona Pride
Paul Radziwill
Emma Turrell-Clarke

Getting the most from this book

Travel can be a great adventure. The purpose of this book is to encourage people to travel – but in safety.

World Wise – your passport to safer travel has its roots in a report commissioned by The Suzy Lamplugh Trust and researched by Oxford Brookes University. The report related the experiences of young travellers and their thoughts on making themselves safer, especially where they felt they had made mistakes and put themselves in danger. Mark Hodson has based the first section of this book upon this report, as well as drawing on his own extensive travel experiences.

Ideally, you should read this book when you are starting to think about travelling. There is a lot of safety advice and information packed into the first section, so reread it to absorb it all.

This book is pocket-sized and lightweight so that you can carry it around, and use it for reference during your journey.

Your passport to safer travel

- Read through all of the first section well before you start out on your travels.
- Note down any points you need to research further or investigate.
- Use the *More information* chapter, which lists useful contacts, as your starting point for your research.
- Then look up any countries in the Directory that you think you might want to travel to.
- Look at our website at www.suzylamplugh.org/worldwise for regular updates.

The Directory

- When you have decided which countries you intend to visit, photocopy these pages and leave them, together with an itinerary, with a member of your family or a friend.

Getting the most from this book

- The Directory is prefaced with an explanation of the symbols and categories used in the country-by-country listing.
- Also explained are health issues and religious observances highlighted in the Directory.

Just before you go...

- Check out updated pages of the Directory on the World Wise website at www.suzylamplugh.org/worldwise before you set off.
- The listings in the Directory section were up to date at time of publication, but the information contained within it is liable to change – so browse the website before for the very latest information.

The Suzy Lamplugh Trust offer their own 'PLAN' to help you remain safe, wherever you travel.

PREPARE YOURSELF
Plan your journey
Wear sensible clothing
Assess the risks
Leave an itinerary with someone

LOOK CONFIDENT
Be alert and have a sense of purpose
Know where you are going and how to get there
Carry a personal alarm

AVOID PUTTING YOURSELF AT RISK
Your aim is to remain safe
Be wary of strangers
Assess the risks as you venture into new territory

NEVER ASSUME
It won't happen to me
They look respectable

Do not ignore your instincts

Your passport to safer travel

Planning your trip

• *Get thinking*

If life was like the movies you would need nothing more than a suitcase, a pair of shades and an open-top sports car. The idea of just hitting the road and leaving behind the monotony of everyday life is enough to get anyone's heart racing. But road movies rarely have happy endings. Think of *Thelma and Louise, Easy Rider, Wild at Heart.* All those films looked like a whole heap of fun in the first reel but they all ended in disaster.

This doesn't mean you should abandon your dreams of going away. Travel is one of the greatest thrills that life has to offer. Few experiences can compare with the head-spinning, eye-popping excitement of arriving for the first time in a foreign country where every sight, sound, taste and smell is new. It's like sex – you never forget your first time.

Travel is easy but it does involve some element of risk. To abandon everything familiar in your life and place yourself in a totally alien environment can be a daunting, unsettling experience. It can also, if you're not careful, be a dangerous one. That's why you need to have your wits about you, to know something about the country you're visiting, to know something about yourself and to understand how local people see you.

While you are gazing at maps and dreaming about your big trip, your parents and friends may be telling you all the things that might go wrong. In reality, there are two major problems you're most likely to run into – getting sick and being robbed. But neither of these need seriously affect your trip provided you're well prepared, and know what to do if they happen to you. That's one way this book will help – with advice on things like money, insurance and health precautions, and what to do if you get in trouble.

Many of the problems that arise on the road are caused by a lack of understanding. Travellers may fail to understand the cultural significance of their actions, or even the way they dress, unaware that they are causing offence. One purpose of this book is to help you avoid these situations by being well prepared and knowing how to cope in tricky situations.

• Where, when and who with?

Before you rush out and buy an air ticket or an Inter-Rail pass, think about the kind of trip you want to take. Don't just follow the crowds – consider which parts of the world really interest you. Start browsing through the internet and reading books, newspapers and magazine articles about the countries you might want to visit. If you're going abroad to work or study, try to learn as much as you can about the area where you'll be staying. If you're interested in art, architecture or food you'll get a lot more out of your trip if you read up on the subject. Don't be just another gormless tourist going from one sight to the next, understanding nothing.

Think whether you want to travel alone, with a group, with a best friend or with a boyfriend or girlfriend. Travelling alone can be a more thrilling experience, giving you maximum exposure to a foreign culture, but it can be more

stressful, especially if you get sick or something goes wrong. It will also be more expensive if you can't find other travellers to share rooms, taxis and organised tours.

> **When I set off around the world most people thought I would be starting a year of loneliness and introspection. All those fears were unfounded. I soon found travelling partners with whom I shared common interests and goals.**

In some countries travelling alone is dangerous, particularly if you're a woman. It's a shame, but in many parts of the world a lone female wearing Western clothes is immediately assumed to be sexually available.

If you travel with a friend you'll probably be safer, but you may have to compromise your own plans. Talk honestly with your intended travel partner about how you each want to spend your time and what you hope to achieve. You might learn that even your best friend has very different ideas about what would make an interesting trip. If you can, go away for a weekend together to see if you would make good travel partners.

If you travel on your own, you need to be extra vigilant – there is no one else to look out for you. Careful planning is even more important.

If you're looking for an adventurous outdoors trip with minimum danger – and if you're a sociable type – you might consider joining an overland truck tour, travelling across Africa, Asia or South America for up to six months. If you want to contribute to a worthwhile project you could try raising enough sponsorship money to join an environmental expedition where you might be drilling wells in Africa or building orang-utan shelters in Indonesia. You'll find contact details for these organisations on pages 96–97.

By doing your own research you'll also learn why there is often a 'wrong' time of year to visit certain countries. For instance, it makes sense to avoid Goa in June and July (the Indian monsoon), and the Caribbean in early September (hurricane season). Don't rely on travel agents or airlines to volunteer this information – check the weather details for each country you intend to visit in the Directory. For the most up-to-date information, visit the

World Wise website at www.suzylamplugh.org/worldwise

> **We arrived by boat at Patras with no Greek money to find the country in the middle of a general strike. All the banks were closed and there were no trains running. If only we had found this out before getting on the boat!**

Cultural and political differences can also affect the timing of your trip. Think twice before visiting a strict Muslim country during the month of Ramadan, when restaurants are closed during the day. In politically unstable areas of Asia, Africa and Latin America it's best to avoid general elections when political rallies and demonstrations can quickly turn to riots. The best way to stay in touch is to read a good newspaper.

If you intend to make an extensive overland tour of an undeveloped country invest in a detailed map – it's usually easier to find them at home than once you arrive – and take a good look at the road and rail network to ensure that your plans are not too ambitious. In some parts of the world it might take all day just to cover 50 miles – and that's without punctures and breakdowns. It's a good rule to try not to see and do too much.

Sadly, some parts of the world remain completely off-bounds to travellers because of war, famine or a risk of kidnapping. These include large parts of central Africa, the Indian states of Jammu and Kashmir, Algeria and some remote regions of Indonesia. You shouldn't assume that just because these areas don't appear on the TV news every night that they're safe. They are not.

Use all the resources at your disposal. Borrow guidebooks from your local library, contact tourist boards and embassies, search the internet and speak to travellers who have recently returned from the countries you intend to visit. You'll also find lots of useful details in the Directory section of this book, including tourist office addresses, hints on currency and transport safety and general information on each country.

For current safety information, use the Foreign Office Travel Advice service which is updated daily and published on both Ceefax and the internet. The address is given on page 95.

• *Buying air tickets*

Before you make a final decision about where and when to go, take a look at how the prices of airline tickets fluctuate throughout the year. You can often save a fortune by delaying the start of your trip by just a few weeks. For instance, a round-the-world ticket from Trailfinders (020 7938 3939) flying London-Singapore-Bali-Perth-Cairns-Sydney-Christchurch-Auckland-Fiji-Los Angeles-London would cost you £1,555 in December. But wait until February 1 and the same ticket will cost you just £961, saving almost £600.

Find a travel agent or ticketing agent with IATA bonding who specialises in selling the kind of tickets you want. There's no point phoning a bucket shop that sells last-minute charter flights to Spain if you want a discounted multistop ticket to Australia. Nor should you go direct to the airline – the fare will almost certainly be a lot higher. Instead, use the experience and expertise of an agent who knows the parts of the world you're interested in, and how to get the maximum available discounts on those routes.

Don't try to cut too many corners on price. An agent who can sell you the same ticket slightly cheaper than a rival probably has to compromise on service, so if you ring back with an urgent query about your ticket you may find the phone permanently engaged. Similarly, don't always opt for the cheapest fare. If you pay a bit extra to fly on a more reputable airline you're not just paying for a more comfortable flight, you're getting a better safety record, better reliability, more direct routing and less chance of delays. Generally speaking, the bigger airlines suffer fewer long delays because they have the capacity to draft in an alternative aircraft if yours develops a fault.

Many budget travellers make the mistake of buying a cheap ticket to somewhere they don't really want to go, often believing that once they arrive there they can buy another cheap ticket to their intended destination. Nine times out of ten they're disappointed. A flight from, say, Rio to Buenos Aires may be cheaper in London than it is if bought in Rio.

Always buy a two-way ticket that allows you to come home at any time – you may run out of money earlier than you thought. If you don't think you can afford a return ticket, then can you really afford to go?

While travel agents are useful sources of advice on ticketing, they won't be able to tell you which countries you should visit. That's something you need to decide on before you call them. And don't let them persuade you to buy tickets you don't need. Some agents will try to sell you air passes within a country, which may offer, say, 30 days of unlimited flights for, say, £300. These deals may look tempting but to make them worthwhile you'd have to charge about the country spending half your time in airports. You may be better off travelling more slowly and getting to know places better.

Finally, you must remember to reconfirm flights as you go, particularly when travelling in developing countries. All tickets carry a warning that you need to reconfirm within 72 hours of the flight and although this isn't strictly necessary on airlines travelling within Europe, it is vital in other parts of the world. If you don't ring the airline within 72 hours of your departure time, you run the risk of losing your reservation. Any travel agent will be able to do it, but, to be doubly sure, make the call yourself.

• *Gearing up*

If you walk into a specialist travel shop you'll see literally hundreds of items – from crampons to travel washing lines – that manufacturers claim you can't live without. Don't believe a word of it. Unless you plan to climb the northwest face of K2 or sail singlehanded across the Bay of Bengal you can dispense with almost all specialist travel products. Most of the clothes you need will already be in your own wardrobe. If you want to waste your money on a four-season sleeping bag, trekking socks, a pump-action wasp killer and half a dozen tubes of clothes-washing gel, go ahead. But you'll have to carry it all. Never forget the first rule of packing – take half the clothes you think you'll need, and twice the money.

> Before I went travelling my friends clubbed together and bought me a good-quality travel pack, the type that zips up into a shoulder bag. It went everywhere with me for two years and is still going strong. I met other travellers with cheap rucksacks that fell apart after a few months.

Rather than buy dozens of small pointless items, invest in a few vital pieces of kit and buy the best you can afford. The most important of these is your backpack. There are dozens of different types of backpacks on the market but in my mind the best option is a 'travel pack', which looks like a big shoulder bag but has one side that zips away to reveal an internal frame that allows it to be worn like a rucksack. This means you can carry a lot of gear on your back in comfort, but you can also look smart when you need to – at immigration checks, police stations or hotel reception desks. Travel packs are easier to lock than conventional rucksacks and they don't tend to get damaged on airport carousels because all the dangling straps and handles that can get caught in machinery are tucked inside the zipped compartment.

Whatever type of pack you decide to buy, make sure it fits you. A good one will have an adjustable frame that can be fitted to your own body shape. The waist strap should sit on your hip bones, not around your waist, and carry most of the weight. Get it right before you leave – don't wait until you're midway through a five-day trek in Thailand or trudging around Athens in mid-August looking for a room.

> Don't overpack a rucksack. That's what I did and, even though it was an expensive one, it split within a month.

WHAT TO PACK

ESSENTIALS

- money belt ☐
- photocopies of all your documents sealed in a watertight bag ☐
- padlocks (combination) and small chain (the sort you would use for a bicycle) ☐
- Maglite-style torch (doubles as a miniature table lamp) ☐
- foam ear plugs, eye shades and inflatable pillow (for long bus journeys and flights) ☐
- Swiss Army knife/pen knife (put in your checked baggage during flights) ☐
- string, rubber bands and masking tape ☐
- alarm clock (for early starts) ☐
- pocket compass ☐
- sunblock ☐
- sunglasses (with UVP protection) ☐
- sunhat or baseball cap ☐
- spare passport-size photos of yourself ☐
- toilet roll ☐
- guidebooks and maps ☐
- universal sink plug ☐
- first-aid kit (see page 30) ☐

You'll need a daypack (a mini backpack) that's comfortable enough to wear all day long, and bulky enough to hold a guidebook, water bottle, sunglasses, sunblock and camera. It should be lockable and anonymous, so avoid designer labels and garish colours. It should also have two strong shoulder straps so you can wear it on your back with both hands free or swing it round so that it sits on your chest. There are two advantages to wearing a daypack on your chest – it helps your balance when you're also carrying a back-pack, and it deters pickpockets.

Some travellers wear a bumbag – called a fanny pack in America – to carry cash, a compact camera and other small items. I don't like them because they look like an invitation to thieves and mark you out as a tourist. Some pickpockets don't even bother trying to get their fingers inside them, they just snip the waistband with scissors or slash it with a knife and whisk the whole thing off before you have time to blink. I've seen it happen.

The safest way to carry valuables is in a money belt worn under the front of your trousers, and preferably under a shirt, too. The best ones are made of thin canvas with a zip at the top. Because they're absorbent they can get soaked with sweat in hot weather, so to avoid ruining your cash, cheques and air tickets, put them first in a small sealable plastic folder, like the type you get when buying travellers cheques.

I imagined it would be a drag having to wear a money belt all the time but I soon got used to it and after a while I would have felt naked without one. Wearing baggy trousers made it a lot more comfortable.

There are dozens of other hidden pockets and wallets on the market, such as neck pouches, invisible pockets and belts with secret zipped compartments, all of which are worth considering. If you're in an area where theft is a very real danger – on some South American bus routes, for instance – you could strap your valuables to one leg with a bandage under long trousers. Some travellers sew $100 bills into the lining of a jacket, which isn't a bad idea so long as you don't lose the jacket or get drenched in a downpour. Others recommend lining your rucksack with chicken wire to deter bag slashers. This isn't a good idea because eventually the wire comes loose and rips your rucksack and your clothes to shreds. I speak from bitter experience on this one. And, yes, I did feel stupid at the time.

You'll need a comfortable pair of walking shoes or boots. It's far better to take one decent pair of shoes rather than two or three shoddy pairs. Wear them in thoroughly before you set off – there are few surer ways of ruining the first couple of weeks of a trip than walking around all day with painful blisters. Don't be tempted to take your favourite trainers as they will make your feet sweat.

When packing clothes, try to stick to lightweight cotton items. Avoid too much black, which absorbs heat, and white, which shows the dirt. In hot climates, lightweight canvas or cotton trousers are a lot more comfortable than jeans. Take at least one jumper or fleece jacket and a set of thermal underwear. If you're going to the tropics this might sound ridiculous but, believe me, you'll need warm clothes, particularly if you spend any time at altitude or in desert areas where nights can be freezing. Air-conditioned buses are often so cold that you'll wake up in the night shivering.

> **One of the most effective ways to ward off mosquitoes at night is to sleep under a fan in a long-sleeved thermal vest and leggings tucked into socks.**

Pack lots of cotton socks and underwear, which are sometimes hard to buy in developing countries, but not too many T-shirts and pairs of shorts which can be picked up anywhere. T-shirts with naff western logos may be highly prized in some countries so they make good gifts. Make sure you have at least one pair of long trousers (or skirt) and a long-sleeved shirt – you may need it to cover up when visiting temples or churches.

> **Arriving at Windhoek in Namibia before dawn, I was shocked because it was freezing cold. Three hours later we were in the scorching sun in the back of trucks and our hats and sun cream were at the bottom of our rucksacks.**

WHAT TO PACK

CLOTHES

- walking shoes or boots ☐
- long cotton trousers and/or skirt ☐
- T-shirts, shorts, socks, underwear ☐
- long-sleeved shirt ☐
- sarong (doubles as a towel and beach mat) ☐
- thermal vest and leggings ☐
- jumper or fleece jacket ☐
- flip-flops, leather sandals or sports sandals (for beaches and communal bathrooms) ☐
- swimming costume ☐

WASH KIT

- toothbrush, toothpaste, soap, shampoo ☐
- watertight soap dish ☐
- shaving kit (stick soap is lighter and longer-lasting than cans of foam) ☐
- washbag (airtight to keep out insects, with a hook for hanging from bathroom doors) ☐
- small towel ☐

Try to pack at least one relatively smart outfit (shirt and trousers or a dress) in case you're invited to somebody's house or need to deal with officials. In some remote areas where tourists are a rarity you may even find yourself invited to official functions where muddy boots and a baggy T-shirt wouldn't go down too well. If you can afford it, invest in a pair of specialist travel trousers such as Rohan Globetrotters which are very light, durable, have secret zipped pockets and fold up to the size of a Coke can. They are expensive but well worth it and come in men's and women's sizes. If you've got a

OPTIONAL ITEMS

- camera, film and spare camera battery ☐
- shortwave radio (to keep in touch with world news and tune into local stations) ☐
- notebook and pens (so you can keep a diary of your travels) ☐
- sleep sack (if staying at hostels where linen isn't provided) ☐
- small calculator ☐
- sewing kit (for repairs to clothes and luggage) ☐
- gifts from home (postcards, souvenirs, photographs of your house and family) ☐
- rubber door wedge (to stop people entering your room at night) ☐
- photo of your travel pack (carry it in your daypack) ☐

pair of combat trousers, leave them at home – in some countries they might get you arrested or mistaken for a paramilitary.

Finally, before setting off try this experiment. Pack everything you plan to take away with you into your rucksack and daypack and put them on, along with your walking shoes and enough layers of clothing to make you feel uncomfortably hot. Now walk for half an hour up and down an unfamiliar crowded street with a map in one hand and a guidebook in the other. Still want to take quite so much stuff? Thought not.

• *Who needs guidebooks?*

You'd be daft to go abroad without guidebooks (although I have done – in Morocco – and got along just fine) but you'd be equally stupid to treat every word they contain as gospel. Still, that is what some travellers do, particularly in countries like India where almost everybody you meet carries the same guidebook (in this case, the Lonely Planet) and dutifully marches from one recommended guest house to the next, all eating at the same restaurants where – amazingly! – they bump

There's a lot of useful information in the Directory section of this book. But do also use guidebooks when planning your trip – to help you work out your budget, choose where to stay that first night, to find out which areas are safe to stay in, and to get hints on local customs, what to tip and so on.

into the same people again and again. I've even met travellers who refused to stay at perfectly good hotels because they were not mentioned in 'the book'. Sad.

> **I got fed up following my guidebook so I kept it in my rucksack and spent two weeks travelling by my own wits. It was tricky at times but much more rewarding and I found places that I would never have visited where I saw no other Westerners.**

Guidebooks are extremely useful for picking up general background information and for orientating yourself in a new place, but try not to become dependent on them. They're not written by gurus or soothsayers, just ordinary people who can make mistakes or have flawed judgment.

Nor are guidebooks always up to date, particularly in developing countries where prices change and restaurants and hotels are continually appearing and disappearing. By the time some books reach the shops some of the information they contain may not be current. If it's an updated or revised edition, the author may not have had time to revisit some remote places since writing the first edition. On the other hand, some guidebooks are published on the internet, so they can be updated regularly.

In my experience, some owners of guesthouses and restaurants recommended in the more popular guidebooks tend to get lazy because they know they're guaranteed a steady stream of custom every day. They may be reluctant to increase their prices which will be written in the book, so instead they allow their standards to drop. Furniture isn't mended, mattresses aren't replaced, the standard of the food falls and the service becomes surly rather than welcoming. If you see a newly-opened rival business down the street that isn't mentioned in the guidebooks it may well be smarter and more friendly, yet empty.

It's possible to dig up vast quantities of travel information on the internet, though you may have to wade through a lot of irrelevant stuff to find it. And remember, because anybody with access to a newsgroup can post information, you should not believe everything you read.

Once you have decided where you want to go, draw up an itinerary that you can leave with your family or a friend. They may need to contact you.

• *A healthy start*

Make sure you're in good shape before you set off. Start jogging or going to a gym because if you're physically fit you'll have more stamina while travelling and be less likely to fall ill. Ask your doctor for a check-up and make a note of your blood group. If you're a citizen of an EU country and are travelling within the EU get hold of a Form E111, which will guarantee you free or reduced cost emergency medical treatment, available at any post office or freephone 0800 555777.

If you are already taking medication, check with your doctor before you go. Get a letter confirming which drugs you take, giving the generic name in case you need a repeat prescription while you are away. If you have an allergy, ensure you have appropriate medication to counteract the allergy and know how to use it. If you have a medical condition, wear a medic-alert bracelet in case of emergency.

"I was climbing Tiger Leaping Gorge in China when my mild toothache became so intense that I almost went to a village dentist to have it pulled. In the end I flew to Hong Kong where the extraction cost almost £500. I later found teeth weren't covered on my insurance policy."

Visit your dentist before you go because you won't want to develop a crippling toothache when you're canoeing up the Amazon or riding a camel across the Sahara. If you plan to travel in developing countries where medical facilities are basic, it's worth investing £17.49 in a pack of sterile needles and swabs, available from MASTA, the Medical Advisory Service for Travellers Abroad (0113 238 7575; www.masta.org). Boots sells its own version, the Medical Emergency Travellers Kit.

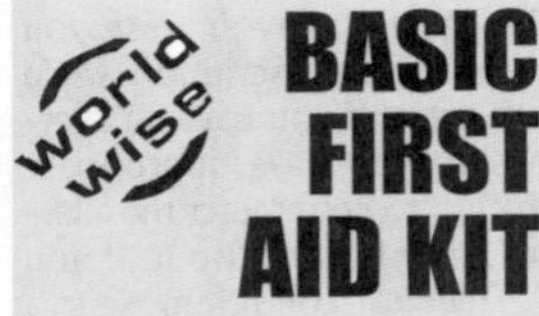

BASIC FIRST AID KIT

- Antiseptic cream ☐
- Plasters ☐
- Soluble aspirin ☐
- Throat lozenges ☐
- Anti-diarrhoea tablets ☐
- Antihistamine cream ☐
- Mosquito repellent ☐

Don't be paranoid about getting sick – the chances of catching a deadly or incurable tropical disease are small. You should see your doctor about two months before travelling to get the various jabs and pills currently on offer. Don't bother with private travel clinics which will give you more or less the same advice but charge a small fortune for it. I found one clinic in London demanding £100 for an armful of jabs that were all available free on the National Health Service.

Most travellers worry about catching malaria and take their daily and weekly tablets with religious adherence. Remember that these pills reduce your chances of catching malaria but they don't make you immune. Malaria is transmitted by mosquitoes and the only sure way to avoid catching the disease is not to get bitten. Mosquito coils, which can be bought almost anywhere, are effective although they're brittle and tend to break when carried in backpacks. Electrical devices that emit a high-pitch note to 'scare off' mosquitoes don't work. If you're planning to get pregnant or already pregnant you might not be able to take malaria tablets – ask your doctor.

Take a good mosquito repellent. I travel with Ultrathon cream, which is used by both the British and US armies and is recommended by Dr Ron Behrens, director of the travel clinic at the Hospital for

Tropical Diseases in London. It contains 33% Deet (the most effective chemical repellent available) which it releases slowly over a 12-hour period, making it particularly effective at night. Look for a similar percentage of Deet (it will be marked on the bottle) if you have to buy repellent abroad. Don't believe people who tell you that malarial mosquitoes only bite at dawn and dusk. Some strains feed from midnight until dawn and those carrying dengue fever can strike at any time during the day.

Because Deet is an unpleasant chemical that dries out your skin and corrodes some types of plastic, some travellers refuse to use it and opt instead for a 'natural' repellent containing an ingredient like citronella or eucalyptus oil. These certainly smell nicer and are more gentle on your skin but there is a problem – they don't work very well.

• Passports, visas and other boring stuff

Dig out your passport at least a couple of months before you set off. Check it's valid for at least six months after your intended return date, and that the photograph still looks like you – if not you can send off a new one to get it changed, but this takes time.

> **I was stopped by an immigration officer who didn't believe that the picture in my passport was of me because my hairstyle had changed. He tried to get me to pay a bribe but I persuaded him I had no money.**

Find out if you need visas to visit any of the countries on your itinerary (use the Directory section and browse the FCO website) and apply for them in plenty of time, particularly if you need to send your passport away. It's usually possible to apply in person at the relevant embassy and collect your visa the following day.

When applying for a visa, you may have to hand over two or three passport-sized photos of yourself, so take a supply away with you. Most countries ask you to state the purpose of your visit (always write 'tourism'), and your occupation. Don't put 'journalist' or 'photographer' here, because these terms often arouse suspicion and some countries – such as Burma and China – may deny you entry. Anything nondescript such as student, office worker, factory worker or computer operator will do fine. (I once wrote 'goalkeeper' on a visa application form, which was stupid because I am 5ft 8in and wear glasses, but I was fortunate enough to get away with it.)

You must take out comprehensive travel insurance. It's expensive and tiresome but it could save you a fortune, particularly if you fall ill and need to be taken to the nearest emergency hospital or flown home. Before you run out and buy the cheapest policy check that it offers medical cover of at least £1million and will cover emergency dental work. The majority of policies do cover watersports and scuba-diving, but you may have to pay an extra premium to cover things like skiing and bungee jumping (if that appeals to you). Additional third-party insurance is essential if you consider hiring a car in the United States. With insurance, as with most things, you get what you pay for.

Finally, make three sets of photocopies of all your documents, including the back page of your passport, insurance documents, immunisation certificate, visa stamps and air tickets. Keep one set in your luggage, give one to a travelling companion (if you are not travelling solo) and leave the third at home with somebody who can fax it to you in an emergency.

Money

If you plan to travel for more than a couple of weeks you should be thinking not just about how much money to take, but how to keep it safe. Traveller's cheques are secure – provided you keep the receipt separately – and are welcomed almost anywhere in the world, particularly if they're made out in US dollars. Check which denominations you should take by looking in the Directory section of this book. A credit card is useful

because it's easy to conceal and can sometimes be used to get a cash advance in an emergency. Two credit cards are even better, provided you keep them separately so that if one is stolen you'll still have the other. If you're away from home for more than a month you can instruct your bank to pay credit card bills by direct debit. Emergency contact numbers are given for the main credit card companies in the Directory.

"My Switch card was handy in the US, Australia, New Zealand, Singapore and Bangkok where it can be used in any cashpoint with the Cirrus symbol. Take out large amounts each time because there is a flat charge."

If you don't have a credit card, your parents or a close friend may be prepared to let you have a second card on their account, to be used in emergencies only. Unfortunately, credit cards can't be used everywhere. Cheap hotels, hostels, guesthouses, bus companies and even railway ticket offices in some countries don't have the facilities to process the payments. Don't rely on cashpoint cards,

Carrying credit and debit cards and traveller's cheques is more secure than carrying money, but you should always treat cards and cheques as carefully as you would cash.

Keep your traveller's cheque sales receipt separate from the cheques themselves. In North America, traveller's cheques are accepted as readily as cash, but in some parts of Europe (such as some regions of France and Spain) banks are not always authorised to handle foreign currencies.

Memorise your PIN (personal identificaton number) and keep it secret. Verify your daily withdrawal limit before travelling, and test your card before you go. Be observant and cautious when you use an ATM machine. Don't let anyone else see the screen and keyboard, and put your cash away immediately.

Don't let your credit card out of you sight during transactions, and keep all the slips. Report lost and stolen cards and traveller's cheques immediately – use the Directory to find the phone number.

WIRING MONEY ABROAD

One way of getting money in an emergency is to have someone wire you the funds. Sending money abroad this way was once considered expensive and time consuming. However, money-wiring services, such as ***MoneyGram*** SM and Western Union, specialise in sending money around the world quickly, easily and inexpensively.

HOW *MoneyGram* SM WORKS

If you run out of money, contact a friend or family member who can help out. They can go to their nearest ***MoneyGram*** SM agent (in the UK, most Post Offices and Thomas Cook branches). The sender will need some form of ID, together with the cash they are sending (plus a service fee). The sender can also include a short message to you at no additional charge.

You can collect the money from any ***MoneyGram*** SM agent in the world 10 minutes after the sender has completed the transaction, or as soon as the local agency opens. You will usually receive the cash in local currency and there are no extra fees. The sender can enquire where the nearest agent is for you, or you can telephone the local number given in the Directory.

You go to any ***MoneyGram*** SM agent with some ID, and collect the cash. If your passport has been lost or stolen, the sender can ask a test question for amounts under $900 as proof of identity – for instance, what is the name of your pet dog? You answer the question correctly and collect the cash.

If you are planning a lengthy trip and want to know that money will be waiting for you later in your journey, or even to receive money on a regular basis, you can ask someone at home to use the ***MoneyGram*** SM service to send money to you.

You can collect the cash from any ***MoneyGram*** SM location anywhere in the world, as long as you do so within 45 days of the money being sent.

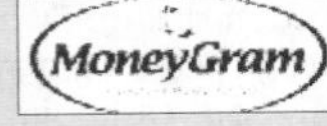

either. Your bank might boast that its cards can be used in ATMs around the world but you're not always likely to see one when you need it. The Directory gives an idea of ATM availability in each country. However, it is no use knowing you can use your card at banks in the capital if you are halfway up a mountain or staying on a remote island.

> **At the national airport in Laos my airline would not accept a credit card so I had to get a taxi into town to get a cash advance at a bank then another taxi back to buy a ticket. I should have carried more cash.**

I find one of the best ways to top up your money supply as you travel is to carry an American Express card which can be used at any of the company's offices around the world as security against a personal cheque. If you're a cardholder you can either buy travellers cheques or get cash simply by writing a cheque drawn on your current account. All you need to carry is your cheque book and the Amex card which works like a cheque guarantee card.

> **In Zimbabwe the banks went on strike for two days and the only way I could get around was by using US dollars cash. Fortunately, I was carrying lots of small notes.**

Another way of carrying money safely is Visa Travel Money. This looks just like a credit card. With a VTM card you can obtain local currency from ATMs. You buy a pre-set limit of money, which is electronically 'loaded' onto the card and is used up as you make withdrawals. Buying several cards spreads the risk of losing one. The remaining value can be replaced if your card is lost or stolen, and unused amounts are refundable.

Whatever cheques and plastic you carry, it's always important to carry some cash. US dollars in small denominations can be used just about anywhere in the world for tips, taxi fares or some purchases. In the 1980s, New Yorkers started carrying a 'mugger's twenty' – a $20 bill that they would hand over without a fuss if they were robbed in the street. Not a bad idea, but make sure first that your 'attacker' isn't simply an enthusiastic beggar.

• *Surviving the flight*

If a bunch of evil scientists were to design a machine to make travellers feel tired, ill, disorientated and bad-tempered when they arrive at their destination, then they couldn't do much better than come up with a modern commercial aircraft. Despite the obvious advantages of being able to jet around the world in a matter of a few hours, planes are not comfortable, relaxing or good for your health. Most people disembark after a long-haul flight feeling jet-lagged, dehydrated and aching all over.

There are reasons for this. In order to keep fares low, airlines cram in as many passengers as is legally possible. Seats are designed to be lightweight, not comfortable, and cabin air is dry and thin, with a low oxygen content - equivalent to being at 8000 ft. Cabin crews ply passengers with drink, even though the alcohol will combine with the thin air to make them dehydrated on arrival.

If you're flying for more than about eight hours, and crossing several time zones, you can expect to arrive feeling tired and spaced out. That's fine if you're going to be met by a taxi and whisked off to a five-star hotel, but not if you're on your own in a strange city, trying to find your way around and get somewhere to stay.

Here's how to survive a long-haul flight. Take some exercise before boarding, even if that means walking up and down the terminal building. Take warm clothes and a large bottle of mineral water (not sparkling, which expands in your stomach giving you indigestion). When you board set your watch to the time at your destination – this helps beat jet lag by warning your body clock about the changing time zones. Drink lots of water but eat lightly, avoiding coffee, chocolate, red wine and cheese, and try to abstain from all alcohol as this will dehydrate you. Take ear plugs and eye shades to help you sleep. Use moisturiser to stop your skin drying out.

If you experience any aches and pains during the flight, or your legs start to tingle, get up and walk about. If you feel breathless or unwell ask for a canister of oxygen which will alleviate most in-flight ills and has to be carried on all

commercial aircraft under international aviation law. Above all, remember that you're a paying customer and deserve the best available treatment, however surly and superior the cabin crew might appear.

• *How airports work*

As soon as the wheels of your plane hit the tarmac you need to be on your guard. First, you'll have to deal with the inevitable confusion and bureaucracy in the airport itself. Don't worry. At all airports, wherever they are, the procedure is essentially the same – first you go through immigration, where you'll need to show your passport and visa, then into the baggage hall to collect your checked luggage, then out through the customs hall where your bag may be searched for illegal contraband.

As a general rule, the bigger the airport the longer all this takes. Countries with strict immigration policies such as the US, the UK and Australia often have the longest queues at immigration for foreign passports holders. Developing countries with a reputation for being inefficient or bureaucratic can be even worse. Ask for a seat near the exit of the aircraft so you can be one of the first passengers off and get straight to the front of the queue.

At the immigration desk you may be asked questions about how long you intend to stay and how much money you're carrying. Often, what they really want to know is whether you plan to work illegally. Be honest about the time you plan to stay, because if you say two weeks instead of two months you may only get a two-week permit stamped into your passport.

Be prepared to prove you have 'sufficient funds' – traveller's cheques and a credit card usually do the trick. You may also need to show an onward or return ticket to satisfy the authorities that you don't intend to stay indefinitely. It always helps to be polite and to dress smartly when dealing with immigration officials. This is serious stuff – if they're not satisfied with your story they can put you on the next flight back home, regardless of whether or not you have a visa.

You may be given an immigration form, which you should fill in before you get to the desk. If it asks you to state where you plan to stay, and you don't have a reservation, copy the name of a hotel from your guidebook. If you have the name and address of a local person, even if it's just a penpal or a friend of your family, that may help. Some immigration forms contain seemingly ridiculous questions, such as your mother's maiden name. Whatever you decide to write, don't leave any blanks.

"I bought a one-way ticket from London to Guatemala City but when I turned up at check-in the airline said I needed a return. I had to sign a form saying I would be liable for repatriation costs if I was turned away on arrival. I got away with it, but next time I'd buy a return ticket."

The next challenge is finding the bag you checked in. Luggage has a mysterious habit of disappearing at airports. Occasionally it's stolen but far more often it's lost or sent to another airport with a similar identification code. It isn't unknown for a bag marked TYO (the code for Tokyo) to land up in Toronto (YTO).

If your bag doesn't appear on the carousel don't go directly through customs but report it lost at the baggage handlers desk in the baggage hall. It's a good idea to carry a photo of your pack and to make sure it's clearly labelled both inside and out. Again, don't panic. From the laid-back attitude of the handlers you'll have guessed that luggage is lost dozens of times each day.

Your bag will probably turn up the next day and the handlers will deliver it to your hotel if you give them the address – check first to confirm this. If you don't know where you'll be staying pick a hotel from your guidebook and try to get a room there. Otherwise, phone later with the address. If your bag hasn't turned up after 24 hours check your insurance documents because you may have to report it lost to the police. Because luggage goes astray so often, experienced travellers always carry their valuables, guidebooks and a change of clothes in their carry-on luggage. Better still, travel light and take only hand luggage. The total dimensions of a piece of hand luggage (height times width times depth) is 45 inches. This is no guarantee, but in practice you can get away with more.

> **If your bag doesn't turn up after 24 hours the airline may give you cash to buy replacement clothes and toiletries.**

The last stage before leaving the airport is customs, which is usually a formality. Most customs officers are looking for large quantities of drugs but on a slow day they may decide to hassle you, particularly if you look like a likely candidate for a shakedown. So it's best not to carry several dozen packets of cigarette papers, or wear a 'Legalise Cannabis' T-shirt.

• *Taxi drivers, touts and other pond life*

Because all sorts of touts, pickpockets and social misfits hang around airports you need to keep on your toes as you go through customs. In my experience, you're at more risk of being fleeced in your first hour in a country than at any other time. Another good reason not to drink all that free booze on the plane.

Hit the ground running

If possible, change money inside the airport. You'll usually find branches of the main foreign exchange companies and banks, which will have good rates, long opening hours and – because they're not used by local people – short queues. It may even be possible to change money before you go through customs, which can save a bit more time. Insist on being given your cash in small-denomination notes, plus a few coins for phones and tips. Keep the receipt and count the money meticulously before you leave the counter because it's not completely unknown for bank tellers at airports to take their own unofficial 'commission'.

> **At Budapest airport I went to one of the banks and changed $500 into local money. When I counted the cash I found I was short-changed. I told the bank clerk and he just shrugged and gave me another note. He obviously knew what he'd done.**

Before leaving the airport building, hide most of your cash in your money belt, leaving enough in your front pocket for bus or taxi fares, drinks, tips and so on. You should already have consulted your guidebook about the best way to get into town. If there is no airport bus you may be able to buy a prepaid taxi voucher at the airport which will save a lot of hassle arguing over a fare. If your plane arrives in the evening or at night it's always worth reserving a hotel room, at least for one night. You may be able to do this, too, in the airport building, although the agent may take a hefty commission.

Most travellers have a horror story about a dodgy taxi driver, particularly those that pick up fares at airports. Some of the cruellest scams are operated at Delhi, where a large number of international flights arrive in the early hours of the morning. Taxi drivers frequently tell new arrivals elaborate lies about riots breaking out across the city, roadblocks going up and shots being fired in the street. They'll offer to take you instead to Agra, the next stop on most travellers' itinerary and some 130 miles away. Some taxi drivers will even tell you the hotel where you have a reservation has just burned down. Of course, he knows another hotel that has vacancies (and will pay him a handsome bribe if he delivers you there). Needless to say, don't listen to a word of it.

> If I'm arriving by air I always ask a local person on the plane how much the taxi fare should be into town. If you get chatting to other travellers you can usually agree to share a cab.

Always try to agree the fare with a taxi driver before setting off. If the cab has a meter, check that it's switched on and working properly, but also ask for an approximate fare. If, when you arrive, the driver demands a lot more, keep calm, stick to your guns and argue your case. Follow your instincts. In some situations you may simply have to hand over the 'correct' fare and walk away, ignoring his protestations. Don't do a runner – if you're in the right tell him where you're staying and say you don't mind if he calls the police (he won't). This is one reason why you should carry plenty of small notes. It's amazing how many taxi drivers around the world apparently carry no change whatsoever.

I always insist on keeping my pack beside me on the back seat of a taxi. I know it's safe there and I won't be charged any mysterious bag supplement. In some parts of the world where theft is rife, such as South America, you should not get out of a taxi leaving your pack inside. Some travellers have lost all their possessions when they have climbed out and paid the fare and the driver has simply sped away with their bags on the back seat.

On the other hand, there is no need to be rude or aggressive towards taxi drivers, or get stressed out arguing over the equivalent of a few pennies. You would not get into a screaming argument with a cabbie at home so don't do so just because you're abroad. Most taxi drivers are poorly paid and they resort to tricks only out of desperation. If you chat to them and treat them with respect you'll find they can be useful sources of information. Just remember that their advice on where to stay (or where to shop) may not be impartial, and don't tell them too many personal details about yourself. If you're a single woman, for instance, you might want to say you're meeting your husband at the hotel.

> **At some airports if you arrive at night there are no buses or taxis and you have to sleep in the airport. I always try to time the flight so I arrive in daylight.**

• *Arriving by train or bus*

Unlike airports, which are usually a long way from the centre of town, train and bus stations tend to be located slap bang in the middle, often in the seediest and most threatening areas. Here, especially, you need to keep a lookout for shady characters, pickpockets and dishonest or unlicensed taxi drivers.

Try not to wander off your train or bus at night with no idea of what to do or where to go next. If you walk around the station looking lost, you may be marking yourself out as a potential victim. Equally, if you start walking down the first street you see with no idea where you are headed, you may find yourself in the middle of a nasty red-light district. Think of the area around King's Cross in London and you'll get the picture.

> **I was waiting on a train at Budapest Keleti station when a man started knocking on the window and beckoned me over. At first I ignored him, but as he persisted I opened the window to see what the problem was. I didn't hear his accomplice open the compartment door and take my bag.**

Forewarned is forearmed. Study your guidebook before you get there, know exactly where you are, have a plan and stick to it. Try to arrive before dusk so you can feel alert, have your wits about you, and stay sober. Save the celebrations until you've found somewhere safe and comfortable to stay.

A shock to the system

It might sound odd to say that going abroad can be a shocking experience. We've all seen so many movies and TV documentaries during our lifetimes that the world seems such a familiar place. And if you've spent any time in a fast modern city like London, New York or Paris you probably think you've seen it all – drugs, poverty, crime, homelessness. You might even consider yourself unshockable.

But stepping into a foreign culture – particularly a developing country with its many different social problems – can still be a disturbing experience. The noises, the smells, the heat and humidity, the constant attention of beggars and touts can all add to a general sense of bewilderment and frustration, particularly when you don't understand the language.

The symptoms of culture shock are not easy to pin down and they don't always come on straight away. Most travellers feel on a high when they first arrive in a foreign country and it's only a few days or weeks later that they start to get worn down by a combination of the heat and the hassle. If you find yourself becoming impatient and stressed out, losing your temper with people and feeling tired and even a little homesick, you may have just caught a mild dose of culture shock.

Try to recognise the symptoms in yourself. Don't be ashamed of them and don't try simply to tough them out. These feelings are perfectly normal and not a sign of weakness. Coming to terms with them is one of the challenges of travelling. Unlike two-week holidaymakers, who might content themselves with a five-star hotel, a pool and a few palm trees, you're having to deal with total immersion into an alien culture. Look at it this way – if you don't experience some form of culture shock you ain't doing it properly.

The trick is to adapt, not to meet difficulties head on. Try not to judge everything you see by your own values and upbringing. Understand that people aren't trying to make your life unpleasant, that's just the way things happen. In some countries – such as India, China and Morocco – the cultural differences are particularly intense and you'll need to try even harder

to go with the flow. But many people agree that these are the countries where the thrill of travel is at its most potent, where those with open minds can learn humility, understanding and empathy with other people. Travel will broaden your mind – if you let it.

One of the best ways of coping with culture shock is to take a short holiday within your trip. Laze around beside a beach with a good book or splash out a bit of money and stay in a nice hotel. Treat yourself to a burger and a movie. Don't feel guilty about not being a 'real traveller' – whatever that means. After a few days you'll probably find your batteries have been recharged.

If you're visiting a series of countries, you could try starting your trip in a country where English is widely spoken, such as the United States, Australia or South Africa.

You are at your most vulnerable when you arrive in a new place and are tired and disorientated. Keep your wits about you. Try to look alert and confident so that you can be in control of any situation.

Most people who buy round-the-world tickets in London start by flying into Delhi or Bombay and finish their trip in New York when, in fact, it would make much more sense to do it the other way round.

> **In my first few days in Asia I rushed around trying to see everything and wore myself out until I got sick. After that I learned to take it easy, to have a siesta after lunch and just visit the sights that interested me.**

If you are travelling to a hot country you may find yourself frustrated at how long it takes people to perform simple tasks, like changing a travellers cheque or fetching a round of drinks. The reason, of course, is that local people have learned to adapt to the heat, conserving their energy and allowing more time for things to happen. Try to relax and do the same. Avoid setting yourself too many tasks or sightseeing trips, and confine your activities to the cooler times of the day. Try getting up early, taking a nap in the middle of the day and doing chores and shopping trips in the early morning or evening.

• *Language*

In most countries with a significant tourist industry you'll be able to get by speaking English, particularly in hotels, bars and taxis. There are exceptions. Travelling in Latin America is extremely difficult if you don't speak some Spanish (or Portuguese in Brazil), and in some parts of West Africa you won't get by without French. In China only a few young people in the bigger cities speak English and many of these may be reluctant to talk to you in case they 'lose face' by pronouncing words wrongly. This is also true in Japan, where young people can often read English but have poor conversational ability.

But even in countries where English is widely spoken it's worth learning at least a few words of the local language. Making an effort is always appreciated and will help you break down barriers, showing that you're interested in people and not stuffy or arrogant.

> **In a small town in Vietnam I met a man who spoke excellent English, which he had learned from listening to the BBC World Service. He invited me to visit the local school where he taught, which turned out to be one of my most amazing experiences in the country.**

If you learn to count in the local language you might find you can avoid paying 'tourist' prices for everything. But more importantly, speaking the language will allow you to communicate with ordinary people rather than just those who work in the tourist industry – like shopkeepers, waiters and taxi drivers – many of whom are understandably cynical or too busy to chat.

Even in obscure parts of the world where English isn't widely spoken, you'll often come across individuals who speak it, many of whom have remarkable stories to tell. Some may introduce themselves if you look like you have a sympathetic ear but others may be happy to sit around and eavesdrop on your conversation. For this reason you should be careful what you say in public. You're bound to get frustrated at times – at the transport system, or the bureaucracy, or the beggars – but when this happens try to vent your feelings in private, not within earshot of local people who may find your remarks deeply offensive. Even if you whisper, your body language may betray your feelings.

You should also be wary about discussing politics in public places, particularly in countries with oppressive governments, such as Burma and Nigeria. It might be fascinating talking to ordinary people about their hopes and fears, but they may be putting themselves at risk by doing so. If you're interested in the politics of these countries – and every tourist should be, in my opinion – then read books and newspapers and try to talk to local journalists and political activists, who will be a lot better informed than people you meet in shops or bars.

How to go with the flow

Understanding a new culture means getting to grips with social convention, manners and body language. It is as much about understanding ourselves as it is about understanding others. For instance, in the West we have a heightened sense of 'personal space' and tend to dislike anybody intruding on it (according to psychologists, our exclusion zone extends to about 18 inches). But in many parts of the world no such laws apply. Touching a stranger's arm or tugging on his shirt may be quite acceptable, and this can take a bit of getting used to.

There are no hard and fast rules, except to learn what's socially acceptable by watching local people. Be aware of the subtle differences in body language, how in India a tilt of the head may signal agreement, or how in Japan you should bow your head when introduced to a stranger. In many parts of the world it may be considered rude for a man to refuse a handshake, but ill advised for a woman to accept one. Kissing in public may be frowned on and nudity on beaches may be illegal.

Be prepared for poor timekeeping, particularly in countries with hot

‘Six hours before I was due to catch an internal flight in India I realised I had no cash. I left the hotel and found a rickshaw driver who said he'd take me to a bank. He couldn't find one. It took an hour to find a bank 300 yards from the hotel. The bank didn't have enough money to give me more than $30 worth of rupees.

I found another bank but that had no credit card facilities, so I had to go to the main branch where they said it would be no problem. After an hour of waiting I asked what was the problem. They said there was no problem. After another hour I asked again and they admitted that the telex machine was broken. (Remember telex?) They said they couldn't confirm my card transaction without the telex. When it was finally fixed they gave my cash to another customer.

Eventually, I got my money and arrived at the airport ten minutes before the flight left. The whole episode had taken six hours.’

climates. Don't get upset if you arrange to meet somebody at a certain time and they're half an hour late. Not everybody in the world wears a watch. Equally, don't rely on transport connections to be bang on time. Most local people won't find this worrying and there's no point in you doing so – try to enjoy the fact that for once your life isn't ruled by the clock.

If you've been brought up in the West you may be shocked at how, in many parts of the world, women seem to be treated as second-class citizens. Women may be excluded from social situations or required to cover their hair in public. Some Hindu temples have signs outside them saying menstruating women are not allowed to enter. These rules and traditions are often the result of thousands of years of complex cultural development and religious belief. Even if they appear to us to be archaic and unfair they should be respected. Certainly, they won't be changed simply because they inconvenience you.

If you're a woman travelling alone you may find that, in order to fend off lecherous men, you have to go out of your way to appear modest and demure. It can also help if you tell a few white lies. Try wearing a ring on your wedding finger and carrying a photo of an imaginary husband. If you're travelling with a man – even just a friend – your life will be made a lot easier if you tell local people you're a married couple. You might consider adopting local dress, but first take sound advice about what is appropriate. You may be sending out the wrong messages by wearing something colourful that actually makes you look like a prostitute in the eyes of local people, or something with religious connotations that you don't fully understand. Some locals may find your attempts to 'go native' condescending or even insulting.

> **In some countries men assume foreign women are loose and available. Since learning this the hard way, I never wear make-up and I dress in a long skirt, long-sleeved shirt and headscarf.**

One of the great lessons to be learned in Asia is the art of avoiding confrontation. In the West we tend to admire people who speak their minds and say what they think. In many parts of the world, particularly in Asia, this is

considered unsophisticated and embarrassing behaviour. To get into a heated argument is undignified and can amount to a loss of face. Losing your temper is seen as a sign of weakness rather than strength. This method of dealing with problems by avoiding confrontation is sometimes called 'the Asian way'. It can be frustrating if all you want is a straight answer to a question, but it can be a revelation, a new way of thinking and behaving that many travellers take home with them and benefit from for the rest of their lives.

Another unexpected delight of foreign travel is experiencing the hospitality and generosity of local people. If you're friendly to others you'll frequently find yourself being asked inside their homes and offered meals, drinks and presents. It may be considered rude to refuse such offers – but be wary. You may need to think on your feet: for instance, is the glass of water you have been given safe to drink? If not, just sip at it politely without swallowing it.

> **Even the poorest people in the Third World are very proud and the fact they let you into their homes is a sign of friendship, not of their acceptance of poverty. Smile, say hello in the local language and leave your camera behind.**

When accepting hospitality, you may feel you want to give something in return. To offer money might be considered offensive so it's worth having a few suitable gifts up your sleeve. There is no need to hand over your Walkman or your Oakley sunglasses, perhaps just a postcard or a souvenir from your home town, or a photograph of your family. Rather than selling your used paperbacks to other travellers, give them to local people who are learning English, or to a school.

If you travel with a camera you'll almost certainly want to take photos of people, whether they're friends you've made or simply ordinary men and women you see in the street. Some travellers might tell you this is intrusive and patronising but I find that most people – particularly children – enjoy having their picture taken and are flattered by your interest. Of course, that's no excuse for behaving like a member of the paparazzi and sneaking up on people with flashguns blazing. *Always* ask permission first and don't try to stage-manage the shot, but allow people to pose in a way that pleases them (think how you would feel if a tourist snatched a photo of you in your home town).

> **I found people in Asia love having their picture taken so long as they have time to compose themselves. They can be embarrassed or angry if taken by surprise.**

Many people you photograph in developing countries will ask you to send them a copy of the picture. You'd be amazed how much it means to some people, so don't promise to do so unless you intend to.

• *Politics, culture and religion*

A few years ago a young British backpacker went missing in the popular tourist town of Kanchanaburi in Thailand. Within a few days the 23-year-old law graduate was found dead, the victim of an apparently random and motiveless murder. The news left travellers stunned and many parents of young backpackers were thrown into a panic at the thought that their children might be on their way to a similar fate. What seemed even more strange was that the killer, who later confessed to the police, was a young Buddhist monk who had made friends with the victim just hours before killing her. If you could not trust a monk in a country famed for its gentle and friendly people, then who could you trust?

This story is not repeated here to create a scare, but to illustrate the danger of making assumptions based on our own cultural backgrounds. In this case the victim may have trusted her killer because he was a monk, the ultimate symbol in the West of peace and abstinence. In Thailand, too, most monks are harmless, but not all of them are. Some young Thai men join a religious order because they have criminal convictions or a history of drug addiction and can't get a regular job. What the victim didn't know was that her killer was an active heroin addict.

Reading newspapers and books both before you leave and while you're away will help you to understand the endlessly fascinating culture that surrounds you. It will also make you aware of your own 'cultural baggage', the collection of assumptions and prejudices that interpret the things you see and guide the way you think and make decisions.

In Buddhist countries you should not point with your feet or touch somebody's head, not even a small child's, because the head is considered sacred and feet unclean.

We all carry cultural baggage, whether we like it or not. One of the best ways of illustrating this is to ask visitors from abroad their impressions of your own country. Many visitors to Britain, for instance, see people spilling out of pubs and conclude that we're a nation of drunkards. The inability of most British people to speak foreign languages makes us seem rude and arrogant, and our reluctance to touch each other in public can make us seem cold and unfriendly. But it's all relative: Italians find us stuffy, yet Japanese complain that we're too informal.

In Thailand it is illegal to climb on a Buddha image. One traveller took photographs of himself on a big statue and was arrested when he went to collect the film from the chemist in Chiang Mai.

Once you recognise your own cultural baggage you can start trying to shed it, or at least work around it. For instance, in the West we tend not to take religion very seriously, thinking that those people who live by their religious beliefs are a little odd. In fact, we are the odd ones because in most countries around the world religion is taken very seriously indeed. So, if you visit a temple and are asked to remove your shoes you should do so. And if a devout Muslim politely declines your offer of a beer he will not appreciate you trying to twist his arm.

> Always accept an offer of tea or coffee in the Middle East, even at a bank or travel agency. People are very persistent and saying no will just seem rude.

Similarly, in many parts of the world people have a greater respect for royalty and politicians than we do. People in Thailand, for instance, will be deeply offended if you insult their royal family and extremely puzzled if you rubbish your own. In some countries, tearing up banknotes or stepping on the national flag are criminal offences. This may seem extreme, but many people around the world have fought and died for democracy and political independence and, unlike us, they don't take it for granted.

• *Being streetwise*

We all like to think we're streetwise – knowing our way about, recognising the danger signs and being able to look cool and confident. As we go through life we develop a sixth sense that works a bit like radar, a funny feeling we get when we know things aren't right. If we're smart we learn to trust this sixth sense. It can steer us out of trouble.

But when we travel abroad we enter a new world where all the little signals and nuances in people's behaviour are slightly different. We may be watchful and cautious but we no longer have our instincts because we don't understand what we should be looking for. We might think we're pretty clever, and we might even think we're pretty tough, but we're no longer streetwise.

> If you agree to meet people do it in a public place. Be wary of going to someone's house. If you must, let someone else know exactly where you are going or take a friend.

Once you realise that you're vulnerable simply because you're in an alien environment you're halfway to being safe. Arrogance and aggression will get you into trouble, not fend it off. In Britain, a survey showed that men are twice as likely as women to be the victims of random street violence.

Some tourists – out of arrogance or stupidity – take risks abroad that they would never consider taking at home, such as wandering around city streets at night or going back to a stranger's house. Obviously, this is pretty daft. Once you've spent a bit of time in a country you'll start to develop a new sixth sense as you subconsciously recognise the danger signals. Until then, it's worth reading newspapers and talking to other travellers, expats and local people and asking advice about where it's safe to go at night, and so on.

• *Haggling and tipping*

In some cultures haggling for goods and services is a way of life. Arguing over prices and playing games of bluff and counter-bluff can be fun at first, particularly if you're buying an interesting souvenir and you enter into the spirit of the deal, taking your time and perhaps sitting down for a cup of tea with a friendly shopkeeper. After a while, however, it can be downright boring. It's one thing haggling over a carpet, but quite another thing arguing over the price of a bottle of water when you're tired and thirsty. Most people find themselves at one time during their travels reduced to a gibbering wreck and screaming: 'Just tell me the right price!'

Local people tend not to understand this reaction. To them, haggling is an enjoyable social experience and fixed prices represent a rip-off. In some countries there are no such things as fixed prices, so it's pointless wandering around a shop demanding to know the price of everything as if you were in your local supermarket. The price is simply the lowest figure the seller will accept or the highest the buyer is prepared to pay.

Don't haggle for something you don't really want because if the seller accepts your offer you may find it very awkward explaining that you've been wasting his or her time. Be firm but calm and keep smiling throughout. Don't feel guilty about paying too little for something – no trader will sell it to you unless he's making a profit, despite what he tells you about his five hungry children.

Don't get obsessive about trying to shave a few pennies off the price of everything. But do take advantage of the laws of supply and demand. If, for instance, you arrive at a hotel that is clearly empty ask for a discount on the price of a room. Even in the West hoteliers will always drop their prices when business is slack.

Tipping can be another area of difficulty. Budget travellers are rarely obliged to tip and some never do because they're obsessed with saving money the whole time. I think this is pretty miserable and I would recommend you get in the habit of leaving small tips at hotels and restaurants. There is usually no need to tip taxi drivers or people running their own businesses, but employees such as waiters and room cleaners are often very poorly paid and will really appreciate your small change.

The purpose of tipping varies around the world. In America, in bars, hotels and restaurants, a tip is considered part of the bill and is almost obligatory. If you leave nothing you can often expect loud sarcastic comments and very poor service if you dare to come back. In Britain and other European countries a tip is thought of as a reward for good service, an opportunity for the customer to feel a bit generous.

But in developing countries a tip – sometimes called baksheesh – is a guarantee that something will be done. It should be given before the event, rather than after. So, when you arrive at a hotel give the room boy a small tip (it may be just a few coins) and you'll find that the service improves by several hundred per cent. A lightbulb is broken in your room? It will be fixed right away. You want a beer after the bar has closed? No problem. Think of tips as small investments that will make your life a lot easier.

• *Dealing with beggars*

There are no hard and fast rules on whether you should give money to beggars. It comes down to a matter of personal choice. But when you come across a beggar it's best to decide immediately whether or not you want to give something because dithering is uncomfortable for both of you and may mean you get hassled even more.

There is usually a clear distinction to be made between the genuinely impoverished – such as widows or disabled people – who rely on the charity of local people, and the opportunistic beggars who seem to target foreigners.

> **Be firm in telling people to go away and ignore all sob stories, but don't be rude as often it is just over-friendliness that makes people so irritating.**

The sight of children begging may have you reaching into your pocket but bear in mind that some of them are controlled by adults and may supplement their income with a bit of pickpocketing on the side. Children in developing countries may be only opportunistic beggars and your 'generous' gift of sweets, pens or coins may be keeping them away from school and undermining their relationship with their parents. If you want to give real help to street children, a donation to an orphanage or homeless charity will be more helpful. Still, there are plenty of travellers who construct all sorts of clever arguments to explain why they should not give to beggars, when very often it's simply because they're too mean or jaded. At the end of the day, we all have to eat.

Not everybody who pesters you will be asking for money. Some will be touts or guides trying to earn a living and others will just be curious to talk to you. Try to get in the habit of being patient and polite. By losing your temper you'll look ridiculous and make your own life more stressful. Remember the essential difference between you and them is that you're there by choice, they by necessity. If you get fed up you can always go home.

• *Where to sleep*

Many first-time travellers dream of sleeping on tropical beaches. It sounds idyllic – turn up at a beautiful stretch of deserted sand, sling a hammock between two trees and doze under the stars. Unfortunately, the reality is rather less appealing. People who have camped out on beaches will tell you horror stories of being robbed, sexually assaulted or arrested in the middle of the night.

If you sleep on a beach you have no protection against thieves, insects or dangerous animals. You'll get drenched if it rains, there will be nowhere to shower and nowhere to leave your backpack during the day. I did it once and woke up at 5am covered in mosquito bites. Never again.

> **My boyfriend and I arrived at St Raphael in the South of France at 10pm. We slept on a secluded part of the beach and I woke at 4am to find a man sexually assaulting me. Our sleeping bags had been burnt at the bottom where he had tried to get at our money. It was a bad idea.**

Sleeping in a railway station or under a bridge – the traditional last resort of the penniless Inter-Railer – is an even worse idea. You might as well hang a sign around your neck inviting all the local criminals, drunks and weirdos to help themselves to your possessions. Think about it: would you sleep rough in your home town? Almost certainly not. If you arrive later in the day than anticipated and cannot find a room for the night, then find somewhere safe, like an all-night café, and stay awake for the night. You can look for somewhere to stay the next morning and catch up on your sleep later.

> **If sleeping in an open place don't put your valuables at the bottom of your sleeping bag. At Salzburg station I saw thieves slashing open sleeping bags with swords.**

You shouldn't ever need to sleep outdoors if you take a few sensible precautions. Firstly, think about what time of day you'll be arriving to look for a place to stay. The best time is mid-morning

when most hoteliers and hostel and guesthouse managers know which of their guests are going to check out that day. Even if the room isn't yet ready you can usually pay up front, leave your bags in a luggage room and wander off to have lunch, happy in the knowledge that you have somewhere to stay. If possible, don't arrive after dark when rooms in your price range may be full and you're left wandering the streets, an easy target for potential thieves.

Tourist Offices can help you find a place to stay, but will charge for booking accommodation. Most towns and cities have good, clean and cheap guesthouses, hotels and hostels to choose from. If there are two of you, take turns to search for rooms while the other waits with the bags at a café or in a busy square. Don't wait in bus and railway stations which always seem to attract dodgy characters. If there are three of you sharing, bear in mind that a hotel room may be no more expensive than a hostel.

It's usually much harder finding rooms at weekends and public holidays and at some popular places – such as Seville during Holy Week, Goa at Christmas, Ko Pha Ngan before a full-moon party – it may be well nigh impossible. Having said that, you'll almost always find somewhere to stay, particularly if you ask around.

If you arrive on an island by ferry – in Greece, Thailand or Indonesia, for instance – you'll often find a crowd of locals offering rooms. Don't barge them aside and stride disdainfully into town – they might be your only hope of finding somewhere to stay. Pick a respectable-looking individual, ask the price, the type of room they have, the distance from the beach and town (if they say 5 minutes, assume it's 10 or 15 minutes) and ask if they have any photos to show you. Once you agree to take the room you should not change your mind when you get there unless you feel you have been seriously misled.

> **It is not worth camping in Africa because rooms are cheap and the ground is often too hard to sleep on. Carrying around a tent, a sleeping bag and all the other gear was a complete nightmare.**

Assuming you have a choice of places to stay, there are several factors to consider. Location is important, so is comfort, but top of your list should be security. Check that doors and windows can be locked from the inside and that there are no mysterious connecting doors. Take your own combination padlock which you'll be able to use when you're out to secure the door from the outside, or to lash your backpack to something solid like a water pipe or bedstead. If you have two padlocks you can do both. If there is a safe at reception, use it. If not, you could tape your valuables to the back of a drawer. At night, if you can't bolt the door from the inside, prop a chair under the handle or balance something behind the door that will wake you up if it's disturbed. Better still, use a rubber wedge under the door. And sleep with your money belt under your pillow.

If you are staying in a hostel you need to take extra precautions. Although sleeping in a dormitory can be fun, and a good way to meet new friends, there is a greater risk of being robbed, particularly by down-at-heel travellers who have run out of money and see you as a likely target. Keep your valuables hidden away, don't flaunt large amounts of cash or travellers cheques and use zip locks on your luggage. If you are given a locker, secure it with your own padlock – at least nobody else in the hostel will have a spare key.

You may decide you want to camp, either to save money or to enjoy the countryside. If so, find an official campsite with security guards, showers and maybe even secure lockers. You are particularly vulnerable in a tent, so think carefully and take advice before pitching up in a deserted spot. You will be safer if you are surrounded by other campers.

Don't assume if you're offered a room with air-conditioning that it will be better than one with a simple ceiling fan. Some air-conditioning units make an unbearable noise and many people wake up in the morning with a sore throat or a cold. This is because nasty infectious microbes tend to lurk in the extractor ducts if they're not serviced properly.

If mosquitoes are a problem, particularly in malarial areas, make sure the room has grilles on the windows or a mosquito net. Check the grilles and nets for tiny holes and ask for another room if you don't like what you see. Burn mosquito coils at night and don't leave lights on in the room once it starts to get dark because these will attract insects. (Mosquitoes are also attracted by the smell of perfume and soap, so one drastic way of keeping them at bay is to forget about washing for a few days. That, at least, is my excuse.)

• *Public Transport*

If you find yourself tempted by the idea of hitch-hiking, consider for a moment the true story of Max Hunter and his girlfriend Charlotte Gibb, both students at Durham University. They were taking a six-week summer break in Israel and hitched from the Red Sea resort of Eilat to Jerusalem. Charlotte had already spent several months in Israel, working in a kibbutz, and felt safe there. The man who stopped to give them a ride was middle-aged and looked perfectly respectable. Nobody could have predicted what would happen next.

Twenty miles into their journey the driver stopped the car for a cigarette break. Then, without a word, he drew a gun and started shooting at his two passengers. Max, 22, was killed instantly. Charlotte, 20, was shot in the face, arm and hand and left for dead. She was found an hour later and rushed to hospital where surgeons managed to save her life.

Such incidents happen only rarely, and Israel remains a relatively safe country, but there is a lesson here about hitch-hiking. It's simple: don't do it. What was once a safe and fun way of travelling is now, sadly, a kind of Russian Roulette. There is simply no way of knowing whether you're getting into a car with a friendly local or a crazed psychopath. In America, drivers are so paranoid about being robbed by hitchers that most sensible people never give rides. Anybody who does stop for you is immediately suspect.

> **I found hitch-hiking in America difficult. People regarded us as strange and some warned us of the kind of people who might pick us up.**

Trains are just about the safest and most comfortable way of getting about, although they're not always the fastest and you may have to book seats in advance. The view from a train is almost always better than the view from a bus – who would choose to breathe fumes while being thrown about on potholed roads when you could be gliding through open countryside in a comfortable carriage?

> **At the end of my six months in Asia I had the option of flying from Calcutta to Bombay but I took a train instead. It took 36 hours but it was an amazing experience and gave me a very real sense of the sheer size of India.**

Trains also tend to be good places to meet local people, particularly on long journeys which can take days rather than hours. Overnight sleepers provide a useful alternative to spending out on hotels, although on some routes you'll have to take precautions against robbery. Lock up your pack and chain it to your seat and keep all valuables in your money belt, worn under your clothes.

In Eastern Europe, take thick metal wire to secure the door of your compartment from the inside. In Russia, particularly on the line between Moscow and St Petersburg, thefts at night are commonplace and many passengers have been knocked out with chloroform before being robbed. If you feel uneasy, sleep in shifts making sure at least one person in the compartment is awake at any one time. Top bunks tend to be safer than bottom bunks.

> **If you need to go to the toilet on a train take your valuables with you. Lock your rucksack to the luggage rack before settling down to sleep.**

Rail networks don't cover every corner of the globe so sooner or later you'll find yourself using buses. These tend to be cheaper than trains and are often more convenient because in most towns the bus station is situated close to the cheapest accommodation. On the down side, buses are often uncomfortable and sometimes dangerous. Overcrowded buses driven at high speed on unmarked roads are a common sight in developing countries.

Night buses are even more of a risk because they often travel extremely fast on unlit roads and the driver may be drunk or too tired to notice obstacles such as abandoned vehicles, bicycles or cattle. Try to avoid sitting near the back of a bus where the ride can be very bumpy – the most comfortable section is midway between the two axles – and stay well away from 'video buses' which ply long-distance routes all across the undeveloped world, keeping their passengers awake for hours on end with endless badly-dubbed B-movies played at top volume.

Another reason to avoid overnight buses is the fact that some crews take the opportunity to rifle through your luggage. The most notorious scam of this type is the 'luxury' tourist coach between Bangkok and Chiang Mai in Thailand, which has a spacious baggage compartment accessible from a trapdoor close to the driver. During the night the bus boy may go down below with a torch and work his way through every bag – picking locks if necessary – looking for valuables. He then neatly repacks the bags so that his victims only discover something is missing when they arrive at their hotel the following evening.

Occasionally, you may decide to take a domestic flight to save time or to avoid retracing your steps. In some countries flying is comparatively cheap but the safety record of domestic airlines may be dire, especially in countries such as China, Burma, India, Vietnam and parts of the former Soviet Union. Check the FCO website (see p. 96) for advice on using domestic airlines.

Ferries can also be dangerous, particularly in developing countries where they're often overcrowded and ill-equipped to deal with storms. The most notorious country for ferry disasters is the Philippines. One August recently – bang in the middle of the typhoon season – 16 tourists died when a sightseeing boat capsized in Manila Bay, and dozens more drowned when a ferry sank in the Visayan Sea. That was just in one day. If you must go island hopping during the monsoon, take flights.

There is one form of transport that, in my view, is simply too dangerous to contemplate, and that is motorcycling. Renting a scooter or a bike is one of the most risky things you can do abroad, particularly if you're not an experienced rider. In many countries it's so easy to rent a bike that you won't even need to show a licence or wear a helmet. Sounds great, but chances are the bike will be in a terrible state of disrepair, the roads will be atrocious and truck drivers will use you for target practice. You may not even be covered on your insurance policy. Please – don't do it. Be careful about getting on the back of a motorcycle taxi with a heavy rucksack, because the weight can topple both you and the driver over. If you're still not convinced, pay a visit to a nearby hospital and check out the conditions in the casualty ward.

• *Finding your way around*

In big cities the key is to look like you know where you're going. Try to memorise your route rather than standing around on a busy street corner grappling with a map. Be confident and walk with purpose. Use a pocket compass, which will at least let you know if you're heading in the right direction. If you do get lost, go into a shop or a café where you can study your map or ask somebody. A good trick in European cities is to carry a local newspaper under your arm so that people will assume you're a local.

> **I found in Egypt that when I asked some people for directions they would start following me. I soon learned to ask people who were working in shops because they wouldn't be able to leave their posts.**

In some parts of the world you'll need to think about how to phrase questions. Local people may be so anxious to help you that they are reluctant to admit their ignorance (it's not because they're stupid – do you know where all the cheap hotels are in your home town?)

If you point down a street and ask somebody: 'Is this the way to the Hotel Fleapit?' they may answer yes even if they haven't got a clue. Instead, you should rephrase your question and simply ask: 'Where is the Hotel Fleapit?' If they know, they'll tell you. If not, ask somebody else. In developing countries it's often useless showing maps and guidebooks to local people. They may not be able to read English – and may not even have seen a map before – but they will happily pass a little time idly thumbing through your guidebook trying to look knowledgeable.

When you eventually find the Hotel Fleapit and get a room, ask the receptionist to give you a business card or write down the address for you. This is particularly important if the local language is in a different script – Arabic, Thai or Chinese, for instance. Keep this piece of paper with you at all times. If you get in trouble you can always jump in a taxi and show it to the driver.

> **In Mexico City I showed the taxi driver a map in my guide book. After saying 'Si' he headed off in the wrong direction and we spent two hours going round in circles until we found a local woman who translated for him.**

In cities you should stick to well-lit roads but in the countryside or beside beaches that isn't always possible. Paths and tracks may be pitch black. It's sensible to carry a torch with you, but try not to use it. Instead, concentrate on developing your night vision. Even when there seems to be no light at all, after a few minutes you'll find you can see enough to get by. It may feel eerie but you'll be a lot less vulnerable than if you advertise your presence with a torch.

• *Food and drink*

Most travellers worry about getting sick from eating infected food. That can happen but you're just as likely to fall ill because you're not eating enough or not drinking enough water. In hot weather you need to drink up to three litres of water a day just to replenish the fluid that your body loses naturally. When you sweat you also lose essential saline so you should add extra salt to your food.

Dehydration can be a nasty experience leading to headaches, muscle cramps, lethargy and nausea. The first signs that you're not drinking enough fluids are mild headaches and a darkening of your urine. If you pick up a stomach bug and suffer from diarrhoea it's particularly important to keep replacing lost fluid. Drink bottled water or flat Coke (for the sugar content). Live yoghurt – known as curd in India – is a proven defence against Delhi Belly. Some people chew cloves of raw garlic which they say prevents diarrhoea although the inevitable smell can make them unpopular roommates.

If you're in a hot and humid climate, you'll probably drink plenty of water because you'll notice that you're sweating profusely, but in somewhere hot and dry such as North Africa or the Australian Outback you won't realise how much fluid you're losing because your sweat will evaporate as soon as it reaches your skin. If a strong wind is blowing you may feel comfortably cool even as your bodily fluid dips to dangerously low levels. In these conditions you need to drink about six litres of water per day. You'll also find that alcohol has a more noticeable affect on you, so drink only in moderation and try to alternate beers with bottles of water.

Don't drink tap water unless you're sure it's safe (check the Directory for guidance) and don't assume that a flask of water left in your room has been boiled or sterilised. If you do attempt to boil water you'll need to do so for 20 minutes. You're much better off with bottled water, which can be bought just about anywhere – but check first that the factory seal hasn't been broken. It has been known for children to refill empty bottles, leaving the seal apparently intact, so it's best to buy from shops or hotels rather than somebody who approaches you in the street. Check the Directory for information on how safe local food and drink is.

I got used to cleaning my teeth without water. After a while it seems quite normal. With practice, I could even take my malaria tablets without swallowing water.

Get into the habit of drinking through a straw, especially from recycled bottles which may not have been properly cleaned in the factory or may have picked up some rust from the cap. If you don't think the tap water is clean enough to drink then you shouldn't brush your teeth with it or wash your hands in it before a meal or if you have a cut.

Avoid ice, which will have been made from tap water, and salad, which will have been washed in tap water, and be very wary of ice cream. Many cautious travellers have succumbed to the temptation of ice cream and spent the next couple of days kneeling over a toilet bowl.

You're less likely to get sick if you eat what the locals eat. The food will usually be well-prepared, fresh, cheap and won't have been lying around on a slab waiting for a customer. For this reason, try to go to restaurants and food stalls that are popular and have a high turnover. Be wary of cold buffets where food may have been sitting around for hours.

Eating at street stalls, where the food is cooked in front of you, is usually safer – and always cheaper – than splashing out on a meal at a five-star hotel. But when you eat on the street always make sure your hands are clean. You're just as likely to pick up a bug from something you've touched as from infected food. The only thing I always avoid at street stalls is seafood, which can make you very ill indeed.

If you're setting off on a long journey stock up on provisions so that you don't arrive feeling tired and undernourished. The best things to pack are mineral water, bananas, biscuits, peanuts and bread. On buses and trains never accept food or drink from strangers, even those that seem incredibly friendly. I've lost count of the number of times I've heard of travellers waking up on a bus with a bad headache to find their new 'friend' and their money belt have vanished into the night. This is not a threat to be taken lightly: in 1997, Edward Bravo, an American tourist, was given a drink of raki spiked with drugs in the Turkish resort of Egirdir. He not only lost his valuables, he never woke up.

• *Staying in touch*

If you're away from home for a long time your family is bound to worry about your safety, and friends will be curious to know what you're up to. Keep in touch. You might be having so much fun that it doesn't occur to you to call them. This is a bit selfish because, like it or not, your parents will worry about you, and your friends might resent the fact that you've 'forgotten' them.

Short frequent phone calls are best but don't make promises that you won't be able to keep. Don't commit yourself to phoning home every Sunday, for instance, and then one week find yourself on a remote beach or on a mountain trek where there's no phone. It might not seem worth you trying to get to a phone, but your parents will be climbing the walls with worry.

> **I promised to phone home every week during my two months away. One time, I was talking to my mother when my money ran out and I walked away without a second thought. A week later I couldn't find a phone that worked. Then the lines went down for a week. By the time I did get through my mum was worried sick and I realised I'd been stupid.**

Phoning from abroad isn't always expensive, particularly if you dial direct and avoid hotel switchboards. International dialling codes are listed by country in the Directory section; when ringing the UK from overseas don't forget to drop the 0 from the area code. If you plan to call your parents in the UK ask them to get you a BT contact card which can be used to dial their number from many places in the world. It's free and the charges appear on their home bill. If you want to be able to make calls to other numbers too, ask for a charge card. Details on 0800 345144.

You should phone somebody at home if you make significant changes to your travel plans or if you've been in an area where there's been a disaster, such as an air crash or an earthquake, just to reassure your folks that you're safe. It might not seem necessary to you but they may be beside themselves with worry.

If friends and relatives want to write to you, give them a list of poste restante addresses where mail will be held until you arrive. A good guidebook will tell you which post offices keep mail and how letters should be addressed. In some countries your first name is treated as your family name so it's best to write to 'SMITH, John' rather than 'John Smith'. When you go to pick up your mail ask the clerk to look under both your surname and your first name and, just to be sure, under 'M' for Mr or Miss.

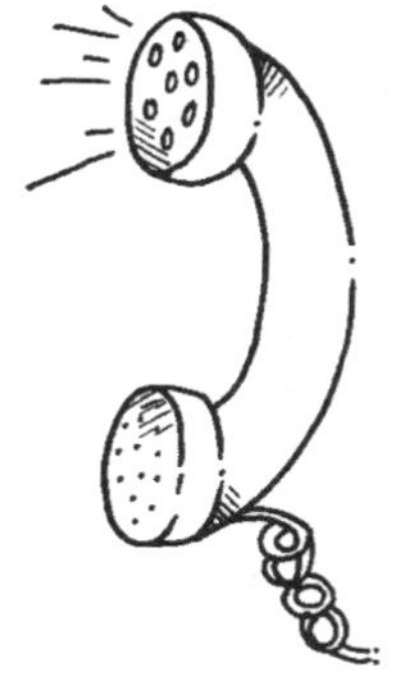

Be cautious about where you tell people to send mail, bearing in mind that letters may take days or weeks to arrive. So if you plan to be in Sydney next week and Melbourne the week after, then Cairns the following week, tell them to write to Cairns. Poste restante mail is officially kept for just a month, but in practice it's often held for longer. When you collect mail you'll need proof of ID, ideally a passport.

American Express also runs a poste restante service for clients, which tends to be more efficient and reliable than local post offices. You don't need to be a cardholder to qualify, providing you have some Amex travellers cheques. Even just one $10 cheque is sufficient. The company won't keep parcels, for security reasons.

When I met other travellers who were about to go home I would give them a letter to send on to my family. One guy even phoned my mum to say I was fine.

Sending mail home can be a hit-and-miss affair. Unless you have the money to use an international courier firm there's no guarantee that your letters and parcels will arrive. Occasionally this is because post office staff steal stamps then pocket the cash, so when you hand over your letter always stick on the stamps yourself, with glue if necessary, and insist on seeing them franked.

Modern technology has made keeping in touch a lot easier. One of the best innovations is the free e-mail service offered by companies such as Hotmail (www.hotmail.com). Anybody can get their own email address – you don't need an Internet connection at home, or even a computer. Go to your college, to a library or a cyber café, and log on. Once online, you will be given a free e-mail address which you can use to pick up messages anywhere in the world. The service is funded by online advertising, so you pay nothing. For a list of cyber cafés around the world where you can send and pick up messages, go to www.netcafeguide.com.

Several websites, including Mail2Web (www.mail2web.com), allow you to pick up email on your own ISP account from any computer terminal in the world, simply by typing in your user name and password. Better still, why not get

Leave an itinerary with a friend back home or a member of your family. If you change your plans, move on earlier than anticipated or decide to stay longer, then let them know.

a free voicemail account with a messaging portal company such as Onebox (www.onebox.com). This allows your friends to leave voice messages for you and means you can receive faxes direct to any computer terminal and dictate emails on the phone.

• *Getting work*

If you find yourself running out of money my advice is to go home. When you're broke and trying desperately to save cash you're at your most vulnerable and travel ceases to be enjoyable. If you insist on staying away, however, you'll probably have to get some sort of job.

It's worth doing some research about finding work before you head off on your travels. Don't believe the first person you meet who says you'll be able to walk into a job waiting tables in Sydney or crewing a yacht in the Caribbean. Find out first if you'll need a work permit and whether you'll be able to work legally. If not, and you're relying on getting some sort of work, you may need to prepare a good story for immigration officials when you arrive. If you're caught and deported you may not be allowed back into the country.

If you are illegal you'll almost certainly be badly paid and you may be at the mercy of unscrupulous employers. Some will try to confiscate your passport and may even withhold your pay if you turn up late or they take a dislike to you. You are powerless to stop them – after all, you're illegal and your employer knows it.

I waitressed in France and did not have any formal agreement with my boss so when we had an argument he refused to pay me. I had been relying on that money to get me home.

If you can't work legally don't agree to be paid more than a few days in arrears. Certainly don't believe any employer who says he will 'look after' your wages to help you save money. Remember, too, that if you are illegal a written agreement may not be worth the paper it's written on. If you feel there's nowhere secure to keep your earnings, open a bank account.

Be especially wary of employers who are looking exclusively for attractive young women. In Japan, foreign women can earn good money working in bars but some customers regard them as little more than prostitutes. The offers can be blatant and generous. Be warned: this is how many a respectable girl has been sucked into prostitution.

I went to America for three months to nanny for friends and arrived with no return flight and no work permit. I was given a gruelling interrogation but fortunately I had a letter from my university in England confirming that I had a place to go back to.

There is an alternative to working abroad. It might not sound very glamorous but it's legal, well-paid and safe. It's working at home. Most young people find they save money more quickly if they get a job at home, partly because the pay is relatively good and partly because their costs are low, particularly if they can live with their parents. Working abroad, on the other hand, can be a treadmill where the money you spend on food, accommodation and the occasional night out means you can never save enough to move on. Eventually you are trapped, until you have to phone home and ask your parents or beg a friend to buy you a plane ticket home. Not very cool.

• *Theft*

Be warned: once you make the decision to go travelling all sorts of people will begin to tell you scare stories about gun-toting, drug-crazed thieves, muggers, bag slashers and white-slave traders. There are two things you can be sure of: (1) the more exotic your intended destination, the more dire the warnings will be; and (2) the people advising you not to go will not have been travelling themselves.

There is no need to panic about the threat of crime, provided you take sensible precautions. Remember that the most common forms of theft are simple pickpocketing and opportunistic bag snatching, both of which are largely confined to big cities. Surprisingly, they're far more common in countries like Spain, Italy and the Czech Republic than in far-away Thailand or Turkmenistan. My own experiences have borne this out. In the six months I spent travelling around 'dangerous' countries like El Salvador, Nicaragua and Guatemala my bags were only broken into once, and that was by baggage handlers at Miami airport.

Don't think that problems only occur in exotic parts of the world. Even on familiar territory and while travelling close to home, it is possible for things to go wrong.

The advice given in this book applies wherever you are in the world.

The Directory section of this book indicates which countries present the highest risk to travellers, or should be totally avoided, but petty crime can happen anywhere.

Most theft is easily preventable and need not ruin your trip. Keep all the items you can't afford to lose in your hotel safe or in your money belt which you should wear under your clothes. Don't take it off because you're hot, or bored with wearing it, and don't dip into it on the street. Keep enough cash in your front pocket to last you through the day but not enough so that losing it would be a tragedy. Put small padlocks on the side pockets of your bags.

Don't be a victim

> **Try not to let your luggage out of your sight. On a long bus journey it is a good idea to get out at stops to check that your bag is not unloaded.**

In cities where there is extensive poverty, particularly in Africa and Latin America, don't wear any kind of jewellery on the street. Don't wear an expensive watch, or even a fake one that might look expensive to a passing thief. Be alert. Don't wear a personal stereo while walking on the street, standing on a crowded bus or in any public place (you wouldn't wear a blindfold so why deprive yourself of your sense of hearing?).

Trust your instincts and that sixth sense you've been developing. If anything weird happens – if you are shoved by a stranger on the street or find yourself suddenly surrounded by screaming children – you may have been targeted by thieves. Think clearly, don't panic and let people know you're aware that something is wrong. This is usually enough to scare them off. If you are with an organised group do not wander off by yourself. Remember it is your responsibility to stay in touch with the group leader.

If somebody offers to wipe some mysterious substance, such as ketchup or bird droppings, from your shoulder or back, congratulations! – you have just come across one of the oldest pickpocketing tricks in the book. As the stranger dabs at you with a handkerchief, either he or his accomplice will try to run off with your wallet or camera in the ensuing confusion. You have a couple of options – walk away briskly, or shout 'Thief!' and watch as your new friend takes to his heels. Don't get angry, because once you lose your cool your defences are down. (Incidentally, a survey of readers in the *Sunday Times* revealed that this mystery-substance-on-your-jacket scam is being used in Paris, Amsterdam, Mexico, Thailand, India, New York, Peru and Hungary. As far as thieves are concerned, it seems the old tricks are the good ones.)

> **People riding pillion on mopeds in Rome may snatch your bag and disappear down a narrow alleyway before you know what's going on. Carrying a rucksack makes you an easily recognisable target.**

Bag snatchers are a problem particularly in Mediterranean countries, Eastern Europe and South America. They are usually unsophisticated and opportunistic, grabbing any bag they see and relying on the element of surprise. If you keep your valuables hidden away and your daypack strapped to your chest they should leave you alone. In all my travels I have only had two encounters with bag snatchers. Both incidents happened on the same day in Barcelona, both outside cafés, both after dark. Neither was successful but I now keep my bag on my lap or hook the straps under the legs of my chair, or both.

> **If you think it is safer to leave your passport and credit cards at your hotel than take them to the beach, wrap them in paper, bind them with masking tape then sign the tape. In this way you will know if someone has tampered with your belongings.**

Despite some people's fears about thieves loitering on every street corner, you're just as likely to have things stolen by other travellers, particularly if you sleep in dorms or share rooms with strangers. Try to keep valuables locked away and get into the habit of taking your money belt to the bathroom with you and sleeping with it under your pillow or around your waist. Keep an eye on travellers who seem to have no money and loiter for hours in hostels and dorms.

HOW PICKPOCKETS POUNCE

1. Gangs operate at airports and bus stations looking for new arrivals knowing they're carrying money, credit cards and passports.

2. Young children are sometimes used to create a diversion. A child falls over and bursts into tears. As you bend to help, an adult accomplice picks your back pocket.

3. A crowded bus or train provides perfect cover for a pickpocket who may use a large scarf or overcoat draped over one arm to shield his roving hand.

4. A thief drops a handful of coins on the ground. As you bend to help pick them up your pocket is picked.

5. A gang member squirts ketchup or sun cream on to your shirt, jacket or shoe. A few minutes later his accomplice offers to wipe it away with a tissue, as your pocket is picked.

6. A man loiters at the side of a queue, reluctant to join it. He is waiting to identify a likely victim.

7. A mother hands her baby to you, so that you have to hold the child. While your hands are full, other children steal whatever they can.

8. Somebody rushes up to you saying you've been robbed. Your hand instinctively reaches for your wallet or money belt. You are about to be robbed.

> **In Nairobi you are more likely to be robbed at the end of the month when workers' salaries are paid and they carry more cash in their pockets.**

If you're unlucky enough to be mugged don't resist and never run after the thief. He might pull a knife, or even a gun, and will probably be a lot more scared and desperate than you are. The experience will be over in a flash but the effects could be long-lasting. Try to stay calm, go back to your room, talk to friends and be aware that you might be in a mild state of shock.

• *Violence*

It's very unlikely that you'll encounter violence of any kind. The reason why the killings of backpackers make headlines across the world is that such incidents happen so rarely. There is a far higher chance of you being involved in a fatal road accident, or being washed out to sea than being the victim of a random killing. In fact, one magazine survey concluded that New Zealand was the most dangerous country for British travellers because of the number of deaths and injuries caused by bungee jumping, skiing and white-water rafting.

By reading newspapers and listening to the radio you can keep up to date with political developments in unstable countries, and be aware of incidents that might put tourists at risk of violence or kidnapping. Don't listen to bogus advice from gung-ho travellers who tell you it's safe to walk around the streets of Port Moresby or surf in shark-infested waters. They're just trying to show off. Again, trust your instincts and don't take risks that you wouldn't take at home. In a city with a reputation for violence take taxis at night, rather than buses.

If you are black or Asian, you may come across racism of a type that you are not familiar with in Britain, even in developed countries. In Prague, for instance, British Asian tourists have been attacked by local skinhead gangs who mistook them for Romanian gypsies. There is no need to be paranoid, but be aware of the potential dangers and perhaps take extra care at night.

One of the best defences against violence is to look confident and walk tall. Be relaxed and alert. If you're trapped and think you're about to be attacked, breathe out to help you relax, adopt a passive stance and try to talk your way out of trouble. If that fails scream or yell at the top of your voice. Use physical self-defence only as a last resort. Remember, you could be accused of assault.

> I was groped whilst walking down a street in Malta. I ran after the man and hit him but in retrospect it would have been wiser to shout, not chase him.

The black market

In countries where currency exchange rates are controlled by the central government a black market often emerges offering a better rate of exchange to tourists. A black market is, by nature, illegal and people caught using it can sometimes face large fines or even short stretches in prison.

Black markets usually exist in countries where the local currency is weak so the exchange rate is already pretty generous. Often the government sets exchange rates in a bid to maintain its foreign currency reserves. Tourists tend to take advantage of the black market because they're greedy, often unaware that they're helping to destabilise the local currency and further adding to the problems of the country they're visiting.

Is it worth it? The advantages of using the black market are usually inversely proportional to the risk. So if you're being offered a generous exchange rate that is, say, 20% better than at the bank, you run a high risk of being caught and fined, jailed or deported. If the rate is only 2% or 3% better than at the bank the risk is probably low, but you might ask yourself whether it's worth taking at all.

I think it's only worth using the black market if you're in a remote area many miles from the nearest bank and it's simply not convenient to use the official methods of exchange. Away from the big cities it's usually possible to make the deal safely and discreetly in a shop or your hotel. In a city you're far more likely to be caught or ripped off. As a rule, don't use the black market until you've spent enough time in the country to know the potential risks and rip-offs.

There are all sorts of elaborate and imaginative rip-offs pulled off by money changers. I've seen calculators wired up wrongly so that they produce false totals and conjuring tricks with wads of notes that any magician would be proud of. But most cons are variations on the old 'Here-comes-a-policeman' trick. In this scenario you follow a money changer into a shop doorway or down a darkened alley (really, how stupid can you get?) and just as you hand over your cash there is a commotion. Usually, the money changer claims he has spotted a policeman and before you have time to blink the money changer runs off with your cash or he is 'arrested' and your money is 'confiscated'. Either way, you lose.

• *Drugs*

The best advice is – don't do them. As well as being illegal (in most places), you put yourself at a disadvantage as soon as you take them. If you want to do drugs while you're away you'll find plenty of opportunities, so don't get overexcited and take undue risks the first time you think you see a chance to get off your face. The most important point to remember is that, compared to most countries, Western Europe is very tolerant of individual drug use. In Britain, for instance, most people arrested with small quantities of cannabis escape with a mild ticking off, rather than face a conviction. But in some countries the penalties are incredibly harsh and, surprisingly, these are often the places where you might think the government would be most relaxed.

> **We met a Scot whose bungalow was raided by police after a full moon party on Ko Pha Ngan. They found a tiny quantity of cannabis and jailed him for two weeks then charged him £500 to get out.**

In Brazil, for instance, you can be jailed for 15 years for possessing small quantities of cocaine. India, where every other person you meet seems to be stoned, has very strict laws covering possession. Stephanie Slater, a British backpacker, was caught with a small quantity of cannabis in the southern Indian state of Kerala, and jailed for 10 years. She was later released, but only after serving two years in a filthy, overcrowded prison.

On a bus in Namibia the man in front of me was offering hash to other passengers. Another man on board turned out to be a plain-clothes policeman who told the driver to stop at a police station and drop them both off.

In June 2001, nearly 3300 British citizens were being held in foreign jails, about 32% of whom were on drugs charges. Most of those were not international smugglers or big-time dealers but ordinary travellers. Many had probably assumed that drug-taking was legal or, at least, widely tolerated. Some would have been reported to the police by the very person who sold them the drugs – dealers often supplement their income by collecting rewards for turning in 'addicts'.

In some countries governments encourage courts to hand down the maximum possible sentences to Western travellers in order to deter others from taking the same risks, and to send out a message to the international community that they're making every effort to 'fight the war on drugs'. In this way they hope their supply of foreign aid won't run dry. If you are arrested for carrying drugs, the Foreign and Commonwealth Office will look after your welfare, but they never interfere with another country's judicial processes. Don't expect any sympathy from your own government, either. Politicians don't like to associate themselves with drug users.

• *Sexual harassment*

Wolf whistles, indecent proposals, lecherous glances, bottom pinching, wandering hands. They all happen and, sadly, in some countries they're a fact of life for Western women and, occasionally, for Western men. You may even decide that the promise of sexual harassment makes it worth avoiding some countries altogether.

There are various ways to defend yourself against sexual harassment but your best protection is an understanding of the local culture. Watch how locals behave. If local women cover their arms, legs and hair and refuse to talk to strange men then that's what you should do. You may have to abandon for a short while your convictions about sexual equality and think purely in terms of how your actions and appearance are seen by others.

> **I got fed up with hassle from men in Egypt so I asked a local woman what to do. She told me to hold my hand to my face and flick it away dismissively. It worked and I never got hassled badly again.**

A few general rules for women. Avoid direct eye contact with men and try not to behave in ways that might be construed as being flirtatious. Don't wear swimsuits, bikinis or high-cut shorts in towns. In the Middle East wearing a sleeveless blouse can be tantamount to going topless in the street. Ignore lewd comments. Talking to strange men – even waving or replying to a friendly 'hello' – might be interpreted as a sexual come-on. If you need to ask directions always approach a woman. If you're followed, don't speed up but find a policeman or go into a shop and explain what's happening. Somebody will help you.

> **In Italy we were followed by a man for three hours who even sat behind us at a cafe blowing smoke in our faces. Eventually we found a policeman who took pity on us and held on to the man for ten minutes while we got a head start.**

• *Get-rich-quick schemes*

Watch out for anybody who claims to know a way of making easy money. Of all the scams and tricks played on travellers get-rich-quick schemes are easily the most effective. It seems the one sure way of persuading people to part with their hard-earned cash is to convince them they can make a big profit out of nothing.

Don't be a victim

The most common scam involves gemstones. Travellers in countries such as India and Thailand will be invited to visit a 'factory' where they can see precious stones being polished. Once there, they will be told that if they buy a stone on their credit card they can make a huge profit by selling it once they get home. A variation on this is the friendly local who approaches you in the street, cheerily says he is off to buy some rubies at rock-bottom prices and generously invites you to come along too. This is particularly common in Bangkok.

I bought a string of pearls in Beijing which seemed cheap but I later found the dealer had added a zero to the total on my credit card slip which I had to pay.

Once you get to the 'factory' you may catch a quick glimpse of somebody polishing a stone then you'll be hustled into a back room and offered a drink which may contain drugs of some kind. You will be told how easy it is to sell the stones for profit and that it's perfectly legal, then you may be shown fake letters from other travellers who have supposedly made large sums of money themselves (though why they should write back to say so is beyond me). You may even be given the addresses of non-existent dealers in your home town who will pay you vast sums of money for the gems.

If you want to meet up with local people and think they are genuine, then arrange to meet in a public place of your choosing, such as a café. If they are genuine in their intentions and want to know more about your country, they should be happy to meet on your terms.

When I witnessed this scam in operation (at Agra in Northern India) a Swedish traveller was then produced who looked heavily sedated and who weakly tried to persuade me to sign credit card slips to the tune of several thousand dollars. If you find yourself in a similar situation, walk away immediately. Don't even admit to carrying a credit card. Some of these people are frighteningly persuasive.

• *Other tricks and scams*

I could fill a whole book with the hundreds of different methods used by crooks and con artists around the world but it would probably only make you needlessly paranoid. Anyway, most scams are easily recognisable once you learn to spot the signs.

The most simple approach – and one that is used the world over – is the stranger who claims to recognise you. 'Don't you remember me, I work at your hotel?' he will say. Or, 'I was your bus driver', or 'I saw you on the plane'. Inevitably, you won't recognise this person because you've not seen him before. But you can guarantee that he'll look offended, hoping you in turn will feel guilty. Be firm. If you pretend to recognise him he'll have won because he now has you in conversation.

In this situation your first thought may be to ask the stranger a question of verification such as 'Where am I staying?' or 'Which bus did I get?' or 'When did I arrive?' This isn't a good idea because any good conman can either make an intelligent guess or will have followed you from your hotel. If he answers correctly he has won you over and made you feel bad for doubting him. Be polite but insist that he's got the wrong person, then make an excuse, perhaps saying you're off to meet a friend. Not all these conmen are clever – one optimistic young man in Kenya tried the same line on me two days running. The second time we met I slapped him on the back and said with a smile: 'Yes, I think I do recognise you!'

Other con artists work by asking you a barrage of questions, most of which are perfectly harmless but a few of which may be more sinister, such as 'Where are you staying?' It might seem rude to refuse to answer this question but you can either say you don't remember the name of the hotel or give the name of another nearby (the cheaper the better, so you don't look too wealthy). If your new friend asks your room number or wants to see your room key you should be very suspicious. Also be wary of answering questions about your friends or fellow travellers. The conman might try to use this information to surprise them by 'knowing' their personal details.

Another type of scam is the good Samaritan who magically pops up just when you need help. He may be able to help you find a cheap

HOW TO SPOT A BOGUS COP

1. Bogus cops operate all over the world from Prague to Pretoria. They usually flash a bit of fake ID and claim to be plain-clothes. Nine times out of ten if you keep your cool and suggest you all go to the nearest police station to discuss the problem they will fade into the crowd.

2. The most common trick is to stop a tourist in the street to check for counterfeit or black market cash. As they inspect your money they may either palm a few notes, confiscate them or just grab the whole wad and run off.

3. If you're driving a car you may be pulled over and robbed or have the car stolen. If you're in Mexico in a car with US plates, even the real police might do this!

4. In Nairobi and other African cities you may be approached by a student asking for money. If you give him anything the bogus cops will pounce, claiming you're funding a political dissident and demanding a large on-the-spot fine.

5. Conmen will occasionally pose as immigration officials claiming to be carrying out random passport checks. They may demand a 'fine' if you aren't carrying your passport. Show them a photocopy and say you're broke. They are unlikely to persist.

room or show you around the kasbah (then present you with a bill for his efforts). At a train station he might offer to help you beat the queues by buying a ticket for you. This is a common trick in Paris where con artists loiter at ticket machines offering change to tourists. Some will take your 49FF for a train ticket to the airport then hand you a Metro ticket that has cost them just 8FF.

In some countries tourists are occasionally drugged and robbed. This happens with alarming frequency in the Philippines where even experienced travellers can be taken in by the most plausible and charming people, sometimes even heavily pregnant women.

One common scam is for a friendly young man to tell you his sister is going to your country the following week to work as a nurse and is desperately anxious to talk to somebody about life there.

DEALING WITH DANGER

All the practical advice given in this book will help if you find yourself in a situation where you feel threatened. Your valuables will be hidden and your hands should be free. If facing a potential danger, this will make you less vulnerable. Follow the cultural advice in this book – you may inadvertently upset someone with a careless remark. We might poke fun at our politicians, but criticising another country's politicians and political history might cause great offence.

IF THINGS GO WRONG, OR IF YOU FEEL THREATENED:

Stay calm. Breathe out slowly, and allow yourself to breathe in slowly, then repeat. This helps you relax.

Follow your instincts. Your intuition is telling you something is not right – don't ignore this feeling, act on it. Think about where you could go where you would feel safer.

Don't become aggressive. You may not be able to speak the language, but you can still sound calm. Body language differs from country to country, so try to remain in a passive stance.

Avoid looking down at your assailant. Maintain eye contact from time to time, but not constantly.

Back away gradually, then walk away as fast as you can – don't run, as this will make you less stable and easier to push over.

Walk away quickly, heading for somewhere safer, where you can ask for help, such as a café or a shop.

Don't be a victim

If someone is determined to take your money or belongings, let them go. Don't risk attack.

Don't assume the only threat comes from men. Women and children participate in, and carry out, attacks and scams (see p. 74).

IF YOU ARE ATTACKED:

If you carry a personal alarm, hold this up to the ear of an attacker and let it off. The Suzy Lamplugh Trust recommend one particular gas shriek alarm (p. 96). Activating an alarm near the ear of an attacker will shock and disorientate, to give you valuable extra seconds to get away. The purpose of the alarm is not generally to attract help. If you have a personal alarm, you may be restricted from carrying it in your hand luggage on an airplane, so it should go with the rest of your baggage in the hold.

Shouting or screaming into an assailant's ear will also disorientate them and give you a few seconds to move away. Pretend to vomit, as your attacker will probably pull away.

If trapped, yell or scream. Shout out for the police.

If you are grabbed, try to break free and walk away as quickly as you can.

Report any incident to the police.

If you have been attacked or sexually assaulted, you may be uncertain about how the local police will respond to your report. Get in touch with the Embassy or the Consul to seek help. In a very few countries there is no British representation, so contact the consul of another EU country for advice.

Diana Lamplugh OBE, The Suzy Lamplugh Trust

Don't be a victim

Once you're in his house you may be offered a cup of coffee or a beer that tastes slightly strange. Next thing you know you wake up in a ditch dressed in only your underpants. I've met two people who've fallen for variations of this trick.

The most common tricks are simply those that involve charming the money from your pocket. Carpet sellers the world over seem to have a near magical ability to persuade tourists to buy rugs that they can't really afford, and don't really want. Some might even tell you their carpets sell for many times over that price in your country. This is almost always untrue. In fact, they may be cheaper at home.

It usually starts with a cup of tea for which you feel slightly indebted. A common trick is to lay out dozens of carpets in front of you, starting with a tiny one and slowly building up to a huge, very expensive one. As each of the carpets is then slowly and laboriously rolled back up, the salesmen look at you pleadingly and you shake your head and say you can't afford it. The salesmen look increasingly downcast, worrying how they will feed their wives and children, until finally the last tiny carpet is revealed. And that is the one you will buy because it seems so cheap compared with the rest. It works every time. My advice is this: if you don't want to buy a carpet, don't go to a carpet shop.

• *Getting sick*

From time to time, you're bound to get sick and spend a few days clutching your midriff and making darting runs to the nearest bathroom. The experience will not be very pleasant but chances are you won't have contracted dysentery or cholera, just a mild stomach bug brought on by a combination of unfamiliar food, heat and poor personal hygiene. Your body will fight it naturally and in the process will build up the various bacteria it needs to prevent you being struck down again.

Once you fall ill, stay out of the sun and drink plenty of water because there's a danger of becoming seriously dehydrated. Slow down and don't make any long journeys. If possible, check into a hotel room with a clean, comfortable bathroom (after all, you'll be spending a lot of time there). If you're travelling alone, try to find another traveller or a friendly hotel worker who will keep an eye on you and deliver food and drink.

If the diarrhoea persists for more than about five days call a doctor or go to a clinic. You might need to provide a stool sample (again, not a fun experience) to check you don't have something more persistent like amoebic dysentery or giardia. These need to be treated with specific drugs and will not simply go away of their own accord.

I got worms in Hanoi from eating pork and went to a chemist who gave me some tablets from an unmarked box. They turned out to be the wrong medicine and made my condition far worse. I should have gone to a doctor.

Don't take antibiotics unless advised by a doctor because these not only attack the infection but also strip away all the 'good' bacteria in your stomach. Eating plenty of yoghurt can help to build them back up again. If you suspect you have malaria (the usual symptoms are headaches, sweats, aches and a high temperature, like a very bad dose of flu that may get better after a couple of days then come on again with greater severity) you need to get to a doctor immediately. Dozens of Western travellers die of malaria every year.

In many countries it's possible to buy strong drugs over the counter. Be careful, unless you know what you're doing. It's better to see a doctor and have the correct drugs prescribed. In Europe, you can often get good advice from pharmacists in an emergency. If you're on medication, or have a recurring health problem, keep a note of the drug's generic name and a copy of your doctor's prescription.

• *Reporting crime*

Don't immediately assume because your passport or travellers cheques have mysteriously vanished that you've been robbed. You may have simply mislaid them. Try not to panic, but think where and when you last saw them. It's very easy to lose things when you travel so get into the habit of checking down the backs of seats, under beds and at the backs of drawers and lockers. I once cleverly hid a sizeable amount of cash inside a hotel wardrobe, then left it there.

It's not a good idea to accuse somebody of stealing from you. If you're wrong, you'll have needlessly insulted them and made yourself look stupid. If you're right, they may turn nasty. Either way, you won't get your things back. If you're convinced you know who's responsible (a hotel worker, for instance) give that person a chance to hand back your possessions without losing face or risking arrest. Go to them, tell them how distraught you are at the loss and that, naturally, you'll be calling the police to have the place searched. Then ask politely whether it's worth them having one last look to check that nobody has handed in your valuables. You may find they magically appear. If they do, smile, say thank you and put it down to experience.

If that doesn't work you'll need to report the theft to the police, not because you expect them to get your things back, but to get a report for your insurers. Go as soon as is realistically possible, preferably within 24 hours. If you can't speak the language try to persuade a friendly local to go with you. Wear your smartest clothes and be patient.

"After my bag was snatched in Saigon the police asked me to go to the station to identify the thief. He was cowering in a corner covered in blood. One policeman showed me the stun gun they had used on him. I felt awful that this had happened because I hadn't taken enough care of my bag."

Don't expect any sympathy from the police and prepare for a mountain of paperwork. Reporting a crime can be a long-winded and infuriating process and you may need to pay a bribe just to get it done. Wait until you're asked – never offer a bribe.

"My camera equipment was stolen from an overhead locker on a flight from London to New York. I reported it stolen on arrival at JFK but because I didn't get a police report as well my insurers wouldn't pay up."

In any dealings with officials you need to be careful not to cause offence or appear arrogant. Watch how other people behave in the queue in front of you – do they sit or stand, do they bow their heads slightly, or hold their hands behind their backs? You don't want to cause yourself more problems by using the wrong body language, such as folding your arms and puffing out your chest. In some countries it is a bad idea for a single woman to visit a police station alone. Take advice from a local person.

> **When my passport, tickets and bank cards were stolen I was treated as if it was my fault. You have to be thick-skinned and don't leave the police station until you have proof of what's been taken, where and when.**

If an official insists on keeping a document ask him to make you a photocopy, sign it and give you a receipt. Don't agree to go off with the police in search of the culprit. This is a pointless public relations exercise occasionally put on to impress tourists. It's a waste of time, you won't get your valuables back and you might just be putting yourself in danger.

Once you have the police report, if it is made out in another language, you may need to get it translated, preferably on paper with an official-looking letterhead, say a local university. Stay in town for a day or two just in case your things turn up, but don't hold out too much hope.

Read your insurance documents carefully. If you need to contact your insurers write or phone (if a toll-free number has been provided) with all the necessary details. Note the name of the person you speak to and get a reference number. Keep all receipts, ticket stubs and a note of all the money you spend that you may be able to claim back later.

> **Having things stolen needn't be the end of the world. Try to minimise the fuss, be patient, get documentation and don't worry.**

Above all, don't let the experience get you down and persuade you into going home. Turn to other travellers for help and support and decide what items you really need to replace and what you can live without. Some victims of theft find the experience strangely liberating – they find they can get by with a lot less stuff than they thought they needed.

• *Getting in trouble with the police*

With the best will in the world it isn't always easy to stay on the right side of the law, particularly when you're moving from one country to another. You may be hauled up for what appears to be a trifling offence – jaywalking or getting on a train without a ticket – and find yourself in all sorts of trouble.

Countries that might at first sight seem the most liberal can have the most petty laws. In the Philippines, a place that seems to be permanently on the brink of outright lawlessness, I was pulled over by three armed policemen on the island of Cebu for 'disembarking from a minibus at an unofficial stop'. It would have been tempting to burst out laughing but the cops seemed to be taking it very seriously indeed. I was interrogated at length, then let off with a fine of 10 pesos (about 25p).

In situations like this the police may be perfectly aware that the charge is ridiculous but they may be waiting to see your response, goading you into an argument that only they can win. Needless to say, you should always be respectful, well-spoken and cooperative. Look suitably shamefaced if you're being told off, even if you know you're in the right. Don't just smile stupidly, because your idea of a charming grin might be their idea of a conceited smirk.

> **In Bangkok you can now be fined up to 2000 baht (£25) just for dropping litter in the street. I was fined for dropping a cigarette butt.**

Paying bribes isn't as common as some people would have you believe. If you offer a policeman or immigration official a backhander you run the risk of insulting them and getting yourself into even deeper trouble. This time you might have to pay a very hefty fine (or an even bigger bribe!). If you do have to hand over money, be careful what you say. Call it a gift, a donation or baksheesh, never a bribe. If an official names a figure do not be afraid to plead poverty and haggle.

> **Paying bribes to policemen in Mexico is so common that Mexicans even have a phrase for it. A bribe is known as *una mordita* – a little bite.**

Be particularly cautious at airports and border crossings where security is often very tight. It may be illegal to take photographs of airports, bridges and military installations. If you're caught doing so, the best course is to apologise immediately and offer to hand over the film. Losing a few pictures is better than being carted off to a police station, strip-searched and fed on a diet of rice soup for three days.

• Embassies and consulates

If you do get in trouble or lose your passport or all your money, you should ask for help at your country's embassy or consulate. Don't expect the red-carpet treatment or a 'Get-out-of-jail-free' card. In some countries, diplomats deal with young, down-at-heel travellers who are simply angling for a free loan. They can see you coming. Again, put on your smartest clothes and be respectful.

In an emergency, a consular officer will contact your family and issue you with a temporary passport, though this is a lot quicker and easier if you have a photocopy of your stolen one. In exceptional circumstances, and when you can show that you're broke and have exhausted all ways of getting money, a consular officer may give you a ticket to get home. However, your passport may be withdrawn until you have repaid the cost.

If you land in prison you must insist on a consul being informed. An official should then visit you to check on the conditions in which you are being held, and pass on a message to your family. However, the consul cannot offer legal advice, pay bail money, intervene in court proceedings or try to investigate the crime. Nor can a consular officer arrange for you to have special treatment – you'll just have to rot there with all the other suspects until your case comes up in court.

• *Back to reality*

If you're on your way home after a long time abroad you probably can't wait to see your friends and family and enjoy a few home comforts. Be prepared for disappointment. Many travellers find that coming home can be a depressing and weird experience. Even the trip from the airport can be deeply unsettling.

Remember all that stuff about culture shock? Well, after several weeks or months abroad you've probably become so adjusted to travel that coming home is a kind of culture shock in itself. Britain can seem very drab and unwelcoming after Asia, Africa or Australia. People at home may seem anxious and stressed all the time, not like the friendly locals you've got used to. And the freedom that you've enjoyed, making decisions about your own life and not having to answer to parents or bosses, is stripped away in an instant. It's little wonder that so many travellers vow to go away again as soon as they save enough money.

> **I found it deflating getting home and realising time had stood still while I'd been having this massive experience. I need to keep reminding myself I've been away.**

If you're prepared for this reaction you can at least put on a brave face when you do get home. Those people close to you who have waited so long to see you again will be upset and confused if you appear unhappy to see them, so try to be positive.

You might want to think about maintaining some of the good things that happened to you while you've been away. Reread your diaries (you did keep diaries, didn't you?) and try to put into practice some of the lessons that travel has taught you. If you've been learning a language while you were away, keep studying it. Perhaps get in touch with people from the countries you've visited

who live near you – after all, you now have a lot in common. And don't forget to send prints to those people you photographed and promised a copy. It's your turn now to repay some of the hospitality you've enjoyed.

There are practical considerations too. If you've recently been in a malarial zone, keep taking the tablets for four weeks after your return. If you develop a fever and flu-like symptoms go immediately to your doctor and tell him or her where you've been. Malaria can develop in travellers up to three months after their return home. Also see your doctor if you have persistent diarrhoea.

• *Have your say*

Finally, let us know how your trip went. Much of the advice in this book comes directly from the experiences of ordinary travellers like you. So if you think I've missed anything out, or got something wrong, or you've got an interesting story to tell, please write to Mark Hodson and The Suzy Lamplugh Trust, care of the Project Editor, Thomas Cook Publishing, PO Box 227, Thorpe Wood, Peterborough, PE3 6PU, or by e-mail at books@thomascook.com, and let me know about it so that I can use your comments and stories in the next edition of this book. Have a great trip!

• Travellers' tips

www.dmoz.org/Recreation/Travel/Backpacking - links to web rings, chatrooms, message boards, etc

www.BootsnAll.com - all-purpose backpacking site

www.lonelyplanet.com - guidebook updates, travellers' tips and email newsletters

www.travel.roughguides.com - *Rough Guides* published online

www.izon.com/news.htm - Backpackers News Wire

www.gapyear.com - advice on taking a gap year

www.noshit.com.au - the unsavoury, and hilarious, side of travel

• Planning ahead

www.thebackpacker.net - advice for first-time travellers

www.worldclimate.com - check weather patterns worldwide

www.wherewillwego.com - inspiration on adventure travel

www.whatsonwhen.com - global events guide

www.infomatch.com/~cdtg - advice from the *Crazy Dog Travel Guide*

• Staying in touch

www.netcafeguide.com - search a worldwide database of internet cafes

www.TotallyFreeStuff.com - find a web-based email account

• Health and safety

www.fco.gov.uk/travel - Foreign Office Travel Advice (also on Ceefax p. 470)

www.tripprep.com - Travel

Health Online

www.24dr.com - personal health advice

www.travel.state.gov - US State Department travel information

Travellers Guide to Health, available free from doctors' surgeries or the Central Office of Information (0800 555777).

Healthy Travel: Bugs, Bites and Bowels by Dr Jane Wilson Howarth (Cadogan, £7.99).

• Uploading data

Safeguard your important documents by uploading them to a secure website before you travel. Lonely Planet's ekno service (www.ekno.lonelyplanet.co.uk) allows you to scan in your passport, air tickets, visas and emergency phone numbers. In an emergency, you simply log on and retrieve the data. British consulates can use the data to issue a replacement passport.

• Personal alarms

The Suzy Lamplugh Trust sells its recommended personal gas shriek alarm (£7.50 plus £1.50 p&p). Tel: 020 8876 0305; fax: 020 8876 0891; or visit our website at www.suzylamplugh.org.

• Overland truck companies

Adventure Bound (020 8742 8612). Africa and South America

Dragoman (01728 861133). Africa, Asia, Middle East, North and South America

Guerba (01373 826611). Africa.

Exodus (020 8675 5550). Africa, Asia and South America

Kumuka (020 7937 8855). Africa, Middle East, Central and South America.

Truck Africa (01986 873124). Africa.

• Expeditions and voluntary work

Africa and Asia Venture (01380 729009; www.aventure.co.uk).

Four-month teaching placements in Africa and Asia.

Frontier Environmental Expeditions (020 7613 1911; www.frontier.ac.uk). Conservation projects in Madagascar, Tanzania and Vietnam.

Gap Activity Projects (0118 959 4914).

Gap Challenge (0181 961 1122).

Kibbutz Representatives (020 8458 9235).

Raleigh International (020 7371 8585).

Trekforce Expeditions (020 7828 2275).

• *Women and travel*

Women Travel, ed. Natania Jansz, Miranda Davies, Emma Drew and Lori McDougall (Rough Guides, £12.99).

• *Working abroad*

Work Your Way Around the World by Susan Griffith (Vacation Work, £12.95).

www.immi.gov.au/allforms/temp-whm.htm - Australian Department of Immigration

www.jobsearch.gov.au - Australian Job Search

• *World Wise Directory*

The need for this Directory was conceived by The Suzy Lamplugh Trust, who commissioned it from Oxford Brookes University with funding from the Prince's Trust.

This section contains information on over 200 countries around the world, including basic safety, health, visa and currency facts, and, where appropriate, the level of risk for travellers to that country. It also provides important cultural information so that you are aware of local codes of dress and behaviour, details that help you to stay safer.

Each page of the Directory is devoted to one country. The country's capital is given first, followed by information plotted against a symbol. What each of these symbols indicate is explained in the key, opposite.

The Directory is also accessible on the World Wise website at www.suzylamplugh.org/worldwise. The listings in the Directory section were up-to-date at the time of publication, but this information is subject to change. Funded by the Foreign and Commonwealth Office, the website is regularly updated, so check this before you embark on your travels.

TIME ZONE
indicates local time zone in relation to Greenwich Mean Time (GMT).

TELEPHONE SERVICES
shows the dialling code FROM UK, followed by the OUTGOING CODE TO UK if you want to make an international call home from that country. The code should be followed by the home STD code minus the first 0. American readers should replace 44 with 1, and similarly, readers from elsewhere should use their own country code in place of 44. All countries now use International Direct Dialing (IDD), but in some places, IDD is available only in upmarket hotels and public telephone centres attached to the main post office.

EMERGENCY TELEPHONE NUMBERS
We list numbers for the emergency services – Ambulance, Fire and Police. In some countries there is a different telephone number for each service.

REPRESENTATION IN THE UNITED KINGDOM
This details the address and phone number of the country's Embassy, Consulate or High Commission in the UK. E-mail and website addresses are also given where appropriate.

UK REPRESENTATION
This gives the address and phone number of the British Embassy or Consulate in the country. E-mail and website addresses are given where appropriate.

TOURIST INFORMATION IN THE UK
The contact point, such as tourist office or Consulate, for more information about the country. A website address may be given as well or instead.

LOCAL TOURIST INFORMATION
indicating contact details within the country itself for tourist information. There is also an e-mail and website address where these are available.

PASSPORT INFORMATION
lists passport and other entry requirements for UK passport holders.

VISA INFORMATION

indicates whether or not a visa is required by a UK passport holder for travel to this country.
NB: Because details vary so widely, the Passport and Visa sections provide information appropriate only to holders of UK passports. Please also note that, because regulations are liable to change, you should double-check the passport and visa requirements with the country's Embassy or Consulate before you go. Don't forget that the World Wise website (www.suzylamplugh.org/worldwise) is updated regularly.

PROHIBITED ITEMS

indicates which articles cannot be brought into (or taken out of) the country, or are not permitted without the appropriate licence or documentation.

AIRPORT TAX
indicates if this is payable and in which currency it should be paid (see note on Euro under 'Currency').

RESTRICTED ENTRY
gives any specific details or requirements that need to be met to allow entry into the country.

HEALTH MATTERS
This shows, firstly, if immunisation against the following is recommended (indicated by 'R' against the disease): HEPATITIS A, POLIO, TYPHOID.
Then, information about the presence of MALARIA is given, followed by recommended precautions against YELLOW FEVER.
Finally, there is a listing of any other health risks that exist in this country.

FOOD AND DRINK
Where there is no indication, the water is regarded as drinkable, and normal precautions should be observed with food. Otherwise, the following applies:
W1 indicates that the water is untreated and not safe to drink. Avoid dairy products as they are not pasteurised. Fruit and vegetables should be peeled before consumption.
W2 indicates that water is untreated and not safe to drink.

CURRENCY
This section starts by indicating the local currency and its units. This is followed by information about foreign exchange, the acceptance of credit cards and travellers cheques, and the preferred currency denomination for travellers cheques. This is concluded with a note on ATM (automatic teller machine/cashpoint) availability within the country.
From January 2002, 12 countries in the European Union are using the single European currency, the Euro. Coins and notes may have national variations in design but are valid throughout the Euro Zone. French Overseas Départements are on the Euro from July 2002. Where a non-European country uses a European currency (e.g. French Francs) as its preferred denomination for travellers cheques, or for hard-currency transactions such as airport taxes, we have continued to show the old currency, as conversion rates and/or acceptability of the Euro are not certain at time of going to press.

MONEY WIRING SERVICES
gives local contact details for MoneyGram and Western Union.

CREDIT CARD EMERGENCY NUMBERS
lists the telephone number to call if your American Express, Diners Club, MasterCard or Visa credit card is lost or stolen.

TRAVELLERS CHEQUES EMERGENCY NUMBERS
gives the telephone number to call (often toll-free/reverse charges) if your American Express, Thomas Cook or Visa travellers cheques are

lost or stolen. These are often local numbers, but a global emergency number may be given.

BANKING HOURS
notes the normal bank opening hours

COST OF LIVING
notes factors that may affect local prices. For instance, in some countries tourists have to pay higher prices for goods and services than local people.

LANGUAGES
details the main languages spoken in the country.

WEATHER
provides brief information on the climate.

RELIGIONS
lists the main religions observed in each country. (See pp. 106-108.)

NATIONAL HOLIDAYS
lists the national holidays for each country. The fixed dates are given with an indication about which moveable date holidays are taken. Religious feast and holidays are decided by reference to the lunar calendar. See pp 106–108.

ELECTRICITY
indicates the local voltage and the type of plug used.

POST
shows approximately how long it will take a letter to reach Europe or the UK.

WOMEN AND SOCIETY
gives information on how women are expected to dress and appropriate cultural information of particular interest to women travellers. This section may also give safety information for lone female travellers, and notes on society in general.

SAFE TRANSPORTATION
looks at road, rail and air travel within the country, highlighting the safer and most appropriate forms of travel. It may also give information about car hire and the documentation needed to either hire a car or take your own car into the country.

SPECIFIC INFORMATION
gives varied cultural information such as modes of behaviour and dress and the importance of religion. Also included is information appropriate to the safety of travellers, such as which crimes are prevalent and which areas should be avoided. It may also indicate what should not be photographed.
Most importantly, this section notes any warnings from the Foreign and Commonwealth Office (FCO) that apply to travellers intending to visit the country. If the FCO has a warning about the level of risk to visitors, then this is indicated. The situation can change without notice and it is prudent to check the latest information about a country:

- on the FCO Country Advice website, at www.fco.gov.uk/travel
- BBC Ceefax page 140

or call the FCO Travel Advice Unit, Tel: 020 7008 0232.

• Abbreviations

A few abbreviations appear throughout the Directory to save space.

FCO	Foreign and Commonwealth Office (Note: usually refers to the Travel Advice Unit of the FCO).
IDD	International Direct Dialling
IDP	International Driving Permit
Jan, Feb	January, February
Mon, Tues	Monday, Tuesday etc
R	Recommended (as in recommended vaccinations)
TO	Tourist Organisation/Tourist Office
Y	Yes

• Health advice

This section details the diseases listed throughout the Directory (where the presence of diseases and other health problems in each country is noted). It also gives advice on immunisation and prevention. Don't forget that health advice is also given on pages 29–31 and 87–88 of this book.

AIDS/HIV

All travellers should be aware of the risk of AIDS, which is present throughout the world. There is no cure for the disease, caused by the HIV virus. This is spread through unprotected sex with an infected person; use of infected needles, medical instruments or tattooing equipment; and transfusions of infected blood. Avoid having sex with anyone other than your usual partner; use a condom if you have sex with a new partner. If you need a blood transfusion while you are away, insist that you are given screened blood.

Bilharzia

Bilharzia (schistosomiasis) is caused by a worm that penetrates the skin. Prevention is by avoiding contact with stagnant water or swimming in waterways in countries where the disease is present.

Cholera

Cholera causes severe diarrhoea, which may lead to dehydration and possibly even death. It is transmitted by contaminated food and water. Immunisation is regarded as ineffective: prevention is by good hygiene and exercising caution with food and drink.

Dengue fever

This is a disease transmitted by the bite of an infected mosquito. There is no immunisation against the disease, which causes flu-like symptoms.

Diptheria

Most adults in the UK will already have been immunised against this disease, caught by contact with a person infected with the disease. Vaccines are available for those who do not already have this protection.

Hepatitis

There are two forms of this viral infection of the liver – hepatitis A and hepatitis B. Hepatitis A is sometimes known as infectious hepatitis, transmitted by contaminated food and water, faeces and from a carrier of the disease. The most appropriate vaccination for this strain depends on the length of time you will spend travelling, so consult your doctor once you have decided on your travel plans.

Hepatitis B is spread in the same way as the HIV virus (see above). You can be vaccinated against this strain of the disease, but it takes six months to become effective.

Japanese encephalitis

Is a viral disease spread by mosquito. Because this disease can be fatal, those intending to spend some time in risk areas of south-east Asia (especially during the monsoon) are advised to seek immunisation.

Malaria

Malaria is spread by bite from infected mosquitoes and causes a fever and other complications. It can be fatal. Precautions are outlined on page 30. Anti-malaria tablets should be taken for a month after returning home. If you develop a fever or flu-like symptoms while you are travelling, or up to three months after your return home, seek medical attention. There are several strains of malaria: falciparum being the most serious. In some parts of the world, falciparum and vivax strains are becoming resistant to anti-malaria treatments. See also p.30

Meningitis

This bacterial disease can be fatal and is transmitted by contact with a carrier. There is an effective vaccination against strains A and C, but no immunisation against the strain most prevalent in the UK.

Polio

Polio (poliomyelitis) is a viral infection that causes meningitis and paralysis. It is transmitted through faeces and contaminated water. If you have been immunised over ten years ago, a booster can be taken. Those who have not received the vaccine before should have the full course of three doses. (This is the vaccine usually given on sugar lumps.)

Rabies

This is an infection of the nervous system, and once symptoms have developed – muscle spasms and delirium – it is usually fatal. The disease is spread by bite or scratch from an infected animal. If bitten, seek treatment immediately. Wash the wound, apply alcohol and go to the nearest doctor or hospital. Treatment is by a course of injections. Vaccinations are available, but you still need to seek the same treatment if bitten.

Tetanus

Tetanus is transmitted through cuts and wounds, and causes

painful muscle spasms. The spores that carry it live in the soil, and can be transmitted by an injury as minor as a scratch from a thorn. Immunisation is by a series of three injections and, if this was within the last ten years, a booster can be given.

Tick-borne encephalitis/ Lyme disease

A vaccination is available for tick-borne encephalitis, but none for Lyme disease. Prevention is by covering up in areas affected by the disease, especially if hiking or camping. Both diseases are transmitted by a bite from an infected tick – encephalitis is inflammation of the brain, whilst Lyme disease produces arthritic pain, swollen joints and a rash. Early treatment of Lyme disease is effective; if left too late, treatment will not work.

Tuberculosis (TB)

Most adults in the UK will already have been vaccinated against this respiratory disease. If not, immunisation is advisable if you are going to work or stay for more than a month in a country where TB is common.

Typhoid

Typhoid fever is transmitted via contaminated food and water. Those travelling to areas where sanitation is poor should be immunised and care should be taken when handling food.

Yellow fever

This is transmitted by mosquito bite. Some countries (see the Directory) require a vaccination certificate in order to gain entry. The vaccination is highly effective, lasting for ten years, but can only be given at a designated centre. Ask your own doctor for advice on obtaining the vaccination.

Religions

This is not the place for a full introduction to the religious cultures you may encounter on your travels. You should learn as much as you can from guidebooks and reference sources for the areas you intend to visit. The purpose of this section is to acquaint you with some considerations about behaviour and sensitivity to the more widespread religions. These will apply to many of the countries in the following Directory – to save repeating them everywhere, they are outlined here.

Always, in any event, be guided by the local customs you observe. In particular, if you wish to visit a place of worship, always ensure that you adhere to appropriate dress codes. For example, women visiting a mosque should always cover their heads. Look for any notices giving guidance about what should be worn, or observe how other worshippers are dressed.

Christianity

The main differences in customs between Christian cultures are less to do with sects and more to do with strictness of observance, which is often connected to how traditionally society is organised. For example, in southern European countries both Roman Catholic and Greek Orthodox communities impose a much stricter dress code on visitors to churches than would be the case in northern Europe. Unless the contrary is obvious from the conduct of other visitors, assume that in churches and other Christian sites bare arms and legs are frowned upon and may result in entry being denied. Women may have to cover their heads, if only with a shawl. In nearly all Christian countries it is still the custom for men to uncover their heads whilst in a church, on the other hand. Entry may also be denied or restricted during religious services, and even when not, visitors are expected to maintain silence.

Be prepared also for a greater deference or respect towards priests in many communities than you would expect in your own country, and take care not to flout it, which will cause offence or worse.

In some Christian countries, the national holidays include important Christian feasts such as Easter, Ascension Day, Pentecost (Whitsun) and Corpus Christi, and these fall on different dates each year. This is because they are determined by reference to the lunar cycle and not the modern calendar. Where countries also mark Mardis Gras as a holiday, this is the day before Lent, forty days before Easter Sunday. Where Easter is indicated in the country profile, it usually means that both Good Friday and Easter Monday are holidays. In countries where the Orthodox Church predominates, Christmas and Easter are celebrated a few days later than in the Western Church.

Buddhism

Originating in India as an offshoot of Hinduism, this religion has spread throughout southern and eastern Asia over the last two millennia. Its most obvious manifestations are statues or images of the Buddha, as well as temples, festivals and communities of priests or monks.

Buddhist monks are invariably treated by the locals with the greatest of respect, which you should emulate. Buddhist monks do not live separately from the community, like Christian monks, and they may in some respects seem quite worldly to an outsider; but they should not be criticised. Nor should you touch a monk, even accidentally. Monks may not accept money directly (put it in their bowl), or anything at all from a woman.

Dress and conduct in Buddhist temples and shrines should resemble that in Muslim and conservative Christian places of worship, i.e. no bare arms and legs, and remove shoes before entering. Respect for the image of the Buddha is important, and this means not climbing on one, or even posing for a photograph with one.

Islam

Islamic belief has its principles in the existence of the one God, Allah. The words of Allah were given to the prophet Mohammed and became known as the Koran. Adherence to Islam permeates all areas of daily life in Muslim countries.

Muslims must perform the five Pillars of Islam: to publicly pronounce 'There is no God but God and Mohammed is the messenger of God'; to pray five times a day; the giving of alms; to fast during the month of Ramadan; to make the Haj – the annual pilgrimage to Mecca.

Prayers may take place anywhere, but the worshipper always faces the direction of Mecca. A visitor should not display embarrassment if prayers are offered in front of him/her, by a shopkeeper on his premises, for instance.

During Ramadan, Muslims abstain from food and drink between the hours of sunrise and sunset. Shops may close afternoons, and some may open again at night. It is usually possible for non-Muslim travellers to obtain food and refreshment, in the main cities and western-style hotels, at any rate, but to eat, drink or smoke in public during Ramadan would be considered insulting.

Muslims abstain from alcohol and from the consumption of pork. Non-Muslim visitors may drink alcohol, with more or less discretion according to the strictness of local observance, but drunkenness is always considered beyond contempt.

Women, even in the more liberal Muslim countries, dress conservatively, generally showing their face and hands only; in stricter cultures faces may be veiled and indeed women may not be visible in public much at all.

Shoes should not be worn inside a house or mosque, and to show the soles of the feet towards another person is considered an insult. In mosques very often there is a barrier beyond which non-believers should not enter. If giving or receiving gifts, always use the right hand. Hospitality towards others is an integral part of Islam; to refuse an offer of hospitality may be considered an insult.

The national holidays of countries with populations of Muslims are determined by the cycle of Islamic festivals. The dates vary from year to year because they are based on the lunar months and not the modern calendar. This also applies to other faiths.

Other religions

A number of significant religions, with worldwide or extensive regional followings, are also noted throughout the Directory, for example Hinduism, Judaism, Sikhism and Taoism. Where these have a major impact on the culture of the country you will be visiting, find out what you can about them beforehand.

Afghanistan

CAPITAL: Kabul

GMT + 4.5

FROM UK: 0093
OUTGOING CODE TO UK: All international calls must go through the operator.

Not present.

Embassy of the Islamic State of Afghanistan, 31 Princes Gate, London SW7 1QQ
Tel: 020 7589 8891. Fax: 020 7581 3452.

British Embassy, Karte Parwan, Kabul, Afghanistan. Tel: 88888. NOTE: At the time of writing the British Embassy is closed. Some consular assistance may be provided by the High Commission in Islamabad, Pakistan.

Refer to Embassy in London.

Afghan Tourist Organisation (ATO), Ansari Wat, Shar-i-Nau, Kabul, Afghanistan.
Tel: 30323.

Return Ticket required. Requirements may be subject to short-term change. Contact the relevant authority before departure.
VALID PASSPORT REQUIRED.

Required by all except travellers holding re-entry permits issued by Afghanistan and travellers holding confirmed onward tickets and continuing their journey to another country by the same aircraft within 2 hours.

Alcohol. The export of antique carpets and furs is prohibited without licence. All valuable goods must be declared on arrival.

Af 200

Nationals of Israel require special authorisation from the Embassy for entry.

POLIO, TYPHOID: R
MALARIA: Exists in the falciparum and vivax varieties.
YELLOW FEVER: A vaccination certificate is required if arriving from endemic or infected areas. Travellers arriving from non-endemic areas should note that vaccination is strongly recommended for travel outside the urban areas.
OTHER:Cutaneous leishmaniasis, cholera, tick-borne relapsing fever, typhus, and rabies are present.

W1

Afghani (Af) = 100 puls. Credit cards and travellers cheques are not accepted.ATM: Unavailable.

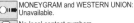

MONEYGRAM and WESTERN UNION: Unavailable.

No local contact numbers

No local contact numbers

Generally 0800-1200 and 1300-1630 Sat to Wed, 0830-1330 Thur. At the time of writing many banks are closed.

Limited accommodation and commodities in Kabul. All are inexpensive.

Pashtu and Dari Persian. English, French, German and Russian are also spoken.

Regions above 2500m are extremely cold. There are considerable differences between temperatures in the summer and winter, and between day and night in lowland regions and the valleys.

Islamic majority (mostly Sunni); Hindu, Jewish and Christian minorities.

Mar 21, Apr 28, May 1, 4, Aug 19, 30 or 31. Islamic festivals

220 volts AC, 50 Hz.

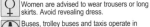

Postal services unavailable.

Women are advised to wear trousers or long skirts. Avoid revealing dress.

Buses, trolley buses and taxis operate in Kabul. It is essential to check these services with the relevant airline offices.

The FCO advises against travel to Afghanistan. Continuing tension between different Afghan groups has led to outbreaks of fighting throughout the country. UN sanctions against the ruling Taliban have provoked anti-Western feeling which could give rise to violent attacks on foreign visitors, including aid workers. Those who propose to travel, despite the warning, are strongly advised to check the situation before setting out. Religion has a strong influence over daily life. Exercise care when taking photographs and do not photograph military installations.

CAPITAL: Tirana

GMT + 1 (GMT + 2 during the summer).

FROM UK: 00355.
OUTGOING CODE TO UK: 0044

Police 24445, Fire 23333, Ambulance 22235

Embassy of the Republic of Albania, 4th Floor, 38 Grosvenor Gardens, London SW1W 0EB.

Tel: 020 7730 5709. Fax: 020 7730 5747.

British Embassy, Rruga Skënderbeu N12, Tirana, Albania. Tel: 00355 42 34973 Fax: 00355 42 247697.

Albturist (Travel Agency) c/o Regent Holidays (UK) Limited, 15 John St, Bristol BS1 2HR. Tel: 01179 211 711. Fax: 01179 254 866.

Albanian Ministry of Construction and Tourism, Marketing and Promotion Department, Bulevardi Dëshmorët e Kombit, Tirana, Albania.

Tel: (42) 28123. Fax: (42) 27931.

Return Ticket required. Requirements may be subject to short term change. Contact the relevant authority before departure.
VALID PASSPORT REQUIRED.

Export permits are required for precious metals, antique rolls and scrolls, books, works of art. NOTE: Passing through customs can take a long time and be a difficult procedure.

US$57 is payable on entry to Albania and US$10 is levied on all foreign departures.

Proof of sufficient funds to finance stay may be required.

POLIO, TYPHOID: R.
YELLOW FEVER: A vaccination certificate is required from travellers over 1 year of age coming from infected areas.
OTHER: Hepatitis A and B, Rabies.

W1

CURRENCY: Lek (Lk) = 100 qindarka. Exch; Banks offer the best rate of exchange. Credit cards are not widely accepted in Albania, although the major international hotels in Tirana accept American Express, Mastercard and Diners Club, but not Visa. US dollars are generally accepted
ATM AVAILABILITY: None.

MONEYGRAM: 00 800 0010 then 800 592 3688.
WESTERN UNION: (42) 34979

AMEX: 0044 1273 696933
DINERS CLUB: no local number
MASTERCARD: 1 314 542 7111.

VISA: no local number
AMEX: 0044 1273 571600
THOMAS COOK: 0044 1733 318650

0700-1500 Mon to Fri.

Albania is one of the poorest countries in Europe, although its economy is improving. Visitors will be charged a far higher rate for services and goods than locals.

Albanian. In the south, Greek is spoken. Italian may also be spoken.

Temperate climate. Warm and dry periods occur between June-Sept. Cool and wet between Oct-May. Best time to visit is May-June and mid Sept.

Mostly Muslim with Greek Orthodox. Protestant and Roman Catholic minorities.

Jan 1, 11, May 1, Nov 28, 29

220 volts AC 50 Hz.

May take up to 2 months. Send recorded delivery to avoid loss.

Women are expected to dress modestly, although attitudes are becoming slightly more relaxed.

RAIL: mainly single track, dilapidated and overcrowded. ROAD: Most are in poor condition and driving standards are low. BUS: The major form of transportation in Albania. TAXIS: Can be found in the capital in front of the main hotels.

The crime rate is steadily rising, and criminal gangs are active throughout the country. Foreign visitors and their vehicles are an attractive target for criminals. Visitors should not overtly display valuables. Avoid large gatherings and street demonstrations, and keep away from remote areas especially at night. It is greatly appreciated if you attempt to speak Albanian.

Algeria

CAPITAL: Algiers

GMT + 1

FROM UK: 00213 OUTGOING CODE TO UK: 0044

Not present.

Embassy of the Democratic and Popular Republic of Algeria, 54 Holland Park, London, W11 3RS. Tel: 020 7221 7800. Fax: 020 7221 0448

British Embassy, 6 Avenue Souidani Boudiemaa, BP08 Alger-Gare 1600, Algiers Tel: 00213 (21) 230068

Algerian Consulate, 6 Hyde Park , London, SW7 5EW. Tel: 020 7589 6885. Fax: 020 7221 0448. Web: www.algeria-tourism.org/

Valid passport and return ticket required – may be subject to change at short notice. Contact the Consulate before travelling.

Visa required.

Personal jewellery weighing more than 100g will be subject to a temporary importation permit which ensures its re-exportation.

AD 1000, payable in local currency.

Evidence of sufficient funds required. Visa not granted for those showing Israeli visas and exit stamps.

HEP A, POLIO, TYPHOID: R.
MALARIA: Limited risk.
YELLOW FEVER: Recommended. Certificate is required if arriving from infected areas.
Bilharzia present

W2

Algerian Dinar (AD) = 100 centimes. NOTE; when exchanging money a receipt is required that should be presented on departure. Foreign money must be declared via a declaration form and stamped at arrival. Very limited acceptance of credit cards. Travellers cheques can only be changed in 4-star hotels. French francs are the preferred currency. ATM AVAILABILITY: Over 100 locations.

MONEYGRAM: Unavailable
WESTERN UNION: Unavailable

AMEX: 0044 1273 696933
MASTERCARD: 001 314 542 7111
VISA: (1) 410 581 9091

AMEX: 0044 1273 571 600
THOMAS COOK: 0044 1733 318950
VISA: 0044 1733 318949

0900-1630 Sun-Thur

Visitors should expect to pay much more than local people.

Arabic, French and English are spoken in tourist centres.

During the summer the temperatures can be very high with humid weather in the North. Travel delays can be caused by sandstorms and coastal towns are also prone to storms.

Islam (mostly Sunni). Few Roman Catholics and Protestants.

Jan 1, May 1, Jun 19, Jul 5, Nov 1. Islamic festivals

127/220 Volts. Plugs = European 2-pin

Airmail from the main cities takes 3-4 days, from elsewhere it takes much longer.

Strict dress codes for women prevail; only one eye can be shown. Women should cover themselves in accordance with Islamic religion.

RAIL: Daily services between the main centres. COACH: Not recommended for long journeys. ROAD: Most are in good condition. NOTE: For desert travel, vehicles must be in good working order as breakdown facilities are virtually non-existent. Water and petrol supplies must be carried. DOCUMENTATION: IDP is required.

The crime rate in Algeria is moderately high, and is increasing. Serious crimes have been reported in which armed men posing as police officers have entered homes , and robbed occupants at gunpoint. Armed car hijacking is also a serious problem.
There have been a number of recent attacks on tourists. The FCO advises against non-essential travel to Algeria. Note that Algiers airport is considered a potential terrorist target. Foreign nationals should ensure they have adequate security protection, and are aware of the current situation. Visitors are advised to stay only in hotels that take security precautions. The land border between Morocco and Algeria is closed.

American Samoa

CAPITAL: Pago Pago

GMT-11

FROM UK: 00684. OUTGOING CODE TO UK: 0044

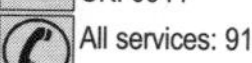
All services: 911.

United States of America, 24-32 Grosvenor Square, London W1A 1AE. Tel: 020 7499 9000. Fax: 020 7629 9124.

No British representation.

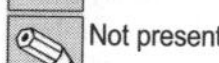
Not present.

Office of Tourism, Convention Centre, Pago Pago, AS 96799. Tel: 6331091. Fax: 6331094.

Return ticket required. Regulations may be subject to change at short notice. Contact the American Embassy before departure. Passports required by all except nationals of the USA with other proof of identity with a valid onward return ticket for stays of up to 30 days. Passports must be valid for at least 60 days beyond the period of stay.

Not required for tourist purposes providing a confirmed reservation and documentation for onward travel is held. Passengers wishing to stay for more than 30 days will be required to obtain special permission.

Narcotics.

US$10 on all international departures.

POLIO, TYPHOID: R
YELLOW FEVER: A vaccination certificate is required by those arriving from infected areas.

W2

US Dollar (US$) = 100 cents. Amex is widely accepted. Other credit cards have more limited use. Travellers cheques, preferably in US dollars, are widely accepted. ATM AVAILABILITY: 4 locations.

MONEYGRAM: Unavailable.
WESTERN UNION: 800 543 4080.

AMEX: 0044 1273 696933
DINERS CLUB: No local number
MASTERCARD: 1 800 307 7309
VISA: (1) 410 581 9091

AMEX: (61) 2 886 0689
THOMAS COOK: 1 800 223 7373
VISA: 1 800 732 1322

0900-1500 Mon to Fri.

Relatively expensive, although local guest-houses are cheaper.

Samoan. English is widely spoken.

Hot tropical climate with heavy rainfall from Dec-Apr. Most comfortable time is May-Sept.

Christian Congregation, Roman Catholicism, Latter day Saints and Protestant.

As USA plus Apr 17

110/220 Volts AC 60 Hz.

1-2 weeks. Poste Restante: General Delivery, Pago Pago, American Samoa, 96799.

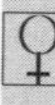
Traditional Samoan society is bound by very strict customs. The government issues a list of behaviour and dress codes for both Western and American Samoa. Traditional clothing is preferred. Samoans' social behaviour conforms to strict and rather complicated rituals.

CAR HIRE: Drivers must be 25 or older (except for a few local companies). DOCUMENTATION: National driving licence is acceptable or IDP. BUS: A local service operates between the airport and capital. TAXI: Plentiful, fixed fare.

Beach wear should be kept for the beach. Local culture should be respected. Do not interrupt evening prayer rituals. Some villages will not allow swimming or fishing on Sundays.

CAPITAL: Andorra-la-Vella

GMT + 1 (GMT + 2 during the summer)

FROM UK: 00376.
OUTGOING CODE TO UK: 044

Emergency medical service: 825 225, Ambulance and Fire: 118, Police: 110

Embassy of Spain, 39 Chesham Place, London, SW1X 8SB. Tel: 020 7235 5555. Fax: 020 7259 5392.

British Consulate, (in Barcelona), 13th Floor, Edificio Torre de Barcelona, Avenida Diagonal 477, 08036 Barcelona, Spain. Tel: (3) 419 9044. Fax: (3) 405 2411. Honorary Consul: britconand@mypic.ad

Andorra Tourist Board, 63 Westover Road, London SW18 2RF. Tel: 020 8874 4806

Sindicat d'Initiative de las Valls d'Andorra, Carrer Dr Vilanova, Andorra la Vella, Andorra. Tel: 820214. Fax: 8825823.

Return ticket required. Requirements may be subject to short-term change. Contact embassy before departure. Passport required except for nationals of France or Spain.

Not required for stays of up to 3 months.

Pornography, radio transmitters, certain foodstuffs, plants, flowers, animals and birds. Items made from endangered species are prohibited.

Nearest airport is Barcelona, Spain.

Rabies

Most currencies are accepted. The main currency in circulation is the Euro. Travellers cheques and all major credit cards are accepted.
ATM: 150 locations.

MONEYGRAM: 0 800 99 0011 then 800 592 3688.
WESTERN UNION: Unavailable.

AMEX: 044 1273 696933
DINERS CLUB: no local number
MASTERCARD: 900 97 1231
VISA: (1) 410 581 9091

AMEX: 044 1273 571 600
THOMAS COOK: 900 99 4403
VISA: 900 97 4447

0900-1300 and 1500-1700 Mon to Fri, 0900-2000 Sat.

Similar prices to the rest of Western Europe.

Catalan, Spanish and French are also spoken.

Summers are generally warm and winters are cold, but the climate is generally temperate. There is rain throughout the year.

Roman Catholic.

Jan 1, 6, Mar 14, May 1, Jun 24, Aug 15, Sep 8, Nov 1,4, Dec 8, 24, 25, 26,31

Sockets 240 volts AC 50 Hz. Lighting 125 volts AC.

Approx. 1 week to Europe. Internal mail services are free.

Similar to other European countries.

ROAD: A good road runs from the Spanish to the French border. DOCUMENTATION: A national driving licence is sufficient.

Usual social courtesies, as in Western Europe, should be applied. Andorra is not a member of the European Union. Adequate insurance cover is essential as the form E111 does not provide health cover in Andorra.

Angola

CAPITAL: Luanda

GMT +1

FROM UK: 00244. OUTGOING CODE TO UK: Calls through the operator are booked in advance

Not present.

Embassy of the People's Republic of Angola, 98 Park Lane, London W1Y 3TA. Tel: 020 7495 1752. Fax: 020 7495 1635. Email: embassyofangola@cwcom.net

British Embassy, CP 1244, Rua Diogo Cão 4, Luanda, Angola. Tel 00244 2334582 Fax: 00244 2333 331. Email: Postmaster@Luanda.mail.fco.gov.uk

Not present.

National Tourist Agency, CP 1240 Palácio de Vidro, Luanda, Angola,. Tel: (2) 372 750.

Return ticket required. May be subject to short-term change. Contact Embassy before departure. Passport required by all.

Visa required and at least six month's validity on the passport.

Firearms and ammunition.

Persons arriving without a visa are subject to possible arrest or deportation.

HEP A and B, POLIO, TYPHOID: R. MALARIA: R. Falciparum variety present. YELLOW FEVER: R. with vaccination certificate if arriving from an infected area. OTHER: Bilharzia, Cholera, Rabies and Polio.

W 1.

New Kwanza (NKW) = 100 lwie (LW). Note: All imported currency should be declared on arrival. Export of local currency is prohibited. Credit cards and travellers cheques are not accepted. ATM AVAILABILITY: Unavailable.

MONEYGRAM: Unavailable.
WESTERN UNION: Unavailable.

AMEX: 44 1273 696933
DINERS CLUB: No local number
MASTERCARD: No local number
VISA: No local number

AMEX: No local number
THOMAS COOK: No local number
VISA: No local number

0845-1600 Mon-Fri

High inflation present due to the country's instability.

Portuguese. African languages are spoken by the majority of the population.

North: Hot and wet in the summer months (Nov to Apr), winter is slightly cooler and mainly dry. South: Hot throughout the year with a slight decrease in the winter months.

Roman Catholic, Protestant and Animist.

Jan 1, Feb 4, Mar 8, 27, Apr 14, May 1, Jun 1, Aug 1, Sep 17, Nov 11, Dec 1, 10, 25.

220 Volts AC, 60 Hz. Plugs are continental 2- pin.

5-10 days for airmail.

Women are generally self-sufficient due to the decimation of most of the male population in civil war.

FLIGHTS: Between main centres. RAIL: Erratic with no sleeping cars or air conditioning. ROAD: Many roads are unsuitable for travel. Local advice is needed. DOCUMENTATION: ID papers to be carried at all times. All travel is strictly controlled and some business travel is prohibited.

The FCO advises against travel to Angola, unless on essential business. There is still a high risk of conflict and civil war outside the capital. Car theft is common. The use of cameras, binoculars and maps near government buildings should be avoided. Travel within Angola remains unsafe due to bandit attacks, undisciplined police and military personnel, sporadic military actions and unexploded land mines in rural areas.
Tourist facilities are non-existent. Severe shortages of lodging, transportation, food, water, medicine and utilities plague Luanda and other cities.

CAPITAL: The Valley

GMT-4

FROM UK: 001264
OUTGOING CODE TO UK: 01144

911

No Embassy in the UK, as Anguilla is a British Overseas Territory.Government House: govthse@anguillanet.com

Anguilla Tourist Office, 7 Westwood Road, London SW13 0LA. Tel: 020 8876 9025

Department of Tourism, The Secretariat, The Valley, Anguilla. Tel: 497 2759 or 497 2451. Fax: 497 3389.

Return ticket required. Requirements may be subject to short term change. Contact embassy before departure.
Valid passport required by all.

May be required by some nationals, check with the Passport office, Clive House, Petty France, London SW7.

Narcotics.

EC$ 13, payable in local currency, for international departures.

POLIO, TYPHOID: R.
YELLOW FEVER: A vaccination certificate is required from passengers over 1 year of age arriving from infected areas

W2

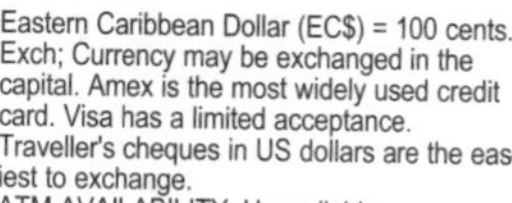
Eastern Caribbean Dollar (EC$) = 100 cents. Exch; Currency may be exchanged in the capital. Amex is the most widely used credit card. Visa has a limited acceptance. Traveller's cheques in US dollars are the easiest to exchange.
ATM AVAILABILITY: Unavailable.

MONEYGRAM: Unavailable
WESTERN UNION: 497 5585
AMEX: 01144 1273 696933
DINERS CLUB: No local number

MASTERCARD: 1-800 307 7309
VISA: 1-800 847 2911
AMEX: (1) 801 964 6665
THOMAS COOK: 1 800 223 7373

VISA: 1 800 732 1322

0800-1500 Mon to Thur. 0800-1700 Fri.

Hotels range from deluxe class to self-catering, but all are expensive.

English.

Generally hot. Oct-Dec is the rainy season, July-Oct hurricanes may occur.

Roman Catholic, Anglican, Baptist, Methodist and Moravian with Hindu, Jewish, and Muslim minorities.

Jan 1, May 1, last Fri in May, first week of Aug, Dec 19,25,26. Christian feast days.

110/220 volts AC, 60 Hz.

4 days to 2 weeks.

Although equality prevails, women are still expected to fulfil traditional housekeeping roles.

ROAD: There is a good but basic network of roads. TAXIS: Are available at the airport and seaports with various fixed prices to hotels and resorts. CAR HIRE: Agencies are present. DOCUMENTATION: A temporary licence can be issued by the police station in the capital on presentation of a valid national driving licence. There is very little public transport.

Relaxed lifestyle with predominant English culture. Beachwear should be confined to the beach and resort areas. NOTE: Hurricanes and tropical storms can strike Anguilla between June and November, and flooding can occur, which can close the airport for several days at a time.

Antigua and Barbuda

CAPITAL: St Johns

GMT–4

FROM UK: 001268 OUTGOING CODE TO UK: 01144

999/911

Antigua and Barbuda High Commission, 15 Thayer Street, London W1M 5LD. Tel: 020 7486 7073. Fax: 020 7486 9970. Web: www.antigua-barbuda.com. Email: ronald@antiguahc.sonnet.co.uk

British High Commission, Price Waterhouse Centre, 11 Old Parham Road, St. John's; Tel: 001268 462 0008; Fax: 001268 562 2124. Email: britishh@candw.ag

Refer to High Commission.

Antigua Department of Tourism, PO Box 363. Long and Thames Streets, St John's, Antigua. Tel: 462 0480. Fax: 462 2483. Email: antbar@msn.com

Return ticket required. Requirements may be subject to short-term change. Contact embassy before departure. Nationals of the USA do not require a passport if they have other documents with proof of their identity. A passport, valid for at least 6 months beyond the intended period of stay. is required by all other nationalities.

Required if stay is longer than 6 months.

Contact the High Commission for a full list.

US$35 foreign national departure tax except children under 16 years of age.

POLIO, TYPHOID: R.
YELLOW FEVER: A vaccination certificate is required from passengers over 1 year of age arriving from infected areas. The dengue fever mosquito is common. HIV/AIDS is prevalent.

W2

Eastern Caribbean Dollar (EC$) = 100 cents. Exch: US$ and Sterling can be exchanged at hotels and larger shops. All credit cards are accepted. Travellers cheques can be exchanged at banks, large hotels and shops. US dollars are the preferred currency. ATM AVAILABILITY: Over 70 locations.

MONEYGRAM: 1 800 543 4080.
WESTERN UNION: 463 0102.

AMEX: 001144 1273 696933
DINERS CLUB: No local number.
MASTERCARD: 1 800 307 7309
VISA: 1 800 847 2911

AMEX: (1) 801 964 6665
THOMAS COOK: 1 800 223 7373
VISA: 1 800 732 1322

0800–1400 Mon to Thur. 0800–1700 Fri.

Can be very expensive, especially in the tourist centres. Accommodation is cheaper in the summer than in the winter.

English. Patois is also spoken.

Tropical, warm climate. Rainfall is minimal.

Anglican, Methodist, Moravian, Roman Catholic, Pentecostal, Baptist and Seventh Day Adventists.

Jan 1, first Mon in May, Jul, Aug, second Sat in Jun, Oct 7, Nov 1, Dec 25,26. Christian feast days.

220/110 volts AC 60 Hz. American style 2-pin plugs are generally used. Some hotels have outlets for 240 volts to be used in which case European type 2-pin plugs are used.

5-7 days.

Usual precautions should be taken. Do not walk alone at night or in quiet areas.

ROAD: Mostly all weather. Buses are irregular. TAXI: Available everywhere charging standard rates, US$ commonly accepted. CAR HIRE: Can be arranged before arrival although is easy to arrange on arrival. DOCUMENTATION: A national driving licence is acceptable but a local licence must be obtained.

Embracing is the common method of greeting friends and family. Dress should be appropriate for the occasion and location; keep beachwear for the beach/pool. It is an offence for anyone, including children, to dress in camouflage clothing. Special events, such as International Sailing Week (Apr/May) and Tennis Weeks (July-Aug), require accommodation to be booked well in advance. June to November is the hurricane season.

CAPITAL: Buenos Aires

GMT-3

FROM UK: 0054 OUTGOING CODE TO UK: 0044

Police 101/107.

Embassy of the Argentine Republic, 53 Hans Place, London, SW1X 0LA. Tel: 020 7584 6494

British Embassy, Casilla 2050, Dr Luis Agote 2412/52, 1425 Buenos Aires, Argentina. Tel: 0054 11 4576 2222; Fax: 0054 11 4803 1731. www.britain.org.ar

Argentine Embassy Consular Section: 27 Three Kings Yard, London W1Y 1FL. Tel: 020 7318 1340; Fax: 020 7318 1349. www.argentine-embassy-uk.org/

Secretaría de Turismo de la Nacíon, Av. Santa Fe 883, 1059 Buenos Aires, Tel. 4312-2232 or 0800 555-0016
www.arecoturismo. com.ar

Return ticket and valid passport required. May be subject to change at short notice: contact the consular authority before going.

Visas required by all for business purposes. Refer to the relevant authority for visa requirements for tourists.

Animals and birds from Africa and Asia (except Japan), parrots and fresh food stuffs. All gold must be declared.

US$ 13. Transit passengers and those under two years of age are exempt. This can not be paid in other currencies.

POLIO, TYPHOID: R. MALARIA: Exists in the vivax variety in rural and areas below 1200m. OTHER: Rabies, noteworthy risk of hepatitis A, trypanosomiasis, gastro-enteritis, intestinal parasitosis and anthrax.

W2

Nuevo Peso (P) = 100 centavos. Diners Club, American Express and MasterCard are accepted. Travellers cheques can be exchanged in larger towns: US$ preferred. ATM AVAILABILITY: Over 800 locations.

MONEYGRAM: 001 800 54288 then 800 592 3688. WESTERN UNION: 1 311 4900.

AMEX: 0044 1273 696933. DINERS CLUB: 0044 1252 513500. MASTERCARD: 0800 555 0507. VISA: No local number.

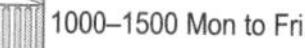

AMEX: 011 800 301 6269. THOMAS COOK: 0044 1733 318950. VISA: 0044 1733 318949

1000–1500 Mon to Fri.

Reasonably priced lodging, food and transport is available. Allow for fluctuating prices between cities and rural areas.

Spanish is the official language. English, German, French and Italian are sometimes spoken.

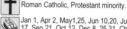

The central area is hot and humid Dec-Feb, cooler in winter. The north has a sub-tropical climate, the south has a sub-arctic climate.

Roman Catholic, Protestant minority.

Jan 1, Apr 2, May1,25, Jun 10,20, Jul 9, Aug 17, Sep 21, Oct 12, Dec 8, 25,31. Christian feast days.

220 Volts AC, 50 Hz. Plugs = older buildings require 2-pin , but 3-pin can be used in more modern buildings.

Airmail to Europe takes between 5 to 10 days. Surface mail can take as long as 50 days, so airmail is advisable.

Women's roles differ greatly between cities and large towns and traditional areas in the lower Andes. Lone women travellers will find Argentina generally safer than most Latin American countries, although caution is still advised, but may encounter some unwanted attention in Buenos Aires.

FLIGHTS: Air travel is the most convenient way to get around the main cities but is often in heavy demand and subject to delay. ROADS: Cross-country highways are well built, although road conditions off the main routes can be unreliable. DOCUMENTATION: IDP is required and this must be stamped at the offices of the Automovil club Argentina. Minor violations are subject to large fines. RAIL: One of the largest domestic rail networks in the world. It has good facilities and lower-class travel can be good value.

Avoid casual discussion of the Falklands/ Malvinas Islands. Avoid poorly-lit areas at night. Theft is rife in Buenos Aires; do not offer resistance if robbery is attempted. Avoid carrying large amounts of cash at all times. Avoid military installations, which usually allow no stopping. Many of the northern provinces of Argentina suffer from seasonal flooding. and disruption to transport.

Armenia

CAPITAL: Yerevan

GMT + 4. (+5 during the summer)

FROM UK: 00374. IDD: Available to Yerevan. Outgoing calls to countries outside the CIS must be made through the operator. Long waits are inevitable.

Not present.

Embassy of the Republic of Armenia, 25A Cheniston Gardens, London W8 6TG. Tel: 020 7938 5435. Fax: 020 7938 2595.

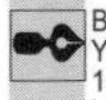
British Embassy, 28 Charents Street, Yerevan, Armenia. Tel: (2) 151 842. Fax: (2) 151 807. www.britemb.am; britemb@arminco.com

Intourist, 219 Marsh Wall, Isle of Dogs, London E14 9PD. Tel: 020 7538 8600. Fax: 020 7538 5967.

Not present.

Requirements may be subject to change at short notice. Contact the relevant authority before travelling. Required by all and must be valid for 3 months from the point of departure.

Visa required.

Pornography, loose pearls and anything owned by a third party to be carried for that third party. Works of art and antiques, lottery and state loan tickets can not be exported. A full list is available from Intourist.

POLIO, TYPHOID: R. OTHER: Rabies

W1

The official currency is the Armenian Dram. The exchange rate is stabilising but rapid inflation is possible. US$ and Russian Roubles are sometimes used in official transactions. The import and export of local currency is prohibited for non-residents. Import and export of foreign currency is unlimited by non-residents if declared on arrival. Credit cards and travellers cheques are not accepted. ATM AVAILABILITY: 2 locations.

MONEYGRAM: Unavailable.
WESTERN UNION: 2 58 9367.

No local contact numbers

No local contact numbers

0930–1730 Mon to Fri.

High inflation: all luxury goods are very expensive and in short supply.

Armenian and Russian.

Continental climate: Summers are hot and dry but temperatures fall at night. Winters are very cold with heavy snowfalls.

Christian (mostly Armenian Apostolic Church). Russian Orthodox and Muslim minority.

Jan 1, 6 (Christmas), Apr 7, 24, Easter, May 9, 28, Jul 5, Sep 21, Dec 7, 31.

220 volts AC, 50 Hz. Power cuts are frequent.

International services are severely disrupted and extremely erratic with infrequent deliveries made. Letters may be more efficiently handled if posted via Paris but may still be subjected to considerable delay.

Women tend to be less retiring than in nearby Muslim areas. There have recently been attacks on single women walking alone in Yerevan at night. Vigilance is recommended.

ROAD: Surfaces can be very poor even in the case of major highways. Supplies of fuel and parts are limited. The general standard of driving is poor. COACHES: Run between major centres of population.

A cease-fire has been in place since May 1994 but the dispute over Nagorny Karabakh remains unresolved and border areas with Azerbaijan should still be avoided. Travel at night outside the capital Yerevan should be avoided if possible. It is not clear whether maintenance procedures for local aircraft are observed. Visitors are advised to travel by an International airline departing from outside Armenia. Visitors should avoid discussing politics with the local population. Travellers should be prepared for a lack of electricity and heat, fuel shortages, and limited availability of consumer goods. The crime rate is low, but petty theft from pockets and bags is on the increase.

CAPITAL: Oranjestad

GMT-4

FROM UK: 00297. OUTGOING CODE TO UK: 0044

Police: 11000, Ambulance: 74300, Fire: 115

No embassy in the UK.

EUROPE: Office of the Minister Plenipotentiary of Aruba, Schimmelpennincklaan 1, 2517 JN The Hague, The Netherlands. Tel: 0031 70 356 6200 or 365 9824. Fax: 0031 70 345 1446.

Not present.

Caribbean Tourism, 42 Westminster Palace Gdns, Artillery Row, London SW1P 1RR. Tel. 020 7222 4335. Fax: 020 7222 4325. www.doitcaribbean.com; cto@carib-tourism.com.
Aruba Tourism Authority, PO Box 1019, L G Smith Boulevard 172, Oranjestad, Aruba. Tel: (8) 21019 or 23777. Fax: (8) 34702.

Return ticket required. Requirements may be subject to short-term change. Contact embassy before departure. Valid passport required.

All nationals may enter for a period of 14 days for tourist purposes providing they have onward or return tickets and proof of sufficient funds for the length of stay.

Duty free is only available to persons over 18 years.

Approx. US$20 per person for all travellers over 2 years of age.

YELLOW FEVER: R. A Yellow Fever vaccination certificate is required from travellers over 6 months of age arriving from infected areas.

W2

Aruba Florin (AFL) = 100 cents. Exch: The US$ is widely accepted. Local currency can not be exchanged outside Aruba. Travellers cheques in US dollars are widely accepted. MasterCard is widely accepted. ATM AVAILABILITY: 10 locations.

MONEYGRAM: 800 1554.
WESTERN UNION: 2978 22473.

AMEX: 0044 1273 696933
MASTERCARD: 800 1561
VISA: 800 1518

AMEX: 1 801 964 6665
Thomas Cook: 1 800 223 7373
VISA: 1 800 732 1322

0800–1200 and 1300–1600 Mon to Fri.

Hotels on the Palm Beach and Eagle Beach resorts are very expensive. Rates for other accommodation are much lower in the summer season.

Dutch. English, Spanish and Papiamento are also spoken.

Warm and dry climate. Average temperature 28ºC. The months of October, November and December experience short showers.

Roman Catholic, Protestant and Jewish minorities.

Jan 1, 25, Mar 18, Apr 30, May 1, Dec 25, 26. Christian feast days.

110 volts AC 60 Hz.

Up to 1 week.

Usual precautions should be taken. Do not walk alone at night or in quiet areas.

FLIGHTS: Air Aruba offers domestic services between other Caribbean islands. ROAD: Very good system of roads throughout the island. BUS: Bus services operate between the towns and hotels. TAXI: Fares are fixed and should be checked before journey. CAR HIRE: The most pleasant way of getting around the island. Many cars are available. DOCUMENTATION: A valid national or IDP is required. Minimum age is 23 for driving.

Beachwear should only be worn around the beach/pool.

Australia

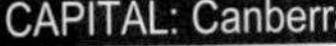

CAPITAL: Canberra

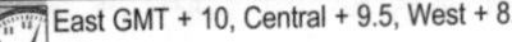

East GMT + 10, Central + 9.5, West + 8.

FROM UK: 0061. OUTGOING CODE TO UK: 001144

Emergency services: 000.

High Commission for the Commonwealth of Australia, Australia House, The Strand, London. WC2B 4LA. Tel: 020 7379 4334. Fax: 020 7465 8218.

British High Commission, Commonwealth Avenue, Yarralumba, Canberra ACT 2600, Australia. Tel: (6) 270 6666. Fax: (6) 273 3236. www.uk.emb.gov.au/ ; bhc.consular@uk.emb.gov.au

Australian Tourist Commission, Gemini House, 10–18 Putney Hill, London, SW1S 6AA. Tel: 020 8780 2227. Fax: 020 8780 1496. atc@acxiom.co.uk

Australian Tourist Commission, PO Box 2721 Level 3, 80 William Street, Woolloomooloo. Sydney, NSW 2011, Australia. Tel: (2) 360 1111. Fax: (2) 331 3385. www.aussie.net.au; www.australia.com

Return ticket required. Regulations may be subject to change at short notice. Contact the embassy before departure. Valid passport required.

Visa required. British nationals can obtain Electronic Travel Authorities (ETAs) from their local travel agent, which will allow travel for up to three months as a visitor.

Strict regulations on non-prescribed drugs, weapons, foodstuffs and potential sources of infection.

YELLOW FEVER: A vaccination certificate will be required if travelling from an infected area. Disease-bearing mosquitos are common in Queensland and Northern Territory and precautions should be taken.

Australian Dollar (A$) = 100 cents. NOTE: Import or export of A$5000 must be reported to customs at entry or departure. All major credit cards and traveller's cheques, in any international currency, are widely accepted. ATM AVAILABILITY: Over 6000 locations.

MONEYGRAM: 0011 800 66639472.
WESTERN UNION: 1 800 649 565.

AMEX: 001144 1273 696933
DINERS CLUB: (3) 8054444
MASTERCARD: 1 800 120 113
VISA: 1 800 125 161

AMEX: 1 800 251 902
THOMAS COOK: 1 800 127 495
VISA: 1 800 450 346

0930–1600 Mon to Thur, 0930–1700 Fri. These hours vary throughout the country.

Cheap compared to the UK and USA. Caters for all.

English and many minority languages.

Extreme varieties of climate from tropical to temperate. Nov-Mar warm or hot everywhere. Apr-Sept occasional rain in the South which can be intense.

Mainly Protestant, Roman Catholic and many minorities.

Jan 1,26, Apr 25, second Mon in June, Dec 25,26. Christian feast days and State holidays.

240/250 Volts AC 50 Hz. Unique 3-pin plugs used – adaptor required.

7–10 days.

Relatively safe for women travellers although a patriarchal culture still prevails, especially in the outback.

FLIGHTS: Vast size of Australia makes this the most convenient form of intercity travel. ROAD: In the outback a full set of spares should be carried, with water, food and petrol. DOCUMENTATION: National licence, valid for 3 months, must be carried whilst driving.
When travelling into the interior, specific precautions should be taken, for instance, take adequate supplies, and leave information of your whereabouts. Special care and respect of natural habitats is recommended.

Always ask permission before photographing aborigines. Tourists should exercise care in Sydney, as a number of backpackers have been attacked. Be cautious when using ATMs.

Austria

CAPITAL: Vienna

GMT + 1 (GMT + 2 during the summer)

FROM UK: 0043. OUTGOING CODE TO UK: 0044

Police: 133, Ambulance: 144, Fire: 122.

Embassy of the Republic of Austria, 18 Belgrave Mews West, London, SW1X 8HU. Tel: 020 7235 3731/4. Fax: 020 7235 8025. www.austria.org.uk; embassy@austria.org.uk

British Embassy, Jauresgasse 10, A-1030 Vienna, Austria. Tel: (1) 71613 5151. Fax: (1) 71613 5900. www.britishembassy.at; britemb@netway.at

Austrian National Tourist Office, PO Box 2363, London W1A 2QB. 30 St George Street, London, W1R 0AL. Tel: 020 7629 0461. Fax: 020 7499 6038. Email: oewlon@easynet.co.uk

Österreich Werbung (ANTO), Margaretenstrasse 1, A-1040 Vienna, Austria. Tel: (1) 58866. Fax: (1) 588 6620. www.austria-tourism.at/; oeinfo@oewwien.via.at

Valid passport required. Requirements may be subject to short-term change. Contact embassy before departure.

Visa required by all except: Nationals of EU countries with a passport or valid ID card.

Rabies. Ticks also pose a problem, and may transmit Lyme disease.

Euro=100cent. Credit cards are not as widely used in Austria as they are in the USA and the United Kingdom, however most major cards will be accepted in large towns. Travellers cheques are accepted in towns and tourist areas. ATM AVAILABILITY: Over 3000 locations.

MONEYGRAM: 022 903 011
WESTERN UNION: (0222) 798 4400

AMEX: 0044 1273 696933
DINERS CLUB: (43) (1) 5046667
MASTERCARD: 0800 21 8235
VISA: 0800 293084

AMEX: 0660 6840
THOMAS COOK: 0660 6266
VISA: 0660 7320

0800–1230 and 1330–1500 Mon, Tues, Wed and Fri. Thur 0800–1230 and 1330–1730. Various provinces will have different opening times.

Relatively expensive, like other Western European countries.

German.

Moderate continental climate. Winter - high snow levels but sunny. Summer - warm days cool nights.

Mostly Roman Catholic, some Protestant.

Jan 1,6, May 1, Aug 15, Oct 26, Nov 1, Dec 8, 25,26. Christian feast days.

220 volts AC 50 Hz. Round 2-pin European plugs are used.

2–4 days within Europe.

RAIL: An efficient rail service operates throughout Austria. Special offers / discounts can often be found. ROAD: Excellent network of roads. There is free assistance from the Austrian motoring association (OAMTC). Visitors using Austrian motorways display a Motorway Vignette on their vehicle. Failure to have one will mean an on the spot fine. Motorway Vignettes are obtainable at all major border crossings and at larger petrol stations. For more information visit the website at www.vignette.at. DOCUMENTATION: Green card is strongly recommended for driving. The British driving licence is usually recognised.

It is customary to greet people with the salute *Grüss Gott!*. Austrians tend to be quite formal. The Church holds a high position in Austrian society, which should be kept in mind by the visitor. It is customary to dress up for the opera or theatre.

Azerbaijan

CAPITAL: Baku

GMT + 4. (GMT + 5 during the summer).

FROM UK: 00994. IDD available to Baku. All international calls must be made through the operator.

Not present.

Embassy of the Azerbaijan Republic, 4 Kensington Court, London W8 5DL. Tel: 020 7938 5482. Fax: 020 7937 1783. www.president.az/ ; sefir@btinternet.com

British Embassy, 2 Izmir Street, 370065 Baku, Azerbaijan. Tel: (12) 985 558. Fax: (12) 922 739. www.britishembassy.az ; office@britemb.baku.az

Refer to the Embassy.

Ministry of Foreign Affairs, Ghanjlar meydani 3, 370004 Baku, Azerbaijan. Tel: (12) 933 012. Fax: (12) 937 969 or 930 743.

Return Ticket required. Requirements may be subject to short-term change. Contact the relevant authority before departure. Passport, required by all, must be valid for at least the length of the visa.

Visa required.

Antiques, works of art, precious metals, state loan certificates, lottery tickets, siaga horns, red deer antlers and deer skins.

MALARIA: Exists exclusively in the vivax variety throughout the year in southern areas of Azerbaijan.
OTHER: Rabies, cutaneous and visceral leishmaniasis occur. Trachoma is common. Diphtheria has been reported.

W1

CURRENCY: 1 Manat (AM) = 100 gyapik. Travellers cheques and credit cards are not accepted. It is generally a cash-only economy. US$ are the favoured foreign currency and can be easily changed into Azeri Manats, provided the dollar bills are clean and not torn. ATM AVAILABILITY: Unavailable.

MONEYGRAM: Unavailable.
WESTERN UNION: Unavailable.

No local numbers.

No local numbers.

0930–1730 Mon to Fri.

Since the dispute with Armenia, shortage of commodities has forced prices to rise.

Azerbaijani.

Continental climate.

Mostly Shia Muslim.

Jan 1,20, Mar 8, 22, May 1, 9 28, Jun 15, Oct 9, 18, Nov 17, Dec 31. Islamic festivals.

220 volts AC 50 Hz.

International postal services are severely disrupted. Long delays are inevitable and may take months. Parcels may not arrive intact.

Local women, especially in rural areas, tend to be retiring. Initially foreign women are treated with courtesy, which may lead to unwelcome attention. Women are advised to dress conservatively and act in a cool manner. Although a Muslim country, women may dress in Western fashion.

ROAD: Most of the road network is paved. Military operations and mass migration of refugees may delay journeys considerably. NOTE: Special permission from the Ministry of Interior will be required to visit regions in restricted areas. Visitors should not try to enter or leave Azerbaijan by the land borders with Russia or Iran as these border crossings are closed to foreigners.

Travel to this region should be avoided. Recent incidents against foreigners have included robberies and have in some cases been violent. Visitors must be vigilant at all times. Use officially marked taxis, which you should not share with strangers. It is not known whether aircraft used on internal flights are subject to thorough maintenance procedures and therefore internal flights should not be used.

CAPITAL: Nassau

GMT–5 (–4 during the summer)

FROM UK: 001242. OUTGOING CODE TO UK: 01144

All services: 911

High Commission of the Commonwealth of the Bahamas, 10 Chesterfield Street, London, W1X 8AH. Tel: 020 7408 4488. Fax: 020 7499 9937.
bahamas.hicom.lon@cablenet.co.uk

British High Commission, Ansbacher House (3rd Floor) East Street, PO Box N516, Nassau Tel: 001242 325 7471; Fax: 001242 323 3871.
www.interknowledge.com/bahamas/

Bahamas Tourist Office, 3 The Billings, Walnut Tree Close, Guildford, Surrey GUI 4UL. Tel: (01483) 448 900. Fax: (01483) 448 990.

Bahamas Ministry of Tourism, PO Box N-3701, Bay Street, Nassau, The Bahamas. Tel: 322 7500 or 322 8634. Fax: 328 8634 or 328 0945.

Return ticket required. Requirements may be subject to short term change. Contact embassy before departure. Passport required by all.

Visa not required by Nationals of EU countries for visits of less than 8 months.

Radio transmitters.

Ba$15, payable in local currency. Children under 3 years of age and transit passengers are exempt.

YELLOW FEVER: A vaccination certificate is required from travellers over 1 year of age arriving within 6 months of visiting an infected area.

W2

Bahamian Dollar (Ba$) = 100 cents. All major credit cards are accepted. Travellers cheques, preferably in US$ or Pound sterling, are accepted. ATM AVAILABILITY: Over 25 locations.

MONEYGRAM: 1 800 543 4080.
WESTERN UNION: 327 5170.

AMEX: 01144 1273 696 933
DINERS CLUB: 01144 1252 513 500
MASTERCARD: 1800 307 7309
VISA: 1800 847 2911

AMEX: 01144 1273 571600
THOMAS COOK: 1 800 223 7373
VISA: 01144 20 7937 8091

0930-1500 Mon to Thur, 0930-1700 Fri.

Avoid the tourist centres when looking for cheaper accommodation and food. Staying in the Bahamas may prove difficult for the budget traveller.

English.

The Bahamas are slightly cooler than other islands in the Caribbean.

Baptist, Anglican and Roman Catholic.

Jan 1, first Fri in June, Jul 10, first Mon in Aug, Oct 12, Dec 25,26. Christian feast days.

120 volts AC, 60 Hz

5 days.

Usual precautions should be taken. Do not walk alone at night or in quiet areas.

SEA: A mail boat serves the outer island which may also be used by passengers. ROAD: Inexpensive and frequent buses are available. TAXIS: Metered. CAR HIRE: Major companies have agencies at the airport and in Nassau. DOCUMENTATION: A valid British driving licence is valid for 3 months.

Bahamas has 700 islands in total. The tourist may consider visiting those that are less commercial. Beachwear is not acceptable in towns, where informal dress should be worn. It is illegal to work without a work permit. Employment is scarce so do not expect to find work to finance your visit. Violent crime is increasing and a number of incidents have taken place in tourist areas. The hurricane season runs from June to November, and visitors should be alert for advice on local radio and from hotel staff.

Bahrain

CAPITAL: Manama

GMT + 3.

FROM UK: 00973. OUTGOING CODE TO UK: 044

All services: 999.

Embassy of the State of Bahrain, 98 Gloucester Road, London SW7 4AU. Tel: 020 7370 5132/3. Fax: 020 7370 7773.

British Embassy, PO Box 114, 21 Government Avenue, Manama, 306, Bahrain. Tel: 534 404 or 534 865/6. Fax: 531 273. www.ukembassy.gov.bh; britemb@batelco.com.bh

Refer to Embassy.

Bahrain Tourism Company (BTC) PO Box 5831, Manama, Bahrain. Tel: 530 530. Fax: 530 867.

Return ticket required. Requirements may be subject to short-term change. Contact the relevant authority before departure. Valid passport required by all.

Visa required by citizens of the UK for a maximum of 4 weeks (providing their full passport is valid for 6 months).

Jewellery and all items originating in Israel may only be imported under licence. Pearls are under strict import regulations. Videotapes may be withheld on arrival at the airport.

BD3 for international departures, payable in local currency.

Holders of Israeli passports. Holders of passports with visas or endorsements for Israel (valid or expired) are permitted to transit Bahrain providing they do so by the same aircraft.

POLIO, TYPHOID: R.
OTHER: Cutaneous leishmaniasis, typhoid fevers and hepatitis A and B occur.

Dinar (BD) = 100 fils. All credit cards and travellers cheques are accepted. US dollars are the preferred currency. ATM AVAILABILITY: Over 60 locations.

MONEYGRAM: 800 010.
WESTERN UNION: 214021.

AMEX: 044 1273 696 933
DINERS CLUB: 532139
MASTERCARD: 01 314 542 7111
VISA: 800 006

AMEX: 044 1273 571 600
THOMAS COOK: 044 1733 318950
VISA: 044 20 7937 8091

0800-1200 and usually 1600-1800 Sat to Wed. 0800-1100 Thur.

Can be relatively cheap if you travel around by foot and make purchases from the souk. Accommodation ranges from the deluxe to cheaper family-run guest houses

Arabic. English may also be spoken.

Summers are very hot. Winters are much cooler. Rainfall is only likely in the winter. Spring and autumn are pleasant.

Muslim (Shia and Sunni). Christian, Bahai, Hindu and Parsee minorities.

Jan 1, Dec 16-17. Islamic festivals.

230 volts AC, single phase and 400 volts, 50 Hz. (Awali-100 volts AC, 60 Hz.) Plugs are normally the 13-amp pin type.

3-4 days to Europe.

Attitudes towards women are more liberal than in many other Gulf states. It is acceptable to wear short dresses. However, it is advisable to avoid wearing revealing clothes. Bahrain is described as one of the friendliest countries in the Gulf to travel in.

SEA: Transport between the smaller islands is by motor boat or dhow. ROAD: Manama is served by an excellent road system. BUS: Routes now serve most towns and villages. TAXI: Identifiable by their orange and red colouring. Those waiting outside hotels may charge more and between midnight and 0500 - fares increase by 50%.

Bahrain is relatively liberal in comparison to other Gulf countries. Non Muslims may not enter mosques except during prayer times. Religious sensitivities should be respected, especially during the religious festivals of the Shia community, when black flags will be displayed. Avoid eating, drinking and smoking during the daytime in the month of Ramadan (usually around November). Offenders may be fined.
Violent crime is quite rare, but visitors should avoid village areas, especially after dark. It is polite to drink 2 small cups of tea when offered.

Bangladesh

CAPITAL: Dhaka

GMT + 6.

FROM UK: 00880. IDD: Limited.
OUTGOING CODE TO UK: 0044

High Commission for the People's Republic of Bangladesh, 29 Queen's Gate, London SW7 5JA. Tel: 020 7584 0081. Fax: 020 7225 2130.

British High Commission, PO Box 6079, United Nations Road, Baridhara, Dhaka 1212. Tel: (2) 882 705 or 883 666 (consular/immigration). Fax: (2) 883 437. www.ukinbangladesh.org; consular@dhaka.mail.fco.gov.uk

Refer to High Commission. www.parjatan.org

Bangladesh Parjatan Corporation (National Tourism Organisation) 33 Old Airport Road, Tejgaon, Dhaka 1215. Tel: 8119192. bpcho@bangla.net

Return ticket and valid passport required by all. Requirements may be subject to short-term change: contact the relevant authority before departure.

Visa required.

Animals.

Tk300, payable in local currency. Passengers in transit are exempt.

POLIO, TYPHOID: R. MALARIA: Exists throughout the year in the whole country, except Dhaka City. The falciparum variety is reported to be highly resistant to chloroquine. YELLOW FEVER: A vaccination certificate is required if arriving from an infected area. OTHER: Cholera, rabies, filariasis, visceral leishmaniasis, dengue fever, dysentery and hepatitis A, B and E are present.

W1

Bangladeshi Taka (Tk) = 100 poisha. EXCHANGE: Many shops in cities offer better rates than banks. NOTE: All currency exchange must be entered on a currency declaration form. Diners Club and Amex accepted. Travellers cheques can be exchanged at Dhaka Airport. ATM: Unavailable.

MONEYGRAM: Single location at capital city. WESTERN UNION: (2) 9554733.

AMEX: 0044 1273 696933. DINERS CLUB: 0044 1252 513 500. MASTERCARD: 001 314 542 7111. VISA: 001 410 581 9994

AMEX: 001 801 964 6665. THOMAS COOK: 0044 1733 318950. VISA: 0044 1733 318949

0900–1500 Sat to Wed, 0900-1300 Thur.

Can be cheap if willing to sacrifice luxuries.

Bengali (Banga). English is spoken in Government and commercial circles.

Generally a hot tropical climate with a monsoon season Apr-Oct when temperatures are highest. The cool season is Nov-Mar.

Mainly Muslim with Hindu, Buddhist and Christian minorities. Since 1988 Islam has been the official state religion.

Jan 1, Feb 21, Mar 26, Apr 14, May 1, first Mon in Jul, Aug 15, Nov 7, Dec 16, 25, 26, 31. Islamic festivals and Hindu feasts.

220/240 volts AC, 60 Hz. Plugs are of the British 5 and 15 amp, round 2- or 3-pin type.

Airmail takes 3-4 days to Europe. Surface mail can take several months.

Women should wear trousers or long skirts especially when attending religious places. Women should not be photographed unless it is clear there will be no objection.

RAIL: A slow but efficient system sometimes limited by the geography of the country. ROAD: It is possible to reach almost everywhere by road, but with frequent ferry crossings; many main roads and bridges are in poor condition. Poor driving and vehicle maintenance as well as unlit buses and lorries cause frequent accidents. BUS: Serve all major towns, fares are generally low. TAXI: Available at airports and major hotels. Agree fares in advance. CAR HIRE: Available at airports and major hotels. DOCUMENTATION: IDP or national licence.

New arrivals should register with the High Commission in Dhaka. Money must not be given as gifts as it causes offence. Religious customs should be respected by all visitors. PHOTOGRAPHY: In rural areas people are unused to tourists and therefore respect should be shown. Do not take photographs of military installations. SPECIAL PRECAUTIONS: Visitors should avoid demonstrations and crowded places where outbreaks of violence have occurred. Major roads between towns are subject to armed banditry at night; trains, ferries and long-distance buses have been targeted by organised gangs of thieves. Widespread flooding Jun–Sept.

Barbados

CAPITAL: Bridgetown

GMT-4

FROM UK: 001246. OUTGOING CODE TO UK: 01144

Police: 112; Ambulance: 115; Fire: 113. All services: 119.

Barbados High Commission, 1 Great Russell Street, London, WC1B 3JY. Tel: 020 7631 4975. Fax: 020 7323 6872. barcomuk@dial.pipex.com

British High Commission, PO Box 676, Lower Collymore Rock, St Michael, Barbados. Tel: 436 6694. Fax: 436 5398.

www.britishhc.org/ ; britishhc@sunbeach.net

Barbados Tourism Authority, 263 Tottenham Court Road, London, W1P AA. Tel: 020 7636 9448. Fax: 020 7637 1496.
www.barbados.org; btauk@barbados.org
Barbados Tourism Authority, PO Box 242 Harbour Road, Bridgetown, Barbados. Tel: 427 2623/4. Fax: 426 4080.

Return ticket and passport, valid for 6 months after date of entry, required.

Visa not required by nationals of EU countries for stays up to 6 months.

Import of foreign rum and ammunition and firearms. Permits are required for plants and animals.

Bds$25 in local currency, for all departures.

POLIO, TYPHOID: R
YELLOW FEVER: A vaccination certificate if required from passengers over 1 year of age coming from infected areas. The dengue fever mosquito is found all over Barbados. HIV/AIDS is prevalent.

Barbados Dollar (Bds$) = 100 cents. All major credit cards are accepted. Travellers cheques, preferably in US dollars and Pound sterling, are accepted. ATM AVAILABILITY: 45 locations.

MONEYGRAM: 1 800 543 4080.
WESTERN UNION: 436 6055.

AMEX: 01144 1273 696933
DINERS CLUB: 01144 1252 513 500
MASTERCARD: 1 800 307 7309
VISA: 1 800 847 2911

AMEX: 01144 1273 571 600
THOMAS COOK: 1 800 223 7373
VISA: 01144 20 7937 8091

0800-1500 Mon to Thur, 0800-1300 and 1500-1700 Fri.

Generally expensive. Avoid the tourist centres if travelling on a budget, although prices throughout the island are quite expensive.

English. Local Bajan dialect is also spoken.

Subtropical climate cooled by sea breezes. Wet season - July till Nov when brief showers occur. Dry season - Dec till June.

Christian (Protestant majority, Roman Catholic minority). Small numbers of Jews, Hindus and Muslims are also present.

Jan 1,21, Apr 28, May 1, Aug 1, first Mon in Aug, Nov 30, Dec 25,26. Christian feast days.

110 volts AC, 50 Hz American style 2-pin plug are used.

Up to 1 week.

Usual precautions should be taken. Do not walk alone at night or in quiet areas.

FLIGHTS: Several operators run flights between neighbouring islands. ROAD: A good network of roads run throughout the island. BUS: Frequent comprehensive coverage of the island. Although cheap buses are crowded during the rush hour. CAR HIRE: Various vehicles can be hired at the airport or large hotels. DOCUMENTATION: A Barbados driving licence is required, a valid national or IDP should be held.

Attacks and thefts are rare although persistent salesmen are likely to continually approach you. Visitors should exercise common sense precautions such as not exhibiting conspicuous signs of wealth and not to visit deserted beaches at night. It is an offence for anyone, including children, to wear camouflage clothing. The hurricane season is from June to November and visitors should be alert to advice on local radio and from hotel staff.

CAPITAL: Minsk

GMT + 2 (+3 during the summer)

FROM UK: 00375. OUTGOING CODE TO UK: 8/10 (wait for second tone) Outside main cities, international calls go through the operator.

Police: 02; Ambulance: 03; Fire: 01.

Embassy of the Republic of Belarus, 6 Kensington Court, London W8 5DL. Tel: 020 7937 3288. www.belemb.freeserve.co.uk/ ; belaru@belemb.freeserve.co.uk

British Embassy, 37 Karl Marx Street 220030 Minsk, Belarus. Tel: 00375 172 105920. Fax: 00375 172 292306. pia@bepost.belpak.minsk.by

Intourist, 219 Marsh Wall, Isle of Dogs, London E14 9FJ. Tel: 020 7538 8600. Fax: 020 7538 5967.

Belintourist, Masherava 19, 220078, Minsk, Belarus. Tel: (172) 269 840. Fax: (172) 231 143.

Return ticket required. Requirements may be subject to short term change. Contact Embassy before departure. Pasport required,: must be valid for 6 months after departure.

Visa required by all except nationals of the CIS republics. Transit visas are required if crossing Belarus to reach Ukraine or the Baltic States. Visas not available on arrival.

Pornography, loose pearls, anything owned by a third party that is to be carried in for that third party.

Not present.

Polio, rabies.

Belarusian Rouble. Exchange should only take place at authorised bureaux and the transaction must be entered on the currency declaration form which will be issued on arrival. Amex and Visa are accepted in larger towns. Travellers cheques are not widely accepted, but are preferable to cash. It is advisable to take hard currency as well. ATM AVAILABILITY: 5 locations.

MONEYGRAM: Unavailable.
WESTERN UNION: 095 119 8250

AMEX: 8/10 44 1273 696933
DINERS CLUB 8/10 44 1252 513 500
MASTERCARD 8/10 1 314 542 7111
VISA: 8/10 1 410 581 9994

AMEX 8/10 44 1273 571 600
THOMAS COOK: 8/10 44 1733 318950
VISA 8/10 44 20 7937 8091

0900-1730 Mon to Fri.

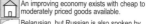

An improving economy exists with cheap to moderately priced goods available.

Belarusian, but Russian is also spoken by 13% of the population.

Temperate continental climate.

Christian, mainly Eastern Orthodox and Roman Catholic with small Jewish and Muslim minorities.

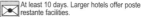

Jan 1, 7, Mar 8, 15, May 1, 9, Jul 3, Nov 2,7 Dec 25. Western and Orthodox Christian feast days.

220 volts AC, 50 Hz, adapters are recommended.

At least 10 days. Larger hotels offer poste restante facilities.

Traditionally, a patriarchal society, but younger women are becoming more liberated.

RAIL: 5590 km of rail track is in use. ROAD: Tourists can only drive on approved routes. Valid visa and passport, insurance certificate and customs form guaranteeing the visitor will not take the car out of the country, Intourist documentation with the approved route and accommodation to be used must be carried at all times. DOCUMENTATION: IDP is required.

The people of Belarus offer a welcoming and friendly hospitality to visitors. It is advisable to take warm clothing in winter and waterproofs throughout the year. Avoid dairy produce and mushrooms, which can carry high levels of radiation. Theft is a problem so exercise caution in major cities.
NOTE: All foreigners visiting Belarus for more than 2 days must register their passports with the local police.

Belgium

CAPITAL: Brussels

GMT +1 (+2 during the summer)

FROM UK: 0032. OUTGOING CODE TO UK: 0044

Police: 101; Fire, Ambulance: 100; From mobile phone: 112

Embassy of the Kingdom of Belgium, 103-105 Eaton Square, London, SW1W 9AB. Tel: 020 7470 3700 (general enquiries) or (0891) 600 255 (recorded message) Fax:020 7259 6213.

British Embassy, 85 rue d'Arlon, B-1040 Brussels, Belgium. Tel: (2) 287 6211. Fax: (2) 287 6355. www.british-embassy.be/

Belgian Tourist Office, 225 Marsh Wall, London E14 9FW. Tel. 020 7531 7390. Brochure line (free) 0800 954 5245. www.belgium-tourism.net Email: infor@belgium-tourism.org

Office de Promotion du Tourisme Wallonie-Bruxelles, 61 rue Marché-aux-Herbes, B-1000 Brussels, Belgium. Tel: (2) 504 0200. Fax(2) 513 6950.

Return ticket required. Requirements may be subject to short-term change. Contact embassy before departure. Valid passport required by all except nationals of EU countries (provided they carry a national ID card.

Unpreserved meat products. Other preserved food stuffs must be declared.

BFr250/530.

Rabies

Euro=100 cents. Credit cards and Travellers cheques are widely accepted. ATM AVAILABILITY: Over 2000 locations.

MONEYGRAM: 0800 7 1173.
WESTERN UNION: 0800 99090

AMEX: 0044 1273 696933
DINERS CLUB: 02 639 4110
MASTERCARD: 0800 15096
VISA: 0800 78465

AMEX: 0800 12112
THOMAS COOK: 0800 12121
VISA: 0800 71645

0900-1200 and 1400-1600 Mon to Fri. Some banks are open 0900-1200 Sat.

Relatively expensive, similarly to other Western European countries.

Flemish and French.

Warm May-Sept, and snow likely during the winter months.

Mostly Roman Catholic with small minorities of Protestants and Jews.

Jan 1, May 1, Jun 11 (Flemish), Jun 21, Aug 15, Sep 27 (French), Nov 1, 11, Dec 25. Christian feast days.

220 volts AC, 50 Hz. Plugs are the 2-pin round type.

2-3 days to other European destinations. Poste restante is available in the main cities.

Similar values to those of the rest of Western Europe.

RAIL: A dense, regular service operates. A reduced-rate card can be purchased for unlimited discounts for 1 month period.

Flemings often prefer to speak English, rather than French, to all foreign visitors.

CAPITAL: Belmopan

GMT–6

FROM UK: 00501. OUTGOING CODE TO UK: 0044

All services: 911

Belize High Commission, 22 Harcourt House, 19 Cavendish Square, London, W1M 9AD. Tel: 020 7499 9728. Fax: 020 7491 4139.

British High Commission, PO Box 91, Embassy Square, Belmopan, Belize, CA. Tel: (8) 22146/7. Fax: (8) 22761. britihicom@btl.net

Caribbean Tourism, 42 Westminster Palace Gdns, Artillery Row, London SW1P 1RR. Tel: 020 7222 4335. Fax: 020 7222 4325. www.doitcaribbean.com; cto@carib-tourism.com

Belize Tourist Board, PO Box 325, 83 North Front Street, Belize City, Belize, CA. Tel: (2) 77213. Fax: (2) 77490, www.travelbelize.org

Return ticket required. Requirements may change at short notice. Contact the High Commission before departure. Passports valid for 6 months beyond the intended length of stay are required by all.

Visa required by all, but it is advisable to contact the High Commission before departure as regulations are subject to change.

Narcotics and firearms.

BZ$22.50 departure tax with BZ$ 2.50 security tax is levied on all passengers except transit passengers and those under 12 years of age. Payable in the local currency.

POLIO, TYPHOID: R.
MALARIA: Exists throughout the year, excluding the urban areas, predominately in the benign Vivax form.
YELLOW FEVER: A vaccination certificate is required for travellers arriving from infected areas.
OTHER: Rabies

W1

Belizean Dollar (BZ$) = 100. Amex and Visa are widely accepted. MasterCard can also be used but to a more limited extent. US Dollar is the preferred currency for travellers cheques. ATM AVAILABLITY: Unavailable.

MONEYGRAM: 555 then 800 592 3688.
WESTERN UNION: (2) 72678.

AMEX: 0044 1273 696933
DINERS CLUB: 0044 1252 513 500
MASTERCARD: 001 314 542 7111
VISA: 001 410 581 9994

AMEX: 0044 1273 571 600
THOMAS COOK: 0044 1733 318950
VISA: 0044 20 7937 8091

0800-1300 Mon to Thur, 0800-1200 and 1500-1800 Fri.

Caters for all travellers and budgets.

English is the official language but Spanish is spoken by over half the population.

Sub-tropical climate, hot and humid. Monsoon season June–Sept.

Roman Catholic, Anglican, Methodist, Mennonite, Seventh Day Adventist, Pentecostal minorities.

Jan 1, Mar 9, May 1,24, Sep 10, 21, Nov 19, Dec 1, 25, 26. Christian feast days.

110/220 volts AC, 60 Hz.

Up to 5 days to Europe.

Culture is influenced by Caribbean, Latin and colonial heritage. Women tend to restrict their activities to simple craft-making and household chores. Visitors may experience pestering from the local men, which should not be a problem if ignored.

FLIGHTS: Charter and scheduled flights operate between the main towns. ROAD: All weather roads link the main towns in the country although torrential rain during the monsoon season often makes these impassable. CAR HIRE: International companies exist in the main cities. DOCUMENTATION: A national driving licence is acceptable.

Petty crime is common and mugging is a problem in Belize City. Keep valuables out of sight.Travel in groups if possible, and take a local guide for trips off the beaten track. Common-sense rules should be applied. It is inadvisable to discuss politics with the locals. A fishing permit must be obtained before going on offshore charter fishing trips. Inland Belize has numerous relics of the Maya civilisation.

Benin

CAPITAL: Porto Novo

GMT +1

FROM UK: 00229. OUTGOING CODE TO UK: 0044

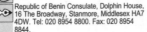

30 14 31 (UK Embassy)

Republic of Benin Consulate, Dolphin House, 16 The Broadway, Stanmore, Middlesex HA7 4DW. Tel: 020 8954 8800. Fax: 020 8954 8844.

The British High Commission in Lagos deals with enquiries relating to Benin.

Refer to Embassy.

Office National du Tourisme et de l'Hôtellerie (ONATHO), BP 89, Contonou, Benin. Tel: 315 402.

Return ticket and valid passport required. May be subject to short term change. Contact the Embassy before departure

Visa required.

Foreign currency.

Departure tax levied CFA 2500 or US$ 9.

POLIO, TYPHOID, Cholera, Hepatitis A.

W1

CFA Franc = 100 centimes. Benin is part of the French Monetary Area. Only currency issued by the Banque des Etats de l'Afrique Centrale is valid. Credit cards are accepted on a very limited basis. French francs are the preferred currency in traveller's cheques. ATM AVAILABILITY: Unavailable.

MONEYGRAM: Unavailable
WESTERN UNION: 31 40 23

AMEX: 0044 1273 696933
DINERS CLUB: No local number
MASTERCARD: 1 314 542 7111
VISA: (1) 410 581 9091

AMEX: No local number
THOMAS COOK: 0044 1733 318950
VISA: 0044 1733 318949

0800–1100 and 1500–1600 Mon to Fri

Moderate growth resulting in continuous rising prices.

French. A variety of languages are also spoken by ethnic groups. Some English is spoken.

South: hot and dry from Jan to Aug. Rainy season is May-July and Sept-Dec. North: hot and dry from Nov to Jun and cooler and very wet July-Oct.

Mostly Animist / Traditional with Muslim and Christian (mainly Roman Catholic).

Jan 1,10, May 1, Aug 1,15, Oct 26, Nov 1,30, Dec 25. Islamic and Christian festivals.

220 volts AC 50 Hz.

3-5 days for airmail.

A predominantly patriarchal society, but with the changing economy, roles are modifying.

RAIL: 600 km of track runs from Contonou to Pobé, Ouidah, Seg boroué and Patakou. ROAD: Roads are reasonably good but most are impassable during the rainy season. It is advisable to clear your itinerary with the authorities. Foreigners travelling outside Contonou are subject to restrictions and visitors are advised to check their position before travelling. TAXI: Settle fares in advance. CAR HIRE: A number of local car hire firms now exist. DOCUMENTATION: International Driving License is required.

Recent attacks and armed robberies require the visitor to be vigilant. Importance is placed on religious beliefs, which should be respected.

Bermuda

CAPITAL: Hamilton

GMT –4

FROM UK: 001441. OUTGOING CODE TO UK: 01144

All services: 911.

British Dependent Territories Visa Section, The Passport Office, 70–78 Clive House, Petty France, London, SW1H 9HD. Tel: 020 7271 8552. Fax: 020 7271 8645

Not present. Government House: depgov@ibl.bm

Bermuda Tourism, 1 Battersea Church Road, London SW11 3LY. Tel: 020 7734 8813. Fax: 020 7352 6501

Bermuda Department of Tourism, Global House, 43 Church Street, Hamilton HM 12, Bermuda. Tel: 292 0023. Fax: 292 7537. www.bermudatourism.com

Return ticket required. Requirements may change at short notice. Contact the Embassy before departure. Valid passport required.

Visas are not required for stays of up to 3 weeks.

Spear guns for fishing, firearms and non-prescribed drugs.

Bda$20. Levied on passengers over 12 years old. Passengers in immediate transit are exempt. This is payable in local currency.

Bermuda Dollar (Bda $) = 100 cents. Export of local currency is usually limited to Bda$ 250. US$ cheques are widely accepted. Mastercard, American Express, Visa and Diners Club are all accepted, in hotels, shops and restaurants. ATM AVAILABILITY: 54 locations.

MONEYGRAM: 1 800 543 4080.
WESTERN UNION: Available.

AMEX: 01144 1273 696933
DINERS CLUB: 800 468 4033
MASTERCARD: 1 800 307 7309
VISA: 1888 412 7709

AMEX: (1) 801 964 6665
THOMAS COOK: 1 800 223 7373
VISA: 1 800 732 1322

0930–1500 Mon to Thur, 0930–1500 and 1630–1730 Fri.

Very expensive. Bermuda is a holiday destination for affluent tourists.

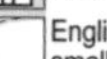
English is the official language. There is a small community of Portuguese speakers.

Semi-tropical climate, with cool sea breezes. Showers can occur at any time of the year.

Anglican, Episcopal, Roman Catholic, Christian.

Jan1 , May 24, third Mon in Jun, first Mon in Sep, Nov 11, Dec 25, 26. Good Friday/ Easter and Cup Match Day (Thur/Fri before first Mon in Aug).

110 volts AC 60 Hz. American flat 2-pin plugs are used.

Airmail: 5-7 days to Europe.

Bermuda has a very English air about it. The pace is relaxed and polite. Usual precautions should be taken. There is no need for additional concern.

ROAD: Visitors are not allowed to drive in Bermuda. TAXI: Official taxis display a small blue flag.

Most hotels and restaurants require jacket and tie in the evening. Social conventions are mostly British influenced. Drinking alcohol in public outside licensed premises is not allowed. Hurricanes and tropical storms can strike Bermuda between June and November.

Bhutan

CAPITAL: Thimphu

GMT + 6.

FROM UK: 00975. IDD: Restricted to main areas. OUTGOING CODE: 0044

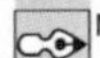
No representation.

No representation. Nearest consulate in Calcutta.

Not present.

Tourism Authority of Bhutan PO Box 126, Thimphu, Kingdom of Bhutan. Tel: 00975 2 23251 TAB@overseas.net.
Bhutan Yod Sel Tours and Treks. PO Box 574, Thimpu, Bhutan. Tel: (2) 23912. Fax: (2) 23589

Return ticket required. Requirements may be subject to short-term change. Contact the relevant authority before departure. Valid passport required by all

Visa required by all except for nationals of India. NOTE: There are two ways of entering Bhutan; by air to Paro Airport or by road to the Bhutanese border town of Phuntosholing. All travellers entering by road must ensure they have the necessary documentation for transiting through India.

Gold and silver bullion and obsolete currency. The export of antiques, religious objects, manuscripts, images and anthropological materials is strictly prohibited.

Nu 300, payable in local currency.

POLIO, TYPHOID: R. MALARIA: Exists throughout the year in the Southern belt. Resistance to chloroquine has been reported in the falciparum variety of the disease. YELLOW FEVER: A vaccination certificate is required if coming from an infected area. OTHER: Cholera, Rabies, Meningitis.

W1

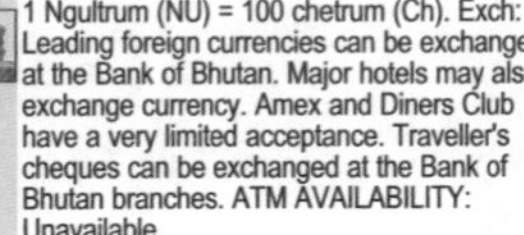
1 Ngultrum (NU) = 100 chetrum (Ch). Exch: Leading foreign currencies can be exchanged at the Bank of Bhutan. Major hotels may also exchange currency. Amex and Diners Club have a very limited acceptance. Traveller's cheques can be exchanged at the Bank of Bhutan branches. ATM AVAILABILITY: Unavailable.

MONEYGRAM: Unavailable/
WESTERN UNION: Unavailable.

AMEX: 0044 1273 696933
DINERS CLUB: Not present.
MASTERCARD: No local number
VISA: No local number

AMEX: (1) 801 964 6665
THOMAS COOK: 0044 1733 318950
VISA: 0044 1733 318949

0900–1700, with an hour's closure at lunchtime, Mon-Fri

Caters for all budgets, but predominantly very inexpensive. Accommodation varies from hotels in the capital to guesthouses and cottages elsewhere.

Dzongkha is the official language. A large number of local dialects are spoken due to the isolation of many villages. Nepali is common in the south of the country.

June-Aug: The temperatures drop dramatically as this is the monsoon period. Nights are cold. Generally Oct, Nov and Apr-mid Jan are the best times to visit when rainfall is slight and temperatures are pleasant.

Mahayana Buddhism is the state religion; the majority of Bhutanese people follow the Drukpa school of the Kagyupa sect.

10–15th day of Second Lunar month (April), Aug 8, Nov 11, Dec 17.

220 volts AC, 50 Hz.

Airmail to Europe can take up to 2 weeks.

Equal rights exist between men and women.

ROAD: The country has a fairly good internal road network. The northern regions of the High Himalayas have no roads. YAKS/PONIES/MULES: The main form of transportation. DOCUMENTATION: IDP required.

Religion has a strong influence on traditional ways of life. Travel to the country has been restricted to visitors for many years and some areas are closed to foreigners.

Bolivia

CAPITAL: La Paz

GMT-4

FROM UK: 00591. OUTGOING CODE TO UK: 01144

Embassy and Consulate of the Republic of Bolivia, 106 Eaton Square, London, SW1W 9AD. Tel: 020 7235 4248 or 235 2257. Fax: 020 7235 1286.

British Embassy, Avienda Arce 2732, Castilla 694, La Paz, Bolivia. Tel: (2) 357 424. Fax: (2) 391 063. ppa@mail.megalink.com

Contact the Embassy or Consulate.

Direccón Nacionale de Turismo, Calle Mercado 1328, Casilla 1868, La Paz, Bolivia. Tel: (2) 367 463. Fax: (2) 374 630. www.bolivia-travel.gov.bo/

Valid passport required by all.

Visa required for all tourist purposes.

Cameras must be declared.

US$20 for all international departures. This cannot be paid in other currencies.

POLIO, TYPHOID: R. MALARIA: Exists in rural and low-lying areas below 2500m in the Vivax variety. Resistance to chloroquine has been reported. YELLOW FEVER: Vaccination is recommended to all. Those arriving from infected areas must have a vaccination certificate.

W2

Boliviano (B) = 100 centavos. Sterling can not be exchanged. Most money is changed at Gambios and Hotels. All major credit cards have very limited acceptance. US$ travellers cheques are the most acceptable form of currency to take with you. Sterling cheques can be changed with difficulty. ATM AVAILABILITY: 70 locations.

MONEYGRAM: 0 800 1112.
WESTERN UNION: (2) 379 422

AMEX: 01144 1273 696933
DINERS CLUB: 001144 1252 513 500
MASTERCARD: 0800 0172
VISA: 0111 410 581 9994

AMEX: 01144 1273 571 600
THOMAS COOK: 1 800 223 7373
VISA: 01144 20 7937 8091

0830–1200 and 1430–1730 Mon to Fri.

Caters for all budgets. Reasonable prices for comfortable accommodation and eating out.

Spanish, English, Inca and other local dialects spoken.

There can be extreme temperature changes between day and night especially in the mountain areas. The wet season is between November and February. La Paz has very thin air due to its high altitude.

Roman Catholic, Protestant.

Jan 1, May 1, Aug 6, Nov 1, Dec 25. Christian feast days, local fiestas, Carnival week before Lent.

110/220 volts AC in La Paz. 220 volts AC in the rest of the country, 50 Hz. Plugs: most houses have 2-pin sockets for both electrical currents. Variations may occur.

3-4 days. A poste restante service is available.

Women's roles are dependent on their geographical location within Bolivia. Women travelling alone will arouse suspicion. Unwelcome attention from men may occur. Dress should be conservative.

During the rainy season all modes of public transport including airlines may suspend services for weeks at a time without explanation. ROAD: Work is in progress to improve the condition of the road network. Standards of driving are often low which may make rail a preferred option. When driving, a full set of spares, tools, extra petrol, food and water should be carried. DOCUMENTATION: IDP is required. When entering Bolivia a circulation card 'Hoja de Ruta' must be obtained from the 'Servicio National de Transito' at the border of Bolivia. These will be presented and stamped at all police posts.

Respect for traditions should be observed. Rural Bolivians should be referred to as campesinos, rather than Indians, which is considered an insult. Petty theft is an occasional problem.

CAPITAL: Kralendijk

GMT–4.

FROM UK: 005997. OUTGOING CODE TO UK: 0044

Police: 11; Ambulance: 14. All services: 5997 8004.

No embassy in the UK.
EUROPE: Office of the Minister Plenipotentiary of the Netherlands Antilles, Badhuisweg 173-175, 2597 JP The Hague, The Netherlands. Tel: 0031 70 306 6111. Fax: 0031 70 351 2722.

The British Consulate in Curacao deals with enquiries relating to Bonaire.

Caribbean Tourism, 42 Westminster Palace Gdns, Artillery Row, London SW1P 1RR. Tel: 020 7222 4335. Fax: 020 7222 4325.
www.doitcaribbean.com
cto@carib-tourism.com

Tourism Corporation Bonaire, Kaya Simon Bolivar 12, Kralendijk, Bonaire, Netherlands Antilles. Tel: 78322. Fax: 78408.
www.infobonaire.com/

Return ticket required. Requirements may be subject to short-term change. Contact Embassy before departure. Valid passport required

Nationals of the UK are allowed to stay for 90 days without a visa providing they have a return or onward ticket. NOTE: Enquire at the Ministers office at the Hague for a complete, up-to-date list of regulations.

Narcotics and firearms.

NAG 22.50 for passengers over two years of age on international flights. US$5.75 for inter-Caribbean flights.

POLIO, TYPHOID: R. YELLOW FEVER: A vaccination certificate is required from travellers over one year of age coming from an infected area.

Netherlands Antilles Guilder or Florin (NAG) = 100 cents. NOTE: Import and export of local currency is limited to NAG 200. Credit cards are accepted in large establishments. Travellers cheques in US currency is the most welcomed. ATM AVAILABILITY: 10 locations approximately.

MONEYGRAM: Unavailable.
WESTERN UNION: Unavailable.

AMEX: 0044 1273 696933
DINERS CLUB: 0044 1252 513 500
MASTERCARD: 001 800 307 7309
VISA: 001 800 847 2911

AMEX: 0044 1273 571 600
THOMAS COOK: 001 800 223 7373
VISA: 0044 20 7937 8091

0830–1200 and 1330–1600 Mon to Fri.

Generally inexpensive goods, especially perfume, jewellery and alcohol.

Dutch. Papiamento, English and Spanish are also spoken.

Hot throughout the year with cooling sea winds. Wet season Oct to Dec.

Roman Catholic. Protestant and a variety of Evangelical church minorities.

Jan 1, 19, Apr 30, May 1, Sep 6, Dec 25, 26. Christian feast days.

127 volts AC 50 Hz.

4-6 days.

Society is heavily influenced by South American culture.

ROAD: Reasonably good but a 4-wheel drive may be required for extensive tourism of the island. CAR HIRE: Firms are located at the airport and large hotels. DOCUMENTATION: A valid national licence will be sufficient but drivers must be 23 years or older. TAXI: A good taxi service exists on the island.

Beachwear is only suitable for the beach or poolside. Most bars and restaurants outside the two main hotel resorts are closed by midnight.

Bosnia-Herzegovina

CAPITAL: Sarajevo

GMT + 1 (GMT + 2 during the summer).

FROM UK: 00387. OUTGOING CODE TO UK: 9944

It is advisable to consult the foreign office in your country of residence before departure, regarding emergency assistance.

Embassy of the Republic of Bosnia-Herzegovina, 320 Regent Street, London W1R 5AB. Tel: 020 7255 3758. Fax: 020 7255 3760.

British Embassy, 8 Tina Ujavica, 7100 Sarajevo, Bosnia-Herzegovina. Tel: 33 444 429. Fax: 33 666 131.
www.britishembassy. ba;
consularenquiries@sarajevo.mail.fco.gov. uk

Not present.

Ministry of Foreign Affairs, Vojvode Putnika 3, 71000 Sarajevo, Bosnia-Herzegovina. Tel: 33 213 777. Fax: 33 653 592.

Check before travelling to the country.

Narcotics.

Euro12 approx.

Rabies

W1

Yugoslav Dinar (YuD) = 100 paras. Croatian Kuna (K) = 100 lipa. In the Serb controlled areas, only the Yugoslav Dinar is legal tender, while in Croat controlled areas only the Kuna is accepted. NOTE: Pound sterling is of little value and rarely used. Credit cards may be used to obtain cash from some banks. ATM AVAILABILITY: Some participating banks.

MONEYGRAM: Unavailable.
WESTERN UNION: 7221418.

AMEX: 9944 1273 696933
DINERS CLUB: 9944 1252 513 500
MASTERCARD: 991 314 542 7111
VISA: 991 410 581 9994

AMEX: 9944 1273 571 600
THOMAS COOK: No local number

VISA: 9944 20 7937 8091
0730–1530 Mon to Fri.

Limited commodities and high inflation as a result of the war.

Serbo-Croat (Serbs) and Croatian (Croats).

The climate is variable with moderate continental conditions. It is usually cold in the winter and hot in the summer.

Slavic Muslims, Serbian Orthodox and a minority of Roman Catholic Croats.

Jan 1, 7, 14, Mar 1, May 1, 6, Jun 28, Jul 12, Aug 2, 15, 28, Sep 8, 21, Nov 1, 2, 8, 25, Dec 25. Western and Orthodox Christian feast days, Islamic festivals and Jewish holidays observed.

220 volts AC, 50 Hz.

1 week to western Europe

Revealing clothes should not be worn.

Transport systems are slowly getting back to normal after civil conflict. Off-road driving should be avoided as there remains a risk of mines over much of the countryside.

The Foreign and Commonwealth Office advises care in planning travel to Bosnia-Herzegovina. Check the situation before travelling.

CAPITAL: Gaborone

GMT +2

FROM UK: 00267. OUTGOING CODE TO UK: 0044

Police: 351161

Botswana High Commission, 6 Stratford Place, London W1N 9AE. Tel: 020 7499 0031. Fax: 020 7495 8595.

British High Commission, Private Bag 0023, Gaborone, Botswana. Tel: 352 841 / 2/ 3. Fax: 356 105. bhc@botsnet.bw

Refer to Embassy.

Dept of Tourism, Ministry of Commerce and Industry. Private Bag, 0047, Gaborone, Botswana. Tel: 353 024 Or 313 314. Fax: 308 675 Web: www.botswanatourism.org

Return ticket required. May be subject to change at short notice. Contact the relevant authority before departure. Valid passport required by all and must be valid for 6 months.

Military clothing and some agricultural products, without obtaining prior permission.

Pula 80, payable in local currency.

POLIO, TYPHOID: R.
MALARIA: Falciparum variety present, especially in the north of Botswana.
OTHER: Bilharzia, cholera, rabies, ticks, hepatitis A, sleeping sickness present. AIDS/HIV is a major problem, with between at least 35 per cent of the population HIV positive.

W1

Pula (P) = 100 thebes Note: Export of local currency is limited to P500. Credit cards are accepted on a limited basis. Travellers cheques are accepted, but the surcharge may be high. ATM AVAILABILITY: 27 locations.

MONEYGRAM: Unavailable
WESTERN UNION: Available.

AMEX: 0044 1273 696933
DINERS: CLUB 0044 1252 513 500
MASTERCARD: 001 314 542 7111
VISA: 001 410 581 9994

AMEX: 0044 1273 571 600
THOMAS COOK: 0044 1733 318950
VISA: 0044 1733 318949

0900–1430 Mon, Tues, Thur and Fri. Wed: 0815-1200 and Sat 0815-1045.

Comparable with Western Europe.

English and Setswana.

Oct-Apr: hot and wet season. May-Sept: cooler and drier.

Mostly traditional with Christian minority. Islam and Bahá'I faith represented.

Jan 1, May 1, Jul 1, 15–16, Sep 30, Dec 25,26. Easter, Ascension Day.

220/240 volts AC, 50 Hz 13-amp sockets.

1-3 weeks by airmail.

Men and women are socially and culturally equal.

AIR, RAIL AND BUS: Major cities are linked by these networks. ROAD: tarmacked roads are limited; most roads are sand tracks. Reserves of water and fuel should always be taken. DOCUMENTATION: IDP is recommended for stays up to 6 months, after which a Botswana driving licence must be obtained.

Casual clothing is acceptable. Respect for the traditional way of life must be displayed. Do not take photographs of airports, official residences and military and defence establishments.

CAPITAL: Brasilia

Spans several time zones: Eastern Standard Time = GMT–3, North East States and East Pará = GMT–3, Western Standard Time = GMT–4, Amapa and West Pará time = GMT –4, Acre State = GMT–5, Fernando de Noronha Archipelago = GMT–2.

FROM UK: 0055. OUTGOING CODE TO UK:0044

All services: 0.

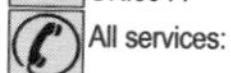

Brazilian Consulate General, 6 St Albans Street, London, SW1Y 020 7930 9055.

British Embassy, Caixa Postal 07-0586, Seto de Embaixadas Sul, Quadra 801, Conjunto K, 70.408 Brasilia DF, Brazil. Tel: (61) 225 2710. Fax: (61) 225 1777. www.reinounido.org.br; britemb@terra.com.br

Brazilian Tourist Office and Embassy of the Federal Republic of Brazil, 32 Green Street, London, W1Y 4AT. Tel: 020 7499 0877. Fax: 020 7493 5105. www.brazil.org.uk; tourism@brazil.org.uk

Centro Brasileiro de Informacao Turistica (CEBITUR), Rua Mariz e Barros 13, 6º andar, Praca de Bandeira, 20.270 Rio de Janeiro. Tel: 21 293 1313. Fax: 21 273 9290.

Return ticket and valid passport required. Requirements may change at short notice. Contact the embassy before departure.

Visas required unless travelling as tourists for stays of under 3 months.

Meat and cheese products from various countries. Contact the consular authority.

US$ 17-18 is levied on international departures, payable in local currency only.

POLIO, TYPHOID: R. MALARIA: Exists throughout the year below 900 m in some rural areas. Falciparum variety has been reported as being highly resistant to chloroquine. YELLOW FEVER: A vaccination certificate is required by all travellers arriving from infected areas. OTHER: Bilharzia, rabies.

W1

'Real' (Rl) = 100 centavos. All banks and Gambios exchange foreign currency. All major credit cards are accepted. Travellers cheques can be easily exchanged. US$ cheques are preferred. ATM AVAILABILITY: Over 10,000 locations.

MONEYGRAM: Limited to larger towns
WESTERN UNION: Unavailable.

AMEX: 0044 1273 696933. DINERS CLUB: (11) 2356628. MASTERCARD: 000 811 887 0553. VISA: 000 811 933 5589

AMEX: 0044 1273 571 600(11) 545 5018. THOMAS COOK: 000 811 870 0553. VISA: 000 811 342 0552

1000–1630 Mon to Fri.

All types of accommodation can be found in main centres of population.

Portuguese. French, German, Italian and English are also spoken.

Climate varies considerably, from arid scrubland in the interior to the impassable tropical rain forest of the northerly amazon jungle and the tropical eastern coastal beaches. Rainy season: south Jan-Apr; north Apr-July; Rio and Sao Paulo Nov-Mar.

Roman Catholic.

Jan 1, 20(Rio only),25(Sao Paulo only) Apr 21, May 1, Jul 9, Sep 7, Oct 12, Nov 1,2,15, Dec 8, 24, 25. Christian feast days, Carnival week before Lent.

Brasilia: 220 Volts AC, 60 Hz. Rio de Janeiro and Sao Paulo: 110 volts AC, 60 Hz. 2-pin plugs are used.

4–6 days. Reasonably reliable. Sending mail registered or franked will eliminate the risk of having stamps steamed off.

Women's roles vary greatly, depending upon location, religion and education. Women travellers will arouse curiosity and possible unwelcome attention from males. Maintaining a low profile is advisable.

TAXI: Recognised by red number plates and fitted with meters. DRIVING: Car hire is possible but parking is difficult, as is driving through the congested city streets. DOCUMENTATION: IDP is required. RAIL: Limited services exist between the major cities but there has been a substantial decline in the number of long-distance trains.

Crime is a growing problem, particularly in Rio de Janeiro and Sao Paulo. Use extreme caution and avoid showing expensive possessions. By law, a passport should be carried at all times. Health conditions vary from region to region. There is a shortage of doctors and hospitals outside the big cities.

British Virgin Islands

CAPITAL: Road Town

GMT–4

FROM UK: 001284. OUTGOING CODE TO UK: 00144

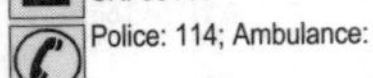

Police: 114; Ambulance: 112.

British Dependent Territories Visa Section, The Passport Office, Clive House, 70-78 Petty France, London, SW1H 9HD. Tel: 020 7271 8552. Fax: 020 7271 8645.

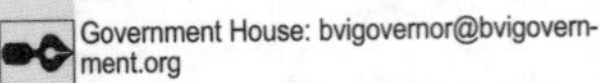

Government House: bvigovernor@bvigovernment.org

British Virgin Islands Tourist Board, 11 St Martins Lane, London, WC2N 4DY. Tel: 020 7240 4259. Fax: 020 7240 4270.

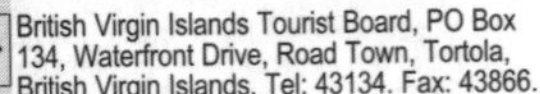

British Virgin Islands Tourist Board, PO Box 134, Waterfront Drive, Road Town, Tortola, British Virgin Islands. Tel: 43134. Fax: 43866.

Return ticket required. Requirements may be subject to short-term change. Contact embassy before departure. Valid passport required

Nationals of Great Britain, Australia, Canada, the USA, and Japan may stay up to 6 months without a visa.

Import licences are needed for some goods, mainly foodstuffs.

US$8 for all international departures.

POLIO, TYPHOID: R

W2

US Dollar (US$) = 100 cents. All major credit cards are accepted. Travellers cheques, preferably in US dollars, are accepted. ATM AVAILABILITY: 6 locations.

MONEYGRAM: Limited availability
WESTERN UNION: 494 5381.

AMEX: 00144 1273 696933
DINERS CLUB: 00144 1252 513 500
MASTERCARD: 0011 314 542 7111
VISA: 0011 800 847 2911

AMEX: 00144 1273 571 600
THOMAS COOK: 0011 800 223 7373
VISA: 00144 20 7937 8091

0900-1500 Mon to Thur, 0900-1700 Fri.

Generally expensive and may prove difficult for the budget traveller.

English.

Tropical climate with cooling winds. Low rainfall and comfortable night temperatures.

Methodist. Also Church of God, Anglican, Adventist, Baptist and Roman Catholic.

Jan 1, second Mon in Mar, second Sat in Jun, Jul 1, first Mon in Aug, Oct 21, Nov 14, Dec 25,26. Easter and Whit Mon.

110/60 volts AC 60 Hz. American 2-pin plugs are used.

Up to 1 week.

Usual precautions should be taken.

ROAD: There is a good road network. TAXI: Usually operate according to fixed rates. CAR HIRE: There are 9 car hire companies. DOCUMENTATION: A temporary British Virgin Islands licence is required which will be issued for a small fee on production of a valid foreign licence.

Backpacking is actively discouraged. Beachwear should be kept for the beach or pool. Sixty islands to explore.

CAPITAL: Bandar Seri Begawan

GMT +8

FROM UK: 00673. OUTGOING CODE TO UK: 0044

Not present.

High Commission of Brunei Darussalam, 19/20 Belgrave Square, London SW1X 8PG. Tel: 020 7581 0521. Fax: 020 7235 9717. Consular Section: 19A Belgrave Mews West, London SW1X 8HT. Tel 020 7581 0521. Fax: 020 7235 9717

British High Commission, PO Box 2197, 3rd Floor, Hong Kong Bank Chambers, Jalan Pemancha, Bandar Seri Begawan, Brunei. Tel: (2) 222 231 or 222 6001 (consular section). Fax: 226 002. www.britain-brunei.org ; brithc@brunet.bn

Refer to High Commission / Consular section.

Information Bureau Section, Information Department, Prime Minister's Office, Bandar Seri Begawan 2041, Brunei. Tel: (2) 240 400. Fax: (2) 244 104.

Return ticket required. Requirements may change at short notice. Contact the embassy before departure. Valid passport required by all, with assured re-entry facilities to country of origin or domicile required by all. Passports must be valid for at least 6 months after entry.

Visa not required by nationals of the UK for stays of up to 30 days. NOTE: All visitors must be able to display proof of sufficient funds on entry.

Pornography, non-prescribed drugs - the penalty for carrying the latter is harsh.

Br$15.

Nationals of Cuba, Israel and North Korea will be refused admission.

POLIO, TYPHOID: R. YELLOW FEVER: A vaccination certificate is required by those who have visited an infected area within the previous six days.

W1

Brunei Dollar (Br$) = 100 sen. Foreign currency and travellers cheques can be exchanged at any bank. Hotels and department stores may also exchange travellers cheques. Credit cards are generally accepted by major establishments. The export of local currency is limited to Br$1000. Preferable currency for travellers cheques is US dollars. All credit cards are generally accepted by major establishments. ATM AVAILABILITY: Over 25 locations.

MONEYGRAM: Unavailable.
WESTERN UNION: Unavailable.

AMEX: 0044 1273 696933
DINERS CLUB: 0044 1252 513 500
MASTERCARD: 001 314 542 7111
VISA: 001 410 581 9994

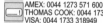

AMEX: 0044 1273 571 600
THOMAS COOK: 0044 1733 318950
VISA: 0044 1733 318949

0900-1200 and 1400-1500 Mon to Fri, 0900-1100 Sat.

Accommodation can be very expensive. Transport and food are comparable with prices in the rest of East Malaysia.

Malay. English and Chinese dialects are also spoken.

Tropical climate most of the year. Monsoon season is Oct–Mar, when there is very heavy rainfall.

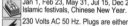

Mostly Sunni Muslims. Also Buddhist, Confucian, Daoist and Christian minorities.

Jan 1, Feb 23, May 31, Jul 15, Dec 25. Islamic festivals, Chinese New Year.

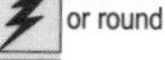
230 Volts AC 50 Hz. Plugs are either square or round 3-pin.

2-5 days.

Women should ensure that head, knees and arms are well covered. Women are not expected to shake hands. Generally safe for women travellers.

BUS: Services operate to main centres. CAR HIRE: Available at the airport and large hotels. DOCUMENTATION: IDP is required. A temporary licence obtainable on presentation of a national licence.

Avoid passing or receiving with the left hand or pointing the soles of the feet towards companions. Shoes should be removed when entering Muslim homes. If offered refreshments by a host it is considered rude to refuse. Accommodation is impossible to find outside the main towns.

Bulgaria

CAPITAL: Sofia

GMT +2

FROM UK: 00359. OUTGOING CODE TO UK: 0044 Some calls go through the international operator.

Ambulance: 150; Fire: 160; Police: 166.

Embassy of the Republic of Bulgaria, 186-188 Queens Gate, London SW7 5HL. Tel: 020 7584 9400 or 584 9433. Visa Information: 0900 117 1208

British Embassy, Boulevard Vasil Levski 65 67, Sofia 1000, Bulgaria. Tel: (2) 885 361/2 or 885 325. Fax: (2) 656 022. www.british-embassy.bg/ : Sofia-Consular@VisaSofia.mail.fco.gov.uk

Balkan Holidays (Travel Agency), Sofia House, 19 Conduit Street, London W1R 9TD. Tel: 020 7491 4499. Fax: 020 7491 7068.

Balkantourist, Boulevard Victosha 1, 1000 Sofia, Bulgaria. Tel: (00359) 287 2990

Requirements may change at short notice. Contact the relevant authority before finalising travel arrangements. A valid passport with at least 6 months remaining validity at time of departure is required.

Visa required by all.

Pornography. NOTE: Many items must be declared e.g. antique rolls and scrolls, books and works of art. Check with embassy for a full list.

US$3 levied on all foreign departures.

An AIDS test may be required if stay is longer than 1 month.

W2

Lev (Lv) = 100 stotinki. Exch: A bordereau receipt will be given and must be kept until departure. NOTE: Import and export of local currency is prohibited. Amounts of currency over US$1000 have to be declared. Diners Club, American Express and Visa have limited acceptance. Travellers cheques can be exchanged in major banks. US$ and Pound sterling are the preferred currency. ATM AVAILABILITY: Over 100 locations (MasterCard/Cirrus only).

MONEYGRAM: 00800 0010 then 800 592 3688.
WESTERN UNION: Unavailable.

AMEX: 0044 1273 696933
DINERS CLUB: 980 2559
MASTERCARD: 001 314 542 7111
VISA: (1) 410 581 9994

AMEX: 0044 1273 571 600
THOMAS COOK: 0044 1733 318950
VISA: +44 20 7937 8091

0800-1130 and 1400-1800 Mon to Fri, 0830-1130 Sat.

Inexpensive when compared with Western Europe.

Bulgarian. English is spoken in resorts. Turkish, Russian, French and German may also be spoken.

Summers are warm, with some rainfall. Winters are cold with snow. Rain falls frequently in the spring and autumn.

Eastern Orthodox Church, Muslim and Roman Catholic minorities.

Jan 1, 6, 7, Feb 14, Mar 1, 3, 25, Apr 23, May 1, 6, 24, Jun 29, Jul 20, Aug 6, 15, Sep 6, 22, Oct 14, 26, Nov 1, 8, Dec 6, 24–27. Easter.

220 volts AC, 50 Hz. Plugs are 2-pin.

4 days to 2 weeks to Western Europe.

FLIGHTS: Air travel is only slightly more expensive than rail and more convenient. RAIL: Reservations are essential, 1st class is advisable. ROAD: Speed limits are strictly enforced, as are drinking and driving penalties. CAR HIRE: Can be arranged through hotels. DOCUMENTATION: An IDP should be obtained although foreign driving licences are acceptable for short journeys. A green card is compulsory.

A nod of the head means 'No' and shaking the head means 'Yes'. Dress should be conservative but casual. It is advisable to register with the police, a hotel or guesthouse within 48 hours of arrival. Do not accept food or drink from strangers. Exercise caution in Sofia, particularly at night.

Burkina Faso

CAPITAL: Ouagadougou

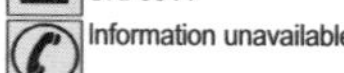

GMT

FROM UK: 00226. OUTGOING CODE TO UK: 0044

Information unavailable.

Honorary Consulate of Burkina Faso, 5 Cinnamon Row, Plantation Wharf, London SW11 3TW. Tel: 01710 738 1800. Fax: 020 7738 2820

British Embassy, 01 BP 2581 Third Floor, Abidjan 01, Cote d'Ivoire. Tel: 2268 50/1/2 and 328209. Fax: 22 32 21. Honorary Consul www.britaincdi.com; britemb.a@aviso.ci

Refer to Consulate

Direction de l'Administration Touristique et Hôtelière, BP 624, Ouagadougou 01, Burkina Faso. Tel: 306 396

Return ticket required. Valid passport required.

Visa required by all.

Sporting guns can only be imported under licence.

US$ 13, is payable on international departures.

HEP A, POLIO, TYPHOID: R. MALARIA: R. Falciparum variety present. YELLOW FEVER: R. with vaccination certificate if arriving from an infected area. OTHER: Bilharzia, rabies, cholera, river blindness and sleeping sickness. HIV/AIDS is prevalent.

W1

CFA Franc (CFA Fr). Visa and MasterCard, and travellers cheques, have limited acceptance. ATM AVAILABILITY: Unavailable.

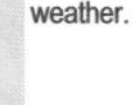

MONEYGRAM: Unavailable.
WESTERN UNION: Unavailable.

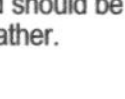

AMEX: 0044 1273 696933
DINERS CLUB: 0044 1252 513 500
MASTERCARD: 001 314 542 7111
VISA: 001 410 581 9994

AMEX: 0044 1273 571 600
THOMAS COOK: 0044 1733 318950
VISA: 0044 20 7937 8091

0730-1130 + 1500-1600 Mon to Thur, 0730-1130 + 1530-1700 Fri.

Burkina Faso is the sixth poorest country in the world.

French with several indigenous languages.

Tropical climate. Dec–Mar are the best months. Rainy season is June–Oct. Winds blow Nov–Feb which brings cool and dry weather.

Animist. With Muslim and Christian (Roman Catholic) minorities.

Jan 1, 3, Mar 8, May 1, Aug 4, 5, 15, Oct 15, Nov 1, Dec 11, 25. Christian feast days and Islamic festivals.

220/380 volts AC 50 Hz. Plugs are 2-pin.

Up to 2 weeks by airmail. There are few post offices. Poste restante is available with a charge for collection of letters.

Society and culture are predominantly patriarchal.

ROAD: Most are impassable during the rainy season. Police checkpoints often cause delay. FLIGHTS: there are few domestic flights. DOCUMENTATION: Temporary driving licences are available from local authorities if you present a valid national driving licence.

Customs should be respected especially in traditional rural areas. Clothing can be casual and should be appropriate for the hot weather.

Burundi

CAPITAL: Bujumbura

GMT +2

FROM UK: 00257. OUTGOING CODE TO UK: 9044

All travellers are advised to consult the foreign office in their country of residence regarding emergency assistance.

No embassy in the UK. Europe: 46 Square Marie-Louise, B-1040 Brussels, Belgium. Tel: (2) 230 4535 or 230 4548. Fax: (2) 230 7883.

British Consulate, BP 1344, 43 avenue Bubanza, Bujumbura, Burundi. Tel: (2) 23711.

Refer to the Embassy in Belgium.

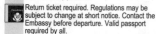

Office National du Tourisme, BP902, 2 ave des Euphorbes, Bujumbura, Burundi. Tel: (2) 24208. Fax: (2) 29390.

Return ticket required. Regulations may be subject to change at short notice. Contact the Embassy before departure. Valid passport required by all.

Visa required by all. Tourist and business passengers arriving at Bujumbura airport will be issued entry stamps, providing they have previously informed their travel agency of their passport number and identity.

All baggage must be declared and duty may be required for cameras, radios and typewriters.

A departure tax equivalent of 5 US$ is levied for alien residents. Transit passengers are exempt.

HEP A, POLIO, TYPHOID: R. MALARIA: R. Falciparum variety exists of which resistance to chloroquine has been reported. The recommended prophylaxis is mefloquine. YELLOW FEVER: Strongly recommended. If arriving from an endemic area a vaccination certificate will be required. OTHER: Cholera, bilharzia, rabies, meningitis present. NOTE: Visitors may be asked to show proof of vaccination against meningococcal meningitis.

W 1

Burundi Franc (BIF) = 100 centimes. Unlimited import of foreign currency, subject to declaration, export limited to amount declared on import. Import and export of local currency is limited to BIF 2000. Limited acceptance of MasterCard and Diners Club. Travellers cheques are not currently accepted. ATM AVAILABILITY: Unavailable

MONEYGRAM: Unavailable
WESTERN UNION: Unavailable.

AMEX: 9044 1273 696933.
DINERS CLUB: 9044 1252 513 500
MASTERCARD: 901 314 542 7111
VISA: 901 410 581 9994

AMEX: 9044 1273 571 600
THOMAS COOK: No local number.
VISA: 9044 20 7937 8091

0800-1130 Mon to Fri. There are banks in Bujumbura and Gitega.

Due to the coup of 1996 the country's economy has been all but wiped out.

French and Kirundi. Kiswahili is also spoken.

The climate is mostly mild and pleasant, although a hot equatorial climate is found near Lake Tanganyika and in the Ruzizi river plain.

Mostly Roman Catholic with local Animist beliefs. Also Anglican and Pentecostalism.

Jan 1, Feb 5, May 1, Jul 1, Aug 15, Sep 18, Oct 13,21, Nov 1, Dec 25. Ascension Day.

220 Volts 50 Hz

There is a main post office in Bujumbura. Delivery times are uncertain.

A volatile tribal culture predominates.

FLIGHTS: There are no regular internal flights. ROADS: Most are sealed but often impassable during the rainy season. DOCUMENTATION: IDP is required.

EXTREME RISK. The FCO advises against all travel to Burundi. People outside the cities may not be used to visitors. Therefore respect should be shown for local traditions. Dress should be conservative. A curfew operates throughout the country from midnight to 5am, but the FCO recommends visitors should avoid any movement out of their accomodation after 10pm.

Cambodia (Kingdom of)

CAPITAL: Phnom Penh

GMT + 7

FROM UK: 00855. OUTGOING CODE TO UK: 0044. Outside Phnom Penh, calls must go through the operator.

Not present.

No embassy in the UK.

British Embassy, 29 Street 75, Phnom Penh, Cambodia. Tel: (23) 427124. Fax: (23) 427125. britemb@bigpond.com.kh

No tourist office in the UK.

Ministry of Tourism, 3 Monivong Boulevard, Phnom Penh, Cambodia. Tel: (23) 26107. Fax: (23) 24607.

Requirements may change at short notice. Contact the embassy before departure. Valid passport required.

Required by all. Tourist and Business types granted. Tourist visas available at airport.

Narcotics.

US$15 levied on international departures.

POLIO, TYPHOID: R.
MALARIA: Exists all year throughout the country in the falciparum variety, which has been reported as being highly resistant to chloroquine. Dengue fever is also widespread.
YELLOW FEVER: A vaccination certificate is required if arriving from an infected area.
OTHER: Bilharzia, plague, polio, rabies.

W1

CURRENCY: Riel (CRI) = 100 sen. Exch: US$ are widely accepted and exchanged. Other currencies are not readily recognised. NOTE: Import and export of local currency is prohibited. Travellers cheques and credit cards are accepted at a small number of hotels and restaurants in Phnom Penh and large cities. Most transactions are in cash. ATM AVAILABILITY: Unavailable.

MONEYGRAM: Unavailable.
WESTERN UNION: Unavailable.

AMEX : 0044 1273 696 933
DINERS CLUB: 0044 1252 513 500
MASTERCARD: 001 314 542 7111
VISA: 001 410 581 9994

AMEX: 0044 1273 571 600
THOMAS COOK: no local number
VISA: 0044 20 7937 8091

0800–1500 Mon to Fri.

Due to civil war, prices fluctuate, although restaurants are in abundance in Phnom Penh.

Khmer. Chinese and Vietnamese are also spoken. French is spoken by older people and English taught to younger generations.

Tropical monsoon climate. May-Oct is the monsoon. Temperatures throughout the country are fairly constant, though winters in the north can be cold.

Mostly Buddhist with a Christian and Muslim minority.

Jan 1, Mar 8, Apr 13–15, May 1, Jun 1, Sep 24, Oct 23, 30–31, Nov 9, Dec 10. Buddhist holidays, Chinese New Year.

220 volts AC 50 Hz. Power cuts are frequent and power is only available in the evenings outside Phnom Penh.

4-5 days.

Mostly servile in nature and custom.

Independent travel is restricted. ROAD: Travel permits are required to cross provincial borders. Most roads are in poor condition. DOCUMENTATION: IDP is required.

HIGH RISK. Foreigners have been kidnapped and others may be targeted. NOTE: The FCO advises against travel outside the capital. If you have to travel outside Phnom Penh you should contact the embassy for advice. There is still a danger from landmines, particularly in remote areas. Venturing outside areas under government control will carry a higher degree of risk and banditry is rife. Slow down when approaching checkpoints. PHOTOGRAPHY: Ask permission before taking photos and extra courtesy should be shown towards monks.

Cameroon

CAPITAL: Yaoundé

GMT +1

FROM UK: 00237. OUTGOING CODE TO UK: 0044

Not present.

Embassy of the Republic of Cameroon, 84 Holland Park, London W11 3SB. Tel: 020 7727 0771. Fax 020 7792 9353.

British High Commission, BP 547, avenue Winston Churchill, Yaoundé, Cameroon. Tel: 220 545 or 220 796. Fax: 220 148. www.brit-cam.org/ ; BHC@yaounde.mail.fco.gov.uk

Refer to the Embassy

Société Camerounaise de Tourisme (SOCA-TOUR) BP 7138, Yaoundé, Cameroon. Tel: 233 219.

Return ticket required. Requirements may be subject to change at short notice. Contact the Embassy before departure. Valid passport required by all.

Visas required. Tourist and business visas issued.

Radios, cameras and alcoholic beverages must be declared on arrival and are usually admitted free of duty if there is only one of each of them.

Departure tax: CFA Fr10,000 for International flights, Fr500 for domestic flights, payable in local currency.

HEP A, POLIO, TYPHOID: R. MALARIA: R. Falciparum variety present, resistance to chloroquine has been reported. YELLOW FEVER: R. A vaccination certificate is required by all visitors over one year of age. OTHER: Bilharzia, cholera, meningitis and rabies present.

W1

CFA Franc (CFA Fr) = 100 centimes. NOTE: Only notes issued by the Banque des Etats de l'Afrique Centrale are valid, but not those issued by Banque des Etats de l'Afrique de l'Ouest. It is better to exchange French Francs or US$ than Sterling. Both have very limited acceptance. French francs are the preferred currency in traveller's cheques, although Pound sterling is also accepted. ATM AVAILABILITY: Unavailable.

MONEYGRAM: Unavailable.
WESTERN UNION: Unavailable.

AMEX: 0044 1273 696 933
DINERS CLUB: 0044 1252 513 500
MASTERCARD: 001 314 542 7111
VISA: 001 410 581 9994

AMEX: 0044 1273 571 600
THOMAS COOK: 0044 1733 318950
VISA: 0044 20 7937 8091

0730–1130 and 1430–1630 Mon to Fri.

The economy has deteriorated due to civil unrest.

French and English are given equal importance in the constitution although French is more commonly spoken. Many local African languages are spoken.

South is hot and dry from Nov to Feb. Rainy season mainly July to Oct although there is some rain Mar to June. Temperatures in the north vary.

Mainly Animist and Christian. A minority with Muslim faith.

Jan 1, Feb 11, May 1,20,21, Aug 15, Dec 25. Easter, Islamic festivals.

110/220 volts AC 50 Hz. Plugs are round 2-pin.

Approximately 1 week.

A patriarchal culture prevails.

FLIGHTS: The most efficient means of internal travel. RAIL: Slow and cheap, a limited few have restaurant facilities and air conditioning. Couchettes are available on some trains.

There has been an increase in violent crime and highway robbery is prevalent in the North. Avoid the north-west of the country. The north is mainly Muslim and traditions and customs should be respected – for example, visitors should never step inside a Muslim prayer circle of rocks. In rural areas traditional beliefs predominate, so it is essential to use tact. Cameras should be used with discretion and permission obtained before taking photographs. Do not take photographs of anything connected with the military.

CAPITAL: Ottawa

6 time zones, from GMT –3.5 in Newfoundland to GMT –8 on the Pacific Coast.

FROM UK: 001. OUTGOING CODE TO UK: 011

911 or 0 (depending on province).

Canadian High Commission, Macdonald House, 1 Grosvenor Square, London, W1X 0AB. Tel: 020 7258 6600. Fax: 020 7258 63333. www.canada.org.uk

British High Commission, 80 Elgin Street, Ottawa, Ontario, K1P 5K7. Tel: (613) 237 1530. Fax: (613) 237 7980. Consulates in Edmonton, Halifax, St Johns, Montreal, Toronto, Vancouver, and Winnipeg. www.britain-in-canada.org/

Visit Canada Centre, 62-65 Trafalgar Square, London WC2N 5DT. Tel: 020 7930 8540 (trade) or (0891) 715 000 (general information). vcc@dial.pipex.com

Tourism Canada, Industry Canada, 4th Floor East, 235 Queens Street, Ottawa, Ontario, K1A 0H5. Tel: (613) 954 3851. Fax: (613) 952 7906. http://info.ic.gc.ca/Tourism/

Return ticket required. Requirements may change at short notice. Contact the embassy before departure. Passport valid for at least one day beyond the intended departure date from Canada is required by all.

Visa not required by British passport holders. Visa regulations are subject to change at short notice; it is advisable to check with the nearest Canadian Consulate, Embassy or High Commission prior to travel.

Firearms and explosives, endangered species of animal and plants, animal products, meat, food and plant material is subject to restrictions. Dogs and cats may be imported from certain rabies-free countries subject to restriction and formalities.

Can $10 levied on international departures, payable in local currency.

Canadian Dollar (Can $) = 100 cents. Credit cards are widely accepted. Travellers cheques in Canadian dollars are preferred. ATM AVAILABILITY: Over 13,000 locations.

MONEYGRAM: 1 800 933 3278.
WESTERN UNION: 800 235 0000.

AMEX: 01144 1273 696 933
DINERS CLUB: 1800 363 3333
MASTERCARD:1800 307 7309
VISA: 1800 847 2911

AMEX: 01144 1273 571 600
THOMAS COOK: 1800 223 7373
VISA: 1800 227 6811

1000–1500 Mon to Fri. Some banks in major centres have extended hours-check locally.

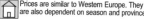

Prices are similar to Western Europe. They are also dependent on season and province.

English and French (the latter principally in Quebec).

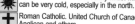

Summers are warm and sunny whilst winters can be very cold, especially in the north.

Roman Catholic. United Church of Canada, Anglican and others.

Jan 1, May 24, Jul 1, first Mon in Aug, Sep, second Mon in Oct, Nov 11, Dec 25,26. Easter. Various Provincial holidays.

110 volts AC 60 Hz. American-style flat 2-pin plugs are standard.

5–7 days.

Equality between men and women is the norm. Culture, generally is influenced by France in Quebec and England/America elsewhere.

FLIGHTS: About 75 airlines operate national services. RAIL: Services are extensive across Canada. ROADS: Extensive covering vast distances. COACH: One of the cheapest and most convenient ways of travelling the country. Each region is well served by networks of coach lines. CAR HIRE: Available in all cities and airports to drivers with full licences over 21 years of age. DOCUMENTATION: Visitors may drive with their national driving licences for up to 3 months in all provinces.

Smoking has been banned in most public places.

Cape Verde

CAPITAL: Cidade de Praia

GMT –1

FROM UK: 00238. IDD: Possible to main cities. Some calls to and from the country must go through the international operator. OUTGOING CODE TO UK: 044. Outgoing calls must go through the local operator.

All services: 87

No embassy in the UK. EUROPE: Koninginnegracht 44, 2514 AD The Hague, The Netherlands. Tel: (70) 346 9623. Fax: (70) 346 7702.

British Consulate, c/o Shell Cabo Verde, Sal Avenue, Amilcar, Cabral, CP4, Sal, Cape Verde. Tel: 314 470 or 314 605 or 314 232. Fax: 314 755

Refer to Embassy

Instituto Nacional do Tourismo-INATUR, CP294, Chã da Areia, Praia, São Tiago, Cape Verde. Tel: 631 173. Fax: 614 475

Return ticket required. Requirements may change at short notice. Contact the Embassy before departure.Passport with a validity of at least 6 months required by all.

Visa required.

HEP A, POLIO, TYPHOID: R. MALARIA: R. YELLOW FEVER: Vaccination certificate required from visitors over one year old arriving from an area where incidents of yellow fever have been reported within the last six years. OTHER: Cholera.

W1

Cape Verde Escudo (CVEsc) = 100 centavos. Note: Import and export of local currency is prohibited. Import of foreign currency unlimited but declaration on arrival required. Maximum export of foreign currency is CVEsc 25000 or the amount declared on arrival, whichever is the larger. Credit cards and travellers cheques are not usually accepted. ATM AVAILABILITY: Unavailable

MONEYGRAM: Unavailable.
WESTERN UNION: Unavailable.

AMEX: 044 1273 696 933
DINERS CLUB: 044 1252 513 500
MASTERCARD: 01 314 542 7111
VISA: 01 410 581 9994

AMEX: 044 1273 571 600
THOMAS COOK: No local number
VISA: 044 20 7937 8091

0800–1400 Mon to Fri.

Tourism is very undeveloped, but this may change with the government's recent decision to promote it.

Portuguese, Creole and some English and French

Temperate with a low rainfall.

Almost entirely Roman Catholic with a Protestant minority.

Jan 20, May 1, Jul 5, Aug 15, Sep 12, Nov 1, Dec 25. Easter.

220 volts 50 Hz

To and from Europe – over 1 week.

Culture is predominantly patriarchal.

ROAD: There are 2250 km of road on the islands, of which one third are paved. There is currently a road improvement programme taking place. BUS: Services are satisfactory. TAXI: Fares should be agreed in advance. DOCUMENTATION: IDP is recommended.

Usual European social courtesies should be observed.

Cayman Islands

CAPITAL: George Town

GMT-5.

FROM UK: 001809. IDD: Possible to North America and Europe. OUTGOING CODE TO UK: 044

Police: 911; Ambulance: 555. All services: 911.

Cayman Islands Government Office and Department of Tourism, 6 Arlington Street, London, SW1A 1RE. Tel: 020 7491 7772, Fax: 020 7491 7944 (Government Office) or Tel: 491 7771, Fax: 409 7773 (Department of Tourism). info-uk@caymanislands.ky

UK Passport Agency, Clive House, Petty France, London, SW1H 9HD. Tel: 020 7279 3434.

At Government Office, see above.

Cayman Islands Department of Tourism, The Cricket Square, Elgin Avenue, PO Box 67, Grand Cayman. Tel: (94) 90623. Fax: (94) 94053. www.caymanislands.ky/

Return ticket required. Requirements may be subject to short-term change. Contact embassy before departure. Valid passport required by all except nationals of Canada, the UK and the USA, if proof of nationality is provided and return or onward tickets show that the visitor will leave the Cayman Islands within 6 months.

Visa not required by UK nationals.

Import of pets requires a permit from the Cayman Islands Department of Agriculture.

CI$ 8 or US$ 10 payable by all travellers over 12 years of age.

POLIO, TYPHOID: R

Cayman Islands Dollar (CI$) = 100 cents. Exch: US currency circulates freely. Major credit cards are widely accepted. Travellers cheques in US dollars are widely welcomed. ATM AVAILABILITY: 4 locations.

MONEYGRAM: 1 800 543 4080.
WESTERN UNION: 949 7822.

AMEX: 01144 1273 696 933
DINERS CLUB: 01144 1252 513 500
MASTERCARD: 1800 307 7309
VISA: 1800 847 2911

AMEX: 01144 1273 571 600
THOMAS COOK: 1 800 223 7373
VISA: 01144 20 7937 8091

0900–1600 Mon to Thur, 0900–1630 Fri.

Extremely expensive.

English. Local dialects are also spoken.

Warm tropical climate throughout the year. Wet season - May to Oct with generally brief showers.

Presbyterian with large numbers of minorities.

Jan 1, third Mon in May, first Mon in Jul, Nov 11, Dec 25,26. Christian feast days.

110 volts 60 Hz. American-style flat 2-pin plugs are used.

5-7 days.

Normal precautions should be followed.

ROAD: A good road network connects the coastal towns of all three main islands. BUS: A cheap but infrequent bus service operates between George Town and the West Bay. CAR HIRE: By far the best way to get around. DOCUMENTATION: An IDP is required in addition to insurance. Drivers must be over 21 years of age.

Beachwear should be kept to the beach or pool.

Central African Republic

CAPITAL: Bangui

GMT +1

FROM UK: 00236. Many calls still go through the operator. OUTGOING CODE TO UK: 1944

Not present.

No embassy in the UK. EUROPE: Embassy of the Central African Republic, 30 rue des Perchamps, 75016 Paris, France. Tel: (1) 42 24 42 56. Fax: (1) 42 88 98 95.

British Consulate, c/o SOCACIG, BP 728, Bangui, Central African Republic. Tel: 610 300 or 611 045. Fax: 615 130

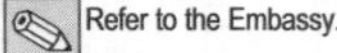

Refer to the Embassy.

Office National Centrafrican du Tourisme (OCATOUR) BP 655, Bangui, Central African Republic. Tel: 614 566

Return ticket required. Requirements may be subject to change at short notice. Contact the embassy before departure. Valid passport required.

Visa required.

Firearms. Animal skins and diamonds must be declared on departure.

Departure tax of US$5 is levied on all international flights.

HEP A, POLIO, TYPHOID: R.
MALARIA: R. falciparum form is prevalent. Resistance to chloroquine has been reported.
YELLOW FEVER: A vaccination certificate is required on arrival, by all travellers over one year of age. OTHER:Cholera. A vaccination certificate is required by all travellers. Bilharzia, meningitis and rabies also present.

W1

CFA Franc (CFA Fr) = 100 centimes. Very limited acceptance of credit cards and travellers cheques, and commission is very expensive. ATM AVAILABILITY: Unavailable.

MONEYGRAM: Unavailable.
WESTERN UNION: Unavailable.

AMEX: 1944 1273 696 933
DINERS CLUB: 1944 1252 513 500
MASTERCARD: 191 314 542 7111
VISA: 191 410 581 9994

AMEX: 1944 1273 571 600
THOMAS COOK: 1944 1733 318949
VISA: 1944 20 7937 8091

0730–1130 Mon-Fri

Tourists can expect to pay high prices.

French is the official language and essential for business. The native language is Sango.

Hot all year round especially in the Northeast. The monsoon in the south is May–Oct.

Animist, Christian and a minority follow Islam.

Jan 1, Mar 29, Jun 30, Aug 13, 15, Nov 1, Dec 1, 25. Easter

220/380 volts AC 50 Hz

Airmail takes 1 week, although it is often much longer. Poste restante is available in Bangui. Postal and telecommunication systems are currently being developed.

Women should respect the Muslim dress code and are segregated in the towns.

FLIGHTS: Domestic flights are limited to chartered planes. RIVER: River-boats operate along the Ubangi but can be very slow. ROAD: Good roads connect the main towns but are impassable during the rainy season. Travellers must carry as much petrol as possible as deliveries to stations outside the towns are infrequent. DOCUMENTATION: IDP is required.

The FCO advise against travel unless essential. The border with Cameroon is closed, and armed guards are targetting visitors. Visitors should dress modestly in Muslim areas and respect customs. Ensure you do not smoke or drink in public places during Ramadan. PHOTOGRAPHY: Be cautious and ask permission before taking photographs.

CAPITAL: N'Djamena

GMT + 1

FROM UK: 00235. It may be necessary to go through the international operator. OUTGOING CODE TO UK: 1544. Calls outside N'djamena and Moudou must go through the operator.

Not present.

No embassy in the UK. Europe: 65 rue des Belles Feuilles, 75116 Paris, France. Tel (1) 45 53 36 75. Fax (19) 45 53 16 09.

British Consulate BP 877, Avenue Charles de Gaulle, N'djamena, Chad. Tel: 513 064. Telex 5234 (a/b ACT KD).

Refer to the Embassy.

Direction du Tourisme, des Parcs Nationaux et Réserves de Faune BP 86, N'djamena, Chad. Tel: 512 303. Fax: 572 261.

Return ticket required. Requirements may be subject to change at short notice. Contact embassy. Valid passport required.

Visa required.

Narcotics.

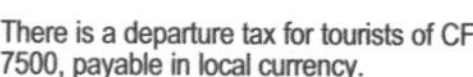
There is a departure tax for tourists of CFA Fr 7500, payable in local currency.

Evidence of sufficient funds may be necessary.

HEP A, POLIO, TYPHOID: R. MALARIA: R: falciparum variety present. YELLOW FEVER: R, with certificate of vaccination. OTHER: Bilharziasis, river blindness, sleeping sickness and meningitis.

W1

CFA Franc (CFAfr) = 100 centimes. Advisable to bring US$ rather than sterling into the country. Credit cards and travellers cheques are not widely accepted outside the capital. ATM AVAILABILITY: Unavailable.

MONEYGRAM: Unavailable.
WESTERN UNION: Unavailable.

AMEX: 1544 1273 696 933
DINERS CLUB: 1544 1252 513 500
MASTERCARD: 151 314 542 7111
VISA: 151 410 581 9994

AMEX: 1544 1273 571 600
THOMAS COOK: no local number
VISA: 1544 20 7937 8091

0900–1400 Mon to Fri

The economy is very unstable, due to civil unrest.

French. Arabic and Sara are also widely spoken. There are over 50 local languages.

The climate is hot and tropical. South has a rainy season from May-Oct. Central has a rainy season from Jun-Sept. The North has little rain. It is often cool in the evenings.

Muslim and Animist with a Christian minority.

Jan 1, Apr 13, May 1, 25, Aug 11, Nov 1, 28, Dec 25. Easter and Islamic festivals.

20 volts AC 50 Hz. Plugs are 3-pin.

Airmail takes about one week.

There is strict segregation of women, especially in towns. Dress should be conservative in respect of Muslim laws.

FLIGHTS: Very limited. ROAD: N'Djamena needs 4-wheel drive and permits are usually required. Due to security conditions and lack of petrol and repair facilities the government have put prohibitions on travel, especially in central and northern areas. Travel outside the capital requires special authorisation from the Ministry of the Interior, which must be obtained on arrival. There may be difficulty obtaining it. Most roads are impassable during the rainy season. DOCUMENTATION: Carnet de passage is required and is issued by the Tourist Association in the country of origin. An IDP is also required and either a green card or All Risks insurance obtained in Chad. Documentation must be obtained at all times, as travellers may encounter roadblocks. Chad's northern provinces bordering Libya constitute a military zone and remain heavily mined. Travel to and from this area is very dangerous and should be avoided.

MODERATE RISK. Visitors to Chad should be vigilant at all times. Respect for traditional beliefs and customs is expected.

CAPITAL: Santiago

GMT–4 (GMT–3 from second Sunday in October to second Sunday in March). Easter Island: GMT–6 (GMT–5 from second Sunday in Oct to second Saturday in March).

FROM UK: 0056. OUTGOING CODE TO UK: 0044

Police: 133; Fire: 132.

Embassy and Consulate of the Republic of Chile, 12 Devonshire Street, London, W1N 2DS. Tel: 020 7580 6392. echileuk@echileuk.demon.co.uk

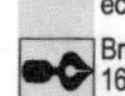
British Embassy, Casilla 72 D or Casilla 16552, Avenida El Bosque Norte 0125, Santiago 9, Chile. Tel: (2) 231 3737. Fax: (2) 231 9771. www.britemb.cl; embsan@britemb.cl

Refer to Embassy.

Servicio Nacionale de Turismo (SERNATUR), Casilla 14082, Avenida Providencia 1550, Santiago, Chile. Tel: (2) 696 7141. Fax: (2) 696081.

Return ticket required. Requirements may change at short notice. Contact the embassy before departure. Valid passport required. Passports have to remain valid for 6 months after departure. NOTE: Passports of children must contain a photo and state the nationality.

As the regulations are always subject to change at short notice, check with the Chilean Consulate for the latest information.

Meat products, flowers, fruit and vegetables.

US$18 or the peso equivalent.

POLIO, TYPHOID: R

W1

Peso (Ch$) = 100 centavos. Exch: Many outlets will exchange currency. NOTE: Visitors should avoid black market exchange rates. All major credit cards are accepted. Travellers cheques in US$ are preferred, but must be exchanged before midday. ATM AVAILABILITY: Over 1000 locations.

MONEYGRAM: 123 0 020 3725.
WESTERN UNION: 800 200 102.

AMEX: 0044 1273 696 933
DINERS CLUB: 800 220 220
MASTERCARD: 1230 020 2012
VISA: 1230 020 2136

AMEX: 0044 1273 571 600
THOMAS COOK: 001800 223 7373
VISA: 0044 20 7937 8091

0900–1400 Mon to Fri.

Chile is no longer a bargain. Modest lodgings, food and transport however are still cheaper than Europe, North America or Argentina.

Spanish. English is also widely spoken.

Roman Catholic, Protestant minority.

Jan 1, May 1,21, Jun 28, Aug 15, first Mon in Sep, Sep 6,18,19, Oct 12, Nov 1, Dec 8,25,31. Easter and Corpus Christi.

220 Volts AC 50 Hz. 3-pin plugs and screw-type bulbs are used.

Daily airmail services to Europe take approximately 3–4 days.

Chile's diverse geographical variants, ranging from arid grasslands to the Atacama desert (the driest in the world) governs women's role and occupation in society. Women should not wear shorts outside rural areas.

FLIGHTS: There are frequent services to main towns. The southern part of the city relies heavily on air links. Reservations are essential. ROADS: Generally in good condition. It is advisable in remoter areas to carry spare parts, and petrol. Tyres must be hard-wearing in the remoter areas. DOCUMENTATION: IDP is required. BUSES: Intercity buses are cheap and reliable. TAXI: Agree the fare in advance.

Violent crimes are rare but purse snatching in Santiago is not unusual. Crime is common in the beach resorts during the summer. Always carry your identification and in the event of an emergency contact your embassy for advice. PHOTOGRAPHY: Avoid taking photographs of anything connected to the military.

People's Republic of China

CAPITAL: Beijing

GMT +8.

FROM UK: 0086. OUTGOING CODE TO UK: 0044

Police: 110; Fire: 119.

Embassy of The People's Republic of China (Consular Section), 31 Portland Place, London, W1 3AG. Tel: 020 7636 5637. Fax 020 7636 9756. www.chinese-embassy.org.uk

British Embassy, 11 Guang Hua Lu, Jian Guo Men Wai, Beijing, People's Republic of China. Tel: (1) 532 1961/5 or 532 1930/1938/9. Fax: (1) 532 1937. www.britain.gov.co; consular-mail@peking.mail.fco.gov.uk

China National Tourist Office, 4 Glentworth Street, London NW1 5PG. Tel: 020 7935 9427. Fax: 020 7487 5842.

China International Travel Service (CITS), Head Office, 103 Fuximgmenni Avenue, Beijing, People's Republic of China. Tel: (1) 601 1122. Fax: (1) 601 2013.

Return ticket and valid passport required by all. Requirements may change at short notice. Contact embassy before departure.

Visa required by all.

Radio transmitters/receivers, exposed but undeveloped film. Baggage declaration forms must be completed on arrival and a copy given to customs when leaving the country.

Yuan 90.

POLIO, TYPHOID: R. MALARIA: Exists throughout the country below 1500 m in the falciparum variety, which has been reported s being highly resistant to Chloroquine. YELLOW FEVER: A vaccination certificate is required by anyone arriving from infected areas. OTHER: Bilharzia, cholera, rabies.

W1

Yuan (Renminbi RMB) = 10 chiao/jiao or 100 fen. EXCHANGE: there is only one national bank, which has 30,000 branches. In hotels and certain stores, luxury items such as spirits may be bought in Western currency. All credit cards are valid in major provincial cities in designated establishments. US dollars are the preferred currency in travellers cheques. ATM AVAILABILITY: Over 60 locations.

MONEYGRAM: 10811 then 800 592 3688. WESTERN UNION: (10) 6318 4313.

AMEX: 0044 1273 696 933
DINERS CLUB: 0044 1252 513 500
MASTERCARD: 10 800 110 7309
VISA: 10 800 110 2911

AMEX: 0044 1273 571 600
THOMAS COOK: 0044 1733 318950
VISA: 0044 20 7937 8091

0930–1200 and 1400–1700 Mon to Fri, 0900–1700 Sat.

China is predominantly an agrarian community in spite of the recent Westernisation of its major cities: prices vary substantially from region to region and city to city.

Mandarin Chinese. Cantonese, Fukienese, Xiamenhua and Hakka. English may sometimes be spoken.

Great variations in climate. North-east: hot and dry summers with very cold winters. North and central: continental rainfall, hot summers and cold winters. South-east: substantial rainfall, with semi-tropical summer and a cool winter.

Buddhism, Daoism and Confucianism. Also Muslim, Protestant and Roman Catholic.

Jan 1,2, Mar 8, May 1,2,4, Jun 1, Jul 1, Aug 1, Oct 1,2. Chinese New Year.

220/240 Volts AC, 50Hz.

Approx. 1 week. Address all postal communications 'People's Republic of China'.

Women in major cities are becoming more culturally free, however this is still limited due to tight censorship legislation. Women in rural areas continue to live a feudal, peasantry existence, in accordance with tradition.

Independent travel is increasingly possible. Further information can be obtained from the Chinese National Tourist Office (address above). ROAD: Most places can be reached by road but many are of poor quality. BUS: Reasonable services operate in main cities.

Visitors are sometimes greeted by applause as a sign of welcome. The usual response is to applaud back. PHOTOGRAPHY: Do not take photos of airports and always seek permission. Personal theft is common. People often stare, and spitting is common. Since 1988 independent travel to Tibet has ceased: China issues approx. 1000 visas a year for guided excursions only.

Colombia

CAPITAL: Santa Fe de Bogota

GMT–5

FROM UK: 0057. Calls to remote areas may have to be made through the international operator. OUTGOING CODE TO UK: 9044

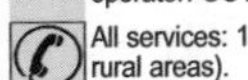
All services: 112 (01 in smaller towns and rural areas).

Embassy of the Republic of Colombia, Flat 3A, 3 Hans Crescent, London, SW1X 0LR. Tel: 020 7589 9177. Fax: 020 7581 1829. www.colombia.demon.co.uk; colombia@colombia.demon.co.uk

British Embassy, Apdo Aereo 4598, Torre Propaganda Sancho, Calle 98, No 9-03, Piso 4, Santa Fe de Bogota DC, Colombia. Tel: (1) 218 5111. Fax: (1) 218 2460. Consulates in Baranquilla, Cali and Medellin. www.britain.gov.co; britain@cable.net.co

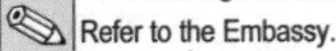
Refer to the Embassy.

Corporacion Nacional de Turismo, Apdo Aereo 8400, Calle 28, No 13A-15, 16º-18º, Santa Fe de Bogota DC, Colombia. Tel: (1) 283 9466. Fax: (1) 284 3818.

Return ticket and passport with 6 months validity required by all. Requirements may change at short notice: contact the Embassy.

Not required by tourists staying less than 90 days. Visitors must show proof of sufficient funds to cover their stay. All visitors must obtain an exit stamp from the security police before leaving (best obtained at the airport or in the main cities.)

Emeralds, gold and platinum require receipts of purchase, to be presented to Customs on departure.

US$17 or the equivalent in pesos. This tax is doubled for stays of more than 60 days.

POLIO, TYPHOID: R. MALARIA: Exists in throughout the year in low-lying and rural areas in the falciparum variety, reportedly resistant to chloroquine. YELLOW FEVER: R. OTHER: Cholera, hepatitis and rabies.

W1

Peso (Col$). Exch: US$ is the easiest to exchange at hotels, banks, shops, travel agencies. All major credit cards accepted. Travellers cheques in US$ are preferred and are easier to exchange in larger towns. ATM AVAILABILTY: Over 2500 locations.

MONEYGRAM: 980 12 0834.
WESTERN UNION: 9800 15690.

AMEX: 9044 1273 696 933
DINERS CLUB: 98 009 100 56
MASTERCARD: 9809 12 1303
VISA: 9809 12 5713

AMEX: 9044 1273 571 600
THOMAS COOK: 1 800 223 7373
VISA: 9044 20 7937 8091

0900–1500 Mon to Fri.

Accommodation and commodities are moderately priced in the cities.

Spanish. Local Indian dialects and English is also spoken.

Hot and humid with a rainy season between May-Nov. Cooler climate in the upland areas.

Roman Catholic. Protestant and Jewish minorities.

Jan1,6, Mar 19, May 1, Jun 29, Jul 20, Aug 7, 15, Oct 12, Nov 1, 11, Dec 8, 25. Christian feast days.

110/120 Volts AC, US 2-pin plugs are used.

Airmail usually takes 5–7 days. International postboxes are yellow.

Travelling alone is not advised, as violent attacks have recently increased. Inequality between men and women can be a problem.

FLIGHTS: There is an excellent network of domestic flights and the large distances between cities makes this method of transport more convenient. ROAD: Highways connecting the main cities have recently been completed. Roads are usually passable except during the rainy season. DOCUMENTATION: An IDP is required. Visitors are strongly advised to avoid driving at night.

HIGH RISK: The FCO advises travellers to be vigilant and to take sensible precautions in Colombia. Violence by drug traffickers, guerrillas, paramilitary groups and other criminal elements affects all parts of the country. The area close to the border with Panama should be avoided in particular.Corruption is commonplace. Personal safety and possessions are at risk at all times. Kidnapping and criminal violence remain problems. Attackers are known to use drugs to subdue their intended victims, sometimes added to take-away food or drinks, so do not accept offers of food, drink or cigarettes from strangers.

CAPITAL: Moroni

GMT +3

FROM UK: 00269. OUTGOING CODE TO UK: 10. Most calls must go via the operator.

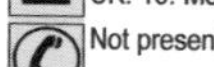

Not present.

No embassy in the UK. Europe: Embassy of he Federal Republic of the Comoros, 20 rue Marbeau, 75106 Paris, France. Tel: (1) 40 67 90 54. Fax: (1) 40 67 72 96.

British Embassy in Madagascar deals with enquiries relating to the Comoro Islands: British Embassy, BP 167, First Floor, Immeuble 'Ny Havana', Cité de 67 Ha, Antananarivo, Madagascar. Tel: (2) 27749 or 27370. Fax (2) 26690. ukembant@simicro.mg

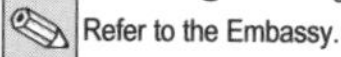

Refer to the Embassy.

Société Comorienne de Tourisme et d'Hôtellerie (COMOTEL) Itsandra Hotel, Njazidja, Comoros. Tel: 732 365.

Return ticket required. Requirements may be subject to short term change. Consult embassy before departure. Valid passport required by all.

Required by all. Transit and tourist. visas are issued by the Immigration officer on arrival. Exit permits are required by all.

Weapons, ammunition and radio transmission equipment. Plants and soil.

Departure tax CFA Fr 500 or Ffr 100.

HEP A, POLIO, TYPHOID: R. MALARIA: R. Falciparum variety present. YELLOW FEVER: If travelling from an infected area a vaccination certificate may be required.

W1

CFA Franc (CFA Fr) = 100 centimes. There is a very limited acceptance of credit cards, restricted mainly to hotels. French Franc travellers cheques are recommended. The Banque Internationale des Comoros is the only bank that will exchange traveller's cheques. ATM AVAILABILITY: Unavailable.

MONEYGRAM: Unavailable.
WESTERN UNION: Unavailable.

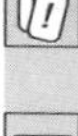

AMEX: 1044 1273 696 933
DINERS CLUB: 1044 1252 513 500
MASTERCARD: 101 314 542 7111
VISA: 101 410 581 9994

AMEX: 1044 1273 571 600
THOMAS COOK 1044 1733 318950
VISA : 1044 20 7937 8091

0730–1300 Mon to Thur, 0730–1100 Fri.

Tourists can expect to pay higher prices than on the mainland.

French and Arabic. The majority speak Comoran and there is a blend of Arabic and Swahili.

Climate is tropical and very warm. Coastal areas are very hot and humid (Dec–Mar) with some rain and cyclones. Upland areas are cooler and have more rain.

Muslim with a Roman Catholic minority.

Mar 18, May 1, 25, 29, Jul 6, Nov 26, Dec 25

220 Volts AC, 50 Hz

At least 1 week.

Culture is predominantly patriarchal.

Private vehicles are the only form of transport on the Islands. 4 wheel drives are needed for the interior and outlying islands, especially in the rainy season. DOCUMENTATION: IDP is required.

Religious customs should be respected, especially during Ramadam. French residents and tourists tend to be quite relaxed about what they wear, although dress should be conservative.

Congo

CAPITAL: Brazzaville

GMT + 1

FROM UK: 00242. OUTGOING CODE TO UK: 0044

Not present.

Honorary Consulate of the Republic of Congo, Alliance House 12 Caxton Street , London SW1H 0QS. Tel: 020 7222 7575. Fax: 020 7233 2087.

Refer to British Embassy in Kinshasa, Zaïre (Democratic Republic of Congo). British Embassy, 83 Avenue du Roi Baudouin (ex Avenue Lemera), Gombe, Kinshasa. Tel: 00243 88 46102 Fax (after GMT 1400 hrs): 00243 88 01738; ambrit@ic.cd.

Europe: Embassy of the Republic of Congo and the Tourist Office, 37 bis rue Paul Valery, 75016 Paris, France. Tel: (1) 45 00 60 57. Fax: (1) 40 67 70 86.

Direction Générale du Tourisme et des loisirs, BP 456, Brazzaville, Congo. Tel: 830 953.

Return ticket required. Requirements may be subject to change at short notice. Consult embassy before departure. Valid passport required by all.

Visa required by all except nationals of Gabon. Tourist and business, 15 or 30 days.

A licence is required for sporting guns.

Departure tax of CFAFr 500, payable in local currency.

HEP A, POLIO, TYPHOID: R. MALARIA: R. Falciparum variety exists, resistance to chloroquine has been reported. YELLOW FEVER: Vaccination is required by all visitors over one year of age.
OTHER: Biharzia, cholera, river blindness and sleeping sickness are also prevalent.

W1

CFA Franc (CFA Fr) = 100 centimes. Credit cards and travellers cheques are not widely accepted. ATM AVAILABILITY: Unavailable.

MONEYGRAM: Unavailable.
WESTERN UNION: Unavailable.

AMEX: 0044 1273 696 933
DINERS CLUB: 0044 1252 513 500
MASTERCARD: 001 314 542 7111
VISA: 001 410 581 9994

AMEX: 0044 1273 571 600
THOMAS COOK: no local number
VISA: 0044 20 7937 8091

0630–1300 Mon to Fri. Counters close at 1130.

Tourists can expect to pay high prices for services.

French. Other languages are Likala and Kikongo. Very little English is spoken.

The climate is equatorial. Rainy season: Oct–Apr. Dry season: May–Sept.

Majority of the population believe in Animism. Also Roman Catholics and a minority of Protestants and Muslims.

Jan 1, Feb 5, 8, Mar 8, 18, May 1, Jun 22, Jul 31, Aug 15, Dec 25, 31

220/230 Volts AC 50Hz

Unreliable internal service

Culture is predominantly patriarchal.

RAIL: Advance booking is recommended. Services can be erratic. ROAD: The roads are mostly tracks and are suitable for 4-wheel drive. Several car-hire firms in Brazzaville. DOCUMENTATION: IDP is required.

The FCO advises against all travel, except to Pointe Noire. Travellers should contact the Consul on arrival, and should exercise caution after dark. PHOTOGRAPHY: Do not photograph public buildings.

Cook Islands

CAPITAL: Avarua

GMT –10

FROM UK: 00682. Operator assistance may be required. OUTGOING CODE TO UK: 0044

Police: 999. Ambulance and hospital: 998. Fire: 996.

Refer to New Zealand High Commission.

The British High Commission, PO BOX 1812, 44 Hill Street, Wellington 1, New Zealand. Tel: (4) 472 6049. Fax: (4) 471 1974.

Tourism Council of the South Pacific, 203 Sheen Lane, London SW 14 8LE. Tel: 020 8878 9876. Fax: 020 8878 9955. info@spto.org

Cook Islands Tourist Authority, PO Box 14, Raratonga, Cook Islands. Tel: 29435. Fax: 21435. www.cook-islands.com/ ; tourism@cookislands.gov.ck

Return ticket required. Regulations may be subject to change at short notice. Contact the embassy before departure. Passport required by all except nationals of New Zealand, valid for 12 months after the intended date of departure.

Visa required for business purposes. Not required for tourist purposes if staying for less than 31 days. NOTE: Proof of arranged accommodation and sufficient funds for length of stay will be required.

Fruit, meat, fireworks, ammunition and gunpowder.

NZ$25, payable in local currency, for passengers over 12 years. NZ$ 10 for passengers between 2 and 12 years.

POLIO, TYPHOID: R

New Zealand Dollar (NZ$) = 100 cents. Both credit cards and travellers cheques are accepted. Australian dollars are the preferred currency in travellers cheques. ATM AVAILABILITY: Unavailable.

MONEYGRAM: Unavailable.
WESTERN UNION: Available.

AMEX: 0044 1273 696 933
DINERS CLUB: 0044 1252 513 500
MASTERCARD: 0800 44 9140
VISA: 001 410 581 9994

AMEX: 0044 1273 571 600
THOMAS COOK: 0800 44 0112
VISA: 0800 44 0110

0900–1500 Mon to Fri.

Can be expensive in the tourist centres. However, accommodation is increasing yearly, which may bring a price decrease in the resorts.

Maori. English widely spoken

Hot throughout the year. Most rain Nov-Apr.

Cook Islands Christian Church. Roman Catholic. Latter Day Saints, Seventh Day Adventists and Assembly of God.

Jan 1, Apr 25, second Mon in Jun, Jul 25, Aug 4, Oct 26, Dec 25, 26, 31. Easter.

240 Volts AC, 50 Hz

Up to 2 weeks.

A conservative Christian society prevails. Cover arms and shoulders in church. Be careful in secluded areas, especially at night.

The cheapest way to travel around the island is on an inter-island cargo ship. On Rarotinga there is a bus service and plenty of taxis. ROAD: Vehicles can be hired from a number of outlets. DOCUMENTATION: A current Cook Islands driving licence is required and available from the police station in Avarua on presentation of a national licence or IDP.

Religious celebrations, for instance Gospel Day in October, are taken very seriously and should be respected. Beachwear should not be worn in the towns. Usual social courtesies should be followed.

Costa Rica

CAPITAL: San Jose

GMT –7

FROM UK: 00506. OUTGOING CODE TO UK: 0044

Police: 104; Fire: 103; Ambulance: 225/1436 and 228/2187.

Embassy and Consulate of the Republic of Costa Rica, Flat 1, 14 Lancaster Gate, London, W2 3LH. Tel: 020 7706 8844. Fax: 020 7706 8655. www.embcrlon.demon.co.uk; info@embcrlon.demon.co.uk

British Embassy, Apartado 815, 11th Floor, Edificio Centro Colón, 1007 San José, Costa Rica. Tel: 221 5566 or 221 5716 or 221 5816. Fax: 233 9938. britemb@sol.racsa.co.cr

Refer to the Embassy.

Instituto Costarricense de Turismo, Apartado 777, Edificio Genaro Valverde, Calles 5 y 7, Avenida 4a 1000 San José, Costa Rica. Tel/Fax: 223 3254. www.tourism-costarica.com/

Return ticket required. Requirements may change at short notice. Contact the embassy before departure. Passport required by all, with a minimum validity of 6 months from date of arrival.

Visas not normally required. Check with the embassy and consulate for latest information.

Narcotics and firearms.

US$ 37 or local equivalent, payable if staying in Costa Rica for longer than 48 hours by everyone.

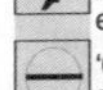
'Gypsies and persons of unkempt appearance will be deported.'

POLIO, TYPHOID: R. MALARIA: Exists throughout the year in the Vivax variety in the rural areas below 700 m. OTHER: Bilharzia.

W2

Costa Rican Colón = 100 centimos. EXCHANGE: Gambios will give the best exchange rates. All major credit cards accepted. Travellers cheques in US dollars only will be accepted. ATM AVAILABILITY: Over 150 locations.

MONEYGRAM: 001 800 824 2220.
WESTERN UNION: 283 6336.

AMEX: 0044 1273 696 933
DINERS CLUB 257 1766 or 257 0121
MASTERCARD 0800 011 0184
VISA: 0800 011 0030

AMEX: 0044 1273 571 600
THOMAS COOK: 001 800 223 7373
VISA: 0044 20 7937 8091

0900–1500 Mon to Fri.

More expensive than other Central American countries but still cheaper than North America. All accommodation is graded.

Spanish. English is also spoken.

Coastal areas are much hotter than inland valleys. The rainy season is May–Nov.

Roman Catholic.

Jan 1, Mar 19, Apr 11, May 1, Jun 29, Jul 25, Aug 2,15, Sep 15, Oct 12, Dec 8, 24–31. Easter, Corpus Christi.

110/220 Volts 60 Hz. 2-pin plugs are standard.

6-10 days.

Roman Catholicism influences all aspects of daily living. Women may receive unwelcome male attention.

FLIGHTS: A number of operators offer domestic flights, but reservations cannot be made out side of San José. ROADS: Generally very good standard but heavy traffic can make driving arduous. DOCUMENTATION: A national driving licence is required. BUS: Services operate between most towns but book in advance because overcrowding is common.

Christian names are preceded by Don for a man and Donna for a woman. Casual dress is acceptable for most occasions but beachwear should be confined to the pool/beach. Muggings and theft from cars are common.

Côte d'Ivoire

CAPITAL: Yamoussoukro

GMT

FROM UK: 00225. OUTGOING CODE TO UK: 0044.

Not present.

Embassy of the Republic of Côte d'Ivoire, 2 Upper Belgrave Street, London SW1X 8BJ. Tel: 020 7235 6991. Fax: 020 7259 5439.

British Embassy, 01 BP 2581, Third Floor Immeuble 'Les Harmonies', angle boulevard, Carde et Avenue Dr Jamot, Plateau Abidjan 01, Côte d'Ivoire. Tel: 226 850/1/2 or 328209. Fax: 223 221. www.britaincdi.com; britemb.a@aviso.ci

Refer to the Embassy.

Office Ivoirien du Tourisme et de l'Hôtellerie, BP V184, Abidjan, Côte d'Ivoire. Tel: 206 528. Fax: 225 924.

Return ticket required. Requirements may be subject to change at short notice. Consult embassy before departure. Valid passport required by all.

Visa required. Tourist and business visas available. Transit visas not usually required by travellers not leaving the airport.

Sporting guns may only be imported under licence. Limits are placed on the importation of certain personal affects. Contact the consulate prior to departure.

Departure tax domestic: CFA Fr 800 International: £5.90. Transit passengers are exempt.

HEP A, POLIO, TYPHOID: R. MALARIA: The falciparum variety is present. Resistance to chloroquine has been reported. YELLOW FEVER: A vaccination certificate is required from all visitors over 1 year of age. OTHER: Bilharzia, meningitis, rabies.

W1

CFA Franc (CFAFr) = 100 centimes. Exchange available in airport, banks and hotels. Amex and MasterCard are widely accepted. Visa and Diners Club are only accepted on a limited basis. Traveller's cheques are accepted in major hotels and some shops. French francs are the preferred currency. ATM AVAILABILITY: Unavailable.

MONEYGRAM: 00 111 11
WESTERN UNION: 22 12 12

AMEX: 0044 1273 696 933
DINERS CLUB: 0044 1252 513 500
MASTERCARD: 001 314 542 7111
VISA: 001 410 581 9994

AMEX: 0044 1273 571 600
THOMAS COOK: 0044 1733 318950
VISA: 0044 20 7937 8091

0800–1130 and 1430–1630 Mon to Fri.

Services and prices are generally expensive.

French. Local dialects of Dioula and Baoule are also spoken.

Dry season : Dec-Apr and Aug- Sept. Rainy season: May-July and Oct-Nov.

Mostly traditional beliefs. Also Muslim and Christian.

Jan 1, May 1, Aug 7,15, Nov 1,15, Dec 7, 25. Christian feast days and Islamic festivals.

220 Volts AC 50 Hz. Plugs are round 2-pin.

Airmail can take up to 2 weeks.

Women can expect to enjoy a more multi-cultural society than in the rest of West Africa.

ROAD: Good road system of tarmac roads with frequent petrol stations in the north. Hire cars are available in the main towns. TAXIS: Available in the main cities. FLIGHTS: Regular domestic flights operate between the main cities. RAIL: Fast, regular trains operate throughout the day between the main cities.

There is extreme ethnic and linguistic variety which distinguishes it from many other African countries. Swimming off the coast is dangerous.

Croatia

CAPITAL: Zagreb

GMT +1 (+2 during the summer)

FROM UK: 00385. OUTGOING CODE TO UK: 9944

Police: 92; Fire: 93; Ambulance: 94.

Embassy of the Republic of Croatia, 21 Conway Street, London W1P 5HL. Tel: 020 7387 1144. Fax: 020 7387 3276.

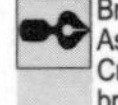
British Embassy, PO Box 454, 2nd Floor, Astra Tower, Tratinska, 41000 Zagreb, Croatia. Tel: 1 334 245. Fax: 1 338 893. ; british-embassy@zg.tel.hr

Croatian National Tourist Office, 2 The Lanchesters, 162-164 Fulham Palace Road, London W6 9ER. Tel: 020 8563 7979. Fax: 020 8563 2616. ; info@cnto.freeserve.co.uk

Ministry of Tourism, Avenija Vukovar 78, 41000 Zargreb, Croatia. Tel: 1 613 9444. Fax: 1 611 3216. www.mint.hr ; info@htz.hr

Return ticket required, may be subject to change at short notice. Contact the Embassy before travelling. Valid passport required.

Visa not required by British passport holders.

US$8 on international flights from Zagreb.

Rabies

W1

Kuna (Kn) = 100 Lipa (Lp). Exch: The only true repositories of value and real medium of exchange locally are the German DM and the US$ (Sterling is rarely used). The import and export of local currency is limited to Kn 2000. All major credit cards are accepted. German DM is the preferred traveller's cheque currency. ATM AVAILABILITY: Over 80 locations.

MONEYGRAM: 99 385 0111 then 800 592 3688
WESTERN UNION: Unavailable.

AMEX: 0044 1273 696 933
DINERS CLUB: 0800 1144 or 4920 501
MASTERCARD: 001 314 542 7111
VISA: 001 410 581 9994

AMEX: 0044 1273 571 600
THOMAS COOK: 0044 1733 318950
VISA: 0044 20 7937 8091

0700-1500 Mon to Fri, 0800-1400 Sat.

The Croatian economy is still recovering after civil war. Visitors may be charged higher prices than locals.

Croat-Serb with the Latin alphabet.

Continental climate in the north and Mediterranean on the Adriatic cost.

Roman Catholic Croats. Eastern Orthodox Serbs.

Jan 1, May 1, Aug 7,15, Nov 1,15, Dec 7, 25. Christian feast days and Islamic festivals.

220 volts AC, 50Hz

May take several days.

ROAD/RAIL: The main road/rail route to and from Western Europe now effectively stops at Zagreb (coming from Ljublijana) with extensive detours via Hungary for international traffic going South to and from Serbia, Republic of Macedonia and Greece. DOCUMENTATION: National or IDP required. A green card should be carried by visitors taking their own car into Croatia.

The situation has now calmed in most parts of Croatia. Avoid travel in the Eastern Slavonia/Baranja area, where tensions remain high. There is, however, a continued risk of a deterioration in the security situation in some areas, so visitors should remain cautious. For up-to-date information, contact the FCO travel advice unit before travelling. Certain restrictions exist on taking photographs in some areas.

CAPITAL: Havana

GMT –4

FROM UK: 0053. OUTGOING CODE: 11944 (From Havana only. All other calls must go through the operator.)

All services: 26811.

Embassy of the Republic of Cuba, 167 High Holborn, London, WC1V 6PA. Tel: 020 7420 3100. Fax: 020 7836 2602. Cuban Consulate, 15 Grape Street, London WC2 8DR. Tel: 020 7240 2488 or 0900 188 0820. Fax: 020 7836 2602. embacuba.lnd@virgin.net

British Embassy, Calle 34, 708 Miramar, Havana, Cuba. Tel: (7) 331 771 or 331 049 (Commercial section). Fax: (7) 338 104. embrit@ceniai.inf.cu

Cuba Tourist Board 154 Shaftesbury Avenue, London WC2. Tel: 020 7240 6655 Brochure line: 0900 160 0295.

Empresa de Turismo Internacional (Cubatur), Calle 23, No 156, entre N y O, Apartado 6560, Vedado, Havana, Cuba. Tel: (7) 324 521. Fax: (7) 333 104. www.cubatravel.cu/ ; promo@mintur.mit.cma.net

Return ticket required. Requirements may be subject to short-term change: contact Embassy. Passport required by all, valid for at least 6 months beyond length of stay.

Visa required by all, except holders of a tourist card.

Natural fruits or vegetables, meat and dairy products, weapons and ammunitions, all pornographic material and drugs.

US$15.

POLIO, TYPHOID: Low risk present. OTHER: Rabies

W2

Cuban Peso (Cub$) = 100 centavos. At official tourist shops purchases can only be made in US$. EXCHANGE: Should only be made at authorised money exchanges, as there are severe penalties for black market transactions. Keep all exchange receipts, which will be required when making purchases. Do not enter the place or date details on any cheque until ready to make the transaction or the cheque will be refused. The import of local currency is prohibited. Generally a maximum of Cub$10 can be reconverted to foreign currency when leaving on presentation of an official exchange form. Visa and MasterCard are widely accepted. US$ (not drawn from a US bank) and Sterling are accepted in traveller's cheques. ATM AVAILABILITY: Unavailable.

MONEYGRAM: Unavailable.
WESTERN UNION: Unavailable.

AMEX: 11944 1273 696 933
DINERS CLUB: 11944 1252 513 500
MASTERCARD: 1191 314 542 7111
VISA: 1191 410 581 9994

AMEX: 11944 1273 571 600
THOMAS COOK: 1191 800 223 7373
VISA: 11944 20 7937 8091

0830-1200 and 1330-1500 Mon to Fri, 0830-1030 Sat.

Not as expensive as some of the other Caribbean Islands.

Spanish. English and French may also be spoken.

Hot all year round. Rainy season May-Oct. Hurricane possible Aug-Nov. Cooler between Nov-Apr.

Roman Catholic majority.

Jan 1, 2, May 1, 20, Jul 25–27, Oct 10.

110/220 volts AC 60 Hz. American-style plugs are used except for large hotels, which may use European-type plugs.

Can take up to several weeks.

Normal precautions should be followed. Avoid venturing out alone at night and keep to busy areas.

FLIGHTS: Cubana operates scheduled services between the main towns. It is essential to book in advance. TAXI: A number of bogus taxis operate at the airports. Be sure to use a registered taxi and not a private car.

The tourist industry is rapidly developing, with growing tolerance of Western influences, following the decline in trade with eastern Europe and the ending of Russian subsidies. Visitors should be on the alert for pickpockets and bag snatching in Havana and tourist sites. Shorts should only be worn at the beach or pool. The penalties for drug trafficking are severe.

Curaçao

CAPITAL: Willemstad

GMT –4

FROM UK: 00599. OUTGOING CODE TO UK: 0044

Police: 114; Ambulance: 112. All services: 444444.

Office of the Plenipotentiary of the Netherlands Antilles, Antillenhuis, Badhuiisweg 173-175, 2597JP The Hague, The Netherlands. Tel: (70) 306 6111. Fax: (70) 351 2722.

British Consulate, Heintje Kool, Z/N, Willemstad, Curaçao, NA. Tel: (9) 695 968. owers@curinfo.an

Caribbean Tourism, 42 Westminster Palace Gdns, Artillery Row, London SW1P 1RR. Tel: 020 7222 4335. Fax: 020 7222 4325. www.doitcaribbean.com; cto@carib-tourism.com

Curaçao Tourism Development Bureau, Pietermaai 19, Willemstad, Curaçao, NA. Tel: (9) 616 000. Fax: (9) 612 305.

Return ticket required. Requirements may be subject to short-term change. Contact embassy before departure. Valid passport required.

Nationals of the UK are allowed to stay for 90 days without a visa provided they have onward or return tickets. Contact the embassy for an up to date complete list of visa regulations, which are complex and may change at short notice.

Narcotics and firearms.

NAG22.50, or US$12.50 per person. Children under 2 years of age and transit passengers are exempt.

POLIO, TYPHOID: R. YELLOW FEVER: A vaccination certificate is required from travellers over 6 months of age arriving from infected areas.

Netherlands Antilles Guilder or Florin (NAG) = 100 cents. Credit cards are accepted in large establishments. US$ travellers cheques are the most welcomed. ATM AVAILABILITY: 10 locations.

MONEYGRAM: 001 800 872 2881.
WESTERN UNION: 5999 9 617472.

AMEX: 0044 1273 696 933
DINERS CLUB: 0044 1252 513 500
MASTERCARD: 001800 307 7309
VISA: 001800 847 2911

AMEX: 0044 1273 571 600
THOMAS COOK: 001800 223 7373
VISA: 0044 20 7937 8091

0830-1130 and 1330-1630 Mon to Fri.

The most expensive of the Netherlands Antilles.

Dutch. English, Spanish Papiamento are also used.

Hot all year round with cooling winds. Rainy season Oct-Dec.

Roman Catholic.

Jan 1, Apr 30, May 1, Jul 2, Oct 21, Dec 25,26. Carnival week before Lent, Easter, Ascension Day.

110/220 volts AC 50 Hz.

4-6 days.

Usual precautions should be taken. Women tend to be conservative, in accordance with the island's dominant religion.

ROAD: An IDP is required. BUS: A good bus service operates throughout the island and many hotels operate their own minibuses to the capital. TAXI and CAR HIRE: Plentiful.

Swimwear is for beach/pool-side only.

CAPITAL: Nicosia

GMT +2 (GMT +3 during the summer)

FROM UK: 00357. OUTGOING CODE TO UK: 0044

All services: 199.

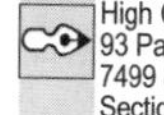
High Commission of the Republic of Cyprus, 93 Park Street, London W1Y 4ET. Tel: 020 7499 8272. Fax: 020 7491 0691. Consular Section Tel: 020 7629 5350. Fax: 020 7491 0691.

British High Commission, PO Box 1978, Alexander Pallis Street, Nicosia, Cyprus. Tel: (2) 771 131. Fax: (2) 781 758. www.britain.org.cy; infobhc@cylink.com.cy

Cyprus Tourism Organisation, 213 Regent Street, London W1R 8DA. Tel: 020 7734 9822 or 734 2593. Fax: 020 7287 6534.

Cyprus Tourism Organisation, PO Box 4535, 19 Limassol Avenue, Melkonian Building, Nicosia, Cyprus. Tel: (2) 337 715. Fax: (2) 331 644. www.cyprustourism.org/

Return ticket required, may be subject to change at short notice. Contact consulate before travelling. Valid passport required by all: must be valid for 3 months after date of departure for visitors not requiring visas. Those requiring visas must have passports valid for at least 6 months from the date of departure.

Visa not required by nationals of Great Britain.

Narcotics.

C(£)7, payable in local currency.

Passports stamped with 'Turkish Republic of Northern Cyprus'.

Cyprus Pound (C£) = 100 cents. Travellers cheques can be cashed in all banks, US dollars, Pound sterling and the Deutsche Mark are all accepted currencies. All major credit cards are accepted. ATM AVAILABILITY: Approx. 200 locations.

MONEYGRAM: Available at all Avis Rent-a-Car locations.
WESTERN UNION: Available.

AMEX: 0044 1273 696 933
DINERS CLUB: 02 660924 or 02 868100
MASTERCARD: 080 90 569
VISA: 001 410 581 9994

AMEX: 0044 1273 571 600
THOMAS COOK: 080 91029
VISA: 0044 20 7937 8091

Generally 0815-1230, in tourist areas 1530 - 1730 (winter) and 1630 -1830 (summer).

Slightly cheaper than Western Europe.

Mostly Greek with some Turkish. English, German and French are also spoken.

Mediterranean climate. Hot dry summers with mild winters. Rainfall is most likely during the winter.

Greek Orthodox and Muslim minorities.

Jan 1,6, Mar 25, Apr 1, May 1, Aug 15, Oct 1,28, Dec 25,26. Mon before Lent, Easter.

240 volts AC 50 Hz.

Approx. 3 days to Europe. Poste restante facilities are available in the main cities and resorts.

Traditional roles persist among the older generation. Around the capital city views are influenced by western culture. Usual precautions should be observed.

BUS: Services are cheap and efficient. CAR HIRE: Widely available and considered to be the best way of seeing the island, but check car is roadworthy. DOCUMENTATION: IDP or National driving licence is accepted.

It is considered impolite to refuse an offer of Greek coffee or a cold drink. Casual wear is usually accepted, but beachwear should be confined to the beach or poolside. Respect should be shown for religious beliefs. Visitors can expect a warm and hospitable reception from Cypriots.

NOTE: It is possible to travel to the north of Cyprus from the south by crossing at the United Nations-controlled Ledra Palace checkpoint in Nicosia. Goods bought in the north may be confiscated at the checkpoint on return to the south. Visitors to Northern Cyprus should not attempt to cross into the south. If they do, they are liable to arrest and possible imprisonment. See next page for Northern Cyprus.

Cyprus, Northern

CAPITAL: Nicosia

GMT+2 (+3 during the summer)

FROM UK: 0090392. OUTGOING CODE TO UK: 0044

Police: 155; First Aid: 112; Fire: 199.

The government of Northern Cyprus has a representative office in the United Kingdom at 28 Cockspur Street, London, SW1Y 5BN Tel: 020 7839 4577 Fax: 020 7839 5282. www.cypnet.com/.ncyprus/tourist.html

The Turkish Republic of Cyprus is not recognized by the British Government.

North Cyprus Tourist Office in UK: 28 Cockspur Street, London, SW1Y 5BN Tel: 020 7930 5069 Fax: 020 7839 5282.

Visitors who do not wish to have their passports stamped by the authorities on arrival in Northern Cyprus may request a stamped visa form, which is loosely inserted into the passport and removed on departure.

Citizens of European Union states do not require a visa.

Each adult visitor is allowed to bring in 200 cigarettes, or their equivalent in cigars or tobacco, together with one bottle of spirits and one bottle of wine and a reasonable quantity of perfume.

The unit of currency in North Cyprus is Turkish Lira (TL). Most businesses will also happily accept payment in Pound sterling, Euro, US$ and other main currencies. There is no restriction for the import of foreign currency into Northern Cyprus, however, the export of currency is restricted to US$3000, or the equivalent in other currencies.
Currency exchange is possible in banks, exchange offices and hotels.
All major international credit and charge cards are accepted by hotels, restaurants, and shops.

Banks in Northern Cyprus are open from 8am to 2pm. Most major banks also have ATMs, which also accept main credit and charge cards.

Turkish is the official language of Northern Cyprus, but English is also widely used and understood.

Summers are hot with July and August averaging over 30ºC. The coolest months are January and February with a mean temperature of 10ºC.The sea temperature ranges from a mean average of about 16ºC in January, to 32ºC in August.

North Cyprus is a secular state with no official religion, although 98% of the population are Muslim. There are also small communities of Baha'is and Maronite and Orthodox Christians.

Jan 1, Apr 23, May 1, Jul 20, Aug 1, 30, Oct 29, Nov 15. There are also religious festivals, Ramazan Bayram and Kurban Bayram, which occur according to the lunar calendar and last for 3 days.

240 Volts AC, 50 Hz. Sockets are the British 3-pin variety.

AIR AND SEA: There are daily scheduled flights from major European capitals and from the major cities of Turkey to Ercan Airport in Northern Cyprus. There are also ferryboats running from the Turkish ports of Istanbul, Antalya, Mersin and Tasucu; from Haifa, Israel; and Lattakia, Syria to the North Cyprus ports of Famagusta and Kyrenia.
ROAD: Traffic in Northern Cyprus drives on the left, as in Britain, with good dual carriageways between major towns. CAR HIRE: Renting a car in Northern Cyprus is easy and cheap (between UK £10 to £15 per day. Car rental services are widely available in the main towns, and petrol is cheap. A current national driving licence along with your passport is all that is needed. The speed limit in urban areas is 30 mph. BUSES: There are frequent bus services between the major towns during the day. After 7pm and at weekends the services are less regular. TAXIS are to be found at taxi stands only. The charges are reasonable, but as there are no meters, it is advisable to agree upon the fare with the driver before setting off.

The United Nations supervises a frontier known as the Green Line, which cuts the island and through the capital, Nicosia. Visitors to the mainly Greek section are allowed across the Green Line only for day trips. Access to Northern Cyprus for a longer stay is allowed only by airline flights to Ercan Airport or by ferry from Istanbul or other ports on the mainland of Turkey.

CAPITAL: Prague

GMT + 1 (GMT + 2 during the summer).

FROM UK: 0042. OUTGOING CODE TO UK: 0044

Ambulance: 155; Fire: 150; Police: 158.

Embassy of the Czech Republic, 26-30 Kensington Palace Gardens, London, W8 4QY. Tel: 020 7243 1115. Fax: 020 7727 9654. www.czech.cz ; london@embassy.mzv.cz

British Embassy, Thunovská 14, 11 800 Prague 1, Czech Republic. Tel: (2) 24 51 04 39. Fax: (2) 539 927. www.britain.cz/ ; info@britain.cz

Czech Tourist Centre 95 Great Portland Street, London W1N. Tel: 020 7291 9925 or 0906 364 0641. www.visitczechia.cz/main-uk.html ; gillespie@czechcentre.org.uk

Czech Tourist Authority (Information Centre), Národní trída 28, 110 01 Prague !, Czech Republic. Tel: (2) 24 21 14 58. cccr-info.cz/ ; visitczech@cccr-cta.cz

Requirements may be subject to short-term change. Contact embassy before departure. Valid passport required. Passports must be valid for at least 8 months at the time of application, and in a reasonable state.

Nationals of EU countries do not require a visa (except those with the endorsement British Overseas Citizen who do require a visa).

Pornography. All items of value, e.g. cameras and tents must be declared on arrival to allow clearance on departure.

W2

Koruna (Kc) or Crown = 100 hellers. Exch: All banks, exchange offices, main hotels and cross border crossings. NOTE: The import and export of local currency is prohibited by non-residents. All major credit cards are accepted in main hotels, restaurants and shops. Travellers cheques are widely accepted. The preferred currencies are US$, Pound sterling and Deutsche Mark. ATM AVAILABILITY: Over 1000 locations.

MONEYGRAM: 00 42 000 101.
WESTERN UNION: (02) 2422 9524.

AMEX: 0044 1273 696 933
DINERS CLUB: 02 671 97 450
MASTERCARD: 001 314 542 7111
VISA: 001 410 581 9994

AMEX: 0044 1273 571 600
THOMAS COOK: 0044 1733 318950
VISA: 0044 20 7937 8091

Generally 0800-1800 Mon to Fri.

Currently cheaper than Western Europe. However as visitors are increasing so are the prices, and it can be expected to become increasingly difficult for the budget traveller.

Czech (spoken with Bohemia and Moravia). Slovak, Russian, German and English are also spoken.

Mild summers and cold winters.

Roman Catholic. Protestant including Methodist, Moravian, Unity of Czech Brethren and Baptist, Judaism.

Jan 1, May 1,8, Jul 5,6, Oct 28, Dec 24-26. Easter.

Generally 220 volts AC 50 Hz.

There is a 24-hour service available at the main post office in Prague. Poste restante is available throughout the country.

Traditional roles are still maintained by the older generation, whereas western values are developing among the younger members of society.

FLIGHTS: Very cheap, quick and convenient. RAIL: Fares are low but supplements are payable for travel by express trains. Reservations should be made in advance for long journeys. BUS: Efficient and comfortable. They are more reliable than the train but it is advisable to book in advance. CAR HIRE: Available from several companies. DOCUMENTATION: A national driving licence will be sufficient.

When using public transport ensure you pay the correct amount, to avoid paying any extra money to persistent train/bus conductors. Pickpocketing is rife. PHOTOGRAPHY: Do not take photographs of anything connected to the military.

CAPITAL: Copenhagen

GMT + 1 (+2 during the summer)

FROM UK: 0045. OUTGOING CODE TO UK: 0044

Police and Ambulance: 112 (in Copenhagen).

Royal Danish Embassy, 55 Sloane Street, London SW1X 9SY. Tel: 020 7333 0200 or 7333 0265. Fax: 020 7333 0270 or 7333 0266. dkembassyuk@compuserve.com; www.denmark.org.uk

British Embassy, Kastelsvej 36-40, DK -2100 Copenhagen Ø, Denmark. Tel: 35 44 5200. Fax: 3 44 5253. info@britishembassy.dk; www.denmark.org.uk

Danish Tourist Board, 55 Sloane Street, London SW1X 9SY. Tel: 020 7259 5958/9. Fax: 020 7259 5955. dtb.london@dt.dk www.dtb.dt.dk/dtr.html

Danmarks Turistråd (Tourist Board), Vesterbrogade 6D, DK-1620 Copenhagen V, Denmark. Tel: 33 11 14 15. Fax: 33 93 14 16. dt@dt.dk www.dt.dk/

Requirements may be subject to short term change. Contact embassy before departure. Valid passport required.

Visa not required by nationals of the UK with full British Passports.

Meat and meat products cannot be imported into Denmark.

Danish Krone (Dkr) = 100 øre. Exchange: Eurocheques are cashed by hotels and banks and may also be used at most restaurants and shops. Personal cheques cannot be used by foreigners in Denmark. Some banks may refuse to exchange large foreign bank notes. All major credit cards accepted. Travellers cheques can be cashed by banks and hotels, and can be used at most hotels and shops. US dollars and Deutschmarks are the preferred forms of currency. ATM AVAILABILITY: Over 2500 locations.

MONEYGRAM: 8001 0010 then 800 592 3688.
WESTERN UNION: 800 10711.

AMEX: 0044 1273 696 933
DINERS CLUB: 36 737373
MASTERCARD: 8001 6098
VISA: 8001 0277

AMEX: 0044 1273 571 600
THOMAS COOK: 800 10110
VISA: 8001 0448

0930-1700 Mon, Tues, Wed and Fri, 0930-1800 Thur. Several exchange bureaus are open until midnight.

Slightly cheaper than other Scandinavian countries but still relatively expensive.

Danish. English, German and French may also be spoken.

Summer June–Aug. Winter, Oct–Mar, is wet with period of frost. Feb is the coldest month. Spring and autumn are generally mild.

Mainly Evangelical Lutheran with a small Roman Catholic minority.

Jan 1, Jun 5, Dec 24,25,26,31. Easter, Ascension Day, Pentecost.

220 volts AC 50 Hz. Continental 2-pin plugs are used.

2–3 days to rest of Europe.

Relatively safe for women in comparison to other countries. There is little inequality between men and women.

PUBLIC TRANSPORT: Extensive service provided. SEA: There are frequent ferry services between the islands. RAIL: The main cities on all islands are connected by the rail network. Express trains operate and 'Inter-Rail' and 'Nord-Tourist' pass (which can be used throughout Scandinavia) can provide good value. CAR HIRE: Available to drivers over the age of 20. DOCUMENTATION: National driving licence is acceptable. Visitors taking their own car are advised to obtain a green card as without will limit their insurance coverage.

Usual social courtesies should be observed. Casual dress is suitable for most places. Railway porters and washroom attendants will expect a tip.

Djibouti

CAPITAL: Djibouti

GMT + 3

FROM UK: 00253. OUTGOING CODE TO UK: 0044

Not present.

No embassy in the UK. Europe: Embassy of the Republic of Djibouti, 26 rue Emile Ménier, 75116, Paris, France. Tel: (1) 47 27 49 22. Fax: (1) 45 53 50 53.

British Consulate, BP 81 Gellatly, Hankey et Cie, Djibouti, Djibouti. Tel: 351 940. Fax: 353 294. martinet@intnet.dj

Refer to the Embassy.

Office Nationale du Tourisme et de l'Artisanat (ONTA), BP 1938, place du 27 juin, Djibouti, Djibouti. Tel: 353 790. Fax: 356 322.

Return ticket required. Requirements may be subject to change at short notice. Contact the appropriate diplomatic or consular authority before finalising travel arrangements. Valid passport required.

Visa required for a maximum stay of 3 months. An extension may be granted in Djibouti on request to the headquarters of the Police Nationale. Entry and transit visas are granted

Gold objects, apart from personal jewellery.

Departure tax DFr5000, payable in local currency.

POLIO, TYPHOID: R.MALARIA: R. Falciparum variety exists throughout the year. Resistance to chloroquine has been reported. YELLOW FEVER: R. A vaccination certificate is required for visitors over one year of age arriving from infected areas. OTHER: Cholera.

W1

Djibouti Franc (DFr) = 100 centimes. Credit cards are accepted by airlines and large hotels only. French franc is the preferred currency in traveller's cheques, but they are only accepted if marked as an External Account or Pour Compte Etranger. Sterling and US$ also accepted. ATM AVAILABILITY: Unavailable.

MONEYGRAM: Unavailable.
WESTERN UNION: Unavailable.

AMEX: 0044 1273 696 933
DINERS CLUB: 0044 1252 513 500
MASTERCARD: 001 314 542 7111
VISA: 001 410 581 9994

AMEX: 0044 1273 571 600
THOMAS COOK: 0044 1733 318950
VISA: 0044 20 7937 8091

0715-1145 Sat to Thur.

Expensive and should be avoided by travellers on tight budgets.

Arabic and French. English is spoken by hoteliers, taxi drivers and traders.

Very hot and dry between June and Aug. Slightly cooler between Oct and Apr with occasional rain.

Muslim with Roman Catholic, Protestant and Greek Orthodox minorities.

Jan1, May 1, Jun 27, Dec 25. Islamic festivals.

220 Volts AC 50 Hz

Approximately 1 week to Europe by airmail.

Due to a predominantly Muslim faith, culture remains patriarchal.

TAXIS: Fares increase 50% after dark. CAR HIRE: 4-wheel drive is recommended. Water and petrol supplies must be carried. RAIL: There is only 1 service to Ethiopia which tourists and business people are prohibited from using.

NOTE: Much of the country is desert, and most people live on a coastal strip. Areas of the country are closed, and risk of banditry and fighting is prevalent in certain areas. Check with the Foreign and Commonwealth Travel Advice unit before departure. Visitors should register with their embassy or consulate shortly after arrival. Despite Djibouti being a Muslim country, casual wear is acceptable. However, beachwear should not be worn in the towns.

Dominica (Commonwealth of)

CAPITAL: Roseau

GMT –4.

FROM UK: 001809. OUTGOING CODE TO UK: 011 (only 1 for the USA, Canada and most Caribbean Islands)

999

Dominica High Commission, 1 Collingham Gardens, South Kensington, London, SW5 0HW. Tel: 020 7370 5195. Fax: 020 7373 8743. highcommission@dominica.co.uk www.dominica.co.uk

The British High Commission in Barbados deals with enquiries relating to Dominica. britishhc@sunbeach.net

Caribbean Tourism, 42 Westminster Palace Gdns, Artillery Row, London SW1P 1RR. Tel: 020 7222 4335. Fax: 020 7222 4325. www.doitcaribbean.com; cto@carib-tourism.com

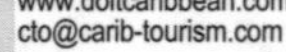

National Development Corporation (NDC)-Division of Tourism, PO Box 73, Valley Road, Roseau, Dominica. Tel: 448 6032. Fax: 448 5840.

Return ticket required. Requirements may be subject to short-term change. Contact embassy before departure. Valid passport required.

Visas not required by nationals of Commonwealth countries for stays of up to 6 months. Enquire at the nearest embassy or High Commission for the latest, complete list of regulations regarding visas.

Narcotics and firearms.

EC$ 25 or US$ 10.

POLIO, TYPHOID: R. YELLOW FEVER: A vaccination certificate is required from travellers over 1 year of age coming from infected areas. The dengue fever mosquito is found throughout Dominica. HIV/AIDS is prevalent.

W2

East Caribbean Dollar (EC$) = 100 cents. Travellers cheques are accepted in most hotels – US$ preferred. All major credit cards have limited acceptance. ATM AVAILABILITY: 1 location.

MONEYGRAM: 800 543 4080.
WESTERN UNION: 448 2181.

AMEX: 01144 1273 696 933
DINERS CLUB: 01144 1252 513 500
MASTERCARD: 1800 307 7309
VISA: 1800 847 2911

AMEX: 01144 1273 571 600
THOMAS COOK: 1800 223 7373
VISA: 01144 20 7937 8091

0800-1500 Mon to Thur, 0800-1700 Fri.

Not as expensive as some of the other Caribbean islands.

English. Creole French is spoken by most of the population.

Hot, subtropical climate all year round. Rainy season June-Oct, which is also the hottest time.

Roman Catholic.

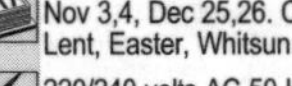
Jan 1,2, first Mon in May, first Mon in Aug, Nov 3,4, Dec 25,26. Carnival week before Lent, Easter, Whitsun.

220/240 volts AC 50 Hz.

Post to Europe takes approximately 14 days. There is no poste restante service.

Women tend to be conservative, in accordance with the dominant religion of the island.

ROAD: There are more than 700 km of well maintained roads on the island, although even these can be difficult when driving. BUS: Service exists but is unpredictable. TAXIS: Are the most efficient means of transport. CAR HIRE: Available but driving can be difficult. DOCUMENTATION: IDP is recommended. A valid foreign licence can be used to get a temporary visitors licence.

Beachwear should be kept to the beach or pool-side. It is an offence for anyone, including children, to dress in camouflage clothing. PHOTOGRAPHY: Permission should be asked before taking photos of local people.

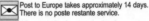

CAPITAL: Santo Domingo

GMT –4

FROM UK: 001809. OUTGOING CODE TO UK: 011 (just 1 to USA and Canada)

711/809 472 7111

Embassy of the Dominican Republic, 139 Inverness Terrace, London W2 6JF. Tel: 020 7727 6285. Fax: 020 7727 3693. general@embajadadom-london.demon.co.uk; www.serex.gov.do

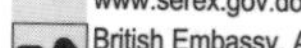

British Embassy, Ave 27 de Fabrero No 233 Edificio Corominas Pepin, Santo Domingo. Tel: 472 7671; Fax: 472 7574. brit.emb.sadom@codetel.net.do

Caribbean Tourism, 42 Westminster Palace Gdns, Artillery Row, London SW1P 1RR. Tel: 020 7222 4335. Fax: 020 7222 4325. www.doitcaribbean.com cto@carib-tourism.com

Dominican Tourism Promotion Council, Desiderio Arias 24, Bella Vista, Santo Domingo, Dominican Republic. Tel: 221 4660. Fax: 682 3806. www.dominicana.com.do

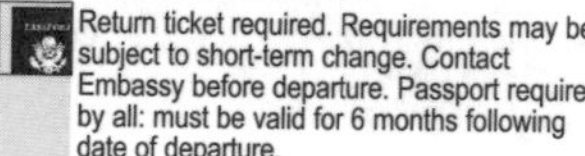
Return ticket required. Requirements may be subject to short-term change. Contact Embassy before departure. Passport required by all: must be valid for 6 months following date of departure.

Visa not required by nationals of the UK, as tourists only for a maximum of 90 days, and foreign nationals who are legal residents of the UK. Refer to the nearest consulate for a complete list of regulations for all countries.

Agricultural or horticultural products.

US$10. Passengers under 2 years of age and those in direct transit are exempt.

POLIO, TYPHOID: R - Polio is endemic. MALARIA: Exists throughout the year in particular areas in the falciparum variety, which has been reported as being highly resistant to chlororquine. OTHER: Rabies, bilharzia and hepatitis.

W1

Dominican Republic Peso (RD$) = 100 centavos. Import and export of local currency is prohibited. All major credit cards are accepted. Travellers cheques, in any international currency, are accepted by some banks. ATM AVAILABILITY: Over 100 locations.

MONEYGRAM: 1 800 543 4080.
WESTERN UNION: 200 1163.

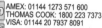

AMEX: 01144 1273 696 933
DINERS CLUB: 01144 1252 513 500
MASTERCARD: 1800 307 7309
VISA: 1 410 581 9994

AMEX: 01144 1273 571 600
THOMAS COOK: 1800 223 7373
VISA: 01144 20 7937 8091

0800-1600 Mon to Fri.

The best buys are the island's own handicrafts, such as amber jewellery and decorative pieces encasing insects, leaves or dewdrops. Other bargains are wood carvings, limestone carvings and Dominican turquoise.

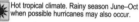

Spanish. English is also spoken.

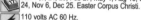

Hot tropical climate. Rainy season June–Oct when possible hurricanes may also occur.

Roman Catholic. Protestant and Jewish minorities.

Jan 1 ,6, 21, 26, Feb 27, May 1, Aug 16, Sep 24, Nov 6, Dec 25. Easter Corpus Christi.

110 volts AC 60 Hz.

7 days. Advisable to post all mail from the central post office in Santo Domingo.

Although a strong Roman Catholic heritage prevails, women are influenced by American culture, highlighted by the high divorce rate. Unaccompanied females should take special care outside hotels especially at night.

ROAD: There is a reasonable network of roads although not all are all-weather and 4 wheel drives are recommended for wet weather. Driving between towns at night is not recommended because of poor lighting. Everyone involved in accident is likely to be arrested while the incident is investigated. BUS: Cheap and efficient service runs from the capital to the main towns. CAR HIRE: Several car-hire companies are present. Credit cards are recommended when paying for car hire. Minimum age for driving is 25. DOCUMENTATION: IDP or national licence.

The Dominican Republic is now a major tourist destination. The FCO advises against excursions across the border to Haiti. Store valuables in hotel safety deposit boxes.

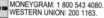

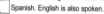

Ecuador

CAPITAL: Quito

GMT –5, Galapagos Island GMT –6

FROM UK: 00593. OUTGOING CODE TO UK: 0044

Police: 101. Ambulance: 131.

Embassy of the Republic of Ecuador, Flat 3B, 3 Hans Crescent, Knightsbridge, London, SW1X 0LS. Tel: 020 7584 1367. Fax: 020 7823 9701.

British Embassy, Citiplaza Building, Naciones Unidas Ave. and Republica de El Salvador. (Consular Section 12th floor) PO Box 1717830, Quito. Tel: (593) (2) 970 800; Fax: 970 807. consular@quito.mail.fco.gov.uk; www.britembquito.org.ec/

Refer to the Embassy.

Asociación Ecuatoriana de Agencias de Viajes y Turismo (ASECUT), Casilla 9421, Edificio Banco del Pacifico, 5º Piso Avenida, Amazonas 720 y Veintimilla, Quito, Ecuador. Tel: (2) 503 669. Fax: (2) 285 872. www-pub4.ecua.net.ec/mintur/. GALAPAGOS: Camara Provincial de Turismo de Galapagos, Avda Charles Darwin, Puerto Ayora, Isla Santa Cruz, Galapagos.Tel: 00593 5 526206 Fax: 00593 5 526609. info@galapagoschamberoftourism.org; www.galapagoschamberoftourism.org/

Return ticket required. Requirements may change at short notice. Contact embassy before departure. Valid passport required.

Visa not required by UK nationals for stays of up to 90 days. All nationals wishing to stay in Ecuador for stays of between 3 and 6 months for business reasons need a visa, US$50.

Fresh and dry meats, plants, vegetables, require special permission prior to the journey.

US$25 payable in dollars.

POLIO, TYPHOID: R. MALARIA: Exists throughout the year below 1500 m in the falciparum variety. Resistance to chloroquine has been reported. YELLOW FEVER: Vaccination is strongly recommended for travellers wishing to leave urban areas; a vaccination certificate is required if arriving from infected areas. OTHER: Cholera, hepatitis, rabies.

W1

The US$ has been the only legal currency in Ecuador since September 2000. All major credit cards are accepted, although some traders will not accept cards issued by foreign banks. Travellers cheques in US$ are accepted. ATM AVAILABILITY: Over 160 locations.

MONEYGRAM: 999 119 then 800 592 5755. WESTERN UNION: (2) 508 085.

AMEX: 0044 1273 696 933
DINERS CLUB: 5932 981 300
MASTERCARD:1 314 542 7111
VISA: 1 410 581 9994

AMEX: 0044 1273 571 600
THOMAS COOK: 1800 223 7373
VISA: 0044 20 7937 8091

0900-1330 and 1430-1830 Mon to Fri, some open 0930-1400 Sat.

Standard prices outside the main towns. Relatively low costs for travelling and food.

Spanish. Indian dialects and English are also spoken.

Warm subtropical climate. Andean areas are cooler. High rainfall in coast and jungle.

Roman Catholic.

Jan 1, May 1,24, last Fri in Jun, Jul 24, Aug 10, Oct 9,12, Nov 2,3, Dec 6, 25,31. Carnival week before Lent, Easter.

110/120 Volts AC, 60 Hz.

Up to 1 week

The Roman Catholic faith plays a major part in daily living. Tribal customs apply in rural areas. Usual precautions are advised for lone female travellers.

FLIGHTS: The usual form of intercity transport. ROAD: Conditions vary due to previous earthquakes and flooding. Improvements are being made to the extensive network. CAR HIRE: Several international companies. DOCUMENTATION: IDP not required. BUS: Can be a convenient way of getting around, but avoid at night.

Ecuador has active volcanoes close to Quito and Banos, and the country is in an earthquake zone. The Panecillo Hill area of Quito should be avoided due to local dispute and Mount Cotopaxi National Park should be visited only after seeking local expert advice. Tourist muggings occur. Register with the Embassy on arrival, and carry a copy of your passport at all times.

CAPITAL: Cairo

GMT +2

FROM UK: 0020. OUTGOING CODE TO UK: 0044

Not present.

Embassy of the Arab Republic of Egypt, 26 South Street, London W1Y 8EL. Tel: 020 7499 2401. Fax: 020 7355 3568

British Embassy, 7 Ahmad Raghab Street, Garden City, Cairo, Egypt. Tel: (2) 794 0850; Fax: 794 0859. consular.cairo@fco.gov.uk; www.britishembassy.org.eg/ Consulates also in Alexandria, Suez, Port Said, and Luxor.

Egyptian State Tourist Office, 170 Piccadilly, London, W1V 9DD. Tel: 020 7493 5282. Fax: 020 7495 5283. Opening hours Mon to Fri 0930-1630. http://touregypt.net/

Egyptian General Authority for the Promotion of Tourism, Misr Travel Tower, Abassia Square, Cairo, Egypt. Tel: (2) 285 4509.

Return ticket required. Requirements may be subject to change at short notice. Contact the appropriate consular authority before finalising travel arrangements. Valid passport required by all, and must be valid for at least 6 months beyond the intended stay in Egypt.

Visa required by nationals of UK. Tourist and business, single or multiple entry types granted.

Check with the embassy or tourist office for a comprehensive list. NOTE: All cash, travellers cheques, credit cards and gold over £E 500 must be declared on arrival.

Departure tax is £E21, payable in local currency.

POLIO, TYPHOID: R. MALARIA: No risk in Cairo or Alexandria but falciparum and vivax varieties exists from June to October in the El Faiyoum area. YELLOW FEVER: A vaccination certificate is required if arriving from infected areas. Check with embassy as to which areas Egypt considers infected. OTHER: Bilharzia, malaria, rabies.

W1

Egyptian Pound (£E) = 100 piastres. There are 5 national banks and 78 branches of foreign banks. All major credit cards are accepted. Travellers cheques in US dollars are the preferred currency. ATM AVAILABILITY: 88 locations.

MONEYGRAM: Available at Thomas Cook and American Express locations
WESTERN UNION: (2)355 5023

AMEX: 0044 1273 696 933
DINERS CLUB: 02 341 8778
MASTERCARD: 001 314 542 7111
VISA: 001 410 581 9994

AMEX:0044 1273 571 600
THOMAS COOK: 0044 1733 318950
VISA: 0044 20 7937 8091

0830-1400 Sun to Thur.

Tourists can expect to pay higher prices than locals.

Arabic, English and French are widely spoken.

Hot and dry during the summer with dry winters with chilly nights. Dusty winds from the Sahara prevail during April.

Islam. All types of Christianity are represented especially the Coptic Church.

Apr 25, May 1, Jun 18, Jul 23, Oct 6,24, Dec 23. Islamic festivals.

220 Volts 50 Hz are most common. 110/380 volts AC may also be used.

Approximately 5 days by airmail. There are poste restante facilities at the main post office in Cairo; a small fee is charged when the mail is collected.

Revealing clothes should not be worn by women, especially in the religious areas.

RAIL: A good rail network exists. ROAD: Local driving conditions are poor especially at night. TAXIS: Available in the cities. Agree the fare in advance.

Following action by extremist groups against tourists, the Egyptian authorities have increased security measures; visitors are advised to be vigilant and heed advice given by guides and the police. Ask permission before photographing people.

El Salvador

CAPITAL: San Salvador

GMT –6

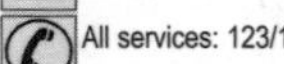

FROM UK: 00503. OUTGOING CODE TO UK: 0044

All services: 123/121.

Embassy of the Republic of El Salvador, Tennyson House, 159 Great Portland Street, London, W1N 5FD. Tel: 020 7436 8282 or 0891 444 580. Fax: 020 7436 8181. consulsalvadoruk@compuserve.com

British Embassy, PO Box 1591, Paeso General Escalón 4828, San Salvador, El Salvador. Tel: 263 6527. Fax: 263 6516. britemb@sal.gbm.net

Refer to the Embassy.

Instituto Salvadoreño de Turismo (ISTU), Calle Rubén Dario 619, San Salvador, El Salvador. Tel: 222 0960. Fax: 222 1208.

Return ticket and valid passport required by all. Requirements may change at short notice. Contact Embassy before departure.

Visa not required by nationals of the UK for stays of up to 90 days.

Narcotics and firearms.

US$24 when leaving the country.

Contact the Embassy for the latest information.

POLIO, TYPHOID: R. MALARIA: Exists all year throughout the country in the Vivax variety. Risk is greater in lowlying areas. YELLOW FEVER: Vaccination certificates are required by travellers over 6 months of age coming from infected areas. OTHER: Rabies, visceral leishmaniasis, mucocutaneous leishmanisis, dengue fever.

W1

Colón Esc (colloquially Peso) = 100 centavos. MasterCard, Visa and Amex are widely accepted. Travellers cheques in US$ are accepted in banks and hotels on production of a passport. Pound sterling is not recognised in El Salvador and cannot be changed into local currency. ATM AVAILABILITY: Over 20 locations.

MONEYGRAM: 1 800 824 2220.
WESTERN UNION: 298 7521

AMEX: 0044 1273 696 933
DINERS CLUB 298 1811
MASTERCARD 1 314 542 7111
VISA: 1 410 581 9994

AMEX: 0044 1273 571 600
THOMAS COOK: 1800 223 7373
VISA: 0044 20 7937 8091

0900-1300 and 1345-1600 Mon to Fri.

The main hotels are in the capital. Prices fluctuate, depending on festivals and national events.

Spanish. English is also widely spoken.

Hot subtropical climate. Rainy season is May-Oct. The upland areas are cooler.

Roman Catholic.

Jan 1, May 1, Jun 30, Aug 4, 6, Sep 15, Nov 2, Dec 25, 31. Easter.

110 Volts AC, 60 Hz

7 days.

Since the civil war ended officially, women have become independent and forthright, due to the mass disappearances of much of the male population at the height of the war. Roman Catholicism continues to influence society.

ROADS: Approx. a third of roads are suitable for all-weather driving. DOCUMENTATION: IDP or national driving licence is required. RAIL: Links main cities. BUS: A good service exists between major towns. TAXI: Are plentiful but are not metered, so agree fare in advance.

El Salvador portrays a more stable political climate than for many years. However, the infrastructure remains fragile, with rival factions contesting territorial supremacy. Travellers should still contact their embassies for current developments. Tourists should exercise great caution, as robberies and kidnapping are common and can occur anywhere in the country. Youths with guns are a growing problem on the streets of towns and cities. Seek advice as to which areas are safe. Extreme political unrest and crime rate. Avoid using cameras around military areas. El Salvador is prone to earthquakes.

Equatorial Guinea

CAPITAL: Malabo

GMT +1

FROM UK: 00240. OUTGOING CODE TO UK: 0044. Operator assistance may be required.

Not present.

No Embassy in the UK. EUROPE: Embassy of the Republic of Equatorial Guinea, 6 rue Alfred de Vigny, 75008 Paris, France. Tel: (1) 47 66 44 33 or 47 66 95 70. Fax: (1) 47 64 94 52.

Consulate in Cameroon now deals with enquiries: British Consulate, Winston Churchill Avenue, BP 547, Yaoundé, Cameroon. Tel: (237) 220 545. Fax: (237) 20 148.

Not present.

The Centro Cultural HispanoGuineano gives out good maps of the island and mainland.

Return ticket required. Requirements may be subject to change at short notice. Contact the relevant consular authority before finalising travel arrangements. Valid passport required by all

Visa required by all.

Spanish newspapers.

POLIO, TYPHOID: R. MALARIA: R. Falciparum strain exists throughout the country and resistance to chloroquine has been reported. YELLOW FEVER: Vaccination certificate required by arrivals from infected areas. How- ever, vaccination is advised for all travellers. OTHER: Bilharzia, river blindness in unchlorinated water, oriental lung fluke (recently reported) and cholera are present.

W1

CFA Franc (CFA Fr) = 100 centimes. NOTE: Export of local currency is limited to CFA Fr3000. CFA Franc can not be easily exchanged outside of the CFA Fr area. Diners Club is accepted on a limited basis in large towns only. Traveller's cheques are not accepted. ATM AVAILABILITY: unavailable.

MONEYGRAM: Unavailable.
WESTERN UNION: Unavailable.

AMEX: 0044 1273 696933
DINERS CLUB: 0044 1252 513 500:
MASTERCARD: No local number.
VISA: No local number.

AMEX: 0044 1273 571 600
THOMAS COOK: No local number.
VISA: No local number.

0800-1200 Mon to Sat.

Tourists can expect to pay high prices for services.

Spanish, African dialects including Fang and Bubi are spoken.

Tropical climate throughout the year. Rainfall throughout the year although less falls between Dec and Feb.

There are no official religions but the majority of the population are Roman Catholic with Animist minority.

Jan 1, May 1,25, Jun 5, Aug 3,15, Oct 12, Dec 10,25. Easter, Corpus Christi.

220/240 Volts. AC

Approximately 2 weeks

Women should take extra precautions if travelling in Equatorial Guinea.

FLIGHTS: Advisable to book in advance. ROADS: There are few tarred roads and car hire companies are unavailable but taxis can be hired. SEA: There is a ferry between Malabo, Bata and Doula, allow 12 hours for the trip.

Although the current situation is calm, caution should be exercised. Travelling after dark should be avoided. Europeans are likely to be met with curiosity and even suspicion. Foreign cigarettes are often accepted as gifts. PHOTOGRAPHY: A photo permit, available from the embassy, is essential. Photography of ports, airports and military installations is forbidden.

Eritrea

CAPITAL: Asmara

GMT + 3

FROM UK: 00291. OUTGOING CODE TO UK: 0044 Operator assistance required for outgoing international calls.

Not present.

Eritrean Consulate, 96 White Lion Street, London N1 9PF. Tel: 020 7713 0096. Fax:020 7713 0161.

British Consulate, PO Box 5584, c/o Mtchell Cotts Building, Emperor Yohnanes Avenue 5, Asmara, Eritrea. Tel: (1) 120 145. Fax: (1) 120 104. alembca@gemel.com.er

Refer to the Consulate.

Eritrean Tour Service (ETS) PO Box 889, 61 Harnet Avenue, Asmara, Eritrea. Tel: (1) 124 999. Fax: (1) 126 366

Return ticket required. Requirements may be subject to change at short notice. Contact the relevant consular authority before finalising travel arrangements. Valid passport required by all

Visa required by all. Business and tourist visas granted. Transit passengers who do not leave the airport do not need a visa.

US$20 for international departures + Br 3 service charge.

POLIO, TYPHOID: R. MALARIA: Exists throughout the year and high resistance to chloroquine has been reported. YELLOW FEVER: A vaccination certificate is required by all arrivals over one year of age arriving from infected areas. However, everyone is advised to have the vaccination for travel outside the urban areas. OTHER: Bilharzia, cholera, hepatitis, rabies, meningitis are present. Tetanus injection is also recommended.

W1

Ethiopian Birr (Br) used in Asmara and the South. The Sudanese Dinar is in circulation in the North and West. US$ in cash is the best form of currency. MasterCard and Diners Club have limited acceptance.ATM AVAILABILITY: Unavailable.

MONEYGRAM: Unavailable.
WESTERN UNION: 1 11 33 57.

AMEX: 0044 1273 696 933
DINERS CLUB: 0044 1252 513 500
MASTERCARD: 001 314 542 7111
VISA: 001 410 581 9994

AMEX: 0044 1273 571 600
THOMAS COOK: 0044 1733 318950
VISA: 0044 20 7937 8091

0800-1200 and 1400-1700 Mon to Fri, 0800-1200 Sat.

Prices are generally lower in Eritrea than in surrounding countries.

Arabic and Tigrinya. English and Italian also spoken.

Hottest period is Apr to Jun but it can be very cold at night. June-Feb rainy season depending on the area of the country.

50% Ethiopian Orthodox and 50% Muslim.

Jan 1, Mar 8, May 24, Jun 20, Sept 1

110 Volts AC in Asmara. Different voltage exists outside the capital. There are occasional power surges.

Delays should be expected.

Women must avoid wearing revealing clothes.

No internal flights or railways. ROADS: Reasonable between tourist and business centres. Improvements are being made. BUSES: Connect all larger towns and cities. TAXIS: Can be found in the capital and at the airport, fares should be agreed in advance.

Travel to the Sudanese border should be avoided. The border with Ethiopia remains a military zone and is also to be avoided. The Hanish islands and their coastlines are also unsafe for travellers. Only take accommodation in the larger towns, as there are many landmines in rural Eritrea. Avoid travel after dark. Casual wear is suitable for most places.

CAPITAL: Tallinn

GMT + 2 (+3 during the summer)

FROM UK: 00372. OUTGOING CODE TO UK: 8/0044 (wait for second dial tone)

Ambulance: 03 (Tallinn: 003); Police: 02 (Tallinn: 002); Fire: 01 (Tallinn: 001).

Embassy of the Republic of Estonia, 16 Hyde Park Gate, London SW7 5DG. Tel: 020 7589 3428. Fax: 020 7589 3430. tvaravas@estonia.gov.uk; www.estonia.gov.uk

British Embassy, Wismari 6, Tallinn 10136. Tel: 667 4700; Fax: 667 4725. information@britishembassy.ee; www.britishembassy.ee/

Not present.

Estonian Tourist Board, Estonian Tourist Board, Mündi 2,Tallinn 10146, Estonia. Tel: 00372 699 0420; Fax: 00372 699 0432. info@tourism.ee; www.visitestonia.com/

Requirements may be subject to short-term change. Contact embassy before departure. Valid passport required by all

Visa not required by nationals of Great Britain. For the latest information contact the relevant authorities at least 3 weeks before finalising travel arrangements.

Pornography.

Rabies.

1 Kroon = 100 sents. Exchange: US$ and Deutsche Marks are widely accepted. Credit cards are accepted on a limited basis. Travellers cheques can be exchanged at most banks. Preferred currency is US$. ATM AVAILABILITY: Over 200 locations.

MONEYGRAM: 8 00 8001001.
WESTERN UNION: 2 640 5023.

AMEX: 8/0044 1273 696 933
DINERS CLUB: 8/0044 1252 513 500
MASTERCARD:8/001 314 542 7111
VISA: 8/001 410 581 9994

AMEX: 8/0044 1273 571 600
THOMAS COOK: 8/0044 1733 318950
VISA: 8/0044 20 7937 8091

0930-1630 Mon to Fri.

Estonian. Some Russian may also be spoken.

There is rainfall throughout the year with the heaviest falling in Aug. Heavy snow falls are likely in the winter months. The climate has large temperature variations. Summer can be quite warm but winter, lasting from Oct-Mar, can be very cold.

Protestant (Lutheran).

Jan 1, Feb 24, May 1, Jun 23,24, Aug 20, Dec 25,26. Easter and Whitsun.

220 volts AC, 50 Hz. European 2-pin plugs are used.

Approx. 6 days.

Traditionally a patriarchal society, but gender roles becoming more equal.

RAIL: The rail system is underdeveloped but the most major cities are connected to the network. SEA/RIVER: Ferries connect the mainland with the main islands. ROAD: There is a dense road network but few major highways. Careful driving is advised and driving at night is not recommended. It is best to remember that spare parts are not always available. CAR HIRE: Hertz agencies are present in Tallinn. DOCUMENTATION: European nationals should be in possession of the new 'European Driving Licence'. BUS: A wide network of routes are operated including express services. Prices are very low and buses are still the most important means of transport. Tickets and passes can be bought from kiosks. TAXIS: Check that a meter is visible, and don't use unmarked cars that claim to be taxis.

There has been an increase in incidents of theft against foreign tourists. Care should be taken, especially at night, in Tallinn Old Town and on the way to and from hotels. It is advisable to take a supply of basic medicines such as aspirin, as they are unlikely to be available. Visitors should take care to respect Estonians' sense of national identity.

Ethiopia

CAPITAL: Addis Ababa

GMT +3

FROM UK: 00251. OUTGOING CODE TO UK: 0044. Most international calls must be made through the operator.

Not present.

Embassy of Ethiopia, 17 Princes Gate, London, SW7 1PZ. Tel: 020 7589 7212. Fax: 020 7584 7054 www.ethioembassy.org.uk/

British Embassy, PO Box 858, Fikre Mariam, Abatechan Street, Addis Ababa, Ethiopia. Tel: (1) 612 354. Fax: (1) 610 588. b.emb4@telecom.net.et

Refer to Embassy.

Ethiopian Commission for Hotels and Tourism, PO Box 2183, Addis Ababa, Ethiopia. Tel: (1) 517 470. Fax: 513 899.

Return ticket required. Requirements may be subject to change at short notice. Consult the relevant consular authority before finalising travel arrangements. Valid passport required by all.

Visa required. Tourist, business and transit visas granted (latter is not required if remaining in the airport before an onward journey).

Narcotics.

US$10 is payable on departure, in US$ only. Entry into Ethiopia can normally only be made by air transport via Addis Ababa international airport. Special permission will be required for alternative entry.

POLIO, TYPHOID: R. MALARIA: R. Resistance to chloroquine has been reported. YELLOW FEVER: Vaccination strongly recommended. A vaccination certificate will be required by all travellers over one year of age arriving from infected areas. OTHER: Bilharzia, cholera, meningitis and rabies.

W1

Ethiopian Birr (Br) = 100 cents. US$ currency is the most convenient. Import and export of local currency is limited to Br100. Foreign currency is unlimited but must be declared on arrival. MasterCard and Diners Club are accepted in the capital only. Travellers cheques have limited acceptance, US$ the preferred currency. ATM AVAILABILITY: Unavailable.

MONEYGRAM: Unavailable.
WESTERN UNION: 1 51 24 37.

AMEX: 0044 1273 696 933
DINERS CLUB: 0044 1252 513 500
MASTERCARD: 001 314 542 7111
VISA: 001 410 581 9994

AMEX: 0044 1273 571 600
THOMAS COOK: 0044 1733 318950
VISA: 0044 20 7937 8091

0800-1200 and 1300-1700 Mon to Thur, 0830-1130 and 1300-1700 Fri.

Prices are generally lower than in surrounding countries

Amharic. English is the second official language. Italian and French are also spoken.

Lowlands hot and humid, warm in the hill country and cool in the uplands. Rain is mostly from June to Sept.

North: mainly Orthodox Christian. East and South: mainly Islam.

Jan 7, 19, Mar 2, May 28, Sept 11 (Ethiopian New Year), Sept 27. Easter and Islamic festivals.

220 Volts AC 50 Hz.

Approximately 2 weeks.

A patriarchal culture exists.

FLIGHTS: Erratic internal flights operate to over 40 towns. ROADS: A good network of all-weather roads exists, though they can become impassable during the rainy season. Frequent fuel shortages can make travel outside Addis Ababa very difficult. TAXI: Fares should be agreed in advance. DOCUMENTATION: A British driving licence is valid for 1 month, after which a temporary Ethiopian licence will be required.

Mugging and hijacking is increasingly posing a threat. Tourists should confine themselves to recognised tourist areas and avoid travel after dark. Border areas should be avoided, as there is still some tension with the military forces of neighbouring Eritrea. The FCO advises against travelling to border regions. Travelling alone is discouraged. Casual wear is suitable for most places. NOTE: Ethiopia uses the pre-Julian Solar Calendar with 12 months of 30 days and the 13th month of 5 or 6 days. It is important to check dates before travelling.

CAPITAL: Port Stanley

GMT–4

FROM UK: 00500. OUTGOING CODE TO UK: 044

All services: 999.

Falkland Islands Government and Tourist Office, Falkland House, 14 Broadway, London, SW1H 0BH. Tel 020 7222 2542. Fax: Fax: 020 7222 2375. rep@figo.unet.com

No British Embassy present.

Government Office, see above.

Falkland Islands Tourist Board, Old Transmitting Station, Stanley, East Falkland. Tel: 22215. Fax: 22619. www.tourism.org.fk

Return ticket required. Requirements may change at short notice. Contact the Government Office before departure. Valid passport required by all.

All nationals must complete visitor forms from the Government Office before, or on, arrival.

Uncooked or cured meat and plants are only allowed under licence. No livestock allowed on any incoming aircraft.

Falkland Islands Pound (Fl£) = 100 pence. EXCHANGE: available in Stanley and the Standard Chartered Bank. Cheques issued by the main UK bank (up to £50) can be cashed with a valid cheque card. Credit cards have only a limited acceptance. ATM AVAILABILITY: Unavailable.

MONEYGRAM: Unavailable.
WESTERN UNION: Unavailable.

AMEX: 044 1273 696 933
DINERS CLUB: 044 1252 513 500
MASTERCARD: 01 314 542 7111
VISA: 01 410 581 9994

AMEX: 044 1273 571 600
THOMAS COOK: 044 1733 318950
VISA: 044 20 7937 8091

0830-1200 and 1330-1500 Mon to Fri.

Comparable with United Kingdom but tends to be more expensive, due to the importation of most requirements.

English.

Temperate climate conditioned by the surrounding sea.

Christianity.

As United Kingdom, plus Jun 14.

240 Volts AC, 50 HZ.

4–7 days.

Same precautions should be taken as in Western Europe.

FLIGHTS: Light aircraft services can be used to travel between most of the Islands. The Chilean national airline, LanChile, operates a weekly flight to Stanley from Santiago, calling also at Rio Gallegos in Argentina twice a month. ROAD: A 4 wheel drive is recommended if travelling outside the capital where vehicles may become bogged down. TAXI: Available in Port Stanley, but need to be booked in advance.

The islands are made up of a small population, living in and around the capital, Port Stanley. The close-knit community means crime is not particularly a problem.On arrival, visitors are warned about landmines in some off-road areas.

CAPITAL: Suva

GMT +12

FROM UK: 00679. OUTGOING CODE TO UK: 0544

All services: 000.

Fiji High Commission, 34 Hyde Park Gate, London, SW7 5DN. Tel: 020 7584 3661. Fax: 020 7584 2838. fijirepuk@compuserve.com

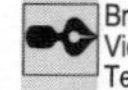
British High Commission, PO Box 1355, Victoria House, Gladstone Road, Suva, Fiji. Tel: 311033. Fax: 301406. www.ukinthepacific.bhc.org.fj ukinfo@bhc.org.fj

Refer to Embassy.

Fiji Visitors Bureau, PO Box 92, Thompson Street, Suva Fiji. Tel: 302 433. Fax: 300 986. infodesk@fijifvb.gov.fj

Return ticket required. Regulations may be subject to change at short notice. Contact the embassy before departure. Valid passport required by all and must be valid for 6 months from the date of entry.

Nationals of the UK do not require a visa.

Fruit and plants may be confiscated on entry.

F$20, payable in local currency. Children under 16 years of age are exempt.

POLIO, TYPHOID: R. YELLOW FEVER: A vaccination certificate will be required of arriving from an infected area (excluding those under 1 year of age). OTHER: The dengue fever season runs from Nov to Apr.

W2

Fijian dollar (F$) = 100 cents. NOTE: Export of local currency is limited to F$100, export of foreign currency as cash is limited to F$500. All major credit cards are accepted in hotels and restaurants. Travellers cheques, preferably in Australian dollars, can be easily exchanged. ATM AVAILABILITY: 10 locations, but not all international cards are accepted.

MONEYGRAM: Unavailable.
WESTERN UNION: 314 812.

AMEX: 0544 1273 696 933
DINERS CLUB: 0544 1252 513 500
MASTERCARD: 051 314 542 7111
VISA: 051 410 581 9994

AMEX: 0544 1273 571 600
THOMAS COOK: 0544 1733 318950
VISA: 0544 20 7937 8091

0930-1500 Mon to Thur, 0930-1600 Fri.

Can be expensive in the tourist centres, but cheaper dormitory-style accommodation is gradually being introduced. Different islands cater for different needs and are budgeted accordingly.

Fijian and Hindi. English is widely spoken.

Tropical climate, rainy season = Dec-Apr.

Methodist and Hindu. Roman Catholic and Muslim minorities.

Jan 1, Feb 16, Mar 7, last Fri in May, second Sat in Jun, Jun 18, Jul 23, Oct 10, Dec 25,26. Easter, Prophet's Birthday, Diwali.

240 Volts AC, 50 Hz.

Up to 10 days.

Fijian society is friendly and open. A multiracial culture prevails. There is no discrimination between men and women. Saris are worn by women.

FLIGHTS: Shuttle services are available between islands, although more expensive than other methods. SEA: Ferries operate inexpensive crossings between islands. Arrangements should be confirmed before the vessel leaves port. TAXI: Metered in towns. BUS: Services operate between large towns and on suburban routes. ROAD: Car hire is available. The roads are poorly lit at night and animals often stray into the path of traffic. DOCUMENTATION: Foreign driving licence is acceptable. TAXI: Metered in towns. BUS: Services operate between large towns and on suburban routes.

Petty crime is on the increase. There are dangerous riptides along the reefs and special safety equipment is available. The cyclone season in Fiji is from November to April.

Finland

CAPITAL: Helsinki

GMT +2 (GMT +3 during the summer)

FROM UK: 00358. OUTGOING CODE TO UK: 0044

Helsinki Police: 002; Doctor: 008; Ambulance and Fire: 000.

Embassy of the Republic of Finland, 38 Chesham Place, London SW1X 8HW. Tel: 020 7838 6200; Fax: 7235 3680. www.finemb.org.uk

British Embassy, Itainen Puistotie 17, 00140 Helsinki, Finland. Tel: (09) 2286 5100; Fax: (09) 2286 5284. info@ukembassy.fi; www.ukembassy.fi/

Finnish Tourist Board, 30-35 Pall Mall, London SW1Y 5LP. Tel: 020 7839 4048 or Fax: 020 7321 0696. mek.lon@mek.fi www.finlandtourism.com

Embassy Matkailun edistämiskeskus (Tourist Board) PO Box 625, Töölönkatu 11, 00101 Helsinki, Finland. Tel: 00358 9 417 6911; Fax: 00358 9 4176 9333. mek@mek.fi

Requirements may be subject to short-term change. Contact embassy before departure. Valid passport required.

Visa not required by nationals of Great Britain (holders of British Hong Kong passports do require a visa). Many other nationals do not require visas - check with the nearest authority for a complete uptodate list of visa requirements for Finland.

Food, plants, medicine, works of art are subject to restrictions. Import of drinks with more than 60% volume of alcohol are prohibited.

Markka (FMK) = 100 penniä. Exch: banks and exchange bureaux at ports, airports, stations. All major credit cards are widely accepted. Travellers cheques are accepted throughout the country: US dollars are the preferred currency. ATM AVAILABILITY: Over 2000 locations.

MONEYGRAM: 0 800 1 115198.
WESTERN UNION: 9 800 20440.

AMEX: 0044 1273 696 933
DINERS CLUB: 0800 9 5555
MASTERCARD: 0800 11 56234
VISA: 0800 11 0057

AMEX: 0044 1273 571 600
THOMAS COOK: 0044 1733 318950
VISA: 0044 20 7937 8091

0915-1615 Mon to Fri.

Relatively expensive, similar to other Scandinavian countries.

Finnish. Swedish and English may also be spoken.

The climate is temperate, but with considerable variation in temperatures. Summers are warm whilst winters, Oct-Mar, are very cold. The north has snow cover from mid Oct to mid May.

Mostly Lutheran with others including; Finnish Orthodox, Baptists, Methodists, Free Church, Roman Catholic, Jews and Muslim.

Jan 1,6, May 1, first Fri/Sat after June 18, Sat after Oct 30, Dec 6, 24–26. Easter, Ascension Day, Whitsun.

220 volts AC, 50 Hz. Plugs are continental 2-pin type.

3 days within Europe.

Women should encounter few problems. Whilst usual precautions should be taken, the crime rate is quite low and there is little inequality between men and women.

FLIGHTS: Cheap tickets can be found to the various airports throughout the country. RAIL: Cheap and efficient, various discount schemes operate depending on status e.g. group travel, Interrail and Scanrail. ROAD: A well-developed road system, use of horns is frowned upon and signs will indicate warnings of reindeer and other wildlife when collisions are possible. BUS: An excellent network of routes are available offering cheap offers to specific groups. CAR HIRE: Normally drivers should have at least 1 year's driving experience. DOCUMENTATION: Usually national or IDP is required with insurance. A green card is recommended.

Finnish people often appear reserved. During the summer mosquitoes and gnats can be a nuisance, especially in the north, where a good supply of repellent is recommended.
PHOTOGRAPHY: Check with the Russian Embassy if you wish to take photos near the Russian border.

CAPITAL: Paris

GMT +1 (GMT +2 during the summer)

FROM UK: 0033. OUTGOING CODE TO UK: 0044.

Police: 17; Fire: 18; Ambulance: 15.

French Embassy, 58 Knightsbridge, London SW1X 7JT. Tel: 020 7201 1000. French Consular Section, 21 Cromwell Road, London SW7 2DQ. Tel: 020 7838 2000. press@ambafrance.org.uk; www.ambafrance.org.uk. The French Embassy and Consulate deal with enquiries about French Overseas Départements and Territories around the world.

British Embassy, 35 rue du Faubourg St Honore, 75383 Paris, Cedex 08, France. Tel: 0033 1 44 51 31 00; Fax: 00 33 1 44 51 31 27 (Consular). www.ambgrandebretagne.fr/

French Government Tourism Office, 178 Piccadilly, London W1V 0AL. Tel: 0891 244 123 (France Information Line). Fax: 020 7493 6594. piccadilly@mdlf.demon.co.uk; www.franceguide.com and www.frholidaystore.co.uk

Maison de la France, 8 avenue de l'Opéra, 75001 Paris. Tel: 0033 1 42 96 10 23. Fax: 0033 1 42 86 80 52. www.maisondelafrance.fr

Advisable to have a return ticket or proof of sufficient funds to finance stay, although this is not an absolute requirement. Requirements may be subject to short-term change. Contact embassy before departure. Valid passport required.

British citizens who have retained Commonwealth passports may require a visa. Check with the visa section of the consulate.

Gold jewellery, other than personal jewellery below 500 g in weight must be declared.

Euro = 100 cents. American Express, Diners Club and Visa credit cards are all widely accepted. Travellers cheques are accepted almost everywhere. ATM AVAILABILITY: Over 25,000 locations.

MONEYGRAM: 00 800 66639472.
WESTERN UNION: 01 43 54 46 12

AMEX: 0044 1273 696 933
DINERS CLUB: 01 49 06 17 50
MASTERCARD: 0800 90 1387
VISA: 0800 90 1179

AMEX: 0044 1273 571 600
THOMAS COOK: 0800 90 8330
VISA: 0800 91 5613

0900-1200 and 1400-1600 Mon to Fri. Some banks close on Mon and close at 1200 the day before a bank holiday.

Similar to other Western European countries. Cities and tourism centres are more expensive than less commercial areas.

French. Basque is spoken in the South-west by some and Breton in Brittany. Some English is spoken by much of the population, but visitors will find they get more cooperation if they speak French.

Temperate climate in the North. Rainfall throughout the year and some snow in the winter. Mediterranean climate in the South. Relatively mild temperatures in the West.

Mostly Roman Catholic with a Protestant minority.

Jan 1, May 1,8, Jul 14, Aug 15, Nov 1,11, Dec 25,26. Christian feast days.

220 volts AC 50Hz. Plugs are the 2-pin type.

2-3 days within the rest of Europe.

Roles vary depending on the region women live. Generally, there is little inequality in urban areas.

RAIL: The Channel Tunnel provides rail connections to France's excellent national rail network and international services to all parts of Europe. ROAD: Mainland France has good roads but tolls are charged on autoroutes. Information about alternative routes is available on the French Transport Ministry web site, www.bisonfute.equipment.gouv.fr/ BUS: Very few long distance bus services exist. CAR HIRE: A list of agencies can be obtained from the tourist information office. DOCUMENTATION: A national driving licence is sufficient. Nationals from the EU are strongly advised to take a green card. The car registration documents must also be carried.

Topless sunbathing is tolerated on most beaches but naturism is restricted to certain beaches. Be aware of pickpockets and bag snatchers at railway stations and tourist areas. Cars rented in France usually carry number plates ending with 51 and are often a target for thieves. Do not expect to find work to finance your stay as France currently has a relatively high rate of unemployment. The medical form E111 provides basic emergency health cover for British visitors to mainland France, but not in the overseas territories.

French Guiana

CAPITAL: Cayenne

GMT –3

FROM UK: 00594. OUTGOING CODE TO UK: 0044.

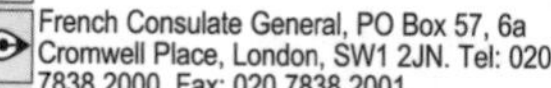
Police: 17; Fire: 18; Ambulance: 15.

French Consulate General, PO Box 57, 6a Cromwell Place, London, SW1 2JN. Tel: 020 7838 2000. Fax: 020 7838 2001.

British Honorary Consulate, 16 ave Président, Nibbervukkem VO211m 97324 Cayenne Cedex; Tel: 311034/304242.

Not present.

Federation des Offices de Tourisme et Syndicats d'Initiative de la Guyane, 12 rue Lallouette, B.P.702, 97336 CAYENNE Cedex. Tel: 00594 30 96 29; Fax: 00594 31 23 41. fotsig@nplus.gf ; www.guyanetourisme.com/

Return ticket required. Requirements may change at short notice. Contact the embassy before departure. Valid passport required by all.

Same as for France. A valid visa for France is also valid for French Guiana, although visitors should make it clear that they intend to visit French Guiana when applying for a visa for France.

Gold jewellery, other than personal jewellery below 500 g in weight must be declared.

US$20, payable in French francs.

POLIO, TYPHOID: R. MALARIA: Exists in the falciparum variety. Resistance to chloroquine has been reported. YELLOW FEVER: A vaccination certificate is required for visitors over 1 year of age arriving from all countries. OTHER: Rabies.

W2

Euro = 100 cents. (French Guiana is an overseas Département of France) Exch: The Banque de la Guyane will exchange money – there are no exchange facilities at the airport. There are two currency exchange offices in Cayenne. All major credit cards are accepted except for Diners Club. Travellers cheques have limited acceptance. ATM AVAILABILITY: Unavailable.

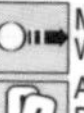

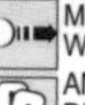
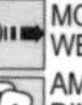

MONEYGRAM: Unavailable.
WESTERN UNION: Unavailable.

AMEX: 0044 1273 696 933
DINERS CLUB: 0044 1252 513 500
MASTERCARD: 1 314 542 7111
VISA: 1 410 581 9994

AMEX: 0044 1273 571 600
THOMAS COOK: 0800 90 8330
VISA: 0044 20 7937 8091

0745-1130 and 1500-1700 Mon to Fri.

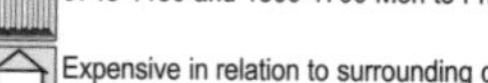
Expensive in relation to surrounding countries.

French. English and Creole are also spoken.

Tropical climate. Rainy season Jan–June. Hot all year with cool nights.

Roman Catholic.

Jan 1, May 1, 8, Jun 10, Jul 14, Aug 15, Oct 15, Nov 1,2,11, Dec 25. Start of Lent, Easter, Ascension Day and Whitsun.

220/127 Volts AC, 50 Hz

5–7 days.

French and indigenous culture coexist.

FLIGHTS: Air Guyane serves the interior of the country from Cayenne. ROAD: There is a road along the coast. DOCUMENTATION: IDP is recommended. TAXI: Available in Cayenne. CAR HIRE: Available at the airport or in Cayenne.

Modest beachwear is preferred. Lying off the coast is the infamous Devil's Island, upon which the book and subsequent film *Papillon* were based.
The medical form E111 provides basic health cover as in mainland France, visitors should still have full travel insurance for emergencies.

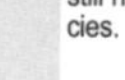

Gabon

CAPITAL: Libreville

GMT +1

FROM UK: 00241. OUTGOING CODE TO UK: 0044

Not present.

Embassy of the Gabonese Republic, 27 Elvaston Place, London SW7 5NL. Tel: 020 7823 9986. Fax: 020 7584 0047.

British Embassy closed in 1991. The West African department of the Foreign and Commonwealth Office handles enquiries for Gabon. Tel: 020 7270 2516. Fax: 020 7270 296. British Honorary Consul in Libreville Tel: 76 22 00.

Refer to the Gabonese Embassy.

Office National Gabonaise du Tourisme, PO Box 161, Libreville, Gabon. Tel: 722 182.

Return ticket required. Requirements may be subject to short-term change. Contact the relevant consular authority before finalising travel arrangements. Valid passport required by all.

Visa required by all. Tourist and business visas are granted.

Guns and ammunition can not be imported without a police permit.

Nationals of Angola, Cape Verde, Cuba, Ghana, Guinea Bissau, Haiti and Israel will be refused admission unless transiting by the same aircraft.

POLIO, TYPHOID: R. MALARIA: R. Falciparum variety prevalent, resistance to cholorquine has been reported. YELLOW FEVER: A vaccination certificate is required by travellers over one year of age. OTHER: Bilharzia, cholera, rabies, river blindness also present.

W1

CFA Franc (CFA Fr) = 100 centimes. NOTE: Import of local currency is limited to CFA Fr 250,000. There is very limited acceptance of any credit cards or travellers cheques. ATM AVAILABILITY: Unavailable.

MONEYGRAM: Unavailable.
WESTERN UNION: 77 33 33

AMEX: 0044 1273 696 933
DINERS CLUB: 0044 1252 513 500
MASTERCARD:001 314 542 7111
VISA: 001 410 581 9994

AMEX: 0044 1273 571 600
THOMAS COOK: 0044 1733 318950
VISA: 0044 20 7937 8091

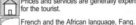

0730-1130 and 1430-1630 Mon to Fri.

Prices and services are generally expensive for the tourist.

French and the African language, Fang.

May-Sept is the dry season, Feb-Apr is rainy season. Trade winds prevail during the dry season.

Mostly Christian, with the remainder Muslim and Animist.

Jan 1, Mar 12, May 1,6, Aug 15, 16, Nov 1, Dec 25. Islamic festivals, Easter, Whitsun.

220 Volts Ac 50 Hz

Airmail at least 1 week to Western Europe.

A patriarchal society exists.

FLIGHTS: Regular domestic flights operate. SEA: River barges and ferries operate along the waterways. RAIL: Currently being expanded connects main cities. ROAD Mostly not tarred and of poor standard, inadvisable during the rainy season. CAR HIRE: Possible from main hotels and airports. DOCUMENTATION: IDP required.

CAPITAL: Banjul

GMT

FROM UK: 00220. OUTGOING CODE TO UK: 0044

495 133 (Embassy)

High Commission of the Republic of the Gambia, 57 Kensington Court, London, W8 5DG. Tel: 020 7937 6316/7/8. Fax: 020 7937 9095.

British High Commission, PO Box 507, 48 Atlantic Road, Fajara, Banjul, The Gambia. Tel: 495 133/4 or 495 578. Fax: 496 134. bhcbanjul@gamtel.gm.

Refer to the High Commission.

The Gambia National Tourist Office, The Quadrangle, Banjul, The Gambia.Tel: 229563 or 227593. Fax: 227753

Return ticket required. Requirements may be subject to change at short notice. Consult the appropriate consular authority before finalising travel arrangements. Valid passport required by all

Nationals of Rep.of Ireland do not require a visa. Nationals of the UK do not require a visa for the purpose of tourism only, for visits no longer than 3 months.

Narcotics.

Domestic and international departure tax is Di150 or US$20, payable in any currency.

POLIO, TYPHOID: R MALARIA: Present throughout the year in the falciparum variety. Resistance to chloroquine has been reported. YELLOW FEVER: A vaccination certificate is required by all visitors over 1 year of age travelling from infected areas. Vaccination is recommended to all visitors planning to travel outside the urban areas. OTHER: Bilharzia, cholera and rabies are present. Meningitis A has been reported around the Basse and a vaccination is advised if intending to visit the area.

W1

Gambian Dalasi (Di) = 100 bututs. Currency must be declared on arrival and export of foreign currency is limited to the amount imported. Black market currency exchange is strongly discouraged. MasterCard and Visa are accepted in large towns only. Travellers cheques are accepted, US dollars and pound sterling are the preferred currency. ATM AVAILABILITY: Unavailable.

MONEYGRAM: Unavailable.
WESTERN UNION: 225 289.

AMEX: 0044 1273 696 933
DINERS CLUB: 0044 1252 513 500
MASTERCARD: 001 314 542 7111
VISA: 001 410 581 9994

AMEX: 0044 1273 571 600
THOMAS COOK: 0044 1733 318950
VISA: 0044 20 7937 8091

0800-1330 Mon to Thur, 0800-1100 Fri.

Services and prices for tourists will generally be expensive.

English

Generally recognised to have the most agreeable climate in West Africa. Mid Nov–mid May is dry in coastal areas. June–Oct is rainy season. Inland the cool season is shorter and daytime temperatures are very hot between March and June.

Mostly Muslim. Remainder are Christian and Animist.

Jan 1, Feb 18, May 1, Aug 15, Dec 25. Easter, Islamic festivals.

220 Volts AC 50Hz. Plugs are either round or square 3-pin.

Due to a predominant Muslim culture a patriarchal society exists.

ROADS: Few paved roads of which most are impassable during the rainy season. Road improvements programmes are in place. TAXIS: Tourist taxis are green. Fares should be settled in advance. CAR HIRE: Possible: check with company before travelling. DOCUMENTATION: IDP is required. RIVER: Ferries operate on a frequent basis along the river which connects Barra Point to Banjul. A weekly ferry operates between Banjul and Basse.

Beware of pickpockets and bag snatchers. Beachwear is not suitable for towns. Visitors should respect local laws and customs and dress conservatively. Do not expect to find work in the country. Sea swimming can be dangerous.

Georgia

CAPITAL: Tbilisi

GMT + 4 (GMT + 5 during the summer).

FROM UK: 00995. OUTGOING CODE TO UK: 8/1044 (wait for second dial tone)

Fire: 01; Police: 02; Ambulance: 03.

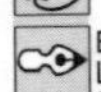
Embassy of Georgia, 3 Hornton Place, London W8 4LZ. Tel: 020 7937 8233; Fax: 020 7938 4108. geoemb@dircon.co.uk; www.embassyofgeorgia.org.uk

British Embassy, Sheraton Palace Hotel, Tbilisi, 38003 Tel: 32988796; Fax: 32001065. british.embassy@caucasus.net.

Not present.

Not present.

Return ticket required. Requirements may be subject to short-term change. Contact the relevant authority before departure. Valid passport required by all: British passports must be valid for at least 6 months after leaving Georgia.

Visa required. Arriving at the airport without a visa incurs a charge of US$80.

Pornography, loose pearls and anything owned by a third party that is to be carried in for that third party. State loan certificates, lottery tickets and works of art antiques can not be exported.

US$10, levied on international travel.

The Consulate/Embassies of the Russian Federation no longer issue tourist visas valid for Georgia.

POLIO, TYPHOID: R OTHER: Rabies.

W2

The national currency the Lari has been introduced and by law it should be used for all local purchases. US$ are readily changed. Credit cards are accepted in some hotels. Travellers cheques are not accepted. ATM AVAILABILITY: Unavailable.

MONEYGRAM: Unavailable.
WESTERN UNION: 32 938921.

AMEX: 0044 1273 696 933
DINERS CLUB: 0044 1252 513 500
MASTERCARD: 001 314 542 7111
VISA: 001 410 581 9994

AMEX: 0044 1273 571 600
THOMAS COOK: no local number
VISA: 0044 20 7937 8091

0930-1730 Mon to Fri.

Accommodation caters for all budgets, but the larger hotels do tend to inflate their prices.

Mostly Georgian. Russian, Ossetian, Abkhazian and Adzharian.

Hot summers with mild winters, particularly in the south-west. Low temperatures are common in Alpine areas and rainfall may be heavy in the subtropical south-west.

Christian, mainly Georgian Orthodox and other denominations; Islam; Judaism.

Jan 1,7,19, Mar 13, May 26, Aug 28, Oct 14, Nov 23. Easter.

220 volts AC, 50 Hz.

International postal services are severely disrupted.

At social occasions foreign women are likely to be the object of flattery. Those who do not like this should be careful not to show signs of encouragement.

ROAD: An adequate supply of fuel must be purchased in Tbilisi if driving around Georgia as fuel may be hard to obtain in other areas. Reliable road maps and signs do not exist, and roads are poorly lit at night. BUS: Provide a reliable if uncomfortable service between towns in the republic. TAXIS: Only use official taxis, which should not be shared with strangers in view of the incidents of crime. NOTE: Travel at night outside Tbilisi should be avoided if possible.

The breakaway regions of Abkhazia and South Ossetia should be strictly avoided as they remain insecure. The Georgia–Russia border is usually closed to Westerners. The Georgians are very friendly and hospitable. It is normal for most men in Georgia to carry firearms. Be vigilant against banditry and street crime. Powers cuts are frequent and this has led to street demonstrations, which should be avoided by visitors. Tap water tends to be contaminated, and bottled water is readily available.

CAPITAL: Berlin

GMT +1 (GMT +2 during the summer)

FROM UK: 0049. OUTGOING CODE TO UK: 0044

Police: 110; Fire: 112.

Embassy of the Federal Republic of Germany, 23 Belgrave Square, 1 Chesham Place, London SW1X 8PZ. Tel: 020 7824 1300. Fax: 020 7824 1435. mail@germanembassy.org.uk

Consulate: Tel: 0891 331 166 (recorded visa information) or 020 7824 1465/6. Fax: 020 7824 1449. Other Consulates in Manchester and Edinburgh.

British Embassy; Wilhelmstrasse 70, 10117 Berlin. Tel: 0049 30 204570; Fax: 0049 30 20457 579; www.britischebotschaft.de. British Consulate General is in Dusseldorf. consular.section@ duesseldorf.mail.fco.gov.uk; www.britishconsulategeneral.de

Consulates also in Berlin, Bremen, Frankfurt/M, Hamburg, Hannover, Kiel, Munich, Nuremberg and Stuttgart.

German National Tourist Office, Nightingale House, 65 Curzon Street, London W1Y 8NE. Tel: 0891 600 100 (recorded information) or 020 7317 0908 (general enquiries). Fax: 020 7495 6129. German_National_Tourist_Office@compuserve.com

Deutsche Zentrale für Tourismus e. V. (DZT), Beethovenstrasse 69, Frankfurt/M, Germany. Tel: 0049 69 974640; Fax: 0049 69 751 903. www.germanytourism.de

Requirements may be subject to short term change. Contact Embassy before departure. Valid passport required by UK Nationals. Republic of Ireland: holders of national ID cards do not require valid passports.

Visas not required by nationals of the UK and Ireland.

Rabies

Euro = 100 cents EXCHANGE: Banks, post offices, travel agencies and hotels. All major credit cards are accepted in 60% of shops, restaurants, hotels and petrol stations. Travellers cheques in all major currencies are accepted everywhere. ATM AVAILABILITY: Over 40,000 locations.

MONEYGRAM: 00 800 66639472
WESTERN UNION: 0180 522 5822

AMEX: 0044 1273 696 933
DINERS CLUB: 05 921 86 12 34
MASTERCARD: 0800 819 1040
VISA: 0800 811 8440

AMEX: 0044 1273 571 600
THOMAS COOK: 0130 85 9930
VISA: 0800 181 4070

Generally 0830-1300 and 1400 or 1430-1600 Mon to Fri, Thur until 1730 in main cities. Main branches do not close for lunch.

East Germany is still slightly cheaper than West Germany in small towns, although prices are reaching Western levels in cities.

German. English and French may also be spoken.

Temperate climate throughout the country. Summers are warm and winters are cold. There is rain throughout the year.

Mostly Protestant and Roman Catholic; other Christian denominations are also present.

Jan 1, 6, May 1, Aug 15, Oct 3, 31, Nov 1, Dec 24, 25, 26, 31. Various Christian feast days.

220 volts AC, 50 Hz. Plugs are continental 2-pin.

An efficient service operates.

There is little inequality between men and women.

RAIL: A modern, sophisticated rail system operates throughout the country. ROAD: Western area is covered by a modern network of motorways. Motorways in the East are of a reasonable standard but this may not be the case for secondary roads. CAR HIRE: Available at most towns and railway stations. DOCUMENTATION: Foreign drivers may use their national driving licence for up to 1 year or IDP. Carry licence, insurance and car registration details. EU citizens taking their own cars are strongly advised to take a green card for full insurance coverage. BUS: Tend to run in towns. There are few intercity services.

Medical form E111 is valid for emergency medical treatment.

German police are entitled to check a person's identity at any time and a passport is the only acceptable form of ID for British visitors.

Casual wear is widely accepted although formal wear may be required in upmarket restaurants. Shops, businesses, schools begin at 0800 or earlier.

Ghana

CAPITAL: Accra

GMT

FROM UK: 00233. OUTGOING CODE TO UK: 0044

221 665 (High Commission)

Ghana High Commission, 13 Belgrave Square, London, SW1X 8PN. Tel: 020 7235 4142; Fax: 020 7245 9552.

British High Commission, PO Box 296, Osu Link, off Gamel Abdul Nasser Avenue, Accra, Ghana. Tel: (21) 221 665 or 669 585. Fax: (21) 664 652.
high.commission@accra.mail.fco.gov.uk

Ghana Tourist Board, PO Box 3106, Tesano, Nsawam Road, Accra, Ghana. Tel: (21) 231 779. Fax: (21) 231 779.

Return ticket required. Requirements may be subject to change at short notice. Consult embassy before departure. Valid passport required by all.

Visa required.

Animals, firearms, ammunition, explosives and milk with a high fat content.

Departure tax is US$10.

POLIO, TYPHOID: R. MALARIA: Precaution advised. Falciparum form exists and resistance to chloroquine has been reported. YELLOW FEVER: A vaccination certificate is required by all. OTHER: Bilharzia, rabies. A vaccination against cholera is strongly recommended; a vaccination certificate is required if arriving from an infected area.

W1

Cedi (c) = 100 pesewas. Only authorised foreign exchange dealers must be used. NOTE: Import and export of local currency is limited to c3000 and should be recorded in passport. Credit cards and travellers cheques have very limited use. ATM AVAILABILITY: Unavailable.

MONEYGRAM: 0191 then 800 592 3688
WESTERN UNION: 21 66 27 58.

AMEX: 0044 1273 696 933
DINERS CLUB: 0044 1252 513 500
MASTERCARD: 001 314 542 7111
VISA: 001 410 581 9994

AMEX: 0044 1273 571 600
THOMAS COOK: 0044 1733 318950
VISA: 0044 20 7937 8091

0830-1400 Mon-Thur, 0830-1500 Fri. A few branches are open 0830-1200 Sat.

Relatively more expensive than surrounding countries.

English and local African languages are spoken.

The climate is hot and humid throughout the year. Average temperature between 25ºC and 29ºC. Apr-July is the rainy season.

Christian, Muslim, and traditional beliefs. All forms of religion have a strong influence on daily life.

Jan 1, Mar 6, May 1, Jun 4, Jul 1, Dec 6,25,26,31. Easter, Islamic festivals.

220 Volts AC 50 Hz Plugs are 3-pin in larger buildings, older buildings have 2-pin plugs.

2 weeks or more to Europe.

Not as patriarchal as surrounding West Africa.

RAIL: Limited. ROAD: In poor condition generally and street lighting virtually nonexistent outside the capital. CAR HIRE: Available but very expensive. DOCUMENTATION: British driving licence valid for 90 days. IDP is recommended. BUSES: Extensive bus services operate in Accra.

Take local advice about security matters. Exercise care with possessions at the main airport. Ghanaians should always be addressed formally. PHOTOGRAPHY: Be discreet with cameras, especially around the Castle in Accra or at the Akosombo Dam. Do not take photos of anything connected with the military.

CAPITAL: Gibraltar

GMT +1 (GMT +2 during the summer)

FROM UK: 00350. OUTGOING CODE TO UK: 0044

All services: 999.

Gibraltar's Foreign Affairs are handled by the UK Foreign and Commonwealth Office, King Charles Street, London SW1A 2AH. Tel: 020 7270 2862. All other enquiries to the Gibraltar Information Bureau.

Gibraltar Information Bureau, Arundel Great Court, 179 The Strand, London WC2R 1EH. Tel: 020 7836 0777. Fax: 020 7240 6612.

Gibraltar Tourist Board, Duke of Kent House, Cathedral Square, Gibraltar. Tel: 74950. Fax: 74943. tourism@gibraltar.gi; www.gibraltar.gov.gi/

Requirements may be subject to change at short notice. Contact Consulate before travelling. Valid passport required by all, except EU nationals in possession of a valid identity card.

Visa not required. Contact the Foreign and Commonwealth office for the latest information.

Gib£10, payable in local currency.

Pound sterling (Gib £) = 100 new pence. It is advisable to change unused currency from Gibraltar before leaving the area as UK banks charge for conversion. All major credit cards and travellers cheques are accepted. Pound sterling is the preferred currency. ATM AVAILABILITY: 3 locations.

MONEYGRAM: 8800 then 800 592 3688
WESTERN UNION: 51 999.

AMEX: 0044 1273 696 933
DINERS CLUB: 0044 1252 513 500
MASTERCARD: 001 314 542 7111
VISA: 001 410 581 9994

AMEX: 0044 1273 571 600
THOMAS COOK: 0044 1733 318950
VISA: 0044 20 7937 8091

0900-1530 (and 1630-1800 on Fri).

Certain goods may be cheaper due to Gibraltar's duty free status. Otherwise similar to Spain.

English and Spanish.

The climate is warm throughout the year. Summers are hot and can be quite humid. Winters are mild.

Mainly Roman Catholic. Church of England, Judaism, Hindu and other minorities are also represented.

Jan 1, second Mon in Mar, May 1, last Mon in May and Aug, second Mon in Jun, Sep 10, Dec 25, 26. Easter.

220/240 volts AC 50 Hz.

1–5 days within Europe. Poste Restante facility available in the Post Office in Main Street.

Usual precautions should be taken. No additional risks apply.

ROAD: Gibraltar's roads are narrow and winding, and traffic drives on the right. Self-drive hire cars are readily available. BUS: There are good local bus services operating at frequent intervals. TAXI: There are plenty of taxis and the drivers are required by law to produce on demand a copy of fares. Taxi drivers are well known for their expertise on conducting tours of the Rock.

Traditional British and Mediterranean customs are upheld. Medical form E111 is valid for emergency medical treatment. Gibraltar's major attractions have difficulty providing access for visitors in wheelchairs. The sovereignty of the United Kingdom over Gibraltar is disputed by Spain; there are often delays and other difficulties involved in crossing the land border.

Greece

CAPITAL: Athens

GMT +2 (GMT +3 during the summer)

FROM UK: 0030. OUTGOING CODE TO UK: 0044

Police: 100; Ambulance: 166; Fire: 199.

Embassy of the Hellenic Republic, 1A Holland Park, London W11 3TP. Tel: 020 7229 3850 or 0891 171 202 (visa information line). Fax: 020 7243 3202. www.greekembassy.org.uk

British Embassy, Odos Ploutarchou 1, 106 75 Athens, Greece. Tel: 727 2600; Fax: 727 2720. britania@hol.gr http://www.britishembassy.gr/
Consulates also on Corfu, Crete, Rhodes, Kos and in other locations on the mainland.

Greek National Tourist Organisation (GNTO), 4 Conduit Street, London W1R 0DJ. Tel: 020 7734 5997. Fax: 020 7287 1369.
EOTgreektouristoffice@btinternet.com
www.antor.com/greece

Ellinikos Organismos Tourismou (EOT), 2, Amerikis Street, 105 64 Athens, Greece. Tel: 0030 13271300/2. info@gnto.gr www.gnto.gr/

Requirements may be subject to change at short notice. Check before travelling. Passport valid for at least 6 months required by all.

Visa not required for a period of 3 months. Visitors using chartered tickets, leaving Greece on an overnight trip to another country, may risk having their return ticket invalidated by the authorities.

Plants. Visitors are allowed one surfboard per person (if entered in passport).The export of antiques is prohibited unless permission is obtained from the Archaeological Service in Athens.

Dr6000 included in ticket price.

YELLOW FEVER: A vaccination certificate is required from visitors over 6 months of age coming from infected areas. OTHER: Rabies.

W2

Euro = 100 cents All major credit cards are accepted. Travellers cheques are accepted in all major currencies, and can be easily changed at banks. ATM AVAILABILITY: Over 1500 locations.

MONEYGRAM: 00 800 11 293 0309.
WESTERN UNION: 01 927 1010.

AMEX: 0044 1273 696 933
DINERS CLUB: 92 90 130
MASTERCARD: 00800 11 887 0303
VISA: 00800 4412 1092

AMEX: 0044 1273 571 600
THOMAS COOK: 00800 4412 8366
VISA: 00800 4412 1863

0800-1400 Mon to Fri. Many of the banks of the larger islands stay open longer, especially during the tourist season.

Tourist centres can be very cheap when compared to other European countries.

Greek. Most people working in tourism speak some English, German, Italian or French.

Warm Mediterranean climate. Nov-Mar is when most rain falls. Winters are mild in the south but much cooler in the north.

Mainly Greek Orthodox, and Muslim and Roman Catholic minorities.

Jan 1, 6, Mar 25, May 1, Aug 15, Oct 28, Dec 25,26. Start of Lent, Easter, Pentecost.

220 volts AC 50 Hz.

All post for overseas will be sent by airmail. Poste restante is available at the post office.

Take usual precautions. Women from Northern and Western Europe may receive unwanted attention from Greek men, but this doesn't usually lead to problems if ignored. Women should not walk alone at night.

RAIL: Regular trains operate between Athens and main cities. There is a 20% discount on return fares and other offers available. ROAD: Good road network. Accidents with scooters and mopeds are common and hiring them is not advisable. BUS: Link Athens and all the main towns in Attica, Northern Greece and Peloponnese. TAXI: Run on a shared basis. Rates are reasonable, on a per-km basis. Extra charge on journeys from/to airports, ports, stations. CAR HIRE: Most firms operate throughout Greece. DOCUMENTATION: A national driving licence is acceptable for EU nationals.

The Greek Orthodox church has an important place in the community. Throwing back the head is a negative gesture. It is an offence to sell your belongings and can lead to arrest. Medical form E111 is valid for free emergency treatment. Visitors seeking work in bars, restaurants and clubs must have a health certificate issued by the Greek local authority.

CAPITAL: St George's

GMT –4

FROM UK: 001473. OUTGOING CODE TO UK: 01144

Police: 112; Ambulance: 434. All services: 911.

Grenada High Commission, 8 Queen Street, Mayfair, London W1X 7PH. Tel: 020 7290 2275; Fax: 020 7409 1031. grenada@highcommission.freeserve.co.uk

British High Commission, Netherlands Building, Grand Anse, St George's Grenada. Tel: 001473 440 3222/; Fax: 001473 440 4939. bhcgrenada@caribsurf.com

Refer to High Commission.

Grenada Board of Tourism, Burns Point, PO Box 293, St. Georges's, Grenada, West Indies. Tel: 001 473 4402279; Fax: 001 473 4406637. gbt@caribsurf.com; www.grenada.org

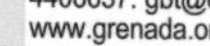

Return ticket required. Requirements may be subject to short-term change. Contact embassy before departure. Valid passport required by all

Visa not required.

Narcotics and firearms.

EC$50 per adult payable in cash, EC$17.50 is charged for children between 5 and 12 years old.

POLIO, TYPHOID: R. YELLOW FEVER: A vaccination certificate is required from those over one year of age coming from infected areas. OTHER: Rabies. Dengue fever mosquito. HIV/AIDS prevalent.

Eastern Caribbean Dollar (EC$) = 100 cents. All travellers cheques and major credit cards are widely accepted. US$ are the preferred currency. ATM AVAILABILITY: Unavailable.

MONEYGRAM: 1 800 543 4080.
WESTERN UNION: 440 2198.

AMEX: 01144 1273 696 933
DINERS CLUB: 01144 1252 513 500
MASTERCARD: 1800 307 7309
VISA: 1800 847 2911

AMEX: 01144 1273 571 600
THOMAS COOK: 1800 223 7373
VISA: 01144 20 7937 8091

0800-1400 Mon to Thur, 0800-1300 and 1400-1700 Fri.

Moderate to expensive. Hotels need to be booked well in advance. Prices may vary with seasonal changes and specific events. Dutyfree shops exist with an international market.

English

Tropical climate. Rainy season June-Dec.

Roman Catholic. Anglican, Methodist and Seventh Day Adventist minorities.

Jan 1, Feb 7, May 1, first and second Mon/Tue in Aug, Oct 25, Dec 25, 26. Easter, Whitsun, Corpus Christi.

220/240 volts AC, 50 Hz.

Post will take approximately 14 days to reach Europe.

Society is influenced by African and colonial heritage, resulting in a conservative and reserved outlook.

SEA: Round island trips are very popular, small to large boats can be hired. ROAD: They are narrow and winding, and traffic drives on the left. CAR HIRE: A large variety of vehicles can be hired. DOCUMENTATION: A full national driving licence must be produced to obtain a local driving permit. BUS: Cheap but slow service operates.

The hurricane season runs from June to November. Beachwear is not acceptable in town. The removal of the bark of trees or taking wildlife from forest or rivers is strictly forbidden.

Guadeloupe

CAPITAL: Basse-Terre

GMT–4.

FROM UK: 00590 OUTGOING CODE TO UK: 0044

Police: 17; Fire and Ambulance: 18.

As French Consulate General (for visa enquiries) or French Embassy (cultural).

Routine consular matters are covered by the British Consulate-General in Paris. In an emergency, contact the Honorary British Consul in Guadeloupe, 23 rue Sadi Carnot, 97110 Pointe-à-Pitre, Guadeloupe. Tel: 00590 82 57 57; Fax: 00590 82 89 33.

Caribbean Tourism, 42 Westminster Palace Gdns, Artillery Row, London SW1P 1RR. Tel: 020 7222 4335. Fax: 020 7222 4325. www.doitcaribbean.com cto@caribtourism.com

Office du Tourisme, BP 1099, 5 Square de la Banque, 97181 Pointe-à-Pitre, Guadeloupe. Tel: 820 930. Fax: 838 922. Also: French National Travel Organisation website: www.franceguide.com/

Return ticket required. Requirements may be subject to short-term change. Contact the Embassy before departure. Valid passport required.

Visa not required of citizens of the EU, USA, Canada.

Ffr 80, payable in local currency, is levied on all foreign nationals.

POLIO, TYPHOID: R. YELLOW FEVER: A vaccination certificate is required from visitors over 1 year of age coming from infected areas. OTHER: Bilharzia is found in fresh water throughout GrandeTerre and in much of Basse-Terre, including Grand Etang lake.

W2

Euro = 100 cents. All major credit cards are accepted. ATM AVAILABILITY: Unavailable.

MONEYGRAM: Unavailable.
WESTERN UNION: Unavailable.

AMEX: 0044 1273 696 933
DINERS CLUB: 0044 1252 513 500
MASTERCARD: 1 314 542 7111
VISA: 1 410 581 9994

AMEX: 0044 1273 571 600
THOMAS COOK: 1800 223 7373
VISA: 0044 20 7937 8091

0800–1600 Mon to Fri

Expensive due to a 15-30% tax levied on services depending on the time of year.

French. Patois and English are widely spoken.

Warm weather all year round. Main rainy season June-Oct. High humidity at times.

Roman Catholic. Evangelical Protestant minority.

Jan 1, May 1, 8, Jul 14, Aug 15, Nov 1, 11, Dec 25, 26. Christian feast days.

110/220 volts AC, 50 Hz.

Approx. 1 week to Western Europe.

Relaxed and equal society.

SEA: Regular ferry services move around the island. ROAD: Well maintained Night driving can be dangerous, especially in the mountains and on winding rural roads. BUS: There is a good bus service. CAR HIRE: Many companies are present. DOCUMENTATION: National driving licence is sufficient. One years driving experience is required. IDP is advised.

Hurricane season runs from June to November. Guadeloupe is a French overseas département and the French culture is clearly evident. Medical form E111 is valid for emergency medical treatment.

Guam

CAPITAL: Agana

GMT +10

FROM UK: 001671. OUTGOING CODE TO UK: 01144

All services: 911.

Refer to the USA entry.

No British representation in Guam.

Refer to USA entry. www.gov.gu/

Guam Visitors Bureau, PO Box 3520, Suite 201-205, Boon's Building, 127 North Marine Drive, Upper Tumon, Agaña, Guam 96911. Tel: 646 5278/9. Fax: 646 8861.

As for the USA. Valid passport required by all except those entering directly from the USA.

See USA entry.

See entry for the USA. Importation of plants, fruits, and animals are restricted without documentation from the point of origin.

See USA entry.

POLIO, TYPHOID: R.

W2

US Dollar (US$) = 100 cents. Credit cards are widely accepted. Travellers cheques in US dollars can be exchanged. ATM AVAILABILITY: Over 30 locations.

MONEYGRAM: 0011 800 821 8192.
WESTERN UNION: Available.

AMEX: 01144 1273 696 933
DINERS CLUB: 01144 1252 513 500
MASTERCARD: 1800 307 7309
VISA: 888 425 0227

AMEX: 01144 1273 571 600
THOMAS COOK: 1800 223 7373
VISA: 01144 20 7937 8091

1000–1500 Mon to Thur, 1000–1800 Fri.

Appropriate to all tastes and budget. The island's duty-free status means that brand-name goods are often less expensive than in the country of origin.

English and Chamorro. Japanese and Tagalog also spoken.

Tropical climate with rains July-Nov.

Roman Catholic.

Jan 1, third Mon in Jan and Feb, first Mon in Mar, last Mon in May, Jul 4, 21, first Mon in Sep, 2nd Mon in Oct, Nov 2, 11, fourth Thur in Nov, Dec 8, 25. Easter.

120 Volts AC 60 Hz.

Up to 2 weeks.

Western culture is widely accepted, due to a large US naval presence. This is reflected in the status of women in Guam. Guam is a melting pot of Chamoru, Micronesian, American, and Asian cultures.

BUS: A reasonable bus service is available on a limited number of routes. TAXI: Fare are metered. CAR HIRE: Available from most major companies. DOCUMENTATION: AN IDP is required.

Guam is the westernmost part of the United States and the travel hub to other Micronesian Islands. Most major Asian cities are only a few hours away. The tourist industry is geared towards the Japanese market, which make up 80% of visitors. As a result other travellers will observe an abundance of Japanese customs in the tourist areas. Usual social courtesies should be observed.

Guatemala

CAPITAL: Guatemala City

GMT –6

FROM UK: 00502. OUTGOING CODE TO UK: 0044

Police: 120 / 137 / 138; Fire: 122 / 123; Ambulance: 125 / 128.

Embassy of the Republic of Guatemala, 13 Fawcett Street, London, SW10 9HN. Tel: 020 7351 3042. Fax: 020 7376 5708. Tourism information: Tel: 020 7349 0346 101740.3655@compuserve.com

British Embassy, Avenida La Reforma 1600, Zona 10, Edificio Torre Internacional, Nivel 11. Tel: 00502 367 5425; Fax: 00502 367 5430. embassy@terra.com.gt

Refer to the Embassy.

Guatemala Tourist Commission, 7 Avenida 1-17, Centro Civico, Zona 4 Guatemala City, Guatemala. Tel: (2) 3311 333. Fax: (2) 318 893. www.inguat.net/

Return ticket and valid passport required by all. Requirements may change at short notice; contact the Embassy.

Those on business from the UK or Republic of Ireland require visas. Tourists from the UK or Republic of Ireland may stay for a maximum of 90 days without a visa – a tourist card will be issued by the authorities at the airport.

Narcotics.

US$30 is levied on all international departures, payable in local currency.

Contact the embassy for an up to date list of countries, which have restricted entry.

POLIO, TYPHOID: R. MALARIA: Exists throughout the year in areas below 1500 m, including popular tourist spots. YELLOW FEVER: A vaccination certificate is required by travellers arriving from infected areas. OTHER: Hepatitis, rabies, onchocerciasis, American trypanosomiasis and altitude sickness can occur in higher areas.

W1

Quetzal (Q) = 100 centavos Visa and Amex are widely accepted. Other cards have only a limited acceptance. Travellers cheques in US$ are recommended. ATM AVAILABILITY: Over 120 locations.

MONEYGRAM: 099 1350.
WESTERN UNION: (02) 312 860.

AMEX: 0044 1273 696 933
DINERS CLUB: 331 60 75 or 331 80 27
MASTERCARD: 1800 999 1480
VISA: 1800 999 0115

AMEX: 0044 1273 571 600
THOMAS COOK: 1800 223 7373
VISA: 0044 20 7937 8091

0900–1500 (certain branches 0900–2000) Mon to Fri.

Accommodation is diverse and priced accordingly. Food and local merchandise, are relatively inexpensive, especially in markets.

Spanish. English and over 20 indigenous languages are also spoken.

Climate varies according to altitude. Lower altitudes being far hotter than highlands. The rainy season is May–Oct.

Roman Catholic and Protestant.

Jan 1, May 1, Jun 30, Aug 15, Sep 15, Oct 20, Nov 1, Dec 24, 25, 31. Easter.

110 Volts AC 60 Hz. There are some regional variations.

7-21 days.

Guatemala is a densely populated country, whose culture is mainly Indian with Spanish influence. Economy is based on bartering and selling home-grown merchandise.

FLIGHTS: Air transport is by far the most efficient means of internal travel; there are over 380 airstrips. RAIL: A daily service between the Pacific and Caribbean coasts. ROAD: There is an extensive road network but only a small number are all-weather. BUS: The bus services are cheap but crowded. TAXI: A flat rate is often charged within the city but prices can be high. CAR HIRE: International companies operate in Guatemala City and rates are low. DOCUMENTATION: A local licence will be issued on presentation of a national driving licence.

Some regions may still be politically volatile. Visitors should register with the Embassy upon arrival. Violent crime is rife throughout the country. Four of Guatemala's volcanoes are currently active and the country also experiences hurricanes, earthquakes and torrential rain leading to mud slides.

CAPITAL: St Peter Port

GMT (GMT + 1 during the summer).

FROM UK: 01481 (calls from overseas must be made using the UK country code: 441481). OUTGOING CODE TO UK: not required.

All services: 999.

Guernsey Tourist Office, PO Box 23, North Esplanade, St Peter Port, Guernsey, Channel Islands GY1 3AN. Tel: 726 611 (administration) or 723 552 (information). Fax: 721 246.
enquiries@tourism.guernsey.net
www.guernseytouristboard.com/
www.guernseymap.com/

Same as those for the UK - see the United Kingdom.

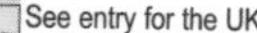
See entry for the UK.

£20, payable in local currency.

Pound sterling (£) = 100 pence. EXCHANGE: Bureaux de change in banks, hotels. Channel Islands notes and coins are not accepted in the UK, although they can be reconverted at parity in UK banks. All major credit cards and travellers cheques are accepted. ATM AVAILABILITY: Over 10 locations.

MONEYGRAM: 0800 018 0104
WESTERN UNION: 0800 833 833.

AMEX: 01273 696 933
DINERS CLUB: 01252 513 500
MASTERCARD: 0800 964767
VISA: 0800 895082

AMEX: 01273 571 600
THOMAS COOK: 0800 622 101
VISA: 020 7937 8091

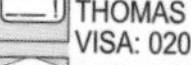
0930-1530 Mon to Fri. Some banks are open later on weekdays and on Saturday morning.

The Channel Islands are largely a duty-free zone.

English. Norman patois is spoken in some parishes.

The most popular holiday season is from Easter to October with temperatures averaging 20-21°C. Rainfall is mainly during the cooler months.

Church of England, Baptist, Congregational and Methodist.

Jan 1, first Mon in May, May 9, last Mon in May and Aug, Dec 25, 26. Easter.

240 volts AC, 50 Hz.

Only Guernsey stamps will be accepted for outgoing mail.

Men and women are deemed equal.

ROAD: BUS: A comprehensive bus service operates. TAXI: Guernsey has a regulated, licensed taxi service, based on two ranks in central St Peter Port, one at St Sampson's (on The Bridge) and one at the airport. It is advisable to book taxis whenever possible, especially if you wish to travel early in the morning or during the evening.
CAR HIRE: Many companies have agencies in Guernsey. DOCUMENTATION: A full national driving licence is required.

Casual wear is acceptable in most places. Usual social courtesies should be observed.
The National Health Service does not operate in Guernsey. Most doctors and dentists are in private practice and patients are required to pay for treatment. There is a reciprocal health agreement in place between the island's authorities and the United Kingdom's Department of Health for immediately necessary treatment of conditions which may arise during your stay.
Alderney can be reached from Guernsey only by air a 15-minute flight.
www.alderney.net/
The island of Sark can be reached only by boat. www.sarktourism.com/
Herm also can be reached only by boat.
www.hermisland.com/.
Lihou Island can be reached only by a causeway which is accessible at certain states of the tide. Times are available from the Information Centre, Tel: 01481 723552.

Guinea Bissau

CAPITAL: Bissau

GMT

FROM UK: 00245. OUTGOING CODE TO UK: 0044 Most outgoing calls must go through the operator

Not present

Embassy of the Republic of Guinea Bissau, 94 Rue St Lazare, Paris 9, France. Tel: 0033 1 452 61851

British Embassy is in Dakar. Honoray Consulate, Mavegro Int, Cp100, Bissau, Guinea Bissau. Tel: 201 224 or 201 216. Fax: 201 265.

Refer to the Embassy.

Centro de Informação e Turismo, CP 294, Bissau, Guinea Bissau.

Return ticket required. Requirements may be subject to change at short notice. Consult embassy before departure. Valid passport required by all

Visa required (can be extended in central police station).

Alcohol.

US$12, levied on international departures.

POLIO, TYPHOID: R. MALARIA: Falciparum variety exists throughout the year; resistance to chloroquine has been reported. YELLOW FEVER: Strongly recommended to all visitors. A vaccination certificate must be provided by visitors arriving from infected areas. OTHER: Bilharzia and Rabies. AIDS/HIV prevalent.

W1

Guinea Bissau Peso (GBP) = 100 centavos. Travellers cheques can be cashed at major banks only. US$ are the preferred currency. Credit cards are not accepted except in the top hotels and some banks. ATM AVAILABILITY: Unavailable.

MONEYGRAM: Unavailable.
WESTERN UNION: Unavailable.

AMEX: 0044 1273 696 933
DINERS CLUB: 0044 1252 513 500
MASTERCARD: 001 314 542 7111
VISA: 001 410 581 9994

AMEX: 0044 1273 571 600
THOMAS COOK: not available
VISA: 0044 20 7937 8091

0730-1430 Mon to Fri.

Guinea Bissau is one of the poorest countries in the world. Some hotels are very expensive.

Portuguese. The majority of the population speak Guinea Creole.

Tropical climate. May-Nov is wet season. Dec-Apr is dry season. Temperatures vary with altitude.

Mostly Animist with Muslim and Christian.

Jan 1, 20, Mar 8, Sep 24, Nov 14, Dec 25. Good Fri, end of Ramadan.

Limited electricity supply on 200 volts AC 50 Hz.

Post to Europe will take over a week.

A patriarchal society exists.

FLIGHTS: The national airline provides regular internal flights. SEA/RIVER: most towns are accessible by ship. Coast-hopping ferries operate from the north coast to Bissau. ROADS: Only a fifth are tarred and suitable for all-weather driving. DOCUMENTATION: IDP is recommended though not legally required. A temporary driving licence can be obtained on presentation of a valid British driving licence.

Tourism is developing in Guinea Bissau. Casual wear is acceptable. Social customs should be respected especially in the Muslim areas. PHOTOGRAPHY: It is forbidden to take photos of any public buildings or anything connected with the military. There are minefields in Guinea Bissau left over from the civil war – visitors should not leave designated roads and pathways. There are frequent power blackouts in the capital.

Guinea Republic

CAPITAL: Conakry

GMT

FROM UK: 00224, OUTGOING CODE TO UK: 0044 Most international calls must be made through the operator.

442 959 (Embassy)

No embassy in the UK. Europe: Embassy of the Republic of Guinea, 51 rue de la Faisanderie, 75016 Paris, France. Tel: (1) 47 04 81 48 or 45 53 85 45. Fax: (1) 47 04 57 65.

British Embassy in Dakar. Honorary British Consul (emergencies only), BP 834, Conakry, Guinea. Tel: 45 58 07; Fax: 45 60 20. brit-con.vat@eti.net.gn

Refer to the Embassy in Paris.

Secrétariat d'Etat au Tourisme et à l'Hôtellerie, BP1304, place des Martyrs, Conakry, Guinea. Tel: 442 606.

Return ticket and valid passport required. Requirements may be subject to change at short notice. Consult embassy.

Tourist, transit or business visa required

Narcotics

Departure tax FG9000 or US$5.

Journalists may visit by government invitation only.

POLIO, TYPHOID: R. MALARIA: Present in the falciparum variety; resistance to chloroquine has been reported. YELLOW FEVER: Vaccination is strongly recommended by to all visitors. Those arriving from infected areas over one year of age are required to have a vaccination certificate. OTHER: Bilharzia, river blindness, hepatitis, meningitis and rabies are present.

W1

Guinea Franc (FG) = 100 centimes. NOTE: Import and export of local currency is prohibited. Foreign currency must be declared on arrival. Credit cards, even in Conakry, are strictly limited to a few of the larger hotels and car rental and air ticket payments. MasterCard has limited acceptance in the capital. Travellers cheques can be changed at banks, French francs are the preferred currency. ATM AVAILABILITY: Unavailable.

MONEYGRAM: Unavailable.
WESTERN UNION: 45 11 10.

AMEX: 0044 1273 696 933
DINERS CLUB: 0044 1252 513 500
MASTERCARD: 001 314 542 7111
VISA: 001 410 581 9994

AMEX: 0044 1273 571 600
THOMAS COOK: 0044 1733 318950
VISA: 0044 20 7937 8091

0830-1230 and 1430-1630 Mon-Fri.

Tourist areas tend to be more expensive.

French and several local languages.

Hot and humid climate. Wet season: May-Oct. Dry season: Nov-Apr.

Mostly Muslim with the remainder Christian and Animist.

Jan 1, Apr 3, May 1, Aug 27, Oct 1, Nov 1, Dec 25. Easter, end of Ramadan.

220 Volts, 50 Hz

Post will take over a week to reach Europe.

Patriarchal values exist.

ROADS: Only a very few are suitable for all-weather conditions. Taxis, buses and minibuses are the way to cross into neighbouring countries by land, and you can enter Cote d'Ivoire, Guinea Bissau, Mali and Senegal overland. DOCUMENTATION: IDP is required. RAIL: None. BOAT: You can reach Mali by river boat when the river is high enough, and a fast and luxurious hydrofoil service may start operating again between Conakry and Freetown when the civil war in Sierra Leone is definitely over.

Tourists should not venture out into Conakry at night due to a high level of street violence. Muslim traditions should be respected. Casual dress is acceptable. PHOTOGRAPHY: Permits are no longer required but taking photos of public buildings, bridges, ports or anything connected to the military is prohibited. NOTE: The FCO advises against all travel near the border region with Liberia and Sierra Leone, and visitors should be extremely cautious if travelling outside Conakry.

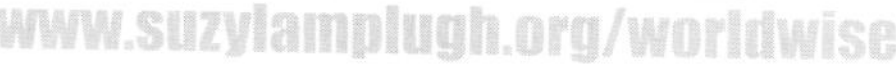

Guyana

CAPITAL: Georgetown

GMT–3

FROM UK: 00592. OUTGOING CODE TO UK: 00144

Ambulance: 56900 (Georgetown only).

High Commission for the Co-operative Republic of Guyana, 3 Palace Court, Bayswater Road, London, W2 4LP. Tel: 020 7229 7684/8. Fax: 020 7727 9809.

British High Commission, PO Box 10849, 44 Main Street, Georgetown, Guyana. Tel: 226 5881. Fax: 225 0671. Consular@georgetown.mail.fco.gov.uk; www.Britaininguyana.org.

Caribbean Tourism, 42 Westminster Palace Gdns, Artillery Row, London SW1P 1RR. Tel: 020 7222 4335. Fax: 020 7222 4325. www.doitcaribbean.com; cto@caribtourism.com

Tourism and Hospitality Association of Guyana, 157 Waterloo Street, Cummingsburg, Georgetown, Guyana. Tel: 225 0807; Fax: 225 0817. thag@networsgy.com

Return ticket and valid passport required. Requirements may change at short notice. Contact the embassy before departure.

Visas not required for full British nationals. Contact the High Commission for an up-to-date list of nationals requiring visas

Narcotics.

GUY$2500, payable in local currency.

POLIO, TYPHOID: R. MALARIA: Exists throughout the year in certain areas in the falciparum variety; resistance to chloroquine has been reported. Sleep under a mosquito net and use insect repellents. YELLOW FEVER: A vaccination certificate is required for travellers arriving from infected countries (contact High Commission for Guyana's list of infected countries). Vaccination is strongly recommended to any traveller planning to travel outside urban areas. Typhoid is present throughout Guyana. Malaria and dengue fever are prevalent in the interior.

W2

Guyana Dollar (Guy$) = 100 cents. Credit cards are not widely accepted in Guyana. Only one bank will issue cash advances against them and only the bigger hotels will accept them. Travellers cheques (in US$) can take a long time to exchange. ATM AVAILABILITY: Unavailable.

MONEYGRAM: 165 then 800 592 3688 WESTERN UNION: (2) 751 41.

AMEX: 00144 1273 696 933 DINERS CLUB: 00144 1252 513 500 MASTERCARD: 1 314 542 7111 VISA: 1 410 581 9994

AMEX: 00144 1273 571 600 THOMAS COOK: 00144 1733 318950 VISA: 00144 20 7937 8091

0800-1200 Mon to Thur, 0800-1200 and 1530-1700 Fri.

Relatively inexpensive. Most accommodation is located in populated areas.

English. Hindi, Urdu, Creole and Amerindian are also spoken.

Hot tropical climate, with the most rain in Nov-Jan and Apr-July.

Christian, Hindu and Muslim.

Jan 1, Feb 23, May 1,5, first Mon in Jul and Aug, Dec 25, 26. Islamic festivals, Easter, Diwali.

110 Volts AC, 60Hz

7-10 days. Recorded delivery is recommended.

A diverse and sometimes volatile mixture of Latin, African and Caribbean cultures.

FLIGHTS: The only reliable means of travelling into the interior. ROAD: All-weather roads are concentrated in the eastern coastal strip. Most journeys will involve ferries, which may create delays. BUS: Regular but crowded services operate in Georgetown. Avoid using minibuses, which are extremely prone to accidents. TAXI: Recommended at night, but only prebooked taxis from reputable firms. Do not hail from the roadside. A supplement is added to evening fares and for long journeys fares should be agreed in advance.

Do not expose valuable possessions at any time and avoid showing signs of wealth. Street crimes take place in the major business and shopping districts of Georgetown, in and around the markets of Stabroek and Bourda, and near hotels used by foreign visitors. The areas adjacent to the sea wall and the National Park in Georgetown have been the scenes of crimes ranging from pickpocketing to violent assaults, and should be considered dangerous, especially at night.

CAPITAL: Port-au-Prince

GMT –5.

FROM UK: 00 509. OUTGOING CODE TO UK: 0044

Police: 114; Ambulance: 118.

No embassy in the UK. EUROPE: Embassy of the Republic of Haiti, BP25, 160a avenue Louise, B1050 Brussels, Belgium. Tel: (2) 649 7381. Fax: (2) 640 6080.

British Consulate, PO Box 1302 Hotel Montana, rue Cardoza, Port-au-Prince, Haiti. Tel: 257 3969; Fax: 257 4048, 573 969, 574 048.

Caribbean Tourism, 42 Westminster Palace Gdns, Artillery Row, London SW1P 1RR. Tel. 020 7222 4335. Fax: 020 7222 4325. www.doitcaribbean.com; cto@caribtourism.com

La Secrétairerie d'Etat au Tourisme, 8, Rue Légitime, Champ de Mars, Port-au-Prince, Haïti. Tel: 00509 2215960; Fax: 00509 2228659. info@haititourisme.org www.haititourisme.org/

Return ticket required. Requirements may be subject to short-term change: contact embassy. Valid passport required by all.

Visa not required by nationals of the UK. Visitors are given a card on arrival, which must be kept for presentation to immigration officials on departure.

Coffee, matches, methylated spirits, pork, all meat products from Brazil and the Dominican Republic.

US$25 or 15 Haitian Gourdes. Transit passengers and children under 2 years are exempt.

POLIO, TYPHOID: R. MALARIA: Exists throughout the year in the falciparum variety below 300 m. Dengue fever and hepatitis are common. YELLOW FEVER: R. A vaccination certificate is required from all passengers coming from infected areas. OTHER: Bancroftian filariasis, rabies.

W1

Gourde (Gde) = 100 centimes. EXCHANGE: US$ accepted and exchanged everywhere. Most credit cards may be used in major hotels, and in some shops and businesses in the capital. Travellers cheques are accepted in banks and major shops. US$ is the preferred currency. ATMS: Unavailable.

MONEYGRAM: 183 then 800 592 3688. WESTERN UNION: 22 7876.

AMEX: 0044 1273 696 933
DINERS CLUB: 0044 1252 513 500
MASTERCARD: 1 314 542 7111
VISA:1 410 581 9994

AMEX: 0044 1273 571 600
THOMAS COOK: 1800 223 7373
VISA: 0044 20 7937 8091

0900-1300 Mon to Fri.

Accommodation is limited in Haiti, varying form luxury hotels to modest small inns and guesthouses.

French and Creole. English is widely spoken in tourist areas.

Tropical climate with high humidity. Intermittent rain throughout the year. Hill resorts are much cooler. The hurricane season lasts from Jun to Nov.

Roman Catholic. Protestant minorities.

Jan 1,2, Apr 7, 14, May 18, 22, Aug 15, Oct 8, 17, 24, Nov 1,2,18, Dec 5, 25. Carnival week before Lent, Easter, Ascension Day, Corpus Christi.

110 volts AC, 60 Hz.

Up to 1 week.

A multicultural heritage ranging from Christianity, Roman Catholicism and Voodoo plays a major part in the roles of women.

ROADS: All-weather roads have been constructed. BUS: Operate on an unscheduled basis. TAXI: Station wagons run between the capital and the large towns. CAR HIRE: Available independently or through the hotels. Petrol can be scarce outside the capital. DOCUMENTATION: Some national licences are accepted but IDP is recommended.

RISK of personal crime and violence, especially for tourists, due to their relative affluence. Be on your guard and do not carry valuables or wear jewellery. It is estimated that 85% of the population live below the poverty line. Do not leave your accommodation after dark and do not travel to rural areas. Avoid large gatherings and political demonstrations. The FCO advises against all holiday and other non-essential travel to Haiti. Visitors who must go are advised to leave travel plans and photocopies of travel documents with friends or relatives in the UK.

Honduras

CAPITAL: Tegucigalpa

GMT –6

FROM UK: 00 504. OUTGOING CODE TO UK: 0044

Police: 119; Fire: 198; Ambulance: 37 8654.

Embassy of the Republic of Honduras and Consulate General, 115 Gloucester Place, London, W1H 3PJ. Tel: 020 7486 4880. Fax: 020 7486 64550.

British Embassy, Apartado Postal 290, Edificio Palmira, 3º Piso, Colonia Palmira, Tegucigalpa, Honduras, CA. Tel: 325 429 or 320 612. Fax: 325 480.

Refer to the Embassy.

Instituto Hondureño De Turismo, Apartado Postal 3261, Centro Guanacaste, Barrio Guanacaste, Tegucigalpa, Honduras. Tel: 383 975. Fax: 382 102.
hondurastips@ honduras.com;
www.hondurastips.honduras.com

Return ticket required. Requirements may change at short notice. Contact the embassy before departure. Valid passport required by all.

Visa not required.

Narcotics.

US$10 is levied on all passengers over 12 years of age.

POLIO, TYPHOID: R. MALARIA: Exists throughout the year in the vivax variety within certain regions. YELLOW FEVER: A vaccination certificate is required from all travellers arriving from infected areas. OTHER: Cholera, rabies

W1

Lempira (L) = 100 centavos. All credit cards are accepted. Travellers cheques in US dollars are recommended. ATM AVAILABILITY: Over 20 locations.

MONEYGRAM: 123 then 800 592 5755 (Spanish).
WESTERN UNION: 39 0037.

AMEX: 0044 1273 696 933
DINERS CLUB: 0044 1252 513 500
MASTERCARD: 1 314 542 7111
VISA: 1 410 581 9994

AMEX: 1801 964 6665
THOMAS COOK: 1 800 223 7373
VISA: 0044 20 7937 8091

0900-1500 Mon to Fri, some open 0900-1100 Sat.

Relatively inexpensive. Accommodation is graded. Food and transport are also inexpensive.

Spanish. English is also spoken.

Tropical climate which is cooler in the mountains. Rainy season is May–Oct. The North coast is usually very hot with rain all year.

Roman Catholic, Evangelist and Mormon.

Jan 1, Apr 14, May 1, Sep 15, Oct 3, 12, 21, Dec 25. Easter.

110/220 Volts AC, 60Hz

7 days.

There are strong Spanish influences but the majority of the population are Mestizo, leading mainly an agricultural way of life. Many rural communities can still be found leading a relatively unchanged traditional lifestyle. Usual precautions should be taken by women travellers.

FLIGHTS: Local airlines operate services between principle towns, which is much more convenient for business visitors. ROAD: Over half the roads are suitable for all weather conditions. BUS: Services operate to most large towns but they are well used and booking in advance is essential. TAXI: Usually unmetered so agree the fare in advance. CAR HIRE: Available at the airport. DOCUMENTATION: Foreign and international licences are accepted.

Exercise caution - beware of bag slashing and muggings. Watch out for poisonous snakes, alligators, scorpions, wasps and other stinging insects. Beachwear should not be worn in towns. Visitors should register with the Embassy or consulate on arrival.

GMT + 8.

FROM UK: 00 852. OUTGOING CODE TO UK: 00144

All services: 999

Chinese Embassy, 4951 Portland Place, London W1N 4JL. Tel: 020 7636 9375. www.chineseembassy.org.uk

British Consulate General, 1 Supreme Court Road, Central Hong Kong. PO Box 528. Tel: 2901 3000; Fax: 2901 3204. consular@britishconsulate.org.hk www.britishconsulate.org.hk/

Hong Kong Tourist Association, 6 Grafton Street, London W1X 3LB. Tel: 020 7533 7100; Fax: 020 7533 7111. hktalon@hkta.org

Hong Kong Tourist Association, 9-11th floor, Citicorp Centre, 18 Whitfield Road, North Point, Hong Kong. Tel: 28 07 65 43. Fax: 28 06 03 03. info@hkta.org www.hkta.org

Valid passport required by all.

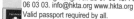

Visitors to Hong Kong can stay for up to six months without a visa. Visitors travelling on a British passport to mainland China via Hong Kong must obtain a Chinese visa before arrival at the border. Visas are not available on arrival at the Chinese border for British passport holders.

Non-prescribed drugs without a doctor's certificate.

Adults pay HK$ 50 in local currency.

POLIO, TYPHOID: R. MALARIA: There may occasionally be a risk in rural areas.

Hong Kong Dollar (HK$) = 100 cents. All credit cards and travellers cheques are widely accepted. Pound sterling and US dollars are the preferred currency. ATM AVAILABILITY: Over 1,000 locations.

MONEYGRAM: 001 800 66639472.
WESTERN UNION: 2528 5631.

AMEX: 00144 1273 696 933
DINERS CLUB: 2860 1888
MASTERCARD: 800 966 677
VISA: 800 967 025

AMEX: 800 963 403
THOMAS COOK: 00161 3 693 2952
VISA: 0044 20 7937 8091

0900-1630 Mon to Fri and 0900-1330 Sat.

Although Hong Kong is a tax haven, commodities and accommodation can be expensive. However, transport is cheap and some luxury items are often cheaper than in Europe.

Chinese and English, Cantonese is most widely spoken.

Winter: influenced by the north-northeast monsoon. Summer: is influenced by the south-west monsoon. Summers are very hot with the rainy season June–Aug. Spring and autumn are warm with occasional rain and cooler evenings. Winters can be cold.

Buddhist, Confucian, Taoist with Christian and Muslim minorities, but there are also places of worship for most other religious groups.

Jan 1, May 1, Jul 1, Oct 1, Dec 25, 26. Chinese New Year and other festivals.

220 volts AC, 50 Hz.

Airmail to Europe takes 3–5 days.

Hong Kong has a unique cultural mix, of Chinese and western ideologies. Women, depending on their heritage, will conform accordingly. Generally all customs coexist. There are no particular dangers for foreign female travellers.

RAIL: More expensive than the ferry, but quicker. BUS: Services are often very crowded. ROAD: Traffic moves on the left in Hong Kong, and the streets are very congested in the daytime. Seat belts are compulsory. The use of handheld mobile phones whilst driving is strictly forbidden. DOCUMENTATION: IDP is recommended but not legally required.

Hong Kong is now part of the People's Republic of China, but it remains a Special Administrative Region with its own immigration controls. Contact the Chinese Embassy or Tourist Office prior to travelling for up-to-date information on passport and visa requirements. Typhoons very occasionally hit Hong Kong between April and October and may cause flooding and landslides. Pickpocketing and other street crime occurs in Hong Kong. British passports are very desirable to thieves, so visitors should take extra care of passports, as well as credit cards and money in crowded areas.

Hungary

CAPITAL: Budapest

GMT +1 (GMT +2 in the summer)

FROM UK: 0036. OUTGOING CODE TO UK: 0044

Police: 107; Ambulance: 104; Fire: 105. Tourists who become victims of crime in Hungary can call a multilingual reporting line, 01 438 8080 from 8am to 8pm, and after hours on 06 8066 0044.

Embassy of the Hungarian Republic, 35 Eaton Place, London SW1X 8BY. Tel: 020 7235 5218. Fax: 020 7823 1348. Consulate Tel: 020 7235 2664 or 0891 171 204 (visa enquiries). www.huemblon.org.uk/front.htm

British Embassy, Harmincad utca 6, Budapest 1051, Hungary. Tel: (1) 266 2888; Fax: (1) 429 6360. info@britemb.hu www.britishembassy.hu

Hungarian National Tourist Office, 46 Eaton Place, London SW18 4XE. Public enquiries in UK only: Tel: 0891 171 200; Fax: 0891 669 970. htlondon@hungarytourism.hu www.hungarytourism.hu/

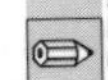
Hungarian Tourism Service, Margit körút 85, 6th floor, H1024 Budapest. Tel: 0036 1 3751682; Fax: 0036 1 3753819. htbudapest@hungarytourism.hu www.hungarytourism.hu/

Requirements may be subject to short-term change. Contact embassy before departure. Valid passport required. All passports must be valid for at least 6 months.

Visa not required by British nationals for a stay of up to 6 months.

Narcotics and firearms.

Rabies

Hungarian Forint (HUF) = 100 fillér. Exchange: banks, hotels, airports, railway stations, some restaurants. Import and export of local currency is limited to HUF 10,000. Retain all exchange receipts. All major credit cards and travellers cheques are widely accepted. Deutsche Mark is the preferred currency. ATM AVAILABILITY: Over 1000 locations.

MONEYGRAM: 00 800 12249.
WESTERN UNION: (01) 267 4282.

AMEX: 0044 1273 696 933
DINERS CLUB: 06 40 CITI 24
MASTERCARD: 06 800 12517

VISA: 06 800 14352
AMEX: 800 11128
THOMAS COOK: 800 11501
VISA: 0044 20 7937 8091

0900-1400 Mon to Fri.

Western Europeans will not experience great disparity in local and Western prices.

Hungarian (Magyar). German is widely spoken. Some English and French may also be spoken, mainly in the West.

June-Aug. is usually very warm. Spring and autumn are mild and winters are very cold. There is rainfall throughout the year.

Mostly Roman Catholic with some Protestant. Eastern Orthodox and Jewish minorities are also present.

Jan 1, Mar 15, May 1, Aug 20, Oct 23, Nov 1,25, Dec 25,26. Easter, Whitsun.

220 volts Ac, 50 Hz.

3-7 days to other European destinations.

Traditional roles persist in rural areas. However, modern influences developing in urban regions.

RAIL: All main cities are connected by regular services but facilities are often inadequate. Concessions are available to groups of six or more and the young and elderly. ROAD: Generally the road system is good. BUS: Services link Budapest with the major provincial towns. CAR HIRE: Available at large hotels and the main airports. DOCUMENTATION: Pink UK licence is accepted, but IDP is required if a green licence is held.

Petty crime is rife in Budapest, especially in tourist areas. Very few people speak English except in large hotels and restaurants. A knowledge of German is very useful. Usual social courtesies apply. Both Christian and surname should be used in introductions. PHOTOGRAPHY: Do not take photographs of anything connected with the military. Other restrictions will be signposted. Under a bilateral agreement British visitors to Hungary are entitled to emergency medical treatment free of charge. You must be able to show some form of identity if requested by the police, so it's advisable to carry your passport at all times. Foreigners may experience problems with excessive billing and a threat of violence at some nightclubs featuring 'adult entertainment'.

CAPITAL: Reykjavik

GMT

FROM UK: 00354. OUTGOING CODE TO UK: 0044

All services: 112

Embassy of the Republic of Iceland, 2 Hans Street, London SW1X 0JE. Tel: 020 7259 3999; Fax: 020 7245 6949.
icemb.london@utn.stjr.is www.iceland.org.uk/

British Embassy, Laufasvegur 49, 121 Reykjavik, Iceland. Postal address: PO Box 460, 121 Reykjavik, Iceland. Tel: 00354 550 5100; Fax: 00354 550 5105.
britemb@centrum.is

Iceland Tourist Bureau, 3rd Floor, 172 Tottenham Court Road, London W1P 0LY.

Iceland Tourist Board/ Ferðamálaráð Íslands, Laekjargata 3, 101 Reykjavik, Iceland. Tel 00354 535 5500. Fax: 00354 535 5501.
info@icetourist.is www.icetourist.is/

Regulations may change at short notice and you are advised to contact the relevant consular authority before finalising travel arrangements. Passports with at least 3 months validity are required.

Visa required.

Uncooked meat.

Icelandic Krona (1Kr) = 100 aurar. The major credit cards are widely accepted. Traveller's cheques are also widely used and the preferred currency is US Dollars. ATM AVAILABILITY: over 500 locations at main banks.

MONEYGRAM: 800 9001 then 800 592 3688
WESTERN UNION: no local number

AMEX: 0044 1273 696 933. DINERS CLUB: 0044 1252 513 500. MASTERCARD: 001 314 542 7111. VISA: 001 410 581 9994

AMEX: 0044 1273 571 600
THOMAS COOK: 0044 1733 502 995
VISA: 0044 20 7937 8091

0915–1600 Mon to Fri.

Can be very expensive, as with other Scandinavian countries.

Icelandic. English and Danish are also widely spoken.

Summers are mild and winters are rather cold. From the end of May to the beginning of August there are nearly 24 hours of perpetual daylight in Reykjavik, whilst in the northern part of the country the sun rarely sets at all. The weather is highly changeable at all times of the year.

Lutheran with a Roman Catholic minority.

Jan 1, Thu after Apr 19, May 1, first Mon in Aug, Dec 24,25,26,31. Easter, Ascension Day, Whitsun.

220 volts AC, 50 Hz.

Efficient airmail service to Europe.

Men and women are considered equal.

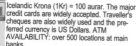

ROAD: Roads serve all settlements. Studded tyres are compulsory on vehicles Oct–Apr. The 900-mile ring road (Highway 1) that encircles the country is tarmacked, but many other roads outside the capital, especially those to the interior, are dirt tracks. Many are impassible until July due to muddy conditions caused by melting snow. Headlights must be kept on even in the daytime, and seat-belts are compulsory. Check with Vegagerdin, the office in charge of roads, Tel: 00354 563 1400, before departure, who can advise on weather and then state of roads. www.vegag.is/indexe.html gives up to date information on all roads in Iceland. RAIL: There is no rail system. FLIGHTS: connect 12 local airports.

People who wish to travel off-road during winter should contact local authorities. Visitors who wish to tour the Skeithararsandur Sands icebergs are advised to do so only in the company of a local guide because of quicksands in the area. Take special care when touring Iceland's natural attractions, which include glaciers, volcanic craters, lava fields, ice caves, hot springs, boiling mud pots, geysers, waterfalls and glacial rivers. There are few warning signs or barriers to alert visitors to the potential hazards.
Casual wear is not suitable for social functions. Visitors should note that downtown Reykjavik can become especially disorderly on weekend evenings. Hotel accommodation in Iceland is very limited and is mostly fully booked in the summer.

India

CAPITAL: New Delhi

GMT +5.30.

FROM UK: 0091. OUTGOING CODE TO UK: 0044

Contact the hotel reception.

Office of the High Commissioner for India, India House, Aldwych, London WC2B 4NA. Tel: 020 7836 8484. Fax: 020 7836 4331. www.hcilondon.org/

British High Commission, Shanti Path, Chanakyapuri, New Delhi 110021, India. Tel: (11) 687 2161. Fax: (11) 687 2161. or (11) 687 2882.
nedel.conqry@NewDelhi.mail.fco.gov.uk
www.ukinindia.com

Deputy High Commissions in Mumbai, Kolkata and Madras.

Government of India Tourist Office, 7 Cork Street, London W1X 2LN. Tel: 020 7437 3677 or 01233 211 999 (brochure request line). Fax: 020 7494 1048.

Government of India Tourist Office 88, Janpath, New Delhi 10001. Tel: 0091 11 3320005.

Requirements may be subject to short-term change. Contact the relevant authority before departure. Valid passport required by all

Visa required by all. Ensure your visa is valid for the areas you wish to travel.

Plants, gold and silver bullion and coins not in current use are prohibited.

RS750 payable, in local currency, on departure.

Entry is refused to nationals of a) Afghanistan if their passport or ticket shows evidence of transit or boarding in Pakistan and b) British passport holders, including those of Indian origin, who are being deported to India without their consent.

POLIO, TYPHOID: R. MALARIA: Exists in the vivax variety throughout the year in the whole country excluding parts of Himachal Pradesh, Jammu and Kashmir and Sikkim. High resistance to chloroquine has been reported in the falciparum variety.YELLOW FEVER: A vaccination certificate is required from everyone coming or who have transited through infected areas.
OTHER: Bubonic plague, meningitis, tick-borne relapsing fever, dengue fever, visceral leishmaniasis, filariasis and hepatitis B.

W1

Rupee = 100 paise. Exchange: At banks or authorised exchangers. Import and export of local currency is prohibited. All major credit cards are accepted. Traveller's cheques can be widely exchanged. Pound sterling and US dollars are the preferred currencies. ATM AVAILABILITY: Over 150 locations.

MONEYGRAM: 000 117 then 800 592 3688.
WESTERN UNION: (022) 838 2038.

AMEX: 0044 1273 696 933
DINERS CLUB: 0044 1252 513500
MASTERCARD: 001 314 542 7111
VISA: 000 117 800 847 2911

AMEX: 011 614 5920
THOMAS COOK: 0044 1733 318950
VISA: 0044 20 7937 8091

1000-1400 Mon to Fri,1000-1200 Sat.

Caters for all visitors and budgets. Accommodation ranges from international standard to youth hostels. All commodities are inexpensive in comparison with other countries.

The universal national language is English. There are 14 official languages in India. About 50% of the population are Hindi speakers. The Muslim population generally speak Urdu.

Hot tropical weather with variations from region to region. Coolest weather lasts Nov–mid Mar, with cool fresh mornings and evenings and dry sunny days. Really hot weather occurs Apr–June. Monsoon rains occur in most regions during the summer.

Most of the population is Hindu. The remainder are Muslim, Sikh, Christian, Buddhist and a minority of others.

Jan 1,26, Aug 15, Oct 2, Dec 25. Hindu and Islamic festivals, Good Friday.

Usually 220 volts AC, 50 Hz. Plugs are of the round 2- and 3- pin type.

Airmail to Western Europe takes up to 1 week. Stamps are sold in hotels.

Women should dress conservatively and respect the religious customs which are practised in the different regions. Usual precautions should be taken and it is inadvisable to walk alone at night. Indian women prefer not to shake hands. Many do not drink alcohol.

AIR: The domestic airline connects over 70 cities. Special fares are available throughout the year.
ROAD: Driving on Indian roads is hazardous, with badly lit and poorly maintained buses and trucks the cause of numerous accidents.
SEA/RIVER: Services are often seasonal and suspended during the monsoon period. One particularly attractive route is the 'backwaters' excursion in the vicinity of Cochin.
RAIL: The network covers much of the country and is relatively inexpensive.

The Foreign and Commonwealth Office advises against travelling to Jammu and Kashmir and the north-east because of civil unrest.
Major tourist destinations are quiet. However, there is a serious risk of kidnapping in the state of Jammu and Kashmir. Foreigners have been held at gunpoint and therefore visitors are advised against travelling to this area. Some travel agents in India claim this area is safe for tourists.
The only official India–Pakistan border crossing point is between Atari, India, and Wagah, Pakistan.
Check with local tourist offices before venturing away from tourist areas, as foreigners are forbidden entry to some parts of the country.
Severe penalties exist for the possession of drugs.
Footwear should be removed when entering houses or places of worship. Hindus are vegetarian. Religion plays a large role in everyday life and visitors are expected to respect the customs and dress code followed by Indian people.
Crime is rife in Delhi, with British passports a particular target for thieves.

Indonesia

CAPITAL: Jakarta

GMT +7 (West); +8 (Central); +9 (East).

FROM UK: 0062. OUTGOING CODE TO UK: 0044

Police:110; Fire: 113; Ambulance: 118.

Embassy of the Republic of Indonesia, Consular Section, 38a Adams Row, London W1X 9AD. Tel: 020 7499 7661; Fax:: 020 7491 4993. kbri@indolondon.freeserve.co.uk www.indonesianembassy.org.uk/

British Embassy, Jalan M. H.Thamrin 75, Jakarta 10310, Indonesia. Tel: (21) 315 6264. www.britainindonesia.or.id/

Indonesian Tourist Promotion Office, 3-4 Hanover Street, London, W1R 9HH. Tel: 020 7493 0030. Fax 020 7493 1747. www.indonesiatourism.com/

Directorate-General of Tourism, 16/19 Jalan Merdeka Barat, Jakarta 10110, Indonesia. Tel: (21) 386 0822. Fax: (21) 386 7589.

Return ticket and valid passport required by all. Requirements may change at short notice. Contact the embassy.

Tourist visas not required, provided your stay does not exceed 60 days.

Television sets, Chinese publications, medicines and pornography. Cameras and jewellery must be declared on arrival.

Varies according to airport Rp25,000, payable in local currency, from Denpasar.

Portuguese nationals will be refused admission under all circumstances. Nationals of Israel will require special approval.

POLIO, TYPHOID: R. MALARIA: Exists in the falciparum variety everywhere except the main tourist resorts of Bali, Java and large cities. YELLOW FEVER: A vaccination certificate is required if arriving from infected areas. OTHER: Bilharzia, rabies.

W1

Rupiah (Rp) = 100 sen. EXCHANGE: Not a problem in tourist areas, may be more difficult in less commercialised places. Import and export of local currency is limited to Rp 50,000. Traveller's cheques are easily exchanged in large hotels and banks. Preferred cheque currency is US dollars. Visa, MasterCard and Amex are all accepted, Diners Club has a more limited use. ATM AVAILABILITY: Over 1300 locations.

MONEYGRAM: 001 800 011 0945
WESTERN UNION: 021 601 5560

AMEX: 0044 1273 696 933
DINERS CLUB: 021 570 1255 or 021 570 6711
MASTERCARD: 001 803 1 887 0623
VISA: 001 803 44 1600

AMEX: 001 803 61005
THOMAS COOK: 0044 1733 318950
VISA: 0044 20 7937 8091

0800-1500 Mon to Fri.

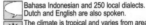

Tourist resorts are more expensive, although cheap accommodation can be found in the form of bungalows in the main resorts. Provisions may be difficult to find in rural areas.

Bahasa Indonesian and 250 local dialects. Dutch and English are also spoken.

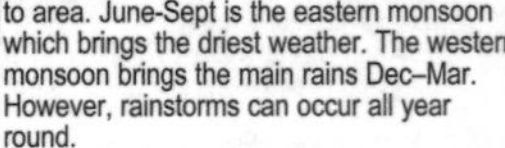
The climate is tropical and varies from area to area. June-Sept is the eastern monsoon which brings the driest weather. The western monsoon brings the main rains Dec–Mar. However, rainstorms can occur all year round.

Mainly Muslim. Christian, Hindu, Buddhism and Animist beliefs.

Jan 1, Aug 17, Dec 25. Islamic festivals, Easter, Ascension Day.

110 Volts AC, 50Hz, but may vary between areas.

Up to 10 days.

Women should dress modestly, although dress in tourist areas is likely to be more relaxed. This is a male-oriented country.

FLIGHTS: Good internal air system. ROADS: Good roads within Java but less so in Bali and Sumatra. The other islands have poor road systems. TAXI: Available in all main cities, all are metered and cheap, but keep to taxis supplied by reputable companies. DOCUMENTATION: IDP is required.

Never pass or accept anything with your left hand. There is very little violent crime but pickpockets are common. Visitors should be alert to the media and avoid large gatherings and political demonstrations. Nightclubs in Jakarta have been the target of bombs in the recent past, and visitors should be ready to leave at the least sign of trouble. The FCO advise against travel to West Timor, where UN workers have been killed. Bali is relatively safe and tourist facilities operate normally.

CAPITAL: Tehran

GMT +3.5 (GMT +4.5 during the summer).

FROM UK: 0098. OUTGOING CODE TO UK: 0044.

Not present.

Iranian Consulate, 50 Kensington Court, Kensington High Street, London W8 5DB. Tel: 020 7937 5225; Fax: 020 7938 1615. info@iranembassy.org.uk www.iranembassy.org.uk/

British Embassy, PO Box 113654474, 143 Ferdowsi Avenue, Tehran 11344, Iran. Tel: (21) 6705011; Fax:: (21) 6710761.

Refer to Consulate.

Return ticket required. Requirements may be subject to short-term change. Contact the relevant authority before departure.Valid passport required by all

Visa required

Alcohol, aerial photographic equipment, transmitter and receiver apparatus, indecent photos, films, records and any fashion magazines.

RL 70,000, payable in local currency. Transit passengers remaining in the airport and those under 7 years of age are exempt.

Nationals of Israel. Women dressed immodestly will be refused entry.

POLIO, TYPHOID: R. MALARIA: Exists in the vivax variety in certain provinces. Resistance to chloroquine has been reported in the falciparum variety. OTHER: Cutaneous leishmaniasis, Tick-borne relapsing fever and bilharzia.

W2

Iranian Rial (RL) = 100 Dinars. Foreign visitors must convert the equivalent of US$ 300 into Iranian Rials. Declare all currency on arrival. Credit cards and traveller's cheques are not accepted. ATM AVAILABILITY: Unavailable.

MONEYGRAM: Unavailable.
WESTERN UNION: Unavailable.

AMEX: 0044 1273 696933
DINERS CLUB: No local number.
MASTERCARD: No local number.
VISA: No local number.

AMEX: 0044 1273 571 600
THOMAS COOK: No local number.
VISA: No local number.

0900-1600 Sat to Wed, 0900-1200 Thur. Closed Fri.

Commodities are quite limited outside the main city of Tehran. The economy is in a state of transition following the war with Iraq and the US embargo on Iranian oil.

Persian (Farsi). Arabic in Khuzestan and Turkish in the Northwest. English, French and German are often spoken by businessmen and officials.

Summers are hot and dry and winters are harsh.

Predominantly Islamic (Shia) with a minority of Sunnis. Also Zoroastrians, Bahais, Armenian and Assyrian Christians.

Feb 11, Mar 20, 21, 25, Apr 1, 2. All Islamic festivals.

220 volts AC, 50 Hz.

At least 2 weeks to Western Europe.

Women travelling alone should be prepared to adjust to the local code if they want to avoid problems. Dress should be discreet and conservative. It is advisable to befriend local women.

ROAD: There is an extensive road network but the quality is unreliable. BUS: Cheap and comfortable although may be erratic. TAXIS: Available in all cities. CAR HIRE: Available in all cities and airports. DOCUMENTATION: IDP and personal insurance is required. All motorists must possess a carnet de passage or pay a large deposit.

Western influences are discouraged. Violent crime is almost unheard of but the usual precautions should still be taken. Particular care should be taken not to offend against the Islamic religion, even the smallest ways, such as a male visitor speaking to an Iranian woman. PHOTOGRAPHY near military installations is strictly prohibited. The FCO advises visitors to avoid the border areas with Afghanistan and Iraq, and against travelling overland to Pakistan.

Iraq

CAPITAL: Baghdad

GMT +3 (GMT +4 during the summer).

FROM UK: 00964. OUTGOING CODE TO UK: 0044

Not present.

Iraqi Interests Section, Jordanian Embassy, 21 Queen's Gate, London SW7 5JG. Tel: 020 7585 7141/6. Fax: 020 7584 7716.

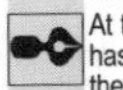
At the time of writing, the United Kingdom has no diplomatic relations with Iraq, and there is no diplomatic or consular service.

Tourists are not permitted to enter to Iraq at the present time.

Return ticket required. Requirements may be subject to short-term change. Contact the relevant authority before departure. Valid passport required by all.

Visa required.

Many types of fruits and plants, souvenirs in amounts considered to be of commercial value and electrical items other than personal effects.

Departure tax ID 2000, payable in local currency.

Holders of Israeli passports or other passports containing Israeli visas. US passports are not currently valid for travel to or in Iraq without special validation being required

POLIO, TYPHOID: R. MALARIA: Exists entirely in the vivax variety between May and November. YELLOW FEVER: A vaccination certificate is required from travellers arriving from infected areas. OTHER: Visceral leishmaniasis, bilharzia, Crimean Congo fever, rabies.

W1

Iraqi Dinar (ID) = 20 dirhams = 1000 fils. NOTE: Import of local currency is allowed up to ID 25. Export of local currency is limited to ID 5. Credit cards and traveller's cheques are not accepted. ATM AVAILABILITY: Unavailable.

MONEYGRAM: Unavailable.
WESTERN UNION: Unavailable.

AMEX: 0044 1273 696933
DINERS CLUB: No local number.
MASTERCARD: No local number.
VISA: No local number.

AMEX: No local number.
THOMAS COOK: No local number.
VISA: No local number.

0800-1200 Sat to Wed, 0800-1100 Thur. Banks close at 1000 during Ramadan.

Since the Gulf War and the imposition of United Nations sanctions, Iraq's economy has become hyperinflated.

Mostly Arabic. Some Kurdish, Turkish and Aramaic.

Summers are hot and dry, winters are warm with some rain.

Sunni Muslim and Shia Muslim with Druze and Christian minorities.

Jan 1, 6, Feb 8, Apr 17, May 1, Jul 14,17, Aug 8. All Islamic festivals.

220 volts AC, 50 Hz.

Usually takes 5-10 days between Europe and Iraq but can take much longer.

Women are greatly influenced by the Muslim religion and are often veiled.

ROAD: BUS: Services run between Baghdad and other main cities. TAXI: Available in the cities. Fares should be agreed in advance. Metered taxis charge twice the amount shown on the meter. CAR HIRE: Available at the airport and in Baghdad. DOCUMENTATION: IDP is required and third-party insurance is necessary.

EXTREME RISK. Travelling to Iraq is strongly discouraged by virtually all governments. Visitors should respect the Islamic religion and act accordingly. Avoid taking photographs.

Ireland (Republic of)

CAPITAL: Dublin

GMT (GMT +1 during the summer)

FROM UK: 00353. OUTGOING CODE TO UK: 0044.

All services: 999 or 112. Medical services Freephone 1800 661 771.

Embassy of the Republic of Ireland, 17 Grosvenor Place, London SW1X 7HR. Tel: 020 7235 2171. Fax: 020 7245 6961. Passports – Tel: 020 7245 9033. Fax: 020 7493 9065.

British Embassy, 29 Merrion Road, Dublin 4, Ireland. Tel: 01 205 3700; Fax: 01 205 3890. bembassy@internetireland.ie www.britishembassy.ie/

Irish Tourist Board, 150-151 New Bond Street, London W1Y 0AQ. Tel: 020 7493 3201. Fax: 020 7493 9065.

Bord Fáilte Eireann, Baggot Street Bridge, Dublin 2, Ireland. Information Service, PO Box 273, Dublin 8. Tel: 00353 1 602 4000; Fax: 00353 1 602 4100. www.ireland.travel.ie

Return ticket required. Requirements may be subject to short term change. Contact the relevant authority before departure.Valid passport required by all except nationals of EU countries provided they carry a national ID card. British nationals visiting Ireland do not require a passport to enter the country, but airlines are insisting that passengers have reliable photographic identification.

Visa not required

Narcotics.

Euro 8, payable on all departures.

Euro = 100 cents. All major credit cards and travellers cheques are accepted throughout Ireland. Pound sterling is the preferred currency. ATM AVAILABILITY: Approx. 1000 locations.

MONEYGRAM: 00 800 66639472
WESTERN UNION: 1 800 395 395

AMEX: 0044 1273 696 933
DINERS CLUB: 0044 1252 513 500
MASTERCARD: 001800 557 378
VISA: 001 410 581 9994

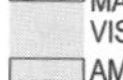
AMEX: 0044 1273 571 600
THOMAS COOK: 0044 1733 318950
VISA: 0044 20 7937 8091

1000–1600 Mon to Fri. Banks may stay open longer in Dublin (till 1700 on Thur) and in other parts of the country.

Food and drink can be quite expensive. However bed and breakfast and campsites offer cheaper accommodation.

Irish (Gaelic) is the official language and is mainly spoken in the west. English is more widely spoken.

Rain falls all year. Spring and autumn are very mild. Summers are warm, winters are much cooler.

Roman Catholic. Protestant minority.

Jan 1, Mar 17, first Mon in May, Jun, Aug, last Mon in Oct, Dec 25,26. Easter, Ascension Day, Corpus Christi.

220 volts AC, 50 Hz.

Irish postage stamps must be used on all mail. Poste restante correspondence is available.

Usual precautions should be followed. No additional problems should be encountered.

RAIL: Extensive network between the main cities. ROAD: The network links all parts of Ireland. TAXI: Services available in the main cities. BUS: A nationwide network of buses serves all the main cities but services to remote areas will be infrequent. CAR HIRE: Available at the major airports and seaports and large hotels. DOCUMENTATION: Owners taking their own cars into Ireland require the vehicles registration book, nationality plates, insurance for the Republic and a full EU licence or IDP. A green card is strongly recommended.

The Irish are a very gregarious people and usually have very close community bonds. Visitors will find people very friendly. Casual wear is acceptable. Dublin is a bustling, booming city with an exciting nightlife. Normal precautions should be taken, as petty thieves operate amidst the otherwise friendly crowds. Theft from cars is on the increase. Medical form E111 is valid for emergency treatment but other health services must be paid for. Full health insurance is therefore recommended.

CAPITAL: Jerusalem

GMT +2 (GMT +3 during the summer).

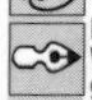
FROM UK: 00972 . OUTGOING CODE TO UK: 0044

Fire / Police: 100; Ambulance: 101.

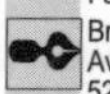
Embassy of Israel, 2 Palace Green, London W8 4QB. Tel: 020 7957 9500. Fax: 020 7957 9577. Consular Section: 15A Old Court Place, London W8 4QB. Tel: 020 7957 9516. Fax: 020 7957 9577.

British Embassy, 192 Rehov Hayarkon, Tel Aviv 63405, Israel. Tel: 3 7251222; Fax: 3 524 3313. bricontv@netvision.net.il www.britemb.org.il/

British ConsulateGeneral, 19 Nashashibi Street, Sheikh Jarrah Quarter, PO Box 19690 East Jerusalem, 97200. Tel: (2) 541 4100; britain@palnet.com; www.britishconsulate.org Consulate also in Eilat.

Israel Government Tourist Office, UK House, 180 Oxford Street, London W1N 9DJ. Tel: 020 7299 1111; Fax: 020 7299 1112. igtouk@dircon.co.uk

Ministry of Tourism, PO Box 1018, 24 King George Street, Jerusalem 91009, Israel. Tel: 2 675 4811. Fax: 2 56 25 34 07 or 56 25 08 90. www.infotour.co.il/

Return ticket required. Requirements may be subject to short-term change. Contact the relevant authority before departure. Passports required by all, valid for 6 months after the date of arrival. All require a stamp on arrival.

Visa not required by EU nationals.

Flowers, plants and seeds (without prior permission). Fresh meat.

Approximately £9.

POLIO, TYPHOID: R. OTHER: Rabies

W2

New Israeli Shekel (NIS) = 100 new agorot. EXCHANGE: Foreign currency can only be exchanged at authorised banks and hotels. Payment in foreign currency exempts tourists from VAT on certain purchases. All major credit cards and traveller's cheques are accepted. ATM AVAILABILITY: Over 1000 locations.

MONEYGRAM: 177 101 2939.
WESTERN UNION: 1 770 222 131.

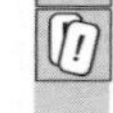
AMEX: 0044 1273 696 933
DINERS CLUB: 03 572 6767
MASTERCARD: 001800 941 8873
VISA: 177 440 8666

AMEX: 0044 1273 571 600
THOMAS COOK: 177 440 8424
VISA: 0044 20 7937 8091

0830–1230 and 1600–1730 Mon, Tues, and Thur. 0830–1230 Wed, 0830–1200 Fri.

Relatively expensive compared with other Middle Eastern countries, excluding Kibbutz.

Hebrew and Arabic. English is spoken in most major centres. French, Spanish, German, Yiddish, Russian, Polish and Hungarian may also be spoken.

Summers are hot with winds from the Mediterranean. Winters can be cool in the North. Spring and autumn are usually pleasant.

Mostly Jewish with Christian and Muslim minorities.

All major Jewish holidays. 2001: Feb 8, Mar 9, 10, Apr 8, 14, 20 ,26, 28, May 11, 21, 28, Jul 29, Sep 18,19, 27, Oct 28, 29,Dec 10,16.
2002: Jan 28, Feb 26, 27, Mar 28, Apr 3, 9, 16, 17, 30, May 10, 17, Jul 18, Sep 7, 8,16, 21, 27, 28, Nov 30, Dec 5.

220 volts AC, 50 Hz. 3-pin plugs are standard.

Airmail to Europe takes up to a week.

Certain areas within religious buildings can only be entered by men.

RAIL: Regular services provided between Tel Aviv and other major centres. All services are closed between sunset on Fri and sunset on Sat and during religious holidays. ROAD: There is a good road network. BUS: Services are cheap, quick and efficient. DOCUMENTATION: Full national driving licence and insurance is required. IDP is recommended.

HIGH RISK: The FCO strongly advises against travel to the West Bank and Gaza and to the Israel/Lebanon and Israel/Gaza border areas. There continues to be a risk of unpredictable terrorist attacks in crowded places, and there is a risk of getting caught up in tension between Israelis and Palestinians. Dress is casual except in holy places. In many restaurants and hotels it is considered an insult to smoke. SPECIAL PRECAUTIONS: Do not drive through the occupied territories.

CAPITAL: Rome

GMT +1 (GMT +2 in summer)

FROM UK: 0039. OUTGOING CODE TO UK: 0044

Police: 112; Ambulance: 113; Fire: 115.

Embassy of the Italian Republic, 14 The Kings Yard, Davies Street, London W1Y 2EH. Tel: 020 7312 2200. Fax: 020 7312 2230. emblondon@embitaly.org.uk www.embitaly.org.uk/

British Embassy, Via XX Settembre 80A, 00187 Rome, Italy. Tel: 06 482 5551 or 482 5441. Fax 06 487 3324. info@rome.mail.fco.gov.uk www.ukinitalia.it Consulates in Bari, Brindisi, Cagliari, Florence, Messina, Milan, Turin, Trieste, Genoa, Venice, Naples and Palermo.

Italian Sate Tourist Office (ENIT), 1 Princes Street, London W1R 8AY. Tel: 020 7408 1254. Fax: 020 7493 6695. enitlond@globalnet.co.uk

Ente Nazionale Italiano per il Turismo, Via Marghera no. 2/6, 00185 ROMA. Tel: 0039 6 49711. Fax: 0039 6 4463379. sedecentrale@enit.it; www.piuitalia2000.it/ and www.enit.it

Requirements may be subject to change at short notice. Valid passport required

Visa not required by Nationals of the EU.

Although there are no legal limits for tobacco and alcohol, travellers may be questioned.

Rabies.

W2

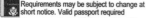

Euro = 100 cents EXCHANGE: banks, railway stations, airports and some hotels. MasterCard, Visa and Diners Club widely accepted. US$ is the preferred travellers cheque currency. ATM AVAILABILITY: Over 20,000 locations.

MONEYGRAM: 167 8 76580.
WESTERN UNION: 1670 16840.

AMEX: 0044 1273 696 933
DINERS CLUB: 800 864064
MASTERCARD: 800 870 866
VISA: 800 819 014

AMEX: 800 872 000
THOMAS COOK: 1678 72050
VISA: 800 874 155

Varies from city to city but in general, 0830–1330 and 1530–1930 Mon to Fri.

Cities and tourist centres can be very expensive, especially at centres of historical or religious importance.

Italian with dialects in different regions. French, German and Slovenian in border provinces. English often spoken in cities and resorts.

Summer is hot, especially in the south. Spring and autumn are mild. Winter is much drier in the south. Mountain regions are colder with heavy snowfalls.

Roman Catholic with Protestant minorities.

Jan 1, 6, Apr 25, May 1, Jun 2, Aug 15, Nov 1, Sun closest to Nov 4, Dec 8, 25, 26. Easter, saints' days in various cities, Carnival in Venice Feb/Mar.

220 volts Ac, 50 Hz.

7-10 days but may be subject to delays. Letters for poste restante should be addressed to 'Fermo Post' and the town. When sending mail, underline the destined country and write the person's surname in capitals.

Religion influences the behaviour of women, especially in the southern rural areas. Extra care should be taken if travelling alone in the south.

RAIL: Cheap and efficient. ROADS: The route to and from France via the Mont Blanc Tunnel is likely to be closed for some time because of a fire: alternative routes are available through Switzerland and along the coast. BUS: Services connect main towns and local services also operate. CAR HIRE: Available in all the main towns. DOCUMENTATION: A green card must be carried or other insurance. A UK licence is valid but 'Green' licences will need to be translated.

The Roman Catholic church holds a high position in Italian society. Visitors must dress conservatively when visiting religious buildings and smaller traditional communities. Theft is quite common, especially in the cities. Pickpockets are active among the crowds in Rome, including religious gatherings in St Peter's Square, and other popular tourist sites. Thieves often work in groups or pairs. There have been reports of theft on trains, where the victim has been offered food or drink spiked with drugs. Form E111 is valid for emergency medical treatment. There continues to be volcanic activity on Mt Etna in Sicily.

CAPITAL: Kingston

GMT –5

FROM UK: 001809. OUTGOING CODE TO UK: 01144

Police: 119; Fire/Ambulance: 110.

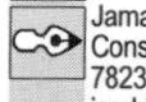
Jamaica High Commission, 12 Prince Consort Road, London, SW7 2BZ. Tel: 020 7823 9911. Fax: 020 7589 5154. jamhigh@jhcuk.com www.jhcuk.com/

British High Commission, PO Box 575, Trafalgar Road, Kingston 10, Jamaica. Tel: 926 9050. Fax: 929 7869. bhckingston@cwjamaica.com

Jamaica Tourist Board (at High Commission in London). Tel: 020 7224 0505. Fax: 020 7224 0551. jtb_uk@compuserve.com

Jamaican Tourist Board, PO Box 360, 2 St Lucia Avenue, Kingston 5, Jamaica. Tel: 929 9200. Fax: 929 9375. www.jamaicatravel.com/

Return ticket required. Requirements may be subject to short-term change. Contact embassy before departure.Valid passport required

Visa not required by nationals of EU countries. (For varying lengths of stay, see the High Commission.)

Fruit, meat coffee, honey, rum, vegetables.

J$500 payable in local currency for all passengers over 2 years of age. Transit passengers are exempt.

Evidence of sufficient funds to finance stay must be available.

POLIO, TYPHOID: R. YELLOW FEVER: A vaccination certificate is required from travellers over one year of age coming from infected areas.

W2

Jamaican Dollar (J$) = 100 cents. EXCHANGE: Visitors should only change money at airport bureaux, banks or hotels. All major credit cards are accepted. US dollar travellers cheques are recommended. ATM AVAILABILITY: Over 45 locations.

MONEYGRAM: 0 800 543 4080
WESTERN UNION: 926 2454.

AMEX: 01273 696 933
DINERS CLUB: 01252 513 500
MASTERCARD: 0800 307 7309
VISA: 0800 847 2911

AMEX: 01273 571 600
THOMAS COOK: 0800 622 101
VISA: 020 7937 8091

0900-1400 Mon to Thur and 0900-1500 Fri.

Expensive in the tourist centres.

English. Local patois is also spoken.

Tropical climate. May-Oct is the rainy season, although showers can occur at any time. Evenings tend to be cooler.

Protestant. Roman Catholic, Jewish, Muslim, Hindu and Bahai minorities.

Jan 1, May 23, Aug 6 and Sun before third Mon in Oct, Dec 25,26, Ash Wed, Good Fri, Easter.

110 volts AC, 50 Hz. American 2-pin plugs are mainly used.

4-5 days.

Extra care should be taken. It is inadvisable to travel alone at night. A multicultural society influenced by colonial rule and Rastafarianism, with its origins in Ethiopia, means that women have a diverse role.

ROAD: One third of the 17,000 km network is tarred. BUS: Reliable in Kingston and Montego Bay, less so for trans-island travel. TAXI: Advice from the FCO is to use only taxis authorised by the Jamaica Union of Travellers Association and ordered from hotels for the sole use of the visitor. Do not share taxis or give lifts to strangers. CAR HIRE: Most major towns and airport have hire facilities. DOCUMENTATION: A full UK licence is valid for up to 1 year.

Over the past few years there has been an increase in violence against tourists, especially in the downtown Kingston area. Gang violence and shootings are usually concentrated in inner city and poor neighbourhoods. These areas are currently subject to curfew and should be avoided. Possession of Marijuana may lead to imprisonment or deportation. Hurricanes may occur in the rainy season between July and October. Visitors should make themselves aware of weather conditions through the local media. Jamaica is also in an earthquake zone.

CAPITAL: Tokyo

GMT +9

FROM UK: 0081. OUTGOING CODE TO UK: 00144

Tokyo English Life Line (TELL): 3403 7106; Japan Helpline: 0120 461 997 (operator service).

Embassy of Japan, 101 Piccadilly, London, W1V 9FN. Tel: 020 7465 6500. Fax: 020 7491 9348. info@embjapan.org.uk www.embjapan.org.uk/

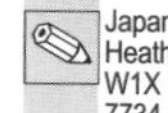
British Embassy, No 1 IchibanCho, ChiyodaKu, Tokyo 1028381, Japan. Tel: (3) 32 5211 1100.; Fax: (3) 52 75 0346. embassy@tokyo.mail.fco.gov.uk www.uknow.or.jp/ Consulate also in Osaka.

Japan National Tourist Organisation, Heathcote, House, 20 Saville Row, London, W1X 1AE. Tel: 020 7734 9638. Fax: 020 7734 4290. jntolon@dircon.co.uk www.jnto.go.jp/english/index.html

Japan National Tourist Association, Tokyo Kotsu Kaikan Building, 2101 Yurakucho, Chiyodaku, Tokyo, Japan. Tel: (3) 32 16 19 01. Fax: (3) 32 14 76 80. www.jnto.go.jp/

Return ticket and valid passport required by all. Requirements may change at short notice: contact the embassy.

Visa not required by nationals of the UK and Republic of Ireland for a stay not exceeding 6 months. Requirements may change at short notice, check with embassy.

Items which infringe copyright, trade marks, patents. Obscene material, some plants, meats and animals without relevant health certificates.

¥ 2650, payable in local currency, depending on airport.

POLIO, TYPHOID: R.

Japanese Yen (¥). EXCHANGE: At authorised banks and moneychangers. Import of local currency is limited to ¥5,000,000. All major credit cards are recognised, but only slowly gaining acceptance in Japan, and few foreign cards can be used in cash machines (ATMs). Most cash machines close after 9pm. Travellers cheques, preferably in US$, can be exchanged in banks and large hotels. ATM AVAILABILITY: Over 700 locations.

MONEYGRAM: 001 800 66639472.
WESTERN UNION: Available.

AMEX: 00144 1273 696 933
DINERS CLUB: 03 3570 1555
MASTERCARD: 00531 11 3886
VISA: 00531 11 1555

AMEX: 0044 1273 571 600
THOMAS COOK: 00531 616531
VISA: 00144 20 7937 8091

0900–1500 Mon to Fri.

Japan can be extremely expensive in comparison with other Asian countries.

Japanese. English may also be spoken in main cities.

Winter: Cold and sunny in the south and around Tokyo. Very cold around Hokkaido. Summer (June-Sept) can be warm to very hot. Spring and autumn are generally mild. Typhoons may occur Sept–Oct.

Shintoist and Buddhist. Christian minority.

Jan 1, 2, 3, second Mon in Jan, Feb 11, Mar 21, Apr 29, May 5 (Golden Week), Jul 20, Sept 15, 23, second Mon in Oct, Nov 3, 23, Dec 23, 31.

100 Volts AC, 60 Hz in the west. 50 Hz in Eastern Japan and Tokyo.

4–6 Days.

Most women still behave in accordance with traditional culture and etiquette in the home, but are influenced by Western culture in the workplace. Strict traditional customs are less apparent in major cities. Usual precautions should be taken by women travellers, although the crime rate is comparatively low.

RAIL: Network is one of the best in the world. ROAD: Driving in Japan is not recommended. TAXI: Expensive. DOCUMENTATION: IDP is required. Public transport is well developed and efficient.

Bowing is the customary form of greeting although handshaking is becoming more common. Remove shoes when entering a host's home. Public toilets are often unsegregated. Blowing your nose in public is frowned upon. Japanese etiquette is very complex but foreign 'ignorance' is tolerated. Common nasal inhalers that can bought over the counter in Europe should not be brought into the country because they contain a substance banned in Japan. Earthquakes occur in Japan each year, some far more serious than others.

Jersey

CAPITAL: St Helier

GMT (+1 in Summer)

FROM UK: 01534. From elsewhere use the UK code 441534. OUTGOING CODE TO UK: 0044

All services: 999.

Jersey Tourism 7 Lower Grosvenor Place, London SW1W 0EN. Tel: 020 7630 8787; Fax: 020 7630 0747. london@jersey.com

Jersey Tourism, Liberation Square, St Helier, Jersey JE1 1BB. Tel: 500 800. Fax: 500 808. www.jersey.com/

See UK entry.

See UK entry.

See UK entry.

£20, payable in local currency.

Pound sterling (£) = 100 pence. EXCHANGE: Bureaux de change, banks and many hotels. Channel Island notes and coins are not accepted in the UK. Notes can be changed at parity in UK banks. All major credit cards and travellers cheques are accepted. Pound sterling is the preferred currency. ATM AVAILABILITY: Over 10 locations.

MONEYGRAM: Limited to St Helier.
WESTERN UNION: Available.

AMEX: 01273 696 933
DINERS CLUB: 01252 513 500
MASTERCARD: 0800 96 4767
VISA: 0800 169 5189

AMEX: 01273 571 600
THOMAS COOK: 01733 318950
VISA: 020 7937 8091

0930-1530 Mon to Fri. Some banks are open on Saturday mornings.

The Channel Islands are a low-duty zone.

English. A dialect of Norman/French is still spoken by some.

Most popular holiday season is May until the end of September, with temperatures averaging 20–21°C. Most rain falls during the cooler months.

Each parish has its own Anglican church.

Jan 1, first Mon in May, May 9, last Mon in May and Aug, Dec 25, 26. Easter.

240 volts AC, 50 Hz.

UK stamps are not valid in Jersey. Generally a very good postal service operates.

There is little inequality between men and women. Usual precautions should, however, be taken.

BUS: Services operate throughout the island. ROAD: A speed limit of 15mph (24 km/h) restricts access along the designated 'green lanes', giving priority to walkers and cyclists. TAXI: Taxi ranks can be found at the airport and St Helier. Different tariffs are applied for day and night hire and on public holidays. CAR HIRE: Generally very cheap as is the petrol. DOCUMENTATION: Visitors who take their own car must have a green card or valid certificate of insurance. Nationality plates must be displayed. Jersey is ideally situated for day trips to France and other Channel Islands. Regular ferry services are available for most of the year, day trips by ferry operate on a seasonal basis.

Similar to the UK but with French influences.

CAPITAL: Amman

GMT +2 (GMT +3 during the summer).

FROM UK: 00962. OUTGOING CODE TO UK: 0044

Police: 192; Fire / Ambulance: 193. All services: 62111 (Jerusalem only).

Embassy of the Hashemite Kingdom of Jordan, 6 Upper Phillimore Gardens, London W8 7HB. Tel: 020 7937 3685. Fax: 020 7937 8795. For visa enquiries Tel: 0891 171 261. lonemb@dircon.co.uk www.jordanembassyuk.gov.jo/

British Embassy, PO Box 87, Abdoun, Amman, 11118 Jordan. Tel: (6) 592 3100. Fax: (6) 592 3759. www.britain.org.jo

Jordan Tourist Information Office, 211 Regent Street, London W1R 7DD. Tel: 020 7437 9465. Fax: 020 7494 0433.

Ministry of Tourism, PO Box 224, Amman, Jordan. Tel: (6) 642 311. Fax: (6) 648 465.

Requirements may be subject to short-term change. Contact the relevant authority before departure.Valid passport required by all.

Visa required. Single entry visas can be obtained on arrival at the airport in Jordan.

JD10 for individual tourists, payable in local currency. Transit passengers are exempt.

Nationals of Bahamas, Bangladesh, India, Pakistan, Sri Lanka and all African countries with the exception of Egypt and South Africa if they have not obtained prior permission from the Ministry of Interior in Amman.

POLIO, TYPHOID: R. YELLOW FEVER: A vaccination certificate is required from all travellers over 1 year of age coming from infected areas. OTHER: Rabies.

W1

Dinar (JD) = 1000 fils. Amex and Visa are accepted widely, but MasterCard and Diners Club have more limited use. Travellers cheques issued by British banks are accepted in authorised bureaux de change. US$ is the preferred currency. ATM AVAILABILITY: Over 50 locations.

MONEYGRAM: 18 800 000 then 800 592 3688.
WESTERN UNION: 616 910.

AMEX: 0044 1273 696 933
DINERS CLUB: 560 1878 or 567 5850
MASTERCARD: 001 314 542 7111
VISA: 001 410 581 9994

AMEX: 0044 1273 571 600
THOMAS COOK: 0044 1733 318 950
VISA: 0044 20 7937 8091

0830–1230 and 1530–1730 Sat to Thur. Hours during Ramadan are 0830–1000, although some banks open in the afternoon.

Jordan is one of the smallest countries in the Middle East. It is also one of the most expensive. Most of the accommodation is in Amman.

Arabic. English and French are also spoken.

Summers are hot and dry with cool evenings. Nov-Mar are the cooler months with rainfall.

Sunni Muslim. Shiite Muslim and Christian minorities.

Jan 1, May 1,25, Jun 10, Aug 11, Nov 14, Dec 25,31. Islamic festivals, Easter.

220 volts AC, 50 Hz.

Packages should be left open for customs officials. Airmail to Western Europe takes 3 to 5 days.

Society in general is less patriarchal than in other Middle Eastern countries. However, women should still dress and act modestly.

ROAD: Good network of roads exists but vehicle needs to be in good working order and plenty of water and supplies should be taken on journeys. Under Jordanian law, the driver is always guilty if a vehicle hits a pedestrian. BUS: Services are efficient and cheap. TAXIS: Shared taxi service to all towns on fixed routes, also available for private hire. CAR HIRE: International companies are available from hotels.

Jordan is safe to travel in. There is always some risk of disturbances relating to the tension between Israelis and Palestinians and visitors should keep alert to the local media for reports of trouble. Avoid large gatherings and political demonstrations. The military keep a low profile and you are unlikely to experience anything but friendliness and hospitality. It is very important that Muslim beliefs and local customs are respected. Beachwear should be confined to the beach/pool.

Kazakhstan

CAPITAL: Almaty / Astana

GMT +6 (GMT +7 during the summer).

FROM UK: 007. OUTGOING CODE TO UK: 8/1044 (wait for second dial tone) International calls are made at reduced rate 2000-0800 local time.

All services: 03.

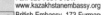

Embassy of the Republic of Kazakhstan, 33 Thurlowe Square, London SW7 2DS. Tel: 020 7581 4646. Consulate: 020 7584 9905. Fax: 020 7584 8481. www.kazakhstanembassy.org

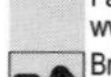
British Embassy, 173 Furmanov Street, Almaty 480110, Kazakhstan. Tel: (3372) 506 192. Fax: (3272) 506 260. britishembassy@kaznet.kz Consulate is at 158 Panfilova Street, Almaty.

See Consulate.

'Proftour' Association (former Kazakh Council for Tourism), 5 Mitina Street, Almaty, Kazakhstan. Tel: (3272) 640 567. Fax: (3272) 531 928. Valid passport and return ticket required.

As regulations are expected to change at short notice, visitors are advised to contact the consulate for current requirements. Carry your passport at all times.

Travellers are advised to contact the consulate for current visa requirements.

Pornography, loose pearls and couriering. Works of art and antiques, lottery and state loan tickets cannot be exported. Contact the Consulate for a full list.

Diphtheria, rabies. TB is endemic. Typhoid is on the increase.

W1

1 Tenge = 100 tigin. Exchange: must be made at authorised bureaux and receipts should be retained for all transactions. US$ are preferred. Major credit cards are accepted in large hotels. US$ travellers cheques are preferred. ATM AVAILABILITY: 3 locations.

MONEYGRAM: Unavailable
WESTERN UNION: 327 2507 106

AMEX: 8/1044 1273 696 933
DINERS CLUB: 8/1044 1252 513 500
MASTERCARD: 8/101 314 542 7111
VISA: 8/101 410 581 9994

AMEX: 8/1044 1273 571 600
THOMAS COOK: 8/10441733 318950
VISA: 8/1044 20 7937 8091

0930-1730 Mon to Fri. All banks close Sat–Sun and for lunch 1300-1400.

Generally inexpensive.

Kazakh, Russian.

Continental climate: Summers are hot and winters are cold. Hottest period: July-Aug.

Mainly Sunni Muslim. Russian Orthodox and Jewish minorities.

Jan 1, Mar 8, 22, May 1, 9, Aug 30, Oct 25, Dec 16

220 volts AC, 50 Hz. Plugs are the 2-pin continental type.

2-3 weeks. Addresses should be laid out from top to bottom: country, postcode, city, street, house number/name, and finally name.

Inside mosques, women observe their own ritual and are separated from the men. Arms and legs must be covered at religious sites.

RAIL: Cost is minimal by Western standards. Regular connections between all major centres. NOTE: There has been an increase in robberies on rail and road. Passengers should travel in groups and compartments should be locked on overnight trains. ROAD: A reasonable network connects all towns. BUS: Reliable connections between all main towns. CAR HIRE: Hertz has agencies at the airport and the large hotels in the centre. DOCUMENTATION: IDP required.

Robberies and personal attacks have increased, especially in the larger cities. Do not walk alone on the streets at night or travel in unmarked taxis. Keep expensive items out of site. Kazakh people are very hospitable. Shorts should not be worn except for sports. Formal dress is often required for evening engagements. Kazakhstan is a newly independent nation in the midst of profound economic and political change. The official capital is Astana; the British Embassy is still located in Almaty, the largest city and former capital. Keep your passport, and carry an Embassy-certified copy of your passport at all times. The police can arrest visitors who cannot produce identification.

CAPITAL: Nairobi

GMT +3

FROM UK: 00254. OUTGOING CODE TO UK: 00044

All services: 336886 / 501280.

Kenya High Commission, 45 Portland Place, London W1N 4AS. Tel: 020 7636 2371/5. Fax: 020 7323 6717.

British High Commission, PO Box 30465, Upper Hill Road, Nairobi. Tel: (2) 714699; Fax: (2) 719942. bhcinfo@iconnect.co.ke; www.britain.or.ke Consulate also in Mombassa.

Kenya Tourist Office, 25 Brooks Mews, off Davies Street, Mayfair, London, W1Y 1LG. Tel: 020 7355 3144. Fax: 020 7495 8656. www.kenyatourism.org/

Kenya Tourism Foundation, Lenana Road, PO Box 51351, Nairobi. Tel: 00254 2 716244. Fax: 00254 2 716246

Return ticket required. Requirements may be subject to change at short notice. Consult embassy before departure. Passport required by all, valid from 6 months from the date of entry.

Visa required. A visa issued on arrival costs US$50.

Gold, diamonds, wildlife skins and game trophies.

US$40 is levied on international flights, usually included in the price of an air ticket.

POLIO, TYPHOID: R. MALARIA: Prevails throughout the year. Falciparum variety is present and high resistance to chloroquine has been reported. YELLOW FEVER: Vaccination is strongly recommended to all visitors travelling outside urban areas. A vaccination certificate is required by anyone arriving from infected areas. OTHER: Bilharzia, rabies, AIDS/HIV is widespread and spreads through substandard medical practices and hygiene.

W1

Kenyan Shilling (Ksh) = 100 cents. NOTE: Import and export of local currency is prohibited. Black market transactions are inadvisable. Diners Club and Visa are accepted. Travellers cheques can be changed at banks. Pound sterling is the preferred currency. ATM AVAILABILITY: 40 locations.

MONEYGRAM: Unavailable
WESTERN UNION: 2 251 696.

AMEX: 00044 1273 696 933
DINERS CLUB: 00044 1252 513 500
MASTERCARD: 0001 314 542 7111
VISA: 0001 410 581 9994

AMEX: 00044 1273 571 600
THOMAS COOK: 00044 1733 318950
VISA: 00044 20 7937 8091

0900-1500 Mon to Fri 0900-1100 on the first and last Saturday of each month. The airport bank is open until midnight every day.

Kenya is greatly influenced by Western European standards of living.

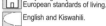

English and Kiswahili.

Coastal areas are tropical and the lowlands are hot and dry. The rainfall can be heavy.

Mostly traditional, with Christian and Muslim minorities.

Jan 1, May 1, June 1, Oct 10,20, Dec 12, 25, 26. Eid Al Fitr, Good Fri, Easter Mon.

220/240 Volts AC 50Hz Plugs are UK type 3 pin.

About 4 days to Europe. Letters can be sent c/o poste restante in any town. Poste restante is well organised in Nairobi and free to collect.

Sexual harassment is far less prevalent in Kenya, though this essentially relates to white women.

ROADS: All major roads are now tarred. TRAIN: Overnight to Mombasa and Nairobi. BUS: Matatus (normally mini buses) are often driven at excessive speed even on poor roads, and are notorious for accidents. BEWARE: Bandits are common on the roads leading to the Somali border. Walking alone at night can be dangerous. DOCUMENTATION: British licence is valid for 90 days but must be endorsed by the police.

Western European habits prevail. Be alert for muggings and armed attacks if travelling in Nairobi or Mombasa. Do not accept food or drink from strangers as it may be drugged. Avoid travelling after dark and isolated places. Game reserves and tourist areas on the coast are generally very safe. The Kenya Tourism Federation operates a Safety and Communication Centre which can give up to the minute advice on tourism matters and provide help in an emergency. Tel: Nairobi 604767, Email safetour@wananchi.com

Kiribati

CAPITAL: Bairiki

GMT +12 except Canton Island. Enderbury Island +11 and Christmas Island +10.

FROM UK: 00686. OUTGOING CODE TO UK: 0044. Most international calls must go through the operator.

All calls are via the operator.

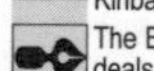
Kiribati High Commission, c/o The Office of The President, PO Box 68, Bairiki, Tarawa, Kiribati.

The British High Commission in Suva (Fiji) deals with enquiries – see Fiji.

Kiribati Visitors Bureau, PO Box 261, Bikenibeu, Bairiki, Tarawa, Kiribati. Tel: 28287. Fax: 26193.

Return ticket required. May be subject to change at short notice. Contact the Consular authority before departure. Valid passport required by all

Visa not required by nationals of the UK (excluding Northern Ireland) for a 28-day stay maximum.

Dogs and cats can only be imported from Fiji, Australia and New Zealand, with an import permit. See the Consulate for up-to-date list.

A$ 10.

POLIO, TYPHOID: R. YELLOW FEVER: A vaccination certificate is required from travellers over 1 year of age arriving from infected areas. OTHER: Filariasis, dengue fever, diarrhoel diseases and helminthic infections are common. Hepatitis A and B are reported. There have been outbreaks of cholera.

W1

Australian Dollar (A$) = 100 cents. US$ can be exchanged for local currency at banks and some shops. Credit cards are not accepted. Travellers cheques are accepted at some hotels and the bank of Kiribati. A$ cheques are preferred, but US$ cheques can also be exchanged. ATM AVAILABILITY: Over 10 locations.

MONEYGRAM: Unavailable.
WESTERN UNION: Unavailable.

AMEX: 0044 1273 696 933
DINERS CLUB: 0044 1252 513 500
MASTERCARD: 001 314 542 7111
VISA: 001 410 581 9994

AMEX: 0044 1273 571 600
THOMAS COOK: 0044 1733 318950
VISA: 0044 20 7937 8091

0930-1500 Mon to Fri.

There are four hotels in Kiribati on each major island. These tend to be more expensive than the resthouses found on all the other islands. Local products can be purchased cheaply, but other items such as imported canned food, which the locals regard as a luxury, are relatively expensive.

Kiribati and English.

Mar-Oct is the most comfortable time to visit. Dec-Mar has the highest rainfall. Nov-Feb is very hot and humid.

Gilbert Islands Protestant and Roman Catholic.

Jan 1, Apr 18, Jul 12–14, Aug 7, Dec 25, 26. Easter.

240 Volts AC, 50 Hz.

Up to 2 weeks.

Like other Pacific Islands people are friendly and hospitable, yet retain their own traditions. Equal status between men and women is considered the norm.

FLIGHTS: Air Tungaru operates an internal scheduled service to nearly all outer islands linking them with Tarawa.

Kiribati is an independent republic and comprises the Gilbert, Phoenix and Line groups of islands. Kiribati aroused worldwide interest and curiosity as a result of its location on the International Date Line, making it arguably the first nation to see in the new millennium. Tourism is largely undeveloped. The islet of Betio where the Battle of Tarawa took place offers a wealth of Second World War relics. If travelling to remote islands it is advisable to bring adequate supplies of essential items. Traditional culture should be respected and beachwear should not be worn away from the beach/pool. The lagoon in South Tarawa is polluted and unsafe for swimming. An informative web site on Kiribati is located at http://members.nbci.com/janeresture/kirricom/

Korea (The Democratic People's Republic of)

CAPITAL: Pyongyang

GMT +9

FROM UK: 00850. OUTGOING CODE TO UK: 0044 Calls go through the operator.

Not present.

No embassy in the UK. EUROPE: General Delegation of the DPRK, 104 boulevard Bineau, 92200 Neuilly-sur-Seine, France. Tel: (1) 47 45 17 97. Fax: (1) 47 38 12 50.

There is currently no British representation. In an extreme emergency, British citizens may approach the Swedish Embassy in Pyongyang, Tel: 2381 7908.

Not present.

National Directorate of Tourism, Central District, Pyongyang, DPR Korea. Tel: (2) 381 7201. Fax: (2) 381 7607.

Return ticket required. Requirements may change at short notice: contact the embassy. Valid passport required by all

Visa required by all. Visitors to North Korea usually obtain their visas at the North Korean Embassy in Beijing, China, which will only issue visas after authorisation has been received from the North Korean Foreign Ministry in Pyongyang.

Binoculars, wireless sets, plants and seeds, groceries without authorisation.

POLIO, TYPHOID: R. OTHER: Rabies

W1

Won (NKW) = 100 jon. NOTE: Import and export of local currency is prohibited. Credit cards and travellers cheques are not accepted. ATM AVAILABILITY: Unavailable.

MONEYGRAM: Unavailable.
WESTERN UNION: Unavailable.

AMEX: No local number.
DINERS CLUB: No local number.
MASTERCARD: No local number.
VISA: No local number.

AMEX: No local number.
THOMASCOOK: No local number.
VISA: No local number.

Economic crisis and the loss of several valuable trading partners has resulted in a shortage of commodities and an increase in prices.

Korean.

Hottest: Jul-Aug, which is also the rainy season. Dec-Jan is the coldest time. Spring and autumn are usually dry and mild

Buddhism. Christian and Chundo Kyo.

Jan 1, Feb 16, Apr 15, 25, May 1, Jul 27, Aug 15, Sept 9, 20–22, Oct 10, Dec 27

110/220 Volts AC, 60 Hz.

Approx. 10 days. Outside the capital services are slow and unlimited.

A communist regime remains in DPR Korea isolating itself from outside influences. Society is totalitarian, but with no discrimination between gender.

ROAD: Quality is good. RAIL: Extensive rail network.

Independent travel is prohibited, however there are official tours available but only in groups of ten persons. Concessions are made for specific business trips. Some moves are being made to encourage educational exchange visits through universities. Travel across the Demilitarized Zone (DMZ) between North and South Korea is not permitted. North Korea has experienced serious shortages of food, electrical power, clean water and medicine.

Korea (Republic of)

CAPITAL: Seoul

GMT +9

FROM UK: 0082. OUTGOING CODE TO UK: 00144

Not present.

Embassy of the Republic of Korea, 60 Buckingham Gate, London SW1E 6AJ. Tel: 020 7227 5500/2; Consular/visa: 020 7227 5505; Fax: 020 7227 5503. www.mofat.go.kr/uk.htm

British Embassy, 4 Chungdong, ChungKu, Seoul 100, Republic of Korea. Tel: (2) 3210 5500; fax: 0082 2 3201 5653). Consular.Seoul@fco.gov.uk. www.britishembassy.or.kr.

Korea National Tourism Organization, 8th Floor, New Zealand House, Haymarket, London SW1Y 4TQ. Tel: 020 7321 2535; Fax: 020 7321 0876. koreatb@dircon.co.uk

Korea National Tourism Organization,10 Dadong, Junggu, Seoul 100180. Tel: 0082 2 7299 600; Fax: 0082 2 7575997. jinhung@www.knto.or.kr www.knto.or.kr and www.visitkorea.or.kr/

Requirements may change at short notice: contact the embassy. Valid passport required.

Visa not required for tourist visit, but a change in status (e.g., to teach English) is not normally granted after arrival in the country.Those wishing to stay for more than one month may be required to provide a certificate proving they are HIV negative, issued within one month of their arrival.

Printed material, films or phonographic material which is regarded to be harmful to national security or public interests. Textile fabrics larger than 5 m². More than 5 foreign phonograph records.

SKW9000, payable in local currency, at the airport.

POLIO, TYPHOID: R. OTHER: Cholera, Japanese encephalitis.

W1

Won (SKW). More than US$ 10,000 in foreign currency must be registered on arrival. Export of local currency is limited to SKW 500,000. All credit cards are widely accepted. Travellers cheques are accepted, but may be difficult to cash in smaller towns. US$ is the preferred currency. ATM AVAILABILITY: Over 1000 locations.

MONEYGRAM: Unavailable.
WESTERN UNION: Unavailable.

AMEX: 00144 1273 696 933
DINERS CLUB: 02 3498 6100/02 3498 6111
MASTERCARD: 00 79 811 887 0823
VISA: 00 81 800 908 8212

AMEX: 0079 8611 1023
THOMAS COOK: 00144 1733 318950
VISA: 00144 20 7937 8091

0930–1630 Mon to Fri, 0930–1330 Sat.

Caters for all types of budget. Hotels are government registered. Travellers usually opt to stay in Yogwans, reasonably priced traditional Korean inns. Self-catering is available.

Korean. The growth in high-tech industries has increased the use of English.

Hottest during the rainy season: Jul–Aug. Coldest: Dec–Jan. Spring and autumn are mild and mainly dry.

Muhayana Buddhism. There is a large Christian minority and also Confucianism, Daoism and Chundo Kyo.

Jan 1, Mar 1, Apr 5, May 1,5, Jun 6, Jul 17, Aug 15, Sep 20–22, Oct 3, Dec 25. Buddha's birthday.

110/220 Volts AC, 60 Hz.

Up to 10 days.

In rural areas women wear traditional costume and perform mainly agrarian tasks.

FLIGHTS: Frequent domestic services between main centres. ROAD: Excellent motorways link all major cities but minor roads may be poorer quality. In all accidents involving a pedestrian, the driver is assumed to be at fault. BUS: Cheap, frequent services operate but are often overcrowded and make no allowances for English speakers. DOCUMENTATION: IDP is required.

Korean culture is unique, with a vivid sense of self-identity. Traditional agrarian culture persists in rural areas whilst the cities are a blend of history and technology. Shoes must be removed when entering someone's house. Use the right hand for passing and receiving. Medical treatment can be expensive. Carry identification at all times.

CAPITAL: Kuwait City

GMT +3

FROM UK: 00965. OUTGOING CODE: 0044

All emergency services: 777

Embassy of the State of Kuwait, 2 Albert Gate, Knightsbridge, London SW1X 7JU. Tel: 020 7590 3400. Fax: 020 7259 5042. Visa information: 0900 160 0160 (premium rate).

British Embassy, PO Box 2, Arabian Gulf Street, 13001 Safat, Kuwait City, Kuwait. Tel: 240 3334/5/6. Fax: 240 5778. consular@britishembassykuwait.org www.britishembassykuwait.org/

Not present.

Department of Tourism, Ministry of Information, PO Box 193, 13002 Safat, asSour St, Kuwait City, Kuwait. Tel: 243 6644. Fax: 242 9758.

Requirements may be subject to change at short notice: contact the relevant authority before travelling. Valid passport required by all.

Visa required. Travellers with Israeli stamps in their passports will be refused entry

Alcohol, pork products, goods from Israel. Penalties are severe and almost everyone's bag is searched at customs.

KWD 2 for international departures. Children under 12 are exempt.

POLIO, TYPHOID: R. OTHER: Cholera

W2

Kuwait Dinar (KWD) = 1000 fils. All credit cards and travellers cheques are accepted. US$ is the preferred cheque currency. ATM AVAILABILITY: 180 locations.

MONEYGRAM: 800 288.
WESTERN UNION: 245 0852.

AMEX: 0044 1273 696 933
DINERS CLUB: 246 6655
MASTERCARD: 001 314 542 7111
VISA: 001 410 581 9994

AMEX: 00973 256 834
THOMAS COOK: 0044 1733 318950
VISA: 0044 20 7937 8091

0800–1200 Sun to Thur.

Expensive and may be difficult for the budget traveller.

Arabic. English is generally widely understood.

Similar to Europe but hotter and dryer. Summer: (Apr–Oct) is hot and humid with little rain. Winter: (Nov–Mar) is cool with limited rainfall.

Mostly Muslim with Christian and Hindu minorities.

Jan 1, Feb 25, 26. Islamic festivals

240 volts AC, 50 Hz single phase. UK-type flat 3-pin plugs are used.

Airmail to Western Europe takes about 5 days.

Harassment of women travellers has been increasing. Do not travel alone in secluded places. Unaccompanied women should not use taxis, especially after nightfall.

ROAD: A good network exists between cities. BUS: Reliable and inexpensive services operate between main cities. TAXI: Popular and reliable service, but fares should always be agreed in advance. CAR HIRE: Available. DOCUMENTATION: IDP required. Temporary licence available on presentation of a valid British licence. Seat belts are compulsory. It is an offence to leave the scene of a road accident before the police arrive.

British nationals should register with the Embassy on arrival, and should not attempt to travel anywhere near the border with Iraq. All Islamic laws should be respected; in particular it is an offence punishable by a fine to eat, drink or smoke in the daytime during the month of Ramadan. Alcohol and pork are forbidden. Women should dress modestly. Men should not wear shorts or go around without a shirt in public. It is greatly appreciated if visitors learn a few words of Arabic. SPECIAL PRECAUTIONS: There is a danger of unexploded land mines throughout the country. Seek advice before using beaches and venturing out of the city. Do not pick up any strange metal, plastic or other objects lying around. Do not souvenir hunt for war memorabilia. PHOTOGRAPHY: In theory a photography permit is required.

Kyrgyz Republic

CAPITAL: Bishkek

GMT +5 (GMT +6 during the summer).

FROM UK: 00996. OUTGOING CODE: 8/1044 (wait for second dial tone). International calls are usually made from a telephone office, attached to a post office.

All services: 03.

Kyrgyz Republic Embassy, 119 Crawford Street, London W1. Tel: 020 7935 1462.

British Embassy in Almaty, Kazakhstan, deals with enquiries relating to the Kyrgyz Republic.

Not present.

State Committee for Tourism and Sport, Togolok Moldo 17, 720033 Bishkek, Kyrgyzstan Tel: (3312) 220 657 Fax: (3312) 212 845.

Requirements may be subject to short-term change. Contact the relevant authority before departure. Passport required by all: must be valid for 1 year after period of stay.

As visa requirements are liable to change visitors are advised to contact the Kyrgyz Embassy.

Pornography, loose pearls and anything owned by a third party being carried for that third party. Works of art and antiques, lottery and state loan tickets can not be exported. Contact the relevant authority for a full list.

POLIO, TYPHOID: R. OTHER: Rabies, diphtheria.

W2. It may be difficult to obtain a balanced diet and it may therefore be wise to take vitamin supplements.

1 Som = 100 Tyn. EXCHANGE: Due to the shortage of change travellers are advised to take small notes. The import and export of foreign currency is prohibited. Credit cards are accepted in some of the large hotels in the capital. Take US$ in cash in preference to travellers cheques. ATM AVAILABILITY: Unavailable.

MONEYGRAM: Unavailable.
WESTERN UNION: Unavailable.

AMEX: 81044 1273 696 933
DINERS CLUB: 8/1044 1252 513 500
MASTERCARD: 8/101 314 542 7111
VISA: 8/101 410 581 9994

AMEX: 8/1044 1273 571 600
THOMAS COOK: 8/1044 1733 318950
VISA: 8/1044 20 7937 8091

Usually 0930-1730 Mon to Fri.

Relatively inexpensive.

Kyrghz and Russian. English may be spoken by those involved with tourism.

Continental climate with little rain. Heavy snowfalls can be expected in the winter.

Sunni Muslim with a Russian Orthodox minority.

Jan 1,7, Mar 8,21, May 1,5,9, Aug 31. Islamic festivals.

220 volts AC, 50 Hz. Round 2-pin continental plugs are standard.

Anything from 2 weeks to 2 months.

Muslim culture prevails, influenced by Northern Asia and the former Soviet Union. Women tend to be conservative. A patriarchal society exists. Usual precautions should be taken. Modest dress is advised.

ROAD: Travel by road is difficult because of the terrain. BUS: There are regular services to many parts of the country but they are often crowded. TAXI: Can be found in all major towns. Many are unlicensed and fares should be agreed in advance. Many street names have changed so it is wise to ask for directions with the old and new street names. DOCUMENTATION: IDP and 2 photos.

The Kyrgyz Republic (formerly known as Kyrgyzstan) is a newly independent nation in Central Asia undergoing profound political and economic change. Tourist facilities are not highly developed. Mugging and theft is increasing in cities and rural areas, some thought to be committed by uniformed police. Exercise caution at all times and keep valuable items out of sight. Do not walk at night.

CAPITAL: Vientiane

GMT +7

FROM UK: 00856. OUTGOING CODE TO UK: 1444 Telephone link exists with Bangkok.

Not present.

No embassy in the UK. EUROPE: Embassy of the Lao People's Democratic Republic, 74 Avenue Raymond Poincare, 75116 Paris, France. Tel: (1) 45 53 02 98. Fax: (1) 47 27 57 89.

The British Embassy in Bangkok deals with enquiries relating to Laos. In an emergency contact the Australian Embassy, Rue J.Nehru; Quartier Phonexay, Vientiane, Laos. Tel: 413 600.

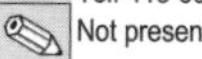
Not present.

National Tourism Authority of Laos People's Democratic Republic, BP 3556, Vientiane, Laos. Tel: (21) 212 248. Fax: (21) 212 769.

Return ticket and valid passport required by all. Requirements may change at short notice: contact the embassy before going.

Visa required (transit passengers exempt).

US$ 5, children under 2 years are exempt.

POLIO, TYPHOID: R. MALARIA: Exists all year throughout the country in the falciparum variety, which has been reported as being highly resistant to chloroquine. YELLOW FEVER: A vaccination certificate is required for travellers arriving from infected areas. OTHER: Rabies.

W1

Laotian New Kip (Kp) = 100 cents. Exchange: Banks and hotels in Vientiane and Luang Prabang. Import and export of local currency is prohibited. Amex cards are gaining acceptance in big hotels, but not travellers cheques. ATM AVAILABILITY: Unavailable.

MONEYGRAM: Unavailable.
WESTERN UNION: Unavailable.

AMEX: 1461 29271 8689
DINERS CLUB: No local number.
MASTERCARD: No local number.
VISA: No local number.

AMEX: No local number.
THOMAS COOK: No local number.
VISA: No local number.

0900–1630 Mon to Fri.

Laos is one of the poorest countries in the world. The foreign traveller can expect to pay very little for local items.As hotels are only located in the capital prices may fluctuate.

Laotian, French, Vietnamese and some English may be spoken.

Cooler weather in the highlands. Most of the country is hot and tropical. May–Oct has the highest temperatures and is the rainy season. Nov-Apr is the dry season.

LaosLum (Valley Laos) people follow the Hinayana (Theravada) form of Buddhism. The religion of the Laos Theung ranges from traditional Confucianism to animism and Christianity.

Jan 1, 6, 20, Mar 22, Apr 13–15, May 1, Jun 1, Aug 13, Oct 12, Dec 2. Chinese New Year, Buddhist festivals.

220 volts AC, 50 Hz.

Restricted to Vientiane.

A subsistence economy prevails. Traditional roles for women exist. Sexual harassment is much less common here than in any other Asian country. Long trousers, skirts, or walking trousers are acceptable attire. Tank-tops, sleeveless blouses and short skirts are not.

FLIGHTS: Domestic air services run from Vientiane to Luang Prabang, Pakse and Savannakhet. ROAD: Few roads are suitable for all-weather driving. BUS: Services link only a few major towns. CAR HIRE: Arrangements can be made through hotels. DOCUMENTATION: IDP is recommended although not legally required.

Laos has only been accessible to foreign visitors since 1988. Tourists should avoid travelling outside the capital independently as bandits are likely to attack. Religious beliefs must be respected. Avoid all topics relating to politics. Lao nationals should not be touched on the head. Dress neatly and remove shoes when entering religious buildings. Buddha objects are religious images so do not pose in front of them and do not drink or sit on them. Common-sense safety precautions should be followed.

CAPITAL: Riga

GMT +2 (GMT +3 in summer).

FROM UK: 00371. OUTGOING CODE TO UK: 0044

Ambulance: 03; Police: 02; Fire: 01.

Embassy of Latvia, 45 Nottingham Place, London W1M 3FE. Tel: 020 7312 0040. Fax: 020 7312 0042.

British Embassy, Alunana iela 5, LV- 1010 Riga, Latvia. Tel: 733 8126. Fax: 733 8132. british.embassy@apollo.lv http://www.britain.lv/

Not present.

National Tourism Board of Latvia, Pils laukums 4, Riga LV 1050, Latvia. Tel: 722 9945. Fax: 722 9945. ltboard@latnet.lv www.latviatravel.com

Return ticket required. Requirements may be subject to short-term change. Contact the relevant authority before departure. Passport required by all: must be valid for 2 months after period of stay.

Visa not required by holders of British passports.

Narcotics, guns and ammunition.

US$12.

Rabies, diphtheria and hepatitis.

1 Latvian Lat (Ls) = 100 santims. Exchange: the banking system is still being developed but there are bureaux de change in most post offices, hotels and railway stations. Credit cards and Travellers cheques are only accepted on a limited basis. The preferred foreign currencies are US$ and the Deutsche Mark. ATM AVAILABILITY: Available in Riga and other big towns.

MONEYGRAM: Riga: 700 7007 then 800 592 3688; outside Riga: 8 2700 7007 then 800 592 3688.
WESTERN UNION: 700 7007

AMEX: 0044 1273 696 933
DINERS CLUB: 0044 1252 513 500
MASTERCARD: 001 314 542 7111
VISA: 001 410 581 9994

AMEX: 0044 1273 571 600
THOMAS COOK: 0044 1733 318950
VISA: 0044 20 7937 8091

1000–1800 Mon to Fri.

Generally less expensive than Western Europe.

Latvian. Russian is increasing. English, German and Swedish may also be spoken.

Temperate climate but with considerable temperature fluctuations. The summer is warm with relatively mild weather in spring and autumn. Winters can be very cold.

Protestant (Lutheran), Roman Catholic and a Russian Orthodox minority.

Jan 1, May 1, second Sun in May, Jun 23, 24, Nov 18, Dec 25, 26, 31. Easter, Whitsun.

220 volts AC, 50 Hz. European style 2-pin plugs are used.

Airmail to Western Europe takes 3–4 days.

Traditionally, a patriarchal society has prevailed, but gender roles are slowly changing.

RAIL: Reasonably developed network connects Riga with the other main towns.
ROAD: There are good connections from Riga to all other parts of the country. BUS: A better form of transport than trains in Latvia.
CAR HIRE: Available through hotels. Reservations are recommended.

Latvians can appear rather reserved and formal, but very welcoming to foreign visitors. Most tourist facilities that one would expect in a Western European city are available in the capital, Riga, but not in the rest of the country. Medical care in Latvia is steadily improving but remains limited.
Tourists should exercise caution as petty crime is a problem. Carry a copy of your passport as ID.

Lebanon

CAPITAL: Beirut

GMT +2 (GMT +3 during the summer).

FROM UK: 00961. OUTGOING CODE TO UK: 0044.

Police: 386 440 425 (Emergency police: 16); Fire: 310 105; Ambulance: 386 675.

Embassy of the Republic of Lebanon, 21 Kensington Palace Gardens, London W8 4QM. Tel: 020 7229 7265. Fax: 020 7243 1699. Consular Section: 15 Palace Gardens Mews, London W8 4RA. Tel: 020 7727 6696. Fax: 020 7243 1699.

British Embassy, Rabieh, rue 8, Beirut, Lebanon. Tel: (1) 405 070 or 403 640. Fax: (1) 402 032.
britishemb@britishembassy.org.lb
www.britishembassy.org.lb/

Lebanon Tourist and Information Office, 90 Piccadilly, London W1V 9HB. Tel: 020 7409 2031. Fax: 020 7493 4929.
abdallah@lebanon.demon.co.uk

Ministry of Tourism, PO Box 115344, 5500 Central Bank Street, Beirut, Lebanon. Tel: (1) 343 196 or 340 940/4. Fax: (1) 340 945.

Return ticket required. Requirements may be subject to short-term change. Contact the relevant authority before departure. Passport required: must be valid for at least 6 months beyond the estimated duration of stay.

Visa required. You will be refused entry to Lebanon if there is an Israeli stamp in your passport.

Firearms and ammunitions require a valid import licence.

POLIO, TYPHOID: R. YELLOW FEVER: A vaccination certificate is required if coming from infected areas. OTHER: Cholera, rabies.

W2

Lebanese Pound (L£) = 100 piastres. Credit cards and Travellers cheques have limited acceptance. ATM AVAILABILITY: Over 30 locations.

MONEYGRAM: 426 801 then 800 592 3688.
WESTERN UNION: 01 511 100

AMEX: 0044 1273 696 933
DINERS CLUB: 01 491 576 or 01 500 636
MASTERCARD: 001 314 542 7111
VISA: 001 410 581 9994

AMEX: 0044 1273 571 600
THOMAS COOK: 0044 1733 318 950
VISA: 0044 20 7937 8091

0830-1200 Mon to Sat.

Relatively expensive. Accommodation can be especially expensive for the traveller looking for a cheap place to stay. Food, however can be cheap if purchased from sandwich and snack bars.

Arabic. French and English are spoken. Kurdish and Armenian are spoken by a small minority.

Summer (June–Sept) is hot along the coast and cooler in the mountains. Winter (Dec–mid Mar) is mostly rainy with snow in the mountains. Spring and autumn are cool and pleasant.

Muslim (mainly Shia) and Christian (mostly Roman Catholic).

Jan 1, 6, 7, Feb 9, May 1, 6, Aug 15, Nov 1, 22, Dec 25. Islamic festivals, Easter.

110/220 volts, AC 50 Hz.

Usually 5–6 days to Europe, up to 8 days to the USA.

Women are likely to encounter rude remarks and leers. The dress code should be obeyed and revealing clothes should not be worn.

BUS: Intercity buses are cheap and efficient but may be uncomfortable. TAXI: Fares should be agreed in advance. They are usually shared and a 50% surcharge will be added after 2200 hours. CAR HIRE: chauffeur-driven cars are recommended although self-drive cars are available. DOCUMENTATION: IDP is recommended although not legally required.

Lebanon has emerged from a long period of civil war, which damaged the economy and the social fabric. The population is composed of both Christians and Muslims from a variety of sects.

Muslim traditions and practices should be respected. Casual dress is suitable for daytime clothing. The main danger spots are in the south, which can be subject to Israeli shelling or air raids. The regional security situation can change rapidly: you should keep aware of events and check the FCO travel website and the local media.

Lesotho

CAPITAL: Maseru

GMT +2

FROM UK: 00266. OUTGOING CODE TO UK: 0044

Police: 123 / 124; Ambulance: 121; Fire: 122

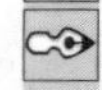
High Commission for the Kingdom of Lesotho, 7 Chesham Place, Belgravia, London SW1 8HN. Tel: 020 7235 5686. Fax: 020 7235 5023.

British High Commission, PO Box Ms 521, Maseru 100, Lesotho. Tel: 323 961. Fax: 310 120. hcmaseru@bhc.org.ls www.bhc.org.ls

Refer to the High Commission.

Lesotho Tourist Board, PO Box 1378 Masseru 100, Lesotho. Tel: 313 760 or 312 896 (information). Fax: 310 108.

Return ticket required. Requirements may be subject to change at short notice. Consult embassy before departure. Valid passport required by all

Required by all non-Commonwealth members.

Departure tax is Lo20, in local currency only, transit passengers and children are exempt.

POLIO, TYPHOID: R. YELLOW FEVER: A vaccination certificate is required by travellers arriving from infected areas. OTHER: Bilharzia and rabies are present.

W1

Loti (Lo) = 100 lisente. Limited acceptance of Visa, MasterCard. Travellers cheques are widely accepted. US$ are the preferred currency. ATM AVAILABILITY: Unavailable.

MONEYGRAM: Unavailable.
WESTERN UNION: 314 255

AMEX: 0044 1273 696 933
DINERS CLUB: 0044 1252 513 500
MASTERCARD: 001 314 542 7111
VISA: 001 410 581 9994

AMEX: 0044 1273 571 600
THOMAS COOK: 0044 1733 318 950
VISA: 0044 20 7937 8091

0830-1530 Mon, Tues, Thur and Fri, 0830-1300 Wed, 0830-1100 Sat.

A developing small African nation with a growing economy.

Sesotho and English.

The climate is temperate. Rain falls mostly between Oct-Apr. The hottest period is between Jan and Feb.

Catholic with Lesotho Evangelical and Anglican.

Jan 1, Mar 12,21, May 2, Jul 4, Oct 4, Dec 25,26. Easter, Ascension Day.

220 volts AC.

7 days.

Women should dress conservatively.

ROADS: Few roads are tarred and are impassable during the rainy season. Lesotho has a high number of road accidents given its small size. Even the previous king died in a road accident in 1996. DOCUMENTATION: IDP is recommended. RAIL: There is no train service in the kingdom.

Inform the head chief if you intend to spend a short stay in a rural village. Dress is casual although stricter in the traditional areas. Religion plays an important part in traditional life. PHOTOGRAPHY: Do not take photos of the palace, police establishments, government offices or anything connected with the military. Lesotho is a very mountainous country. Visitors should bring clothing suitable for cold weather. In the mountains, weather conditions can deteriorate rapidly. In winter (Jun-Oct), snow will often close mountain passes, and temperatures often drop below freezing during the night. Medical facilities in Lesotho are very basic, and many medicines are not available. There is no reliable ambulance service. Good medical care is available in Bloemfontein, South Africa, 90 miles to the west of Maseru.

CAPITAL: Monrovia

GMT

FROM UK: 00231. OUTGOING CODE TO UK: 0044

Not present.

Embassy of the Republic of Liberia, 2 Pembridge Place, London W2 4XB. Tel: 020 7221 1036.

The British Embassy in Abidjan deals with enquiries relating to Liberia (see Côte d'Ivoire).

Refer to the Embassy.

Bureau of Tourism, Sinkor, Monrovia, Liberia. Tel: 222 229.

Return ticket required. Requirements may be subject to change at short notice. Consult embassy before departure. Valid passport required by all.

Visa required.

Import of safety matches.

Departure Tax of L$20, except those under 12 years and those transiting within 24 hours. Tax is payable in local currency.

POLIO, TYPHOID: R. MALARIA: R. Falciparum variety present. High resistance to choloroquine has been reported. YELLOW FEVER: A vaccination certificate must be presented with all visa applications. OTHER: Bilharzia, rabies, cholera and meningitis. HIV/AIDS is widespread.

W1

Liberian Dollar (L$) = 100 cents. Limited acceptance of MasterCard and Visa. Travellers cheques are not accepted. ATM AVAILABILITY: Unavailable.

MONEYGRAM: Unavailable.
WESTERN UNION: Unavailable.AMEX: 0044 1273 696933

AMEX: 0044 1273 696 933
DINERS CLUB: 0044 1252 513 500
MASTERCARD: 001 314 542 7111
VISA: 001 410 581 9994

AMEX: 0044 1273 571 600
THOMAS COOK: 0044 1733 318 950
VISA: 0044 20 7937 8091

0900-1200 Mon to Thur, 0800-1400 Fri. The Bank of Monrovia, Tubman Boulevard, Sinkor, is open 0800-1100 Sat.

Unpredictable due to an unstructured economy and civil unrest.

English and various African languages.

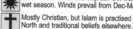

The climate is hot and tropical. Oct-May is wet season. Winds prevail from Dec-Mar.

Mostly Christian, but Islam is practised in the North and traditional beliefs elsewhere.

Jan 1, Feb 11, Mar 8, 15, Apr 12, 14, May 6, 14, 25, Jul 26, Aug 24, Oct 29, Nov 2, 6, 7, 29, Dec 25. Easter.

110 volts AC, 60 Hz

Airmail takes 5-12 days to Europe.

Women should respect Muslim dress codes.

RAIL: Limited services. ROADS: Many of the smaller roads are untarred. Difficulty in bridging river estuaries along the coast.

Visitors are advised by the FCO not to travel to the north-west of Liberia and to any of its borders. The capital Monrovia is calm generally, but tourist facilities are nonexistent. Electricity is in short supply and comes from generators. Heavy rain can last for months at a time in the season from May to October.

CAPITAL: Tripoli

GMT +2

FROM UK: 00218. OUTGOING CODE TO UK: 0044

Not present.

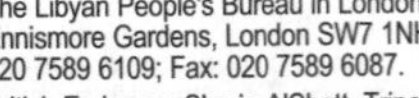

The Libyan People's Bureau in London, 61/62 Ennismore Gardens, London SW7 1NH. Tel: 020 7589 6109; Fax: 020 7589 6087.

British Embassy, Sharia AlShatt, Tripoli. Consular Section: 24th floor, Burj AlFatih,Tripoli, Libya.Tel: 00218 21 335 1422; Fax: 00 218 21 335 1425. belibya@hotmail.com www.britaininlibya.org/

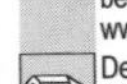

Department of Tourism and Fairs, PO Box 891, Sharia Omar Mukhtar, Tripoli, Libya. Tel: (21) 333 2255.

Return ticket and valid passport required. Requirements may be subject to change at short notice. Consult embassy before going.

Visa required. It is very difficult to obtain tourist visas.

All alcohol, goods made in Israel or manufactured by companies who deal with Israel, and any kind of food are prohibited.

Departure tax of LYD3, payable in local currency, except children under 2 years.

Holders of Israeli and South African passports containing a valid or expired visa for Israel or South Africa, will be refused entry or transit. Women married to, and children of, citizens of Arab League countries will be refused entry if they are travelling alone, unless they are met at the airport by their husband/father.

POLIO, TYPHOID: R. MALARIA: A small risk exists in certain areas. YELLOW FEVER: A vaccination certificate is required for visitors arriving from infected areas. OTHER: Bilharzia, cholera and rabies are present.

W2

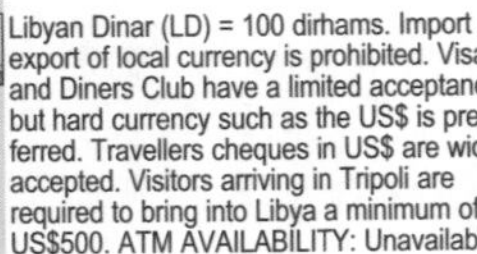

Libyan Dinar (LD) = 100 dirhams. Import and export of local currency is prohibited. Visa and Diners Club have a limited acceptance, but hard currency such as the US$ is preferred. Travellers cheques in US$ are widely accepted. Visitors arriving in Tripoli are required to bring into Libya a minimum of US$500. ATM AVAILABILITY: Unavailable.

MONEYGRAM: Unavailable.
WESTERN UNION: Unavailable.

AMEX: 0044 1273 696 933
DINERS CLUB: 0044 1252 513 500
MASTERCARD: 001 314 542 7111
VISA: 001 410 581 9994

AMEX: 0044 1273 571 600
THOMAS COOK: 0044 1733 318950
VISA: 0044 20 7937 8091

0800-1200 Sat to Wed (winter), 0800-1200 Sat to Thur and 1600-1700 Sat and Wed (summer).

Libya has great internal wealth, but due to its foreign policy cannot form constructive trade links with UN. states.

Arabic, some English and Italian.

The climate is warm all year round. It can be cool in the evenings. Some rainfall Nov-Feb.

Muslim (Sunni).

Mar 3, 28, Jun 11, Jul 23, Sept 1, Oct 7. Islamic festivals.

150/220 volts AC, 50 Hz. There are many power cuts.

Takes approximately 2 weeks to Europe, can be erratic and unreliable.

Women do not attend Arab gatherings. Dress modestly in religious buildings and small towns. Many people advise against women travelling alone in Libya.

ROAD: Petrol is available but spare parts are difficult to obtain. Driving standards are poor. TAXI: Fares should be agreed in advance. CAR HIRE: Available in Tripoli and Benghazi.

Islamic ideals and beliefs provide the conservative foundation of the country's laws and customs. Alcohol is banned absolutely. Tourist facilities are not widely available. Security personnel may place foreign visitors under surveillance: hotel rooms, phones and faxes may be monitored, and personal possessions in hotel rooms searched. Basic modern medical care and medicines may not be available in Libya. If you are a British national visiting for more than two weeks, register with the Consular Section of the British Embassy. The Embassy operates a network of volunteer British Wardens who can keep in touch with the Embassy in a general emergency.

CAPITAL: Vaduz

GMT +1 (GMT +2 during the summer).

FROM UK: 00423. OUTGOING CODE TO UK: 0044

Ambulance: 144; Fire: 118; Police: 117.

Liechtenstein represents very few overseas missions and is generally represented by Switzerland.

British Consulate General, Dufourstrasse 56, CH8008 Zürich, Switzerland. Tel: 91) 261 1520 - 6. Fax (1) 252 8351.

Swiss National Tourist Office (SNTO), Swiss Centre, Swiss Court, London W1V 8EE. Tel: 020 7734 1921 (general enquiries) or 020 7734 4577 (trade). Fax: 020 7437 4577.

Liechtenstein National Tourist Office, Postfach 139, Kirchstrasse 10, FL9490 Vaduz, Liechtenstein. Tel: 232 1443. Fax: 392 1618.

See Switzerland. Valid passport required by all

See Switzerland.

See Switzerland.

See Switzerland

Swiss Franc (SFr) = 100 centimes. All major credit cards and Travellers cheques are accepted. ATM AVAILABILITY: Over 50 locations.

MONEYGRAM: Available in large towns.
WESTERN UNION: Available.

AMEX: 0044 1273 696 933
DINERS CLUB: 0044 1252 513 500
MASTERCARD: 0800 89 7092
VISA: 0800 89 4732

AMEX: 0044 1273 571 600
THOMAS COOK: 0800 55 0130
VISA: 0044 20 7937 8091

0800-1630 Mon to Fri.

Moderate to expensive.

German. A dialect of Alemannish is widely spoken. English may also be spoken.

Temperate climate with wet, warm summers and cool to cold winters.

Christian, mainly Roman Catholic.

Jan 1, 2, 6, Feb 2, Mar 19, May 1, Aug 15, Sep 8, Nov 1, Dec 8, 24, 25, 26, 31. Major Christian feast days.

220 volts AC, 50 Hz.

3-4 days.

Women are unlikely to encounter many problems while travelling in Liechtenstein.

RAIL: The best rail access is via the Swiss border stations at Buchs or Sargans or Feldkirch. BUS: Local buses operate between the local villages. ROAD: A national driving licence is sufficient. Although many roads are mountainous and winding, road safety standards are high. In some mountain areas, vehicle snow chains are required in winter. Road travel can be more dangerous during summer, winter holidays, and Whitsunday weekend (late spring) because of increased traffic.

Lithuania

CAPITAL: Vilnius

GMT +2 (GMT +3 during the summer).

FROM UK: 00370. OUTGOING CODE TO UK: 8/1044 (wait for second dial tone)

Ambulance: 03; Fire: 01; Police: 02.

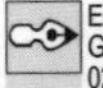
Embassy of the Republic of Lithuania, 84 Gloucester Place, London W1U 6AU. Tel: 020 7486 6401/2. Fax: 020 7486 4603. lralon@globalnet.co.uk

British Embassy, PO Box 863, Antakalnio 2, 2600 Vilnius, Lithuania. Tel: (2) 222 070/1. Fax: (2) 727 579. bevilnius@britain.lt www.britain.lt/

Refer to the Embassy.

Lithuanian State Department of Tourism, Vilnius 4/35, 2600 Vilnius, Lithuania. Tel: 00370 262 26 10; Fax: 00370 2 22 68 19. tb@tourism.lt

Requirements may be subject to short-term change. Contact the relevant authority before departure. Valid passport required by all

Visa regulations are in a state of change. Contact the Embassy for an up to date list.

Narcotics.

US$7.

Rabies, hepatitis A and B and diphtheria are present.

Litas = 100 centas. EXCHANGE: Currency can be exchanged at banks and exchange bureaux. NOTE: The import of local and foreign currency is unlimited but must be declared on arrival. All major credit cards are accepted in large hotels, shops and restaurants. Most banks will cash travellers cheques, but commission rates are high. US$ are the preferred currency. ATM AVAILABILITY: Over 10 locations.

MONEYGRAM: Unavailable.
WESTERN UNION: 22 232 613.

AMEX: 8/1044 1273 696 933
DINERS CLUB: 8/1044 1252 513 500
MASTERCARD: 8/101 314 542 7111
VISA: 8/101 410 581 9994

AMEX: 8/1044 1273 571 600
THOMAS COOK: 8/1044 1733 318950
VISA: 8/1044 20 7937 8091

0900-1700 Mon to Fri.

Tourists can expect to pay higher prices than the locals.

Lithuanian and a large number of dialects.

Temperate climate but with considerable temperature variations. Summers are warm and spring and autumn are usually mild. Winters can be very cold.

Roman Catholic. Minorities of Evangelical Lutheran, Evangelical Reformism and Russian Orthodox.

Jan 1, Feb 16, Mar 11, May 1, Jul 6, Aug 15, Nov 1, Dec 25, 26. Easter.

220 volts Ac, 50 Hz. European 2-pin plugs are used.

To Western Europe takes up to 6 days.

Traditionally a patriarchal society, but gender roles are slowly changing.

RAIL: There are good connections from Vilnius to the other main cities. ROAD: There is a good network of roads. Drivers must always be alert to hazards, especially slow-moving horse carts or trucks travelling at night without tail-lights or reflectors. BUS: Generally more frequent and quicker than domestic trains and serve almost every town and village. CAR HIRE: Several local firms provide car hire services. DOCUMENTATION: European nationals should be in possession of the new European driving licence. Otherwise, a national driving licence is sufficient.

Lithuanians appreciate a show of respect for their culture and national heritage. Do not accept food and drink from strangers. Petty crime is rife on public transport. Do not accept food and drinks from strangers in bars and nightclubs; some visitors have been drugged and robbed this way.

CAPITAL: Luxembourg-Ville

GMT +1 (GMT +2 during the summer).

FROM UK: 00352. OUTGOING CODE TO UK: 0044

Ambulance / Fire: 112; Police: 113.

Embassy of the Grand Duchy of Luxembourg, 27 Wilton Crescent, London SW1X 8SD. Tel: 020 7235 6961. Fax: 020 7235 9735.

British Embassy, 14 boulevard Roosevelt, L2450 Luxembourg-Ville, Luxembourg. Tel: 229 864/5/6. Fax: 229 867. britemb@pt.lu

Luxembourg Tourist Office, 122 Regent Street, London W1R 5FE. Tel: 020 7434 2800. Fax: 020 7734 1205. tourism@luxembourg.co.uk www.luxembourg.co.uk

Office National du Tourisme BP 1001, 77 rue d'Anvers, L1010 Luxembourg-Ville, Luxembourg. Tel: 400 8081. Fax: 404 748. Tel: 00352 42 82 8210; Fax: 00352 42 82 8238. tourism@ont.smtp.etat.lu www.etat.lu/tourism

Requirements may be subject to short-term change. Contact the relevant authority before departure. Valid passport required

Visa not required by nationals of EU member states.

Narcotics and firearms.

US$10 is levied on all foreign departures.

Rabies.

Euro = 100 cents. Credit cards and travellers cheques are widely accepted. ATM AVAILABILITY: Over 250 locations.

MONEYGRAM: Available at single American Express location.
WESTERN UNION: 0800 4040.

AMEX: 0044 1273 696 933
DINERS CLUB: 22 76 36
MASTERCARD: 0800 4533
VISA: 0800 2012

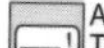
AMEX: 0800 3276
THOMAS COOK: 0800 2123
VISA: 0800 2119

Generally 0900–1200 and 1330–1630 Mon to Fri, but may vary greatly.

Similar to other Western European countries.

Letzeburgesch, a German-Frankish dialect. French and German are usually used for administrative purposes. Many also speak English.

May–Sept is warm. Snow is common during the winter months.

Mostly Roman Catholic with Protestant, Anglican and Jewish minorities.

Jan 1, May 1, Jun 23, Aug 15, Sep 1, Nov 1, Dec 25, 26. Major Christian feast days.

220 volts AC, 50 Hz.

2–4 days to other European destinations.

Women enjoy a liberated culture, similar to the rest of Western Europe. Usual precautions apply. No additional problems should be encountered.

RAIL: Efficient service and fully integrated with the bus service. Reductions can often be found. ROAD: Excellent network. BUS: Cross-country buses are punctual and operate between all major towns. TAXI: Metered, but cannot be hailed in the street – a 15% tip is usual. CAR HIRE: All the main agencies operate. DOCUMENTATION: Third-party insurance is necessary. A green card is strongly recommended. A valid national licence is sufficient.

Western European social courtesies should be followed. Casual dress is widely acceptable, but formal clothing is required by some restaurants and social functions.

Macau

CAPITAL: Macau

GMT +8

FROM UK: 00853 . OUTGOING CODE TO UK: 0044

Fire, Police and Ambulance: 999.

Embassy of the People's Republic of China, 49-51 Portland Place, London W1N 4JL. Tel: 020 7631 1430. Macau is a Special Administrative Region of China.

British nationals in Macau needing assistance should contact the British ConsulateGeneral in Hong Kong. Tel: 2901 3204.

Macau Tourism, 1 Battersea Church Road, London SW11. Tel: 020 7771 7006. bernstein@cibgroup.co.uk

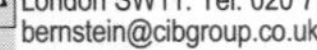
Macau Government Tourist Office, 9 Largo do Senado, PO Box 3006 Macau. Tel: 00853 315566; Fax: 00853 510104. www.macau-tourism.gov.mo/index_en.htm

Requirements may change at short notice. Contact the embassy before departure. Valid passport required by all.

Visa not required by nationals of Great Britain for stays of less than 20 days. Visas may be obtained on arrival in Macau.

Narcotics, firearms, endangered species of animal and plants and pesticides.

Departure tax of MOP130 per person.

Diarrhoel diseases, hepatitis A and B, Oriental liver and oriental lung fluke and haemorrhagic fever with renal syndrome may occur in this area.

W1

Pataca (MOP) = 100 avos. MasterCard is accepted. Travellers cheques may be changed at hotels, banks and bureaux de change. US$ is the preferred currency ATM AVAILABILITY: Over 20 locations.

MONEYGRAM: 0800 111 then 800 592 3688. WESTERN UNION: Unavailable.

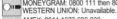

AMEX: 0044 1273 696 933
DINERS CLUB: 0044 1252 513 500
MASTERCARD: 001 314 542 7111
VISA: 882 3002 8561

AMEX: 0044 1273 571 600
THOMAS COOK: 0044 1733 318950
VISA: 0044 20 7937 8091

0930–1600 Mon to Fri, 0930–1200 Sat.

Macau is a free port, offering a variety of bargains. There is a wide range of accommodation, suitable for all budgets.

Portuguese and Cantonese. English may be spoken by those involved in tourism.

Subtropical climate with very hot summers. There is a rainy period during the summer months. Winds can reach gale force and typhoons are not unheard of.

Roman Catholicism, Buddhism, Daoism and Confucianism.

Jan 1, Apr 25, May 1, Jun 10, 24, Oct 1, 5, Nov 2, Dec 1, 8, 25. Easter, Chinese Festivals.

Usually 220 Volts AC 50 Hz.

3–5 days.

Travel is as safe as in any Western country. Revealing beachwear, however is likely to arouse attention.

ROAD: Traffic drives on the left in Macau. Roads are narrow and winding, and generally congested throughout the day.There are 5 bus routes in the city. TAXI: Taxis are plentiful and inexpensive, Fares should be agreed in advance. CAR HIRE: Available. DOCUMENTATION: IDP not required from drivers from the UK.

Macau is a mixture of Portuguese, Chinese and Western culture. Following the handover to China, Macau has retained its character and autonomy in local matters, including currency, laws, and border controls. Facilities for tourism are well developed. Gambling and tourism are major factors in Macau's economy. Violent crime is quite rare and is usually associated with the gambling industry. Although most of the violence has been aimed at police or rival gangs near casinos in the early hours, visitors should be vigilant and take particular care in and around casinos. Pickpockets are more of a problem for tourists, who should be on their guard in crowded places. Cotton or light clothing is recommended for the summer. It is usually casual even in the casinos. Woollen clothing and occasionally even a topcoat is required for the winter. Sweaters and jackets are sometimes necessary for the cooler evenings in Mar–May and Sept–Nov.

Macedonia

CAPITAL: Skopje

GMT +1 (GMT +2 during the summer).

FROM UK: 00389 . OUTGOING CODE TO UK: 0044

Police: 92; Fire: 93; Ambulance: 94.

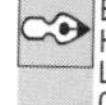
Embassy of the Republic of Macedonia, 10 Harcourt House, 19A Cavendish Square, London W1M 9AD. Tel: 020 7499 5152; Fax: 020 7499 2864. mkuk@btinternet.com

British Embassy, Dimitrija Chupovski 26, 4th Floor, Skopje 91000, Macedonia.
Tel: 00389 91 116 772; Fax: 00389 91 117 005. beskopje@mt.net.mk
www.britishembassy.org.mk

Not available.

Not present.

Requirements may be subject to short-term change. Contact embassy before departure. Valid passport required by all.

Visa not required by nationals of EU countries.

Narcotics and firearms.

Rabies, tick-borne encephalitis.

Macedonian Denar = 100 deni. Credit cards are accepted on a limited basis, in the capital only. Travellers cheques, preferably in US$, are easily exchanged. ATM AVAILABILITY: 7 locations.

MONEYGRAM: Unavailable.
WESTERN UNION: Unavailable.

AMEX: 0044 1273 696 933
DINERS CLUB: 091 113 628
MASTERCARD: 001 314 542 7111
VISA: 001 410 581 9994

AMEX: 0044 1273 571 600
THOMAS COOK: 0044 1733 318950
VISA: 0044 20 7937 8091

0730-1530 Mon-Fri.

Macedonia is the poorest of the former Yugoslav republics. Tourists can expect to pay more for goods than the locals.

Macedonian. Albanian, Turkish, Roma and Serbo-Croat are also used by ethnic groups.

Continental climate with hot summers and very cold winters.

Eastern Orthodox Macedonians, Muslim Albanians, Muslim Turks, Serbian Orthodox Serbs.

Jan 1, 6, 7, 14, Mar 8, May 1, 24, Aug 2, Sep 8. Easter, Eid Al Fitr, Eid Al Adha.

220 volts AC, 50 Hz.

2-3 days within Europe, except for Serbia and Greece, with which communications are currently uncertain.

Due to religious restrictions, women play fairly traditional roles within society. Muslim dress is worn by about 20% of women.

With the recent socio-economic collapse of the republic, day-to-day business often moves very slowly or not at all, due to the local bureaucracy.

There have been recent incidents of violence between the Macedonian and Albanian communities in urban areas including the towns of Tetovo and Bitola. The Macedonian authorities have appealed to the population to show restraint but have also warned that similar outbreaks of violence might occur in other ethnically mixed towns.
The FCO advises against all non-essential travel to Macedonia. The situation is subject to change at short notice due to political uncertainty. Contact the Foreign and Commonwealth Travel Advice Unit for up-to-date information.

Madagascar

CAPITAL: Antananarivo

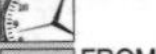
GMT +3

FROM UK: 00261 . OUTGOING CODE TO UK: 0044

Not present.

Consulate of the Republic of Madagascar, 16 Lanark Mansions, Pennard Road, London W12 8DT. Tel: 020 8746 0133. Fax: 020 8746 0134.

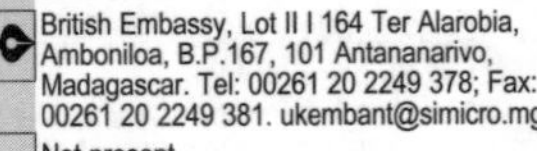
British Embassy, Lot II I 164 Ter Alarobia, Amboniloa, B.P.167, 101 Antananarivo, Madagascar. Tel: 00261 20 2249 378; Fax: 00261 20 2249 381. ukembant@simicro.mg

Not present.

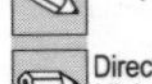
Direction du Tourisme de Madagascar, Ministry of Tourism, BP 610, Tsimbazaza, 101 Antananarivo, Madagascar. Tel: (2) 26298. Fax: (2) 26710.

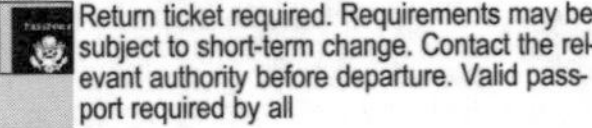
Return ticket required. Requirements may be subject to short-term change. Contact the relevant authority before departure. Valid passport required by all

Visa required.

All vegetables must be declared and animals require a detailed veterinary certificate and must be vaccinated against rabies.

FRF100, or US$2, on most international flights.

POLIO, TYPHOID: R. MALARIA: Exists in the faliciparum variety all year. The highest risk is along the coast. Resistance to chloroquine has been reported. YELLOW FEVER: A vaccination certificate is required from everyone arriving from areas considered by the Malagasy authorities to be infected. OTHER: Bilharzia, cholera, rabies, hepatitis A, B and E are endemic. Dysentery and many viral diseases have been reported.

W1

Malagasy Franc (MGFr) = 100 centimes. Non-residents cannot export local currency. Credit cards are accepted in the capital's major hotels. Travellers cheques can be exchanged at banks and major hotels, French francs preferred. ATM AVAILABILITY: A few have been installed in Antananarivo.

MONEYGRAM: Unavailable.
WESTERN UNION: Unavailable.

AMEX: 0044 1273 696 933
DINERS CLUB: 0044 1252 513 500
MASTERCARD: 001 314 542 7111
VISA: 001 410 581 9994

AMEX: 0044 1273 571 600
THOMAS COOK: 0044 1733 318950
VISA: 0044 20 7937 8091

0800–1300 Mon to Fri.

Relatively inexpensive. Hotels vary from international prices to cheaper guesthouses.

Malagasy and French. Local dialects are also spoken. Very little English is spoken.

Generally hot and subtropical. Nov–Mar: rainy season; Apr–Oct: dry season. The South and West are hot and dry. Dec–Mar: the monsoon may cause storms and cyclones. Mountainous regions are hot and thundery Nov-Apr, dry, cool and windy the rest of the year.

Mostly animist and Christian with the remainder Muslim.

Jan 1, Mar 29, May 1, Jun 26, Sep 27, Nov 1, Dec 30.

Mostly 220 volts AC, 50 Hz. Plugs are generally 2-pin.

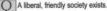

Poste restante at the main post office is the most reliable option. Airmail to Europe takes at least 7 days, surface mail 3 to 4 months.

A liberal, friendly society exists.

FLIGHTS: Most places can be reached by air. Air Madagascar's 'Air Tourist Pass' allows unlimited travel for certain periods. SEA/RIVER/CANAL: Many coastal transport services. RAIL: Services operate in the East, North and South. ROAD: The road network is need of repair. Many are impassable during rainy season. BUS: Services are often unreliable. A flat fare is charged. TAXI/RICKSHAW/STAGECOACH: Available.

The locals are very welcoming and have a very relaxed attitude towards time. To offer money for board and lodging could be considered an insult, tact is required. Respect should always be paid to local taboos. PHOTOGRAPHY: Do not take photographs of military establishments or the police.

Malawi

CAPITAL: Lilongwe

GMT +2

FROM UK: 00265 . OUTGOING CODE TO UK: 10144

Not present.

High Commission for the Republic of Malawi, 33 Grosvenor Street, London W1X 0DE. Tel: 020 7491 4172/7. Fax: 020 7491 9916.

British High Commission, PO Box 30042, Capital City, Lilongwe 3, Malawi. Tel: 00265 772 400. Fax: 00265 772 657. bhc@wiss.co.mw

Refer to the High Commission.

Department of Tourism, PO Box 402, Blantyre, Malawi. Tel: 620 300. Fax: 620 947.

Return ticket required. Requirements may be subject to change at short notice. Consult embassy before departure. Valid passport required by all

On arrival a 3-month visa will be issued. Extensions will not normally be granted in Malawi.

Departure tax US$20, payable in US currency unless a holder of a national passport when local currency will be accepted.

POLIO, TYPHOID: R. MALARIA: Exists throughout the year in the falciparum variety. Resistance to chloroquine has been reported. YELLOW FEVER: A vaccination certificate is required by visitors travelling from infected areas within the last 6 days. OTHER: Bilharzia, cholera and rabies. There is a very high prevalence of AIDS/HIV in Malawi.

W1

Kwacha (Mk) = 100 tambala. EXCHANGE: Lesser-known currencies are difficult to exchange. There is limited acceptance of credit cards. American Express, MasterCard and Diners Club are accepted in the capital city and main hotels. US$ and Pound sterling are the preferred currencies in travellers cheques. ATM AVAILABILITY: Unavailable.

MONEYGRAM: Unavailable.
WESTERN UNION: Unavailable.

AMEX: 0044 1273 696 933
DINERS CLUB: 0044 1252 513 500
MASTERCARD: 01 314 542 7111
VISA: 001 410 581 9994

AMEX: 0044 1273 571 600
THOMAS COOK: 0044 1733 318950
VISA: 0044 20 7937 8091

0800–1300 Mon to Fri

Malawi's economy fluctuates with developments in the climate. Currently the cost of living is reasonable due to the country's heavy borrowing.

English, Chichewa and various other African languages.

Winter: May-July and gets cold at night. Mid Oct–Apr is the rainy season. May–Oct is dry.

Animist with Christian, Hindu and Muslim minorities.

Jan 1, 15, Mar 3, May 6, Jun 14, Jul 6, second Mon in Oct, Dec 25, 26. Easter.

220/240 volts AC, 50 Hz Various types of plug are used. Most modern buildings use square 3-pin.

10 days to Europe.

Women should cover their knees with appropriate clothing.

RAIL: Regular but slow and expensive services. ROAD: All major and most secondary are all-weather roads. Malawi is a very dangerous place to drive. The fatal accident rate is very high. There have been cases of car theft, mainly of 4 x 4 vehicles in Lilongwe. DOCUMENTATION: UK licence is sufficient.

Dress codes should be observed and respected, even though Malawi is more relaxed than in the past. Long hair for men is disliked. Bag snatching is a problem in the main towns and cities. Be cautious of people who offer to act as guides.

Malaysia

CAPITAL: Kuala Lumpur

GMT +8

FROM UK: 0060 . OUTGOING CODE TO UK: 0044

All services: 999.

Malaysian High Commission, 45 Belgrave Square, London SW1X 8QT. Tel: 020 7235 8033. Fax: 020 7235 5161. mwlondon@btinternet.com

British High Commission, 185 Jalan Ampang, 50450 Kuala Lumpar, Malaysia. Tel: (03) 248 2122 or 248 7122 (consular section). Fax: (03) 248 0880.
bhckulppa@ppp.nasionet.net
www.britain.org.my/

Tourism Malaysia, 57 Trafalgar Square, London WC2N 5DU. Tel 020 7930 7932. Fax: 020 7930 9015.

Tourism Development Corporation of Malaysia, 24-27th Floors, Menara Dato'Onn, Putra World Trade Centre, 45 Jalan Tun Ismail, 50480 Kuala Lumpur, Malaysia. Tel: (3) 293 5188. Fax: (3) 293 5884.

Return ticket required. Requirements may change at short notice. Contact the embassy. Passport required: must be valid for 6 months beyond the intended stay. All visitors must have proof of adequate funds for stay.

Most nationals do not require a visa providing the stay is less than a month and for social, business purposes. A visit pass is required, which will be issued at the point of entry.

Visitors must declare valuables and may be required to pay a deposit. It is prohibited to import goods from Israel, pornography or any material including verses from the Koran.

R40 for international departures.

Women in an advanced state of pregnancy and people of a scruffy appearance will not be allowed entry.

POLIO, TYPHOID: R. MALARIA: Exists in certain inland regions e.g. Sabah where there is a risk in the falciparum variety, reported as being highly resistant to chloroquine.

YELLOW FEVER: A vaccination certificate is required if arriving from infected areas.
OTHER: Cholera, rabies.

W1

Ringgit (R) = 100 sen. All credit cards are accepted. Travellers cheques are accepted by all banks, hotels and department stores. US$ cheques are preferred. ATM AVAILABILITY: Over 2000 locations.

MONEYGRAM: Unavailable
WESTERN UNION: Unavailable.

AMEX: 0044 1273 696 933
DINERS CLUB: 03 216 11 266
MASTERCARD: 001800 804 594
VISA: 001800 800 159

AMEX: 0044 1273 571 600
THOMAS COOK: 0044 1733 318950
VISA: 0044 20 7937 8091

1000–1500 Mon to Fri, 0930–1130 Sat. Banks in Sabah usually open 0800 and close for lunch 1200–1400.

Can be reasonably cheap. Wide range of accommodation available. Goods and luxury items vary in price, depending on location. Malaysia prides itself on an extensive range of cuisines.

Bahasa Malaysian. English is also widely spoken.

Tropical without extremely high temperatures. Days are very warm whilst nights are fairly cool. Aug is the wettest time on the West coast. East Malaysia has heavy rains Nov-Feb. Rainfall differs in the East and West coast according to the monsoon wind.

Muslim majority. Buddhist, Taoist, Confucianists, Hindu and Animist.

Jan 1, Feb 1, second Sat in Mar, Apr 8, 15, 19, May 1, 7, 30, 31, June 12, first Sat in Jun, second Sat in July, Jul 19, Aug 31, second Sat in Sep, Sep 16, second Sat in Oct, Dec 25. Islamic, Hindu, Buddhist and Chinese festivals, Good Fri.

220 volts AC, 50 Hz. Square 3- pin plugs are used.

There are post offices in the commercial centres of all towns.

Malaysia is a multiracial society. Although predominantly Muslim, other cultures influence women's status in society. Women travellers must respect the Muslim dress code where this applies. Do not walk alone at night on empty streets or beaches.

ROAD: Most roads are paved. BUS: Services are extensive. TAXI: There is a surcharge between 2400 and 0600 of 50%.

Respect religious beliefs – take off your shoes at the door and wear the appropriate clothing. Smoking is prohibited in a number of public places. There are severe penalties for driving offences.

Street crime is on the increase, particularly bag snatching. Passports are a particular target for thieves in the airport. Credit card fraud is also rife. The FCO also reports that conmen have lured tourists into gambling games and forced them to put up large amounts of money.

The authorities are strict about illegal drugs. The death penalty is still on the statute book for serious cases. Visitors should be aware that they could be asked for a urine test on arrival and be deported if the test is positive.

Maldives Republic

CAPITAL: Malé

GMT +5

FROM UK: 00960 . OUTGOING CODE TO UK: 0044

Police: 119; Fire: 118; Ambulance: 102.

Maldives High Commission, 22 Nottingham Place, London W1M 3FB. Tel: 020 7224 2135. Fax: 020 7224 2157. maldives.high.commission@virgin.net

The British High Commission in Colombo deals with enquiries relating to the Maldives (see the entry for Sri Lanka).

Refer to the High Commission for tourist information.

Maldives Tourism Promotion Board, 4th fl, Bank of Maldives Building, Malé 2005, Republic of Maldives, Tel: 00960 323228; Fax: 00960 323229 www.visitmaldives.com

Return ticket required. Requirements may be subject to short-term change. Contact the relevant authority before departure. Valid passport required by all.

Tourist visas for 30 days will be issued to all visitors in possession of valid travel documents. NOTE: Visitors must be in possession of US$10 per day of stay.

Alcoholic beverages, pornographic literature, idols of worship and non-Islamic religious artefacts (personal Bibles are permitted). Pork products and certain other animal products may not be imported.

US$10 is levied on all international departures.

POLIO, TYPHOID: R. MALARIA: Malaria is disappearing. The last two incidents reported were in 1983. YELLOW FEVER: A vaccination certificate is required from travellers coming from infected areas. OTHER: Rabies, hepatitis A, B and E can occur.

W2 (the water in resort areas is generally safe).

Maldivian Rufiya (Rf) = 100 laari. Most major island resorts will accept Amex, Visa, MasterCard, and Diners Club. Travellers cheques are generally accepted in US$. ATM AVAILABILITY:Unavailable.

MONEYGRAM: Unavailable
WESTERN UNION: Unavailable.

AMEX: 0044 1273 696 933
DINERS CLUB: 0044 1252 513 500
MASTERCARD: 001 314 542 7111
VISA: 001 410 581 9994

AMEX: 0091 11 614 5920
THOMAS COOK: 0044 1733 318950
VISA: 0044 20 7937 8091

0900–1300 Sun to Thur.

As a luxury holiday destination the Maldives can be very expensive in the tourist centres.

Dhivehi. English spoken in Malé and resorts.

The climate is hot and tropical. There are two monsoons, the south-west monsoon from May to Oct and the Northeast monsoon from Nov to Apr. The temperature rarely falls below 25ºC, even during the night. The best time to visit is November to Easter.

Sunni Muslim.

Jan 1, Jul 26, 27, Nov 3, 11, 12. Islamic festivals.

220 volts AC, 50 Hz. Round 2-pin plugs are used, although square-pin plugs are becoming more common.

Airmail to Western Europe takes about 1 week.

Women who are not involved in the tourist industry live in isolated communities on remote islands. The government enforces a strict Muslim code.

SEA: Island-hopping ferry services are available. ROAD: Travel on individual islands creates few problems since few of them take longer than half an hour to cross on foot. Many of the islands are not big enough to need roads.

The Republic of Maldives consists of 1200 islands south-west of Sri Lanka in the Indian Ocean. Tourist resorts are self-contained, catering for the visitors' needs. Backpacking is prohibited. The government enforces standards restricting beachwear outside the resorts. Dress code is informal but nudism is an offence in the Maldives, and topless bathing is not allowed, even on otherwise uninhabited islands. There are severe penalties for drug offences.

CAPITAL: Bamako

GMT

FROM UK: 00223. OUTGOING CODE TO UK: 0044

Not present.

No embassy in the UK. EUROPE: Embassy of the Republic of Mali, Ave Molière 487, 1050 Brussels, Belgium. Tel: 0032 2 345 7432. Fax: 0032 2 344 5700.

British Consulate, BP 2069, rue 111, porte 89, Badalabougou, Bamako. Tel/Fax: 00223 23 34 12, britcon@spider.toolnet.org.

Refer to the Embassy in Belgium.

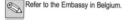

Ministry of Industry, Handicrafts and Tourism BP 1759, Bamako, Mali. Tel: 228 058. Fax: 230 261.

Return ticket required. Requirements may be subject to change at short notice. Consult embassy before departure. Valid passport required

Visa required.

Cameras and film must be declared on arrival.

XO 6000, for destinations in Africa. XOF4500 or US$12 for international flights. Children under two years are exempt.

POLIO, TYPHOID: R. MALARIA: Exists throughout the year in the falciparum variety. Resistance to chloroquine has been reported. YELLOW FEVER: A vaccination certificate is required by travellers over one year of age arriving from all countries. OTHER: Bilharzia, cholera and rabies.

W1

XOF Franc (XOF Fr) = 100 centimes
EXCHANGE: should be available from most banks, however sufficient time must be allowed. French Franc notes are sometimes accepted in cash transactions. Limited use of MasterCard and Visa – they are accepted in the capital city only. Travellers cheques: French francs are the preferred currency.
ATM AVAILABILITY: Unavailable.

MONEYGRAM: Unavailable.
WESTERN UNION: 22 50 89.

AMEX: 0044 1273 696 933
DINERS CLUB: 0044 1252 513 500
MASTERCARD: 001 314 542 7111
VISA: 001 410 581 9994

AMEX: 0044 1273 571 600
THOMAS COOK: 0044 1733 318950
VISA: 0044 20 7937 8091

0730–1200 and 1315–1500 Mon to Thur, 0730–1230 Fri.

Mali is one of the poorest countries in the world and is looking to develop a tourist industry.

French and some African languages are also spoken.

June–Oct is the rainy season. Oct–Feb is the cool season. Mar-May is the hot season.

Muslim with Christian and Animist minorities.

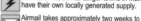

Jan 20, May 25, Sep 22, Nov 19.

220 volts AC, 50 Hz. Larger towns in Mali have their own locally generated supply.

Airmail takes approximately two weeks to Europe. International post is limited to main towns and central post offices.

Women must dress modestly. Women travelling alone will arouse the attention of locals, even if visiting with a guide.

FLIGHTS: Limited provision. ROADS: Range from moderate to very bad. Driving can be difficult during the rainy season. Police checkpoints frequently interrupt journeys.

Religious customs should be respected. The people are very proud of their traditions. Discussion of politics should be avoided. Travel to the north of the country should be avoided, and in some cases visitors should only travel in groups. There have been reports of visitors to Timbuktu being attacked and robbed by armed gangs intent on stealing vehicles. While the level of violent crime remains low, petty crimes, such as pickpocketing and simple theft, are common.

Malta

CAPITAL: Valletta

GMT +1 (GMT +2 during the summer).

FROM UK: 00356. OUTGOING CODE TO UK: 0044

Police: 191; Ambulance: 196; Fire: 199.

High Commission of Malta, Malta House, 36-38 Piccadilly, London W1V 0PP. Tel: 020 7292 4800. Fax 020 7734 1832.

British High Commission, PO Box 506, 7 St Anne Street, Floriana, Malta GC. Tel: 233 134. Fax: 242 001. bhc@vol.net.mt www.britain.com.mt/

Malta National Tourist Office, Malta House, 36-38 Piccadilly, London W1V 0PP. Tel: 020 7292 4900. Fax: 020 7734 1880. office.uk@visitmalta.com www.visitmalta.com

National Tourism Organisation – (NTOM), 280 Republic Street, Valetta CMR 02, Malta. Tel: 224 444. Fax: 224 401.

Return ticket required. Requirements may be subject to short-term change. Contact the relevant authority before departure. Valid passport required.

Visa not required by nationals of the EU.

Pets are not allowed into Malta without prior approval from the Director of Agriculture and Fisheries. It is advisable to declare any large electronic equipment (e.g. video cameras, portable televisions) on arrival as this will prevent duty being levied on them on departure.

YELLOW FEVER: A vaccination certificate is required from travellers over 9 months of age arriving from infected areas. OTHER: A cholera vaccination certificate may be required from travellers arriving from infected areas.

Maltese Lira (MTL) = 100 cents = 100 mils. EXCHANGE: Money can be exchanged at banks, some hotels and shops. NOTE: The import of local currency is limited to MTL 50. The export of local currency is limited to MTL 25. Credit cards and Travellers cheques are accepted. The preferred currency for cheques is Pound sterling. ATM AVAILABILITY: Over 100 locations.

MONEYGRAM: 0800 890 110.
WESTERN UNION: 235 751.

AMEX: 0044 1273 696 933
DINERS CLUB: 0044 1252 513 500
MASTERCARD: 001 314 542 7111
VISA: 001 410 581 9994

AMEX: 0044 1273 571 600
THOMAS COOK: 0044 1733 318950
VISA: 0044 20 7937 8091

0800–1200 Mon to Thur, 0800–1200 and 1430–1600 Fri, 0800–1130 Sat.

Relatively inexpensive.

Maltese. English and Italian may also be spoken.

Mediterranean climate. Hot summers especially July-Sept, although there are cool breezes. Rain falls for very short periods. Winters are mild.

Roman Catholic.

Jan 1, Feb 10, Mar 19, 31, May 1, Jun 7, 29, Aug 15, Sep 8, 21, Dec 8, 13, 25. Carnival week before Lent, Easter.

240 volts AC, 50 Hz.

Good postal services exist within the island.

Revealing clothes should not be worn away from the beach / pool.

ROAD: Traffic drives on the left. Many roads are narrow and winding, with poor visibility around bends. BUS: Good local services operate from Luqa, Valletta, Sa Maison and Victoria (Gozo) to all towns. TAXI: Meter-operated under government control. CAR HIRE: A number of firms are present and rates on Malta are amongst the cheapest in Europe. DOCUMENTATION: Full national driving licence is required.

Visitors should note the importance of the Roman Catholic church, e.g. modest dress should be adopted (legs and shoulders covered) when visiting churches. Malta and Gozo have a low rate of crime. Incidents of pickpocketing and purse-snatching are relatively rare; however, break-ins and thefts from parked vehicles and thefts of cars are on the increase.

CAPITAL: Fort-de-France

GMT –4.

FROM UK: 00596. OUTGOING CODE TO UK: 0044

Police: 17; Fire/Ambulance: 18.

Martinique is an overseas territory of France; see under France.

British Consulate, Route du Phare, 97200 Fort-de-France, Martinique. Tel: 615 630. Fax: 613 389.

French West Indies Tourist Office, 178 Piccadilly, London, W1V 0AL. Tel: 020 7629 2869. Fax: 020 7493 6594.

Office du Tourisme de la Martinique, Rue Ernest Deproge, 97200 Fort-de-France, Martinique. Tel: 00596 63 79 60. Fax: 00596 73 66 93. www.martinique.org/

Return ticket required. Requirements may be subject to short-term change. Contact embassy before departure. Valid passport required: As for France.

As for France.

Same as for France.

FFr 75 payable in local currency is levied on all foreign nationals.

As for France.

POLIO, TYPHOID: R. YELLOW FEVER: A vaccination certificate is required from travellers over 1 year of age coming from infected areas. OTHER: Bilharzia, tuberculosis.

W2

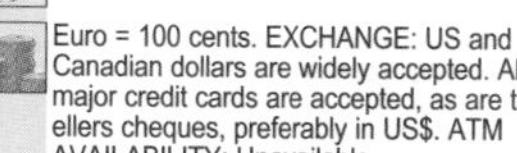
Euro = 100 cents. EXCHANGE: US and Canadian dollars are widely accepted. All major credit cards are accepted, as are travellers cheques, preferably in US$. ATM AVAILABILITY: Unavailable.

MONEYGRAM: Unavailable.
WESTERN UNION: Unavailable.

AMEX: 0044 1273 696 933
DINERS CLUB: 0044 1252 513 500
MASTERCARD: 1 314 542 7111
VISA: 1 410 581 9994

AMEX: 1801 964 6665
THOMAS COOK: 609 987 7300
VISA: 0044 20 7937 8091

0800–1600 Mon to Fri.

Expensive, especially in the tourist centres.

French (Creole dialect).

Warm all year round with most rain falling during the autumn, although showers can occur all year round. Upland areas are cooler.

Roman Catholic.

Jan 1, May 1, 8, Jul 14, Aug 15, Nov 1, 11, Dec 25, 26. Christian feast days.

220/380 volts AC, 50 Hz.

1 Week. Airmail must be sent from post offices.

Usual precautions should be taken. Do not travel alone at night.

SEA: Scheduled ferries operate between the main ports. ROAD: The system is well developed and surfaced. BUS: A limited service operates. TAXI: Government controlled, plentiful, safe and reasonably cheap if shared. CAR HIRE: Excellent car hire facilities are available. Bicycles can also be hired. DOCUMENTATION: An IDP is recommended, but a national driving licence is sufficient providing the driver has at least one year's experience.

The French influence is clearly evident. The usual social courtesies should be observed. Martinique has the best medical care in the Eastern Caribbean, with 13 hospitals, though not all doctors speak or understand English. The hurricane season runs from June to November.

Mauritania

CAPITAL: Nouakchott

GMT

FROM UK: 00222. OUTGOING CODE TO UK: 0044 Most international calls go through the operator

Not present.

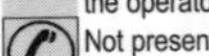

Embassy of the Islamic Republic of Mauritania, 140 Bow Common Lane, London E3 4BH. Tel: 020 8980 4382. Fax: 020 8980 2232.

The British Embassy in Rabat, Morocco handles all enquiries to Mauritania : British Embassy, BP 45, 17 Boulevard de la Tour Hassan, Rabat, Morocco.

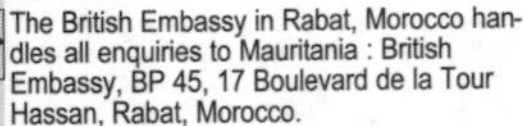

Refer to the Honorary Consulate.

Société Mauritanienne de Tourisme et d'Hôtellerie (SMTH), BP 552, Nouakchott, Mauritania. Tel: 53351.

Return ticket required. Requirements may change at short notice. Contact the embassy before departure Valid passport required

Visa required

Alcohol cannot be imported.

US$ 2, payable on all international departures.

POLIO, TYPHOID: R. MALARIA: Risk exists throughout the year in the falciparum variety. YELLOW FEVER: A vaccination certificate is required for all travellers above one year of age, except travellers arriving from noninfected areas and staying less than two weeks in the country. OTHER: Bilharzia, cholera, rabies.

W1

Mauritanian Ougiya (U) = 5 khoums. NOTE: Import and export of local currency is prohibited. Credit cards and travellers cheques (in French Francs) have limited acceptance. ATM AVAILABILITY: Unavailable.

MONEYGRAM: Unavailable
WESTERN UNION: 25 36 36.

AMEX: 0044 1273 696 933
DINERS CLUB: 0044 1252 513 500
MASTERCARD: 001 314 542 7111
VISA: 001 410 581 9994

AMEX: 0044 1273 571 600
THOMAS COOK: 0044 1733 318950
VISA: 0044 20 7937 8091

0700–1500 Sun to Thur.

Very inexpensive.

Arabic and French. English is rarely spoken.

Most of the country is dry and hot with little rain. In the south, the rainy season is July–Sept. The deserts are cool and windy in March and April.

Islam.

Jan 1, Mar 8, May 1, 25, Jul 10, Nov 28. Islamic festivals.

127/220 volts AC, 50Hz. Round 2-pin plugs are usually used.

2 weeks to Europe. Postal facilities limited to main cities.

Women should dress modestly due to the Islamic Influence.

RAIL: 1 line operates between Nouadhibou and Nouakchott which serves passengers for free, however this is not recommended as journeys are often long and arduous. ROADS: Adequate but require 4-wheel drives. Sandstorms may obscure vision in the dry season and may be impassable in the wet season.

Respect should be paid to the Islamic traditions. Dress modestly and don't drink alcohol unless it is served in a restaurant.
The weather can be very hot and dry, so it is important to drink plenty of water and restore the body's salts.

CAPITAL: Port Louis

GMT +4.

FROM UK: 00230. OUTGOING CODE TO UK: 0044

114 for Service Aide Medicale Urgence (SAMU)

Mauritius High Commission, 32 Elvaston Place, London SW7 5NW. Tel: 020 7584 3666; Fax: 020 7225 1135.

British High Commission, Les Cascades Building, Edith Cavell Street, Port Louis, Mauritius. Tel: 211 1361. Fax: 211 1369. bhc@intnet.mu

Mauritius Tourist Promotion Authority, 32 Elvaston Place, London SW7 5NW. Tel: 020 7584 3666; Fax: 020 7225 1135. mtpa@btinternet.com www.mauritius.net/

Mauritius Tourism Promotion Authority, Emmanuel Anquetil Building, Sir Seewoosagur Ramgoolam Street, Port Louis, Mauritius. Tel: 201 1703. Fax: 212 5142.

Return ticket required. Requirements may be subject to short-term change. Contact the relevant authority before departure. Valid passport required by all: The passport must be valid for 6 months.

Visa issued on arrival to nationals of EU countries for stays up to 3 months.

Narcotics and firearms.

Mre300, or US$7. Transit passengers departing within 48 hours and those under 2 years of age are exempt.

MALARIA: Exists in the vivax variety in the Northern rural areas, except on Rodrigues Island. YELLOW FEVER: A vaccination certificate will be required from travellers over 1 year of age coming from infected areas. OTHER: Bilharzia.

W1

Mauritian Rupee (Mre) = 100 cents. All major credit cards are accepted. Travellers cheques, preferably in US$ or Pound sterling, can be exchanged at banks and hotels. ATM AVAILABILITY: Over 125 locations.

MONEYGRAM: Unavailable.
WESTERN UNION: Unavailable.

AMEX: 0044 1273 696 933
DINERS CLUB: 0044 1252 513 500
MASTERCARD: 001 314 542 7111
VISA: 001 410 581 9994

AMEX: 0044 1273 571 600
THOMAS COOK: 0044 1733 318950
VISA: 0044 20 7937 8091

0930–1430 Mon to Fri, 0930–1130 Sat (except for the Bank of Mauritius).

It is possible to live relatively cheaply by shopping away from the main tourist centres.

English is the official language. The most widely spoken languages are Creole, Hindi, and Bhojpuri. French, Urdu and Chinese are also spoken.

Warm coastal climate, especially from January to Apr. Tropical storms are likely to occur in the cyclone season (Dec-Mar). Sea breezes occur throughout the year.

Hindu with Christian and Muslim minorities.

Jan 12, Mar 12, May 1, Sep 9, Nov 1, Dec 25. Chinese New Year, Islamic festivals, Good Fri.

220 volts AC, 50 Hz. UK-type 3-pin plugs are often used in hotels.

Airmail to Western Europe takes approx. 5 days. Surface mail takes 4 to 6 weeks.

Women's roles are defined by whichever religion they follow. The usual precautions should be taken.

ROAD: There is a good network of paved roads covering the island, though some are narrow and uneven. Traffic drives on the left. BUS: There are excellent and numerous bus services to all parts of the island. CAR HIRE: There are numerous car hire firms. DOCUMENTATION: IDP is recommended, although a foreign licence is accepted.

Visitors should always respect local customs and traditions. The hospitality received by visitors will be dependent on the religion and social customs of the host. Some medicines available on prescription in Britain are banned in Mauritius, so keep medication in the maker's packaging with proof that it is prescribed to you. Cyclones may strike Mauritius between November and May.

CAPITAL: Mexico City

Spans 3 time zones from GMT –6 to –8

FROM UK: 0052. OUTGOING CODE TO UK: 0044.

All services 08.

Embassy of Mexico, 42 Hertford Street, Mayfair, London W1Y 7TF. Tel: 020 7499 8586. Fax: 020 7495 4035. www.demon.co.uk/mexuk

British Embassy, Rio Lerma No. 71, Colonia Cuauhtemoc, 06500 Mexico City. Tel: 0052 5 207 2089; Fax 0052 5 242 8517. consular.section@mail.fco.gov.uk. www.embajadabritanica.com.mx/

Mexico Government Tourist Office, 41 Trinity Square, Wakefield House, London EC3N 4DJ. Tel: 020 7488 9392; Fax: 020 7265 0705. uk@visitmexico.com

Fondo Nacional de Fomento al Turismo (FONATUR), 17th Floor, Insurgentes Sur 800, Colonia de Valle, 03100 México DF. Tel: (5) 687 2697. www.mexicotravel.com/

Return ticket required. Requirements may change at short notice. Contact the embassy before departure. Passport required by all: must be valid for at least 6 months from the date of entry.

Visa usually required. Check the requirements with the appropriate consular authority.

Any uncanned foods, pork or pork products, plants, fruits, vegetables and their products. Firearms and ammunition and all pets and birds require an import permit.

US$ 13.37 for international departures. Children under 2 years of age are exempt.

POLIO, TYPHOID: R. MALARIA: Exists in the vivax variety in rural areas of certain states. YELLOW FEVER: A vaccination certificate is required for travellers over 6 months of age arriving from infected areas. OTHER: Rabies. Cholera is a serious risk, precaution is strongly recommended. Travellers arriving within 2 weeks of having visited an infected area are required to have a vaccination certificate.

W1

Nuevo Peso (MXN) = 100 cents. All credit cards are accepted. US dollar Travellers cheques are preferred. ATM AVAILABILITY: Over 9000 locations.

MONEYGRAM: 001 800 824 2220.
WESTERN UNION: 5 721 3080.

AMEX: 0044 1273 696 933
DINERS CLUB: 258 3220
MASTERCARD: 001800 307 7309
VISA: 001800 847 2911

AMEX: 001800 828 0366
THOMAS COOK: 00180000 2237 3373
VISA: 001800 257 3381

0900–1330 Mon to Fri, some banks are open Sat afternoon.

Relatively inexpensive. Caters for all travellers and budgets.

Spanish is the official language. English is widely spoken.

Climate varies according to altitude. Lowland are hot and humid whilst higher areas have a more temperate climate.

Roman Catholic.

Jan 1, Feb 5, Mar 21, May 1, 5, Sep 1, 16, Oct 12, Nov 2, 20, Dec 12, 25. Easter.

110 volts AC, 60 Hz. US flat 2-pin plugs are standard.

5–7 days to Europe, surface mail is slow.

There is inequality between men and women.

FLIGHTS: There is an excellent network of daily scheduled flights between commercial centres. RAIL: Mexico has a good rail network, which connects the major towns. ROAD: Slightly less than half is paved. BUS: Mexico is linked by an excellent and very economical bus service. CAR HIRE: Available at airports, city centres and resorts. DOCUMENTATION: IDP or national driving licence is acceptable. TAXI: Call taxis from your hotel and make a note of the licence plate number. Robbery assaults on passengers in taxis are frequent and violent, with passengers subjected to beating, shootings and sexual assault. Visitors to Mexico City should avoid taking any taxi not summoned by telephone. Don't hail taxis in the street or outside nightclubs.

The Popocateptl volcano is closed off to the public because of the danger of eruption.

CAPITAL: Chisinău

GMT +2

FROM UK: 00373. OUTGOING CODE TO UK: 8/1044 (wait for second dial tone) Most international calls go through the operator.

Consult hotel on arrival.

No embassy in the UK. EUROPE: Embassy of the Republic of Moldova, 175 avenue Emile Max, 1040 Brussels, Belgium. Tel: 0032 2 732 9659. Fax: 0032 2 732 9660.

British nationals in need of consular assistance should contact the German Embassy, Hotel Jolly Alon, Shada M Chibdaro 37, Chisinau, 27012. Tel: 00373 2 234607.

British Embassy Romania, 24 Jules Michelet Street, 70154 Bucharest. Tel: 0040 1 2104657; Fax 0040 1 3129652. Consular@bucharest.mail.fco.gov.uk

Not present.

Moldova-Tur, 4 Stefan cel Mare, 2058 Chisinău, Moldova. Tel: (2) 262 569. Fax: (2) 262 586.

Requirements may be subject to short-term change. Contact the relevant authority before departure. Valid passport required by all: must be valid for 6 months from date of arrival. In certain cases additional documentation may be required.

Visa required.

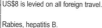

The import of local currency is prohibited by all foreign visitors.

US$8 is levied on all foreign travel.

Rabies, hepatitis B.

1 Leu (l) = 100 bani. Foreign currencies can be exchanged in hotels or bureaux de change. Moldova is essentially a cash-only economy. US$ are the preferred foreign currency. Credit cards and travellers cheques are not widely accepted. ATM AVAILABILITY: Unavailable.

MONEYGRAM: Unavailable.
WESTERN UNION: 095 119 8250.

AMEX: 8/10044 1273 696 933
DINERS CLUB: 8/1044 1252 513 500
MASTERCARD: 8/101 314 542 7111
VISA: 8/101 410 581 9994

AMEX: 8/1044 1273 571 600
THOMAS COOK: 8/1044 1733 318950
VISA: 8/1044 20 7937 8091

0900–1200, Mon to Fri.

Reasonably inexpensive.

Russian. Romanian.

The climate is pleasant and mild. The autumns are crisp and sunny and there is sometimes snow in the winter.

Eastern Orthodox Christian and other Christian denominations. Some Jews are also present.

Jan 1, 7, 8, Mar 8, May 1, 9, Aug 27, 31. Easter.

220 volts AC, 50 Hz.

All mail to and from Moldova is subjected to long delays of up to 6 weeks. It is advisable to send recorded delivery to avoid loss.

Women enjoy equal status with men.

ROAD: The road network covers 10, 000km. TAXI: These can be found in front of the main hotels accommodating foreigners. Fares should be negotiated in advance, although drivers prefer to charge per hour. Taxis run mostly on liquid gas and the bottles, which are stored in the boot, leave little room for luggage. CAR HIRE: Is available. DOCUMENTATION: IDP is required.

Dress should be casual but conservative. Expensive jewellery and cameras should be kept out of sight. Travel to Transdniestria should be avoided, since it is not under Moldovan government control and the security situation is unstable.

Monaco

CAPITAL: Monaco-Ville

GMT +1 (GMT +2 during the summer)

FROM UK: 00377. OUTGOING CODE TO UK: 0044

Police: 17; Fire/Ambulance: 18.

Monaco Embassy and Consulate General, 4 Cromwell Place, London SW7 2JE. Tel: 020 7225 2679. Fax: 020 7581 8161.

British Consulate, BP 265, 33 boulevard Princesse Charlotte, MC98005 Monaco, Cedex. Tel: 93 50 99 66. Fax: 93 50 14 47.

Monaco Government Tourist and Convention Office, 3-18 Chelsea Garden Market, Chelsea Harbour, London SW10 0XE. Tel: 020 7352 9962. Fax: 020 7352 2103.

Direction du Tourisme et des Congrès de la Principauté de Monaco 2a boulevard des Moulins, MC 98030 Monaco, Cedex. Tel: 92 16 61 16 (admin.) or 92 16 61 66 (information). Fax: 92 16 60 00. mgto@monaco1.org www.monacotourism.com/

Valid passport required: See France.

Not required.

See France.

Rabies.

Euro = 100 cents. See France for more details. All major credit cards are widely accepted. Travellers cheques should be exchanged in banks or exchange offices because very few businesses will accept them directly for payment. ATM AVAILABILITY: Over 40 locations.

MONEYGRAM: Single location in Monte Carlo.
WESTERN UNION: (05) 5542 5396.

AMEX: 0044 1273 696 933
DINERS CLUB: 0044 1252 513 500
MASTERCARD: 0800 901387
VISA: 0800 901179

AMEX: 0800 908 600
THOMAS COOK: 0800 908 330
VISA: 0044 20 7937 8091

0900–1200 and 1400–1630 Mon to Fri.

Very expensive, especially around the fashionable coast and social areas.

French. Monegasque (mixture of French Provencal and Italian Ligurian). English and Italian may also be spoken.

Mild climate throughout the year. The hottest months are July–Aug and the coolest Jan–Feb. There is an average of only 60 days rain a year, usually during winter.

Roman Catholic with Anglican minorities.

Jan 1, Feb 26, 27, May 1, Aug 15, Nov 1, 18, 19, Dec 8, 24, 25, 31. Easter, Ascension day, Whitsun, Corpus Christi.

220 volts AC, 50 Hz. Round 2 pin plugs are in use.

2–3 days.

Similar culture to the rest of Western Europe. However, usual precautions should be taken by women travellers.

RAIL: An extensive network runs through the principality connecting all the major towns. ROAD: COACH: There is a direct service connecting Nice airport with Monaco. BUS: There are good connections with the surrounding areas. DOCUMENTATION: A national driving licence will suffice.

Kissing on both cheeks is the usual form of greeting. Formal wear is expected in restaurants, clubs and casinos, but casual clothing is acceptable elsewhere. Apart from on the beaches and bathing areas, it is forbidden to walk about in swimsuits, stripped to the waist or barefoot.

For receptions or the casino, a jacket and tie should be worn. For gala events, black tie (dinner jacket) is required.

CAPITAL: Ulaanbaatar

GMT +8

FROM UK: 00976 (Followed by 1 for Ulaanbaatar). OUTGOING CODE TO UK: 0044

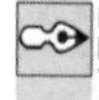
Embassy of Mongolia, 7 Kensington Court, London W8 5DL. Tel: 020 7937 0150 or 020 7937 5238. Fax: 020 7937 1117. Visa section: 020 7937 5238 ext. 29. embmong@aol.com

British Embassy PO Box 703, 30 Enkh Taivny Gudamzh, Ulaanbaatar 13, Mongolia. Tel: 00976 11 458133; Fax: 00976 11458036. britemb1@magicnet.mn

Mongolian Tourism Board, Chinggis Avenue 11, Ulaanbaatar 28, Mongolia 210628. Tel. 311102; Fax. 318492. ntc@mongol.net www.mongoliatourism.gov.mn/

Requirements may be subject to short-term change. Contact the relevant authority before departure. Valid passport required by all

Visa required, must be obtained in advance. It is no longer possible to obtain visas at Mongolian borders or at the airport on arrival.

Long list of prohibited items: contact Embassy. Customs declaration form must be completed on arrival and kept until departure.

US$8.

POLIO, TYPHOID: R. OTHER: Rabies.

W1

Tugrik (MNT) = 100 mongos. EXCHANGE: Commercial banks in Ulaanbaatar and bureaux de change at certain hotels. Credit cards are accepted by main banks and large hotels: US$ is the preferred currency. ATM AVAILABILITY: Unavailable.

MONEYGRAM: Unavailable
WESTERN UNION: Unavailable.

AMEX: 0044 1273 696 933
DINERS CLUB: 0044 1252 513 500
MASTERCARD: 001 314 542 7111
VISA: 001 410 581 9994

AMEX: 0044 1273 571 600
THOMAS COOK: 0044 1733 318950
VISA: 0044 20 7937 8091

1000–1500 Mon to Fri.

Independent travel can be relatively cheap, although visitors are expected to pay ten times the prices charged to locals. Ask the price before you eat.

Khalkha Mongolian. Many dialects are spoken.

Cool climate with short, mild summers and longer severe winters.

Buddhist Lamaism is the main religion. Shamanism is also widespread.

Jan 1, 24, Jun 1, Jul 11–13, Nov 26. Chinese Lunar New Year.

220 volts AC, 50 Hz, European-style 2-pin plugs.

Airmail to Europe takes up to 2 weeks.

Women have a minor role in society but this does not apply to foreigners.

FLIGHTS: Internal flights are operated by Air Mongol. It is not known whether maintenance procedures are properly carried out. RAIL: The main route runs north–south. ROAD: Paved roads can only be found in or near major cities. TAXIS: There are few taxis in town and no regulation of the industry. Most people simply wave down a vehicle and negotiate a price with the driver. BUS: Services run between towns. CAR HIRE: Available through tourism companies. It is sometimes possible to hire a car and driver. NOTE: Visitors may only enter Mongolia by air or train. The TransSiberian Express train is an increasingly popular way to reach Ulaanbaatar. Entry by road is not permitted.

Religious customs should be respected. Mentioning death, divorce or accidents is considered a bad omen and will be taken seriously. Street crime is on the increase in Ulaanbaatar and visitors should exercise caution; do not go out on foot after dark. Dogs, both stray and domestic, should be avoided: many are vicious and some are rabid. The Mongolian Tourist Board appeals to visitors not to give money to beggars in the street, but to donate to projects that help them. Vodka is causing an alcohol problem. Most hotels in Ulaanbaatar have IDD facilities. Alternatively, calls can be made from telephone exchanges around the city: the Central Post Building is the largest, and has e-mail and fax. PHOTOGRAPHY: Not allowed in monasteries or temples.

Montserrat

CAPITAL: Plymouth

GMT –4

FROM UK: 001664. OUTGOING CODE TO UK: 01144.

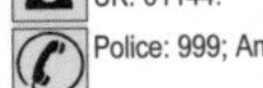
Police: 999; Ambulance: 911.

UK Passport Agency, Visas to British Dependant Territories, Room 203, Clive House, Petty France, London SW1H 9HD. Tel: (0990 210 410).

No embassy present. In extreme emergency the Governor's Office may be able to help. The Governor's Office, Lancaster House, Olveston, Montserrat; Tel: 001 664 491 2688. Fax: 001 664 491 8867. govoff@candw.ag

Montserrat Tourist Board, Suite 433, High Holborn House, 52-54 High Holborn, London WC1V 6RB. Tel: 020 7242 3131. Fax: 020 7242 2838.

Montserrat Tourist Board, PO Box 7, Marine Road, Plymouth, Montserrat. Tel: 2230 or 8730. Fax: 7430. mrattouristboard@candw.ag

Return ticket required. Requirements may be subject to short-term change. Valid passport not required by nationals of the UK and its colonies, who may enter as tourists with a form of identity for a maximum stay of 6 months.

Visa not required.

Firearms. Cats and dogs require a veterinary certificate.

US$6 or equivalent in any international currency.

Visitors must have sufficient funds to finance stay and be in possession of onward or return tickets.

POLIO, TYPHOID: R. OTHER: Bilharzia, dengue fever, dysentery and hepatitis A are present.

W2

East Caribbean Dollar (EC$) = 100 cents. Visa is widely accepted. Travellers cheques are accepted in tourist areas. Pound sterling or US$ are the preferred currencies. ATM AVAILABILITY: 1 location only.

MONEYGRAM: Unavailable.
WESTERN UNION: 491 2361.

AMEX: 01144 1273 696 933
DINERS CLUB: 01144 1252 513 500
MASTERCARD: 1800 307 7309
VISA: 1800 847 2911

AMEX: 01144 1273 571 600
THOMAS COOK: 1800 223 7373
VISA: 01144 20 7937 8091

0800–1500 Mon, Tues and Thur, 0800–1300 Wed, 0800–1700 Fri.

Following the volcanic eruption in 1996, the economy and the tourist industry have suffered.

English.

Subtropical climate and warm all year round. Most rain falls between Sept and Nov. The heavy cloudbursts refresh the climate and once cleared the sun reappears.

Roman Catholic, Anglican, Methodist, other Christian denominations.

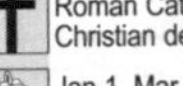
Jan 1, Mar 17, first Mon in May and Aug, Dec 25, 26, 31. Easter, Whitsun.

120/220 volts AC, 60 Hz.

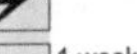
1 week.

A blend of West Indian and British culture has resulted in a pleasant, relaxed society.

ROAD: A good network exists connecting all towns, but driving can be difficult for those not use to winding mountain roads. BUS: Scheduled buses run hourly. CAR HIRE: Available at the airport and hotels and is often included in the price of accommodation. DOCUMENTATION: A valid foreign licence can be used to purchase a temporary licence either at the airport or Plymouth police station.

Access to some parts of the island coastal waters is forbidden because of volcanic activity. Volcanic ash poses health problems. Although volcanic eruptions have abated, the volcano appears still to be active and dangerous. Consult the Governor's Office for further information. Residents are concentrated in the northern designated safe zones. While the airport is closed, visitors to the island travel by ferry from Antigua. The hurricane season runs from June to November.

CAPITAL: Rabat

GMT

FROM UK: 00212. OUTGOING CODE TO UK: 00/44 (wait for second dial tone)

Police: 19; Fire and Ambulance: 15.

Embassy of the Kingdom of Morocco, 49 Queens Gate Gardens, London, SW7 5NE. Tel: 020 7581 5001. Fax: 020 7225 3862.

British Embassy, BP 45, 17 Boulevard de la Tour Hassan, Rabat, Morocco. Tel: 00212 037 729696; Fax: 00212 037 704 531. Consulates also in Casablanca and Tangier.

Moroccan National Tourist Office, 205 Regent Street, London, W1R 7DE. Tel: 020 7437 0073; Fax: 020 7734 8172.

Office Nationale Marocain de Tourisme, 31 angle rue Oued Fès, Avenue Al Abtal, Agdal, Rabat. Tel: (7) 775 171. Fax: (7) 777 437.

Return ticket required. Requirement may change at short notice. Contact the embassy before departure. Valid passport required.

Visa not required. Contact embassy for the most recent list. Single entry, multiple entry and transit visas are granted.

A permit is required for sporting guns and ammunition. Obtainable from police authorities if a permit is already held in the passenger's country of residence.

Israeli passport holders are prohibited from entering, as are those of scruffy appearance.

POLIO, TYPHOID: R. MALARIA: A minimal risk of becoming infected exists at certain times of the year, in rural areas. OTHER: Bilharzia and rabies.

W2

Moroccan Dirham (DH) = 100 Centimes. Import and export of local currency is prohibited. Bank transfers can take up to 6 weeks. Travellers cheques and all major credit cards are accepted. ATM AVAILABILITY: Over 250 locations.

MONEYGRAM: 002 11 0011 then 800 592 3688.
WESTERN UNION: (2) 20 8080.

AMEX: 00/44 1273 696 933
DINERS CLUB: 02 29 94 55 or 02 20 80 80
MASTERCARD: 00/1 314 542 7111
VISA: 00/1 410 581 9994

AMEX: 00/44 1273 571 600
THOMAS COOK: 00/44 1733 318950
VISA: 00/44 20 7937 8091

0830–1130 and 1430–1700 Mon to Fri (winter), 0800–1530 Mon to Fri (summer). These hours may vary during Ramadan.

Savings can be made at souks. Bargaining is essential and can lead to purchases costing a third of the original asking price.

Arabic with some Berber. French and Spanish are widely spoken, and English is understood, in the North.

Mostly dry, with high temperatures. The mountains and inland are cooler.

Mainly Muslim, with Jewish and Christian minorities.

Jan 1, 11, May 1, Jul 30, Aug 14, 20, Nov 6, 18. Islamic festivals.

110–120 volts AC, 50Hz.

Up to 1 week, but can be unreliable

Women should dress modestly, covering arms and legs. Unescorted women may experience verbal abuse or find themselves pestered by the local men: take a low profile and continue on your way if approached.

RAIL: Limited but cheap. Most have air conditioning, sleepers and restaurant cars. ROADS: Major roads are all-weather. Travelling in the mountains is difficult. CAR HIRE: Available but expensive. DOCUMENTATION: Third-party insurance is required and a green card. A UK licence is sufficient.

Mainly French social customs, but with an increasingly Islamic influence. Alcohol is forbidden, except in private bars in hotels. Most restaurants are closed in the daytime during the month of Ramadan. Do not try to distribute non-Islamic religious materials. Be courteous but wary of young boys selling goods or acting as guides. Local advice is to learn an Arabic phrase meaning 'please go away' to deter them. Hire only official tour guides through hotels and travel agencies. Beachwear should be confined to the beach and pool-side. PHOTOGRAPHY: Ask permission before taking photos.
NOTE: Travel in Western Sahara is restricted and travellers may be turned back at the border. There are thousands of landmines in the region.The area south of Tan Tan is a military zone.

Mozambique

CAPITAL: Maputo

GMT +2

FROM UK: 00258 . OUTGOING CODE TO UK: 0044 Most international calls must go through the operator.

All services: 493924 (Maputo only); Police: 119; Ambulance: 117; Fire: 198.

High Commission of the Republic of Mozambique, 21 Fitzroy Square, London W1P 5HJ. Tel: 020 7383 3800. Fax: 020 7383 3801.

British High Commission, Caixa Postal 55, Avenida Vladimir I Lénine 310, Maputo. Tel: (1) 420 111/1/2/5/6/7. Fax: (1) 421 666. consular@maputo.mail.fco.gov.uk

Refer to the Embassy.

Empresa Nacionale de Tourismo (ENT) CP 2446, Avda 25 de Setembro 1203, Maputo, Mozambique. Tel: 421 794.

Return ticket required. Requirements may change at short notice. Contact the embassy before departure. Valid passport required by all: with a minimum validity of 6 months.

Visa required.

Narcotics.

US$20, or US$10 if travelling within Africa.

POLIO, TYPHOID: R. MALARIA: Risk exists throughout the years across the whole country in the Falciparum variety. Reported as being highly resistant to chloroquine. YELLOW FEVER: A vaccination certificate is required by all travellers over one year of age arriving from infected areas. OTHER: Bilharzia, cholera and rabies. HIV/AIDS.

W1

Mozambique Metical (M) = 100 centavos. NOTE: import and export of local currency is prohibited. Credit cards can now be used in some places in Maputo, and banks will change travellers cheques. ATM AVAILABILITY: Unavailable.

MONEYGRAM: Unavailable.
WESTERN UNION: 1 455 155.

AMEX: 0044 1273 696 933
DINERS CLUB: 0044 1252 513 500
MASTERCARD: 001 314 542 7111
VISA: 001 410 581 9994

AMEX: 0044 1273 571 600
THOMAS COOK: 0044 1733 318950
VISA: 0044 20 7937 8091

0745–1115 Mon to Fri.

Although civil war has ended, economy remains unstable.

Portuguese and many African languages.

The climate varies according to the area. Inland is cooler with most rain between Jan and Mar. The coast is warm and dry Apr–Sept. Hottest and wettest Oct–Mar.

Christian (mainly Roman Catholic) with Muslim, Hindu and traditional beliefs.

Jan 1, Feb 3, Apr 7, May 1, Jun 25, Sep 7, 25, Nov 10, Dec 25.

220 volts AC, 50Hz.

Approximately 1 week by air to Europe. Available from main cities.

A higher population of women than men exists due to civil war.

FLIGHTS: Air taxi services are available and are the safest means of travel outside the main cities due to the internal fighting. RAIL: All rail services are liable to disruption at present. BUS: Buses are available but plenty of food and water should be taken since journeys are frequently interrupted by checkpoints to examine documents. DOCUMENTATION: IDP is required. Heavy flooding in central and southern Mozambique has disrupted roads and railways and travellers should check the conditions before setting out on cross-country journeys.

Armed robbery and other violent crimes are prevalent. There is also the risk of unexploded mines. Travel between major cities should only be undertaken in daylight. Casual wear is acceptable. Formal dress is seldom required. PRECAUTIONS: Ensure all food is fully cooked and drink only bottled or boiled water. Diseases caused by poor hygiene are common.

Myanmar/Burma

CAPITAL: Yangoon (Rangoon)

GMT +6.30

FROM UK: 0095. OUTGOING CODE TO UK: 044. IDD available only at Government offices, some companies and hotels.

Embassy of the Union of Myanmar, 19a Charles Street, Berkeley Square, London, W1X 8ER. Tel: 020 7499 8841. Fax: 020 7629 4169. www.myanmar.com

British Embassy, PO Box 638, 80 Strand Road, Yangoon, Myanmar. Tel: (1) 95300. Fax (1) 89566.

Myanmar Tourist Board, 36c Sisters Avenue, London SW11 5SQ. Tel/Fax: 020 7223 8987. info@burmah.co.uk; www.burmah.co.uk

No tourist office. Refer to web site: www.myanmar.com

Return ticket required. Requirements may change at short notice: contact embassy before going. Valid passport required by all.

Visa required, which must be obtained in advance.

Playing cards, gambling antiques, archaeological equipment and pornography. Jewellery must be declared.

US$8. Passengers in transit are exempt.

POLIO, TYPHOID: R. MALARIA: Exists in certain areas, especially below 1000m, in the falciparum variety, reported as being highly resistant to chloroquine. YELLOW FEVER: A vaccination certificate is required if arriving from an infected area. OTHER: Cholera, Japanese encephalitis, plague, rabies.

W1

Kyat (MMK) = 100 pyas. Import and export of local currency is prohibited. Only 25% of foreign currency changed to Kyats can be re converted on exit. The currency is unstable. Keep receipt for Customs checks on exit. Credit cards are accepted in the larger hotels in Rangoon and Mandalay. Travellers cheques can be exchanged at some banks. ATM AVAILABILITY: Unavailable.

MONEYGRAM: Unavailable.
WESTERN UNION: Unavailable.

AMEX: 044 1273 696 933
DINERS CLUB: 044 1252 513 500
MASTERCARD: not accepted
VISA: 01 410 581 9994

AMEX: 044 1273 571 600
THOMAS COOK: 044 1733 318950
VISA: 044 20 7937 8091

1000–1400 Mon to Fri.

Can be high by South-east Asian standards. Tourist facilities are very limited outside Rangoon, Bagan, Taunggyi and Mandalay.

Burmese. Over 100 district languages are spoken. English is often spoken in business.

Monsoon climate with 3 main seasons: Feb-May is the hottest month with little or no rain. Rainy season is from May to Oct. Oct-Feb is cooler.

Mostly Therevada Buddhist. Hindu, Muslim, Christian and Animist minorities.

Jan 4, Feb 12, Mar 2, 27, Apr 17, May 1, Jul 19, Dec 25. Buddhist festivals, Eid Al Adha, Diwali (Deepavali).

220/230 volts AC, 50 Hz.

Up to 1 week to Europe. Correspondence should be taken to the post office and registered for a small fee.

Women must cover shoulders in religious buildings and should not wear shorts and short skirts.

Keep to officially designated tourist areas. Cycling is strongly discouraged. FLIGHTS: The most efficient mode, but delays are frequent and scheduled flights are limited. SEA/RIVER: Regarded as the best way to see Myanmar but as delays are frequent: allow plenty of time. BUS: Long-distance buses are not recommended, due to their condition and that of the roads. RAIL: Several good services operate. Tickets should be purchased 2 hours in advance. Flooding in the rainy season tends to disrupt services. DOCUMENTATION: IDP required.

Respect towards religious beliefs should be shown. Avoid discussion of politics. Political tension is high, causing risk of sectarian violence. The government suppresses expression of opposition to its rule. Visitors have been deported for distributing pro-democracy literature, photographing sites and activities, and visiting Burmese pro-democracy leaders. Newspapers are censored. Internet access is illegal: tourists have had laptops with modems confiscated and held at the airport until their departure. Crossing the border into Thailand requires official approval.

Namibia

CAPITAL: Windhoek

GMT +2

FROM UK: 00264. OUTGOING CODE TO UK: 0944

Police: 1011; Ambulance: 2032276 Fire: 2032270.

High Commission for the Republic of Namibia, 6 Chandos Street, London, W1M 0LQ. Tel: 020 7636 624. Fax: 020 7637 5694. namibia.hicom@btconnect.com

British High Commission, 116 Robert Mugabe Avenue, PO Box 22202 Windhoek Tel 00264 61 274800. Fax 00264 61 228895. bhc@mweb.com.na

Namibia Tourism, 6 Chandos Street, London W1M 0LQ. Tel: 020 7636 2924. Fax: 020 7636 2969. namibia@globalnet.co.uk www.tourism.com.na/

Namibia Tourism, Private Bag 13346, Windhoek, Namibia. Tel: (61) 284 2111. Fax: (61) 221 930.

Return ticket required. Requirement may change at short notice. Contact the embassy before departure. Valid passport required by all: must be valid for 6 months after the date of leaving Namibia.

Visa not required by nationals of EU countries for stays of up to 3 months.

Hunting rifles need a permit. The import of obscene literature, second-hand military clothing is prohibited without special authorisation.

POLIO, MALARIA: Exists in certain areas during periods of the year in the falciparum variety. YELLOW FEVER: A vaccination certificate is required by those arriving from infected areas excluding those under 1 year of age. If arriving by scheduled flights and are in transit a certificate will not be required if passengers do not leave the airport. OTHER: Bilharzia, cholera, rabies. PRECAUTION: The FCO points out that Namibia has the third highest rate of HIV/AIDS infection in the world. Visitors should avoid casual unprotected sex.

W2

Namibian Dollar (N$). All currency must be declared at the point of entry. Import and export of local currency is limited to N$500. Credit cards and travellers cheques are widely accepted. ATM AVAILABILITY: 34 locations.

MONEYGRAM: Unavailable.
WESTERN UNION: 461 246 970.

AMEX: 0944 1273 696 933
DINERS CLUB: 0944 1252 513 500
MASTERCARD: 091 314 542 7111
VISA: 091 410 581 9994

AMEX: 0944 1273 571600
THOMAS COOK: 09441733 3188950
VISA: 0944 20 7937 8091

0900–1530 Mon to Fri, 0830–1100 Sat.

Moderately expensive in urban areas, but reasonably inexpensive in rural locations.

English, Afrikaans, German and African languages are spoken.

The coast is cool and rain free most of the year. Inland rain falls between Oct and Apr. December is the hottest month. The rainy season is from Jan to Apr.

Christian majority.

Jan 1, Mar 21, May 1, 4, 25, Aug 26, Oct 7, Dec 10, 25, 26. Easter, Ascension Day.

220/240 volts AC. Plugs are of the 3-pin type.

4 days to 2 weeks. Good airmail service available.

Equal or higher social standing exists for women in Namibia.

ROADS: Are well maintained. Wildlife and stray farm animals are a hazard to drivers. FLIGHTS: Are often the most economic way to travel. The national airline links all the major cities. RAIL: Trains operate between the main cities, and offer first class and sleeping facilities. DOCUMENTATION: IDP is required.

Western customs prevail. Do not enter the Sperrgebeit (prohibited diamond area). Take advice locally on which areas to avoid. Do not enter the townships at night. Avoid the area near the border with Angola. Avoid purchasing diamonds and other protected resources outside of licensed retail establishments. The purchase and exportation of other protected resources, such as elephant ivory, is prohibited by Namibian and international law.

CAPITAL: Yaren

GMT +12

FROM UK: 00674. OUTGOING CODE TO UK: 0044 Most calls must be made through the international operator.

Contact local operator.

Refer to Fiji High Commission

The British High Commission in Suva (Fiji) deals with enquiries relating to Nauru. www.ukinthepacific.bhc.org.fj

No office in UK. Refer to web site: www.tcsp.com: uk@spto.org

Tourism Council of the South Pacific, PO Box 13119, Suva, Fiji Islands. Tel: 00679 304 177; Fax: 00679 301 995. info@spto.org www.tcsp.com/

Return ticket required. Regulations may be subject to short-term change. Contact the embassy before departure. Valid passport required by all.

Visa required, apart from those in transit providing they hold tickets for immediate travel to a third country.

Nauruan artefacts may not be exported without a licence.

A$10 per person over 12 years, on departure.

POLIO, TYPHOID: R. YELLOW FEVER: A vaccination certificate is required from travellers over 1 year of age arriving from infected areas.

W2

Australian Dollar (A$) = 100 cents. Credit cards are widely accepted. Travellers cheques, preferably in A$, can be exchanged. ATM AVAILABILITY: None.

MONEYGRAM: Unavailable.
WESTERN UNION: Unavailable.

AMEX: 0044 1273 696 933
DINERS CLUB: 0044 1252 513 500
MASTERCARD: 001 314 542 7111
VISA: 001 410 581 9994

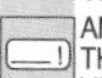
AMEX: 0044 1273 571 600
THOMAS COOK: 0044 1733 318950
VISA: 0044 20 7937 8091

0900–1500 Mon to Thur, 0900–1630 Fri.

The absence of taxes means some goods are cheaper e.g. electrical goods, cigarettes and alcohol. Visitors should buy essential goods in advance as shops are rather limited.

Nauruan and English.

A maritime, equatorial climate tempered by Northeast trade winds from Mar to Oct. The wettest period is from Mar to Oct. Hot all year round. Monsoon season runs from Nov to Feb.

Christian, most Nauruan Protestant Church.

Jan 1, 31, May 17, Oct 26, Dec 25, 26. Easter.

110/240 volts AC, 50 Hz.

Up to 1 week.

Western and Nauru culture co-exist.

ROAD: A sealed road 19 km long circles the island and there are several miles of road running inland to Buada and the phosphate areas. Buses provide public transport. CAR HIRE: Available. DOCUMENTATION: A national driving licence is sufficient.

The Republic of Nauru, with a coastline of 30 kilometres, is just one island located north of the Solomon Islands and just south of the equator. It became independent from Australia in 1968 and can claim to be the world's smallest republic. The island has a casual atmosphere in which diplomacy and tact are preferable to confrontation. Nauru is making an effort to develop tourism based mainly on game fishing, although there is only one hotel on the island. It's a prosperous little country with an economy based on the mining and export of phosphate, and cultivation of coconut, bananas and pineapples. See website: www.tbc.gov.bc.ca/cwgames/country/Nauru/nauru.html

CAPITAL: Kathmandu

GMT +5.45

FROM UK: 00977. OUTGOING CODE TO UK: 0044

Not present.

Royal Nepalese Embassy, 12a Kensington Palace Gardens, London W8 4QU. Tel: 020 7229 1594. Fax: 020 7792 9861. www.nepembassay.org.uk

British Embassy, PO Box 106, Lainchaur, Kathmandu, Nepal. Tel: (1) 410 583. Fax: (1) 411 789. britemb@wlink.com.np www.britain.gov.np

Refer to website: www.welcomenepal.com/

Nepal Tourism Board, Po Box 11018, Bhrikuti Mandap. Tel: 00977 256229; Fax: 00977 256910. info@ntb.wlink.com.np

Requirements may be subject to short-term change. Contact the relevant authority before departure. Valid passport required.

Visa required.

All baggage must be declared on arrival. Restrictions on the import of goods such as cameras, videos and electronic goods. Objects of archaeological or historical interest cannot be exported.

NPR700, or US$8, for international flights.

POLIO, TYPHOID: R. MALARIA: Exists in the vivax variety in many rural areas. The falciparum variety has also been reported and is highly resistant to chloroquine. YELLOW FEVER: A vaccination certificate is required from travellers coming from infected areas. OTHER: Cholera, altitude sickness, Japanese encephalitis, hepatitis A and B, meningitis.

W1

Nepalese Rupee (Rs) = 100 paisa. EXCHANGE: Obtain 'Foreign Exchange Encashment' receipts when changing currency – they may be needed when making transactions. Import of local and Indian currency is prohibited. Export of local currency is prohibited. Import of foreign currency must be declared. Amex is widely accepted. MasterCard has a more limited acceptance. Travellers cheques are accepted at banks and major hotels. US$ is the preferred currency. ATM AVAILABILITY: Unavailable.

MONEYGRAM: Unavailable.
WESTERN UNION: (1) 223 530.

AMEX: 0044 1273 696 933
DINERS CLUB: 0044 1252 513 500
MASTERCARD: 001 314 542 7111
VISA: 001 410 581 9994

AMEX: 0091 11 614 5920
THOMAS COOK: 0044 1733 318950
VISA: 0044 20 7937 8091

1000–1450 Sun to Thur. 1000–1230 Fri.

Caters for all travellers and budgets.

Nepali, with Maithir and Bhojpuri.

Jun-Oct: Summer and monsoon. Rest of the year is dry. Spring and autumn is the most pleasant time. Temperatures drop dramatically in the winter.

Mostly Hindu and Buddhist, with a small Muslim minority.

Jan 11, 29, Feb 19, Mar 8, Apr 13, Dec 15, 29. Hindu feasts.

220 volts AC, 50 Hz.

Services are available at most centres. Post boxes should not be used for important communications.

Women play a traditional role.

FLIGHTS: A network of domestic flights links major towns. ROAD: The road system is of unpredictable quality. BUS: Services operate, but poor state of roads and high incidence of accidents make long-distance bus travel inadvisable. CAR HIRE: Hertz and Avis are present. NOTE: Driving and vehicle maintenance is poor and the cause of frequent accidents. DOCUMENTATION: An IDP is valid in Nepal for 15 days. A temporary licence can be obtained on presentation of a national licence.

The locals are superstitious and religious. Visitors are considered to be 'polluted' and are likely to be treated by the locals accordingly. Shoes should be removed before entering a local's home.

SPECIAL PRECAUTIONS: Do not trek on your own without a professional guide. Make sure you use a reputable agency for trekking expeditions. Comprehensive travel insurance is essential and should cover all physical activities and medical evacuation, which is expensive. Beware of the dangers of high altitude sickness. Flooding occurs during the monsoon season and can disrupt travel. Nepal is in an earthquake zone. Travellers should register their presence with the British Embassy in Kathmandu.

The political situation is generally calm but demonstrations may occur and should be avoided. There have been recent outbreaks of political violence in the mid-west region. The situation in Nepal can change rapidly; Maoists are extending their influence into popular trekking regions. Read carefully the latest travel advice on the FCO website before going to Nepal, and keep well-informed locally.

The Netherlands

CAPITAL: Amsterdam

GMT +1 (GMT +2 during the summer).

FROM UK: 0031. OUTGOING CODE TO UK: 0044.

All services: 0611.

Royal Netherlands Embassy, 30 Hyde Park Gate, London, SW7 5DP. Tel: 020 7590 3200. Fax: 020 7581 3458. Visa information line 0900 171 217 (Premium rate charges apply). london@netherlands-embassy.org.uk www.netherlands-embassy.org.uk/

British Embassy, Lange Voorhout 10, 2514 ED The Hague, The Netherlands. Tel: 0031 70 427 0427; Fax: 0031 70 427 0345. www.britain.nl Consulate-General, Koningslaan 44, 1075 Amsterdam. Tel 020 676 4343; Fax 020 675 8381.

Netherlands Board of Tourism, PO Box 523, 18 Buckingham Gate, London SW1E 6NT. Tel: 0906 871 777. www.goholland.co.uk/

Nederlands Bureau voor Toerism PO Box 458, 2260 MG Leidschendam, The Nederlands. Tel: 0031 70 3705 705; Fax: 0031 70 3201 654. info@nbt.nl www.visitholland.com/

Valid passport required: must be valid for at least 3 months after the last day of the intended visit.

Visa not required by EU nationals.

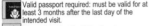

Cats and dogs cannot be imported, except from Luxembourg or Belgium, without a health certificate and a rabies certificate. Firearms and ammunition can only be imported with a licence.

Euro = 100 cents. EXCHANGE: Offices are indicated with the letters GWK. All major credit cards are accepted. Travellers cheques, in any major international currency, are easily exchanged. ATM AVAILABILITY: Over 6000 locations.

MONEYGRAM: 0800 022 3392.
WESTERN UNION: 0800 023 0161

AMEX: 0044 1273 696 933
DINERS CLUB: 020 654 5511
MASTERCARD: 0800 022 5821
VISA: 0800 022 3110

AMEX: 0800 022 0100
THOMAS COOK: 0800 022 8630
VISA: 0800 022 5484

0900–1600 Mon to Fri.

Similar to other Western European countries.

Dutch. French and German are also spoken. English is widely spoken and many locals will willingly use it.

Mild, maritime climate. Summers are generally warm with changeable periods but excessively hot weather is rare. Winters can be fairly cold with the possibility of some snow. Rainfall is prevalent all year.

Roman Catholic and Protestant. Approx. 26% do not profess any religion.

Jan 1, Apr 30, May 1, 5, Dec 25, 26. Easter, Ascension Day, Whitsun.

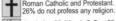

220 volts AC, 50 Hz.

Approx. 5 days within Europe.

The women's movement is strong and has a firm foothold in society.

RAIL: The highly developed rail network is efficient and cheap. ROAD: Excellent road system. BUS: Extensive regional bus services exist. Long-distance coach services operate between cities. TAXI: It is less usual to hail a taxi in the street in Holland. They are usually metered. CAR HIRE: Available from airports and main hotels. DOCUMENTATION: An international driving licence is not required as long as the licence from the country of origin is held. A green card is advisable but not compulsory.

Casual clothes are acceptable everywhere. Pickpockets and conmen are active in Amsterdam, around the Centraal Station, the red-light area and on public transport, especially the trams to the Museum District.

CAUTION: Narcotics remain illegal in the Netherlands, but the authorities operate a policy that if cannabis is allowed in certain places, the users will be less likely to seek harder drugs. In practice this means that the sale and smoking of cannabis is permitted in specially licensed coffee shops in central Amsterdam. Elsewhere the possession of more than 30 grams of the drug could lead to a fine or jail sentence. Possession of hard drugs can result in immediate imprisonment and deportation.

CAPITAL: Noumea

GMT +11

FROM UK: 00687. OUTGOING CODE TO UK: 0044

Emergency medical treatment: 15; Police: 17; Ambulance and Fire: 18.

Refer to the French Embassy

Refer to British Embassy in Paris. In emergency, contact the Honorary British Consul in New Caledonia, BP 362, 98845, Noumea Cedex. Tel: 00687 282153.

Refer to French Tourist Office or Website: www.new-caledonia-tourism.nc/

New Caledonia Tourism, 20 rue Anatole France – Immeuble Nouméa-Centre, Place des Cocotiers, BP 688 – 98845, Noumea. Tel: 00687 24 20 80; Fax: 00687 24 20 70. tourisme@offratel.nc

Return ticket required. Regulations may be subject to short-term change. Contact the embassy before departure. Valid passport required.

Visa not required by nationals of EU countries for a maximum of 3 months.

Contact the French Embassy for an up-to-date list.

POLIO, TYPHOID: R. YELLOW FEVER: A vaccination certificate is required from those over 1 year of age arriving from infected areas.

W2

French Pacific Franc (CFP Fr) = 100 centimes. Foreign exchange facilities available at the airport and trade bank. Credit cards are widely accepted. Australian dollar travellers cheques are accepted. ATM AVAILABILITY: 8 locations.

MONEYGRAM: Unavailable.
WESTERN UNION: Unavailable.

AMEX: 0044 1273 696 933
DINERS CLUB: 020 654 5511
MASTERCARD: 0800 022 5821
VISA: 0800 022 3110

AMEX: 0800 022 0100
THOMAS COOK: 0800 022 8630
VISA: 0800 022 5484

0730–1545 Mon to Fri.

Accommodation varies from moderate to expensive. There is a youth hostel situated outside the city. Locally made food and other commodities are sold cheaply, but imported goods are expensive to buy.

French. Polynesian, Melanesian and English are also spoken.

Warm subtropical climate. Cool season is from June to Sept and the hottest period from Oct to May. The main rains are between Jan and Mar. Climate is tempered by trade winds.

Roman Catholic and Protestant.

Jan 1, May 1, 8, Jun 1, Jul 13, 14, Aug 15, Sep 24, Nov 1, 11, Dec 25, 26. Christian feast days.

220 volts AC 50 Hz

Up to 1 week to Western Europe.

Local traditions and European culture co-exist. Usual precautions should be followed. Beachwear should be confined to the beach.

FLIGHTS: Services are operated by the national airline from the capital to various airfields on the island. SEA: There are regular sea links to the other smaller islands from Grande Terre. ROADS: Limited. BUS: Available throughout the island. CAR HIRE: Major and smaller companies have agencies in the capital. DOCUMENTATION: IDP is required.

Local traditions should be respected. New Caledonia houses the only casino in the South Pacific, situated at Anse Beach.

New Zealand

CAPITAL: Wellington

GMT +12 (GMT +13 from the first Sunday in Oct to the third Sunday in Mar the next year)

FROM UK: 0064. OUTGOING CODE TO UK: 0044.

All services: 111.

New Zealand High Commission, New Zealand House, 80 Haymarket, London, SW1Y 4TQ. Tel: 020 7930 8422. Fax: 020 7839 4580. www.newzealandhc.org.uk

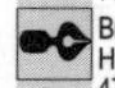
British High Commission, PO Box 1812, 44 Hill Street Wellington 1, New Zealand. Tel (4) 472 6049. Fax: (4) 471 1974. bhc.wel@xtra.co.nz www.britain.org.nz Consulates in Auckland (postmaster@auckland.mail.fco.gov.uk), Christchurch and in the Cook Islands (mckegg@oyster.net.ck).

New Zealand Tourist Board, 80 Haymarket, London SW1Y 4TQ. Tel: 020 7930 1662; Holiday information: 0839 300 900 (Premium rate charges apply).

Fletcher Challenge House, 89 The Terrace, PO Box 95, Wellington, New Zealand. Tel: 0064 4 472 8860. Fax: 0064 4 478 1736. enquiries@nztb.govt.nz www.nztb.govt.nz/

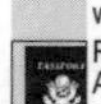
Return ticket required (except for nationals of Australia). Regulations may be subject to short-term change. Contact the High Commission before departure. Valid passport required.

Visa not required by nationals of the UK and other British Passport holders for visits of up to 6 months provided they have proof of the right of abode.

Visitors are advised not to take fruit or plant material with them. The New Zealand Government produces a full list of personal items which may be imported.

NZ$ 20, payable in local currency, on all departures. Transit passengers and children under 2 years are exempt.

New Zealand Dollar (NZ$) = 100 cents. All major credit cards accepted. travellers cheques in any international currencies, are widely accepted. ATM AVAILABILITY: Over 1500 locations.

MONEYGRAM: 00 800 66639474.
WESTERN UNION: 09 270 0050

AMEX: 0044 1273 696 933
DINERS CLUB: 0800 657 373
MASTERCARD: 0800 449 140
VISA: 0800 443 019

AMEX: 0800 441068
THOMAS COOK: 0800 440112
VISA: 0044 20 7937 8091

0900–1630 Mon to Fri.

It is possible to travel relatively cheaply in New Zealand.

English and Maori.

Subtropical in the North Island, temperate in the South Island. The North has no extremes of heat or cold, but winter can be quite cool in the South with snow in the mountains. Rainfall is distributed throughout the year.

Anglican and Roman Catholic. Other Christian denominations are present.

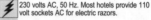

Jan 1, 2, Feb 6, Apr 25, first Mon in Jun, fourth Mon in Oct, Dec 25, 26. Easter. Anniversary days observed locally on nearest Mon.

230 volts AC, 50 Hz. Most hotels provide 110 volt sockets AC for electric razors.

4–5 days to Western Europe, slightly less to the USA.

Common-sense precautions should be followed (e.g. not walking alone at night).

FLIGHTS: The national airline operates flights between the main airports. RAIL: Reliable but limited. TRAVEL PASSES: Allow unlimited travel on New Zealand Railways' train, coach and ferry services. COACH: Modern coaches operate scheduled services throughout the country. It is advisable to make reservations for seats. Contact the tourism board for details. BUS: Regional bus services serve most parts of the country. TAXI: Metered taxis operate throughout the country. CAR HIRE: Major international and local firms have agencies at airports and most major cities. Minimum age for driving a rental car is 21 years.

Should a visitor be invited to a Maori occasion, the pressing of noses is common.

Nicaragua

CAPITAL: Managua

GMT –6

FROM UK: 00505. OUTGOING CODE TO UK: 0044

Police: 118, Fire: 265 0162, Ambulance: 265 1761.

Consulate General of Nicaragua, Vicarage House, 58–60 Kensington Church Street, London W8 4DB. Tel: 020 7938 2373. Fax: 020 7937 0952. emb.ofnicaragua@virgin.net http://freespace.virgin.net/emb.ofnicaragua/

British Embassy, Reparto Los Robles, De la Entrada Principal, 4ta Casa a Mano Derecha, Managua. Tel: 00505 2 278 0014; Fax: 00505 2 278 4085. abritemb@ibw.com.ni.

Not present.

Instituto Nicaragüense de Turismo (INTUR), Apartado Postal A-122, Managua, Nicaragua. Tel: 00505 222 2962; Fax: 00505 222 66 10. www.intur. gob.ni/

Return ticket required. Requirements may change at short notice. Contact the embassy before departure. Valid passport required: must be valid for a further 6 months (minimum).

Visa not required by nationals of Republic of Ireland, or by nationals of the UK for up to 90 days.

Canned meats, dairy products, medicines without prescriptions and military uniforms.

US$18 on all departures; children under 2 years are exempt.

POLIO, TYPHOID: R. MALARIA: Exists in the vivax variety Jun–Dec in the rural areas and the outskirts of towns. YELLOW FEVER: A vaccination certificate is required by travellers over one year of age arriving from infected areas. OTHER: Rabies.

W1

Nicaraguan Gold Córdobe (NIO) = 100 centavos. Credit cards have limited use. Travellers cheques are accepted, preferably in US$. ATM AVAILABILITY: Unavailable.

MONEYGRAM: 001 800 220 0038.
WESTERN UNION: (02) 668 126.

AMEX: 0044 1273 696933
DINERS CLUB: 0044 1252 513 500
MASTERCARD: 001 314 542 7111
VISA: 001 410 581 9994

AMEX: 00 1800 220 1213
THOMAS COOK: 0044 1733 318950
VISA: 0044 20 7937 8091

0800–1600 Mon to Fri, 0840–1130 Sat.

Relatively inexpensive but accommodation is in short supply.

Spanish. English is also spoken along the Mosquito Coast.

Tropical climate. Rainy season: Jun–Nov. The mountains in the north are much cooler.

Roman Catholic.

Jan 1, May 1, 30, Jul 19, Aug 1, Sep 14, 15, Nov 2, Dec 8, 25. Easter.

110 Volts AC, 60 Hz

Up to 2 weeks. Poste restante is available in Managua.

Some towns and cities run women's centres (casa de mujer), mainly consisting of women's clinics. There are no specific dangers facing women travellers in Nicaragua but the normal precautions should be taken.

ROADS: Tarred roads exist to San Juan del Sur and Corinto. CAR HIRE: Available in Managua or at the airport. This is the most convenient way of travelling because public transport is often overcrowded. DOCUMENTATION: National licences are only valid for 30 days. BUS: There is a service to the main towns, booking seats in advance is recommended. TAXI: Fares should be agreed in advance.

Nicaragua lacks an extensive tourist infrastructure. Violent outbursts can take place during political gatherings and demonstrations, so they are best avoided. Be alert to pickpocketing in crowded places. Nicaragua is prone to a wide variety of natural disasters, including earthquakes, hurricanes and volcanic eruptions. PHOTOGRAPHY: Avoid taking photos of military installations. Do not walk alone at night.

Niger

CAPITAL: Niamey

GMT +1

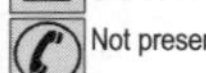

FROM UK: 00227. OUTGOING CODE TO UK: 0044

Not present.

No embassy in the UK. EUROPE: Embassy of the Republic of Niger, 154 rue du Longchamp, 75116 Paris, France. Tel: 0033 1 45 04 80 60. Fax: 0033 1 45 04 62 26.

The British Embassy in Abidjan, Cote d'Ivoire, covers Niger. In an emergency, contact the British Honorary Consul in Niamey, Tel: 724676 or 752459; Fax: 724676.

Not present.

Office Nationale du Tourisme, Bp 612, avenue du Président H Luebke, Niamey, Niger. Tel: 732 447.

Return ticket required. Requirement may change at short notice. Contact the embassy before departure. Valid passport required.

Visa required.

Pornography is prohibited. A licence is required for sporting guns.

US$9, levied on all international flights.

POLIO, TYPHOID: R. MALARIA: Exists throughout the country in the falciparum variety. Resistance to chloroquine has been reported. YELLOW FEVER: A vaccination certificate is required by all travellers arriving from all countries, over one year of age. OTHER: Bilharzia, cholera and rabies.

W1

CFA Franc. (CFA Fr) = 100 centimes. Access and Mastercard are accepted on a limited basis. Hotels, restaurants and most shops exchange travellers cheques. French francs are the preferred currency. ATM AVAILABILITY: Unavailable.

MONEYGRAM: Unavailable.
WESTERN UNION: 73 31 01.

AMEX: 0044 1273 696 933
DINERS CLUB: 0044 1252 513 500
MASTERCARD: 001 314 542 7111
VISA: 001 410 581 9994

AMEX: 0044 1273 571 600
THOMAS COOK: 0044 1733 318950
VISA: 0044 20 7937 8091

0800–1100 and 1600–1700 Mon to Fri.

Moderately expensive for tourists.

French, Hausa – spoken widely in addition to other African languages.

Summers are very hot from Oct to May. Heavy rains and high temperatures are common from July to Aug.

Mostly Muslim, the remainder Christian or Animist.

Jan 1, Apr 24, May 1, Aug 3, 15, Dec 18, 25. Islamic festivals, Easter.

220/380 Volts AC, 50 Hz

Up to 2 weeks. Poste restante operates.

Women are advised not to wear revealing clothes.

ROAD: Many are impassable during the rainy season. It is prohibited to travel on any other route than the one entered on your passport by the police in the previous town. BUS: Daily buses operate between the cities although can be unreliable. DOCUMENTATION: IDP, Carnet de Passage and 2 photos are required. The min age to drive is 23.

Niger is an inland African nation whose northern area includes a part of the Sahara Desert. Tourism facilities are minimal outside the capital, Niamey. Travel in the northern and eastern areas of Niger is dangerous and should be undertaken only by air or in a protected convoy.
HIGH RISK. Contact the FCO Travel Advice Unit for up to date information. Niger remains politically unstable and travellers should be careful when visiting rural areas. Traditional Muslim beliefs prevail and should be respected. Those travelling outside the capital should contact the Embassy first. PHOTOGRAPHY: Permits are required from the police.

CAPITAL: Lagos

GMT +1

FROM UK: 00234. OUTGOING CODE TO UK: 00944.

Not present.

High Commission for the Federal Republic of Nigeria, Nigeria House, 9 Northumberland Avenue, London, WC2N 5BX. Tel: 020 7839 1244. Fax: 020 7839 8746. www.nigeriahouseuk.com

British Deputy High Commission, 11 Walter Carrington Crescent, Victoria Island. (Private Bag 12136). Tel: (1) 2625930; Fax: (1) 2625940. chancery@lagos.mail.fco.gov.uk

Refer to www.lagos-online.com/

Nigerian Tourist Board, PO Box 2944, Trade Fair Complex, Badagry Expressway, Lagos, Nigeria. Tel: (1) 618 665.

Return ticket required. Requirements may change at short notice. Contact the embassy before departure. Valid passport required.

Visa required.

The import of champagne or sparkling wine will result in a heavy fine or imprisonment.

US$20. Transit passengers and those under two years old are exempt.

POLIO, TYPHOID: R. MALARIA: Exists throughout the year mainly in the falciparum variety. Resistance to chloroquine has been reported. YELLOW FEVER: A vaccination certificate is required from passengers over one year of age arriving from infected areas. Travellers are advised to have the vaccination if travelling outside the urban areas. OTHER: Bilharzia, cholera and rabies.

W1

Naira (N) = 100 Kobo. NOTE: Import and export of local currency is limited to N50 in notes. Credit cards have a limited acceptance, and due to a prevalence of credit card fraud, their use is ill-advised. Travellers cheques are accepted but expect to pay a high commission. US$ and Pound sterling are the preferred currencies. ATM AVAILABILITY: Unavailable.

MONEYGRAM: Available.
WESTERN UNION: 1 266 35 62.

AMEX: 0044 1273 696 933
DINERS CLUB: 0044 1252 513 500
MASTERCARD: 001 314 542 7111
VISA: 001 410 581 9994

AMEX: 0044 1273 571 600
THOMAS COOK: 0044 1733 318950
VISA: 00944 20 7937 8091

0800–1500 Mon, 0800–1330 Tues-Fri.

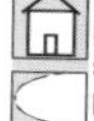
Local produce can be bought inexpensively, but accommodation and foreign imports, such as spirits, are very expensive.

English. There are over 250 local languages.

The southern coast is hot and humid with rainy season Mar-Nov. The north's rainy season Apr-Sept. Nights are cold between Dec and Jan.

Islamic majority with Christian minority and many local religions.

Jan 1, May 1, Oct 1, Dec 25, 26. Islamic festivals, Easter.

210/250 Volts AC, 50Hz.

Unreliable and takes about 3 weeks.

Women should dress modestly and should not wear trousers.

FLIGHTS: Operate between the main cities. It is advisable to book in advance and account for delays which frequently occur. ROADS: Secondary roads are often impassable during the rainy season. Caution is required when travelling in the South. DOCUMENTATION: IDP is required.

Armed robberies are prevalent in Lagos. Visitors are advised not to travel after dark outside the main tourist areas. Casual clothing is suitable. Smoking in public places is illegal. Do not be taken in by scams that promise to make you rich by helping out a businessman or charity worker to move money in or out of Nigerian bank accounts. They pose a danger of serious financial loss or blackmail, with threats of physical harm to you or relatives back home. Any promise of entry into Nigeria without a visa is an indicator of a fraudulent scheme.

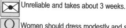

CAPITAL: Alofi

GMT –11

FROM UK: 00683. OUTGOING CODE TO UK: 0044 Most international calls go through the operator.

Police: 999, Fire: 4133, Hospital: 998

Contact the New Zealand High Commission in London.

Not present.

Refer to the New Zealand Tourism Board, New Zealand House, 80 Haymarket, London SW1Y 4TQ. Tel: 020 7973 0363. Fax: 020 7839 8929, or www.niueisland.com or www.niueisland.nu/

Niue Tourism Office, PO Box 42, Alofi, Niue Tel: 4224. Fax 4225. niuetourism@mail.gov.nu

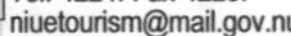

Return ticket required. Regulations may be subject to short-term change. Contact the embassy before departure. Valid passport required

Visa not required by bona fide tourist staying less than 30 days with return or onward tickets and sufficient funds to finance stay. An entry permit is granted on arrival. Visas are required for all nationals staying over 30 days, except those from New Zealand.

Visitors are allowed to import 1 radio cassette player, 1 radio, 1 record player, 1 typewriter, 1 pair of binoculars, 1 camera, 1 movie camera or video.

NZ$20, payable in local currency. Children under 5 year of age are exempt

POLIO, TYPHOID: R. YELLOW FEVER: A vaccination certificate is required from all travellers over 1 year of age arriving from an infected area.

New Zealand Dollar (NZ$) EXCHANGE: The Westpac Bank in Alofi can exchange currency. Credit cards are accepted in most restaurants and tour agencies. Travellers cheques are not accepted. ATM AVAILABILITY: Unavailable.

MONEYGRAM: Unavailable.
WESTERN UNION: Unavailable.

AMEX: 0044 1273 696 933
DINERS CLUB: 0044 1252 513 500
MASTERCARD: 001 314 542 7111
VISA: 001 410 581 9994

AMEX: 0044 1273 571 600
THOMAS COOK: 0061 3696 2952
VISA: 0044 20 7937 8091

0900–1400 Mon to Thur. 0830–1400 Fri.

Moderate to expensive. Accommodation, ranging from modern hotels to guest houses, is affordable to the budget traveller.

Niuean and English.

Average temperature from Dec to Mar is 27ºC., Apr to Nov 24ºC. The weather is generally pleasant all year round.

Mostly Ekalesai Niue, Latter-Day Saints, Roman Catholics, Seventh Day Adventists and Jehovah's Witnesses.

Jan 1, 2, Feb 6, Apr 25, first Mon in Jun, fourth Mon in Oct, Dec 25, 26. Easter.

230 Volts AC, 50 Hz. Plugs are the standard 3-pin type.

1–2 weeks.

Niuean women are regarded for their quality weaving, of hats, baskets, handbags and mats produced from indigenous plants, such as pandanus. Children are bestowed with gifts of money or handmade mats from their relatives upon coming of age. Girls also have their ears pierced, and boys receive their first haircut.

There is no organised public transport. ROAD: Badly damaged by a cyclone in 1990, some of the roads are paved. CAR HIRE: Can be hired on arrival although it is better to arrange it in advance. BIKES: Mountain bikes, motorbikes and motor scooters can also be hired on the island. DOCUMENTATION: As well as a national driving licence visitors will have to obtain a local licence from the Niue police station.

Niue island is an emerged atoll with a coastline of 64 km, and a former reef and lagoon uplifted to about 60m above sea level. It consists of limestone. The interior is a plateau featuring a jagged surface, slightly depressed towards the centre. Niue has no surface water but artesian bores enable the subterranean reservoir of fresh water to be tapped.
Sunday is taken seriously as a day of rest and activities such as boating and fishing are not allowed.

CAPITAL: Oslo

GMT +1 (GMT +2 during the summer).

FROM UK: 0047 OUTGOING CODE TO UK: 0044

Oslo Police: 002, Ambulance: 003.

Royal Norwegian Embassy, 25 Belgrave Square, London SW1X 8QD. Tel: 020 7235 7151. Fax: 020 7245 6993. emb.london@mfa.no www.norway.org.uk

British Embassy, Thomas Heftyesgate 8, 0244 Oslo, Norway. Tel 2313 2700; Fax: 2313 2738. www.britain.no. Consulates also in Bergen, Stavanger, Tromsø and Trondhiem.

Norwegian Tourist Board, Charles House, 5 Lower Regent Street, London SW1Y 4LR. Tel: 020 7839 6255. Fax: 020 7839 6014. greatbritain@nortra.no or infouk@ntr.no. www.norway.org.uk/travel.htm

NORTRA (Norwegian Tourist Board) PO Box 2893 Solle, Drammensveien 40, 0230 Oslo, Norway. Tel (22) 925 200. Fax: (22) 560 505. norway@ntr.no; www.ntr.no

Requirements may be subject to change at short notice. Contact the relevant authority before travelling. Valid passport required. NOTE: Expired passports cannot be considered as valid travel documents.

Visa not required by nationals of the EU.

Spirits over 60% volume and wine over 22% volume alcohol. Certain foodstuffs. Birds and animals.

Rabies is present on the island of Savlbard.

Norwegian Krone (Nkr) = 100 øre. NOTE: Import and export of local currency is limited to Nkr 25, 000. All major credit cards are accepted. Travellers cheques, preferably in US$, can be exchanged in banks, hotels and shops. ATM AVAILABILITY: Over 2000 locations.

MONEYGRAM: 800 12419.
WESTERN UNION: Unavailable.

AMEX: 0044 1273 696 933
DINERS CLUB: 023 00 11 00
MASTERCARD: 800 12697
VISA: 800 11 570 or 800 12052

AMEX: 800 11000
THOMAS COOK: 800 11005
VISA: 800 11815

0900–1700 Mon to Thur in major cities and 0900–1530 Fri.

Relatively expensive as in the other Scandinavian countries.

Norwegian. Lappish is spoken by Sami people in the North. The majority of people also speak English.

Coastal areas have a moderate climate. Inland areas are more extreme, with hot summers and cold winters.

Mostly Evangelical Lutherans with other Christian denominations.

Jan 1, May 1, 17, Dec 24, 25, 26, 31. Major Christian feast days.

220 volts AC, 50 Hz. Plugs are the continental 2-pin type.

2–4 days within Europe.

There is very little inequality between men and women in Norway.

RAIL: Connects main cities and Sweden. Substantial reductions can be gained through the Scanrail pass. ROAD: The road system is of variable quality, especially in the North during freezing conditions. BUS: Efficient service. DOCUMENTATION: IDP or national driving licence is required along with the vehicles log book. A green card is strongly recommended.

Punctuality is very important, especially if invited to someone's home. Lunch is the main meal of the day, but it is often eaten as late as 1700. Casual dress is acceptable everywhere during the day. Northern Norway (above the Arctic Circle) experiences the midnight sun during May and June, as the sun doesn't set below the horizon; conversely, there are long dark winters with no sunshine at all for two months, as the sun doesn't rise above the horizon. Northern Norway offers some of the world's best cross-country skiing locations.

Oman

CAPITAL: Muscat

GMT +4.

FROM UK: 00968. OUTGOING CODE: 0044.

All services: 999.

Embassy of the Sultanate of Oman, 167 Queen's Gate London SW7 5HE. Tel: 020 7225 0001. Fax: 020 7589 2505.

British Embassy, PO Box 300, 113 Muscat, Oman. Tel: 693 077. Fax: 693 087. becomu@omantel.net.om; www.britishembassyoman.org

Not present. See www.oman.org/tourism.htm

Directorate General of Tourism , PO Box 550, 113 Muscat, Oman. Tel: 774 253. Fax: 794 238. www.omanet.com/

Return ticket and valid passport required. Requirements may be subject to change: contact relevant authority before going.

Tourist and business visas are required. Allow seven days to process applications.

Fresh foods, pornography. All animals need an import licence.

OMR3 for all departures: transit passengers and those under 12 years of age are exempt.

Holders of Israeli passports will be refused entry and transit.

POLIO, TYPHOID: R. MALARIA: Exists in the falciparum variety throughout the country. Resistance to chloroquine has been reported. YELLOW FEVER: A vaccination certificate is required from travellers arriving from infected areas. OTHER: Cholera, rabies.

W1. Mains tap water in Muscat is safe to drink but may taste of chlorine.

Omani Rail (OR) = 100 baiza. Amex and Diners Club accepted. Travellers cheques, preferably in US$ or Pound sterling, exchanged easily. ATM AVAILABILITY: 50 locations.

MONEYGRAM: Unavailable.
WESTERN UNION: 787 220

AMEX: 0044 1273 696 933. DINERS CLUB: 706 007 or 704 251. MASTERCARD: 001 314 542 7111. VISA: 001 410 581 9994

AMEX: 0044 1273 571600. THOMAS COOK: 001733 318950. VISA: 0044 20 7937 8091

0800–1200 Sat-Wed and 0800–1130 Thur.

It is impossible to travel on a tight budget. There are few middle-range hotels and restaurants.

Arabic and English.

June-July are very hot. Rainfall varies according to the region.

Ibadi Muslim with Sunni and Shia minorities.

Jan 1, Nov 18, 19, Dec 31. Islamic festivals.

220/240 volts AC, 50 Hz.

Up to 2 weeks to Western Europe.

Although Oman is more tolerant than its neighbouring states, women should still dress modestly. The preferred outfit is loosely cut trousers or a long dress; a headscarf is necessary only in rural areas.

If you are travelling in remote areas, make sure that you carry plenty of water and sunblock. Visitors are not allowed to travel into the interior further up the coast than Seeb. ROAD: Traffic drives on the left. Seat belts are compulsory and hand-held mobile phones are banned while driving. The roads outside Muscat at night can be dangerous, as there is a risk of hitting camels. There is a mandatory three nights in jail for traffic offences. BUS: Services exist in Muscat and North Oman. TAXI: Prices are high and should be agreed in advance. DOCUMENTATION: Those on tourist visas can use their driving licence for up to 7 days; after that a local licence is required, available from a police station.

Oman has only been open to the outside world for a short period and visitors should be sensitive to this. Do not dress in a provocative way, e.g. sports clothing when not obviously engaged in sport. It is legal to drink alcohol only in licensed establishments. Non-Muslims are not allowed into mosques. Drug laws are strict and the death penalty is available for serious cases. PHOTOGRAPHY: Signs will indicate areas where it is prohibited. Be careful when photographing people, especially women, and always ask permission. Collecting seashells, abalones, corals, crayfish and turtle eggs is forbidden.

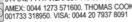

CAPITAL: Islamabad

GMT +5.

FROM UK: 0092. OUTGOING CODE TO UK: 0044

Not present.

High Commission of the Islamic Republic of Pakistan, 35-36 Lowndes Square, London SW1X 9JN. Tel: 020 7664 9200. Fax: 020 7664 9224.
informationdivision@ highcommission-uk.gov.pk; www.pakmission-uk.gov.pk

British High Commission, PO Box 1122, Diplomatic Enclave, Ramna 5, Islamabad Pakistan. Tel: 051 2822131; Fax: 051 2279356. bhcmedia@isb.comsats.net.pk
British Deputy High Commission, Shahrah-E-Iran, Clifton, Karachi 75600; Tel: 021 5872431; Fax: 021 5874328.
bdhc@crestarnet.net.

No tourism office in UK. See www.tourism.gov.pk/

Pakistan Tourism Development Corporation, 2nd Floor, 22/A Saeed Plaza, Jinnah Avenue, Blue Area (P.O. Box 1465), Islamabad 44000. Tel: 0092 51 2877039; Fax: 0092 51 274507. tourism@isb.comsats.net.pk

Return ticket required. Requirements may be subject to short-term change. Contact the relevant authority before departure. Valid passport required.

In place of a visa, a Landing Permit will be issued to tourists on arrival, and allows a maximum 30–day stay.

Import of alcohol, matches, plants, fruit and vegetables and export of antiques is prohibited.

Rs 200 for economy class, payable in local currency (Rs 300 and 400 respectively for club and first class). There is an additional Foreign Travel Tax of Rs 700 on tickets issued within Pakistan. Transit passengers and those under 2 years of age are exempt.

POLIO, TYPHOID: R. MALARIA: Exists in the falciparum variety in all areas below 2000 m. It has been reported as being highly resistant to chloroquine. YELLOW FEVER: A vaccination certificate is required from all travellers coming from an infected area. Children under 6 months of age are exempt if the mother has proof of vaccination before the child was born. OTHER: Cholera, rabies.

W1

Pakistani Rupee (Rs) = 100 paisa. Pakistan is largely a cash economy. Credit cards are accepted by only a few establishments in the larger cities. Travellers cheques are generally accepted at most banks, 4- and 5-star hotels and major shops. US$ are the preferred currency. ATM AVAILABILITY: 3 locations.

MONEYGRAM: Available in major cities.
WESTERN UNION: (21) 586 8261.

AMEX: 0044 1273 696 933
DINERS CLUB: 0044 1252 513 500
MASTERCARD: 001 314 542 7111
VISA: 001 410 581 9994

AMEX: 021 262 1989
THOMAS COOK: 0044 1733 318950
VISA: 0044 20 7937 8091

0900–1300 and 1500–2000 Sun to Thur, closed Fri. Some banks open on Sat.

Staying in Pakistan can be relatively cheap if you are willing to shop at the markets and sacrifice luxuries.

Urdu and English. There are regional languages of Sindhi, Baluchi, Punjabi and Pashtu, and numerous local dialects.

Three seasons: Winter (Nov–Mar) – warm but cooled by sea breezes. Summer (Apr–Jul) – extreme temperatures. Monsoon (Jul-Sept) - the highest rainfall on the hills.

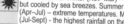

Mostly Muslim with Christian and Hindi minorities.

Jan11, Feb 7, Mar 23, May 1, Aug 14, Sep 6, 11, Nov 9, Dec 25, 26. Islamic festivals. Easter (Christian minority).

220 volts AC, 50 Hz. Round 2-or 3-pin plugs are in use.

Airmail takes 4–5 days to reach Western Europe.

Women should not wear tight or revealing clothing and should make sure arms and legs are covered. Strict Muslim rules always apply.

FLIGHTS: Many daily flights from Karachi to commercial centres. The quickest and most efficient means of travel. RAIL: Extensive rail network. Travel in air-conditioned coaches is advised along with reservations for longer journeys. ROAD: The highway network between cities is well made and maintained. Driving without experienced local drivers or guides is not recommended. For specific current information on road conditions along the Karakoram Highway, visitors can call the Frontier Works Organization in Rawalpindi, Tel: 92 51 566639.

BUS: Regular services between most towns and villages. Air-conditioned coaches are recommended for longer journeys. Advance booking is advised. TAXI: By far the most efficient mean of urban travel, being reasonably priced and widely available. CAR HIRE: Available in major cities. DOCUMENTATION: An IDP will be issued on presentation of a national driving licence.

!

Punjab region should be avoided as tourists are often targeted for political reasons. Muslim traditions and beliefs should be respected at all times. Mutual hospitality and courtesy are of great importance. Rallies, demonstrations and processions occur from time to time throughout Pakistan at very short notice and have occasionally taken on anti-Western character.

Visitors wishing to trek in Gilgit, Hunza, Chitral and the upper Swat valley should use only licensed guides and tourist agencies. Substantial areas within the Northwest Frontier Province are designated tribal areas and are outside the normal jurisdiction of government law enforcement authorities. Because of dangerous security conditions, extreme caution is advised if travelling overland to the Khyber Pass. However, the monthly steam train excursion through the Khyber Pass for tourists is well protected by the authorities.

Crime is a serious concern for foreigners throughout Pakistan: Lahore and Karachi, in particular, experience high levels of crime.

Homosexuality is illegal, as is the co-habitation of a non-married couple.

CAPITAL: Koror

GMT +9

CODE FROM UK: 00680. OUTGOING CODE TO UK: 01144.

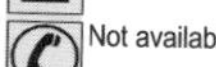
Not available.

Palau has no diplomatic mission in the UK. The Palau Embassy in Washington can be contacted. Tel: 001 202 452 6814. ambkyota@erols.com

The British High Commission in Suva, Fiji, deals with consular matters in Palau. In an emergency, contact the Honorary Consular Agent, C/o NECO Marine Corporation, PO Box 3045, Koror, Republic of Palau 96940, Western Caroline Islands.Tel: 00680 488 2600; Fax: 00680 488 4514.

Palau Visitors Authority Representative for Europe: Simone Rosel Tourism Consulting (SRTC), Fasanenstr. 2, 25462, Rellingen, Germany.Tel: 0049 4101 370732; Fax: 0049 4101 370733. palau@srtc.de Also see: www.destmic.com/palau.html

Palau Visitors Authority, PO Box 256, Koror, Republic of Palau 96940. Tel: 00680 488 1930; Fax: 00680 488 1453. pva@palaunet.com www.visit-palau.com/dest.html

Passport required.

Visa not required. Visitors must have a return or onward travel ticket. An entry permit is issued on arrival. Visitors who want to stay more than 30 days need an approval by the Chief of Immigration for an extended stay.

Firearms, ammunition and narcotics.

US$20

YELLOW FEVER, CHOLERA immunisation certificates required of visitors arriving from infected areas. Smallpox immunisation required of all travellers from outside the USA. HEPATITIS B is endemic. Hepatitis A and dengue fever can occur. Mosquito protection is recommended.

Mains water in Koror is safe but may cause mild stomach upsets at first. Elsewhere, boiled water is advisable. Bottled water is available.

US$. Credit cards are accepted at tourist facilities, including hotels and boat charters and diving centres. Travellers cheques can be changed at banks.

MONEYGRAM: 0011 800 821 8192.
WESTERN UNION: Available.

AMEX: 01144 1273 696 933
DINERS CLUB: 01144 1252 513 500
MASTERCARD: 1800 307 7309
VISA: 888 425 0227

AMEX: 01144 1273 571 600
THOMAS COOK: 1800 223 7373
VISA: 01144 20 7937 8091

0800–1600 Monday to Thursday; 0800–1700 Friday. The Peleliu branch bank is open from high tide Friday until high tide Saturday on the payday weekend.

Palau has a range of accommodation from budget no-frills hotels to mid-range and luxury beach resort complexes.

English and Palauan.

Tropical, hot and humid all year. Rainy season July to October. Typhoons are rare.

Roman Catholic, other Christian denominations and Modoknei, an indigenous religion of Palau.

Jan 1, Mar 15, May 5, Jun 1, Jul 9, first Mon in Sep, Oct 1,24, last Thur in Nov, Dec 25.

230 volts AC, 60 Hz; some premises are on 115 volts.

Palau is a matriarchal society, with a tradition of great respect for women. In the past a council of women would advise the village chiefs on issues concerned with land and money.

AIR: Palau is 2 hours flying time from Guam. There twice-weekly flights to and from Manila. BOAT: Several companies offer charter boats for touring the islands and diving. ROAD: Side roads in Koror and on Babelthaup Island are in poor condition. Overtaking slow-moving vehicles is not allowed. The speed limit is 40kph (25mph). TAXI: There is a standard $2 flat rate for a single journey within Koror. It's also possible to hire bicycles and scooters. CAR HIRE: Several firms operate in Koror. A 4 x 4 vehicle is recommended. DOCUMENTATION: A national driving licence is required.

Crime is not a problem for visitors so long as sensible precautions are taken to avoid petty theft. Cool, loose clothing is best. Hats and sunscreen are recommended. Beachwear is not appropriate in towns and villages.

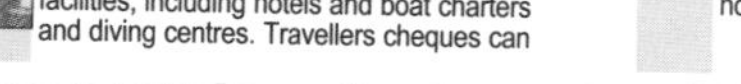

Panama

CAPITAL: Panama City

GMT –5

UK: 00507. OUTGOING CODE TO UK: 044.

Police: 104, Fire: 103, Ambulance: 225 1436/ 228 2187.

Embassy of the Republic of Panama, 40 Hertford Street, London W1Y 7TG. Tel: 020 7493 4646. Fax: 020 7493 4333.

British Embassy, Apartado 889, Zona 1 4th and 5th Floor, Torre Banco Sur, Calle 53 Este, Panama 1, Republic of Panama. Tel: 269 0866. Fax: 223 0730. britemb@cwp.net.pa

No tourist office in UK. See www.ipat.gob.pa/

Instituto Panameño de Turismo (IPAT), Apartado, 4421, Centro de Convenciones ATLAPA, Via Israel, Panamá 5, Republic of Panama. Tel: 226 7000 or 226 4614. Fax: 226 3483.

Return ticket required. Requirements may change at short notice. Contact the embassy before departure. Valid passport required

Visa not required by UK passport holders for a stay of up to 30 days.

Fruit, vegetables and animal products.

US$ 20 except for children under 2 years who are exempt.

Refer to the relevant Consular authority.

TYPHOID: R. MALARIA: Exists in the Vivax variety in certain areas. The Falciparum variety is also present in certain areas and is reported to be highly resistant to chloroquine. YELLOW FEVER: Vaccination is strongly recommended for those planning to travel outside the urban areas. A vaccination certificate is recommended for those planning to visit the province of Darien. OTHER: Rabies. Dengue fever in rural areas.

W2

Balboa (Ba) = 100 centesimos. EXCHANGE: Banks and Gambios. All major credit cards are accepted. Only US dollar travellers cheques are accepted. ATM AVAILABILITY: Over 150 locations.

MONEYGRAM: 001 800 543 4080.
WESTERN UNION: 2 69 1055.

AMEX: 044 1273 696 933
DINERS CLUB: 044 1252 513 500
MASTERCARD: 01 800 307 7309
VISA: 01 800 111 0016

AMEX: 044 1273 571 600
THOMAS COOK: 044 1733 318950
VISA: 044 20 7937 8091

0800–1330 Mon-Fri, 0830–1200 Sat.

Caters for all travellers and budgets.

Spanish. English is also spoken.

Hot all year with a dry season Jan-Apr and a rainy season Apr-Dec.

Roman Catholic.

Jan 1, 6, 9, Mar 11, May 1, Jun 16, Aug 15, Nov 1, 2, 3, 4, 5, 10, 28, Dec 8, 24, 25, 31. Carnival in week before Lent, Easter.

120 volts AC, 60 Hz. Plugs are flat 2-pin American type.

5–10 days.

A vibrant mixture of Spanish and American lifestyles dictates much of the culture. Inequality can still be a problem between men and women.

FLIGHTS: Internal air services are operated by local companies which link Panama City with all centres in the interior. ROAD: Good road system. Front seat belts compulsory. Many local drivers do not have insurance. The Pan-American Highway is only single lane in Panama. BUS: Services between most large towns although they are very slow. TAXI: Often not metered, so agree fare in advance. CAR HIRE: Available in city centres and airports. DOCUMENTATION: A national driving licence will be sufficient.

The economy is based mainly on services related to the Canal, and there are few tourist facilities. Avoid the area close to the border with Colombia. Crime is rife in areas of the city. In the San Felipe district most of the cheap accommodation can be found, but it is not safe to venture out at night in this area. Colon is renowned for danger. Common-sense precautions should be taken; deposit valuables in the hotel safe.

Papua New Guinea

CAPITAL: Port Moresby

GMT +10

FROM UK: 00675. OUTGOING CODE TO UK: 0544

Police, Fire and Ambulance: 000. (NOTE: this is not accessible in some areas.)

Papua New Guinea High Commission, 14 Waterloo Place, London, SW1Y 4AR. Tel: 020 7930 0922. Fax: 020 7930 0828.

British High Commission, PO Box 212, Kiroki Street, Waigani, Boroko, Port Moresby, Papua New Guinea. Tel: 325 1677 Fax 325 3547. bhcpng@datec.com.pg

No tourism office in UK. See www.interknowledge.com/papua-newguinea/

Tourism Promotion Authority, PO Box 7144, Boroko, Papua New Guinea. Tel: 272 310 Fax: 259 119.

Return ticket required. Contact the embassy before departure. Valid passport required: Passports should be valid for one year after entry.

Visa required. Tourists may obtain visas on arrival.

Plants and soil, uncanned food of animal origin, unless from Australia or New Zealand, and all pig meat from New Zealand. Animals cannot be imported except for cats and dogs, which may be subject to lengthy quarantine.

PGK 15, in local currency, on all international flights. Children under 2 years and passengers not leaving the airport are exempt.

POLIO, TYPHOID: R. MALARIA: Exists all year throughout the country below 1800m. Falciparum is the dominant variety and reported to be highly resistant to chloroquine. YELLOW FEVER: A vaccination certificate is required from travellers over one year of age arriving from infected areas. OTHER: Cholera – serious risk. Hepatitis A and B are endemic. HIV/AIDS is increasing.

W1

Kina (PGK). Export of local currency is prohibited. Amex is widely accepted. Travellers cheques are widely accepted in shops and hotels. Australian dollar cheques are preferred. ATM AVAILABILITY: Unavailable.

MONEYGRAM: Unavailable.
WESTERN UNION: Unavailable.

AMEX: 0544 1273 696 933
DINERS CLUB: 0544 1252 513 500
MASTERCARD: 051 314 542 7111
VISA: 051 410 581 9994

AMEX: 0544 1273 571 600
THOMAS COOK: 0544 1733 318950
VISA: 0544 20 7937 8091

0900–1500 Mon to Thur, 0900–1700 Fri.

Although accommodation varies from international hotels to basic huts, everything is very expensive.

English. 700 local dialects are also spoken.

Tropical climate, hot and humid, but cooler at high altitude. Most rain falls Dec–Mar.

Christian.

Jan 1, second Sat in Jun, Jul 23, Sep 29, Dec 25, 26. Easter, traditional feasts (Kavieng) in Apr and Jun.

240 volts AC, 50 Hz. Australian-style 3-pin plugs are in use.

7–10 days.

The anthropological diversity found in Papua New Guinea is wide. Indigenous tribes inhabit the interior, whilst modern and cultural tolerance is found in the main cities. Women dress conservatively. It is unsafe for women to venture out alone in Papua New Guinea since there is a serious risk of sexual assaults near the main towns.

FLIGHTS: Services which operate are expensive. Internal services should be booked between November and February. ROAD: Traffic drives on the left. Travel on highways outside of major towns can be hazardous. There is no country-wide road network, roads are generally in poor repair, and flat tyres occur routinely as a result of debris on the roadways. Public motor vehicles (PMV) are very efficient and provide a good way of meeting the locals. DOCUMENTATION: A national driving licence is sufficient. RIVERS: Commonly used as a thoroughfare.

Law and order remains poor. Incidents of rioting, looting and shooting occur without warning in major towns. Increase in violent crime requires extra care to be taken. Do not use public transport. Travellers should be met at Port Moresby upon arrival.

Paraguay

CAPITAL: Asuncion

GMT –4

FROM UK: 00595. OUTGOING CODE TO UK: 0044

All services: 00.

Embassy of the Republic of Paraguay, Braemar Lodge, Cornwall Gardens, London, SW7 4AQ. Tel: 020 7937 1253; Fax: 020 7937 5687. embapar@londresdy.freeserve.co.uk

British Embassy, Avda. Boggiani 5848, C/R I6 Boqueron, Asunción, Paraguay. Tel: 021 612 611. Fax: 021 605 007. brembasu@rieder.net.py

No tourist office in UK. See www.paraguaysp.com.br/

Direccion General de Turismo, Ministerio de Obas, Pulicas Y Communicaciones, Palma 468, Asuncion, Paraguay. Tel: (21) 441530. Fax: (21) 491230.

Return ticket required. Requirements may change at short notice. Contact the embassy before departure. Valid passport required.

Visa not required by nationals of EU countries entering as tourists for stays up to 90 days.

Narcotics.

US$15 levied on all international departures excluding transit and those passengers who are under 2 years of age.

POLIO, TYPHOID: R. MALARIA: Exists in the vivax variety in some rural areas from Oct-May. YELLOW FEVER: A vaccination certificate is required for visitors arriving from endemic areas. A certificate is also required from travellers leaving Paraguay to endemic areas. OTHER: Rabies, dengue fever.

W2

Guarani (G). Many of the expensive hotels will accept credit cards and exchange travellers cheques. US$ are preferred to sterling travellers cheques. Major credit cards are widely accepted, although Diners Club has a more limited acceptance. ATM AVAILABILITY: Over 26 locations.

MONEYGRAM: 008 11 800 then 800 592 5755 (Spanish).
WESTERN UNION: (21) 211 060.

AMEX: 0044 1273 696 933
DINERS CLUB: 0044 1252 513 500
MASTERCARD: 001 314 542 7111
VISA: 001 410 581 9994

AMEX: 001 801 964 6665
THOMAS COOK: 0044 1733 318950
VISA: 0044 20 7937 8091

0845-1215 Mon to Fri.

Accommodation is limited to the city and needs to be booked, in writing, well in advance. Other commodities tend to be moderately expensive.

Spanish. Guarani.

Subtropical climate. Hottest and wettest period is Dec–Mar.

Roman Catholic.

Jan 1, 6, Mar 1, May 1, 15, Jun 12, Aug 15, 16, Sep 29, Dec 8, 25. Easter.

220 volts AC, 50 Hz

5 days by airmail.

Culture is dominated by Roman Catholicism.

FLIGHTS: Several visitor flights operate providing a popular view of local sites. RAIL: Services are unreliable and irregular. ROAD: Roads serving the main centres are in good condition. Approx. 10% of roads are unsurfaced and therefore impassable in poor weather. DOCUMENTATION: IDP and national driving licences are all accepted. BUS: The cheapest method of transport NOTE: For longer distances advance booking is necessary. Express links to major cities operate.

Beware of poisonous snakes. Paraguay is generally safer than its neighbours but common-sense precautions should be followed. There are few facilities for tourists outside the capital.

CAPITAL: Lima

GMT –5

FROM UK: 0051. OUTGOING CODE TO UK: 0044.

All services: 011 / 5114.

Embassy of the Republic of Peru, 52 Sloane Street, London, SW1X 9SP. Tel: 020 7235 1917 or 020 7838 9223 (visa section). Fax: 020 7235 4463. postmaster@peruembassy-uk.com; www.peruembassy-uk.com

British Embassy, Natalio Sanchez 125, Edificio El Pacifico, Pisos, 11 y 12, Plaza Washington, Lima 100. Tel: 01 433 4738; Fax: 01 433 4735. britemb@terra.com.pe

No tourist office in UK. See www.virtualperu.net/

Fondo de Promoción Turística, Calle Uno, s/n Urb, Corpac, Lima 27. Tel: (1) 224 3142 or 224 3408. Fax: (1) 224 3133 or 224 3396. postmaster@foptur.gob.peru

Return ticket required. Requirements may change at short notice. Contact the embassy before departure. Valid passport required.

Refer to the embassy for the latest visa information.

It is forbiden to export handicrafts made from insects, feathers or other natural products, or artifacts from pre-colonial civilisations.

US$ 17.70 is levied on all international departures except transit and those passengers under 2 years of age.

POLIO, TYPHOID: R. MALARIA: Exists in rural areas below 1500m in the Vivax variety. The falciparum variety exists sporadically near national borders and where petroleum is being exploited; resistance to chloroquine has been reported. YELLOW FEVER: A vaccination certificate is required by visitors over 6 months travelling from infected areas. Vaccination is strongly recommended to all travellers who plan to journey out of the urban areas. OTHER: Cholera, rabies, dengue fever in northern Peru. Visitors to Andes locations may need time to adjust to the altitude, which can affect blood pressure, digestion and energy level.

W2. Street vendor food is not recommended.

Nuevo Sol = 100 centimos. EXCHANGE: Changing currency other than US$ can be difficult. Outside Lima, credit cards have limited acceptance and cashing travellers cheques can prove a complex process. US dollar cheques are recommended. ATM AVAILABILITY: Over 430 locations.

MONEYGRAM: 001 800 824 2220.
WESTERN UNION: (1) 422 9723.

AMEX: 0044 1273 696 933
DINERS CLUB: 01 221 2050
MASTERCARD: 0800 307 7309
VISA: 001 410 581 9994

AMEX: 001 801 964 6665
THOMAS COOK: 0044 1733 318950
VISA: 0044 20 7937 8091

0930–1600 Mon to Fri. (Some banks open 0930–1230 Sat.)

Costs have increased dramatically in the last few years. Budget travellers can still find cheap accommodation, although the cities are much more expensive than rural areas.

Spanish and Quechua. English may also be spoken.

Oct–Apr is summer in coastal areas but the rainy season in the mountainous regions, which are best visited in May-Sept.

Roman Catholic.

Jan 1, May 1, Jun 29, Jul 29, Aug 30, Oct 8, Nov 1, Dec 8, 25. Easter. Various traditional festivals observed locally.

200 volts AC, 60 Hz.

Up to 2 weeks. Postal facilities are limited outside Lima.

RAIL: Can provide a scenic view of the landscape and sections are among the highest railway in the world. Connections are limited. ROAD: A recently built highway connects Lima with other cities. Landslides are common in the rainy season. A Customs Duty Payment badge must be displayed at all times. BUS: Greyhound-type buses operate along the Pan-American highway. TAXIS: Unmetered, so agree fare in advance. CAR HIRE: International companies have outlets in the major cities and airport. DOCUMENTATION: IDP is required.

Register with your embassy when you arrive in Lima. Travel in groups: terrorist action may occur and street crime is common. Unscrupulous traders may try to sell articles that cannot legally be exported from Peru. Peru is in an earthquake zone.

CAPITAL: Manila

GMT +8

FROM UK: 0063. OUTGOING CODE TO UK: 0044 International calls from smaller towns must go through the operator.

Embassy of the Republic of the Philippines, 9a Palace Green, London W8 4QE. Tel: 020 7937 1600. Fax: 020 7937 2925. embassy@philemb.demon.co.uk www.philemb.demon.co.uk

Embassy of the Philippines, Cultural and Tourism Office, 146 Cromwell Road, London SW7 4EF. Tel: 020 7835 1100; Fax: 020 7835 1926. tourism@pdot.co.uk

British Embassy, 15th - 17th Floors, L V Locsin Building, 6752 Ayala Avenue Makati, Metro Manila 3116. Tel (2) 8167116. Fax: (2) 819 7206.

Philippine Department of Tourism, 17 Albermarle Street, London W1X 7HA. Tel: 020 7499 5443 (general enquiries) or 020 7499 5652 (incentive travel). Fax: 020 7499 5772.

Philippine Department of Tourism, Department of Tourism Building, Teodoro Valencia Circle, Rizal Park, Ermita, Manila. Tel: (2) 599 031. Fax: (2) 501 567.

Return ticket required. Requirements may change at short notice. Contact the embassy before departure. Valid passport required.

Visa not required by transit passengers, or by tourists and business travellers staying for not more than 21 days, if they have a valid passport for at least one year and onward tickets. NOTE: Certain nationalities will require pre-arrival approval by the authorities in Manila before visas can be issued. Check with the embassy before making travel arrangements.

Pornographic material, seditious or subversive material.

PP500 for international departures, payable in local currency. Children under 2 years of age and transit passengers are exempt.

POLIO, TYPHOID: R. MALARIA: Exists in certain areas below 600 m in the falciparum variety, reported as being highly resistant to chloroquine. OTHER: Bilharzia, cholera and rabies. The dengue fever mosquito is found all over the Philippines, including Manila.

W1

Philippine Peso (PP) = 100 centavos. EXCHANGE: Always use authorised money changers or banks in Manila Metro area. Credit cards are accepted in larger cities. Travellers cheques are widely accepted: US$ is the preferred denomination. ATM AVAILABILITY: Over 800 locations.

MONEYGRAM: 1 800 111 0223
WESTERN UNION: (02) 811 1687.

AMEX: 0044 1273 696 933
DINERS CLUB: 88 791 88
MASTERCARD: 001800 1111 0061
VISA: 001800 1111 9015

AMEX: 001800 1611 0087
THOMAS COOK: 0044 1733 318950
VISA: 0044 20 7937 8091

0900–1600 Mon to Fri.

Can be cheap by Western standards, and a haven for shoppers, especially in the markets. Hotels range from the deluxe to small guest houses and prices vary accordingly.

Filipino. English is widely spoken and Spanish may also be spoken.

Tropical climate with constant sea breezes. Rainy season: Jun–Sept. Oct–Feb is the cool dry season. Mar–May is usually hot and dry. Occasional typhoons June-Sept.

Mainly Roman Catholic. Muslims, Christians, Buddhism and Taoists are also present.

Jan 1, Feb 22, Apr 9, May 1, Jun 12, 24, Aug 31, Nov 1, 30, Dec 25, 30, 31. Easter.

220 volts AC, 60 Hz. 110 volts is available in most hotels. Plugs: flat and round 2- and 3-pin.

At least 5 days.

Filipino women tend to be fairly conservative. Filipino men may make persistent advances to female visitors.

FLIGHTS: The Philippines consist of over 7000 islands. Charter planes may be hired to visit the most remote. Internal services are operated by several companies. Reservations should be confirmed before departure date. BUS: Widely available and cheap. ROAD: Travel off national highways and paved roads, especially at night, is particularly dangerous.

All Western tourists are considered wealthy by the host population. Stick to the main tourist areas. Casual dress is acceptable except in Muslim areas, where visitors will be required to cover up. There are more than 200 volcanoes; Mount Kanlaon near Bacolod City is still active.

CAPITAL: Warsaw

GMT +1 (GMT +2 during the summer).

FROM UK: 0048. OUTGOING CODE TO UK: 0/0 (wait for second dial tone)

Police: 997, Fire: 998, Ambulance: 999.

Embassy of the Republic of Poland, 47 Portland Place, London W1N 4GH. Tel: 020 7580 4324/9. Fax: 020 7323 4018. polishembassy@polishembassy.org.uk www.poland-embassy.org.ukmn

British Embassy, Aleja Roz 1, 00–556 Warsaw, Poland. Tel: (22) 628 1001/2/3/4/5. Fax: (22) 621 7161. britemb@it.com.pl www.britishembassy.pl/

Polish National Tourist Office, First Floor, Remo House, 310–312 Regent Street, London W1R 5AJ. Tel: 020 7580 8811. Fax: 020 7580 8866. pnto@dial.pipex.com www.poland.net/travelpage/

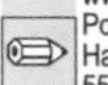
Polish Tourism Centre, 246 King Street, Hammersmith, London W6. Tel: 020 8741 5541.

Warsavawfie Centrum Informacji Gurwstycznej (Warsaw Information Centre), Zankowy Square 1/13, 00–26 Warsaw. Tel: (22) 635 1881. Fax: (22) 310 464.

Requirements may be subject to short-term change. Contact the relevant authority before departure. Valid passport required.

Visa not required by UK nationals for tourist or business visits not exceeding 6 months.

Works of art and antiques cannot be exported.

US$ 10 levied on all international travel.

Rabies. Tick-borne encephalitis.

Zloty (Zl) = 100 grozy. EXCHANGE: Border crossing points, hotels. Import and export of local currency by non-residents is prohibited. All major credit cards and travellers cheques accepted. ATM AVAILABILITY: Over 500 locations.

MONEYGRAM: Single location in the capital. WESTERN UNION: (22) 636 5688.

AMEX: 0044 1273 696 933
DINERS CLUB: 022 513 30 00
MASTERCARD: 001 314 542 7111
VISA: 001 410 581 9994

AMEX: 00800 44 11200
THOMAS COOK: 0044 1733 318950
VISA: 0044 20 7937 8091

0800–1800 Mon to Fri.

Prices are no longer as cheap as they once were.

Polish. There is a German-speaking minority. English and French may also be spoken.

Temperate climate with warm summers and cold winters. Rain falls throughout the year.

Mainly Roman Catholic. The remaining are mainly Polish Orthodox.

Jan 1, May 1, 3, Aug 15, Nov 1, 11, Dec 25, 26. Easter, Corpus Christi.

220 volts AC, 50 Hz. Continental sockets are used.

4 days. Poste restante facilities are available throughout the country.

Conservatism prevails among older women, but younger women have a broader liberal outlook on society. If travelling alone, foreign women may attract curiosity from local men. Take the usual safety precautions.

ROAD: Major roads can be narrow and carry a lot of heavy goods vehicles on east-west transit routes. BUS: There are good regional bus and coach services. CAR HIRE: Various car rental agencies operate and rental also available at the airport. DOCUMENTATION: Travellers using their own cars should have car registration cards, proof of ownership and valid insurance documents. An IDP is compulsory for driving in Poland.

Visitors are made welcome by the Poles, who are very hospitable. Roman Catholicism plays an important role in daily rural life. Conservative casual wear is acceptable for the day. More formal attire is suitable for social evenings out.

Visitors are advised to register with a hotel or local authorities within 48 hours of arrival. There is a serious risk of personal robbery on trains and at main rail stations. Passengers are at most risk when boarding trains. Never leave property unattended. Thieves are known to target the buses and trams serving Warsaw airport. Theft of foreign cars is common, sometimes by gangs posing as police in rural areas.

Portugal

CAPITAL: Lisbon

GMT (GMT +1 during the summer)

FROM UK: 00351. OUTGOING CODE TO UK: 0044

All services: 115.

Embassy of the Portuguese Republic, 11 Belgrave Square, London SW1X 8PP. Tel 020 7235 5331; Fax: 020 7245 1287. www.portembassy.gla.ac.uk/
Portuguese Consulate, Silver City House, 62 Brompton Road, London SW3 1BJ. Tel: 020 7581 8722. Visa information: 0900160 0202 (Premium rate charges apply).

British Embassy, Rua de São Bernardo 33, 1200 Lisbon, Portugal. Tel (1) 396 1191 or 396 1147 or 396 3181. Fax (1) 397 6768. Consulates in Funchal (Madeira), Oporto, Ribeira Grande (Azores) and Portimão.

Information and Tourism Office, 4th Floor, 22/25A Sackville Street, London W1X 1DE, Tel: 020 7494 1441. 24-hour information line: 0900 160 0370 (Premium rate charges apply). www.portugal.org/tourism/index.html

ICEP Portugal - Investimento, Comércio e Turismo, Av. 5 de Outubro, nº 101, PT-1050–051 Lisboa, Portugal. Tel: 00351 217 909 500; Fax: 00351 217 935 028; In Portugal: 808 214 214. turismo@icep.pt www.PortugalinSite.com
Turismo de Lisboa / Lisbon Visitors and Convention Bureau, Tel: 00351 21 361 03 50; Fax: 00351 21 361 03 59. atl@atl-turismolisboa.pt www.atl-turismolisboa.pt

Requirements may be subject to short-term change. Contact the relevant authority before departure. Valid passport required (exceptnationals of Republic of Ireland holding national ID cards).

Visa not required by nationals of EU countries for stays up to 3 months.

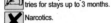

Narcotics.

YELLOW FEVER: A yellow fever vaccination certificate is required from travellers over 1 year of age coming from infected areas arriving in or destined for the Azores or Madeira.

W2

Euro = 100 cents All credit cards are accepted and travellers cheques are easily exchanged. ATM AVAILABILITY: Over 5000 locations.

MONEYGRAM: 0501 8 11 435.
WESTERN UNION: (02) 207 2102.

AMEX: 0044 1273 696 933
DINERS CLUB: 21 315 98 56
MASTERCARD: 0800 811 272
VISA: 0800 811 824

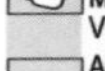
AMEX: 0800 844 080
THOMAS COOK: 0800 844 095
VISA: 0800 844 857

Generally 0830–1500 Mon to Fri. Some Lisbon banks are open 1800–2300 Mon–Fri.

Relatively inexpensive and offers excellent value in transport, accommodation and food.

Portuguese.

North-west: mild winters with a high rainfall and fairly short summers. North-east: longer winters and hot summers. South: Summers are hot with little rain, high temperatures are moderated by a permanent breeze.

Roman Catholic.

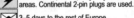

Jan 1, Apr 25, May 1, Jun 10, 13, Aug 15, Oct 5, Nov 1, Dec 1, 8, 24, 25. Easter, Corpus Christi. Various local festivals.

220 volts AC, 50 Hz, may vary in other areas. Continental 2-pin plugs are used.

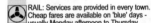

3–5 days to the rest of Europe.

Women who are travelling alone should not encounter many problems.

RAIL: Services are provided in every town. Cheap fares are available on 'blue' days - usually Monday afternoon to Thursday. Tourist tickets providing a period of unlimited travel are also available. ROAD: Every town can be reached by an adequate system of roads. TAXI: Charged according to distance and are metered. CAR HIRE: Available from main towns and airports. DOCUMENTATION: IDP or foreign licence accepted. Third-party insurance is compulsory and a green card must be obtained.

Politeness is essential. Beachwear should not be worn in towns. It is offensive to smoke at mealtimes.

CAPITAL: San Juan

GMT –4

FROM UK: 001787. OUTGOING CODE TO UK: 01144.

Emergencies: 911; Police: 787 343 2020, Fire: 787 343 2330.

Puerto Rico is a commonwealth state of the USA, and is represented abroad by US Embassies and Consulates.

British Consulate, Royal Bank Centre, Suite 807, 225 Ponce De Leon Avenue, Hato Rey, Puerto Rico 00917-1929. Tel: 001787 758 9828; Fax: 001787 758 9809. btopr1@coqui.net

United States Information Service, 55-56 Upper Brook Street, London W1A 2LH. Tel: 020 7499 9000.
http://welcome.topuertorico.org/tinfo.shtml

Puerto Rico Hotel and Tourism Association, Suit 702, Plaza Centre, 954 Ponce de León Avenue, Miramar, Sancturce 00907, Puerto Rico. Tel: 721 2400. Fax 725 2913.
Puerto Rico Tourism Company, Box 4435, Old San Juan Station, San Juan PR 00905. Tel: 001787 721 2400, 1800 223-6530

See USA. Valid passport required: same as the USA.

Same as the USA.

Same as for the USA.

POLIO, TYPHOID: R. OTHER: Bilharzia and rabies.

Tap water is safe to drink. Milk is pasteurised. Local meat, poultry, seafood, fruit and vegetables are generally considered safe to eat.

US Dollar (US$) = 100 cents. All major credit cards accepted. US$ are preferred for travellers cheques. ATM AVAILABILITY: Over 630 locations.

MONEYGRAM: Unavailable.
WESTERN UNION: Unavailable.

AMEX: 01144 1273 696 933
DINERS CLUB: 01144 1252 513 500
MASTERCARD: 1800 307 7309
VISA: 1800 847 2911

AMEX: 01144 1273 571 600
THOMAS COOK: 01144 1733 318950
VISA: 1800 227 6811

0900–1430 Mon to Thur, 0900–1430 and 1530–1700 Fri.

Accommodates all types of travellers.

Spanish. English is widely spoken.

Hot tropical climate. The temperature varies little throughout the year. Cooler in upland areas.

Roman Catholic, other Christian denominations and a Jewish minority.

Jan 1, 6, 11, third Mon in Jan and Feb, Mar 22, Apr 16, last Mon in May, Jun 24, July 4, 25, 27, first Mon in Sept, second Mon in Oct, Nov 11, 19, fourth Thu in Nov, Dec 25. Good Fri, Easter. Various Saints' Days locally.

120 volts AC, 60 Hz.

Up to 1 week.

Spanish and American manners and customs exist side by side. Usual precautions should be taken. Do not travel alone at night.

ROAD: Driving is on the right-hand side of the road. The same rules of the road apply as in any part of the United States, except that the signs are in Spanish, and the distances marked in kilometres. TAXI: A special service called a Linea will pick up and drop off passengers where they wish. They operate between San Juan and most towns at a fixed rate. CAR HIRE: Available at the airport and city agencies. DOCUMENTATION: An IDP is required. BUS: Services operate in the cities although usually stop at 2100. RAIL: There are no passenger trains. A narrow-gauge railway is used for hauling sugar cane.

As well as offering lavish entertainment, notably casinos and a variety of nightlife, in the interior there are anthropological sites of interest, such as a replica of a Taino Indian village, near Guayama. There are no nudist facilities (camps and/or beaches) as nudism is illegal in Puerto Rico. A municipal statute forbids alcohol consumption on the streets of Old San Juan.

CAPITAL: Doha

GMT +3

FROM UK: 00974. OUTGOING CODE TO UK: 044

All services: 999

Embassy of the State of Qatar, 1 South Audley Street, London W1Y 5DQ. Tel: 020 7493 2200; Fax: 020 7493 2661

British Embassy, PO Box 3, Doha, Qatar. Tel: 4421991. Fax: 4438692.

No tourist office in UK. www.qatar-info.com/ and www.arab.net/qatar/qatar_contents.html

Ministry of Tourism and Culture, PO Box 1836, Doha, Qatar. Tel: 831 333. Fax: 831 518.

Return ticket, valid passport and sufficient funds for stay are required. Requirements may be subject to short-term change. Contact the relevant authority before departure.

Visa required and must be obtained in advance, through a sponsor resident in Qatar. For tourists this means a hotel.

All alcohol and pork products are prohibited. Animals cannot be imported.

QR20, payable in local currency.

Those with passports containing a visa for Israel or holders of Israeli passports.

POLIO, TYPHOID: R. YELLOW FEVER: A vaccination certificate will be required from travellers over 1 year of age arriving from infected areas. OTHER: Cholera, rabies.

W1

Qatar Riyal (QR) = 100 dirhams. All credit cards and travellers cheques are widely accepted. US$ and Pound sterling are the preferred currency in travellers cheques. ATM AVAILABILITY: Over 30 locations.

MONEYGRAM: Unavailable.
WESTERN UNION: 424 373.

AMEX: 044 1273 696 933
DINERS CLUB: 044 212 74
MASTERCARD: 01 314 542 7111
VISA: 01 410 581 9994

AMEX: 973 256834
THOMAS COOK: 044 1733 318950
VISA: 044 20 7937 8091

0730–1130 Sat–Thur.

Qatar is one of the richest countries in the world. Accommodation is hotel-based only, ranging from international to standard.

Arabic. Some English may be spoken.

Summers (Jun–Sept) are very hot with low rainfall. Spring and autumn are warm and pleasant.

Muslim

Jun 27, Sep 3, Dec 31. Islamic festivals.

240/415 volts AC, 50 Hz.

Up to a week to Europe.

Strict Muslim rules apply to all women. Single women may find they are unwelcome in some restaurants and hotels. Women should dress conservatively with the knees covered, and only travel in the back seat when taking a taxi. Qatari women, especially older ones, wear the full abayah and the veil. However, Western women are allowed a certain amount of liberty with regard to dress and freedoms, e.g. they may drive cars.

ROAD: Conditions can be poor when it rains, and local driving is fast and erratic. Excursions to the desert can be dangerous unless undertaken in a well-equipped 4 x 4 vehicle. Travel in convoy with other cars and take plenty of water.TAXI: Taxis have meters, but there is a tendency for the meter to be running before you get in. CAR HIRE: Available from hotels and at the airport. DOCUMENTATION: A 90 day temporary driving permit will be granted on presentation of a national driving licence or IDP. If you have an accident, it is important that you do not move your vehicle from the point of impact until the police have checked it, even if the incident blocks a main road.

Qatar is more liberal than Saudi Arabia but not as liberal as Dubai or Bahrain. Extra care has to be taken on the roads. It is important to respect Muslim traditions and local customs – dress modestly and behave courteously. During the holy month of Ramadan (Oct/Nov), don't eat, drink or smoke in the daytime hours of fasting. Most people live along the coastline; the interior of the country is arid and flat, either sandy desert, salt flats or rocky plains.

CAPITAL: St Denis

GMT +4

FROM UK: 00262. OUTGOING CODE TO UK: 0044

Police: 17, Fire: 18, Ambulance: 15.

La Réunion is an overseas Département of the Republic of France. See the entry for France to find the address of the French Embassy.

British Consulate, Kohjenta, 94B avenue Leconte de Lisle, 97490 Sante-Clotide, Réunion. Tel: 291 491. Fax: 293 991.

Refer to the French Consulate General in London or Comité du Tourisme de la Réunion, 90 rue la Boétie, 75008 Paris, France. Tel: (1) 40 75 02 79. Fax: (1) 40 75 02 73.

Office du Tourisme, 48 rue Saint-Marie, 97400 Saint-Denis, Réunion. Tel: 418 300. Fax: 213 776.

Contact the French Consular authority for up to date information as passport/visa requirements are subjected to constant change. Valid passport required: See France.

Visa requirements are constantly changing. It is advisable to contact the French Consular authority for current information.

See France.

Ffr10.

POLIO, TYPHOID: There is a risk of Typhoid. YELLOW FEVER: A vaccination certificate is required for travellers coming from infected areas. OTHER: Rabies.

W1

Euro = 100 cents, as from Jul 2002. Major cards are widely accepted although MasterCard has a more limited acceptance. ATM AVAILABILITY: Unavailable.

MONEYGRAM: Unavailable.
WESTERN UNION: Unavailable.

AMEX: 0044 1273 696 933
DINERS CLUB: 0044 1252 513 500
MASTERCARD: 001 314 542 7111
VISA: 001 410 581 9994

AMEX: 0044 1273 571 600
THOMAS COOK: 0044 1733 318950
VISA: 0044 20 7937 8091

0800–1600 Mon to Fri.

Wide range of hotels, inns and guest-houses, all of which are expensive.

French. Local Creole is also spoken.

The climate is hot and tropical but temperatures are cooler in the hills. The cyclone season is from Jan to Mar and brings hot but wet weather.

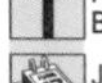
Roman Catholic, with Hindu, Muslim and Buddhist minorities.

Jan 1, May 1, 8, Jul 14, Aug 15, Nov 1, 11, Dec 20, 25, 26. Christian feast days.

220 volts AC, 50 Hz.

Airmail to Western Europe takes up to 3 weeks.

Similar to Western Europe.

SEA: Four shipping lines run services around the island. ROADS: Fair and many of the highways are tarred. The island can be crossed easily by bus, taxi, or hired car. CAR HIRE: Available from the airport and Saint-Denis.

The locals follow French fashion. Licensing laws are unrestricted. Sugar cane has been the primary crop and source of export revenue. The government is encouraging the development of a tourist industry. Health facilities in Réunion are excellent. The medical form E111 is for basic emergency treatment. La Réunion is subject to devastating cyclones between Jan and March. Piton de la Fournaise, on the south-eastern coast, is an active volcano.

Romania

CAPITAL: Bucharest

GMT +2 (GMT +3 during the summer)

FROM UK: 0040. OUTGOING CODE TO UK: 0044 Dial 971 for international operator.

Ambulance: 961, Police: 955, Fire: 981.

Embassy of Romania, Arundel House, 4 Palace Green, London W8 4QD. Tel: 020 7937 9666; Fax: 020 7937 8069. Visa Information: 020 7376 0683 (24 hours). romaina@roemb.demon.co.uk

British Embassy, Strada Jules Michelet 24, 70154 Bucharest, Romania. Tel: (1) 312 0303/4/5/6. Fax: (1) 312 9652. Press@bucharest.mail.fco.gov.uk

Romanian National Tourist Office (Carpati), 83A Marylebone High Street, London W1M 3DE. Tel: 020 7224 3692. 0906 555 8860 (premium rate). www.rezq.com/ronto/

National Tourist Office (Carpati) Boulevard Magheru 7, Bucharest 1, Romania. Tel: (1) 614 5160.

Return ticket required. Requirements may be subject to short-term change. Contact the relevant authority before departure. Passports, required by all, must have a minimum validity of 3 months after return.

Visa not required by EU passport-holders for a tourist stay up to 30 days.

Ammunition, explosives, narcotics, pornographic material, uncanned meat and animal and dairy products.

POLIO, TYPHOID: R. OTHER: A number of cases of cholera have been reported and travellers may want to take precautions. Hepatitis A. Rabies is endemic; visitors should avoid all contact with stray dogs.

W2

Leu (plural Lei) = 100 bani. EXCHANGE: Visitors are advised to take hard currency, particularly US$. Money should be changed in recognised exchange shops, banks and hotels; it is illegal to change it on the streets. Dollar notes must be in a clean condition. The import and export of local currency is prohibited. Credit cards are accepted in large hotels in Bucharest only. Travellers cheques can only be used at the tourist office and for paying hotel bills. US$ cheques are preferable. ATM AVAILABILITY: Over 60 locations.

MONEYGRAM: 01 800 4288 then 800 592 3688.
WESTERN UNION: (1) 321 1609.

AMEX: 0044 1273 696 933
DINERS CLUB: 0044 1252 513 500
MASTERCARD: 001 314 542 7111
VISA: 001 410 581 9994

AMEX: 0044 1273 571 600
THOMAS COOK: 0044 1733 318950
VISA: 0044 20 7937 8091

0900–1200 Mon to Fri. 1300–1500 Mon to Fri (currency exchange only).

Romania remains relatively inexpensive, despite a modernising economy.

Romanian. Hungarian and German in border areas. English and French may be spoken by those involved with tourism.

Summer: inland is hot but the coast is cooled by a sea breeze and has milder winters. Snow can fall throughout the country.

Romanian Orthodox, Roman Catholic. Lutheran, Muslim and Jewish minorities.

Jan 1, 2, 6, May 1, Dec 1, 25, 26. Easter.

220 volts AC, 50 Hz. Plugs are 2-pin.

Airmail to Western Europe takes up to 2 weeks.

Women tend to be conservative in their behaviour in rural areas.

RAIL: Romanian State Railways run efficient and cheap services. Seats must be reserved in advance for express and rapid trains. BUS: Local services operate to most towns and villages. TAXI: Can be hailed in the street or called from hotels. Prices are relatively low but drivers expect a tip. Most older taxis do not have seat belts. CAR HIRE: Available at hotels and the airport. Driving is very erratic so it may be wise to hire a driver. DOCUMENTATION: National driving licence or IDP and green card insurance is required.

Romania has undergone profound political change and is in a period of economic transition. Most tourist facilities, while being upgraded, have not yet reached Western European standards. Petty crime is on the increase in Romania, particularly in Bucharest. Some tourist attractions charge visitors for photographs. Dress tends to quite conservative but casual clothes are usually suitable.

Russian Federation

CAPITAL: Moscow

Moscow and St Petersburg +3 (GMT +4 during the summer). Other regions vary.

FROM UK: 007. When dialling from abroad the 0 of the area code must not be omitted. OUTGOING CODE TO UK: 8/1044(wait for second dial tone). In smaller cities international calls go through the operator.

Fire: 01, Police: 02, Ambulance: 03.

Embassy of the Russian Federation, 13 Kensington Gardens, London W8 4QX. Tel: 020 7229 3628. Fax: 020 7727 8625. Consular Section: 5 Kensington Palace Gardens, London W8 4QS. Tel: 020 7229 8027. Fax: 020 7229 3215.

British Embassy, Smolenskaya Naberezhnaya 10, Moscow 121099, Russia. Tel: (095) 956 7200. Fax: (095) 956 7201; bemppas@online.ru www.britemb.msk.ru/ Consulate in St Petersburg, Tel: (812) 320 3200. bcgspb@peterlink.ru www.britain.spb.ru

Intourist Travel Limited, Intourist House, 219 Marsh Wall, London E14 9PD. Tel: 020 7538 8600. Fax: 020 7538 5967. Russian National Tourist Office, 70 Piccadilly, London W1J 8HP. Tel: 020 7495 7570. www.russia-travel.com/

Intourist, ulista Mokhovaya 13, 103009 Moscow, Russian Federation. Tel: (095) 292 3786 or 292 2300. Fax (095) 292 2034.

Return ticket required. Requirements may be subject to short-term change. All travellers are advised to contact the nearest Russian Embassy or Consulate for up-to-date details. Valid passport required

Visa required. It must be supported by a sponsor, usually a tour company or employer.

Intourist provides a list of articles that must not be brought into Russia. Travellers should obtain receipts for all high-value items purchased in Russia. Any article that could appear old to Customs officers, including icons, samovars, rugs and other antiques, must have a certificate from the vendor or from the Russian ministry of culture indicating that it has no historical value.

US$ 10 payable on international departures.

POLIO, TYPHOID: R. OTHER: Cholera has been reported in Dagestan. Rabies is present.

W1

Rouble (Rub) = 100 kopeks. EXCHANGE: Only at official bureaux. All transactions must be recorded on the currency declaration form issued on arrival. Keep your receipts. Import and export of local currency is prohibited. Major credit cards are accepted in hotels and banks in Moscow and St Petersburg, but in very few other parts of Russia. US dollar travellers cheques are recommended, but you should also take some hard currency. ATM AVAILABILITY: Over 350 locations.

MONEYGRAM: Unavailable.
WESTERN UNION: (095) 119 8250.

AMEX: 8/1044 1273 696 933
DINERS CLUB: 912 00 09 or 745 8407
MASTERCARD: 8/101 314 542 7111
VISA: 8/101 410 581 9994

AMEX: 956 0829 (Moscow only); otherwise: 8/1044 1273 571 600
THOMAS COOK: 877 8298710
VISA: 8/1044 20 7937 8091

0930–1730 Mon to Fri.

Moderate to expensive, since the change to free-market economy.

Russian. English, French or German are spoken by some people.

North and Central European Russia: variable climate. Winters can be very cold. Siberia: very cold winter. Considerable seasonal temperature variation. Summers are usually short and wet. Southern European Russia: winters are shorter than in the North.

Mainly Christian with the Russian Orthodox church being the largest Christian community. Muslim, Buddhist and Jewish minorities.

Jan 1, 2, 7, Feb 23, Mar 8, May 1, 2, 9, 12, Nov 7, Dec 12. Easter.

220 volts AC, 50 Hz.

Airmail to Western Europe takes over 10 days.

A mix of modern and traditional ideologies affect the way women are perceived. Despite the move to democracy, old communist ideas persist especially amongst the older generation.

Russian Federation

AIR: Aeroflot runs services from Moscow to major cities. RIVER: Many companies offer cruises along several rivers. RAIL: The rail network is vital because of the poor road system. Only a few long-distance routes are open to use by visitors and reservations must be made on all journeys. When travelling by train, store valuables in the compartment under the bed/seat. Do not leave the compartment empty. Ensure the door is quite secure from the inside. Do not leave possessions unattended. ROAD: The European part of the Russian Federation depends heavily on its road network. The few roads in Siberia and further East are impassable in winter. It is worth planning your route in advance and arranging motoring holidays through Intourist or another reputable agency.

While good tourist facilities exist in Moscow, St. Petersburg and some other large cities, they are not developed in most of Russia. Each specific region has its own code of dress and traditions, which may be very different from those in the West. NOTE: Carry ID at all times. Incidents of violent mugging, theft and pickpocketing in all cities continue to occur. Keep all valuables out of sight. There has been an increase in racist-syle harassment of foreigners by skinhead groups. All travellers, but particularly those of Asian and African descent, are advised to be cautious in places frequented by skinheads, such as the *rynoks* or open markets.

DANGER: Due to continued civil and political unrest throughout most of the Caucasus Region of Russia, the FCO advises against travel to the Chechen Republic, Ingushetia, Dagestan, North Ossetia, Karachai-Cherkassia, Kabardino-Balkaria (including the Elbrus area), and to the eastern and southern parts of Stavropol Krai, particularly where it borders Chechnya and North Ossetia.

CAPITAL: Kigali

GMT +2

FROM UK: 00250 OUTGOING CODE TO UK: 0044 Most international calls must go through the operator.

Not available

Embassy of the Republic of Rwanda, Uganda House, 58-59 Trafalgar Square, London WC2N 5DX. Tel: 020 7930 2570; Fax: 020 7930 2572. ambarwanda@compuserve.com

British Embassy, Boulevard de 1'Umuganda (opposite Windsor Umubano Hotel), Kacyiru, Kigali Tel : 00250 84098; Fax : 00250 82044. britemb@rwandaone.com.

No tourist office in UK.

Office Rwandais du Tourisme et des Parcs Nationaux (ORTPN), BP 905, Kigali, Rwanda. Tel: 76514. Fax: 76512.

Return ticket required. Requirements may be subject to change at short notice. Contact the embassy before departure. Valid passport required.

Visa required by all nationalities, generally valid for 3 months, and must be obtained in advance.

Departure tax US$20.

POLIO, TYPHOID: R. MALARIA: Exists throughout the year. Resistance to chloroquine has been reported. YELLOW FEVER: A vaccination certificate is required by all travellers arriving over one year of age. OTHER: Bilharzia, rabies. HIV/AIDS is widespread.

W1

Rwandese Franc (RwFr) = 100 centimes. NOTE: Import and Export of local currency is limited to RwFr5000 Credit cards are accepted at a few hotels in Kigali and then only to settle hotel bills. Travellers should expect to pay most expenses, including air tickets, in cash. Travellers cheques have limited acceptance. ATM AVAILABILITY: Unavailable.

MONEYGRAM: Unavailable
WESTERN UNION: Several Kigali banks can now arrange cash transfers.

AMEX: 0044 1273 696 933
DINERS CLUB: 0044 1252 513 500
MASTERCARD: 001 314 542 7111
VISA: 001 410 581 9994

AMEX: 0044 1273 571 600
THOMAS COOK: 0044 1733 318950
VISA: 0044 20 7937 8091

0800–1200 and 1400–1800 Mon to Fri, 0800–1300 Sat.

Due to the recent civil war, the economy has been decimated.

Kinyarwanda and French. Kiswahili is also spoken.

Rwanda is cool due to its high latitude, but warmer in the lowlands. Mid Jan-Apr and mid Oct-Dec are the rainy seasons.

Christian (mainly Roman Catholic) with Islam and Animist minorities.

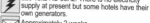

Jan 1, Apr 7, May 1, July 1, 4, 5, Aug 15, Sep 25, Oct 1, Nov 1, Dec 25. Eid Al Fitr, Easter.

220 volts AC 50Hz. There is no electricity supply at present but some hotels have their own generators.

Approximately 2 weeks.

A volatile and patriarchal tribal culture exists.

FLIGHTS: Internal flights are operated by the national airline to the main towns. ROADS: Most roads in bad condition. BUS: Services operate and a timetable is available. DOCUMENTATION: An IDP is required.

Supplies of water, fuel and power and accommodation are hard to find. Normal social courtesies apply. Hotels in Kigali are adequate, but limited in remote areas.

NOTE: Because of attacks by insurgents based in the neighbouring Democratic Republic of Congo, against rural communities of Gisenyi and Ruhengeri, the FCO advises against non-essential travel to north-west Rwanda. This includes the Virunga National Park, home of Rwanda's mountain gorillas. The Government of Rwanda has reopened the Parc National des Volcans, and provides military escorts for visitors with official passes to track gorillas.

Saba

CAPITAL: The Bottom

GMT –4

FROM UK: 00599. OUTGOING CODE TO UK: 0044.

Police: 5994 63237

No representation in UK. Refer to Kabinet van de Gevolmachtigde Minister van de Nederlanse Antillen, Badhuisweg 173-175, 2597 JP's-Gravenhagen, Holland. Tel: 0031703512811; Fax: 0031703512722. Alternatively, contact The Royal Netherlands Embassy, 38 Hyde Park Gate, London SW7 5DP. Tel: 020 7590 3200. london@netherlands-embassy.org.uk or the Saba Government Information Service: sabagis@hotmail.com

British Consulate in Willemstad, Curaçao, deals with enquiries relating to Saba.

Caribbean Tourism, 42 Westminster Palace Gdns, Artillery Row, London SW1P 1RR. Tel. 020 7222 4335. Fax: 020 7222 4325. cto@carib-tourism.com www.doitcaribbean.com See also www.sabatourism.com/sainfo.html

Saba Tourist Bureau, PO Box 527, Windwardside, Saba. Tel: 00599 4 62231. Fax 005994 62350. iluvsaba@unspoiledqueen.com www.turq.com/saba/

Valid passport and return ticket required.

Visa not required.

Parrots, parakeets, dogs and cats from South and Central America. Import of souvenirs and leather goods from Haiti is not advisable.

US$2 to other Netherlands Antilles destinations, US$5 to other destinations.

POLIO, TYPHOID: R. YELLOW FEVER: A vaccination certificate is required from all travellers over 6 months of age coming from infected areas. OTHER: Dengue fever from mosquitoes.

Netherlands Antilles Guilder or Florin (NAG) = 100 cents. Import and export of local currency is restricted to NAG200. MasterCard and Visa are accepted in large establishments. Travellers cheques in US$ are preferred. ATM AVAILABILITY: 10 locations approximately.

MONEYGRAM: Unavailable.
WESTERN UNION: Unavailable.

AMEX: 0044 1273 696933
DINERS CLUB: 0044 1252 513500
MASTERCARD: 001800 3077309
VISA: 001800 847 2911

AMEX: 001801 964 6665
THOMAS COOK: 0044 1733 318950
VISA: 0044 20 7937 8091

0830–1130 and 1330–1630 Mon to Fri.

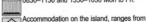

Accommodation on the island, ranges from guest houses around the area called The Bottom, to the more expensive at the coast.

English is usually used. Dutch, the official language of the Netherlands Antilles, is used for legal documents.

Hot with cool sea breezes. Temperatures vary little throughout the year.

Roman Catholic. Anglican and Wesleyan minorities.

Jan 1; Feb 22; Apr 2, 5, 30; May 1, 21; Dec 25, 26. Easter, Ascension Day, Whitsun.

110 volts AC, 60 Hz.

4–6 days.

ROAD: Saba has one road 15 km long. TAXIS: Are available. CAR HIRE: May be hired at Douglas Johnson's The Square Nickel. BOAT: Ferry services connect Saba with St Maarten.

Saba is a five square mile island in the north-eastern Caribbean. The government of Saba is promoting the island for eco-tourism and scientific study. The Saba Conservation Foundation maintains a national park on the slopes of Mount Scenery, and the Saba National Marine Park for the study of marine life. There are paths and trails for trekking and exploring the volcanic island's rainforest.

St Eustatius

CAPITAL: Oranjestad

GMT –4

FROM UK: 00599. OUTGOING CODE TO UK: 01144

All services: 599 382211

No representation in UK. Refer to Kabinet van de Gevolmachtigde Minister van de Nederlanse Antillen, Badhuisweg 173-175, 2597 JP's-Gravenhagen, Holland. Tel: 0031703512811; Fax: 0031703512722. Alternatively, contact The Royal Netherlands Embassy, 38 Hyde Park Gate, London SW7 5DP. Tel: 020 7590 3200. london@netherlands-embassy.org.uk

British Consulate in Willemstad, Curaçao, deals with enquiries relating to St Eustatius.

Caribbean Tourism, 42 Westminster Palace Gdns, Artillery Row, London SW1P 1RR. Tel. 020 7222 4335. Fax: 020 7222 4325. cto@carib-tourism.com www.doitcaribbean.com

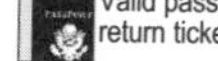
St Eustatius Tourist Bureau, Fort Oranjestad z/n. Orangestad z/n, Oranjestad, St Eustatius, no local number. Tel/Fax: (3) 82433. www.doitcaribbean.com/steustatius/

Valid passport required. Visitors must have a return ticket.

Visa not required.

Parrots, parakeets, dogs and cats from South and Central America. Import of souvenirs and leather goods from Haiti is not advisable.

US$3 to other Netherlands Antilles, US$4 for other international departures.

POLIO, TYPHOID: R. YELLOW FEVER: A vaccination certificate is required from all travellers over 6 months of age coming from infected areas.

Netherlands Antilles Guilder or Florin (NAG) = 100 cents. Import and export of local currency is restricted to NAG 200. Visa and MasterCard are accepted in large establishments. Travellers cheques, preferably in US$, are accepted. ATM AVAILABILITY: 10 locations approximately.

MONEYGRAM: 001 800 872 2881 then 800 592 3688
WESTERN UNION: Unavailable.

AMEX: 0044 1273 696933
DINERS CLUB: 0044 1252 513500
MASTERCARD: 001800 3077309
VISA: 001800 847 2911

AMEX: 001801 964 6665
THOMAS COOK: 0044 1733 318950
VISA: 0044 20 7937 8091

0830–1200 and 1300–1530 Mon to Fri.

Despite the island's small size it has a variety of restaurants and accommodation at moderate prices.

English is the official language. Papiamento, French and Spanish are also spoken.

Hot climate with cooling sea breezes.

Dutch Reformed Church and other Christian denominations, Jewish

Jan 1, Apr 30, May 1, 5, Jul 1, last Mon in July, Oct 21, Nov 16, Dec 25, 26. Easter, Ascension Day, Whitsun.

110/220 volts AC, 60 Hz.

4–6 days.

ROAD: A very small island with very few roads. The whole island can be walked around in a few hours. CAR HIRE and TAXI: Companies operate in Oranjestad. DOCUMENTATION: National licence is sufficient.

Tourism facilities are not well developed. There are just 100 beds on the island, in small hotels and guest houses. There are 12 trails, one of which runs up to the rim of the island's extinct volcano – the Quill – and down into its pit, where there's a rainforest. Twice a year sea turtles clamber onto the volcanic black sand to lay their eggs, and giant land crabs hunt on the beaches every night. Part of old Oranjestad has been reclaimed by the sea – on calm days, the foundations can be seen from the shore-line. A marine park has been established to protect sea life and historical artifacts. There are 33 dive sites featuring coral reefs, canyons and wrecks. The islanders are serious about conserving their underwater treasures – divers in the park must be accompanied by dive operators and anchoring is not permitted.

St Kitts & Nevis

CAPITAL: Basseterre

GMT –4

FROM UK: 001869. OUTGOING CODE TO UK: 01144

911

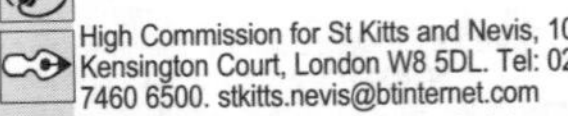
High Commission for St Kitts and Nevis, 10 Kensington Court, London W8 5DL. Tel: 020 7460 6500. stkitts.nevis@btinternet.com

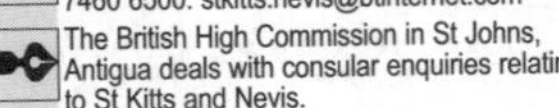
The British High Commission in St Johns, Antigua deals with consular enquiries relating to St Kitts and Nevis.

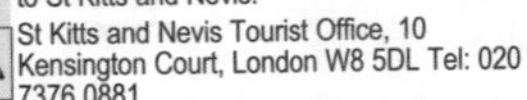
St Kitts and Nevis Tourist Office, 10 Kensington Court, London W8 5DL Tel: 020 7376 0881

St Kitts & Nevis Ministry of Tourism, Culture and the Environment, Bay Road, Pelican Mall, PO Box 132, Basseterre, St. Kitts. Tel: 001869 6478970. mintc&e@caribsurf.com www.geographia.com/stkitts-nevis/index.htm

Valid passport required. Visitors must have a return ticket.

Visa not required.

US$17 Children under 12 are exempt.

POLIO, TYPHOID: R YELLOW FEVER: A vaccination certificate is required from travellers over 1 year of age coming from infected areas. OTHER: Dengue fever from mosquitoes. HIV/AIDS prevalent.

W2

Easter Caribbean Dollar (EC$) = 100 cents. Amex and Visa are the only credit cards accepted. Travellers cheques in US$ are preferred. ATM AVAILABILITY: 2 locations.

MONEYGRAM: 1 800 543 4080
WESTERN UNION: 465 8758

AMEX: 0044 1273 696933
DINERS CLUB: 0044 1252 513500
MASTERCARD: 001800 3077309
VISA: 1800 847 2911

AMEX: 1800 828 0366
THOMAS COOK: 0044 1733 318950
VISA: 0044 20 7937 8091

0800–1500 Mon to Thur, 0800–1500/1700 Fri, 0830–1100 Sat.

Very expensive, especially accommodation, although this is reduced in the low season.

English.

Hot tropical climate with cooling sea breezes. Possibility of hurricanes Aug-Oct. Most rainfall during the summer May-Oct. Showers may occur throughout the year.

Anglican Communion Church. Other Christian Denominations.

Jan 1, 2, first Mon in May, second Sat in Jun, first Mon/Tue in Aug, Sep 19, Dec 25, 26. Easter, Whitsun.

230 volts AC, 60 Hz.

5-7 days.

A fairly relaxed culture prevails. Usual precautions should be taken. Do not walk alone at night.

SEA: There is a regular ferry service between St Kitts and Nevis. ROAD: Traffic in St. Kitts and Nevis drives on the left. A good road network on both island makes anywhere accessible within minutes. BUS: There are private, regular but unscheduled buses, which provide a comfortable service. TAXIS: Services on both islands have set fares. CAR & MOPED HIRE: Several agencies provide hire services. It is best to book cars through the airline well in advance. DOCUMENTATION: A local temporary licence must be obtained from the police Traffic Department before driving any vehicle. This is readily issued on presentation of a valid national licence and a fee of EC$ 30.

Tourism is on the increase, especially on Nevis. The islands are now commercialised and all visitors are readily welcomed. Suitable clothes should be worn for towns and hotel/restaurants. It is an offence for anyone, including children, to dress in camouflage clothing. St. Kitts and Nevis is in the hurricane belt. June to November is the official hurricane season. Visitors should get advice from hotel staff and on local radio.

CAPITAL: Castries

GMT –4

FROM UK: 001758. OUTGOING CODE TO UK: 01144

999

High Commission for St Lucia, 1 Collingham Gardens, South Kensington, London SW5 0HW. Tel: 020 7370 7123; Fax: 020 7370 1905.

British High Commission, Francis Compton Building, PO Box 227, Waterfront, Castries, St Lucia. Tel: 001758 45 22484; Fax: 001 758 45 31543. britishhc@candw.lc

St Lucia Tourist Board, 421A Finchley Road, London NW3 6HJ. Tel: 020 7431 3675. Fax: 020 7431 7920. stlucia@pwaxissm.com www.stlucia.org/

St Lucia Tourist Board, PO Box 221, Sure Line Building, Vide Bouteille, Castries, St Lucia. Tel: 00758 452 4094. Fax: 00758 453 1121. slutour@candw.lc

Valid passport required. Visitors must have a return ticket.

Visa not required by British nationals.

Narcotics and firearms, fresh meat.

EC$54 (or US$20). Transit passengers and children under 12 years of age are exempt.

POLIO, TYPHOID: R. YELLOW FEVER: A vaccination certificate is required from travellers over 1 year of age coming from infected areas.

W2 It is generally advisable to boil all tap water before drinking. Never drink water from rivers or streams, no matter how clear it seems. Bottled water is widely available.

Eastern Caribbean Dollar (EC$) = 100 cents. EXCHANGE: US$ gain a better rate. All major credit cards are accepted. Travellers cheques in US$ are preferred. ATM AVAILABILITY: Most banks have cash machines.

MONEYGRAM: 1 800 872 2881 then 800 592 3688
WESTERN UNION: 452 4191

AMEX: 01144 1273 696933
DINERS CLUB: 01144 1252 513500
MASTERCARD: 1800 3077309
VISA: 1800 847 2911

AMEX: 1800 828 0366
THOMAS COOK: 01144 1733 318950
VISA: 01144 20 7937 8091

Generally 0800–1500 Mon to Thur, 0800–1700 Fri, 0800–1200 Sat.

Caters for all types of budgets, with deluxe to self-catering accommodation.

English. Local French patois is spoken.

Hot tropical climate with cool sea breezes. Most rainfall occurs during the summer.

Roman Catholic, Anglican, Methodist, Seventh Day Adventist, Baptist minorities.

Jan 1, 2, Feb 22, May 1, first Fri in Aug and Oct, Nov 1, 2, 22, Dec 13, 25, 26. Carnival in week before Lent, Easter, Whitsun, Corpus Christi.

220 volts AC, 50 Hz.

Up to 1 week.

A multicultural society with colonial heritage exists. Usual precautions should be taken. Do not walk alone at night.

ROAD: All major centres are served by a reasonably good road network. Traffic drives on the left. BUS: Services connect rural areas with the capital. TAXI: Cheap and easy to use – tipping is unnecessary. CAR HIRE: Available in the towns or at the airport. DOCUMENTATION: On presentation of a national or IDP a local licence will be issued.

Casual resort clothing is appropriate year-round on St Lucia, although a wrap or pullover may be needed on cooler winter evenings. Some of the larger restaurants require men to wear jackets and sometimes ties. St. Lucia is an island of contrasts with lush, green, volcanic vegetation in the interior, and long, unspoilt, white, sandy beaches. Recent laws have been passed to protect St Lucia's rich natural resources. Most coastal waters surrounding the island are now protected areas and no spearfishing or collecting live fish are permitted.The island is in the hurricane belt. June to November is the official hurricane season. Visitors should get advice from hotel staff and on local radio.

St Maarten/St Martin

CAPITAL: Philipsburg/Marigot

GMT –4

FROM UK: 00599. OUTGOING CODE: 0044

Police: 222222 Ambulance: 22111

St Martin/St Maarten is one island with two distinct colonial states; one side is Dutch and the other is French. Philipsburg on Great Bay is the capital of St.Maarten. Marigot is the capital of St Martin.

No representation in UK. Refer to Kabinet van de Gevolmachtigde Minister van de Nederlanse Antillen, Badhuisweg 173-175, 2597 JP's-Gravenhagen, Holland. Tel: 0031703512811; Fax: 0031703512722. Alternatively, contact The Royal Netherlands Embassy, 38 Hyde Park Gate, London SW7 5DP. Tel: 020 7590 3200. london@netherlands-embassy.org.uk St Martin is part of the French West Indies and is represented by the French Embassy.

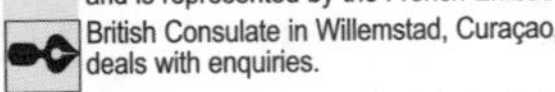

British Consulate in Willemstad, Curaçao, deals with enquiries.

Caribbean Tourism, 42 Westminster Palace Gdns, Artillery Row, London SW1P 1RR. Tel. 020 7222 4335. Fax: 020 7222 4325. cto@carib-tourism.com; www.doitcaribbean.com and sxm-info.com/info.html

St Maarten Tourist Board, Vineyard Park Bldg, W.G. Buncamper Rd #33, Philipsburg, St. Maarten, Netherlands Antilles Tel: 00599 54 22337 Fax: 00599 54 22734. www.st-maarten.com/
French side: Office du Tourisme, Port de Marigot , 97150 Marigot, St. Martin. Tel: 00590 87 57 21; Fax: 00590 87 56 43

Valid passport required. Visitors must have a return ticket.

Visa not required.

Parrots, parakeets, dogs and cats from South and Central America. Import of souvenirs and leather goods from Haiti is not advisable.

US$ 20 for all international departures. US$ 6 for departures to other Caribbean islands. Transit passengers and those under 2 years of age are exempt.

POLIO, TYPHOID: R. YELLOW FEVER: A vaccination certificate is required from travellers over 1 year of age coming from infected areas.

US$ widely accepted on both the Dutch and the French sides of the island. Official currencies are the Netherlands Antilles guilder (NAF), Dutch side, and the Franc, French side. Credit cards accepted in large establishments. ATM AVAILABILITY: 10 locations.

MONEYGRAM: 001 800 872 2881 then 800 592 3688
WESTERN UNION: 5995 22403.

AMEX: 0044 1273 696933
DINERS CLUB: 0044 1252 513500
MASTERCARD: 001800 3077309
VISA: 001800 847 2911

AMEX: 001800 828 0366
THOMAS COOK: 0044 1733 318950
VISA: 0044 20 7937 8091

0830–1530 Mon to Fri.

Good variety of duty-free shops, especially in Philipsburg, offering cheap spirits and imported luxury goods.

English. Dutch is the official language for legal documents. French is also spoken.

Hot tropical climate with cool sea breezes.

Protestant. Roman Catholic and Jewish minorities.

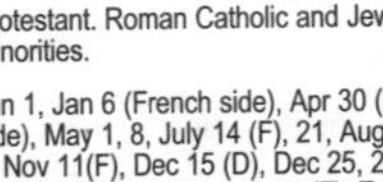

Jan 1, Jan 6 (French side), Apr 30 (Dutch side), May 1, 8, July 14 (F), 21, Aug 15, Nov 1, Nov 11(F), Dec 15 (D), Dec 25, 26. Carnival in week before Lent (F), Easter, Carnival Apr/May (D), Ascension Day, Pentecost.

110/220 volts AC, 60 Hz.

4–6 days.

SEA: Small boats may be chartered for fishing trips and scuba-diving. ROAD: Most roads are good, but damaged by recent hurricanes. TAXI: Available at the airport and hotels. Unmetered, but drivers must follow official rates throughout the island. Cruise ship passengers have reported aggressive behaviour of taxi drivers. CAR HIRE: Agencies at the airport and in the city. DOCUMENTATION: National licence acceptable.

St. Maarten is the most popular of the Netherlands Antilles, with an estimated 900,000 tourists visiting each year. Usual social courtesies should be observed. The island is subject to hurricanes and severe storms from July to Oct.

St Vincent and the Grenadines

CAPITAL: Kingstown

GMT –4

FROM UK: 001784. OUTGOING CODE TO UK: 01144

All services: 999

High Commission for St Vincent and the Grenadines, 10 Kensington Court, London W8 5DL. Tel: 020 7565 2874. highcommission.svg.uk@cwcom.net

British High Commission, PO Box 132, Granby Street, Kingstown, St Vincent. Tel: 457 1701/2. Fax: 456 2750. bhcsvg@caribsurf.com

St Vincent and the Grenadines Department of Tourism, 10 Kensington Court, London W8 5DL. Tel: 020 7937 6570; Fax: 020 7937 3611. svgtourismeurope@aol.com

St Vincent and the Grenadines Department of Tourism, PO Box 834, Bay Street, Kingstown, St Vincent. Tel: 457 1502. Fax: 456 2610. tourism@caribsurf.com www.svgtourism.com/

Valid passport required, except by UK nationals holding a driver's licence or birth certificate. Visitors must have a return ticket.

Visa not required.

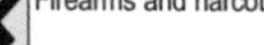
Firearms and narcotics.

EC$30 Children under 12 are exempt.

POLIO, TYPHOID: R. YELLOW FEVER: A vaccination certificate is required from travellers over 1 year of age coming from infected areas. OTHER: HIV/AIDS is prevalent. Dengue fever mosquito found all over the country.

W2. Tap water is safe to drink. Do not drink from rivers or streams. Bottled water is available

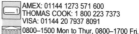

Eastern Caribbean Dollar (EC$) = 100 cents. All major credit cards are widely accepted. All major currencies are accepted in travellers cheques. ATM AVAILABILITY: Unavailable.

MONEYGRAM: Available in St Vincent only.
WESTERN UNION: Available

AMEX: 01144 1273 696 933
DINERS CLUB: 01144 1252 513 500
MASTERCARD: 1 314 542 7111
VISA: 1 410 581 9994

AMEX: 01144 1273 571 600
THOMAS COOK: 1 800 223 7373
VISA: 01144 20 7937 8091

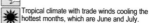

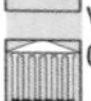
0800–1500 Mon to Thur, 0800–1700 Fri.

Caters for all types of budget. Accommodation varies from luxury hotels to rugged log cabins in the interior.

English.

Tropical climate with trade winds cooling the hottest months, which are June and July.

Roman Catholic. Anglican, Methodist and other Christian minorities.

Jan 1, 22, first Mon in May and Jul, first Tue in Jul, first Mon in Aug, Oct 27, Dec 25, 26. Easter, Whitsun.

220/240 volts AC, 50 Hz.

Up to 2 weeks.

The culture, generally, is a mixture of English and West Indian, and is very relaxed.

SEA: Yacht chartering is easily arranged and one of the bet ways to explore the Grenadines. BUS: Services run regularly throughout St Vincent. TAXI: These are shared and charge standard rates (fixed by the government) CAR HIRE: Easily arranged by a number of national and international firms. DOCUMENTATION: A local driver's permit is required and can be obtained on presentation of a national licence at the airport or the police station in Bay Street, Kingstown, for a fee of EC$75 or about US$28. Traffic drives on the left.

St Vincent island is forested and has an active volcano, Mount Soufriere. Tourism is an increasing part of the local economy. There are 32 islands in the group. June to November is the official hurricane season.

CAPITAL: Apia

GMT –11

FROM UK: 00685. OUTGOING CODE TO UK: 044 Most international calls must be made through the operator.

All services: 999.

Embassy of the Independent State of Samoa, avenue Franklin D Roosevelt 123, B-1050 Brussels, Belgium. Tel: 0032 2 220 8454. Fax: 0032 2 675 0336.

The British High Commission in Wellington, New Zealand covers Samoa. In emergency, contact the Honorary British Consul, c/o Apia Kruse, Enari and Barlow, PO Box 2029, Apia, Samoa. Tel: 21895. Fax: 21407. barlow@samoa.ws

No tourist office in UK.

Samoa Visitor Bureau, PO Box 2272. Apia, Samoa. Tel: 00685 63500; Fax: 00685 20886; info@visitsamoa.ws www1.visitsamoa.ws/home.htm

Onward travel documentation and passport, valid for 6 months beyond the intended stay in Samoa, required.

Visa not required by tourists for stays of up to 30 days. For longer stays visas should be obtained before arrival.

Live animals and plants require prior approval.

SAT$30, payable in local currency, for adults.

POLIO, TYPHOID: R. YELLOW FEVER: Vaccination certificate required from travellers over 1 year old arriving from infected areas.

W2

Samoan Tala (SAT$) = 100 sene. Foreign exchange available at airport or through trade banks. Limited acceptance of all credit cards. Travellers cheques accepted in major hotels and tourist shops. Australian $ cheques preferred. ATM AVAILABILITY: Unavailable.

MONEYGRAM: Unavailable.
WESTERN UNION: Offices on both Upolu and Savaii to process money transfers.

AMEX: 044 1273 696 933
DINERS CLUB: 044 1252 513 500
MASTERCARD: 01 314 542 7111
VISA: 01 410 581 9994

AMEX: 044 1273 571 600
THOMAS COOK: 61 3 696 2952
VISA: 044 20 7937 8091

0900–1500 Mon to Fri. Some open 0830–1130 Sat.

Hotel accommodation is expensive, whilst self-catering beach pensions are moderately priced.

Samoan is the national language but English is the official language of business. Most Samoans are competent English speakers.

Warm, tropical climate with cool nights. The rainy season is from Oct to Mar and the dry season May to Oct.

Congregational Church, Roman Catholic, Methodist and Latter-Day Saints.

Jan 1, 2; Apr 25; May 11; June 1, 2; Aug 3; Oct 12; Nov 6; Dec 25, 26. Easter.

240 volts AC, 50 Hz. Hotels can provide conversion to US 110 volts.

Up to 3 weeks.

Samoans adhere to traditional codes of behaviour. Life in each village is still regulated by a council of chiefs, consisting of mostly men. This extended family social system is inclusive of all society. Outside resorts it is preferable for women to wear dresses. Women are recommended to wear a lavalava (sarong) or dress rather than shorts or trousers if they attend church.

FLIGHTS: Polynesian airlines operate domestic flights between main centres. SEA: Passenger/vehicle ferries operate. BUS: Public transport covers most of the island TAXI: Cheap and readily available in the capital. CAR HIRE: Available from several agencies, deposit and insurance is required. DOCUMENTATION: IDP is required for persons over 21 years or a valid national licence. A local licence will be issued by the transport ministry, for a small fee.

Traditional moral and religious codes are very important. Avoid walking or driving through villages during evening prayer (usually between 6pm and 7pm). This usually lasts for 10–20 minutes and is often marked at the beginning and end by a bell or the blowing of a conch shell. Beachwear should be kept for the beaches. Nude or topless swimming or sunbathing is completely unacceptable anywhere in Samoa. Always ask before swimming at a village beach.

CAPITAL: San Marino

GMT +1 (GMT +2 during the summer).

FROM UK: 00378. OUTGOING CODE TO UK: 0044

Police: 112, Fire: 116, Ambulance: 113.

No embassy in the UK.

British Consulate, Lungarno Corsini 2, 50123 Florence, Italy. Tel: (55) 284 133. Fax: (55) 219 112. bcflocom@tin.it

No tourist office in UK. See www.inthenet.sm/homepage.htm

Ufficio di Stato per il Turismo, Palazzo del Turismo, Contrada Omangnano 20, 47031, Republic of San Marino. Tel: 882 412. Fax: 882 575.

You must comply with Italian passport / visa requirements as entry is via Italy. Valid passport required: See Italy.

See Italy.

See Italy.

See Italy.

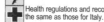

Health regulations and recommendations are the same as those for Italy.

Euro for day-to-day purchases. San Marino mints its own coins, mainly for trading as collectors' items. All major credit cards are accepted. Travellers cheques are widely accepted. ATM AVAILABILITY: Over 20 locations.

MONEYGRAM: Unavailable.
WESTERN UNION: Unavailable.

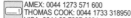

AMEX: 0044 1273 696 933
DINERS CLUB: 0044 1252 513 500
MASTERCARD: 800 870 866
VISA: 800 819 014

AMEX: 0044 1273 571 600
THOMAS COOK: 0044 1733 318950
VISA: 0044 20 7937 8091

0830–1300/1320 and 1430–1530 Mon to Fri.

Accommodation varies from international to budget class.

Italian.

Climate is temperate. Moderate snow in winter, some brief rain showers in the summer.

Roman Catholic.

Jan 1, 6, Feb 5, Mar 25, Apr 1, May 1, Jul 28, Aug 15, Sep 3, Oct 1, Nov 1, 2, Dec 8, 24, 25, 26, 31. Easter, Corpus Christi, Ascension Day, Whitsun.

220 volts AC, 50 Hz.

Good postal service.

Similar to Italy. Usual safety precautions should be observed.

RAIL: The nearest railway station is Rimini. A cable railway, 1.5 km long, connects the city of San Marino to Borgo Maggiore.

Normal European courtesies and codes of conduct should be observed. The crime rate is low. Exercise normal safety precautions and ensure valuables are secure.

San Marino is a small landlocked independent European state, dominated by the Apennines in northern Italy. It's Europe's third smallest state and the world's oldest republic. The local economy is supported by banking, tourism, wine and cheese production, ceramics and the income from postage stamp sales. If philately is your interest, a website is devoted to promoting San Marino stamps; see www.aasfn.sm/english/english.htm

São Tomé and Principe

CAPITAL: São Tomé

GMT

FROM UK: 00239 OUTGOING CODE TO UK: 0044. Most international calls must go through the operator.

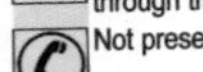
Not present.

Embassy of the Democratic Republic of São Tomé and Principe, Square Montgomery 175, Avenue de Tervuren, 1150 Brussels, Belgium. Tel: 0032 2 734 8966; Fax: 0032 2734 8815

British Consulate, c/o Hull Blythe (Angola) Ltd, BP 15 São Tomé, São Tomé and Principe.

No tourist office.
See www.stome.com/english.html

Valid passport required.

Visa required. Transit visas are not required by those with tickets for onward journeys on the same day. Visas are easily obtained from a consulate in west Africa before crossing the sea.

US$20 adults, US$10 children except those under two years of age, who are exempt.

POLIO, TYPHOID: R. MALARIA: Exists throughout the year in the falciparum variety. Resistance to chloroquine has been reported. YELLOW FEVER: Vaccination is strongly recommended to all travellers. A certificate is required for travellers arriving from infected areas. OTHER: Bilharzia, rabies.

W1

Dobra (Db) = 100 centimes. Credit cards are rarely accepted. Travellers cheques can be cashed at major local banks. US$ are widely accepted at tourist establishments. ATM AVAILABILITY: Unavailable.

MONEYGRAM: Unavailable.
WESTERN UNION: Unavailable

AMEX: 0044 1273 696 933
DINERS CLUB: 0044 1252 513 500
MASTERCARD: 001 314 542 7111
VISA: 001 410 581 9994

AMEX: 0044 1273 571 600
THOMAS COOK: 0044 1733 318950
VISA: 0044 20 7937 8091

0730–1130 Mon to Fri.

Very inexpensive, with little tourist industry and unspoilt by external influences.

Portuguese and native dialects are most widely spoken. French and English are also spoken.

Dry season: June to Sept and Dec to beginning of Feb. The south is wetter than the North.

Roman Catholic majority.

Jan 1, Feb 3, May 1, Jul 12, Sep 6, 30, Dec 21, 25.

220 volts AC.

Up to 2 weeks.

A patriarchal tribal society prevails.

FLIGHTS: There are 3 flights a week from São Tomé to Principe. ROADS: Generally deteriorating therefore a 4 wheel drive is required to get around. BUSES: A bus service is in operation. TAXIS: Services operate.

The Republic of São Tomé and Principe comprises two islands in the Gulf of Guinea, West Africa, straddling the Equator. Both islands are volcanic and covered in forest. Most people live on São Tomé, the larger of the two islands. Cocoa and coffee production are the main export earners. The republic is now encouraging tourism by exploiting its natural assets of forest, extinct volcano, clean beaches, a 12-month summer climate and a society that is more stable than that of its African mainland neighbours.
Usual social courtesies should be shown. Portuguese influence is still dominant.
Medical facilities are extremely limited. Many medicines are not available.

CAPITAL: Riyadh

GMT +3

FROM UK: 00966. OUTGOING CODE TO UK: 0044

Not present.

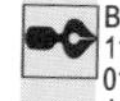
Royal Embassy of Saudi Arabia, 30 Charles Street, London W1X 7PM. Tel: 020 7917 3000.

www.saudiembassy.org.uk/

British Embassy, PO Box 94351, Riyadh 11693, Saudi Arabia. Tel: 01 488 0077. Fax: 01 488 2373. Consulate-General in Jeddah.Tel: 02 622 5550.

Saudi Arabia Information Centre, Cavendish House, 18, Cavendish Square, London W1M 0AQ. Tel: 020 7629 8803. Fax: 020 7629 0374.

Saudi Hotels and Resort Areas Co (SHARACO) PO Box 5500, Riyadh 11422, Saudi Arabia. Tel: (1) 465 7177. Fax: (1) 465 7172.

Valid passport required: valid for 6 months beyond the intended period of stay.

Visa required. Visas are not granted for holiday tourism. Visa applicants must have a Saudi-based sponsor. Hajj visas allow travel to the holy cities but not stopovers in Jeddah or onward travel to Riyadh or other places in Saudi Arabia not connected with the pilgrimage.

Pork, pornography, contraceptives, pearls, children's dolls, jewellery, statues in the form of an animal or human, musical instruments, items considered broadly contrary to Islam (including Christmas decorations, videotapes and fashion magazines). Duty is levied on cameras and typewriters.

Those with passports with Israeli stamps in them. Passengers not complying with Saudi conventions of dress and behaviour, including those who appear to be in a state of intoxication. Those of the Jewish faith.

POLIO, TYPHOID: R. MALARIA: Exists in the falciparum variety throughout the year within certain areas. YELLOW FEVER: A vaccination certificate is required from all travellers arriving from countries where any parts are infected. OTHER: Rabies, bilharzia, meningococcal meningitis.

W1

Saudi Arabian Rial (SAR) = 100 halalah. All major credit cards accepted. Travellers cheques, preferably in US$, accepted. ATM AVAILABILITY: Over 1000 locations.

MONEYGRAM: Unavailable.
WESTERN UNION: (2) 667 2468.

AMEX: 0044 1273 696 933
DINERS CLUB: 800 244 0244
MASTERCARD: 001 314 542 7111
VISA: 001 410 581 9994

AMEX: 00973 256834
THOMAS COOK: 0044 1733 813950
VISA: 0044 20 7937 8091

0830–1200 and 1700–1900 Sat to Wed, 0830–1200 Thur.

Generally expensive. Prices increase by 25% during the summer and hotel charges double in Medina and Mecca during the pilgrimage season. Cheap accommodation and food can be found by the budget traveller.

Arabic. English is spoken in business circles.

Desert climate. Jeddah is warm most of the year. Riyadh is hot in the summer and cooler during the winter. This is one of the driest countries in the world.

Sunni Muslim is the majority. Shiites predominate in the Eastern province.

Sep 24. Eid Al Fitr, Eid Al Adha. Other Islamic festivals.

125/215 volts AC, 50/60 Hz.

Airmail to Europe takes up to 1 week.

Saudi culture is based on the fundamentalist aspects of the Muslim religion and so strict rules apply. Men and women are segregated. Unaccompanied women cannot check into a hotel without a letter from a sponsor. Unaccompanied women must be met at the airport by their husband or sponsor. There are restrictions on women travelling by car with men who are not related by blood. Women are not permitted to drive, or ride bicycles.

Women who are arrested for socialising with a man who is not a blood relative may be charged with prostitution. Some restaurants will not serve women who are not the guests of a close male relative.

Women who look as though they may be of Arab or Asian origin face a greater risk of harassment and officials in some areas will try to force them to wear the abaya or total veil in public places.

FLIGHTS: 19 domestic airports. Flying is the most convenient method of travelling. ROAD: The system is continually being updated and expanded; however, standards of driving are erratic and many driving offences carry an automatic prison sentence. TAXI: Available in all centres but very expensive. Few have meters and fares should be agreed in advance. CAR HIRE: The major international companies have agencies in Saudi Arabia. Minimum driving age is 25. DOCUMENTATION: A national driving licence is valid for up to 3 months. An IDP with translation is recommended. NOTE: Travel to Makkah (Mecca) and Medina, the holy cities of Islam, is forbidden to non-Muslims.

Dress codes and behavioural codes are strictly adhered to. Penalties for drug offences are severe. Non-political criminal activity is minimal, mainly due to the strict implementation of Saudi law. Extreme care must be taken when driving as the blame for accidents may be apportioned wrongly. Visitors should be aware that innocent contact with veiled women can be misinterpreted. Homosexual activity is treated as a criminal offence and a conviction can mean a lashing or a prison sentence; the death penalty is still available to the courts. The penalties are also severe for importing, possessing or consuming alcohol. The display of non-Islamic religious articles such as crosses and Bibles is not allowed.

CAPITAL: Dakar

GMT

FROM UK: 00221. OUTGOING CODE TO UK: 0044

237 392 (Embassy).

Embassy of the Republic of Senegal, 39 Marloes Road, London W8 6LA. Tel: 020 7937 7237; Fax: 020 7938 2546

British Embassy, BP 6025, rue du Docteur Guillet, Dakar, Senegal. Tel: 8237 392 or 8239 971. Fax: 8232 76. britemb@telecomplus.sn

No tourist office in UK. See www.senegal-tourism.com/ and www.le-senegal.com/

Ministry of Tourism and Air Transport, BP 4049, 23 rue Calmette, Dakar, Senegal. Tel: 821 1126; Fax: 822 9413. mtta@primature.sn www.au-senegal.com/index.htm

Valid passport required.

Visa not required by UK citizens, provided they have a return or onward ticket.

There is no free import of alcoholic beverages.

CFA Fr5000 or US$ 7.

POLIO, TYPHOID: R. MALARIA: Exists throughout the country in falciparum variety. Resistance to chloroquine has been reported. YELLOW FEVER: A vaccination certificate is required by travellers arriving from endemic areas. OTHER: Bilharzia, cholera, meningitis, rabies

W1

CFA Franc (CFA Fr) = 100 centimes. Credit cards are accepted in hotels, restaurants and tourism centres. Travellers cheques are accepted and readily changed into local currency in most banks. ATM AVAILABILITY: 9 locations.

MONEYGRAM: Unavailable.
WESTERN UNION: 23 10 00.

AMEX: 0044 1273 696 933
DINERS CLUB: 800 244 0244
MASTERCARD: 001 314 542 7111
VISA: 001 410 581 9994

AMEX: 00973 256834
THOMAS COOK: 0044 1733 813950
VISA: 0044 20 7937 8091

0800–1115 and 1430–1630 Mon to Fri.

Accommodation is expensive, especially in the capital city and surrounding areas.

French. Many local languages are also spoken.

Tropical climate with a hot rainy season from May to Nov, and a hot dry season with harmattan winds from Dec to April.

90% Muslim, 5% Catholic and Protestant and a minority of other beliefs.

Jan 1, Apr 4, May 1, 11, 20, Aug 15, Nov 1, Dec 25. Islamic festivals. Easter, Ascension Day, Whitsun. Carnival in Dakar, late Feb/early Mar.

220 volts AC, 50 Hz

7–10 days to Europe.

Beachwear should be confined to the beach.

ROADS: Many are impassable during the rainy season. There are frequent check points and speed restrictions are strict. TAXI: Available at airport and hotels. 'Bush Taxis', which are mini-vans and station wagons, provide links to every part of the country. DOCUMENTATION: IDP is required. Avoid travel to the Casamance region.

It is polite to pay respect to the headman or schoolteacher of any village you visit. Tipping regarded as discourteous. Pickpocketing and petty crime is common in Dakar.

Seychelles

CAPITAL: Victoria

GMT +4.

FROM UK: 00248. OUTGOING CODE TO UK: 0044 Most international calls must go through the operator.

Not present.

High Commission for the Republic of the Seychelles, 2nd Floor, Eros House, 111 Baker Street, London W1M 1FE. Tel: 020 7224 1660. Fax: 020 7487 5756.

British High Commission, PO Box 161, 3rd Floor, Oliaji Trade Centre, Victoria, Mahé. Tel: 225225; Fax: 225127. bhcsey@seychelles.net; www.bhcvictoria.sc

Seychelles Tourist Office, 2nd floor Eros House, 111 Baker Street, London W1M 1FE. Tel: 020 7224 1670; Fax: 020 7486 1352. sto@seychelles.uk.com www.seychelles.uk.com

Seychelles Tourism Marketing Authority, PO Box 1262, Victoria, Mahé. Tel: 00248 620 000; Fax: 00248 620 620. seychelles@aspureasitgets.com www.aspureasitgets.com

Valid passport required. Visitors must have a return ticket.

Visa not required.

The import of animals, food and other agricultural produce is controlled and subject to licensing.

US$40

POLIO, TYPHOID: Y. YELLOW FEVER: A visitors permit is required from visitors arriving within 6 days of leaving or transiting affected areas. OTHER: Rabies.

Seychelles Rupee (Srs) = 100 cents. EXCHANGE: Airport and banks. Amex and Visa are widely accepted. Travellers cheques, preferably in US$, are accepted in hotels, guest houses and most shops. Most tourism-related costs such as hotels, car hire and diving must be paid for in hard currency, preferably US$ or Euros. Change is often given in Rupees, and these can be spent only in local shops and in bars not connected with hotels. ATM AVAILABILITY: 3 locations.

MONEYGRAM: Unavailable.
WESTERN UNION: Unavailable

AMEX: 0044 1273 696 933
DINERS CLUB: 0044 1252 513 500
MASTERCARD: 001 314 542 7111
VISA: 001 410 581 9994

AMEX: 0044 1273 571 600
THOMAS COOK: 0044 1733 318950
VISA: 0044 20 7937 8091

0830–1430 Mon to Fri, 0830–1100 Sat.

The island is a luxurious getaway for affluent holidaymakers. Prices are often very high.

Creole. English and French.

Monsoon, Nov-Feb, brings hot and humid weather. Temperatures rarely fall below 24ºC.

Mostly Roman Catholic with Anglican. 7th Day Adventists, Muslim and other minorities are also present.

Jan 1, 2, May 1, Jun 5, 29, Aug 15, Nov 1, Dec 8, 25. Easter, Corpus Christi.

240 volts AC, 50 Hz. British 3-pin plugs are in use.

Airmail to Western Europe takes up to 1 week.

Men and women enjoy equal status.

FLIGHTS: An efficient network of scheduled and chartered services operate. SEA: Privately owned schooners provide regular inter-island connections. ROAD: There are paved roads only on the two largest islands. BUS: A regular service is operated on Mahè. Fares of buses and coaches are very reasonable. TAXIS: Government controlled. Rates on Praslin are 25% higher. CAR HIRE: Should be booked in advance. Minimum age is 21. DOCUMENTATION: A national licence is sufficient.

Casual wear is acceptable but beachwear should be confined to the pool or beach. Tourism in the Seychelles is regulated to ensure that the character and natural beauty of the islands remain unspoilt. Topless bathing is tolerated on some beaches.

CAPITAL: Freetown

GMT

FROM UK: 00232. OUTGOING CODE TO UK: 0044. Most international calls must be made through the operator.

223 961/5 (Embassy).

High Commission for the Republic of Sierra Leone, 33 Portland Place, London W1N 3AG. Tel: 020 7636 6483/6. Fax: 020 7323 3159. www.sierra-leone.gov.sl/

British High Commission, Standard Chartered Bank Building of Sierra Leone Ltd, Lightfoot Boston Street, Freetown, Sierra Leone. Tel: 223 961/5.

Refer to the High Commission.

National Tourist Board of Sierra Leone, International Conference Centre, Aberdeen Hill, PO Box 1435, Freetown , Sierra Leone. Tel: 272 520 or 272 396. Fax: 272 197.

Return ticket required. Requirements may be subject to change at short notice. Contact the Embassy before departure. Valid passport required.

Visa required, and it must be obtained in advance.

Narcotics.

Le5000 or US$20 on international departures. Transit passengers are exempt.

POLIO, TYPHOID: R. MALARIA: Exists all year throughout the country in the falciparum variety. Resistance to chloroquine has been reported. YELLOW FEVER: Vaccination is strongly recommended to all visitors if planning to journey into rural areas. A vaccination certificate is required for travellers arriving from infected areas. OTHER: Bilharzia, cholera, rabies.

W1

Leone (Le) = 100 cents. NOTE: Import and export of local currency is limited to Le50000. Amex is accepted, but all other credit cards are only slowly becoming accepted by larger hotels and international businesses. Travellers cheques are accepted by banks. ATM AVAILABILITY: Unavailable.

MONEYGRAM: 1100 then 800 592 3688.
WESTERN UNION: 22 22 27 92.

AMEX: 0044 1273 696 933
DINERS CLUB: 0044 1252 513 500
MASTERCARD: 001 314 542 7111
VISA: 001 410 581 9994

AMEX: 0044 1273 571 600
THOMAS COOK: 0044 1733 318950
VISA: 0044 20 7937 8091

0800–1330 Mon to Fri, 0800–1400 Fri.

Expensive.

English Krio (widely spoken) other local dialects.

Climate is tropical and humid all year round. May-Nov is the rainy season.

Animist with Muslim and Christian minorities.

Jan 1, Apr 27, Dec 25, 26. Easter. Eid Al Fitr, Eid Al Adha, Prophet's Birthday.

220/240 volts AC, 50 Hz. Supply subject to variations.

5 days to Europe

A patriarchal, tribal culture still prevails in most of the country.

ROADS: Secondary roads are impassable during the rainy season. There are road blocks at night on major roads near the centres of population. There is a major petrol shortage with up to 48-hour waits at petrol stations. DOCUMENTATION: IDP is required. BUS/TAXI: Public transport is erratic, and generally not recommended.

The government of Sierra Leone is promoting eco-tourism. There are 21 protected wildlife areas around the country. Although Sierra Leone lacks the big game of the East African plains, wildlife is diverse and the forest and nature reserves support most wildlife species of interest. There are also opportunities for beach, sport and sightseeing holidays. However the security situation is unstable and travel outside the capital, Freetown, is dangerous because numerous anti-government military groups have not been disarmed or demobilized.

Singapore

GMT +8

FROM UK: 0065. OUTGOING CODE TO UK: 00144 Other IDD codes available from phone companies.

All services: 999

High Commission for the Republic of Singapore, 9 Wilton Crescent, London SW1X 8SA. Tel: 020 7235 8315 or 020 7235 5441 (visa). Fax: 020 7245 6583.

British High Commission, Tabglin Road, Singapore 1024. Tel: 473 9333. Fax: 475 2320.

Singapore Tourism Board, 1st Floor, Carrington House, 126-130 Regent Street, London W1R 5FE. Tel: 020 7437 0033. Fax: 020 7734 2191.

Singapore Tourism Board, Tourism Court, 1 Orchard Spring Lane, Singapore 247729. Tel: 0065 736 6622; Fax: 0065 736 9423. www.travel.com.sg/sog/

Valid passport required, with at least six months validity.

Visa not required. All visitors require a 14-day social visit pass which is issued on arrival, provided they have a valid passport and return tickets and sufficient funds to cover their expenses during their stay. This may be extended to 3 months on application to the Singapore immigration department, at their discretion.

Pornographic film and literature, and chewing gum.

Sing$15 at Changi Airport, payable in local currency. Transit passengers and those under 2 years of age are exempt.

Women more than 6 months pregnant must obtain a social visit pass prior to arrival.

POLIO, TYPHOID: There may be a risk of Typhoid. OTHER: Cholera.

W2

Singapore Dollar (Sing$) = 100 cents. The currency of Brunei is also legal tender. All credit cards are widely accepted. Travellers cheques are accepted; US$ are the preferred currency. ATM AVAILABILITY: Over 1000 locations.

MONEYGRAM: 800 1100 560.
WESTERN UNION: Unavailable.

AMEX: 0044 1273 696 933
DINERS CLUB: 29 27 75 66 or 29 44 222
MASTERCARD: 800 1100 113
VISA: 800 1100 344

AMEX: 800 616 1389
THOMAS COOK: 800 448 1115
VISA: 0044 20 7937 8091

1000–1500 Mon to Fri. 1100–1600 Sat. Certain banks are open on Sun on Orchard Road.

Much more expensive than other SE Asian countries. Hotels range from the new high-class to international standard. Prices start at US$ 100. Singapore is known as a shopping capital, where all types of luxury items can be purchased inexpensively.

Chinese (Mandarin). English, Malay and Tamil.

Warm and humid throughout the year. No particularly wet or dry seasons. Most rain falls during the Northeast monsoon (Nov-Jan) and showers can be sudden and heavy.

Confucian, Taoist, Buddhism, Christian, Hindu and Muslim.

Jan 1, May 1, Aug 9, Dec 25. Chinese New Year, Eid Al Fitr, Good Fri, Eid Al Adha, Buddha Purnima, Diwali.

220/240 volts AC, 50 Hz. Plugs are flat 3 pin.

Up to 1 week.

The crime rate is much lower than other countries and sexual harassment is very rare. Women enjoy much more freedom and sexual equality than in other parts of Asia.

SEA: Ferry runs frequent service. ROAD: DOCUMENTATION: IDP is required. BUS: Cheap and efficient. TAXI: Numerous and cheap. METRO: Cheap and efficient.

Singapore has a very low crime rate and very severe penalties for those who break the law. The death penalty is applied to some drug offences. Smoking is illegal in public places. Chewing gum is banned. Dropping litter, spitting, failing to flush public lavatories and many more trivial indiscretions are punishable by an on-the-spot fine in Singapore.

CAPITAL: Bratislava

GMT +1 (GMT +2 during the summer).

FROM UK: 00421. OUTGOING CODE TO UK: 0044

Fire: 150, Ambulance: 155, Police: 158; Rescue: 154.

Embassy of the Slovak Republic, 25 Kensington Palace Gardens, London, W8 4QY. Tel: 020 7243 0803. Passport section: 020 7243 0803. Fax: 020 7727 5824. mail@slovakembassy.co.uk www.slovakembassy.co.uk

British Embassy, Panska 16, 811 01 Bratislava. Tel: 00421 75441; Fax: 00421 75441 0002. bebra@internet.sk www.britemb.sk

Czech and Slovak Tourist Centre, 16 Frognal Parade, Finchley Road, London NW3 5HG. Tel: 020 77943 263/4 also 0800 026 7943; Fax: 0207 7943265. cztc@cztc.demon.co.uk www.czech-slovak-tourist.co.uk/

Slovak Agency for Tourism, 2 Námestie slobody, PO Box 497, 974 01 Banská Bystrica, Námestie, Banská, Slovak Republic. Tel: 00421 88 746 626 or 45890. Fax: 00421 88 746 626.
Slovak Tourist Board, Namestie L. Stura 1 (PO Box 35), 974 05 Banská Bystrica 5, Slovak Republic. Tel: 00421 88 413 6146 or 413 61 47 or 413 61 48; Fax: 00421 88 413 61 49. sacr@sacr.sk www.sacr.sk/

Valid passport required: Passports must be valid for 8 months from the point of entry.

British passport holders do not need a visa for or transit through the Slovak Republic, or for tourism and business visits for up to six months. Nationals of the USA and certain other countries require a visa for visits longer than 30 days.

Materials which promote war, fascism, Nazism or racism. All forms of pornographic literature. All items of value must be declared on arrival to allow clearance on departure.

US$7.40 is payable on all international departures.

Rabies. Tick-borne encephalitis, especially in forests.

Koruna (Sk) or Slovak Crown = 100 halierov. EXCHANGE: Exchange offices, SATUR offices, main hotels, road border crossings as well as some post offices and some travel agencies. Import and export of local currency is prohibited. All major credit cards can be used to exchange currency and are also accepted in large hotels, restaurants and shops. Travellers cheques are widely accepted, preferably in US$. ATM AVAILABILITY: Over 650 locations.

MONEYGRAM: Unavailable
WESTERN UNION: (17) 830 790.

AMEX: 0044 1273 696 933
DINERS CLUB: 0044 1252 513 500
MASTERCARD: 001 314 542 7111
VISA: 001 410 581 9994

AMEX: 0044 1273 571 600
THOMAS COOK: 001733 318950
VISA: 0044 20 7937 8091

Generally 0800–1700 Mon to Fri.

Since the Slovak Republic became an independent state in 1993, the transition to a Western-style economy has increased the standard of living greatly. Tourism is on the increase and more accommodation is being built in remote regions.

Slovak, Czech, Hungarian, German and English may also be spoken.

Cold winters and mild summers.

Roman Catholic, with the remainder being Protestant – Reformed, Lutheran, Methodist – and Jewish.

Jan 1, 6, May 1, 8, Jul 5, Aug 29, Sep 1, 15, Nov 1, Dec 24, 25, 26. Easter.

Generally 220 volts AC, 50 Hz.

Poste restante services are available.

Traditional ideas and values persist in rural areas, especially amongst the older generation.

RAIL: There are several daily express trains between Bratislava and main cities and resorts. Reservations should be made in advance on major routes. Fares are low but supplements are charged on express trains. ROAD: Well-maintained road system including Western-standard motorways. BUS: The extensive network covers areas not accessible by train, and is efficient and comfortable. In towns, single-journey tickets for buses and trams can be bought from machines at stops or from news-stands.
CAR HIRE: May be booked through the

tourist office in main towns and resorts. DOCUMENTATION: A valid national driving licence is sufficient for car hire. Seat belts compulsory. RIVER: Regular passenger services to Vienna and Budapest as well as entertainment and sightseeing river cruises on the Danube and connecting rivers, the Rhone and Main.

The Slovak Republic is the eastern part of the former Czechoslovakia. It has historical towns, magnificent castles, numerous sporting opportunities and areas of breathtaking natural beauty. Dress should be casual but conservative. Take sensible precautions to avoid pickpockets in Bratislava and other tourist areas. There have been reports about harrassment of tourists by skinheads and members of the Roma community. It is an offence to be without identification (usually a passport) and can lead to a fine or 24 hours in custody. The FCO has issued a warning about bogus plain-clothes policemen who may ask to see your foreign currency and passport. If approached, decline to show your money. Offer instead to go with them to the nearest police station or to the British Embassy.

CAPITAL: Ljubljana

GMT +1 (GMT +2 during the summer).

FROM UK: 00386. OUTGOING CODE TO UK: 0044.

Police: 113; Fire and Ambulance: 112; AMZS breakdown service: 1987 or 01 530 5353. Ambulance: 94, Fire: 93, Police: 92.

Embassy of the Republic of Slovenia, Suite 1, Cavendish Court, 11–15 Wigmore Street, London W1H 9LA. Tel: 020 7495 7775. Fax: 020 7495 7776. slovene-embassy.london@virgin.net: www.embassy-slovenia.org.uk

British Embassy, Consular Section, Trg Republike 3, Ljubljana; Tel: 00386 1 200 39 10; Fax: 00386 425 01 74. info@british-embassy.si; www.british-embassy.si/

Slovenian Tourist Office, 49 Conduit Street, London W1R 9FB. Tel: 020 7287 7133; Fax: 020 7287 5476. slovenia@cpts.fsbusiness.co.uk
www.touristlink.com/slovenia.htm

Slovenian Tourist Board, Dunajska 156, 1000 Ljubljana, Slovenia. Tel: 00386 61 189 1840. Fax: 00386 61 189 1841.
www.slovenia-tourism.si/

Valid passport required, except for nationals of EU countries with a valid ID card. Visitors must have a return or onward travel ticket.

Visa not required by nationals of EU countries.

Narcotics and firearms.

US$ 16 or DM 25 is payable on international flights.

POLIO, TYPHOID: R. OTHER: Rabies.

Slovene Tolar (SiT) = 100 stotins. Major cards accepted by hotels, shops, restaurants, and some petrol stations, although motorway tolls may only be paid in cash – local or foreign. Travellers cheques exchangable at banks. ATM AVAILABILITY: Widely available at branches of Banka Slovenije. Tel: 01 5834184 for assistance.

MONEYGRAM: Unavailable.
WESTERN UNION: (061) 140 1223.

AMEX: 0044 1273 696 933
DINERS CLUB: 061 18 96 133
MASTERCARD: 001 314 542 7111
VISA: 001 410 581 9994

AMEX: 0044 1273 571 600
THOMAS COOK: 001733 318950
VISA: 0044 20 7937 8091

0800–1800 Mon to Fri. Some branches are open 0800–1200 Sat.

Slovenia is marginally more expensive than the other former Yugoslav states.

Slovene, which is closely related to Serbo-Croat. Some Hungarian and Italian spoken.

Mediterranean climate on the coast, continental climate with mild to hot summers and cold winters in the uplands to the east.

Mostly Roman Catholic. Eastern Orthodox with Muslim and Jewish minorities.

Jan 1, 2, Feb 8, Apr 27, May 1, Jun 25, Aug 15, Oct 31, Nov 1, Dec 25, 26. Easter, Whitsun.

220 volts AC, 50 Hz.

Reasonable internal service. 4–6 days for letters to UK.

More traditional values persist among the older generation, particularly in the rural areas.

SEA: There are regularly scheduled trips across the Adriatic between Venice and Izola. RAIL: Intercity trains operate and are relatively cheap. ROAD: There is a good network of high quality roads. Petrol stations are generally open from 0700 to 2000 hours, Mon–Sat; those near border crossings, on motorways and near large towns are open 24 hours a day. One spare can of petrol or diesel, up to 10 litres, may be imported into Slovenia duty-free. DOCUMENTATION: Full national driving licences are accepted. International insurance is mandatory for all foreign vehicles with a few exceptions.

Tourist facilities are widely available throughout the country. Normal social conventions apply. Informal dress is acceptable. The mountain region to the north-west of Slovenia has summer resorts and over 50 winter sports centres, of which Kranjska Gora is the best known. SPECIAL PRECAUTIONS: Travellers can become targets of pickpockets and purse snatchers, especially at railway stations and airports. The Sava River is polluted with domestic and industrial waste; and there is evidence of pollution of coastal waters with heavy metals and toxic chemicals originating from metallurgical and chemical plants.

Solomon Islands

CAPITAL: Honiara

GMT +11

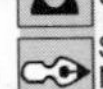
FROM UK: 00677. OUTGOING CODE TO UK: 0044.

Solomon Islands Embassy, 1st Floor, Bvd St Michel 28, 1040 Brussels, Belgium. Tel: 0032 2732 7085. Fax: 0032 2732 6885.

British High Commission, Telekom House, Mendana Avenue, Honiara, Solomon Islands. Tel: (00677) 21705/6. Fax: (00677) 21549. bhc@solomon.com.sb

No tourist office in UK. http://members.nbci.com/janeresture/solhome/index.htm

Solomon Islands Visitors Bureau, PO Box 321, Honiara, Solomon Islands. Tel: 00677 22442; Fax: 00677 23986; visitors@solomon. com.sb www.commerce.gov.sb/Tourism/ index.htm

Passport valid for at least 6 months required by all. Proof of sufficient funds for period of stay and onward or return tickets required.

Visa not required for stays of up to 3 months. 7-day transit visa is available on arrival. Visitors may require a multi-entry visa from Australian authorities for travel via Australia. Visitors intending to work need a permit.

Plants and animals are subject to restrictions.

SI$ 30, payable in local currency, for all departures. Transit passengers and children under 2 years are exempt.

POLIO, TYPHOID: R. MALARIA: Exists throughout the year in some areas, in the falciparum variety, which is reported to be highly resistant to chloroquine. YELLOW FEVER: A vaccination certificate is required from travellers arriving within 6 days of leaving or transiting infected areas,

W2. Water is safe in the main resorts, but in others areas drink only boiled water.

Solomon Islands Dollar (SI$) = 100 cents. Export of local currency limited to SI$ 250. Credit cards accepted only in the main resort areas. Aus$ travellers cheques can be exchanged at banks. ATM AVAILABILITY: Unavailable.

MONEYGRAM: Unavailable.
WESTERN UNION: Unavailable.

AMEX: 0044 1273 696 933
DINERS CLUB: 0044 1252 513 500
MASTERCARD: 001 314 542 7111
VISA: 001 410 581 9994

AMEX: 0044 1273 571 600
THOMAS COOK: 001733 318950
VISA: 0044 20 7937 8091

0830–1500 Mon to Fri.

Accommodation can be quite expensive due to the small number of hotels. However, in the Reef accommodation is cheaper, and more basic.

English, Pidgin English and over 87 local dialects are spoken.

Mainly hot and humid with little variation throughout the year. Monsoon season Jan–Apr.

More than 95% of the population are Christian.

Jan 1, second Sat in Jun, Jul 7, Dec 25, 26. Easter.

240 volts AC, 50Hz, Australian-type, flat, 3-pin plugs are commonly used.

Approx. 7 days to Europe.

European and local traditions and customs co-exist.

FLIGHTS: Solomon Airlines runs services between main islands and towns. Western Pacific Air Services flies to smaller, more isolated island airfields. SEA: Large and small ships provide the best means of travelling between the islands. Services are run by the government and a host of private operators. ROAD: General condition is poor, resulting in limited use. A good road runs east and west from Honiara. TAXI: Flagged down in the street; no meters and no advance booking.

Visitors from the UK must register with the British High Commission, usually through hotel reception. Always seek permission before taking photographs of locals. Tipping is not encouraged. Swearing is a serious offence. Permission is required before use of beaches, footpaths, etc. Informal light clothing is appropriate for day and evening wear. Beachwear should be kept for the beach. Check with local people about where to swim. Swimming is not advised in the sea around Honiara, because of the presence of sharks, bristle-worms, stinging corals and sea urchins. There are no decompression facilities on the islands for divers. Earthquakes, tidal waves and volcanic activity can occur at any time. Hurricanes occur during the rainy season, Nov to Mar.

CAPITAL: Mogadishu

GMT +3

FROM UK: 00252. OUTGOING CODE TO UK: 1944 Most international calls must go through the operator.

All travellers are advised to consult the FCO or foreign ministry in their country of residence before departure regarding emergency assistance.

There is no diplomatic representation in the UK.

British Embassy, Waddada Xasan Geedd Abtoow 7/8 (P O Box 1036), Mogadishu, Somalia. Tel: 00252 1 20288/9. Closed at the time of writing. British Embassies in Djibouti and Kenya may be able to advise on the current situation but can offer little consular or emergency support to visitors in Somalia.

No tourist office.

No tourist office.

Return ticket and valid passport required. Requirements may be subject to change at short notice: contact embassy before going.

Visa required. Transit visas are not required by visitors with reserved onward travel.

The equivalent of US$20 is levied on all international departures. Transit and passengers under two years are exempt.

POLIO, TYPHOID: R. MALARIA: Exists throughout the year in the Falciparum variety. Resistance to chloroquine has been reported. YELLOW FEVER: Vaccination is strongly recommended to all travellers. A vaccination certificate is required by those arriving from infected areas. OTHER: Bilharzia, cholera (vaccination required) and rabies.

W1

Somali Shilling (SoSh) = 100 cents. Import and export of local currency is limited to SoSh 200. Diners Club has limited acceptance. US$ cash is preferred to travellers cheques. ATM AVAILABILITY: Unavailable.

MONEYGRAM: Unavailable.
WESTERN UNION: 1 215 036.

AMEX: No local number
DINERS CLUB: No local number.
MASTERCARD: No local number
VISA: No local number

AMEX: 0044 1273 571600
THOMAS COOK: 0044 1733 318950
VISA: 0044 1733 318949

0800–1130 Sat to Thur.

Economy decimated by political strife and drought, resulting in high inflation and a scarcity of products.

Somali and Arabic. Some English. Somalis use the Roman rather than Arabic script for writing.

Jan-Feb hot and dry, Mar-June is the first rainy season, monsoon winds occur between July and Aug. The second rainy season occurs Sept–Dec.

Mostly Sunni Muslim, with a Christian minority.

Jan 1, 30, Apr 7, May 1, Jun 26, Jul1, 6, Oct 21.

220 volts AC, 50 Hz.

Up to 2 weeks.

Women are advised to cover arms and legs in accordance with the Muslim religion.

ROAD: It is difficult to travel outside of Mogadishu by car because of poor road conditions. DOCUMENTATION : IDP is required.

A number of hotels were built when a new deep-water port was opened in Mogadishu with the help of the World Bank. However, until the security situation improves, tourism is a risky matter not to be embarked upon lightly. Many parts of Somalia remain insecure. Inter-clan and inter-factional fighting can flare up with little warning, and kidnapping, murder, and other threats to foreigners can occur unpredictably in many regions.
The FCO advises against travel to Southern Somalia. The north-west of Somalia, is generally stable but the situation could change without warning. Advice should be taken from the British Embassy in Djibouti before travelling to this area.
In addition to the problems caused by civil war, Somalia is subject to recurring droughts; frequent dust storms over eastern plains in summer; floods during rainy season, and grave shortages of vital supplies such as food and clean water.
PHOTOGRAPHY: People with cameras must have a permit.

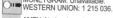

South Africa

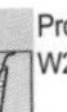
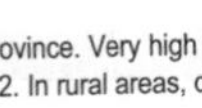

CAPITAL: Pretoria

GMT +2

FROM UK: 0027. OUTGOING CODE TO UK: 0944 or 09144

Police: 1011, Ambulance: 10222, Fire: 1022

High Commission of the Republic of South Africa, South Africa House, Trafalgar Square, London WC2N 5DP. Tel: 020 7451 7299; Fax: 020 7451 7284. general@southafricahouse.com www.southafricahouse.com

British High Commission, 255 Hill Street, Arcadia, Pretoria 0002, South Africa. Tel: 0027 12 4831 402. Fax: 0027 12 483 1444. Consular section: Liberty Life Place, Block B 1st Floor 256, Glyn Street, Hatfield 0083, Pretoria. www.britain.org.za/
British Consulate-General, 15th Floor, Southern Life Centre, 8 Riebeek Street, Cape Town 8001. Tel: 0027 21 409 5900; Fax: 0027 21 419 6877. britcons@cyberhost.co.za

South African Tourism, 5/6 Alt Grove, Wimbledon, London SW19 4DZ. Tel 020 8971 9350. 24-hr brochure request line: 0870 155 0044. london@southafricantourism.com www.southafricantourism.com

South African Tourism, Bojanala House, 12 Rivonia Road, Illovo, Johannesburg 2196. Postal Address: Private Bag X10012, Sandton 2146, South Africa. Tel: 0027 11 778 8000. Fax: 0027 11 778 8001. jhb@southafricantourism.com

Valid passport required: must be valid for 6 months after departure. Visitors must have return or onward travel ticket.

Visa not required for a stay up to 3 months.

Obscene literature and second-hand military clothing is prohibited.

Rand 60, inclusive of international return fare.

POLIO, TYPHOID: R. MALARIA: Exists throughout the year in the falciparum variety. Resistance to chloroquine has been reported. YELLOW FEVER: A vaccination certificate is required from all passengers over one year of age travelling from infected areas. Passengers arriving by unscheduled flights at airports other than those used by scheduled airlines must possess a certificate. OTHER: Bilharzia, cholera and rabies. Cholera in rural areas of KwaZulu Natal and Northern Province. Very high level of HIV/AIDS.

W2. In rural areas, drink only bottled water.

South African Rand (R) = 100 cents. NOTE: Import and export of local SA Reserve Bank notes is limited to R500. Foreign currency must be declared on arrival. All major credit cards are widely accepted. Travellers cheques in all currencies are accepted. ATM AVAILABILITY: Widely available.

MONEYGRAM: 0 800 996 048.
WESTERN UNION: 0800 126 000

AMEX: 0944 1273 696 933
DINERS CLUB: 11 358 8406
MASTERCARD: 0800 990 418
VISA: 0800 990 475

AMEX: 0944 1273 571 600
THOMAS COOK: 0800 998175
VISA: 0800 99 8174

0830–1530 Mon to Fri, 0800–1130 Sat.

Accommodation and other tourist facilities in the cities can be expensive. Avoid short trips in city taxis which are sometimes more expensive than long-distance journeys.

English and Afrikaans with 9 other African languages.

Generally warm and sunny. Winters are usually mild.

Dutch Reformed Church, Anglican, Roman Catholic, Jews, Hindu, Muslim and many others.

Jan 1, Mar 21, Apr 27, Family Day (Apr), May 1, Jun 16, Aug 9, 10, Sep 24, Dec 16, 25, 26. Easter.

250 volts AC, in Pretoria. 220/230 volts AC, elsewhere.

Up to 7 days for airmail to Europe.

Political reforms have redefined the role of women. Cultural sociological and economic differences continue to cause tension. There is a very high incidence of rape in the townships and rural areas.

FLIGHTS: Regular domestic flights operate between main cities. SEA: 'Starlight' cruises operate between the major ports. ROADS: A well maintained network of roads exists. NOTE: Fines are imposed for speeding. It is illegal to carry petrol unless in built-up petrol tanks. DOCUMENTATION: IDP is required.

!

Casual remarks should not be made about the political situation, which is complex. It is unwise for outsiders from any race to enter into a black township without a guide. The crime rate is quite high, and passport theft is common. Visitors should carry only a photocopy of their passport for identification purposes. Daylight muggings are not uncommon, especially in parts of Johannesburg and in railway and bus stations, where tourists are an easy target for petty, and sometimes violent, thieves. Visitors should refrain from changing large sums of money in circumstances where they can be readily observed, and keep jewellery, cameras and other valuables out of sight. There is a risk of armed robbery, and car-hijacking is common, especially on the approach roads to the Kruger Park.

The lack of significant arterial rivers or lakes requires extensive water conservation and control measures; growth in water usage threatens to outpace supply. Pollution of rivers results from agricultural runoff and urban discharge.

Spain

CAPITAL: Madrid

Mainland Spain and Balearics GMT +1 (GMT +2 during the summer).

FROM UK: 0034. OUTGOING CODE TO UK: 0744 or 0044

Emergency services: 112. Police: 91

Embassy of the Kingdom of Spain, 39 Chesham Place, London SW1X 8SB. Tel: 020 7235 5555; Fax: 020 7235 9905.

British Embassy, Calle de Fernando el Santo 16, 28010 Madrid, Spain. Tel: 0034 91 700 8200; Fax: 0034 91 700 8272. www.ukinspain.com

(Gran Canaria) British Consulate, Edificio Cataluña, C/Luis Morote 6-3º, PO Box 2020, 35080 Las Palmas de Gran Canaria. Tel: 92 826 2508; Fax: 92 826 7774. britconsul.laspalmas@canarias7.com

(Tenerife) British Consulate, Plaza Weyler 8-1, Santa Cruz de Tenerife 38003, Tel: 92 2286863; Fax: 92 2289903. tenerifeconsulate@ukinspain.com

Consulates also in Seville, Alicante, Barcelona, Tarragona, Bilbao, Granada, Malaga, Palma, Ibiza, Santander, Menorca and Vigo.

Spanish National Tourist Office, 22-23 Manchester Square, London W1U 3PX. Tel: 0207 486 8077; 24-hour Brochure Request Line: 0900 166 9920 (Premium rate charges apply); Fax: 0207 486 8034. info.londres@tourspain.es www.tourspain.co.uk This web site has links to sites on various cities and resorts.

Direccion General de Turespaña, Jose Lázaro Galdiano 6, 28036 Madrid, Spain. Tel: (1) 343 3500. Fax: (1) 343 3446.

Valid passport required.

Visa not required. For stays of over 90 days, a residence permit must be obtained from the provincial police station.

Narcotics and firearms, metal detectors, some household goods.

Euro = 100 cents.All major credit cards are accepted. Travellers cheques in Sterling pounds can be easily exchanged. ATM AVAILABILITY: Over 35000 locations.

MONEYGRAM: 900 96 1218.
WESTERN UNION: 900 63 3633

AMEX: 0044 1273 696 933
DINERS CLUB: 91 701 5900
MASTERCARD: 900 97 1231
VISA: 900 99 1124

AMEX: 900 99 4426
THOMAS COOK: 900 99 4403
VISA: 900 97 4414

0900–1400 Mon to Fri, 0900–1300 Sat (except during the summer).

Similar prices to other Western European countries.

Spanish (Castilian), Catalan, Galician and Basque.

Varies from temperate in the North to hot and dry in the South. The best months are Apr-Oct, although it can be excessively hot July-Aug except at coastal regions. The central plateau can be very cold during winter.

Roman Catholic in the majority.

Jan 1, 6, May 1, Jun 24, Jul 25, 31, Aug 15, Sep 8, 11, 24, Oct 12, Nov 1, Dec 6, 8, 25. Easter. City and regional fiestas on various dates in addition. See www.map.es

220 volts AC, 50 Hz. In some buildings there is still 110 or 125 volts. Plugs are 2-pin.

5 days. Poste restante facilities are available at main post offices. Stamps are bought from post offices, tobacconists and some hotels.

Spanish women retain traditional values in rural areas, but many of the formerly strict religious and social customs are becoming slightly more relaxed, particularly in urban and tourist regions. Spain is one of the safest countries for women to travel in.

RAIL: Most cities are well served. It is mainly a radial service with connections between Madrid and all major cities. It is one of the cheapest in Europe, with discounts and special concessions. ROAD: Motorways are well maintained and connect North and South. Trunk roads between major cities are general well maintained. BUS: Services are cheap and efficient. Good intercity coach services. Reservations for seats on long-distance coaches may be made only one or two days in advance. CAR HIRE: All major companies have agencies. DOCUMENTATION: An EU national driving licence is accepted for driving in Spain. If your current licence does not comply with the EU format, you must obtain an International Driving Permit. The vehicle registration document and adequate insur-

ance are also required. Third party insurance is compulsory in Spain. Visitors are advised to obtain a green card from their own insurance company.

Spaniards are very hospitable, and value courtesy. Conservative casual dress is suitable, but some larger hotels may insist that men wear a jacket. Beachwear should be confined to the beach/pool. Bathers should be aware of pollution of the Mediterranean from raw sewage and effluents from the offshore production of oil and gas. Street crime can be a problem in some of the tourist areas and large cities.

Metal detecting is a strictly controlled activity in Spain and its practice in public places requires a permit from the relevant local council. Permits are normally granted for investigation purposes only. Admission to museums in Spain is free to students or teachers if booked in advance with the Cultural Office of the Spanish Embassy or the Ministry of Culture, Tel: 0034 91 532 5089. Students must hold an International Student card for this concession. The medical form E111 is valid for free emergency treatment. There is a continuing threat that the Basque separatist organisation, ETA, may try to disrupt the Spanish economy by attacking tourist centres. This is only a small risk, but the situation could change without warning, and visitors are advised to be alert to developments in the media, and report anything suspicious, such as unattended luggage, to the police.

Sri Lanka

CAPITAL: Colombo

GMT +5.30

FROM UK: 0094. OUTGOING CODE TO UK: 0044

All services: 1 691095/699935.

High Commission of Sri Lanka, 13 Hyde Park Gardens, London W2 2LU. Tel: 020 7262 1841. Fax: 020 7262 7970. mail@slhc. globalnet.co.uk; www.users.globalnet.co.uk/~slhc

British Embassy, PO Box 1433, 190 Galle Road, Kollupitiya, Colombo 3, Sri Lanka. Tel: 0094 1437 336. Fax: 0094 1430 308. bhc@eureka.lk

Sri Lanka Tourist Board, 22 Regent Street, London SW1Y 4QD. Tel: 020 7930 2627. Fax: 020 7930 9070.

Sri Lanka Tourist Board, PO Box 1504, 78 Stewart Place, Colombo 3, Sri Lanka. Tel: (1) 437 059. Fax: (1) 437 953. Sri Lanka Tourist Board, Travel Information Center, 72 Victoria Drive, Kandy, Sri Lanka. Tel: 0094 822661. srilanka@cerbernet.co.uk or srilankatourism@aol.com; www.lanka.net/ctb/

Passport (valid for 3 months) and return or onward travel ticket required.

Nationals of EU countries will be issued a visa free of charge on arrival at Colombo airport for a maximum stay of 30 days.

Precious metals must be declared on arrival.

SLRs500, payable in local currency. Transit and passengers under 2 years are exempt.

POLIO, TYPHOID: R. MALARIA: R. YELLOW FEVER: Vaccination certificate required from travellers over 1 year old coming from infected areas. OTHER: Cholera, rabies.

W1

Sri Lankan Rupee (SLRe, SLRs plural) = 100 cents. EXCHANGE: An exchange form is issued on arrival, which must be stamped for all exchange transactions. Banks, hotels exchange currency. All major credit cards widely accepted. Travellers cheques accepted, better exchange rate than cash. US$ is the preferred cheque currency. ATM AVAILABILITY: Over 12 locations.

MONEYGRAM: 430 430 then 800 592 3688.
WESTERN UNION: (1) 320 671.

AMEX: 0044 1273 696 933
DINERS CLUB: 0044 1252 513 500
MASTERCARD: 001 314 542 7111
VISA: 001 410 581 9994

AMEX: 0044 1273 571 600
THOMAS COOK: 001733 318950
VISA: 0044 20 7937 8091

0900–1500 Tues to Fri, 0900–1300 Sat to Mon.

Suitable for all travellers and budgets.

Sinahala, Tamil and English.

Tropical climate. The coastal areas are cooled by the sea winds. The monsoons are May–Jul and Dec–Jan.

Buddhist with Hindu, Christian and Muslim minorities.

Jan 12, 14, Feb 4, May 1, Jul 6, 7, Sep 8, Oct 5, 19, Dec 3, 25. Good Fri, Hindu, Buddhist and Islamic festivals. Full Moon Day each month.

230/240 volts AC, 50 Hz. Round 3-pin plugs are usual.

Airmail to Western Europe takes up to 1 week.

Hindu customs prevail. Traditional saris are worn. It is considered impolite to refuse the offer of tea. Punctuality is considered important. Arms and legs should be covered when visiting religious sites and shoes and hats must be removed.

RAIL: Connects Colombo with all tourist towns. New fast service runs on principal routes. Rail services to the northern area have been greatly reduced because of violent disruptions. ROAD: Most roads are tarred. BUS: An extensive network of reasonable quality. CAR HIRE: Available from several international agencies. DOCUMENTATION: Obtain an IDP before departure.

Fighting between the security forces and the Tamil Tigers (LTTE) continues in the North and East. Do not visit these areas. There have been terrorist attacks resulting in fatalities in Colombo and its airport. The possibility of further civil disturbances is a continuing threat. At the time of writing, FCO advises against all holiday and non-essential travel to Sri Lanka. Intending travellers can get up-to-date information from the FCO website and from the Sri Lanka High Commission.

CAPITAL: Khartoum

GMT +2

FROM UK: 00249. OUTGOING CODE TO UK: 0044 Most international calls must go through the operator.

Embassy of the Democratic Republic of Sudan, 3 Cleveland Row, St James Street, London SW1A 1DD. Tel: 020 7839 8080. Fax: 020 7839 7560. zb24@pipex.com

British Embassy, (PO Box 801) 31 10th St. off Baladia Street 32. Khartoum Central; Tel: 00249 11 777105; Fax: 00249 11 776457 35. British@sudanmail.net.

http://lexicorient.com/m.s/sudan/index.htm and www.i-cias.com/m.s/sudan/ have useful information on travelling in Sudan.

Public Corporation of Tourism and Hotels PO Box 7104, Khartoum. Tel: (11) 781 764.

Passport required. There must be no indication of a prior visit to Israel.

Visa required (including transit passengers) and issued for one month. Extensions can be obtained in Khartoum.

Import of foodstuffs is prohibited.

US$20 is levied on international departures. Transit passengers and those under two years of age are exempt.

POLIO, TYPHOID: R. MALARIA: Exists in the falciparum variety throughout the year. High resistance to chloroquine has been reported. YELLOW FEVER: Vaccination certificate required for passengers over 1 year old arriving from infected areas and may be required from travellers leaving Sudan. Vaccination is strongly recommended if you plan to travel outside urban areas. OTHER: Bilharzia, cholera, rabies and visceral leishmaniasis, guinea worm.

W1. Bottled water is not easy to find outside the main towns.

Sudanese Dinar. Exchange rates are volatile and US$ bills are preferred. Import and export of local currency is prohibited. Only Amex is widely accepted. Travellers cheques are accepted in larger centres only. ATM AVAILABILITY: Unavailable.

MONEYGRAM: Unavailable.
WESTERN UNION: Unavailable.

AMEX: 0044 1273 696933
DINERS CLUB: No local number
MASTERCARD: No local number
VISA: No local number

AMEX: 0044 1273 571 600
THOMAS COOK: 0044 1733 318950
VISA: 0044 1733 318949

0830–1200 Sat to Thur.

Inexpensive, apart from the larger hotels in Khartoum. Most places have basic hotels and government resthouses, which are like boarding houses. Outside Khartoum, there is comfortable accommodation in Wadi Halfa, Kassala and Wadi Medani.

Arabic, English, Local dialects are widely spoken.

Extremely hot with sandstorms from Apr-Sept in the Sahara region. Wet season in the south from May-Oct.

Muslim in the north, Christian and animist in the south.

Jan 1, Mar 3, Apr 6, May 25, Jun 30, Dec 25. Islamic festivals.

240 volts AC, 50 Hz.

Up to 1 week to Europe.

Women should respect the Muslim dress code and not wear revealing clothes. Islamic Sharia law applies, while Western women are not required to be veiled, over-enthusiastic officials can be a nuisance about it. Women should take care not to provoke conservative Sudanese, and be aware that a female travelling is unusual. There can be harassment or general lack of consideration in restaurants and hotels.

NOTE: Travellers must register with the police headquarters within 3 days of arrival, and police permission must be obtained before moving to another location within Sudan. FLIGHTS: Sudan Airways serves 20 national airports. RAIL: Extensive network but services have been disrupted by the civil war. The trains that do run are very slow and uncomfortable. The train from Wadi Halfa to Khartoum cuts through the Nubian Desert. ROADS: Outside the main towns roads are usually in very poor condition and unsuitable for travel during rainy season. Vehicles must be in good condition, with a supply of spare parts, water, food, fuel. Most road transport is by bus, lorry and boksi. Boksi is a shared

taxi, usually a minibus vehicle. Visitors' vehicles are usually those involved in media, science or relief work. DOCUMENTATION: Carnet de Passage, adequate finance, a road worthiness certificate (from embassy) required. IDP recommended. Trailers and cars less then 1500cc are refused entry. Permits are required for all travel outside Khartoum.

The Arab culture predominates in the North. In the South the people belong to a number of tribes. Under Islamic law, alcohol is banned. Sudan is a country of unreliable power supplies, unskilled and slow bureaucracy, civil war, rebel militias, drought and poverty. Sudan is one of the most difficult countries in Africa to travel in, and yet it can offer some of the greatest scenery, well away from the fighting. The border with Egypt is open at Wadi Halfa, but there is fighting near the borders with Eritrea and Ethiopia. HIGH RISK. It is inadvisable to travel to any of the southern provinces due to civil war. Contact the FCO Travel Advice Unit or refer to the FCO website for the latest information.

CAPITAL: Paramaribo

GMT –3

FROM UK: 00597. OUTGOING CODE TO UK: 0044.

Contact hotel operator.

No representation within the UK. EUROPE: Embassy of the Republic of Suriname, Alexander Gogelweg 2, 2517 JH The Hague, The Netherlands. Tel: 0031 70 365 0844. Fax: 0031 70 361 7445.

The British Embassy in Georgetown covers Suriname. British Honorary Consulate, c/o VSH United Buildings, PO Box 1860, Van't Hogerhuys- straat 9-11, Paramaribo, Suriname. Tel: 402 558; Fax: 403 515. united@sr.net

No tourism office in UK. See www.surinfo.org/indexeng.htm

Suriname Tourism Foundation, Upstairs, Dr JF Nasslaan 2, Paramaribo, Suriname. Tel: 410357; Fax: 410357. stsur@sr.net

Valid passport required: valid for 6 months after intended period of stay.

Visa required, and must be obtained in advance. Visa application form can be downloaded on the Internet from www.surinfo.org/indexeng.htm

Fruit, vegetables and meat products.

US$5, children under 2 are exempt.

POLIO, TYPHOID: R. MALARIA: Exists throughout the country all year round in the falciparum variety which has been reported as being highly resistant to chloroquine. YELLOW FEVER: A vaccination certificate is required if arriving from infected areas. OTHER: Bilharzia, rabies. HIV/AIDS

W2. Tap water is purified. Do not drink river water.

Suriname Guilder (SGld) = 100 cents. EXCHANGE: Some banks and hotels are authorised to exchange money. Credit cards are accepted only in the larger hotels. Travellers cheques in US$ can be exchanged in some banks. Generally a cash society. ATM AVAILABILITY: Unavailable.

MONEYGRAM: Unavailable.
WESTERN UNION: 42 11 52.

AMEX: 0044 1273 696933
DINERS CLUB: No local number
MASTERCARD: No local number
VISA: No local number

AMEX: 001 801 964 6665
THOMAS COOK: 001 800 223 7373
VISA: 001 800 732 1322

0730–1400 Mon to Fri.

Hotels are generally located in the city and fairly expensive. A youth hostel and campsite are outside the city. Travellers should bring their own hammock and food.

Dutch (the official language), Taki-Taki, Hindi, Javanese, Chinese, French and Spanish. Students and people in the travel industry generally also speak English.

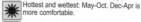

Hottest and wettest: May-Oct. Dec-Apr is more comfortable.

Christian, Hindu and Muslim.

Feb 25, May 1, Jul 1, Nov 25, Dec 25.

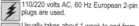

110/220 volts AC, 60 Hz European 2-pin plugs are used.

Usually takes about 1 week to and from Europe.

A diversity of ethnic cultures. The Maroons and Amerindian tribes live a village lifestyle untouched for centuries. Women should wear long trousers for trips to the interior. If travelling alone they will get a lot of provocative attention, but this is meant to be flattering rather than a threat.

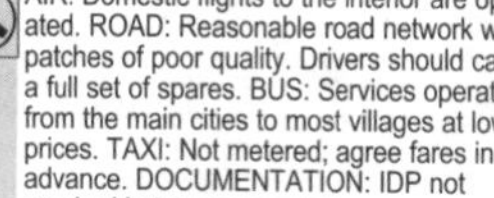
AIR: Domestic flights to the interior are operated. ROAD: Reasonable road network with patches of poor quality. Drivers should carry a full set of spares. BUS: Services operate from the main cities to most villages at low prices. TAXI: Not metered; agree fares in advance. DOCUMENTATION: IDP not required but recommended.

Beachwear should not be worn away from beach/pool. Sunblock and a layer of light clothing are essential. Use established tour companies for journeys into the jungle interior. There are few police outside Paramaribo, so independent travel is not advised. Even in Paramaribo, the Palm Garden area is best avoided because of the threat of robbery and other illegal activity, mainly prostitution. PHOTOGRAPHY: Avoid public, police and military subjects. Seek permission before taking.

Swaziland

CAPITAL: Mbabane

GMT +2

FROM UK: 00268. OUTGOING CODE TO UK: 0044 Most international calls must go through the operator.

Not present.

Kingdom of Swaziland High Commission, 20 Buckingham Gate, London SW1E 6LB. Tel: 020 7630 6611. Fax: 020 7630 6564. Ministry of Tourism www.mintour.gov.sz/

British High Commission, 2nd floor, Lilunga House, Gilfillan Street, Mbabane, Swaziland. Tel: 404 2581 Fax: 404 2585. bhc@realnet.co.sz

No tourist office in UK. See www.sntc.org.sz/tourism/toursd.html

Swaziland National Trust Commission, PO Box 100, Lobamba, Swaziland. Tel: 00268 416 1481; Fax: 00268 416 1875. www.sntc.org.sz/tourism/toursntc.html

Valid passport required.

Visa not required by British passport holders and Commonwealth citizens. Visitors are given a 14-day entry permit on arrival at the border.

Duty-free for married couples is restricted to one quota.

Departure tax is E20, payable in local currency.

POLIO, TYPHOID: R. MALARIA: Exists throughout the year in lowland areas, in the falciparum variety. Resistance to chloroquine has been reported. YELLOW FEVER: A vaccination certificate is required for travellers arriving from infected areas. OTHER: Bilharzia, meningitis, rabies, cholera. HIV/AIDS is highly prevalent.

W1

Lilangeni (E) = 100 cents. South African Rand is also accepted as legal tender. Major credit cards are gaining acceptance at hotels, larger restaurants and other tourist businesses. Travellers cheques are accepted at banks. ATM AVAILABILITY: Some banks have ATMs; they accept only some credit cards.

MONEYGRAM: Unavailable.
WESTERN UNION: Unavailable

AMEX: 0044 1273 696 933
DINERS CLUB: 0044 1252 513 500
MASTERCARD: 001 314 542 7111
VISA: 001 410 581 9994

AMEX: 0044 1273 571 600
THOMAS COOK: 001733 318950
VISA: 0044 20 7937 8091

0830–1430 Mon to Fri, 0830–1100 Sat.

Hotels and recreational facilities in the Holiday Valley complex in Ezulwini is expensive, but there is plenty of moderate and cheap accommodation all over the kingdom.

English and Siswati.

Weather can be changeable due to the high altitude. Lowlands are the hottest and the higher lands have the most rain between Oct-Mar.

Christian and Animist minority.

Jan 1, Apr 25, Jul 22, Sep 6, Dec 25, 26. Easter, Ascension Day, Reed Dance Day (end Aug/early Sep).

20 volts AC, 50 Hz Plugs = 15amp round pin.

Up to 2 weeks.

A patriarchal and tribal culture prevails. Traditional ceremonies involve men and women dancing together in celebration of their spiritual relationship to the King.

ROADS: Generally in good condition in towns. 4 x 4 vehicles are needed to explore off-road trails outside the nature reserves. Watch out for wildlife straying on to roads. There are good road links to cities in South Africa. Traffic drives on the left. BUS: Numerous buses connect various parts of the country some of which are non-stop. There are bus services to Durban, Cape Town and Jo'burg, and to Maputo. Minibus taxis run a regular service between Mbabane and Jo'burg. CAR HIRE: A number of companies operate. DOCUMENTATION: National driving licences are valid for up to 6 months, provided they are printed in English. IDP is recognised.

Do not camp near houses without being granted permission from the village chief. PHOTOGRAPHY: Permission should be asked. Photos of national buildings and the royal family are prohibited.

CAPITAL: Stockholm

GMT +1 (GMT +2 during the summer).

FROM UK: 0046. OUTGOING CODE TO UK: 0044.

All services: 90 000/112.

Royal Swedish Embassy, 11 Montagu Place, London W1H 2AL. Tel 020 7917 6400. Fax 020 7724 4174. embassy@swednet.net www.swednet.org.uk/embassy

British Embassy, PO Box 27819, Skarpögatan 6-8, 115 93 Stockholm, Sweden. Tel 0046 8671 3000. Fax: 0046 8662 9989. britishembassy@telia.com www.britishembassy.com

Consulates in Gothenburg, Malmö, Luleå and Sundsvall.

Swedish Travel and Tourism Council, 11 Montagu Place, London W1H 2AL. Tel: 020 7870 5600; Fax: 020 7724 5872. info@swetourism.org.uk www.gosweden.org

Swedish Travel and Tourism Council, PO Box 3030, 103 61 Stockholm, Sweden. Tel: (8) 725 5500. Fax (8) 725 5531. Stockholm Information Service, www.stockholmtown.com

Valid passport required: Not required by EU citizens holding a valid national ID card.

Visa not required by nationals of EU countries.

Most meat and dairy products, plants, eggs and endangered species.

Skr14 is payable on international departures.

Risk of tick-borne encephalitis, especially in coastal areas.

Swedish Krone (Skr) = 100 øre. Personal cheques can be cashed in Swedish banks through the Eurocheque system. All major credit cards are accepted. Travellers cheques, preferably in US$, are widely accepted. ATM AVAILABILITY: Over 2000 locations.

MONEYGRAM: 009 800 66639472.
WESTERN UNION: 020 741 742.

AMEX: 0044 1273 696933
DINERS CLUB: 08 146 878
MASTERCARD: 020 791 324
VISA: 020 793 146

AMEX: 020 795 155
THOMAS COOK: 020 795 110
VISA: 020 793 108

Generally 0930–1500 Mon to Fri but in many large cities banks close at 1800.

Expensive – similar to other Scandinavian countries.

Swedish. Lapp and English are also spoken.

The climate is mild, which varies according to its great length. Summers can be very hot but get shorter further north. The midnight sun can be seen between mid- May and mid-June above the Arctic circle. Winters can be bitterly cold particularly in the North.

Swedish State Church (Evangelical Lutheran). Other Protestant minorities.

Jan 1, 5, 6, Apr 30, May 1, Jun 6, 19, Nov 1, Dec 24, 25, 26, 31. Easter, Ascension Day, Whitsun.

220 volts 3 phase AC, 50 Hz. 2-pin plugs are used.

3–4 days. Poste restante is widely available.

There is little inequality between men and women, and few problems should be encountered.

RAIL: There is an extensive rail network, denser in the south. Scanrail cards give you the freedom of the rail network. The new Öresund Bridge links Malmö and the resorts of southern Sweden directly with Copenhagen. ROAD: Sweden's roads are well maintained and relatively uncrowded. Seat belts are compulsory. BUS: Cheap and efficient services are available to all towns. TAXI: Available in all towns and airports. CAR HIRE: Available in most towns and cities.

Normal social courtesies should be observed. Casual dress is acceptable for social occasions. Sweden is regarded as one of the safest countries in the world and crimes against foreigners are rare, but sensible precautions should be taken to prevent petty theft, such as from bags and pockets in crowded places.

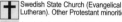

CAPITAL: Bern

GMT +1 (GMT +2 during the summer).

FROM UK: 0041. OUTGOING CODE TO UK: 0044

Ambulance : 144. Police : 117. Fire : 118.

Embassy of the Swiss Confederation, 16-18 Montagu Place, London W1H 2BQ. Tel: 020 7616 6000; Visa Enquiry line: 0906 833 1313 (Premium rate). vertretung@lon.rep.admin.ch www.swissembassy.org.uk

British Embassy, Thunstrasse 50, 3005 Bern. Tel: 0041 31 359 7741 (Consular); Fax: 0041 31 359 7765. info@britain-in-switzerland.ch www.britain-in-switzerland.ch/index2.htm (Geneva) British Consulate-General, 37-39 rue de Vermont (6th Floor), 1211 Geneva 20. Tel: (0041) 22 918 2400; Fax (0041) 22 918 2322.

Switzerland Travel Centre, Swiss Centre, 10 Wardour Street, London W1D 6QF. Tel: 020 7734 1921. Freephone: 00800 100 200 30; Fax: 020 7437 4577; Free fax: 00800 100 200 31. stc@stlondon.com

National Tourist Office, Bellariastrasse 38, CH-8027 Zürich. Tel: (1) 288 1111. Fax: (1) 288 1205.

Passport required, valid for 6 months after intended period of stay.

Visa not required by EU citizens.

All meat products.

Sfr15, inclusive of ticket price.

Swiss Franc (Sfr) = 100 rappen or centimes. Exch: Eurocheques are accepted. Major credit cards are accepted. Travellers cheques are accepted at airports, railway stations and banks. Cheques in Swiss francs are preferred. ATM AVAILABILITY: Over 4000 locations.

MONEYGRAM: 0 800 89 5973.
WESTERN UNION: 0512 22 33 58.

AMEX: 0044 1273 696 933
DINERS CLUB: 01 835 4444
MASTERCARD: 0800 89 7092
VISA: 0800 89 2733

AMEX: 0044 1273 571 600
THOMAS COOK: 0800 55 0130
VISA: 0800 55 8450

0830–1630 Mon to Fri.

Relatively expensive. Prices vary according to popularity of the resort.

Mostly German in Central and Eastern parts. French in the West, some Italian in the South. Raeto-Romansch is spoken in the south-east by 1%. English is spoken by many.

Climate varies throughout Switzerland. The Alpine regions tend to be cooler. The lower land of the northern areas has higher temperatures and warmer summers.

Roman Catholic and Protestant.

Jan 1, 2, Aug 1, Mar 1, May 1, Jun 23, Aug 1, 15, Nov 1, Dec 8, 25, 26, 31. Easter, Ascension Day, Whitsun. Local holidays in Cantons.

220 volts AC, 50 Hz.

3 days. Poste restante facilities available at post offices.

The independence of lone women travellers is respected and few problems are likely to be encountered.

ROAD: Road quality is generally good but mountain roads can be narrow and winding. Many are closed during the winter because of poor conditions. In some areas snow chains are required in winter. Road travel can be more hazardous during holiday periods because of the increased volume of traffic. RAIL: Excellent services, often more efficient than driving. Cheap fares are available through the Swiss Pass and leaflets and timetables are available from the railway company. BUS: Postal motor coaches provide services to even the remotest villages but few long-distance coaches are permitted to operate. TAXI: All taxis are metered although it is advisable to agree the fare in advance. CAR HIRE: All the major companies are present. DOCUMENTATION: A national driving licence is sufficient. Green card is recommended.

This is a very law-abiding nation. Dropping litter can cause offence. The medical form E111 is not valid in Switzerland, nor is travel insurance designed specifically for EU countries. Skiers should note that mountain rescue can be expensive and winter sports premiums may need to be paid for adequate insurance cover.

Syrian Arab Republic

CAPITAL: Damascus

GMT +2 (GMT +3 during the summer).

FROM UK: 00963. OUTGOING CODE TO UK: 0044

Contact hotel operator.

Embassy of the Syrian Arab Republic, 8 Belgrave Square, London SW1X 8PH. Tel: 020 7245 9012. Fax: 020 7235 4621.

British Embassy, Kotob Building, 11 Mohammad Kurd Ali Street, Malki (PO Box 37), Damascus, Syria. Tel: 00963 11 373 9241; Fax: 00963 11 373 1600. Consulate in Aleppo.

No tourist office in UK.
See www.syriatourism.org/

Tourist Information Bureau, rue du 29 Mai, Damascus. Tel: 2222 388, and at Damascus Airport.

Valid passport required. It must not contain any indication of a prior visit to Israel or an Israel–Jordan border crossing.

Visa required. It must be obtained in advance.

All gold jewellery must be declared on arrival. Restrictions apply to the import of alcohol, tobacco, cheese, pharmaceuticals, cosmetics, electrical appliances and modems. It is wise to declare anything contentious and get the Customs to write them down on a page in your passport.

S£200, payable in local currency. Transit passengers are exempt.

MALARIA: Exists in the vivax variety in tiny pockets of the northern border areas May–Oct. YELLOW FEVER: A vaccination certificate is required from passengers arriving from infected areas. OTHER: Bilharzia, visceral leishmaniasis and hepatitis A and B.

W2. Tap water in towns and cities is safe to drink.

Syrian Pound (S£) = 100 piastres. NOTE: The export of local currency is prohibited. Travellers should declare all foreign currency in their possession on arrival. It is illegal to change money on the street or black market. Credit cards are accepted at larger hotels and car hire companies but not widely in shops. Foreign currency and travellers cheques can be exchanged at Damascus Airport, at the frontier posts, in the larger hotels and at banks. ATM AVAILABILITY: Unavailable.

MONEYGRAM: Unavailable.
WESTERN UNION: Unavailable.

AMEX: 0044 1273 696 933
DINERS CLUB: 0044 1252 513 500
MASTERCARD: 001 314 542 7111
VISA: 001 410 581 9994

AMEX: 0044 1273 571 600
THOMAS COOK: 001733 318950
VISA: 0044 20 7937 8091

0800–1400 Sat to Thur (banks tend to close early on Thursday).

Can be expensive in the high season, especially in Damascus. Savings can be made by purchasing local food from the markets.

Arabic. French and English may also be spoken.

Summers are hot and dry; nights are often cool. Sandstorms can be a hazard. Winter is cold, with snow occasionally in Damascus and in the Euphrates and Khabur valleys.

Mostly Muslim. Christian (mainly Greek Orthodox and Greek Catholic).

Jan 1, Feb 22, Mar 8, 21, Apr 17, May 1, 6, Oct 6, Dec 25. Islamic festivals, Easter.

220 volts AC, 50 Hz.

Up to 1 week. Parcels sent from Syria should be packed at the post office.

Muslim customs apply. Modest dress is recommended at all times. Wearing a wedding ring will make one appear more respectable. If rude remarks are made it is advisable to ignore them and make no eye contact.

ROAD: Well over half the roads are tarred. Those that aren't are unsuitable for the wet season. There are motorways to Beirut and into Jordan and a modern highway runs from Palmyra to Damascus across the desert. The Ministry of Tourism has produced a road map of Syria which is more up to date than those published in Europe. BUS: Orange and white air-conditioned buses serve terminals in city centres. Seats must be booked in advance. TAXIS: Shared taxis operate and are available to all parts of the country. DOCUMENTATION: IDP required. Insurance is required by law.

Syrian Arab Republic

! Syria is one of the safest places to travel in and most people are friendly and hospitable, but travellers should keep informed about the situation in the Middle East generally. Entry into Syria is not allowed by the land border with Israel. You may be asked for identification at any time by officials, so it's wise to carry your passport or national ID card at all times. Beachwear should not be worn away from the pool or beach. Conservative casual clothes are suitable. Shoes must be removed before entering a mosque and it is forbidden to pass beyond the ikonostasis in an Orthodox church. Laws concerning illegal drugs are severe; anyone convicted in Syria for growing, processing, or smuggling drugs faces the death penalty, which may be reduced to a minimum of 20 years imprisonment. PHOTOGRAPHY: Ensure you do not photograph anything connected with the military.

Tahiti (French Polynesia)

CAPITAL: Papeete

Ranges from GMT –9 to –10, depending on the island.

FROM UK: 00689. OUTGOING CODE TO UK: 0044 (operator's assistance may be required.)

Dial operator.

Refer to French Embassy. Tahiti is a French overseas territory.

Routine consular matters are covered by the British Consulate-General in Paris. In an emergency, contact the Honorary British Consul in French Polynesia, Proprete Boubee, Route Tuterai Tane, Pirae Tane, Pirae-Tahiti, BP 1064, 98714 Papeete. Tel: 00689 419841; Fax: 00689 412700).

Tahiti Tourisme, 1 Battersea Church Road, London SW11 3LY. Tel: 020 7771 7023; Fax: 020 7771 7181. tahiti@cibgroup.co.uk www.tahiti-tourisme.com/

Tahiti Tourisme Paofai Building, Entry D, Pomare Boulevard, Postal Address: PO Box 65, Papeete, Tahiti. Tel: 505 700 or 505 703. Fax: 436 619. tahiti-tourisme@mail.pf www.tahiti-tourisme.com

Valid passport required: See France.

Visa not required.

Plants, cats, dogs and dangerous goods. Baggage from Brazil, Samoa and Fiji will be fumigated, allow at least 2 hours.

CFP Fr 920, payable in local currency.

See France.

POLIO, TYPHOID: R. YELLOW FEVER: A vaccination certificate is required for those over 1 year old arriving from infected areas.

W2

French Pacific Franc (CFP Fr) = 100 centimes. Exchange facilities are available at the airport, major banks and authorised hotels and shops. Amex is the most widely accepted credit card, while others have only limited acceptance. Travellers cheques are accepted, in any international currency. ATM AVAILABILITY: 11 locations.

MONEYGRAM: Unavailable.
WESTERN UNION: Unavailable.

AMEX: 0044 1273 696 933
DINERS CLUB: 0044 1252 513 500
MASTERCARD: 001 314 542 7111
VISA: 001 410 581 9994

AMEX: 0044 1273 571 600
THOMAS COOK: 001733 318950
VISA: 0044 20 7937 8091

0745–1530 Mon to Fri.

Caters for all types of budgets. Accommodation ranges from hotels to thatched-roof bungalows.

Tahitian and French. English and other Polynesian languages are spoken.

Hot and wet Dec-Feb. Cool and dry Mar-Nov.

Protestant and Roman Catholic.

Jan 1, Mar 5, May 1, Jul 14, Aug 15, Sep 8, Nov 1, 11, Dec 25. Easter, Ascension Day, Whitsun. Chinese New Year.

110/220 volts AC, 50 Hz.

Up to 2 weeks by airmail to Western Europe.

Local women wear traditional dress in bright pareos, reflecting the country's history.

FLIGHTS: Domestic flights connect Tahiti with neighbouring islands, which make up French Polynesia. SEA: Daily connections to neighbouring islands can be made. ROAD: BUS: Basic buses offer an inexpensive service, no schedule is operated. CAR HIRE: Major and local agencies rent cars in the main islands. DOCUMENTATION: National driving licence will be sufficient.

French Polynesia comprises 130 islands divided into 5 archipelagos, Tahiti being the most popular. Tipping is not practised. The medical form E111 does not provide any health cover in French Polynesia. Visitors should have full travel and medical insurance.

CAPITAL: Taipei

GMT +8

FROM UK: 00886. OUTGOING CODE TO UK: 00244

Police: 110 (in Chinese only)

Taipei Representative Office in the UK, 50 Grosvenor Gardens, London SW1 0EB. Tel: 020 7396 9152. Fax: 020 7396 9145. Visa information line: 0900 160 0315 (premium rate).

Refer to Representative Office.

Tourism Bureau of the Republic of China, 9th Fl, 280 Jungshiau E Road, Section 4, Taipei 106, Taiwan, ROC. Tel: 00886 2 2349 1635; Fax: 00886 2 2773 5487.
tbroc@tbroc.gov.tw www.tbroc.gov.tw/

Passport required, valid for 6 months. Visitors must have a return or onward travel ticket.

Visa not required by UK nationals of previous good character for stays of 14 days or less.

Canned meat products. Toy pistols and gambling articles.

NT$300 is levied on international departures, payable in local currency. Children under 2 years and transit passengers are exempt.

Passengers holding passports issued by the People's Republic of China.

POLIO, TYPHOID: R. YELLOW FEVER: Vaccination certificate required if arriving from an infected area. OTHER: Cholera, rabies.

W1

New Taiwan Dollar (NT$) = 100 cents. Import and export of local currency is limited to NT$ 40000. All exchange receipts must be retained. Export of foreign currency is limited to the equivalent of US$ 5000 for passengers leaving within 6 months of arrival. Credit cards and travellers cheques are widely accepted: US$ are the preferred currency. ATM AVAILABILITY: Over 1400 locations.

MONEYGRAM: 0080 10 3678.
WESTERN UNION: Unavailable.

AMEX: 0044 1273 696933
DINERS CLUB: 0044 1252 513 500
MASTERCARD: 0800 10 3400
VISA: 001 410 581 9994

AMEX: 0044 1273 571 600
THOMAS COOK: 0044 1733 318950
VISA: 0044 20 7937 8091

0900–1530 Mon to Fri, 0900–1230 Sat.

It is possible to live relatively cheaply by shopping at markets. Good quality, cheap accommodation may be more difficult to find.

Mandarin (Chinese), English and Japanese.

Subtropical climate with moderate temperatures in the North where there is a winter season. June-Oct is the typhoon season.

Buddhism, Taoism, Christianity, (Roman Catholic and Protestant) and Muslim.

Jan 1, 2, 3, Mar 29, May 30, Jul 1, Sep 28, Oct 5, 10, Nov 12. Chinese festivals.

110 volts AC, 60 Hz.

Up to 10 days.

A patriarchal culture prevails. Women play a traditional role in society.

ROAD: Some roads in central and southern Taiwan, including the cross-island highway, have been blocked by landslides after an earthquake in 1999. Check local conditions before setting out on road journeys, especially after typhoons or rainstorms, as some roads also become impassable because of mudslides. BUS: Local and long-distance bus services operate, and are generally safe. TAXI: There are many inexpensive taxis, but beware of drivers. Women should exercise caution when travelling alone in taxis late at night. DOCUMENTATION: IDP is required.

Taiwan has had thousands of tremors since a major earthquake in September 1999. In the event of an emergency or an approaching typhoon, warnings are broadcast in English on the International Community Radio Taipei (ICRT), FM 100.7. There are very good medical facilities in Taiwan, but doctors expect to be paid immediately for treatment.

Taiwan is sensitive to political discussions regarding neighbouring China, but is still heavily influenced by Chinese culture. It has adopted Western free-market practices and tourism facilities are well developed and expanding. Be cautious about going into massage parlours, illicit nightclubs and illegal barbershops, all fronts for criminal activities.

Tajikistan

CAPITAL: Dushanbe

GMT +5.

FROM UK: 007 (then 3772 for Dushanbe). OUTGOING CODE TO UK: 8/10 (wait for second dial tone). International calls may require operator assistance.

Honorary Consulate of Tajikistan, 33 Ovington Square, London SW3 1LJ. Tel: 020 7584 5111.

The British Embassy is in Tashkent, Uzbekistan. Tel: 00998 71 120 6288; Fax: 00998 71 120 6549. Brit@emb.uz

Intourist, Intourist House, 219 Marsh Wall, Isle of Dogs, London E14 9PD. Tel: 020 7538 8600. Fax: 020 7538 5967. Also see www.traveltajikistan.com/

Intourist Tajikistan, c/o Hotel Tajikistan, ulitsa Shotemur 22, Dushanbe 734001, Tajikistan. Tel: (3772) 274 973. Fax: (3772) 275 155.

Valid passport required: 10-year passport valid for at least 6 months prior to departure.

Visa required. Visa also required for overland re-entry to neighbouring countries, Russia, Kazakhstan or Uzbekistan.

All valuable items and foreign currency should be declared on arrival.

US$10 is levied on all foreign travellers.

POLIO, TYPHOID: R. MALARIA: Reports have indicated there may be a risk of malaria near the southern border, in the vivax variety. OTHER: There is a diphtheria epidemic. Cholera and rabies are also present. NOTE: Medical advice should be sought before travelling bearing in mind the potential medical risk when travelling in Tajikistan.

W1

Rouble. EXCHANGE: The preferred hard currency is the US$, although others are acceptable. All bills are usually settled in cash. Import of local currency is prohibited. Visa has limited acceptance in some hotels in the capital. Travellers cheques are not accepted. ATM AVAILABILITY: Unavailable.

MONEYGRAM: Unavailable.
WESTERN UNION: Unavailable.

AMEX: 0044 1273 696 933
DINERS CLUB: 0044 1252 513 500
MASTERCARD: 001 314 542 7111
VISA: 001 410 581 9994

AMEX: 0044 1273 571 600
THOMAS COOK: 001733 318950
VISA: 0044 20 7937 8091

0900–1730 Mon to Fri. Closed Sat.

High inflation has resulted in lower prices.

Tajik. Russian and English (by those involved in tourism) are also spoken.

Temperatures vary between 12ºC min in the winter to 45ºC max in the summer.

Mainly Sunni Muslim with a large Ishmaeli minority and a smaller Russian Orthodox minority.

Jan 1, Feb 23, Mar 8, 20–22, May 1, 9, Sep 9. Some Islamic festivals.

220 volts AC, 50 Hz.

Mail can take anything between two weeks and two months to reach Western Europe or the USA.

A conservative society prevails in accordance with religious beliefs. Be vigilant and dress down. Shorts are rarely seen and if worn by females are likely to create unwanted attention from local men.

ROAD: In poor weather conditions the roads are mainly impassable. During winter the roads from the capital are often closed because of snow. TAXI: Agree the fare in advance and use the old and new street names, which have been created since independence. Officially marked taxis are safe but avoid sharing with strangers. BUS: There are services between the major towns when the roads are open. DOCUMENTATION: IDP and insurance are required.

Tajikistan is a small, mountainous republic in central Asia. It is recovering from civil war in the 1990s. The situation remains unstable, with conflict between government forces and armed opposition. The FCO advises against all travel to the central mountains and the border areas. Outbursts of fighting continue and the potential for terrorist incidents continue to exist. As a precaution, foreigners living in Dushanbe have imposed a voluntary curfew from 0200 to 0700. Travellers are advised to check local conditions with the German Embassy. Do not travel alone or on foot after dark. It is unwise to travel out of Dushanbe or Khojand unless with persons from an international organisation.

Tanzania

CAPITAL: Dodoma

GMT +3

FROM UK: 00255. OUTGOING CODE TO UK: 0044 International calls may require operator assistance.

Not present.

High Commission for the United Republic of Tanzania, 43 Hertford Street, London, W1Y 8DB. Tel 020 7499 8951. Fax: 020 7491 9321. tanzarep@tanzania-online.gov.uk www.tanzania-online.gov.uk

British High Commission, PO Box 9200, Social Security House, Samor Avenue, Dar-es-Salaam, Tanzania. Tel: 00255 51 117659; Fax: 00225 51 112952. bhc.dar@dar.mail.fco.gov.uk

No tourist office in UK. See www.tanzania-online.gov.uk/tourism/tourism.html and TTC web site.

Tanzania Tourist Corporation, IPS Building, PO Box 2485, Dar-es-Salaam, Tanzania. Tel: 00255 51 26680; Fax: 00255 51 46780. 100711.3161@compuserve.com www.tanzania-web.com/

Zanzibar Tourism Commission, PO Box 1410, Zanzibar, Tanzania. Tel: 00255 (0) 54 233485/6; Fax: 00255 (0) 54 23344. zanzibartourism@zanzibartourism.net

Valid passport required

Visa required in advance of arrival. Visa application form can be downloaded from the Tanzania High Commission's website.

Narcotics.

US$20. Transit passengers and those under two years of age are exempt.

POLIO, TYPHOID: R. MALARIA: Exists all year round throughout the country in the falciparum variety. High resistance to chloroquine has been reported. YELLOW FEVER: Vaccination certificate required for all travellers over 1 year old travelling from infected countries. OTHER: Bilharzia, rabies.

W1

Tanzanian Shilling (Tsc) = 100 cents. Currency can be exchanged at banks, authorised hotels or bureaux de change Credit cards are accepted by top tourist hotels around the country. Visitors are expected to pay their expenses in hard currency. Travellers cheques, in Pounds sterling, US$ or Rand, are accepted. ATM AVAILABILITY: Unavailable.

MONEYGRAM: Unavailable.
WESTERN UNION: 51 382 12

AMEX: 0044 1273 696 933
DINERS CLUB: 0044 1252 513 500
MASTERCARD: 001 314 542 7111
VISA: 001 410 581 9994

AMEX: 0044 1273 571 600
THOMAS COOK: 001733 318950
VISA: 0044 20 7937 8091

0830–1600 Mon to Fri, 0830–1300 Sat.

Hotels and accommodation generally are expensive.

Swahili and English. Other languages are also spoken.

Tropical climate. The rainy season is Mar–May along the coast. Highlands rainy season is from Nov–Dec and Feb–May. Cooler season: Jun–May. The best time to visit Tanzania is between June and March.

Muslim, Hindu, Christian, and traditional beliefs.

Jan 1, 12, Feb 5, Apr 26, May 1, Jul 7, Aug 8, Dec 9, 25, 26. Easter. Islamic festivals.

240 volts AC, 50 Hz. Plugs are British-style.

5 days by airmail to Europe.

Zanzibar is a predominantly Muslim society. Women should dress appropriately, especially in Stone Town. Risk of sexual attack when walking alone on quiet beaches.

FLIGHTS: Air Tanzania runs regular flights between the main towns. RAIL: Regular trains run between the main cities. ROADS: The road network is good, although the rainy season makes minor roads impassable. It is inadvisable to drive at night because of the wild animals. There are often petrol shortages and a lack of spare parts. The country is best explored in a 4 x 4 vehicle. CAR HIRE: Companies operate but are very expensive. DOCUMENTATION: IDP is recommended.

Tourism is a growing industry. Petty crime is common. Travellers should avoid border areas and refugee camps.

CAPITAL: Bangkok

GMT +7.

FROM UK: 0066. OUTGOING CODE TO UK: 001

Royal Thai Embassy, 29-30 Queens Gate, London SW7 5JP. Tel: 020 7589 2944; 24-hour Visa information line: 0900 160 0150 (premium rate). Fax: 020 7823 9695.

British Embassy, Wireless Road, Bangkok 10330, Thailand. Tel: 0066 2 305 8333; Fax 0066 2 255 8619 or 255 6051. britemb@loxinfo.co.th; www.britishemb.or.th/

Honorary Consulate at Chiang Mai. Tel: 053 263015. ukconsul@loxinfo.co.th

Tourism Authority of Thailand, 49 Albermarle Street, London W1X 3FE. Tel: 0906 364 066.

Tourism Authority of Thailand, 372 Bamrung Muang Road, Bangkok 10100. Tel: 0066 2 226 0060. Fax 0066 2 224 6221. www.tat.or.th

Valid passport required.Visitors must possess a return or onward travel ticket.

Check current regulations with your consulate prior to travel.

Images of Buddha and articles of historical value cannot be exported.

Bt500 for all passengers above 2 years old and not in immediate transit.

POLIO, TYPHOID: R. MALARIA: Exists in the falciparum variety in rural areas throughout the year. Resistance to chloroquine has been reported. YELLOW FEVER: Vaccination certificate is required by those over 1 year of age arriving from infected areas. OTHER: Cholera, Japanese encephalitis, rabies, dengue fever, dysentery, hepatitis A and E.

W1

Baht (Bt) = 100 satang. Export of local currency is limited to Bt 50000. All credit cards accepted. Travellers cheques, preferably in US$ or Pounds sterling, accepted in large hotels and shops. ATM AVAILABILITY: Over 2300 locations.

MONEYGRAM: 001 800 12 066 0542
WESTERN UNION: (02) 254 9161.

AMEX: 0044 1273 696 933
DINERS CLUB: 02 232 41 00 or 02 232 36 60
MASTERCARD: 001 800 11 887 0663
VISA: 001 410 581 9994

AMEX: 0044 1273 571 600
THOMAS COOK: 001733 318950
VISA: 001 800 11 342 0662

0830–1530 Mon to Fri.

Relatively inexpensive, especially outside Bangkok.

Thai. English, Malay and Chinese are also spoken.

Generally hot, particularly mid Feb–Jun. The monsoon season is mid May–Oct. The most comfortable time for travelling is Nov–Feb.

Buddhism. Muslim and Christian minorities.

Jan 1, Feb 11, Apr 6, 13-16, May 1, 5, 11, Jul 1, 9, Aug 12, Oct 23, Dec 7, 10, 31. Buddhist festivals. Chinese New Year.

220 volts AC, 50 Hz. A variety of plugs are used.

Up to 1 week.

Be vigilant if travelling alone. It may be advisable to travel around Thailand with a companion.

FLIGHTS: There are services between main towns. ROAD: A reasonable network – all the major roads are paved. DOCUMENTATION: IDP required. BUS: Very cheap but very crowded. There is a good bus service between the airport and Bangkok city. Otherwise use only airport limousines or official taxis. Privately owned buses are more comfortable and moderately priced. When taking the bus in the city, leave the back seat free for the Saffron-robed monks. BOAT: Good services. Get a good map, as finding your way around can be confusing.

The Thai/Burmese border area is unstable, and travellers should get advice before setting out. There are only two legal crossing points into Cambodia overland. The possession of even small quantities of illegal drugs can lead to long prison terms: tourists should be vigilant of any packages or gifts given. The monarchy and religion are sacred: insults to either, such as climbing on statues of Buddha, are not tolerated. Beachwear should be confined to the beach/pool. Shoes should be removed before entering houses. Discretion should be used and permission obtained before taking photos. Do not hand over your passport, even to hotel reception or car hire firms. Theft of passports is common. Avoid black-market jewellery salesmen.

Togo

GMT

FROM UK: 00228 OUTGOING CODE TO UK: 0044

Not present.

No embassy in the UK. EUROPE: Embassy of the Republic of Togo, 8 rue Alfred Roll, 75017 Paris, France. Tel: 0033 1 42 80 12 13. Fax: 0033 1 43 80 90 71.

The British Embassy in Accra deals with routine consular matters. In emergency, contact the British Honorary Consulate, BP 20050, British School of Lomé, Lomé, Togo. Tel: (00228) 264606; Fax: (00228) 264989. admin@bst.tg

No tourist office in UK. See www.afrika.com/togo/

Direction des Professions Touristiques, BP 1289, Lomé, Togo. Tel 215 662. Fax: 218 927.

Valid passport required.

Visa required in advance of arrival in Togo.

Narcotics.

POLIO, TYPHOID: R. MALARIA: Exists throughout the year in the falciparum variety reported to be highly resistant to chloroquine. YELLOW FEVER: Vaccination certificate required if the visitor has been to an infected country. OTHER: Bilharzia, cholera, meningitis, rabies.

W1

CFA Franc (CFA Fr) = 100 Centimes. Amex is widely accepted, but all other credit cards are unacceptable. Travellers cheques are only accepted in the capital city, The preferred currency is French Francs. ATM AVAILABILITY: Unavailable.

MONEYGRAM: Unavailable.
WESTERN UNION: (228) 21 6411.

AMEX: 0044 1273 696 933
DINERS CLUB: 02 232 41 00 or 02 232 36 60
MASTERCARD: 001 800 11 887 0663
VISA: 001 410 581 9994

AMEX: 0044 1273 571 600
THOMAS COOK: 001733 318950
VISA: 001 800 11 342 0662

0800–1600 Mon to Fri.

Hotels are of international standard, but accommodation in general is in short supply. Consequently prices are high.

French and local African languages. English is spoken very little.

Rainy season: Apr–Jun. Hottest months: Feb–Mar. Short rains: Oct–Nov.

Mainly Animist, Christian and Muslim.

Jan 1, 13, 24, Apr 27, May 1, Jun 21, Aug 15, Dec 25.

220 volts AC, 50Hz single phase. Plugs are square or round 2 pin.

Up to 2 weeks by airmail to Europe. Postal facilities are limited to the main towns. Post restante is available and very reliable

FLIGHTS: Air Togo runs flights to the main cities. ROAD: Are generally impassable during the rainy season. RAIL: Services operate between Lomé and main cities. BUS/TAXI: Most are efficient and cheap. CAR HIRE: Available in Lomé. Overland travel outside the towns, is best done in a 4 x 4 vehicle. DOCUMENTATION: IDP is required. If it is necessary to travel at night, go out in a convoy of at least two cars. Visitors should stop at all checkpoints upon request, and expect frequent identity checks. Tourism facilities are non-existent outside Lomé.

Beachwear to be worn only at the pool/beach. Voodoo is still practised in some areas, which also serve the tourist industry. Theft and harassment of foreigners, particularly women, is common on the beach and in the market areas of Lomé. An occasional method of extorting money from foreigners is to stage a mock road accident. Motor cyclists cut in front of cars and cause a minor collision, which draws a crowd that can turn nasty when you try to get on your way. Parts of Togo can be affected by political and military conflict in neighbouring states, particularly Sierra Leone.

CAPITAL: Nuku'alofa

GMT +13

FROM UK: 00676. OUTGOING CODE TO UK: 0044

All services: 911.

Tonga High Commission, 36 Molyneux Street, London, W1H 6AB. Tel: 020 7724 5828. Fax: 020 7723 9074. fetu@btinternet.com

British High Commission, PO Box 56, Vuna Road, Nuku'alofa, Tonga. Tel: 21020/1. Fax: 24109. britcomt@kalianet.to

South Pacific Tourism Organisation / SPTO UK, Postal address: 48 Glentham Road, Barnes, London. SW13 9JJ. Tel: 020 8741 6082; Fax: 020 8741 6107. spto@iiuk.co.uk www.spto.org

Tonga Visitor's Bureau, PO Box 37, Vuna Road, Nuku'alofa, Tonga. Tel: 00676 21 733; Fax: 00676 22 129. tonga@value.net www.vacations.tvb.gov.to.

Valid passport required. Visitors need to have a return or onward travel ticket and have proof of adequate funds for duration of stay.

Visa not required.

Arms, ammunition and pornography are prohibited. Birds, animals, fruit and plants are subject to quarantine regulations. Valuable artefacts and certain flora and fauna cannot be exported.

T$20, payable in local currency. Infants are exempt.

POLIO, TYPHOID: R. YELLOW FEVER: Vaccination certificate required if the visitor has been in an infected country.

W2 Tap water in towns is chlorinated and safe to drink.

Pa'anga (T$) = 100 seniti. Credit cards have limited use. Travellers cheques are accepted at some hotels and tourist shops. Australian dollar cheques are preferred. ATM AVAILABILITY: Unavailable.

MONEYGRAM: Unavailable.
WESTERN UNION: 24345.

AMEX: 0044 1273 696 933
DINERS CLUB: 02 232 41 00 or 02 232 36 60
MASTERCARD: 001 800 11 887 0663
VISA: 001 410 581 9994

AMEX: 0044 1273 571 600
THOMAS COOK: 001733 318950
VISA: 001 800 11 342 0662

0930–1530 Mon to Fri. 0830–1130 Sat.

Relatively cheap.

Tongan. English is spoken widely and used in meetings.

Marginally cooler than most tropical areas. The best time is May–Nov. Heavy rains occur between Dec and Mar.

Wesleyan Church, Roman Catholic, Anglican.

Jan 1, Apr 25, May 4, Jun 4, Jul 4, Nov 4, Dec 4, 25, 26. Easter.

240 volts AC, 50 Hz.

10 days.

Generally considered safe for women travellers, although the islanders may think it strange if a woman is travelling alone. Single women should avoid deserted beaches in the evenings. Women are often required to wear long dresses for evening functions

FLIGHTS: Royal Tongan Airlines operate regular flights between the main cities. SEA: Ferries sail between all the island groups. Schedules are subject to change according to demand and the weather. ROAD: A good network of metalled roads exists. Horses are often used. CAR HIRE: May be arranged through a number of agencies. DOCUMENTATION: A local licence is required from the police traffic department on production of a valid international or national driving licence, the fee and a passport. Minimum driving age is 18. Traffic drives on the left in Tonga. Wild animals and livestock wandering onto roads are a hazard to drivers, especially at night.

Shorts are not acceptable in towns. Casual wear is recommended for most occasions. Tonga law prohibits any person from appearing in a public place without a shirt. Visitors are not expected to tip. The crime rate is low, but sensible precautions should be taken to avoid petty theft in crowded places. The Tonga government is promoting tourism to contribute to the economy, which is based mainly on agriculture. The season for tropical cyclones is November to April. For weather information Tel: 23401.

Trinidad and Tobago

CAPITAL: Port of Spain

GMT –4

FROM UK: 001868. OUTGOING CODE TO UK: 01144.

Police: 9, Ambulance/Fire: 990

High Commission for the Republic of Trinidad and Tobago, 42 Belgrave Square, London SW1X 8NT. Tel: 020 7245 9351. Fax: 020 7823 1065. trintogov@tthc.demon.co.uk

British High Commission, PO Box 778, 19 St Clair Avenue, St Clair, Port of Spain, Trinidad. Tel: 622 2748. Fax: 622 4555. ppabhc@opus.co.tt

No tourist office in UK. See www.tidco.co.tt/

Tourism and Industry Development Corporation of Trinidad and Tobago (TIDCO), 10–14 Phillip Street, Port of Spain, Trinidad. Tel: 00868 623 6022; Fax 00868 624 8124. tourism-info@tidco.co.tt; www.tidco.co.tt/

Valid passport required. Visitors must have sufficient funds to cover their stay.

Visa not required by nationals of EU countries for stays not exceeding 3 months.

Forms of declaration of items must be completed on arrival.

TT$75, payable in local currency, is levied. Children under 5 years of age and passengers in transit are exempt.

POLIO, TYPHOID: R. YELLOW FEVER: A vaccination certificate is required from travellers over 1 year of age coming from infected areas. OTHER: Rabies, dengue fever in the wet season May–Dec. High prevalence of HIV/AIDS.

W2 Drinking water should be boiled or filtered.

Trinidad & Tobago Dollar (TT$) = 100 cents. EXCHANGE: Foreign currency can be exchanged only at authorised banks and some hotels. The export of local currency is limited to the amount declared on arrival. Both credit cards and travellers cheques are widely accepted. Any international currency is acceptable. ATM AVAILABILITY: Over 100 locations.

MONEYGRAM: 1 800 543 4080.
WESTERN UNION: 623 6000.

AMEX: 01144 1273 696 933
DINERS CLUB: 01144 1252 513 500
MASTERCARD: 1800 307 7309
VISA: 1800 847 2911

AMEX: 1800 828 0366
THOMAS COOK: 0111733 318950
VISA: 01144 20 7937 8091

0900–1400 Mon to Thur, 0900–1200 and 1500–1700 Fri.

Caters for all types of traveller whatever their budget.

English. French, Spanish, Hindi and Chinese are also spoken.

Tropical climate with cooling trade winds. Hottest June-Oct.

Roman Catholic, Hindu, Anglican, Muslim and Christian denomination minorities.

Jan 1, Feb 22, Mar 30, May 30, Jun 19, Aug 1, 31, Dec 25, 26. Carnival week before Lent, Easter, Corpus Christi, Eid Al Fitr, Diwali.

115-220 volts AC, 60 Hz. Continental 2 pin plugs are standard but variations may occur.

Up to 2 weeks

Women are influenced by a mixture of Calypso and Latin culture.

SEA: A regular passenger service operates between Port of Spain and Tobago. ROAD: The network of roads between major towns is good but traffic around Port of Spain can be difficult. Traffic drives on the left. BUS: Services operate in most towns. They are cheap but can become crowded. TAXI: Official taxis can be identified by 'H' symbol. Not all taxi fares are fixed rate, so it is advisable to find out the price before undertaking the journey. CAR HIRE: Available from the city or hotels. DOCUMENTATION: National driving licences are valid for 3 months. NOTE: Travel documents stating date of entrance to Tobago should be carried when driving. Front seat belts are compulsory.

Attacks on travellers, especially in Trinidad and around Port of Spain in Tobago, have risen over recent years. Take sensible precautions, do not carry large amounts of cash, and avoid deserted beaches and poorly lit areas if you go out at night. Topless sunbathing is not advised.

CAPITAL: Tunis

GMT +1

FROM UK: 00216. OUTGOING CODE TO UK: 0044

Embassy of the Republic of Tunisia, 29 Prince's Gate, London SW7 1QG. Tel: 020 7584 8117; Fax: 020 7225 2884.

British Embassy, Consular section, 141 Ave de la Liberté, Tunis. Tel: 00216 1 84 61 84, 79 33 22; Fax: 00261 1 792 644. british.emb@planet.tn; www.british-emb.intl.tn/

Tunisian National Tourist Office, 77a Wigmore Street, London W1H 9LJ. Tel: 020 7224 5561. Fax: 020 7224 4053. tntolondon@aol.com; www.tourismtunisia.com/

Office Nationale du Tourism Tunisien, 1 Ave Mohamed V, 1002 Tunis, Tunisia. Tel: (1) 341 077. Fax: (1) 350 997. info@tourism-tunisia.com

Valid passport required.

Visa required.

Obscene material and any material which may be regarded as dangerous to public security, health or morality, including non-Islamic religious materials.

POLIO, TYPHOID: R. YELLOW FEVER: Vaccination certificate required for visitors over 1 year old travelling from infected areas. OTHER: Rabies.

W1

Tunisian Dinar (TD) = 1000 millimes. EXCHANGE: All banks and most hotels (3-star and above). Export of local currency prohibited. Visitors are required to declare on entry any large amounts of money: this usually means anything over £500. Major credit cards, and travellers cheques in major international currencies, accepted in tourist areas. ATM AVAILABILITY: Over 35 locations.

MONEYGRAM: Unavailable.
WESTERN UNION: 1 34 07 33

AMEX: 01144 1273 696 933
DINERS CLUB: 01144 1252 513 500
MASTERCARD: 1800 307 7309
VISA: 1800 847 2911

AMEX: 01144 1273 571 600
THOMAS COOK: 0111733 318950
VISA: 01144 20 7937 8091

0830–1200 and 1300–1700 Mon to Fri.

Tourists can expect to pay more than locals but bargains can be found at the souks. Traditionally Tunisia has been considered inexpensive, but large hotels rates are now comparable with northern Mediterranean.

Arabic, English and French are widely spoken.

Warm climate throughout the year with higher temperatures inland which can be very hot. Winter has the highest rainfall.

Islam with Roman Catholic and Protestant minorities.

Jan 1, 18, Mar 20, 21, Apr 9, May 1, Jul 25, Aug 13, Sep 3, Oct 15, Nov 7. Islamic festivals.

220 volts AC, 50Hz. Plugs: 2-pin continental.

3-5 days airmail to Europe. Poste restante operates in the main cities.

Harassment of unaccompanied women is quite frequent and can be avoided by travelling in groups of two or three and dressing conservatively.

FLIGHTS: Regular daily domestic flights. ROAD: Extensive road network. The Garde Nationale will assist breakdowns free of charge. It is forbidden to drive in the Sahara without first contacting the Garde Nationale. Local drivers tend to ignore rules of the road unless there are police around. DOCUMENTATION: Log books, valid national driving licence and green cards are required. RAIL: Regular trains operate between Tunis and the major cities. Tickets not purchased before the journey will be at double the fare.

Dress can be informal but Islamic conventions must be respected when visiting religious monuments. PHOTOGRAPHY: Do not take photos of military installations or crowds of people. Visitors should avoid political-style gatherings, and take sensible precautions about their bags and pockets in crowded places. Tunisia tolerates non-Islamic religious practices, but do not get involved in activities that could be seen as trying to convert people to another faith. The FCO advises against travelling to the border with Algeria and to take advice from the Embassy about independent travel to the desert areas. Carry a photocopy of your passport for identification, and keep the passport securely in a hotel safe.

Turkey

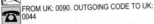

CAPITAL: Ankara

GMT +2 (GMT +3 during the summer).

FROM UK: 0090. OUTGOING CODE TO UK: 0044

Ambulance: 112, Fire: 111, Police: 155.

Embassy of the Republic of Turkey, 43 Belgrave Square, London SW1X 8PA. Tel: 020 7393 0202. info@turkishembassy-london.com; www.turkishembassy-london.com
Turkish Consulate-General, Rutland Lodge, Rutland Gardens, London SW7 1BW.

British Embassy, Ersan Caddesi 46A, Cankaya, Ankara, Turkey. Tel: 0090 312 455 3344; Fax: 0090 312 455 3353.
britembank@fco.gov.uk
www.britishembassy.org.tr

Turkish Tourist Office, First Floor, 170–173 Piccadilly, London W1V 9DD. Tel: 020 7629 7771; Brochure line: 09001 88 77 55; Fax: 020 7491 0773.
tto@turkishtourism.demon.co.uk
www.tourist-offices.org.uk/turkey

Ministry of Tourism, Ismet Inönü Bulvar 5, Bahçelievler, Ankara, Turkey. Tel: 00312 212 8300; Fax: 00312 213 6887.
http://antor.com/turkey/index.html

Valid passport required.

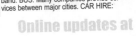

Visa required. Tourist visas are issued on arrival in Turkey, and are not available in advance. Visas for residence, student exchange, work or study trips and multiple entry business visas must be obtained in advance from the Turkish Consulate-General. Transit visas are not required if the traveller has an onward ticket and does not leave the airport.

More than two sets of playing cards. Export of souvenirs such as carpets are subject to regulations. Export of antiques is forbidden. Breaking the customs regulations carries very serious penalties.

US$ 12 payable on all international departures.

POLIO, TYPHOID: R. MALARIA: Potential risk in the vivax form exists during period throughout the year in various areas.
OTHER: Cholera incidents have not been evident over recent years but simple precautions when eating and drinking are advised. Rabies is present.

W2 Tap water is safe to drink in large cities.

Turkish Lira (TL). Certificates of exchange must be retained to prove that legally exchanged currency was used. Money can be exchanged at all PTT branches. Major credit cards are accepted. Travellers cheques in US$ can be easily exchanged.
ATM AVAILABILITY: Over 5000 locations.

MONEYGRAM: 00800 13 293 0909.
WESTERN UNION: 0800 211 63 63

AMEX: 0044 1273 696 933
DINERS CLUB: 00800 261 8903 or 444 0 556
MASTERCARD: 00800 13 887 0903
VISA: 00800 13 535 0900

AMEX: 00800 4491 4820
THOMAS COOK: 00800 4491 4895
VISA: 0044 20 7937 8091

0830–1200 and 1300–1700 Mon to Fri.

Relatively inexpensive.

Turkish, Kurdish. French, German and English are also spoken.

The coasts have a hot Mediterranean climate with hot summers and mild winters.

Muslim with small Christian minority.

Jan 1, Apr 23, May 19, Aug 30, Oct 29. Islamic festivals.

220 volts AC, 50 Hz.

Airmail to Europe takes 3 days.

Muslim laws and cultures apply. However Turkey does not discriminate against non-Muslim beliefs. Women may receive harassment from some local men. Women should cover their heads and arms and not wear short skirts.

RAIL: Fares are comparatively cheap.
ROAD: An extensive road development and maintenance programme. Care must be taken if driving, as accidents can lead to serious complications and delay your travels.
TAXI AND DOLMUS: Taxis are numerous in all Turkish towns. Meters are used. A Dolmus is a collective taxi plying along specific routes and recognisable by a yellow band. BUS: Many companies provide services between major cities. CAR HIRE:

Available in all main towns. DOCUMENTATION: IDP is required for visits over 3 months.

Respect Islamic customs. Informal wear is accepted but confine beachwear to the beach/pool. Drunkenness is not tolerated. PHOTOGRAPHY: Do not take photographs of anything connected with the military.

Petty crime and street robbery is common in Instanbul, and sexual assaults have been reported in tourist areas on the coast. In most cases the threat is from foreigners rather than Turkish people. One technique is for them to befriend tourists and drug their food or drinks.

Although the PKK (Kurdistan Workers Party) has kept a low profile recently, this may alter at any time. There are terrorism risks, but these tend to be in more remote regions of the south-east, rather than popular tourist areas. Do not try to climb Mt Ararat in Eastern Turkey.

The use of metal detectors and export of cultural artifacts is restricted and visitors may be asked for a vendor's receipt and museum export certificate.

Several geological fault lines cross Turkey making it vulnerable to tremors. The earthquake in 1999 devastated Izmit and Duzce.

Turkmenistan

CAPITAL: Ashgabat

GMT +5.

FROM UK: 00993 OUTGOING CODE TO UK: 8/1044 (wait for second dial tone)

All services: 03

Turkmen Embassy, 2nd Floor South, St George's House, 14/17 Wells Street, London, W1P 3FP. Tel: 020 7255 1071; Fax: 020 7323 9184.

British Embassy, Four Points Ak Altin Hotel, 301-308 Office Building, Ashgabat, Turkmenistan. Tel 0993 12 510861; Fax: 00993 12 510868. beasb@online.tm www.britishembassytm.org.uk/

Intourist, 219 Marsh Wall, Isle of Dogs, London E14 9PD. Tel: 020 7538 8600. Fax: 020 7538 5967.

Turkmenintour, U1. Makhtumkhuli 74, Ashgabat, Turkmenistan. Tel: (1) 225 6932 or 225 5191. Fax: (1) 229 3169. Also see Nisa-Service Co, Tour operator. http://valera.8m.com/departure.

Valid passport required

Visa required. Visitors are usually asked to produce hotel bookings or a letter of invitation if on business. The Nisa-Service tour operator can process visa applications online at web page http://valera.8m.com/visa.htm.

Loose pearls, pornography, anything carried for a third party. A complete list is available from Intourist. A customs declaration form should be completed on arrival and retained until departure. Customs inspection can be detailed, it is advisable to ask for a certificate from shops when purchases have been made which state that goods have been paid for in hard currency.

Tax is variable and must be paid in hard currency, preferably US$.

POLIO, TYPHOID: R. MALARIA: R. OTHER: Cholera is a particular risk, medical advice is recommended. Diphtheria and rabies are also potential dangers. Hepatitis A is endemic.

W1 Drink only boiled or bottled water, but lots of it in the summer.

1 Manat = 100 tenge. The preferred hard currency is US$, and then only clean new notes; visitors may find it hard to change other currencies. A cash-only economy exists. Several new hotels accept credit cards. Only Vnesheconombank, the Turkmen National Bank, cashes travellers cheques or accepts Visa, MasterCard and Eurocards for cash advances. ATM AVAILABILITY: Unavailable.

MONEYGRAM: Unavailable.
WESTERN UNION: Available.

AMEX: no local number
DINERS CLUB: no local number
MASTERCARD: no local number
VISA: no local number

AMEX: 0044 1273 571 600
THOMAS COOK: 001733 318950
VISA: 0044 20 7937 8091

0900–1300 Mon to Fri. Closed on Sat.

Exploitative for the traveller.

Turkmen. Russian is also spoken.

Extreme Continental climate. Summers are very hot and dry and winters are very cold.

Mainly Sunni Muslim with a small Russian Orthodox minority.

Jan 1, Feb 19, Mar 8, 21, May 9, 18, Oct 6, 27, 28, Dec 12. Islamic festivals.

20 volts AC, 50 Hz. Plugs are usually the round 2-pin type.

Mail to the USA and Western Europe can take anything from two weeks to two months.

Usual precautions should be taken. Conservative clothing should be worn. Shorts are rarely seen – if worn by women they may attract unwelcome attention.

BUS: Services are available to all major towns. TAXI: They can be found in all major towns. Many are unlicensed and fares should be agreed in advance. As many of the street names have changed since independence it is advisable to use both old and new names. DOCUMENTATION: When car hire is available an IDP will be required.

Shoes must be removed on entering someone's home. The summer sun can be intense, and cause dehydration and sunburn. Carry identification at all times. Earth tremors can occur in eastern Turkmenistan. Some areas of the country are restricted and travellers must get permission to visit them at the time of applying for a visa.

Turks and Caicos Islands

CAPITAL: Cockburn Town

GMT –5 (GMT –4 during the summer).

FROM UK: 001649. OUTGOING CODE TO UK: 01144

All services: 911

Office of the Governor, Waterloo, Grand Turk, Turks and Caicos Islands, British West Indies. Tel: 001 649 946 2308/2309; Fax: 001 649 946 2903.
Consular Section, British High Commission, Ansbacher House (3rd Floor), East Street, PO Box N7516, Nassau, Bahamas. Tel: 001 242 325 7471; Fax: 001 242 323 3871.

No tourist office in UK. See web sites:
http://milk.tciway.tc/ and
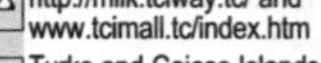
www.tcimall.tc/index.htm

Turks and Caicos Islands Tourist Board, PO Box 128, Front Street, Grand Turk, Turks and Caicos Islands. Tel: 001649 946 2321. Fax: 001649 946 27233. tci.tourism@tciway.tc
www.turksandcaicostourism.com/

Valid passport required.

Visa not required.

Firearms and spear-guns.

US$20. Children under 12 years of age are exempt.

POLIO, TYPHOID: R.

W1

US Dollar (US$) = 100 cents. All major credit cards are accepted. Travellers cheques are widely accepted, preferably in US$. ATM AVAILABILITY: Unavailable.

MONEYGRAM: Unavailable.
WESTERN UNION: 941 3702.

AMEX: 0044 1273 696 933
DINERS CLUB: 0044 1252 513 500
MASTERCARD: 1800 307 7309
VISA: 1800 847 2911

AMEX: 0044 1273 571 600
THOMAS COOK: 001733 318950
VISA: 0044 20 7937 8091

0830–1430 Mon to Thur, 0830–1230 and 1430–1630 Fri (Barclays Bank), 0830–1430 Mon to Thur and 0830–1630 Fri (Scotia Bank).

Extremely expensive. Hotels range from standard to 2 luxury and 2 deluxe, with private beaches and moorings.

English.

Tropical climate with cool winds. Nights are cool with rain in the winter.

Roman Catholic, Anglican, Methodist, Baptists, Seventh Day Adventist and Pentecostal minorities.

Jan 1, second Mon in Mar, second Sat in Jun, Aug 30, Sep 30, Oct 17, Dec 10, 25, 26. Easter. National Heroes' Day (end of Jun).

110 volts AC.

5 days.

Influenced by British colonialism, variants depending on island.

ROAD: Less than a quarter of the roads are tarred. TAXI: Available at the airport but may have to be shared if scarce. CAR HIRE: Limited selection available from local firms. Hire cars are left-hand drive, but traffic drives on the left. DOCUMENTATION: A local licence is obtainable on presentation of a national or IDP licence.

The Turks and Caicos is an archipelago of eight major islands and numerous uninhabited cays. Most tourist facilities are located on Providenciales (Provo) and Grand Turk islands.

Access is primarily by boat, although the larger islands have airports. Divers should leave details of their activity and expected time of return with friends or the hotel reception. There is a small public hospital on Grand Turk, and a private clinic on Provo which has a hyperbaric chamber facility.

The crime rate is low, but visitors should take sensible precautions and avoid carrying large amounts of money. The hurricane season runs from July to November and storms can disrupt roads and air transport.

CAPITAL: Funafuti

GMT +12

FROM UK: 00688. OUTGOING CODE TO UK: 0044 International calls may need operator assistance.

Emergency services: 911

Refer to High Commission of the Fiji Islands, 34 Hyde Park Gate, London SW7 5DN. Tel: 020 7582 2838. IN EUROPE: Honorary Consulate of Tuvalu, Klovensteenweg 115 A, 22559 Hamburg, Germany. Tel: 0049 40 810 580. Fax: 0049 40 811 016.

Consular matters are covered by the British High Commission, Victoria House, 47 Gladstone Road, Suva, Fiji Islands. Tel: 00679 311 033; Fax: 00679 301 406; www.ukinthepacific.bhc.org.fj

South Pacific Tourism Organisation / SPTO UK. 48 Glentham Road, Barnes, London. SW13 9JJ. Tel: 020 8741 6082; Fax: 020 8741 6107. spto@iiuk.co.uk www.spto.org

Ministry of Tourism, Trade and Commerce, Vaiaku, Funafuti, Tuvalu. Tel: 00688 20182; Fax: 00688 20829 mttc@tuvalu.tv

Valid passport required.

Visa not required. Visitors must have a return or onward travel ticket and proof of enough money for the length of stay.

Pornography, pure alcohol, narcotics, arms and ammunition are prohibited imports. Animal and plant materials are subject to quarantine. Export of artifacts and certain flora and fauna is restricted.

AS$ 10 is levied on all international departures.

POLIO, TYPHOID: R.

Australian Dollar is used for transactions over one dollar but Tuvaluan (Dollar) currency may also be used. Credit cards are not accepted although Mastercard is accepted by the national bank. Travellers cheques in Australian dollars can be cashed at the national bank only. ATM AVAILABILITY: Unavailable.

MONEYGRAM: Unavailable.
WESTERN UNION: Unavailable

AMEX: 0044 1273 696 933
DINERS CLUB: 0044 1252 513 500
MASTERCARD: 001 314 542 7111
VISA: 001 410 581 9994

AMEX: 0044 1273 571 600
THOMAS COOK: 001733 318950
VISA: 0044 20 7937 8091

0930–1300 Mon to Thur, 0830–1200 Fri.

There is only one main hotel which offers moderate facilities, whilst other guest houses offer basic accommodation. All are inexpensive. Commodities are scarce, due an undeveloped tourist industry.

Tuvaluan and English are the main languages.

Hot and humid, with little variation throughout the year. Mar to Oct tends to be slightly cooler and therefore more pleasant. Nov - Feb is the wet season, when the climate may be uncomfortable.

Mainly Protestant.

Jan 1, second Mon in Mar, May 13, second Sat in Jun, Aug 5, Oct 1, 2, Nov 11, Dec 25, 26. Easter.

110 volts AC

Up to 10 days, but the service can be erratic.

Culture and tradition play a strong part in Tuvalun life. Religious holidays are taken very seriously. Women are conservative in behaviour.

SEA: The islands are served by passenger and cargo-vessels. ROAD: Mainly dirt tracks TAXIS: Limited. BIKES: Pushbikes and motorbikes can be hired at hotels. Traffic drives on the left.

Men must wear shirts in public places. Sunday is regarded as a sacred day and should be respected along with local customs. Tuvalu is one of the world's smallest and most isolated nations, with a population of 8000 living on a group of atolls in the South Pacific. Tuvalu's economy is based on agriculture, a coconut product called copra, tourism and fishing. Postage stamps, prized by collectors, are a major export.

CAPITAL: Kampala

GMT +3

FROM UK: 00256. OUTGOING CODE TO UK: 0044. International calls may need operator assistance.

High Commission of the Republic of Uganda, Uganda House, 58-59 Trafalgar Square, London, WC2N 5DX. Tel: 020 7839 5783. Fax: 020 7839 8925.

British High Commission, PO Box 7070, 10/12 Parliament Avenue, Kampala, Uganda. Tel: 00256 41 257054/9; Fax: 00256 41 344084. bhcinfo@starcom.co.ug

Refer to the High Commission. See http://ugandaweb.com/

Uganda Tourist Board, PO Box 7211, Parliament Avenue, Kampala, Uganda. Tel: (41) 242 196. Fax: (41) 242 188.

Valid passport and return ticket required. Requirements may change at short notice. Contact the embassy before departure.

Visa required. Visas can be obtained in advance or on arrival in Uganda.

Import of foreign currency must be declared.

US$20 is levied on international departures. Transit and passengers under 2 years of age are exempt.

Passengers not holding sufficient funds.

POLIO, TYPHOID: R. MALARIA Exists all year throughout the country. Resistance to chloroquine has been reported. YELLOW FEVER: Vaccination is strongly recommended to all passengers and a vaccination certificate is required by passengers arriving from infected areas. OTHER: Bilharzia, meningitis, rabies. HIV/AIDS is widespread.

W1

Uganda Shilling (Ush) = 100 cents. EXCHANGE: Central bank, commercial banks and exchange bureaux. NOTE: Import and export of local currency is prohibited. Visa is widely accepted, but other credit cards have limited acceptance. Travellers cheques, preferably in US$, are accepted. ATM AVAILABILITY: Unavailable.

MONEYGRAM: Unavailable.
WESTERN UNION: 41 234 570

AMEX: 0044 1273 696 933
DINERS CLUB: 0044 1252 513 500
MASTERCARD: 001 314 542 7111
VISA: 001 410 581 9994

AMEX: 0044 1273 571 600
THOMAS COOK: 001733 318950
VISA: 0044 20 7937 8091

0830–1400 Mon to Fri.

Since a new privatisation programme was introduced in the last few years, the cost of living has risen.

English and Luganda. Kiswahili is also widely spoken.

The higher altitudes can be quite cool. There is heavy rain: Mar–May, Oct–Nov.

Majority Christian, with Animist and Muslim.

Jan 1, 26, Mar 8, May 1, Jun 3, 9, Oct 9, Dec 25, 26. Easter, main Islamic festivals.

240 volts AC, 50 Hz.

Airmail to Europe can take 3 days to several weeks.

FLIGHTS: Domestic flights operate regularly between major cities. ROAD: Vary in quality and are sparse in the north. Robbery and hijacking of vehicles has increased in Kampala: keep doors and windows locked in urban areas. DOCUMENTATION: A national driving licence or IDP is required. RAIL: Passenger facilities are limited and timetables can be erratic although regular services operate. BUS: Services are often overcrowded and unreliable.

Consult the Embassy before travelling outside Kampala. The FCO advises against any travel to border areas, particularly with Sudan, Rwanda and the Democratic Republic of the Congo. Security measures have been stepped up to protect visitors. The Ugandan army accompanies tourists on gorilla tracking and has greatly increased its presence in the national parks. The government periodically closes tourist areas that it considers to be at risk. Violence in south-west Uganda affects the area around the Bwindi Impenetrable Forest National Park and Mgahinga Gorilla Park, and visitors should get up-to-date local advice before going there or staying overnight in the parks. Taking photos of anything connected to the military is prohibited.

Ukraine

CAPITAL: Kyiv

GMT +2 (GMT+3 during the summer).

FROM UK: 00380. OUTGOING CODE TO UK: 8/1044 (wait for second dial tone)

Embassy of Ukraine, 78 Kensington Park Road, London W11 2PL. Tel: 020 7727 6312; Visa information line: 0900 188 7749. Fax: 020 7243 8923.

British Embassy, vul, Desyatinna 9, 252025 Kyiv, Ukraine. Tel 0380 44 462 0011; Fax: 00380 44 462 0013. ukembinf@sovam.com
British Consulate, 6 Sichnevoho Povstannya Street, Kyiv. Tel: 44 290 7317.
VisaConsular.Section@kievc.mail.fco.gov.uk

Intourist, 219 Marsh Wall, Isle of Dogs, London E14 9PD. Tel: 020 7538 8600/5902.

Ministry of Foreign Affairs, vul. Mykhailoivska pl. 1, 252018 Kyiv, Ukraine. Tel: 00380 44 226 3379. Fax 00 380 44 226 3169.
www.ukremb.com/
Ukranian travel Information System, www.utis.com.ua/index2.html

Valid passport required.

Visa required.

Contact the consular authority for up to date information. Travellers must declare all money in their possession on arrival.

Cholera and diphtheria.

W2

Currency: Hryvnya. Banks and currency offices will exchange money. Ukraine is a cash society, but credit cards and cash machines (ATMs) are beginning to appear in the capital and tourist areas. Travellers cheques can be exchanged at banks. ATM AVAILABILITY: only a handful.

MONEYGRAM: 8 then 100 11
WESTERN UNION: (044) 295 2552

AMEX: 8/1044 1273 696 933
DINERS CLUB: 8/10044 1252 513 500
MASTERCARD: 8/101 314 542 7111
VISA: 8/101 410 581 9994

AMEX: 8/1044 1273 571 600
THOMAS COOK: 8/101733 318950
VISA: 8/1044 20 7937 8091

0900–1600 Mon to Fri.

Less expensive than Western Europe.

Ukrainian is the official state language. Russian is also widely spoken.

Temperate with warm summers, crisp, sunny autumns and cold, snowy winters.

Ukrainian Orthodox. A type of Catholicism exists in the Western part of the country.

Jan 1, 7, Mar 8, May 1, 2, 9, last Sat/Sun in May, Jun 28, Aug 24. Nov 7. Easter.

220 volts AC, 50 Hz

Services are erratic. Letters to Western Europe can take up to 2 weeks.

Usual common-sense precautions should be taken.

FLIGHTS: Not recommended, as flights are far from comfortable and buying tickets is extremely difficult. RAIL: As buying tickets is difficult it is advisable to pre book through Intourist in London. ROAD: Buses exist but are not recommended. TAXIS: Aavailable; fares should be agreed in advance.

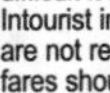

A room in a private home is an excellent accommodation option in the Ukraine as the people are friendly and hospitable. The UK has an agreement that emergency medical treatment will be provided free to visitors to Ukraine.

Crime levels are increasing, and people of African or Asian ethnic origin may be subjected to harassment by racist skinhead groups. Precautions should be taken to avoid crowds and political-style gatherings. Western European cars are a particular target for thieves. Visitors to Ukraine are advised to register their presence in the country with the Embassy.

United Arab Emirates

CAPITAL: Abu Dhabi

GMT +4

FROM UK: 00971. OUTGOING CODE TO UK: 0044.

All services: 344 663 (only Abu Dhabi).

Embassy of the United Arab Emirates, 30 Prince's Gate, London SW7 1PT. Tel: 020 7581 1281. Fax: 020 7581 9616. embinfo@cocoon.co.uk

British Embassy, PO Box 248, Abu Dhabi. Tel: 00971 2632 6600. www.britain-uae.org/ Consular.Section@abudhabi.mail.fco.gov.uk. British Embassy, PO Box 65, Dubai. Tel: 00971 4397 1070. ConsularDubai@dubai.mail.foc.gov.uk.

No tourist office in UK. http://dubaitourism.co.ae/ or www.dubai-online.com/

Federal Ministry of Tourism and Culture, PO Box 5053, Dubai, UAE. Tel: (4) 615 500. Fax: (4) 615 648.

Passport required, valid for at least 6 months from date of arrival.

Visa not required by nationals of the UK with the endorsement 'British Subject Citizen of the UK and Colonies' or 'British Citizen' for visits of up to 30 days.

Loose pearls.

POLIO, TYPHOID: R. MALARIA A risk exists in the valleys and the lower slopes of mountainous areas of the Northern States. OTHER: Cholera, rabies.

W2

UAE Dirham (UAE Dh) = 100 fils. EXCHANGE: Most hotels. All credit cards are accepted. Travellers cheques, preferably in US$, can be easily exchanged. ATM AVAILABILITY: Over 280 locations.

MONEYGRAM: 800 121 then 800 592 3688. WESTERN UNION: 800 2001, 800 2828

AMEX: 0044 1273 696 933. DINERS CLUB: 0800 4080. MASTERCARD: 001 314 542 7111. VISA: 001 410 581 9994

AMEX: 0044 1273 571 600
THOMAS COOK: 001733 318950
VISA: 0044 20 7937 8091

0800–1200 Sat to Wed and 0800–1100 Thur.

Relatively expensive although the budget traveller will be able to find cheaper hotels and food, away from the main tourist areas. Prices are constant throughout the year.

Arabic. English is widely spoken.

Jun–Sept is the hottest period, with little rainfall. Oct–May is more comfortable to visit.

Mostly Sunni Muslim.

Jan 1, Apr 7, 16, 28, Aug 6, Nov 17, Dec 2, 3. Islamic festivals.

220/240 volts AC, 50 Hz. Square 3-pin plugs are widespread.

Airmail takes about 5 days to reach Western Europe.

In general this is one of the more liberal Muslim countries in the Middle East, incorporating many Western traditions. Women face little discrimination and, contrary to the policies of neighbouring countries, are able to drive and walk around unescorted. Foreign female travellers should still be vigilant, especially when looking for cheaper accommodation in the cities.

SEA: Passenger services serve all coastal ports. ROAD: There are good roads running along the West Coast. BUS: A limited service links most towns. However most hotels run their own scheduled service to the airport, city centre and beach. TAXI: Most travellers find taxis to be the most convenient and quickest method of transport. Taxis are metered and there is a surcharge for air-conditioned taxis. CAR HIRE: Most international companies have agencies at the airport and hotels. DOCUMENTATION: Renters must produce 2 photographs, passports and either a valid international or national licence. IDP is recommended.

This is one of the most liberal countries in the Gulf, although it is still very conservative by Western standards. Foreigners are free to practice their own religion, alcohol is served in hotels and the dress code is liberal. Western entertainment is available in the form of cocktail bars, public houses and cinemas. All the same, visitors should respect Muslim traditions, for example by refraining from smoking and drinking in public places during the holy month of Ramadan (Oct/Nov).

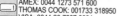

United Kingdom

CAPITAL: London

GMT (+1 during the summer time).

FROM UK TO OVERSEAS: 00 + country code. INCOMING CODE TO UK: National IDD code + 44.

Police, Ambulance, Fire: 999

British Tourist Authority and British Tourist Board, Thames Tower, Black's Road, Hammersmith, London W6 9EL. Tel: 020 8846 9000; Fax: 020 8563 0302 www.visitbritain.com/
Northern Ireland: www.ni-tourism.com
Scotland: www.holiday.scotland.net/
Wales: www.visitwales.com

Valid passport required by all except: nationals of EU countries with a valid ID card for tourist visits not exceeding 3 months; nationals of Iceland Liechtenstein, Monaco, Norway and Switzerland with valid ID cards for tourist/social visits of not less than 6 months and in possession of a British Visitor's guide available from travel agencies.

Visa not required by EU nationals and citizens of Australia, Canada, USA and Japan, for stay up to 6 months.

All cats and dogs must spend 6 months in quarantine on arrival in the country. An import licence is required for all pets.

£20 is payable on all departures, normally included in ticket price.

Pound (£) = 100 pence. Banks, Thomas Cook offices, exchange bureaux and many hotels will exchange currency. All major credit cards are accepted. Travellers cheques are widely accepted. Banknotes issued in Scotland, Northern Ireland are equal in value to Bank of England notes but may not be accepted for payments in England. Some large stores in London accept the Euro, US$ bills and certain other currencies. ATM AVAILABILITY: Extensive network.

MONEYGRAM: 800 66639472.
WESTERN UNION: 800 833 833.

AMEX: 01273 696 933
DINERS CLUB: 0800 46 0800
MASTERCARD: 0800 964767
VISA: 0800 895 082

AMEX: 0800 521 313
THOMAS COOK: 0800 622101
VISA: 0800 895078

0900–1730 Mon to Fri. Main branches are open on Sat mornings.

London and major tourist centres are especially expensive.

English. Welsh is spoken in areas of Wales. Gaelic is spoken in parts of Scotland and N. Ireland. There is a wide range of ethnic minority languages.

The climate is temperate with warm, wet summers and mild, wet winters. It is variable throughout the year and the country.

Protestant; Roman Catholic, Jewish, Muslim, Hindu and other minorities.

Jan 1, Jan 2 (Scotland), Mar 17 (Northern Ireland), first Mon in May, last Mon in May, Jul 12 (Northern Ireland), first Mon in Aug, last Mon in Aug, Dec 25, 26. Jun 3 2002 (Queen's Golden Jubilee). Easter.

240 volts AC, 50 Hz. Square 3 pin plugs are used.

Post destined for overseas should be sent airmail.

RAIL: There is a comprehensive nationwide rail network. Fast trains also run directly from London to Paris and Brussels. ROAD: Buses operate over the whole country, local and intercity routes. London has a range of night buses from midnight to 0600. TAXIS: Metered and strictly regulated by the police and local municipal authorities. 'Mini-cabs', by contrast are not subject to the same regulation; they are best avoided by women on their own. CAR RENTAL: Full range of companies in most cities. DOCUMENTATION: National driving licence is accepted. IDP required from countries using non-Roman alphabet.

Some political tension remains in Northern Ireland. Visitors there are welcomed warmly and are unlikely to be targets of politically motivated violence. Avoid discussions on religion and politics.

Common-sense precautions regarding personal security should be taken everywhere. Pickpockets and purse-snatchers operate on public transport and in tourist areas. Take care especially to avoid being jostled in crowds. Using public transport at night is generally safe, but women should travel where there are other people, to avoid the possibility of an isolated attack. Do not leave baggage unattended.

Normal social courtesies apply. Casual clothing of any style is acceptable in most places; people usually dress up for the opera or high-class restaurants.

United States of America

CAPITAL: Washington DC

USA has 6 time zones ranging from GMT –5 on the East coast to –10 in Hawaii.

FROM UK: 001. OUTGOING CODE TO UK: 01144

911

Embassy of the United States of America, 24-31, Grosvenor Square, London, W1A 1AE. Tel: 020 7499 9000; Visa information line: 09068 200290 (Premium rate). www.usembassy.org.uk

British Embassy, 3100 Massachusetts, NW, Washington DC, 20008. Tel: (202) 588 6500. Fax: (202) 588 7850. www.britainusa.com/ Consulates in major cities.

United States Information Service, 55-56 Upper Brook Street, London W1A 2LH. Tel: 020 7499 9000.

United Sates Travel and Tourism Administration, 14th Constitutional Avenue, NW, Washington, DC 20230. Tel: (202) 482 3811 or 482 2000. Fax (202) 482 2887.

Valid passport required.

Visa not required by EU citizens under the visa waiver program, for which the excluded categories below are ineligible.

Some seeds, fruits and plants, pornography, switchblade knives, narcotic drugs unless with prescription, and hazardous items.

US$10 is levied on all foreign travellers.

Anyone with communicable diseases, a criminal record, narcotic addicts and drug traffickers and anyone who has been deported or denied admission within the previous 5 years.

Rabies, Lyme disease.

US Dollar (US$) = 100 cents. Not all hotels exchange foreign currency. It is advisable to take US$. Credit cards and travellers cheques, preferably in US$, are widely accepted. ATM AVAILABILITY: Over 135000 locations.

MONEYGRAM: 1 800 926 9400.
WESTERN UNION: 800 325 6000

AMEX: 0044 1273 696 933
DINERS CLUB: 1800 234 6377
MASTERCARD: 1800 307 7309
VISA: 1800 847 2911

AMEX: 1800 221 7282
THOMAS COOK: 1800 223 7373
VISA: 1800 227 6811

Variable but generally 0900–1500 Mon to Fri.

Food, accommodation and petrol are cheaper than Western Europe.

English. Many other languages are also spoken.

Varies considerably by region.

Protestant, Roman Catholic, Jewish and many minorities.

Jan 1, 20, third Mon in Jan, Feb, last Mon in May, Jun 14, July 4, first Mon in Sep, second Mon in Oct, Nov 11, fourth Thu in Nov, Dec 25. Various State holidays.

110/220 volts 60 HZ. Plugs are of the flat 2-pin type.

Up to 1 week.

AIR: Extensive network of domestic and international flights. RAIL: Regional commuter trains and long-distance Amtrak services. Subway trains in cities are best avoided late at night. ROAD: Buses and taxis available in cities. Greyhound Buses operate intercity routes. CAR RENTAL: A wide range of agencies available around the country. US driver's licences and most foreign licences are recognised for self-drive. Licences printed in unusual alphabets or languages must be supported by IDP.

If your car is bumped from behind, indicate to the other driver to follow you to the nearest public area and call for police assistance. Do not sleep in your car on the roadside or in rest areas, and avoid driving on unlit side roads at night. Try to keep to main highways and well-lit public areas.

Crime rates vary from state to state. New York City, which was once a by-word for muggings and harassment, has been extensively cleaned up by the City Hall authorities and police. Sensible precautions should be taken, especially at night on subways and in poorer areas of big cities.

US Virgin Islands

CAPITAL: Charlotte Amalie

GMT –4

FROM UK: 001340. OUTGOING CODE TO UK: 01144

All services 911

The US Virgin Islands are an American territory and are represented abroad by US Embassies. See USA Entry.

No British Embassy is present.

US Virgin Islands Division of Tourism, Molasses House, Clove Hitch Quay, Plantation Wharf, York Place, London SW11 3TW. Tel: 020 7978 5262. Fax: 020 7924 3171. usvi@destination-marketing.co.uk See also http://usvi-info.com/

US Virgin Islands Division of Tourism, PO Box 6400, Charlotte Amalie, St Thomas, VI 00804-6400. Tel: 774 8784. Fax: 774 4390. www.usvi.org/tourism/index.html

Valid passport required: See the USA entry.

See the USA entry.

See USA entry.

US$ 10 is levied on all foreign nationals.

See the USA entry.

POLIO, TYPHOID: R.

US Dollar (US$) = 100 cents. All major credit cards and Travellers cheques, preferably in US$ are accepted. ATM AVAILABILITY: 10 locations approximately.

MONEYGRAM: Single location.
WESTERN UNION: Unavailable.

AMEX: 01144 1273 696 933
DINERS CLUB: 01144 1252 513 500
MASTERCARD: 1800 307 7309
VISA: 1800 847 2911

AMEX: 01144 1273 571 600
THOMAS COOK: 011 1733 318950
VISA: 1800 227 6811

0900–1430 Mon to Thur, 0900–1400 and 1530–1700 Fri.

Expensive, especially in the tourist centres. However, luxury items up to $1200 are cheaper, as they are duty-free.

English, Spanish, Creole is widely spoken.

Hot climate with cool winds. Aug-Oct is the wettest period.

Christian, mainly Protestant.

Jan 1, 6, third Mons in Jan and Feb, Mar 31, last weekend in Apr, last Mon in May, Jun 20, Jul 3, 4, 25, first Mon in Sep, Oct 17, Nov 1, 11, 13, fourth Thur in Nov, Dec 26. Easter.

120 volts AC, 60 Hz.

Up to 1 week.

Usual precautions should be followed.

SEA: Ferries operate services between islands. ROAD: Well-maintained roads connect all main towns but not much else. TAXI: Available on all the islands. They follow set routes and their prices are published. CAR HIRE: There are international agencies operating at the airport and in the main towns. DOCUMENTATION: A national licence is acceptable.

The islands have more hotels per square mile than any other in the Caribbean.

CAPITAL: Montevideo

GMT –3

FROM UK: 00598. OUTGOING CODE TO UK: 0044

All services: 999 (Police: 109, Ambulance: 105, Fire: 104, in Montevideo only)

Embassy of the Oriental Republic of Uruguay, 2nd Floor, 140 Brompton Road, London, SW3 1HY. Tel: 020 7589 8835 or 589 8735 (visa section). Fax: 020 7581 9585. emb@urubri.demon.co.uk

British Embassy, PO Box 16024, Calle Marco Bruto 1073, 1130 Montevideo, Uruguay. Tel: (2) 622 3650. Fax: (2) 622 7815. bemonte@internet.com.uy www.britishembassy.org.uy

No tourist office in UK. See www.geocities.com/rocheireland/uruguay.html

Dirección Nacionale de Turismo, Agraciado 1409, 4º, 5º y 6º, Montevideo, Uruguay. Tel: (2) 904 148. www.turismo.gub.uy/ (in Spanish)

Valid passport required.

Visa not required by nationals of Great Britain for stays not exceeding 3 months.

Imported duty-free goods are not to exceed US$30, and exported goods are not to exceed US$150.

US$12 is levied on international departures. Children under 2 years of age are exempt.

Vaccination recommended for typhoid. OTHER: Rabies.

W2

Uruguayan Peso = 100 centesimos. Foreign exchange: Hotels not recommended as they tend to give unfavourable rates – use gambios and banks. Inflation tends to lead to wide fluctuations in exchange rates. All credit cards are accepted. Travellers cheques in US$ are acceptable. ATM AVAILABILITY: Over 60 locations.

MONEYGRAM: 000 413 598 2083.
WESTERN UNION: 0800 2024/2026.

AMEX: 0044 1273 696 933
DINERS CLUB: 02 902 0207
MASTERCARD: 001 314 542 7111
VISA: 001 410 581 9994

AMEX: 000 413 598 2332
THOMAS COOK: 001733 318950
VISA: 0044 20 7937 8091

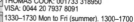

1330–1730 Mon to Fri (summer). 1300–1700 Mon to Fri (winter).

Coastal resorts tend to be more expensive than the capital. It is advisable to book well in advance. More people visit Uruguay than any other South American country.

Spanish. English may also be spoken.

Mild summers and winters. Summer is Dec-Mar and the most pleasant time. Nights are often cool.

Roman Catholic.

Jan 1, 6, Feb 24, Apr 19, May 1, 18, Jun 19, Jul 18, Aug 25, Oct 12, Nov 1, Dec 25. Carnival week before Lent. Easter.

220 volts AC, 50 Hz. Plugs are continental flat 3-pin or round 2-pin.

Airmail to Europe takes 3–5 days. Postal rates are reasonable but the service can be unreliable. It is recommended that important items are sent by registered mail.

Inequality between men and women prevails. This is mostly seen in the overpopulated capital city.

FLIGHTS: Domestic flights are operated between major centres but can be very expensive compared to other modes of transport. RAIL: Services operate between the capital and the major towns. Buffet service is available, air conditioning isn't. ROAD: 80% of roads are suitable for all weather. BUS: Services connect all the main towns and border points. CAR HIRE: Available in Montevideo. DOCUMENTATION: IDP is recommended but not required. A temporary driving licence must be obtained from the town hall.

Uruguay is arguably the most European of South American countries in lifestyle and customs. It has one of South America´s most interesting capitals in Montevideo, several charming colonial towns and a cluster of internationally renowned beach resorts. Uruguayans are very hospitable and like to entertain at home as well as in restaurants. Shaking hands is the usual social greeting. Normal social courtesies should be applied. The best time to visit is between September and April.

Uzbekistan

CAPITAL: Tashkent

GMT +5

FROM UK: 00998. OUTGOING CODE: 8/1044 (wait for second dial tone)

All services: 03

Embassy of the Republic of Uzbekistan, 41 Holland Park, London W11 3RP. Tel: 020 7229 7679. Fax: 020 7229 7029.

British Embassy, 67 Gogolya Street, Tashkent 700 000, Uzbekistan. Tel: 00998 712 1206822. Fax: 00998 712 1206549. brit@emb.uz; www.britain.uz

Uzbektourism, 13 Marylebone Lane, London W1. Tel: 020 7935 1899. Fax: 020 7935 9554. See also www.samarkand.uz/city.html

Ministry of Tourism, 47 Khorezmakaya Street, Tashkent 700047, Uzbekistan. Tel: (3172) 336 475. Fax: (3712) 391 517. For information on Tashkent, see www.tashkent.org/

Requirements may be subject to short-term change. Contact the relevant authority before departure. Passport required, must be valid for 6 months prior to departure date.

Visa required. Visas must be supported by a letter of invitation, which can be arranged through a hotel or tour company.

Items over 100 years old or anything of cultural importance cannot be exported.

US$10 is levied on all foreign travellers.

POLIO, TYPHOID: R. MALARIA Risk exists near the Afghan border. OTHER: Diphtheria is endemic. Rabies and cholera are also health risks. Vaccinations for hepatitis A are also recommended.

W1

The Som is now the official currency, introduced in 1994. Cash is the only real form of currency; US$ is the preferred foreign currency. EXCHANGE: Use banks and official bureaux de change. The import and export of local currency is prohibited. Credit cards and travellers cheques are not accepted. ATM AVAILABILITY: Unavailable.

MONEYGRAM: Unavailable.
WESTERN UNION: Unavailable.

AMEX: No local number
DINERS CLUB: No local number
MASTERCARD: No local number
VISA: No local number

AMEX: No local number
THOMAS COOK: No local number
VISA: No local number

0900–1700 Mon to Fri.

The limited variety of goods that are available are extremely inexpensive.

Uzbek. Russian, Tajik, Kazakh and English are also spoken.

Continental climate. The south is the warmest. Summer temperatures can be very hot. The most comfortable time to visit is during the spring or autumn.

Mainly Sunni Muslim with Shia, Russian Orthodox and Jewish minorities.

Jan 1, 2, Mar 8, 20–22, May 1, 9, Sep 1, Nov 18, Dec 8. Islamic festivals, Orthodox Easter.

220 volts AC, 50 Hz. Round 2 pin continental plugs are standard.

Letters to Western Europe and the USA take between 2 weeks and 2 months.

Conservative dress should be worn in accordance with religious beliefs. Usual precautions should be taken and maintaining a low profile is advised. Shorts are rarely worn and women should be prepared for unwelcome attention from the local male population if they wear them.

ROAD: A reasonable road network exists. BUS: Services connect the major towns and cities. TAXIS: Can be found in all major centres. Many are unlicensed and should be avoided. Travellers are advised to agree the fare in advance and not share with strangers. Use the old and new (since independence) street names when asking for directions. DOCUMENTATION: IDP will be required when car hire is introduced.

Keep valuables out of sight. Long-distance travel by train should be avoided. Do not leave the compartment unattended and lock the door. It is not recommended to use local airlines as they are not always regularly maintained.

The FCO advises caution about travelling to the area near the border with Kyrgyzstan and Tajikistan, where armed rebel groups are active in the mountains.

CAPITAL: Port Vila

GMT +11

FROM UK: 00678. OUTGOING CODE TO UK: Calls must be made through the International operator.

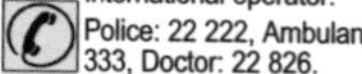
Police: 22 222, Ambulance: 22 100, Fire: 22 333, Doctor: 22 826.

British High Commission, PO Box 567, KPMG House, rue Pasteur, Port Vila, Vanuatu. Tel: 23100. Fax: 23651.

South Pacific Tourism Organisation: 48 Glentham Road, Barnes, London. SW13 9JJ. Tel: 020 8741 6082; Fax: 020 8741 6107. spto@iiuk.co.uk www.spto.org

Vanuatu National Tourism Office, PO Box 209. Kumul Highway, Port Vila, Vanuatu. Tel: 22515 or 22685 or 22813. Fax: 23889. www.vanuatutourism.com/intro.htm tourism@vanuatu.com.vu

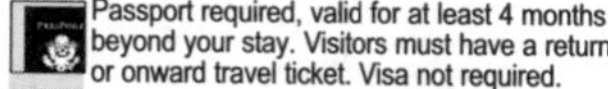
Passport required, valid for at least 4 months beyond your stay. Visitors must have a return or onward travel ticket. Visa not required.

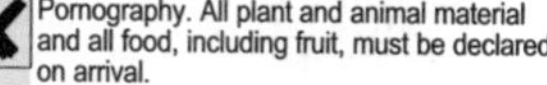
Pornography. All plant and animal material and all food, including fruit, must be declared on arrival.

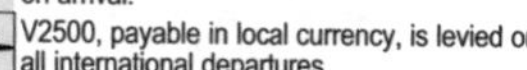
V2500, payable in local currency, is levied on all international departures.

Persons of dubious morality and persons who may become a public charge.

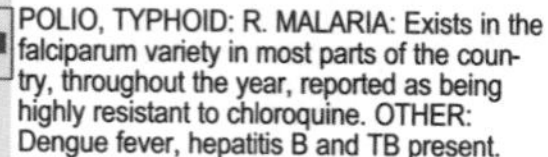
POLIO, TYPHOID: R. MALARIA: Exists in the falciparum variety in most parts of the country, throughout the year, reported as being highly resistant to chloroquine. OTHER: Dengue fever, hepatitis B and TB present.

W2. The town water supply is safe. Boiled water is also available.

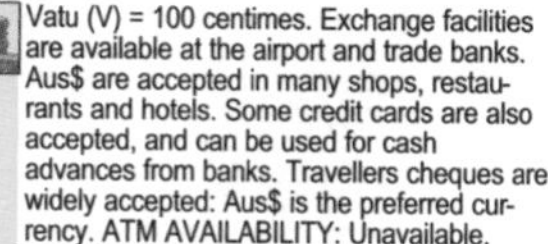
Vatu (V) = 100 centimes. Exchange facilities are available at the airport and trade banks. Aus$ are accepted in many shops, restaurants and hotels. Some credit cards are also accepted, and can be used for cash advances from banks. Travellers cheques are widely accepted: Aus$ is the preferred currency. ATM AVAILABILITY: Unavailable.

MONEYGRAM: Unavailable.
WESTERN UNION: Available.

AMEX: 0044 1273 696 933
DINERS CLUB: 0044 1252 513 500
MASTERCARD: 001 314 542 7111
VISA: 001 410 581 9994

AMEX: 0044 1273 571 600
THOMAS COOK: 001733 318950
VISA: 0044 20 7937 8091

0800–1500 Mon to Fri.

Inexpensive. Affordable accommodation in smaller resorts and self-contained apartments and bungalows around Port Vila.

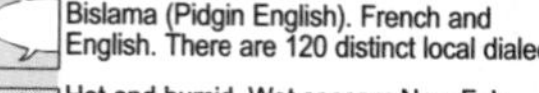
Bislama (Pidgin English). French and English. There are 120 distinct local dialects.

Hot and humid. Wet season: Nov–Feb. Jan–Mar is very hot.The best time to visit is Apr–Oct.

Presbyterian, Anglican, Roman Catholic, Seventh-Day Adventists, Apostolic Church and Church of Christ.

Jan 1, Mar 5, May 1, Jul 24, 30, Aug 15, Oct 5, Nov 29, Dec 25, 26. Easter, Ascension Day.

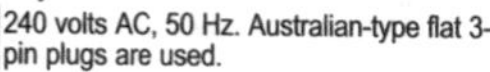
240 volts AC, 50 Hz. Australian-type flat 3-pin plugs are used.

7 days.

Western influences are tolerated around tourist areas, but customs on remote islands and in rural areas remain traditional.

FLIGHTS: The government's airline operates domestic flights, as do private airlines. There are regular flights from New Zealand, Australia and Fiji. SEA: Inter-island ferries operate from Port Vila and Espiritu Santo to the northern and southern islands. BUS: Limited minibus service. You can get on one going in your direction and tell the driver where you want to go. TAXI: Plentiful and not expensive. CAR HIRE: Major car hire operators in Port Vila. DOCUMENTATION: A national driving licence is acceptable.

Tipping and bartering are not considered civilised ways of doing business, and could cause offence. Gratitude is best expressed by sending a postcard from home after your visit. Beachwear should be confined to the pool/beach side. Consumption of alcohol is not permitted outside licensed premises. Make sure scuba-dives are supervised by reputable guides; a recompression chamber is located in Luganville on Espiritu Santo Island. The Yasur volcano on Tanna Island is safe to climb. The season for tropical cyclones is from November to April. NOTE: Turtle, giant clam and trumpet shells can be bought in the markets, but many countries have banned their import.

Vatican City

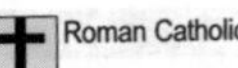

CAPITAL: Vatican City

GMT +1 (GMT +2 during the summer)

FROM UK: 0039 066982. OUTGOING CODE TO UK: 0044

Police: 112, Ambulance: 113, Fire: 115

Apostolic Nunciature, 54 Parkside, Wimbledon, London SW19 5NE. Tel: 020 7486 4880; Fax: 020 7486 4550. www.vatican.va/

British Embassy, Via Condotti 91, 1-00187 Rome, Italy. Tel: 0039 6 699 23561; Fax: 0039 6 6994 0684.

See Vatican web site: www.christusrex.org/www1/citta/0–Citta.html

No entry formalities are required by the Vatican City, but entry will be via Rome and subject to Italian visa/passport requirements.

See Italy.

See Italy.

See Italy.

See Italy for Health Recommendations.

See Italy.

Euro = 100 cents for ordinary purchases. The monetary system is distinct from that of Italy, and Vatican coins are collector's items. Limited acceptance of credit cards and travellers cheques. ATM AVAILABILITY: Unavailable.

MONEYGRAM: Unavailable.
WESTERN UNION: 800 22 00 55

AMEX: 0044 1273 696 933
DINERS CLUB: 0044 1252 513 500
MASTERCARD: 800 870 866
VISA: 001 410 581 9994

AMEX: 0044 1273 571 600
THOMAS COOK: 001733 318950
VISA: 0044 20 7937 8091

There are no taxes and no customs/excise duties in the Vatican City. Accommodation is unavailable to the public.

Italian.

See Italy.

Roman Catholic.

Jan 1, 6, Apr 25, May 1, Jun 2, Aug 15, Nov 1, Sun closest to Nov 4, Dec 8, 25, 26. Major Christian feast days and anniversaries.

220 volts, 50 Hz.

Stamps issued in the Vatican City are valid only within its boundaries.

Revealing clothing should not be worn.

RAIL: Vatican City has its own railway station. The trains are reasonably priced and offer discounts. There is a speed limit of 30 kph in the Vatican City.

The Vatican City is the world's smallest sovereign state, with about 450 citizens and territory that is little more than a private estate on a hill within the city of Rome. Visitors are admitted only to the public areas: St.Peter's Basilica, the Sistine Chapel and certain other church buildings, the Vatican Museum, souvenir shops, cafés and a post office. The post office is of special interest for the sale of Vatican City stamps, which are prized as gifts and souvenirs, but are valid for mail if the letters are posted within the boundaries of the Vatican City. Mail will be postmarked 'Vatican City'.

Arms, shoulders and legs should be kept covered out of respect when visiting religious buildings. Beware of pickpockets and other thieves, especially when crowds gather in St Peter's Square for Papal ceremonies.

CAPITAL: Caracas

GMT –4

FROM UK: 0058. OUTGOING CODE TO UK: 0044

Doctor: 02 483 7021, Ambulance: 02 545 4545.

Embassy of the Republic of Venezuela, 1 Cromwell Road, London SW7 2HW. Tel: 020 7584 4206/7. Fax: 020 7589 8887. venezlon@venezlon.demon.co.uk www.venezlon.demon.co.uk
Venezuelan Consulate, 56 Grafton Way, London W1P 5LB. Tel: 020 7387 6727. Fax: 020 7383 3253.

British Embassy, 3rd floor, Torre Las Merceded, Avenida La Estancia, Chauo, Caracas, Venezuela. Tel: 0058 212 993 4111. britishembassy@internet.ve www.britain.org.ve

No tourist office in UK.

Torre Oeste Piso 35, Parque Centrale, Caracas, Venezula. Tel: (2) 507 8815/16. Fax: (2) 573 8983.

Return ticket required. Requirements may change at short notice. Contact the embassy before departure. Passport required, must be valid for at least 6 months.

Visa not required by EU citizens. Travellers will be given a tourist card by airline staff.

All organic substances.

B5400 is levied on all international departures. Children less than 2 years and transit passengers are exempt.

POLIO, TYPHOID: R. MALARIA: Exists in the falciparum variety, reported as being highly resistant to chloroquine. YELLOW FEVER: Vaccination is not required as a condition of entry but is recommended to all visitors who plan to travel outside the urban areas. OTHER: Bilharzia.

W2

Bolívar (B) = 100 centimos. Visa, MasterCard and Amex are widely accepted. Travellers cheques in US$ are easily exchanged. ATM AVAILABILITY: Over 1500 locations.

MONEYGRAM: 800 11 120 then 800 592 3888.
WESTERN UNION: 800 34598

AMEX: 0044 1273 696 933
DINERS CLUB: 02 202 2323
MASTERCARD: 800 1 2902
VISA: 800 1 2169

AMEX: 001 801 964 665
THOMAS COOK: 8001 2475
VISA: 0044 20 7937 8091

0830–1130 and 1400–1630 Mon to Fri.

Caters for all travellers and budgets.

Spanish. English, French, German and Portuguese may be spoken.

Most pleasant time is Jan–Apr. Rainy season is May–Dec.

Roman Catholic.

Jan 1, 6, Feb 24, Mar 19, Apr 19, May 1, Jun 24, 29, Jul 5, 24, Aug 15, Oct 12, Nov 1, Dec 8, 25, 31. Easter, Ascension Day, Corpus Christi.

110 volts AC, 60 Hz. American-type 2-pin plugs are used.

3–7 days to Europe. Internal mail can often take longer and surface mail to Europe may take up to one month.

Culture is a mixture of Latin, Caribbean and Spanish, all co-existing. In the interior traditional tribal rituals persist.

FLIGHTS: Connect all major centres and regarded as the most convenient form of internal transport. They are in heavy demand and may be overbooked; confirm seats well in advance. ROADS: Of a high standard between main cities. TAXI: Only use licensed taxis bearing a clearly identifiable number. The Ticketaxi service at Caracas Airport avoids having to negotiate a fare with taxi drivers. Prices are reasonable. It can be booked for the return journey to the airport by calling 0800 243 8373. CAR HIRE: Available at the airport and in major cities but expensive. DOCUMENTATION: IDP required.

Crime is on the increase and foreign visitors have been targeted. Cross-border violence, kidnapping, smuggling and drug trafficking are frequent in remote areas along the Venezuela–Colombia border. Caracas can be dangerous. Take care at night and in crowded places. Visitors should avoid political gatherings, and keep informed of developments by following the local media. Frequent ID checks: carry your passport.

CAPITAL: Hanoi

GMT +7

FROM UK: 0084. OUTGOING CODE TO UK: 0084. International calls may need operator assistance.

Police: 13, Fire: 14, Ambulance: 15.

Embassy of the Socialist Republic of Vietnam, 12–14 Victoria Road, London W8 5RD. Tel: 020 7937 1912. Fax: 020 7937 6108. vp@dsqvnlondon.demon.co.uk

British Embassy, Central Building, 31 Hai Ba Trung, Hanoi. Tel: 0084 4 8252510; Fax: 0084 4 8265762. behanoi@fpt.vn. www.uk-vietnam.org.
British Consulate General, 25 Le Duan, District 1, Ho Chi Minh City. Tel: 0084 8 8232862; Fax: 0084 8 8295257. bcghcmc@hem.vnn.vn.

No tourist office in UK. See www.vnstyle.vdc.com.vn/traveldirectory/

The Vietnam Tourism Company, 20 Ly Thuong Kiet Street, Hanoi. Tel: 0084 4 8264 4154; Fax 84 4 825-7538. vntourism2@hn.vnn.vn
VTC, 234 Nam Ky Khoi Nghia Street, District 3, Ho Chi Minh City. Tel: 0084 8 921 0776; Fax: 0084 8 829 0775. vietnamtourism@hcm.vnn.vn

Valid passport and visa required.

Non-prescribed drugs, pornography, firearms, knives and ammunition.

US$ 8 is levied on all foreign nationals.

POLIO, TYPHOID: R. MALARIA: Exists in certain areas in the falciparum variety, reported being highly resistant to chloroquine. Dengue fever is also common. YELLOW FEVER: Vaccination certificate required for travellers arriving from infected areas. OTHER: Bilharzia, cholera, Japanese encephalitis, plague, rabies, TB.

W1. Drink only boiled or bottled water.

New Dong (D) = 100 hao. US$ is the most favoured currency. Limited acceptance of MasterCard and Visa. Amex and Thomas Cook US$ travellers cheques are accepted at hotels and banks. ATM AVAILABILITY: A few locations.

MONEYGRAM: Available in all major cities.
WESTERN UNION: Available

AMEX: 0044 1273 696 933
DINERS CLUB: 0044 1252 513 500
MASTERCARD: 001 314 542 7111
VISA: 001 410 581 9994

AMEX: 0044 1273 571 600
THOMAS COOK: 001733 318950
VISA: 0044 20 7937 8091

0800–1630 Mon to Fri.

Caters for all budgets.

Vietnamese, French, Russian, English, Chinese.

Tropical. The monsoon season is May–Sept. The remainder of the year is dry.

Buddhist, Taoist, Confucian, Hoa Hao, Caodist, Christian (mainly Roman Catholic).

Jan 1, Feb 3, Apr 30, May 1, 19, Sep 2, Dec 25. Vietnamese New Year, Eve of Tet (late Jan/early Feb).

110/220 volts AC, 50 Hz.

Usually takes up to 3 weeks. Correspondence should be taken to a post office personally, to prevent theft and tampering.

FLIGHTS: Regular services operate between the main cities. RAIL: Longer-distance trains are more reliable than shorter routes. ROAD: Reasonable road network but driving can be hair raising. DOCUMENTATION: A local driving licence must be obtained from the Vietnamese Road Administration in Hanoi. BUS: Services are poor and overcrowded.

Some parts of the country are closed to visitors. Exercise caution if travelling in border areas. Be vigilant for street theft, including bag-snatching by young men on motorcycles in Ho Chi Minh City. Keep spectacles on a cord around the neck; don't carry large amounts of money; keep your passport in the hotel safe and carry a photocopy. Footwear should be removed when entering Buddhist Pagodas. Avoid wearing shorts. Vietnamese people should not be touched on the head. The authorities are likely to seize documents and media which they deem to be religious, pornographic, or political in nature. Security officials may put visitors under surveillance and can search hotel rooms and luggage without notice or consent. PHOTOGRAPHY: Restricted at ports, airports and harbours.

CAPITAL: Sana'a

GMT +3.

FROM UK: 00967. OUTGOING CODE TO UK: 0044.

Embassy of the Republic of Yemen, 57 Cromwell Road, London SW7 2ED. Tel: 020 7584 6607. Fax: 020 7589 3350.

British Embassy, PO Box 1287, 129 Haddah Road, Sana'a. Tel: 00967 1 264 081. Fax: 00967 1 263 059. British Consulate, 20 Miswat Road, Aden. Tel: 00967 2 232712.

Yemen Tourist Company, PO Box 1526, Sana'a, Republic of Yemen. Tel: (1) 330 039.

Valid passport and return ticket required. Requirements may be subject to short-term change: contact relevant authority. Visa required.

Obscene literature and all products of Israeli origin.

US$10 on international departures.

Holders of passports with Israeli visa stamps, valid or expired, will be refused entry.

POLIO, TYPHOID: R. MALARIA Exists in the falciparum form throughout the year. Resistance to chloroquine has been reported. YELLOW FEVER: A vaccination certificate is required if coming from infected areas. OTHER: Cholera, bilharzia, rabies.

W1

Yemeni Riyal is preferred (YR) = 100 fils. Yemeni Dinar is also in circulation. Import and export of local currency is limited to YR 5000 or equivalent. Diners Club and Amex widely accepted. US$ travellers cheques can be exchanged in most banks and hotels. ATM AVAILABILITY: Unavailable.

MONEYGRAM: Single location in capital city. WESTERN UNION: Unavailable.

AMEX: 0044 1273 696 933
DINERS CLUB: 0044 1252 513 500
MASTERCARD: 001 314 542 7111
VISA: 001 410 581 9994

AMEX: 0044 1273 571 600
THOMAS COOK: 001733 318950
VISA: 0044 20 7937 8091

0800–1200 Sat to Wed, 0800–1100 Thur.

If you conform to traditional Yemeni lifestyle you can live relatively cheaply, but Western food and en-suite facilities are expensive. Book all accommodation in advance.

Arabic and English.

Highland is warmer in summer, but nights can be very cold Oct–Mar. Summer can be very hot. The best time to visit is Oct–Apr.

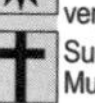
Sunni Muslim (especially in the North). Shia Muslim and small Christian communities.

Jan 1, May 1, 22, Jul 7, Sep 26, Oct 14, Nov 30, Dec 31. Islamic festivals.

220/230 volts AC, 50 Hz.

From Sana'a about 4 days; mail to and from other towns may take longer.

Local women are veiled. Western women cannot visit Yemen without a male companion. Dress modestly, do not look or smile at local men and avoid sunbathing, except at recognised tourist resorts.

SEA: Local ferries connect ports. ROAD: The network is mainly limited to desert track. Use of 4 x 4 vehicles with a guide is recommended. There remains some danger from mines laid during the civil war in the Southern and Eastern provinces. Off-road travel is not recommended. BUS: Regular intercity bus services. TAXI: Sharing taxis is the cheapest transport between cities. Negotiate fares beforehand. CAR HIRE: Available in main towns. DOCUMENTATION: IDP is required.

Most Yemenis are very friendly and welcoming. Do not photograph religious or military sites, and respect local sensitivities. Beachwear and shorts should be confined to the beach/pool. Smoking is forbidden in public during Ramadan. Do not drink alcohol in public places. The security situation in Yemen is improving, though still potentially unstable. Armed theft of vehicles is common. More than 100 kidnappings have been carried out by armed tribesmen in the past ten years. There have been fewer cases since the Yemeni government introduced tougher penalties; nevertheless, the FCO advises against all holiday and non-essential travel to Yemen for the time being. Check the FCO Travel Advice web site. for up-to-date information. All British visitors should register their presence in the country with the British Embassy. Where possible travel in organised groups with well-established tour agents.

Yugoslavia (Federal Republic of)

CAPITAL: Belgrade

GMT +1 (GMT +2 during the summer).

FROM UK: 00381. OUTGOING CODE TO UK: 0044

Police: 92, Fire: 93, Ambulance: 94.

Embassy of the Federal Republic of Yugoslavia, 5-7 Lexham Gardens, London W8 5JJ. Tel: 020 7370 6105. Fax: 020 7370 3838. 24-hour visa information line: 0900 160 0279 (premium rate).

British Embassy, General Zdanova 46, 11000 Belgrade. Tel: 00381 11 645 055; Fax: 00381 11 659 651. Emergency Honorary Consulate in Podgorica, Montenegro, Tel: 00381 81 625 816; Fax: 00381 81 622 166.

Yugoslav Airlines, 7 Dering Street, London W1. Tel: 020 7629 6629.

National Tourism Organisation of Serbia, Dobrinjska 11, 11000 Belgrade. Tel: 00381 11 361 2754; Fax: 00381 11 68 6804. ntos@eunet.yu; www.serbia-tourism.org/ National Tourism Organisation of Montenegro. tourism@cg.yu; www.visit-montenegro.com/english/default.htm

Valid passport required.

Visa required. The Yugoslav authorities have experimented with lifting the visa requirements. The Montenegrin authorities lifted visa requirements some time ago, but this did not allow visitors to cross into Serbia without a visa. Check with the Yugoslav Embassy for current requirements.

Narcotics. All currency brought into the country must be declared on arrival. Failure to do so can risk a fine and confiscation of all remaining cash on departure.

YuD80 is payable on international departures.

POLIO, TYPHOID: R. OTHER: Rabies.

W2

Yugoslav Dinar (Yu D). Euro and US$ are accepted by traders, who give change in dinars. Credit cards are accepted only at larger hotels and international car hire firms. Travellers cheques can be exchanged at major banks only. Yugoslavia is a cash society. ATM AVAILABILITY: Unavailable.

MONEYGRAM: Unavailable.
WESTERN UNION: Available at some banks but the money is slow coming through.

AMEX: 0044 1273 696 933
DINERS CLUB: 0044 1252 513 500
MASTERCARD: 001 314 542 7111
VISA: 001 410 581 9994

AMEX: 0044 1273 571 600
THOMAS COOK: 001733 318950
VISA: 0044 20 7937 8091

0700–1500 Mon to Fri. Some branches are open on Sat for payment and withdrawals.

Very cheap when compared with Western Europe. Limited commodities available outside Belgrade. Accommodation is scarce.

Serbian. Hungarian is also spoken in the autonomous region of Vojvodina, and Albanian in Kosovo.

Serbia has cold winters and warm summers. Montenegro is mainly the same but with alpine conditions in the mountains.

Mostly Eastern Orthodox Serbs, with a large Muslim ethnic Albanian minority (especially in the province of Kosovo) and a small Roman Catholic ethnic Hungarian minority (mainly located in the province of Vojvodina).

Jan 1, 6, 7, 27, Mar 28, Apr 27, May 1, Jul 7, 13, Oct 20, Nov 29.

220 volts AC, 50 Hz.

Postal services within Serbia are reasonable, but slow.

RAIL: Internal rail services are generally poor, often overbooked and unreliable. International trains are often held up for long customs and passport checks at Subotica, on the border with Hungary. ROAD: Main roads in Serbia are reasonable but side roads and lanes are badly pot-holed and require careful negotiation. BUS: Good, efficient services connect towns, faster than the trains. DOCUMENTATION: Full national driving licence. Insurance and green card also necessary.

The situation in Yugoslavia is calm. The country is picking itself up and promoting tourism and cultural visits. Violent crime has increased and places all visitors in danger. Theft of cars is becoming a growing problem and personal theft is particularly common on trains. Register with your Embassy when you arrive and inform them of any change of address. Up-to-date information on Yugoslavia from the FCO travel advice website.

Zaire (Democratic Republic of the Congo)

CAPITAL: Kinshasa

Kinshasa and Mbanaka GMT +1. Haut Zaïre, Kasai, Kivu and Shaba GMT +2

FROM UK: 00243. OUTGOING CODE TO UK: 0044.

Embassy of the Democratic Republic of the Congo, 38 Holne Chase, London N2 0QQ. Tel: 020 8458 0254; Fax: 020 8458 0254.

British Embassy/Ambassade Britanique, 88 Avenue du Roi Baudoin, Kinshasa. Tel: 00243 88 46101. ambrit@ic.cd Consulates in Lubumbasi, Goma, Kisangani.

No tourist office in UK.

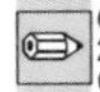
Office Nationale du Tourisme, BP 9502, 2a/2b avenue des Orangers, Kinshasa-Gombe, Zaïre. Tel: (12) 30070.

Valid passport required.

Visa required. Obtain prior to travel.

Arms and ammunition require an import licence.

Travellers entering the DRC with visas and/or entry/exit stamps from Uganda, Rwanda or Burundi may experience difficulties at the airport or other ports of entry, and refused entry.

POLIO, TYPHOID: R. MALARIA: Exists all year round in the falciparum variety throughout the country. Reported to be highly resistant to chloroquine. YELLOW FEVER: A vaccination certificate is required for travellers over one year of age. OTHER: Bilharzia, cholera, plague, rabies.

W1

Zaïre (Z) = 100 makuta. EXCHANGE: There is a large illegal market for exchanging money. Import and export of local currency is prohibited. The purchase of airline tickets can only be made with officially exchanged money. All major credit cards are accepted on a limited basis in Kinshasa, only. Travellers cheques are accepted in large towns and cities: US$ is the preferred currency. ATM AVAILABILITY: Unavailable.

MONEYGRAM: Unavailable.
WESTERN UNION: Unavailable.

AMEX: 0044 1273 696933
MASTERCARD: 001 314 542 7111
VISA: (1) 410 581 9091

AMEX: 0044 1273 571600
THOMAS COOK: 0044 1733 318950
VISA: 0044 1733 318949

0800–1130 Mon to Fri.

All travellers are considered extremely wealthy by local people and will be charged accordingly.

French and many local dialects.

North: dry season is Dec–Mar. South: dry season is May–Oct. It can be humid throughout the year.

Mainly Roman Catholic with Protestant and Animist minorities.

Jan 1, 4, May 1, 20, Jun 24, 30, Aug 1, Oct 14, 27, Nov 17, 24, Dec 25.

220 volts AC, 50 Hz.

Post takes 4–18 days to reach Europe.

Due to the civil war and unrest women have been left as sole earners within the family.

There are indefinite restrictions on tourist travel within DRC. Overland journeys by local public transport or foreign vehicle are forbidden. Anyone who wishes to travel outside Kinshasa must obtain advance written permission from the Ministry of the Interior. Nothing runs on time. ROADS: These are amongst the worst in Africa. Don't take any roads marked on a map as anything other than a possibility. DOCUMENTATION: IDP is recommended. RIVER: This is one of the best ways to travel, although can be unreliable.

The security situation remains unpredictable, and the FCO advises against all holiday and non-essential travel. Political developments have brought about a ceasefire but the foreign troops are only just across the border and there have been reports of sporadic fighting in violation of the negotiated ceasefire. Armed groups operate in parts of the country and are responsible for pillaging, vehicle thefts, violent settling of differences, ethnic tension, and paramilitary operations. Travellers run the risk of attack or detention, and should avoid any area where crowds have gathered. People who must go to DRC should remain in Kinshasa and ensure that they get all necessary local permits to carry out their work.

CAPITAL: Lusaka

GMT +2

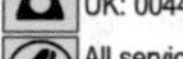
FROM UK: 00260. OUTGOING CODE TO UK: 0044

All services: 1 2 25067/254798.

High Commission for the Republic of Zambia. 2 Palace Gate, London W8 5NG. Tel: 020 7589 6655. Fax: 020 7581 1353.

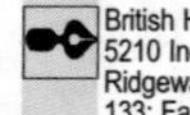
British High Commission, PO Box 50050, 5210 Independence Avenue, 15101 Ridgeway, Lusaka, Zambia. Tel: 00260 1 251 133; Fax: 00260 1 253798. brithc@zamnet.zm

Zambia National Tourist Board, 2 Palace Gate, London W8 5NG. Tel: 020 7589 6343; Fax: 020 7225 3221. zntb@aol.com

Zambia National Tourist Board, PO Box 30017, Century House, Cairo Road, Lusaka, Zambia. Tel: (1) 229 087. zntb@zamnet.zm www.zamnet.zm/zamnet/zntb/zntb.html

Valid passport required Visa not required by UK and Ireland citizens. Visitors from other EU states require visas.

US$20. Transit passengers are exempt.

POLIO, TYPHOID: R. MALARIA Exists in the falciparum variety throughout the whole country al year. Resistance to chloroquine has been reported. YELLOW FEVER: Vaccination is strongly recommended. Those arriving from infected areas will require a vaccination certificate. OTHER: Bilharzia, cholera, rabies, and Africa's worst record of HIV/AIDS.

W1

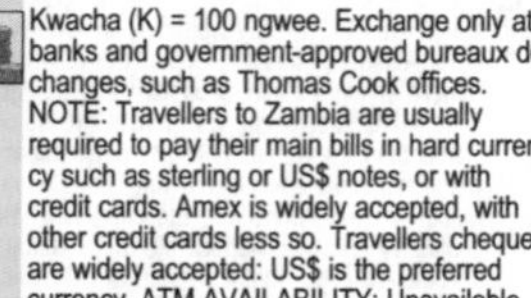
Kwacha (K) = 100 ngwee. Exchange only at banks and government-approved bureaux de changes, such as Thomas Cook offices. NOTE: Travellers to Zambia are usually required to pay their main bills in hard currency such as sterling or US$ notes, or with credit cards. Amex is widely accepted, with other credit cards less so. Travellers cheques are widely accepted: US$ is the preferred currency. ATM AVAILABILITY: Unavailable.

MONEYGRAM: Unavailable.
WESTERN UNION: Unavailable.

AMEX: 0044 1273 696 933
DINERS CLUB: 0044 1252 513 500
MASTERCARD: 001 314 542 7111
VISA: 001 410 581 9994

AMEX: 0044 1273 571 600
THOMAS COOK: 001733 318950
VISA: 0044 20 7937 8091

0815–1430 Mon to Fri.

High inflation means that prices for tourists tend to be expensive.

English and over 73 local dialects.

High altitudes prevent very high temperatures. Cool and dry May–Sept, hot and dry Oct–Nov and hot and rainy Dec–Apr.

Officially Christian with Animist, Muslim and Hindu minorities.

Jan 1, Mar 11, May 1, 25, first Mon/Tue in Jul, first Mon in Aug, Oct 24, Dec 25. Easter.

220 volts, AC, 50 Hz.

7–14 days to Europe.

FLIGHTS: There are over 127 airstrips in the country and several charter companies operate domestic flights. ROADS: A good network exists but they can be dangerous in the rainy season. DOCUMENTATION: IDP is recommended. Traffic drives on the left. BUS: Services are often unreliable and can be very overcrowded. Inter-city bus travel, except by 'luxury coaches', is dangerous because of poor maintenance and bad driving. RAIL: Zambia Railways serves Livingstone and has a connection across the Victoria Falls to Bulawayo and Harare in Zimbabwe.

Tourism is growing in importance to the Zambian economy but the authorities have yet to deal effectively with crime and disorder that deters tourists. Travellers to remote areas will be met with curiosity and particular care should be taken. African culture and traditions dominate. Traditional dancing is popular throughout the country and many colourful annual ceremonies take place. Tourists at famous sites such as Victoria Falls are often the targets for theft, so sensible precautions should be taken to safeguard money and bags.

Zimbabwe

CAPITAL: Harare

GMT +2

FROM UK: 00263. OUTGOING CODE TO UK: 0044

Police: 995, Ambulance: 994, Fire: 993, General emergencies: 999.

High Commission for the Republic of Zimbabwe, Zimbabwe House, 429 Strand, London WC2R 0SA. Tel: 020 7836 7755. Fax: 020 7379 1167.
zimlondon@callnetuk.com
www.zimbabwelink.com

British High Commission, Corner House, Samora Machel Avenue/Leopold Takawira Street (PO Box 4490) Harare. Tel: 00263 4 772990; Fax: 00263 4 774617.
www.britainzw.org

Address as High Commission. See www.gta.gov.zw/
and www.africaonline.com/site/zw/

Zimbabwe Tourist Development Corporation (ZTDC), PO Box 8052, corner of Jason Moyo Avenue and Fourth Street, Causeway, Harare, Zimbabwe. Tel: (4) 793 666. Fax: (4) 793 669.

Return ticket required. Requirements may change at short notice. Contact the embassy before departure. Passport required by all, valid at least 6 months from date of entry.

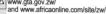

Visa not required by nationals of EU countries.

Indecent film and publications, various food products, various agricultural products, birds and bee-keeping equipment.

Departure tax of US$ 20 for non-residents, or Z$ 20 for residents.

POLIO, TYPHOID: R. MALARIA: Exists in certain areas throughout the year in the falciparum variety. Resistance to chloroquine has been reported. YELLOW FEVER: A vaccination certificate is required for travellers arriving from infected areas. OTHER: Bilharzia, cholera and rabies.

W1

Zimbabwe Dollar (Z$) = 100 cents.
EXCHANGE: Major currencies at hotels and banks. Import and export of local currency is limited to Z$250. American Express, Diners Club and Visa are widely accepted. Banks and major hotels will exchange travellers cheques: US$ is the preferred currency.
ATM AVAILABILITY: Over 75 locations.

MONEYGRAM: Unavailable
WESTERN UNION: Available.

AMEX: +44 1273 696933
DINERS CLUB: No longer number.
MASTERCARD: No local number
VISA: (1) 410 581 9091

AMEX: 0044 1273 571 600
THOMAS COOK: 0044 1733 318950
VISA: 0044 1733 318949

0800–1500 Mon, Tues, Thur and Fri.
0800–1300 Wed and 0800–1130 Sat.

Lower prices can be found away from the tourist centres if you are willing to live simply.

English, Shona and Ndebele.

Sept–Oct is hot, dry season. Rainy season is Nov to Mar. Best time to visit is Apr–May and Aug–Sept.

Christianity, Hindu and Muslim minorities. Traditional beliefs in rural areas.

Jan 1, Apr 18, May 1, 25, Aug 11, 12, Dec 22, 25, 26. Easter.

220/240 volts AC, 50 Hz.

Up to 1 week to Europe by airmail.

Although apartheid has ceased in, some racism still persists in Zimbabwe.

FLIGHTS: Domestic flights run between the main cities. ROADS: Excellent road network. DOCUMENTATION: IDP and vehicle identification required. BUS: Services in most parts of the country. White travellers using the bus may provoke attention. RAIL: Daily between the main cities.

Urban culture in Zimbabwe is greatly influenced by Western culture and education, but in rural areas traditional values continue. Casual dress is suitable for daytime, but jackets and ties are expected in smart hotels and restaurants. Petty crime is prevalent in Harare. Backpackers are at risk in the main tourist areas.

Visitors should avoid political gatherings, which can turn into riots without warning. In rural areas, farms and some conservation parks are occupied illegally by liberation war veterans, and intending visitors should take advice locally before they set out.

Conversion tables

DISTANCES (approx. conversions)

1 kilometre (km) = 1000 metres (m) 1 metre = 100 centimetres (cm)

Metric	Imperial/US		Metric	Imperial/US	Metric	Imperial/US	Metric	Imperial/US
m	ft	in	km	miles	km	miles	km	miles
0.01 (1cm)		3/8	0.75	0.50	20	12.43	200	124.27
0.50 (50cm)	1	8	1	0.62	30	18.64	300	186.41
1	3	3	2	1.24	40	24.85	400	248.45
2	6	6	3	1.86	50	31.07	500	310.69
3	10	0	4	2.49	60	37.28	600	372.82
4	13	0	5	3.10	70	43.50	700	434.96
5	16	6	6	3.73	80	49.71	800	497.10
7	23	0	7	4.35	90	55.92	900	559.23
9	29	0	8	4.97	100	62.14	1000	621.37
10 (11yd)	33	0	9	5.59	125	77.67	1100	683.54
20 (22yd)	66	0	10	6.21	150	93.21	1200	745.68
50 (54yd)	164	0	15	9.32	175	108.74	1300	807.82
100 (110yd)	330	0					1400	869.96
200 (220yd)	660	0					1500	932.10
300 (330yd)	984	0					2000	1242.74
500 (550yd)	1640	0					3000	1864.11

1 kilometre = 0.6214 miles
1 mile = 1.609 kilometres

LADIES' CLOTHES

UK	France	Italy	Rest of Europe	US
10	36	38	34	8
12	38	40	36	10
14	40	42	38	12
16	42	44	40	14
18	44	46	42	16
20	46	48	44	18

MENS' CLOTHES

UK	Europe	US
36	46	36
38	48	38
40	50	40
42	52	42
44	54	44
46	56	46

MENS' SHIRTS

UK	Europe	US
14	36	14
15	38	15
15½	39	15½
16	41	16
16½	42	16½
17	43	17

MENS' SHOES

UK	Europe	US
6	40	7
7	41	8
8	42	9
9	43	10
10	44	11
11	45	12

LADIES' SHOES

UK	Europe	US
3	36	4½
4	37	5½
5	38	6½
6	39	7½
7	40	8½
8	41	9½

TEMPERATURE

°C	°F	°C	°F	°C	°F	°C	°F
-20	-4	-5	23	10	50	25	77
-15	5	0	32	15	59	30	86
-10	14	5	41	20	68	35	95

FLUID MEASURES

Litres	Imp.gal.	US gal.	Litres	Imp.gal.	US gal.
5	1.1	1.3	30	6.6	7.8
10	2.2	2.6	35	7.7	9.1
15	3.3	3.9	40	8.8	10.4
20	4.4	5.2	45	9.9	11.7
25	5.5	6.5	50	11.0	13.0

WEIGHT

Kg	lbs	Kg	lbs	Kg	lbs
1	2¼	5	11	25	55
2	4½	10	22	50	11
3	6½	15	33	75	165
4	9	20	45	100	220

24 HOUR CLOCK

0000	=	Midnight	1415	=	2.15 pm
0600	=	6.00 am	1645	=	4.45 pm
0715	=	7.15 am	1800	=	6.00 pm
0930	=	9.30 am	2000	=	8.00 pm
1200	=	Noon	2110	=	9.10 pm
1300	=	1.00 pm	2345	=	11.45 pm

Index

This index details the subjects covered in this book. As the Directory section lists countries in alphabetical order, these have not been included. However, a few countries may be more familiar by another name or might be difficult to find, so these are given below for ease of reference.

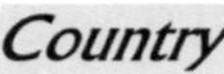

Your Feedback . . .

Return comments to:

The Project Editor, World Wise
Thomas Cook Publishing, PO Box 227
Thorpe Wood, Peterborough PE3 6PU, United Kingdom

Your Feedback . . .

Country

Your Feedback . . .

Please return comments to:

The Project Editor, World Wise
Thomas Cook Publishing, PO Box 227
Thorpe Wood, Peterborough PE3 6PU, United Kingdom

Your Feedback . . .

Country

Your Feedback . . .

Please return comments to:

The Project Editor, World Wise
Thomas Cook Publishing, PO Box 227
Thorpe Wood, Peterborough PE3 6PU, United Kingdom

Your Feedback . . .